CONDITION AND EDITION ARE VERY IMPORTANT

Important: The section on First Edition Identification by publisher (Appendix E) is applicable to each entry unless otherwise stated. Check the date on the title page carefully. If the entry herein does not have the date in parentheses, the date must be on the title page. Compare your book's condition with the conditions listed below. All prices in this volume are for books in the following condition:

Books published before 1800: Rebound in the nineteenth century unless otherwise stated. Copies in original bindings (even extensively repaired) or contemporary bindings would have a much higher value.

Books published from 1800 to 1839: Rebound at some early date after the date of publication unless otherwise stated. Binding is clean and intact. The original binding would greatly increase the value.

Books published from 1840 to 1919: In original leather, cloth (cloth-covered boards), boards (paper-covered boards), or wraps unless otherwise stated. Books published from 1840 to 1879 are in good to very good condition with only minor edge wear or loss and still tight and clean. Books published from 1880 to 1919 are clean and bright with no loss or tears on the edges. Copies in fine to very fine condition would bring much more.

Books published from 1920 to 1949: Must be in very good to fine condition with only minimal (if any) soiling. In original dustwrapper (unless in wraps or in limited-edition slipcase) that is clean, with only minimal soiling or fading, and only a few *small* chips and closed tears. If the dustwrapper is missing, the value is greatly reduced (75 percent on fiction and 20 percent or more on nonfiction).

Books published after 1950: Those published from 1950 to 1975 must be in fine condition, in original dustwrapper that shows only very minor wear, fading, or soiling and that may or may not be price-clipped. Those published from 1975 until the present must, like their dustwrapper, look new, and the dustwrapper must not be price-clipped.

Book

A COMPREHENSIVE GUIDE

ALSO BY ALLEN AND PATRICIA AHEARN

Book Collecting: A Comprehensive Guide (1989 and 1995)

Collected Books: The Guide to Values (1991 and 1998)

Book Collecting 2000

A COMPREHENSIVE GUIDE

Allen and
Patricia Ahearn

G. P. PUTNAM'S SONS

NEW YORK

G. P. Putnam's Sons
Publishers Since 1838
a member of
Penguin Putnam Inc.
375 Hudson Street
New York, NY 10014

Library of Congress Cataloging-in-Publication Data

Ahearn, Allen.
Book collecting 2000 : a comprehensive guide / Allen and
Patricia Ahearn
p.   cm.
Rev. ed. of: Book collecting. 1995.
Includes bibliographical references.
ISBN 0-399-14574-5
1. Book collecting—United States.   2. English imprints—
Collectors and collecting—United States.   3. First editions—
United States.   4. Books—Prices—United States.
I. Ahearn, Patricia.   II. Ahearn, Allen.   Book collecting.
III. Title.   IV. Title: Book collecting two thousand.
Z987.5.U6A35   2000   99-27244 CIP
002'.075—dc21

Printed in the United States of America

1   3   5   7   9   10   8   6   4   2

This book is printed on acid-free paper. ∞

The text of this book is set in Garamond.
Book design by Marysarah Quinn

The authors may be reached at Quill & Brush,
1137 Sugarloaf Mountain Road, Dickerson MD 20842.
E-mail: firsts@qb.com   Homepage: www.qb.com

In memory of
a book lover and our friend

JOSEPH MICHAEL HAYES

Acknowledgments

WE WANT ESPECIALLY TO THANK the following people for providing corrections, suggesting authors for inclusion, and/or providing their opinion on prices for particular titles in this edition or previous editions: Alan Abrams, Bart Auerbach, John Ballinger, Daniel Baranow, Steve Bernard, George Bixby, William Boozer, Andreas Brown, Lew Buckingham, Nigel Burwood, Andy Cahan, Henry Campbell, Pat Cather, Clark Chambers, Tom Congalton, Allan Covici, Lloyd Currey, Joseph Dermont, Steve Deutsch, Larry Dingman, Bob Fleck, Nelson Freck, Beth and Paul Garon, Willard Goodwin, Chan Gordon, Terry Halladay, Jack Hanrahan, Josh Heller, John Hildebrand, David Holloway, David Holmes, Peter Howard, James Jaffe, Priscilla Juvelis, Gary Kane, Norman Kane, Susan Klein, John Knott, Ralph Kristiansen, Richard Lackritz, Mark Samuels Lasner, Ann Lehr, Bill Loesser, Ken Lopez, Edmund Miller, George Robert Minkoff, Edward Moore, Larry Moskowitz, Rusty Mott, Maurice Neville, Al Newgarden, Tom Nicely, Doug O'Dell, Gary Oleson, Al Palanker, Otto Penzler, Jim Pepper, John Ptak, Jo Ann Reisler, Hank Salerno, John Sanderson, Joel Sattler, Steve Schwartz, Richard Shue, Darrell Simmons, Ralph Sipper, Dan Smith, Charles Stecy, Peter Stern, James Taylor, Henry Turlington, Chris Volk, Stephen Weissman, Dick Wilson, Robert Wilson, Clarence Wolf, Howard Woolmer, and John Wronowski. These people were not asked their opinions on values for all of the books (no friend is that good a friend), but if a value is on target it must be something they were asked about. On the other hand, if the price estimate is way off, chances are we did it. Many of the titles included have not appeared in catalogs or at auction in recent years.

In addition, we want to acknowledge all of the dealers listed in Appendix B herein, who have kept Quill & Brush on their mailing lists. Their catalogs have all provided first-book entries and price estimates, and this book is very much dependent on those reference works.

A special thanks to Elizabeth Ahearn, Suzanne Regan, Dyanne Ryan, Carl Hahn, and Sharon Cramer for all the help they have given us.

Contents

Introduction

THIS BOOK has been prepared to provide information for book collectors as well as librarians and book dealers.

It attempts to show that book collecting is enjoyable and a reasonably good investment over the long run. It explains some of the terms used in the trade and how to identify, purchase, care for, and sell first editions. Also included is an interpretation of the rationale that drives collecting interests, which admittedly may be an attempt to explain the unexplainable.

For those actively involved in the trade, the book includes our opinion on the current retail value of first editions of about 6,000 books. These price estimates are not intended to be projections but to be representative of what are, one hopes, realistic current retail values based on the catalogs received, Internet listings, our own experiences in selling first editions, and discussions with collectors and dealers more knowledgeable on values for books that have not appeared for sale in recent years.

This is the third edition of this book to be published by G. P. Putnam's Sons, but we published precursors in 1975, 1978, 1983, and 1986. In 1975, the book was a pamphlet with 1,000 first books and very little text. As the reader can see, it has grown over the years.

This is the first edition of this book to make use of the Internet in establishing estimated prices. The Internet—through providers such as ABE, Bibliofind, and others—has revealed the actual current supply of collectible (and uncollectible) books. As prices in this market are heavily influenced by supply and demand, the Internet has affected prices. It appears that the prices of more common titles have been lowered and the prices of scarcer titles have been pushed up. But the final impact of the Net on book collecting is still the subject of much debate. We have included a new section on the Internet and its impact on book collecting, which gives our current views.

The values listed are estimates of retail prices for very good to fine copies of the books, with the criteria for condition by age as shown prior to the First-Book List and on the endpapers of this book (unless otherwise indicated).

We believe this book can be of help in getting a feel for the value of many more than the 6,000 titles included, because we think the price of the first edition of the first book often sets an upper limit on an author's first editions, and therefore the estimated prices in this book for first books can assist in determining prices for later books by the authors listed.

The prices in this book are intended only as guides. We are not trying to be as specific as it appears. We are more concerned with indicating that a certain title in a certain condition is $50 rather than $500 than with indicating whether it is $50 versus $60.

Most dealers in collectible books do not handle rare books *per se;* they handle scarce books. Very fine copies of scarce books are rare, however. These fine copies command high prices from knowledgeable collectors and libraries because these buyers realize the true relative scarcity of such material. We are certainly not particularly knowledgeable about other collecting fields, such as coins or stamps, but our impression is that if an individual wanted five very fine examples of a certain "rare" coin or stamp and was willing to pay the going price, they could be found within a few weeks. On the other hand, if an individual wanted to buy five very fine copies of a certain edition of a particular title, it might take a few years. And this is not just for books costing hundreds or thousands of dollars; it is equally true of books that sell for only a few dollars.

We have attempted to make the contents as complete and accurate as possible. Our comments or perceptions on book collecting are, of course, our own.

Errors and omissions are normal in projects such as this, and correspondence about them is always appreciated.

Preface to the Millennium Edition

IT SEEMS APPROPRIATE at this important time to make a few comments on book collecting and the trade. We've been around the book trade about half the century. We started as collectors in the 1950s, issued a few catalogs every year in the 1960s and early 1970s (under the name Allen Ahearn–First Editions), and opened the Quill & Brush as a book and art store in 1976.

Initially, our goal was not to make money but to support our own collection by selling duplicates or books we found on scouting expeditions. We achieved this goal—at least the part about not making any money.

With the opening of the Quill & Brush, in 1976, we had a short-term goal to actually support ourselves selling books and art. We met that goal in 1985.

Over the years that we've been associated with the book trade, it has gone through many changes. Gone are the great stocking-of-the-libraries days of the 1950s and 1960s when, we are told, a bookseller could go to huge bookstores in major cities with a libraries wants list and spend days accumulating books on the list, then go back to shop or home, mark them up, mail them to the institution, and go look for more.

By the 1970s, when *we* became more involved in the trade, not only were the great stocking-of-the-libraries days over but most of the large stores were gone. Locally, Lowdermilks in Washington closed at the end of the 1960s, and there was no successor. In most cases smaller shops moved into the area, but there was no longer a large central establishment.

In those days, catalogs were the primary means of selling to a far-flung clientele. Book fairs, which are a good way for booksellers to meet new collectors, existed, but the number per year was relatively small. During the

1970s and 1980s the number of fairs increased, so that now, at century's end, we've gone from perhaps a few fairs a year to few a week.

Over the past few decades, the book trade was slowly evolving, but nothing could have prepared us for the changes in the last two years. The Internet has drastically and irrevocably changed the way we sell books and the way collectors purchase books. Although the Internet has been around awhile (we have been on it with a home page since 1995), it has only been in the past two years that the number of books on line has increased dramatically. Books that previously may have taken years to track down can often be located in an instant using the Internet. At the beginning of 1998, Advance Book Exchange (www.abebooks.com) had 1,500 "dealers" or subscribers on line, listing a cumulative total of approximately 4,000,000 out-of-print books. By April 1999, the numbers were up to 4,500 and 12,000,000, respectively, with about 250 new subscribers and 600,000 books being added monthly. (For more on this subject, see our section "Sources for Books.")

We often hear that the Internet is lowering prices, and in some cases it is, but our perception is that the last time we had such relatively high auction and retail sale prices was in 1929, the end of what Nick Basbanes, in his book *A Gentle Madness,* called the Golden Age of book collecting, sixty years when the building of great libraries became an emblem of wisdom and accomplishment. Book collecting was *in,* and prices were sky-high. The stock market crash, followed by the Depression and World War II, left a large time period in this century when it appears book collecting, at least for the general public, was dormant. Interest stayed low until the 1950s when our economy started to get on its feet. This is not to say that book collecting and perhaps even some high prices did not continue during this period, only that the type of general interest in book collecting we see today did not exist.

In fact, from our view, the high level of general interest we see today was not prevalent throughout the sixties, seventies, or early eighties. Having done price guides for first books from 1975 through 2000, we noted a marked increase in prices and interest starting in 1987, after the stock market downturn—the opposite of the 1929 reaction. We'll leave it to others to explain why, but the prices of first books, which include many *high spots* (books considered classics or rarities), started increasing dramatically. Perhaps 25 to 50 percent a year in 1988. We had done guides in 1978 and 1983 and saw a normal inflation adjustment during this period. In the 1986 edition the prices were just about flat from 1983, with very few exceptions. During 1986 and 1987 the market stayed flat, but in 1988 prices for *high spots* started escalating. It's not that other prices didn't go up too, but not at the same rate. Our estimates for a fine copy of the first edition of Salinger's *Catcher in the Rye* in the dustwrapper was $100 in 1978, $500 in 1986, and $7,500 in 2000; Harper Lee's *To Kill a Mockingbird* was $50 in 1978, $250 in

1986, and $7,500 in 2000 (although we're told a really nice copy sold for $12,500.)

The only thing we know for sure is that for fifty years we've been told that the first-edition market will never hold up, and for almost that long we've been told that many of our books were priced too high. In fact, we know the first statement has not turned out to be true, as the first-edition marketplace is strong, and as to the second comment, we were just ahead of our time.

But as the century begins, we do have a serious problem. What are we to do now that it's a new century and all the twentieth-century books are from the last century—by definition, a hundred years old? What are we dealers in "modern first editions" to do with these books from the last century, and still in their dust jackets?

We in the modern first trade have a sense that the general antiquarian dealers don't feel we're real antiquarians. We're a little sensitive about this. We ourselves thought we understood the term, and when asked to define the difference between an antiquarian book and a modern first edition we always used the example of a Churchill first edition, perhaps *My Early Life,* published in 1930. If it is a very nice copy in the original cloth in a fine dustwrapper, we would consider it a modern first edition, but if the dustwrapper was missing and the book was pretty beat up, or if the covers were gone and it was bound in full leather, we understood it to be an antiquarian book.

We understand eighteenth-century-and-earlier books as being antiquarian and assume if we sell a Dickens, Melville, or Twain that maybe we are dabbling in the antiquarian world. But what of a Jack London first, particularly in a dustwrapper. It's quite old, a hundred years now. Is it an antiquarian book, or is to be forever a modern first edition? Are Hemingway, Faulkner, Fitzgerald, and Steinbeck forever to be "modern"? They've lasted as "modern" throughout almost the whole of the twentieth century. Will they be able to hold on to the title throughout all of the twenty-first century? And what of those recent books—the ones we refer to as the hypermoderns, books published in the last decade or so of the twentieth century? Are they all a century old now?

What to do, what to do? It is curiouser and curiouser.

Book Collecting 2000

A COMPREHENSIVE GUIDE

Book Collecting

BOOK COLLECTORS start as readers. This may seem obvious, but it is important to keep it in mind, for the majority of book collectors collect authors or subjects that they are currently reading or have read and enjoyed. In fact, perhaps "enjoyed" is really not descriptive enough. Collectors do not just enjoy these books; they feel an affinity with the author and admire the author as one of the best in the field. The author expresses the collector's thoughts and inchoate insights and expresses them in ways the collector would if he or she had the talent. Or the books may take him or her to a time and place the collector is interested in or to a setting that removes the collector from his or her current world and cares.

Book readers become book collectors when they find that books have become important as objects that they wish to own, admire, and enjoy at their leisure. This is an important point, for most readers are content with reading a library copy or a paperback reprint and have no desire to go beyond this point. In order to understand the drive of a book collector, one must understand that most people are attracted to book collecting for three reasons: the true enjoyment or fun of the search, the love of the book as an object, and the economics or investment potential. From our experience with collectors—and most dealers for that matter—all three motivations exist in varying degrees.

For the Fun of It

To us, book collecting seems to be more enjoyable than other collecting hobbies, because the scope is broad and the availability of material is large.

One can find bookstores in just about every town, and reasonably priced books and even bargains can be found in most of them. But that's just the beginning, for there are also book fairs; garage sales; school, church, and charity book sales; friends' attics and basements; antique shops; and remainder sales (new books marked down to sell), and now, of course, the Internet.

We haven't done any research, but we suspect that the quantity, variety, and availability far exceeds any other collecting field, such as stamps, coins, glassware, or furniture. And there is another plus for hardback books: even with the Internet as a massive resource for pricing, there are fewer price guides in this field than in any other, which means it is not as regimented as coins, stamps, comic books, or even paperback books, all of which have price guides covering the majority of the material. We are publishing price guides (these will be discussed later), this book is a price guide, and there are others, but cumulatively all these guides cover only a very small portion of the out-of-print book market, and most of their prices require a fair amount of interpretation in order to arrive at a reasonable conclusion on a particular copy in hand. This absence of consistency and regimentation is an attractive feature for book collectors.

There is a vast array of personalities in the book field, including dealers, book scouts, other collectors, librarians, and the authors themselves. You will meet many of them, and the experience will, we hope, add to your enjoyment. Certainly, there will be few towns you visit in the future where you won't find a bookstore where you can spend a few hours and learn something about the owner, prices, editions, and so on.

In his book *The Book-Collecting Game,* A. Edward Newton puts it as well as anyone has:

> Book-collecting. It's a great game. Anybody with ordinary intelligence can play it: there are, indeed, people who think that it takes no brains at all; their opinion may be ignored. No great amount of money is required, unless one becomes very ambitious. It can be played at home or abroad, alone or in company. It can even be played by correspondence. Everyone playing it can make his own rules—and change them during the progress of the game. It is not considered "cricket" to do this in other games.

In his *Modern Book Collecting for the Impecunious Amateur,* Herbert Faulkner West describes collectors in general thus:

> Some collectors desire beetles, while others have divergent and decided propensities for empty bottles, full bottles . . . silhouettes, tea

caddies . . . horseshoes, guns, stuffed owls, stuffed animals, stuffed shirts, candlesticks, trademarks, first editions. . . . Although it is quite evident that collectors are not entirely "all there," I have always found them to be nice, harmless people, whom any of my readers could invite home without danger of being disinherited.

And from *Book-Collecting as a Hobby,* by P. H. Muir:

Book-collecting is not exclusively a hobby for rich and leisured people. It is less a matter of money than of method. I know many people of quite modest means who have gathered valuable and important collections with no greater expenditure than casual book buying might entail.

The point is that the greatest pleasure for the collector is in the chase, and if you can afford to buy an occasional new book, you can also afford to buy an occasional old book.

Books as Objects

It would seem that the transition from reader to collector occurs when the book itself is perceived as an object, akin to art perhaps. Certainly, if you are going to pay $25, $50, or $100 for a first edition when you could borrow a copy from the library or purchase a paperback reprint, you have bought an object that you want to own and actually look at occasionally, just as you want to own an original painting or a signed limited print when there are copies available at significantly lower prices.

Economics

When we started buying first editions years ago, the decision was based (rationalized) on a simple fact. If we bought a reprint or a book-club edition of a book by an author whose work we believed would stand the test of time, we knew that the most we would ever get for it when we sold it was a dollar or perhaps even less, if it was wanted at all. Whereas if we bought a first edition, we believed we would always be able to get back one half of the cost, and there was a good chance that we might eventually get all of our cost back and even more. Therefore, if we were going to buy a copy of Salinger's *Franny and Zooey* at $4, and we had a choice between a first and second printing, obviously we would buy a first. The economics of buying the second printing made absolutely no sense to us. But admittedly, we enjoyed owning a first edition of the book as an object on our shelves, because we had made the transition from readers to collectors. Today a first edition of *Franny and Zooey* is selling for $150 to $200.

Now the second step was a bit harder. We'd enjoyed Salinger's *Catcher in the Rye* and wanted a hardbound copy, but a first edition in the early 1960s was selling for $15 or $20, four to ten times what a hardback reprint would cost. This was a lot of money at the time, at least in our circumstances, but there still seemed little choice, given our feelings about the importance of the book, so we sprang for it. It turned out to be a good investment relative to the purchase of a reprint. Today a nice copy of *Catcher* is selling for $7,500. Whether it was a good investment relative to other investments, such as stock or real estate, is certainly questionable, but we wouldn't have made those investments anyway, so it's a moot point for us.

Three things seem clear to us:

1 Two people can buy the same titles over a ten-year period and each accumulate a library of 500 volumes, 50 a year, a book a week on average, and the person who was selective as to edition and condition will have a collection that is worth considerably more than the other, probably at no greater overall cost. It is no secret that very good to fine copies of recent books turn up on antiquarian bookstore shelves, as remainders in new bookstores, or at book sales for a fraction of their published price.

2 We are talking about a relatively long period of time, probably five years at a minimum and probably ten to twenty years, for real growth in value.

3 Collectors can set their own financial limits. They can spend $100 or $100,000 a year or anything in between. They can collect books that few people are currently collecting and are low-priced, or go for the big-name authors and "high spots," where the competition is the keenest and the prices reflect it.

In summary, if you are looking for a good investment for the short term, don't buy books, but if you want to spend a certain amount of money for books, or already spend a certain amount for books every year, we believe that a collection of good books will not only give you pleasure over the years but will also not disappoint you or your heirs when the time comes to sell them.

Investment

Ever since we started collecting first editions we have been asked how many collected authors lose popularity over the years and have been told that first edition collecting is a fad that will fade; that the market is false, the price inflated, and the bubble will burst any day. We've always wondered about these questions and comments ourselves, and so we've tried to find an answer.

From 1938 to 1941 the R. R. Bowker Company of New York published *Trade Prices Current of American First Editions,* which was subtitled "An indexing service for the American rare book trade." The authors included were all those listed in Merle Johnson's *American First Editions,* fourth edition, edited by Jacob Blanck. There were 209 authors included, and to see how many of these authors are still collected, we checked to see how many were still included in this book. The fact is that all but eight of these authors are still collected. The authors not included were:

Ray Stannard Baker (David Grayson)
Charles Egbert Craddock (M. N. Murfree)
Mazo de la Roche
Edgar Fawcett
Morgan Robertson
Susan Rowson
Harriet Prescott Spofford
Henry Van Dyke

At the time, the average price for these eight authors' first books was $4. Some of these authors may not belong on this list, as there may still be interest in their work, but we have not included them to date. Eight out of 209 is less than 4 percent, leaving more than 96 percent of the authors being collected after more than fifty years.

The next question is whether the market prices for these 201 authors have held up over the years. *Trade Prices Current* indexed dealer catalog prices of the authors' books from 1937 to 1941. Given that the prices in this book represent estimates of dealer retail prices, it seemed reasonable to compare the prices for the first books in *Trade Prices Current* to the prices in this book. A complete comparison could not be made, because *Trade Prices Current* did not record any first books for sale during this period for 35 of the authors on the list, but that still left 166 authors, which we believe is a representative sample. The comparison was actually made on 182 books by the 166 authors, because there were sixteen cases where either separate editions of the first book or first and second books were covered by both reference works. The results are as follows:

Adams, Andy. THE LOG OF A COWBOY.	$ 4	$ 300
Ade, George. ARTIE, A STORY . . .	5	100
Aiken, Conrad. EARTH TRIUMPHANT	5	250
Alcott, Louisa May. FLOWER FABLES	10	3,500
Aldrich, T. B. THE BELLS	5	750
Allen, Hervey. WAMPUM . . .	5	125
Allen, James Lane. FLUTE AND VIOLIN	6	60
Anderson, Sherwood. WINDY MCPHERSON'S SON	15	500
Atherton, Gertrude. WHAT DREAMS . . . (Cloth)	57	350
(Wraps)	44	750
Audubon, John J. BIRDS OF NORTH AMERICA (1840–1844)	500	40,000
Austin, Jane G. FAIRY DREAMS . . .	4	150
Austin, Mary. LAND OF LITTLE RAIN	8	500
Bacheller, Irving. MASTER OF SILENCE	5	100
Bancroft, George. POEMS	10	300
Bangs, J. K. THE LORGNETTE	5	500
Beebe, William. TWO BIRD LOVERS . . .	15	1,750
Bellamy, Edward. SIX TO ONE	7	500
Benét, Stephen V. FIVE MEN AND POMPEY	40	250
Benét, William Rose. MERCHANTS FROM CATHAY	10	50
Bierce, Ambrose. FIEND'S DELIGHT (New York)	5	1,000
Bird, Robert Montgomery. CALAVAR	35	500
Boyd, James. DRUMS	2	350
Bradford, G. TYPES OF AMERICAN CHARACTER	14	100
Bradford, Roark. OL' MAN ADAM . . .	7	125

Bromfield, Louis. GREEN BAY TREE	13	350
Buck, Pearl. EAST WIND, WEST WIND	8	400
Bunner, H. C. A WOMAN OF HONOR	5	200
Burgess, Gelett. THE PURPLE COW	38	500
Burroughs, John. NOTES ON WALT WHITMAN . . .	60	1,250
Bynner, Witter. AN ODE TO HARVARD	6	75
Byrne, Donn. STORIES WITHOUT WOMEN	55	100
Cabell, J. B. EAGLE'S SHADOW	16	150
Cable, George W. OLD CREOLE DAYS	30	300
Caldwell, Erskine. THE BASTARD	6	900
Carman, Bliss. LOW TIDE . . . (Toronto)	88	4,500
(New York)	16	500
Cather, Willa. APRIL TWILIGHTS	160	2,500
Chambers, Robert W. IN THE QUARTER	2	750
Churchill, Winston (U.S.). THE CELEBRITY	7	100
Clemens, Samuel L. CELEBRATED JUMPING FROG	230	17,500
Cobb, Irwin. BACK HOME	3	75
Cooke, John Esten. LEATHERSTOCKING AND SILK	35	300
Cooper, James F. PRECAUTION	210	5,000
Crane, Stephen. MAGGIE	225	750
Crapsey, Adelaide. VERSE	6	125
Cummings, E. E. THE ENORMOUS ROOM	8	3,000
Curtis, George Wm. NILE NOTES OF A HOWADJI	3	250
Dana, Richard H. TWO YEARS BEFORE THE MAST	83	5,000
Davis, Richard Harding. GALLEGHER	15	400
Day, Clarence. DECENNIAL RECORD . . .	8	75
Deland, Margaret. THE OLD GARDEN	15	200
Dickinson, Emily. POEMS	92	7,500

Dodge, Mary Mapes. IRVINGTON STORIES	13	250
Dos Passos, John. ONE MAN'S INITIATION (London)	7	1,000
Drake, Joseph Rodman. THE CULPRIT FAY	18	125
Dreiser, Theodore. SISTER CARRIE	150	6,000
Dunbar, Paul L. OAK AND IVY	25	6,000
Dunne, Finley Peter. MR. DOOLEY . . .	3	75
Farrell, James T. YOUNG LONIGAN	10	1,000
Faulkner, William. MARBLE FAUN	43	25,000
SOLDIER'S PAY	9	20,000
Ferber, Edna. DAWN O'HARA	9	125
Ficke, Arthur. THEIR BOOK	20	1,000
FROM THE ISLES	4	400
Field, Eugene. TRIBUNE PRIMER (Brooklyn)	26	7,500
Fisher, Vardis. SONNETS TO . . .	6	350
Fox, John. A CUMBERLAND VENDETTA	5	250
Frederick, Harold. SETH'S BROTHER'S WIFE	16	300
Frost, Robert. A BOY'S WILL	10	7,500
Gale, Zona. ROMANCE ISLAND	6	100
Garland, Hamlin. MAIN-TRAVELLED ROADS	12	400
Glasgow, Ellen. THE DESCENDANT	6	300
Guiney, Louise I. SONGS AT THE START	12	125
Halleck, Fitz-Greene. FANNY	65	1,500
Harris, Joel Chandler. UNCLE REMUS	50	2,500
Harte, Bret. OUTCROPPINGS	5	350
Hawthorne, Nathaniel. FANSHAWE	850	35,000
Hay, John. JIM BLUDSO	18	150
Hearn, Lafcadio. STRAY LEAVES	70	850
Hecht, Ben. HERO OF SANTA MARIA	3	200

Hemingway, Ernest. THREE STORIES . . .	100	25,000
IN OUR TIME	75	22,500
Herbert, Henry W. THE BROTHERS	70	450
Herford, Oliver. ARTFUL ANTICS	25	50
Hergesheimer, Joseph. THE LAY ANTHONY	7	100
Heyward, DuBose. CAROLINA CHANSONS	6	175
SKYLINE AND HORIZONS	2	150
Holmes, Oliver Wendell. POEMS	19	500
Hough, Emerson. THE SINGING MOUSE STORIES	20	125
Hovey, Richard. POEMS	75	1,000
Howells, William Dean. POEMS OF TWO FRIENDS	10	750
LIVES AND SPEECHES OF ABRAHAM LINCOLN . . .	9	500
VENETIAN LIFE . . . (New York)	3	500
Huneker, James. MEZZOTINTS . . .	5	75
Irving, Washington. HISTORY OF NEW YORK	100	1,500
Jackson, H. H. VERSES	4	300
James, Henry. A PASSIONATE PILGRIM	10	2,000
James, Will. COWBOYS NORTH AND SOUTH	4	600
James, William. PRINCIPLES OF PSYCHOLOGY	20	1,750
Janvier, Thomas. COLOR STUDIES	5	200
Jeffers, Robertson. FLAGONS AND APPLES	33	1,500
Jewett, Sarah Orne. DEEPHAVEN	9	750
Johnston, Mary. PRISONER OF HOPE	4	75
Kennedy, John P. SWALLOW BARN	63	1,200
Kent, Rockwell. WILDERNESS	20	600
Kilmer, Joyce. SUMMER OF LOVE	10	350
Lanier, Sidney. TIGER-LILIES	45	500
Lardner, Ring. BIB BALLADS	45	250
Lewis, Sinclair. HIKE AND THE AEROPLANE	95	6,000

Lindsay, Vachel. THE TRAMP'S EXCUSE	100	1,500
London, Jack. SON OF THE WOLF	22	1,500
Longfellow, Henry W. OUTRE-MER	17	3,000
Lowell, Amy. DREAM DROPS (Cloth)	200	3,000
(Wraps)	135	2,250
Lowell, James R. CLASS POEM	63	1,500
MacLeish, Archibald. TOWER OF IVORY	10	200
Markham, Edwin. THE MAN WITH THE HOE		
(San Francisco)	67	400
(New York)	9	100
Marquis, Don. DANNY'S OWN STORY	5	75
Masters, Edgar Lee. A BOOK OF VERSES	12	1,000
McCutcheon, George Barr. GRAUSTARK	30	100
McFee, William. LETTERS FROM AN OCEAN TRAMP	38	200
Melville, Herman. TYPEE . . .	200	10,000
Mencken, H. L. VENTURES INTO VERSE	150	10,000
Millay, Edna St. V. RENASCENSE (Vellum)	1,150	7,500
Mitchell, S. Weir. WONDERFUL STORY		
(Large-paper copy)	35	1,250
(Trade)	10	450
Moody, Wm. Vaughn. THE MASQUE OF JUDGEMENT		
(Limited edition)	6	100
(Trade)	2	50
Nathan, Robert. PETER KINDRED	8	150
Neihardt, John G. DIVINE ENCHANTMENT	18	1,000
Newton, A. Edward. AMENITIES OF BOOK COLLECTING	17	500
Norris, Frank. YVERNELLE	70	2,500
O'Neill, Eugene. THIRST	40	400
Page, Thomas Nelson. IN OLE VIRGINIA	18	175
Parker, Dorothy. MEN I'M NOT MARRIED TO	10	750

Parkman, Francis. THE CALIFORNIA AND OREGON TRAIL	85	20,000
Paulding, James K. THE DIVERTING HISTORY OF . . .	15	600
Porter, Wm. S. (O. Henry). CABBAGES AND KINGS	32	350
Pound, Ezra. A LUME SPENTO	125	60,000
Pyle, Howard. THE MERRY ADVENTURES OF ROBIN HOOD . . . (Leather)	15	1,000
Remington, Frederic. PONY TRACKS	30	1,000
Repplier, Agnes. BOOKS AND MEN	3	100
Riley, James W. THE OLD SWIMMIN' HOLE	175	1,000
Roberts, Eliz. Madox. UNDER THE TREE	4	350
Robinson, Edw. A. THE TORRENT AND THE NIGHT . . .	227	2,500
CHILDREN OF THE . . . (Vellum)	275	2,000
(Trade)	50	750
Robinson, Rowland E. UNCLE 'LISHA'S SHOP	18	75
Roosevelt, Theodore. NAVAL WAR OF 1812	7	1,250
Saltus, Edgar. BALZAC	4	125
Sandburg, Carl. IN RECKLESS ECSTASY	150	8,500
CHICAGO POEMS	8	250
Santayana, George. SONNETS +	11	750
Smith, Thorne. BILTMORE OSWALD	3	100
Steinbeck, John. CUP OF GOLD	30	10,000
Stockton, Frank B. TING-A-LING	26	350
Stribling, T. S. CRUISE OF THE DRY DOCK	15	150
Tabb, John B. POEMS	135	400
Tarkington, Booth. GENTLEMAN FROM INDIANA	27	150
Teasdale, Sara. SONNETS TO DUSE +	25	750
Thompson, David P. ADVENTURES OF TIMOTHY PEACOCK	7	750
Thompson, Maurice. HOOSIER MOSAICS	9	100

Thoreau, H. D. A WEEK ON THE CONCORD AND MERRIMACK RIVERS	40	15,000
Van Loon, H. THE FALL OF THE DUTCH REPUBLIC	3	350
Van Vechten, Carl. MUSIC AFTER THE GREAT WAR	6	100
Wallace, Lew. THE FAIR GOD	6	300
Wescott, Glenway. THE BITTERNS	16	600
Westcott, Edward Noyes. DAVID HARUM	18	75
Wharton, Edith. THE DECORATION OF HOUSES	3	1,500
Whistler, James. WHISTLER VS. RUSKIN	15	600
White, Stewart Edward. THE CLAIM JUMPERS. (Wraps)	16	150
(Cloth)	20	200
White, William Allen. RHYMES . . .	12	150
Whitman, Walt. FRANKLIN EVANS	50	25,000
Whittier, John A. LEGENDS OF NEW ENGLAND	67	350
Wilder, Thornton. THE CABALA	6	400
Wilson, Harry Leon. ZIG ZAG TALES	27	300
Wilson, Woodrow. CONGRESSIONAL GOVERNMENT	17	350
Wolfe, Thomas. LOOK HOMEWARD, ANGEL	25	7,500
Wylie, Elinor. NETS TO CATCH THE WIND	14	250
	$8,944	$509,585

This seems to us to be a fair representation of the average increase in value for these titles and, by extension, for first editions generally over a sixty-year period. The above comparisons show that few authors go completely out of favor and that the prices of first editions have shown steady increases over the years.

We have been asked to compare the increase to normal inflation. We took the Consumer Price Index (all items, 1982–84 = 100) prepared by the U.S. Bureau of Labor Statistics for 1940 = 14, and for 1999 = 166.2, or an increase of 1,189 percent. This would have meant the $8,944 in 1940 would have increased to $106,165 with normal inflation (for what it's worth).

If your only concern is making sure the books you buy go up in value, you probably shouldn't collect books. But if you decide to collect anyway, you should stick with proven winners that have withstood the test of time. There are still no guarantees, but it is doubtful that the major masterpieces in fine condition will fall in value. None of them will be cheap, either. You can make your own list, but books such as Crane's *Red Badge of Courage,* London's *Call of the Wild,* Fitzgerald's *The Great Gatsby,* Faulkner's *The Sound and the Fury,* Steinbeck's *Grapes of Wrath,* Mitchell's *Gone With the Wind,* Huxley's *Brave New World,* Graves's *Goodbye to All That,* Orwell's *1984,* Salinger's *Catcher in the Rye,* Merton's *Seven Storey Mountain,* or Bradbury's *Martian Chronicles* will very probably hold a continuing interest for collectors in the fore-seeable future; if you have a hundred or more of these classics in fine condition in dustwrappers and are tired of them, please call us immediately.

If you don't have much money, you might consider collecting some of the authors first published in the 1970s or early 1980s that you like. If ten years ago you had bought books by the authors whose first books were listed in the first edition of this book and were published in the 1950s or early 1960s, you would find that most have increased in value. It makes sense that it would take ten to twenty-five years for the collectors and critics to agree on the important authors, and that some more recent authors tend to become overvalued because of the success of their first books, but then go down in value when they publish a few bombs.

Who knows whether the trend will continue. In this edition of *Book Collecting* we have included the values as they appeared in the 1986 and 1995 editions as well as the new estimated values for 2000, so that a comparison could be readily made.

The biggest risk would seem to be paying a good deal of money ($200 and up) for relatively recent trade editions. There are some that will be worth these sums, and more, but many of the recent first books may fade in popularity as later works fail to live up to the author's initial performance.

What to Collect

BOOK COLLECTING allows you a wide choice. Most subjects have been covered by a number of authors. If you are interested in the labor movement, farming, espionage, chess, Americana, law, medicine, a foreign country, a state, a county, a city, railroads, wars, the military, artists, westerns, philosophy, sociology, grammar, writing, cooking, animals, cars, general or specific histories, the future, science fiction, utopias, detectives, or slavery, you will find that hundreds if not thousands of novels, poetry, and nonfiction books have been written about the subject. And if you are interested in a nonfiction area, don't overlook the fiction that has been written using the subject as a vehicle, because you will find interesting additions to your knowledge and library. If there is only one book in your life that you really enjoyed, don't overlook the possibility of collecting all the different editions of that book. There are really interesting collections of *The Rubaiyat, The Compleat Angler,* and other classics.

If you've found a subject or author that interests you, the next decision is which edition to collect. You could decide to collect paperback editions because you have little money and the cover art interests you, or

- hardback editions with dustwrappers, but not necessarily first editions
- first editions without dustwrappers
- first editions with dustwrappers
- hardback editions signed by the author
- all first editions in English, including American, British, Canadian, Australian, etc.
- All editions of an author's work, including reprints, foreign editions, and specially illustrated editions

As you can see, there are many avenues, and you should give some consideration to choices before starting, although it is likely that you will modify your initial decision as your collection grows.

First Editions

A first edition is the first printing of a book. It's true that a first edition may have one or more printings and that a second edition will normally be noted only if there are actual changes, usually major, in the text. But for a collector, a first printing is the only true first edition.

Within the first printing there can be differences that make the earlier books in the printing more valuable than the later books in the same printing. These differences are identified by "points," which are discussed elsewhere.

If it's difficult to explain book collecting in general, the reason for collecting first editions is even more difficult to explain to those who are not afflicted with the mania. Bob Wilson, in his book *Modern Book Collecting,* deals with the question when he comments on book collecting in general:

> A great many people over a great number of decades, have written pamphlets, whole books even, to justify the collecting of books. This seems to me to be an unnecessary exercise. If you are predisposed to collect books, you don't need any *ex post facto* justification for having done so. And on the other hand, if you are not convinced before you start, the chances are that no argument is going to win you over.

Now, we believe there is a little more logic and reason in book collecting than this, but Wilson's argument is not without merit. At any rate, for a collector, the first edition/first printing is the most desirable. It's the edition the author actually saw through production and the closest in time to the writing, and therefore the edition most likely to represent the author's intent. This may seem a minor point, but one has only to read Ray Bradbury's Afterword to a later edition of his book *Fahrenheit 451* to become aware of what can happen to later printings or editions.

> Some five years back, the editors of yet another anthology for school readers put together a volume with 400 (count 'em) short stories in it. How do you cram 400 short stories by Twain, Irving, Poe . . . into one book?
>
> Simplicity itself. Skin, debone, demarrow, scarify, melt, render down and destroy. . . .

Every story, slenderized, starved, blue-penciled, leeched and bled white, resembled every other story . . .

Only six weeks ago, I discovered that, over the years, some cubbyhole editors at Ballantine Books, fearful of contaminating the young, had, bit by bit, censored some 75 separate sections from the novel. . . .

All you umpires, back to the bleachers. Referees, hit the showers It's my game, I pitch, I hit, I catch, I run the bases. . . .

And no one can help me. Not even you.

I can only assume that many first-edition collectors do not want to take a chance with their favorite authors.

First editions are normally identified by publishers. Each publisher has its own method of identification. Many publishers have changed their method of identification over the years; a few have been so inconsistent that one has to resort to individual author bibliographies to be sure one has the true first.

For information on how to identify first editions by publisher, turn to Appendix E. At present we are aware of only two books on the market (other than this one) that include a list of publishers and how each identifies first editions. They are *First Editions: A Guide to Identification,* edited by Edward N. Zempel and Linda A. Verkley (The Spoon River Press, 2319C West Rohmann Avenue, Peoria, IL 61604); and *A Pocket Guide to the Identification of First Editions,* by Bill McBride (585 Prospect Avenue, West Hartford, CT 06105). In addition, *Firsts* magazine includes in its issues a collector's guide to publishers, as well as bibliographic checklists of collected authors with price estimates in many cases. This magazine is a must for collectors (*Firsts: The Book Collector's Magazine,* 4493 N. Camino Gacela, Tucson, AZ 85718).

Proofs and Advance Review Copies

The publication date of a book is normally set sufficiently far after the printing to allow the publisher to distribute copies of the book to reviewers, bookstore owners, store managers, and others, and to actually ship an initial order to bookstores so that the book will be available to customers when the reviews appear.

Prior to the trade edition and the limited edition, if one is published, a book will take different forms. The most common forms that become available on the first edition market are galley proofs, uncorrected proofs, advance reading copies, and the normal trade edition with evidence that the particular book has been sent out in advance. The latter would usually contain a slip of paper or letter from the publisher stating that the copy is sent for advance review, or perhaps a publication date stamped on one of the preliminary pages.

As discussed previously, a first-edition collector is always anxious to obtain the first issue within the first printing; therefore, it should come as no surprise that proofs or advance review copies of the first printing are also collected and bring a premium.

It is difficult to place a value on these "prepublication" copies, because there does not seem to be any consistent formula, but generally we find that trade editions containing advance review slips or other advance publication evidence will sell for perhaps 50 percent more than the regular trade edition; the advance review/reading copies in paperwraps will sell for twice the trade value; the uncorrected proofs (also in paperwraps but with "uncorrected" indicated) for somewhat more than the advance review copies; and the galley proofs (normally on long sheets either bound or unbound) would be the most highly valued, although this form has been rarely used in recent years.

The recent "galleys," run off on copiers, are so easily duplicated that we don't feel they have much monetary value above duplication cost, but this is a personal view; and we must admit that they will prove very valuable to researchers, as they do contain numerous errors and other passages that are later corrected. This is an important consideration in forming a collection. If you are interested in the evolution of a writer's thoughts, the page proofs and uncorrected proofs could prove very useful. If the collection is being formed with the thought in mind of eventual donation to a library, we believe the proofs should be included if at all possible. The number of proof copies actually produced is normally relatively low, 50 to 500 copies, and if eventual scarcity is a determinant of future value, a proof that was printed in an edition of 200 copies (and is very fragile by nature) will certainly have more value than the first trade printing, which for popular authors can run from 75,000 to 800,000 copies. Some recent examples are Tom Clancy's *Debt of Honor* (2,000,000 copies), James Clavell's *Whirlwind* (850,000 copies), Norman Mailer's *Harlot's Ghost* (186,000 copies), and Tim O'Brien's *In the Lake of the Woods* (75,000 copies).

It should be noted that many publishers do not bother with paperbound proofs and only send out copies of the trade edition with review slips.

One example of a limited proof is James Clavell's *Noble House*. We understand the publisher photocopied four copies on one side of the page only, and then sixteen copies on both sides of the page. These copies were put in large three-ring binders, but after assembling twenty copies the publisher stopped. We assume they changed to sending out copies of the regular trade edition with review slips. We believe we know why they changed, as we handled one of the sixteen copies. It was about three inches thick and very unwieldy.

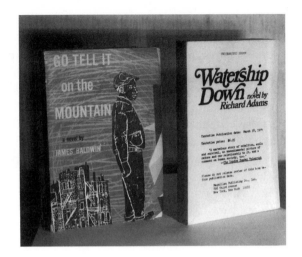

Shown above are two prepublication copies. On the left is a proof of James Baldwin's first book, which is of special interest because the cover differs from the one finally selected for the book (the first trade edition is shown on page 129), and on the right is an uncorrected proof of the first American edition of Adams's *Watership Down* (the true first edition is the English edition).

Limited Editions

The limited edition comes in varying forms, as discussed below. A limited edition of a new book is usually signed, numbered, and in a slipcase and costs three to five times the cost of the regular first edition, which is referred to as the trade, or first trade, edition. The first printing of the trade edition is still considered the first edition, so the collector must decide if both the limited signed and the first trade are required or if only one is necessary for the collection.

Limited editions of 200 copies are usually still available when one has a hard time finding fine copies of first trade editions from the same period that were published in an edition of 5,000 copies. This is because there is an aversion to throwing away a book signed and numbered by an author, even if one has never heard of the author, but no aversion at all to throwing away novels, poetry, drama, detective stories, medical books, and scientific books by an author one has never heard of.

Limited Editions Club (LEC). George Macy started the LEC in 1929. The books were printed on good paper and bound in various interesting and attractive covers, illustrated and signed by famous artists of the period, numbered and limited to 1,500 copies (later 2,000). The books were issued in boxes or slipcases. They're very attractive and actually easy to read. The LEC issued one book a month until recent years, when it changed hands a number of times (it is currently issuing books at a cost of $400 and up per volume). If we look at the total output, we find that one or two titles a year have gone up significantly in price and the balance can be purchased at reasonable prices, particularly at auction.

If you are interested in well-bound illustrated books, you should not overlook the LEC.

Heritage Press. These editions are not limited, but are mentioned because the Heritage Press was an offshoot of the LEC. It produced the trade edition, so to speak. The Heritage editions were printed on good paper, nicely bound, and issued in slipcases. They contained the same illustrations as the comparable LEC editions but were not signed or limited. We believe you can still subscribe to the Heritage Press (for under $25 a volume) and buy most of the earlier editions in the series in used bookstores in the $5 to $25 range. If you like the classics in a very readable form, attractively bound, and at reasonable price, it would be hard to go wrong collecting these editions, although it must be remembered they are reprints.

Franklin Press. The Franklin Mint is a truly interesting phenomenon. Franklin publishes leather-bound "limited editions." What we find interesting is that they publish literary titles and seem to have a bigger clientele than all the specialist literary bookdealers in the country combined. The publishers do not usually disclose the quantities printed, but a John Updike bibliography included a quantity of 12,600 for a reprint of *Rabbit, Run* in 1977, and Ray Bradbury informed a collector that he had signed about 13,000 sheets for *Death Is a Lonely Business* in 1985.

When the Franklin Press started advertising its Pulitzer Prize editions of fiction, a friend asked for advice on whether to purchase them. We told him that for less money he could probably buy first editions, in very good condition, of not only the fiction but also the poetry and drama winners. He bought around 150 titles and it probably didn't cost him $4,000. A nice copy of only one of the books he bought (*Gone With the Wind*) would probably sell for $6,000.

Another publisher bringing out leather-bound editions along the same lines as Franklin is the Easton Press.

Trade Book Publishers. When an author becomes popular, the publisher may decide to issue a signed, numbered limited edition. This edition is usually 300 copies, plus or minus 50, but can be as few as 100 copies or as many as 1,000 copies. These books are normally composed of the first trade edition sheets bound up in a binding different from the trade edition binding and in a slipcase. Most people are very happy with the trade edition. But if you think that Patrick O'Brian is an important writer, and you could buy one of 200 signed and numbered copies of the U.S. edition of *The Commodore* for $125, versus a copy of the trade edition at $25, we'd advise you to buy the signed limited, which is currently selling for $200 or more. Of course, if the choice is between a first edition and a second printing for the same price, always buy the first edition.

Private Press Publishers. When an author becomes popular with book collectors, there are a number of small presses that will publish signed limited editions of his or her work. Sometimes it is new material that has not been published before, or it may be a short story, novella, or poetry that appeared previously in magazine or short-story anthologies, and its publication by the press is considered the first separate edition or publication. These present real problems for the collector, because these books may come out in different states, for example:

10 signed and numbered copies for presentation
26 signed and lettered copies
300 signed and numbered copies
700 hardbound (not signed) copies
1,000 paperbound copies

All of the above are legitimate first editions, usually printed on the same paper at the same time, only bound differently, and in the case of the first three, with an extra leaf with the limitation and signature. If you must have one of each, you can see the problem and expense involved. If the author continues to remain popular, the prices would probably rise proportionally; thus, if one of the twenty-six copies sold at $100 and one of the three hundred copies at $50, their respective values in the future might be $200 and $100.

Fine Press Books. These are also private presses, similar to the last category, but concentrating more on the classics and on the quality of the paper, binding, and illustrations. Their books often contain the signed work of an artist of note. We have made them a separate group because there is significant difference in the published price of these books, usually ranging from $200 to $2,000, but sometimes significantly higher.

Paperbacks or Paperwraps

The bindings of most books published in this century vary from paper covers weighing only slightly more than the pages of the book (paperwraps) to stiffer, heavier paper covers that are flexible (stiff paperwraps) to completely stiff paper covers (boards), and finally to cloth and/or leather-bound covers. Recent books in paperwraps are normally published after the original edition and are not particularly valuable in the first-edition market; however, if the paper edition contains a new introduction, or some major changes in the text, the value could approach that of the regular first edition.

It should be noted that the first printings of these paper reprint editions have found a market of their own, which operates separately from the hardback market. This market is very interested in the cover art as well as the content. There are paperback price guides covering practically all of the field available at local new book stores.

In some cases the paper edition is the true first edition, because no hardback edition was published. We had thought this might become more common in the future as publishing costs continue to increase, but we have been told by our copyeditor (and she seems to be correct) that publishers experimented in the eighties but found they could make more money doing the hardback edition first. One can pick up these paperback first editions cheaply if the seller thinks they are reprints. There was also a move to print the same sheets and bind some in hardback and some in paperwraps. This was done in the seventies and stopped for the same reason. Publishers could make more money selling the hardback. At this time, the standard practice is to discount the hardback best-selling titles heavily, at 40 percent off, while at the same time increasing the cover price of the paperbacks; this makes the hardbacks, for these titles at least, a bargain.

Literary Prize Winners

Some collectors center their collecting on categories of major prize winners: the Booker, Caldecott, Edgar, Hugo, National Book, Nebula, Newbery, PEN/Faulkner, Pulitzer prizes, or on lists of high spots compiled by knowledgeable authors, such as the Connolly 100, Queen's Quorum, and on and on. The following are some of these award winners, the years the awards were won, and the books for which they won. A more comprehensive list of literary awards, in some cases with the runners-up or short-listed authors, was published by Charlene Coffield in 1998. The title is *Notable Literary Awards for Fiction* and is available from her at 1401 Emerald Circle, Southlake, TX 76092. In addition, the American Library Association Web site (ALA.Org) has links to many of the award sites. Also see www.bookwire.com/index/ book~awards.html.

Note that we have listed the books in the year of publication, although in most cases the prizes were awarded the next year (i.e., the 1992 Hugo Award is for the Best Novel Published in 1991).

THE BOOKER PRIZE

The award annually honors the best literature in the British Commonwealth.

1969: P. H. Newby. SOMETHING TO ANSWER FOR
1970: Bernice Rubens. THE ELECTED MEMBER
1971: V. S. Naipaul. IN A FREE STATE
1972: John Berger. G
1973: J. G. Farrell. SIEGE OF KRISHNAPUR
1974 (tie): Nadine Gordimer. THE CONSERVATIONIST
Stanley Middleton. HOLIDAY
1975: Ruth Prawer Jhabvala. HEAT AND DUST
1976: David Storey. SAVILLE
1977: Paul Scott. STAYING ON
1978: Iris Murdoch. THE SEA, THE SEA
1979: Penelope Fitzgerald. OFFSHORE
1980: William Golding. RITES OF PASSAGE
1981: Salman Rushdie. MIDNIGHT'S CHILDREN
1982: Thomas Keneally. SCHINDLER'S ARK
1983: J. M. Coetzee. LIFE AND TIMES OF THOMAS K
1984: Anita Brookner. HOTEL DU LAC
1985: Keri Hulme. THE BONE PEOPLE
1986: Kingsley Amis. THE OLD DEVILS
1987: Penelope Lively. MOON TIGER
1988: Peter Carey. OSCAR AND LUCINDA
1989: Kazuo Ishiguro. THE REMAINS OF THE DAY
1990: A. S. Byatt. POSSESSION
1991: Ben Okri. THE FAMISHED ROAD
1992 (tie): Michael Ondaatje. THE ENGLISH PATIENT
Barry Unsworth. SACRED HUNGER
1993: Roddy Doyle. PADDY CLARKE HA HA HA
1994: James Kelman. HOW LATE IT WAS, HOW LATE
1995: Pat Barker. THE GHOST ROAD
1996: Graham Swift. LAST ORDER
1997: Arundhati Roy. THE GOD OF SMALL THINGS
1998: Ian McEwan. AMSTERDAM

1999: _____

2000: _____

2001: _____

2002: _____

2003: _____

THE CALDECOTT MEDAL

The Caldecott Medal is awarded annually by the Association for Library Service to Children (a division of the American Library Association) for the most distinguished picture book for children. The award was named in honor of Randolph Caldecott, a nineteenth-century illustrator whose work is still delighting children.

1938: Helen Dean Fish. ANIMALS OF THE BIBLE
Illustrated by Dorothy P. Lathrop
1939: Thomas Handforth. MEI LI
1940: Ingri and Edgar Parin. ABRAHAM LINCOLN
1941: Robert Lawson. THEY WERE STRONG AND GOOD
1942: Robert McCloskey. MAKE WAY FOR DUCKLINGS
1943: Virginia Lee Burton. THE LITTLE HOUSE
1944: James Thurber. MANY MOONS
Illustrated by Louis Slobodkin
1945: Rachel Field. PRAYER FOR A CHILD
Illustrated by Elizabeth Orton Jones
1946: THE ROOSTER CROWS . . . (Traditional Mother Goose)
Illustrated by Maud and Miska Petersham
1947: Golden MacDonald. THE LITTLE ISLAND
Illustrated by Leonard Weisgard
1948: Alvin Tresselt. WHITE SNOW, BRIGHT SNOW
Illustrated by Roger Duvoisin
1949: Berta and Elmer Hader. THE BIG SNOW
1950: Leo Politi. SONG OF THE SWALLOWS
1951: Katherine Milhous. THE EGG TREE
1952: Will Lipkind. FINDERS KEEPERS
Illustrated by Nicolas Mordvinoff
1953: Lynd Ward. THE BIGGEST BEAR
1954: Ludwig Bemelmans. MADELINE'S RESCUE
1955: Charles Perrault (translator). CINDERELLA,
OR THE LITTLE GLASS SLIPPER. Illustrated by Marcia Brown
1956: John Langstaff. FROG WENT A-COURTIN'
Illustrated by Feodor Rojankovsky
1957: Janice May Udry. A TREE IS NICE
Illustrated by Marc Simont
1958: Robert McCloskey. TIME OF WONDER
1959: CHANTICLEER AND THE FOX. Adapted from Chaucer
and illustrated by Barbara Cooney
1960: Marie Hall Ets and Aurora Labastida. NINE DAYS TO CHRISTMAS
Illustrated by Marie Hall Ets

1961: Ruth Robbins. BABOUSHKA AND THE THREE KINGS
Illustrated by Nicolas Sidjakov
1962: Marcia Brown. ONCE A MOUSE . . .
1963: Ezra Jack Keats. THE SNOWY DAY
1964: Maurice Sendak. WHERE THE WILD THINGS ARE
1965: Beatrice Schenk de Regniers. MAY I BRING A FRIEND?
Illustrated by Beni Montresor
1966: Sorche Nic Leodhas. ALWAYS ROOM FOR ONE MORE
Illustrated by Nonny Hogrogian
1967: Evaline Ness. SAM, BANGS & MOONSHINE
1968: Barbara Emberley. DRUMMER HOFF
Illustrated by Ed Emberley
1969: Arthur Ransome. THE FOOL OF THE WORLD AND THE FLYING SHIP
Illustrated by Uri Schulevitz
1970: William Steig. SYLVESTER AND THE MAGIC PEBBLE
1971: Gail E. Haley. A STORY—A STORY
1972: Nonny Hogrogian. ONE FINE DAY
1973: Ariene Mosel. THE FUNNY LITTLE WOMAN
Illustrated by Blair Lent
1974: Harve Zemach. DUFFY & THE DEVIL
Illustrated by Margot Zemach
1975: Gerald McDermott. ARROW TO THE SUN
1976: Verna Aardema. WHY MOSQUITOES BUZZ IN PEOPLE'S EARS
Illustrated by Leo Dillon
1977: Margaret Musgrove. ASHANTI TO ZULU
Illustrated by Leo and Diane Dillon
1978: Peter Spier. NOAH'S ARK
1979: Paul Goble. THE GIRL WHO LOVED HORSES
1980: Donald Hall. OX-CART MAN
1981: Arnold Lobel. FABLES
1982: Chris Van Allsburg. JUMANJI
1983: Blaise Cendrar. SHADOW
Illustrated by Marcia Brown
1984: Alice and Martin Provenson. THE GLORIOUS FLIGHT:
ACROSS THE CHANNEL WITH LOUIS BLÉRIOT
1985: Margaret Hodges. SAINT GEORGE AND THE DRAGON
Illustrated by Trina Schart Hyman
1986: Chris Van Allsburg. POLAR EXPRESS
1987: Arthur Yorinks. HEY, AL
Illustrated by Richard Egielski
1988: Jane Yolen. OWL MOON
Illustrated by John Schoenherr

1989: Stephen Gammell. SONG AND DANCE MAN
1990: Ed Young. LON PO PO
1991: David Macauley. BLACK AND WHITE
1992: David Weisner. TUESDAY
1993: Emily McCully. MIRETTE ON HIGH WIRE
1994: Allen Say. GRANDFATHER'S JOURNEY
1995: Eve Bunting. SMOKY NIGHT
Illustrated by David Diaz
1996: Peggy Rathmann. OFFICER BUCKLE AND GLORIA
1997: David Wisniewski. GOLEM
1998: Paul O. Zelinsky. RAPUNZEL
1999: Jacqueline Briggs Martin. SNOWFLAKE BENTLEY
Illustrated by Mary Azarian

2000: _____

2001: _____

2002: _____

2003: _____

THE EDGAR

The Edgar is an annual award named in honor of Edgar Allan Poe.

The Edgar for Best (Mystery) Novel

1954: Charlotte Jay. BEAT THE BONES
1955: Raymond Chandler. THE LONG GOODBYE
1956: Margaret Millar. BEAST IN VIEW
1957: Charlotte Armstrong. A DRAM OF POISON
1958: Ed Lacy. ROOM TO SWING
1959: Stanley Ellin. THE EIGHTH CIRCLE
1960: Celia Fremlin. THE HOURS BEFORE DAWN
1961: Julian Symons. THE PROGRESS OF A CRIME
1962: J. J. Marric. GIDEON'S FIRE
1963: Ellis Peters. DEATH AND THE JOYFUL WOMAN
1964: Eric Ambler. THE LIGHT OF DAY
1965: John le Carré. THE SPY WHO CAME IN FROM THE COLD
1966: Adam Hall. THE QUILLER MEMORANDUM
1967: Nicolas Freeling. KING OF THE RAINY COUNTRY
1968: Donald E. Westlake. GOD SAVE THE MARK
1969: Jeffrey Hudson. A CASE OF NEED
1970: Dick Francis. FORFEIT
1971: Maj Sjöwall and Per Wahlöö. THE LAUGHING POLICEMAN

1972: Frederick Forsyth. THE DAY OF THE JACKAL
1973: Warren Kiefer. THE LINGALA CODE
1974: Tony Hillerman. DANCE HALL OF THE DEAD
1975: Jon Cleary. PETER'S PENCE
1976: Brian Garfield. HOPSCOTCH
1977: Robert B. Parker. PROMISED LAND
1978: William Hallahan. CATCH ME KILL ME
1979: Ken Follett. THE EYE OF THE NEEDLE
1980: Arthur Maling. THE RHEINGOLD ROUTE
1981: Dick Francis. WHIP HAND
1982: William Bayer. PEREGRINE
1983: Rick Boyer. BILLINGSGATE SHOAL
1984: Elmore Leonard. LA BRAVA
1985: Ross Thomas. BRIARPATCH
1986: L. R. Wright. THE SUSPECT
1987: Barbara Vine (Ruth Rendell). DARK-ADAPTED EYE
1988: Aaron Elkins. OLD BONES
1989: Stuart M. Kaminsky. A COLD RED SUNRISE
1990: James Lee Burke. BLACK CHERRY BLUES
1991: Julie Smith. NEW ORLEANS MOURNING
1992: Lawrence Block. A DANCE AT THE SLAUGHTERHOUSE
1993: Margaret Maron. BOOTLEGGER'S DAUGHTER
1994: Minette Walters. THE SCULPTRESS
1995: Mary Willis Walker. THE RED SCREAM
1996: Dick Francis. COME TO GRIEF
1997: Thomas H. Cook. THE CHATHAM SCHOOL AFFAIR
1998: James Lee Burke. CIMARRON ROSE

1999: _____

2000: _____

2001: _____

2002: _____

2003: _____

The Edgar for Best First (Mystery) Novel

1946: Julius Fast. WATCHFUL AT NIGHT
1947: Helen Eustis. THE HORIZONTAL MAN
1948: Fredric Brown. THE FABULOUS CLIPJOINT
1949: Mildred Davis. THE ROOM UPSTAIRS
1950: Alan Green. WHAT A BODY!

1951: Thomas Walsh. NIGHTMARE IN MANHATTAN

1952: Mary McMullen. STRANGLE HOLD

1953: William Campbell Gault. DON'T CRY FOR ME

1954: Ira Levin. A KISS BEFORE DYING

1955: Jean Potts. GO, LOVELY ROSE

1956: Lane Kauffman. THE PERFECTIONIST

1957: Donald McNutt Douglass. REBECCA'S PRIDE

1958: William Rawle Weeks. KNOCK AND WAIT

1959: Richard Martin Stern. THE BRIGHT ROAD TO FEAR

1960: Henry Sleasar. THE GREY FLANNEL SHROUD

1961: John Holbrook Vance. THE MAN IN THE CAGE

1962: Suzanne Blanc. THE GREEN STONE

1963: Robert L. Fish. THE FUGITIVE

1964: Cornelius Hirschberg. THE FLORENTINE FINISH

1965: Harry Kemelman. FRIDAY THE RABBI SLEPT LATE

1966: John Ball. IN THE HEAT OF THE NIGHT

1967: Ross Thomas. THE COLD WAR SWAP

1968: Michael Collins. ACT OF FEAR

1969 (tie): E. Richard Johnson. SILVER STREET

Dorothy Uhnak. THE BAIT

1970: Joe Gores. A TIME OF PREDATORS

1971: Lawrence Sanders. THE ANDERSON TAPES

1972: A. H. Z. Carr. FINDING MAUBEE

1973: R. H. Shimer. SQUAW POINT

1974: Paul E. Erdman. THE BILLION DOLLAR SURE THING

1975: Gregory McDonald. FLETCH

1976: Rex Burns. THE ALVAREZ JOURNAL

1977: James Patterson. THE THOMAS BERRYMAN NUMBER

1978: Robert Ross. A FRENCH FINISH

1979: William L. DeAndrea. KILLED IN THE RATINGS

1980: Richard North Patterson. THE LASKO TANGENT

1981: Kay Nolte Smith. THE WATCHER

1982: Stuart Woods. CHIEFS

1983: Thomas Perry. THE BUTCHER'S BOY

1984: Will Harriss. THE BAY PSALM BOOK MURDER

1985: R. D. Rosen. STRIKE THREE, YOU'RE DEAD

1986: Jonathan Kellerman. WHEN THE BOUGH BREAKS

1987: Larry Beinhart. NO ONE RIDES FOR FREE

1988: Deidre Laiken. DEATH AMONG STRANGERS

1989: David Stout. CAROLINA SKELETONS

1990: Susan Wolfe. THE LAST BILLABLE HOUR

1991: Patricia Daniels Cornwell. POSTMORTEM

1992: Peter Blauner. SLOW MOTION RIOT
1993: Michael Connelly. THE BLACK ECHO
1994: Laurie King. A GRAVE TALENT
1995: George Dawes Green. THE CAVEMAN'S VALENTINE
1996: David Housewright. PENANCE
1997: John Morgan Wilson. SIMPLE JUSTICE
1998: Joseph Kanon. LOS ALAMOS

1999: _____

2000: _____

2001: _____

2002: _____

2003: _____

THE HUGO AWARD FOR BEST SCIENCE FICTION ACHIEVEMENT

The Hugo was named in honor of Hugo Gernsback, the founder of the first professional science-fiction magazine. The winner is chosen by a mail vote by the attending and supporting members of each World Science Fiction Convention.

1953: Alfred Bester. THE DEMOLISHED MAN
1954: No award
1955: Frank Riley and Mark Clifton. THEY'D RATHER BE RIGHT
1956: Robert A. Heinlein. DOUBLE STAR
1957: No award
1958: Fritz Leiber. THE BIG TIME
1959: James Blish. A CASE OF CONSCIENCE
1960: Robert A. Heinlein. STARSHIP TROOPERS
1961: Walter M. Miller, Jr. A CANTICLE FOR LEIBOWITZ
1962: Robert A. Heinlein. STRANGER IN A STRANGE LAND
1963: Philip K. Dick. THE MAN IN THE HIGH CASTLE
1964: Clifford D. Simak. WAY STATION
1965: Fritz Leiber. THE WANDERER
1966: (tie) Roger Zelazny. THE DREAM MASTER
Frank Herbert. DUNE
1967: Robert A. Heinlein. THE MOON IS A HARSH MISTRESS
1968: Roger Zelazny. LORD OF LIGHT
1969: John Brunner. STAND ON ZANZIBAR
1970: Ursula K. Le Guin. THE LEFT HAND OF DARKNESS
1971: Larry Niven. RINGWORLD

1972: Philip José Farmer. TO YOUR SCATTERED BODIES GO
1973: Isaac Asimov. THE GODS THEMSELVES
1974: Arthur C. Clarke. RENDEZVOUS WITH RAMA
1975: Ursula K. Le Guin. THE DISPOSSESSED
1976: Joe Haldeman. THE FOREVER WAR
1977: Kate Wilhelm. WHERE THE SWEET BIRDS SANG
1978: Frederik Pohl. GATEWAY
1979: Vonda N. McIntyre. DREAMSNAKE
1980: Arthur C. Clarke. THE FOUNTAINS OF PARADISE
1981: Joan D. Vinge. THE SNOW QUEEN
1982: C. J. Cherryh. DOWNBELOW STATION
1983: Isaac Asimov. FOUNDATION'S EDGE
1984: David Brin. STARTIDE RISING
1985: William Gibson. NEUROMANCER
1986: Orson Scott Card. ENDER'S GAME
1987: Orson Scott Card. SPEAKER FOR THE DEAD
1988: David Brin. THE UPLIFT WAR
1989: C. J. Cherryh. CYTEEN
1990: Dan Simmons. HYPERION
1991: Lois McMaster Bujold. THE VOR GAME
1992: Lois McMaster Bujold. BARRAYAR
1993 (tie): Vernor Vinge. A FIRE UPON THE DEEP
Connie Willis. THE DOOMSDAY BOOK
1994: Kim Stanley Robinson. GREEN MARS
1995: Lois McMaster Bujold. MIRROR DANCE
1996: Neal Stephenson. THE DIAMOND AGE
1997: Kim Stanley Robinson. BLUE MARS
1998: Joe Haldeman. FOREVER PEACE
1999: Connie Willis. TO SAY NOTHING OF THE DOG

2000: _____

2001: _____

2002: _____

2003: _____

THE NATIONAL BOOK AWARD

An annual award ($10,000) given by the National Book Foundation for best fiction.

1950: Nelson Algren. THE MAN WITH THE GOLDEN ARM
1951: William Faulkner. THE COLLECTED STORIES

1952: James Jones. FROM HERE TO ETERNITY
1953: Ralph Ellison. INVISIBLE MAN
1954: Saul Bellow. THE ADVENTURES OF AUGIE MARCH
1955: William Faulkner. A FABLE
1956: John O'Hara. TEN NORTH FREDERICK
1957: Wright Morris. THE FIELD OF VISION
1958: John Cheever. THE WAPSHOT CHRONICLE
1959: Bernard Malamud. THE MAGIC BARREL
1960: Philip Roth. GOODBYE, COLUMBUS
1961: Conrad Richter. THE WATERS OF KRONOS
1962: Walker Percy. THE MOVIEGOER
1963: J. F. Powers. MORTE D'URBAN
1964: John Updike. THE CENTAUR
1965: Saul Bellow. HERZOG
1966: Katherine Anne Porter. THE COLLECTED STORIES
1967: Bernard Malamud. THE FIXER
1968: Thornton Wilder. THE EIGHTH DAY
1969: Jerzy Kosinski. STEPS
1970: Joyce Carol Oates. THEM
1971: Saul Bellow. MR. SAMMLER'S PLANET
1972: Flannery O'Connor. THE COMPLETE STORIES
1973 (tie): John Barth. CHIMERA
John Williams. AUGUSTUS
1974 (tie): Thomas Pynchon. GRAVITY'S RAINBOW
Isaac Bashevis Singer. A CROWN OF FEATHERS
1975 (tie): Robert Stone. DOG SOLDIERS
Thomas Williams. THE HAIR OF HAROLD ROUX
1976: William Gaddis. JR
1977: Wallace Stegner. THE SPECTATOR BIRD
1978: Mary Lee Settle. BLOOD TIES
1979: Tim O'Brien. GOING AFTER CACCIATO
1980: John Irving. THE WORLD ACCORDING TO GARP
1981: Wright Morris. PLAINS SONG
1982: John Updike. RABBIT IS RICH
1983: Alice Walker. THE COLOR PURPLE
1984: Ellen Gilchrist. VICTORY OVER JAPAN
1985: Don DeLillo. WHITE NOISE
1986: E. L. Doctorow. WORLD'S FAIR
1987: Larry Heinemann. PACO'S STORY
1988: Pete Dexter. PARIS TROUT
1989: John Casey. SPARTINA
1990: Charles Johnson. MIDDLE PASSAGE

1991: Norman Rush. MATING
1992: Cormac McCarthy. ALL THE PRETTY HORSES
1993: E. Annie Proulx. THE SHIPPING NEWS
1994: William Gaddis. A FROLIC OF HIS OWN
1995: Philip Roth. SABBATH'S THEATER
1996: Andrea Barrett. SHIP FEVER AND OTHER STORIES
1997: Charles Frazier. COLD MOUNTAIN
1998: Alice McDermott. CHARMING BILLY

1999: _____

2000: _____

2001: _____

2002: _____

2003: _____

THE NEBULA AWARD

The Nebula is awarded annually by the Science Fiction Writers of America (SFWA).

1966: Frank Herbert. DUNE
1967 (tie): Samuel R. Delany. BABEL-17
Daniel Keyes. FLOWERS FOR ALGERNON
1968: Samuel R. Delany. THE EINSTEIN INTERSECTION
1969: Alexei Panshin. RITE OF PASSAGE
1970: Ursula K. Le Guin. THE LEFT HAND OF DARKNESS
1971: Larry Niven. RINGWORLD
1972: Robert Silverberg. A TIME OF CHANGES
1973: Isaac Asimov. THE GODS THEMSELVES
1974: Arthur C. Clarke. RENDEZVOUS WITH RAMA
1975: Ursula K. Le Guin. THE DISPOSSESSED
1976: Joe Haldeman. THE FOREVER WAR
1977: Frederik Pohl. MAN PLUS
1978: Frederik Pohl. GATEWAY
1979: Vonda N. McIntyre. DREAMSNAKE
1980: Arthur C. Clarke. THE FOUNTAINS OF PARADISE
1981: Gregory Benford. TIMESCAPE
1982: Gene Wolfe. THE CLAW OF THE CONCILIATOR
1983: Michael Bishop. NO ENEMY BUT TIME
1984: David Brin. STARTIDE RISING
1985: William Gibson. NEUROMANCER

1986: Orson Scott Card. ENDER'S GAME
1987: Orson Scott Card. SPEAKER FOR THE DEAD
1988: Pat Murphy. THE FALLING WOMAN
1989: Lois McMaster Bujold. FALLING FREE
1990: Elizabeth Ann Scarborough. THE HEALER'S WAR
1991: Ursula K. Le Guin. THE LAST BOOK OF EARTHSEA
1992: Michael Swanwick. STATIONS OF THE TIDE
1993: Connie Willis. THE DOOMSDAY BOOK
1994: Kim Staney Robinson. RED MARS
1995: Greg Bear. MOVING MARS
1996: Robert J. Sawyer. THE TERMINAL EXPERIMENT
1997: Nicola Griffith. SLOW RIVER
1998: Vonda N. McIntyre. THE MOON AND THE SUN
1999: Joe Haldeman. FOREVER PEACE

2000: _____

2001: _____

2002: _____

2003: _____

THE NEWBERY MEDAL

The Newbery is awarded annually by the Association for Library Service to Children (a division of the American Library Association) to the author of the most distinguished contribution to American literature for children. It is named for eighteenth-century British bookseller John Newbery.

1923: Hugh Lofting. THE VOYAGES OF DOCTOR DOLITTLE
1924: Charles Hawes. THE DARK FRIGATE
1925: Charles Finger. TALES FROM SILVER LANDS
1926: Arthur Bowie Chrisman. SHEN OF THE SEA
1927: Will James. SMOKY, THE COWHORSE
1928: Dhan Gopal Mukerji. GAYNECK, THE STORY OF A PIGEON
1929: Eric P. Kelley. THE TRUMPETER
1930: Rachel Field. HITTY, HER FIRST HUNDRED YEARS
1931: Elizabeth Coatsworth. THE CAT WHO WENT TO HEAVEN
1932: Laura Adams Armer. WATERLESS MOUNTAIN
1933: Elizabeth Foreman Lewis. YOUNG FU OF THE UPPER YANGTZE
1934: Cornelia Meigs. INVINCIBLE LOUISA
1935: Monica Shannon. DOBRY
1936: Carol Brink. CADDIE WOODLAWN

1937: Ruth Sawyer. ROLLER SKATES
1938: Kate Seredy. THE WHITE STAG
1939: Elizabeth Enright. THIMBLE SUMMER
1940: James Daugherty. DANIEL BOONE
1941: Armstrong Sperry. CALL IT COURAGE
1942: Walter D. Edmonds. THE MATCHLOCK GUN
1943: Elizabeth Janet Gray. ADAM OF THE ROAD
1944: Esther Forbes. JOHNNY TREMAIN
1945: Robert Lawson. RABBIT HILL
1946: Lois Lenski. STRAWBERRY GIRL
1947: Carolyn Sherwin Bailey. MISS HICKORY
1948: William Pène du Bois. TWENTY-ONE BALLOONS
1949: Marguerite Henry. KING OF THE WIND
1950: Marguerite de Angeli. THE DOOR IN THE WALL
1951: Elizabeth Yates. AMOS FORTUNE
1952: Eleanor Estes. GINGER PYE
1953: Ann Nolan Clark. SECRET OF THE ANDES
1954: Joseph Krumgold. . . . AND NOW MIGUEL
1955: Meindert DeJong. THE WHEEL ON THE SCHOOL
1956: Jean Lee Latham. CARRY ON, MR. BOWDITCH
1957: Virginia Sorensen. MIRACLES ON MAPLE HILL
1958: Harold Keith. RIFLES FOR WATIE
1959: Elizabeth George Speare. THE WITCH OF BLACKBIRD POND
1960: Joseph Krungold. ONION JOHN
1961: Scott O'Dell. ISLAND OF THE BLUE DOLPHINS
1962: Elizabeth George Speare. THE BRONZE BOW
1963: Madeleine L'Engle. A WRINKLE IN TIME
1964: Emily Cheney Neville. IT'S LIKE THIS, CAT
1965: Maia Wojciechowska. SHADOW OF A BULL
1966: Elizabeth Borten de Trevino. I, JUAN DE PAREJA
1967: Irene Hunt. UP A ROAD SLOWLY
1968: E. L. Konigsburg. FROM THE MIXED-UP FILES
OF MRS. BASIL E. FRANKWEILER
1969: Lloyd Alexander. THE HIGH KING
1970: William H. Armstrong. SOUNDER
1971: Betsy Byars. SUMMER OF THE SWANS
1972: Robert C. O'Brien. MRS. FRISBY AND THE RATS OF NIMH
1973: Jean George. JULIE OF THE WOLVES
1974: Paula Fox. THE SLAVE DANCER
1975: Virginia Hamilton. M. C. HIGGINS, THE GREAT
1976: Susan Cooper. GREY KING
1977: Mildred D. Taylor. ROLL OF THUNDER, HEAR MY CRY

1978: Katherine Paterson. BRIDGE TO TERABITHIA
1979: Ellen Raskin. THE WESTING GAME
1980: Joan Blos. A GATHERING OF DAYS
1981: Katherine Paterson. JACOB HAVE I LOVED
1982: Nancy Willard. A VISIT TO WILLIAM BLAKE'S INN:
POEMS FOR INNOCENT AND EXPERIENCED TRAVELERS
1983: Cynthia Voigt. DICEY'S SONG
1984: Beverly Cleary. DEAR MR. HENSHAW
1985: Robin McKinley. THE HERO AND THE CROWN
1986: Robin MacLachlan. SARAH, PLAIN AND TALL
1987: Sid Fleischman. THE WHIPPING BOY
1988: Russell Freedman. LINCOLN: A PHOTOBIOGRAPHY
1989: Paul Fleischman. JOYFUL NOISE: POEMS FOR TWO VOICES
1990: Lois Lowry. NUMBER THE STARS
1991: Jerry Spinelli. MANIAC MAGEE
1992: Reynolds Naylor. SHILOH
1993: Cynthia Ryland. MISSING MAY
1994: Lois Lowry. THE GIVER
1995: Sharon Creech. WALK TWO MOONS
1996: Karen Cushman. THE MIDWIFE'S APPRENTICE
1997. E. L. Konigsburg. THE VIEW FOR SATURDAY
1998: Karen Hesse. OUT OF THE DUST
1999: Louis Sachar. HOLES

1999: _____

2000: _____

2001: _____

2002: _____

2003: _____

THE PEN/FAULKNER AWARD

PEN/Faulkner was founded in 1980 by writers to honor their peers, and is now the largest juried award for fiction in the United States. It is named in honor of William Faulkner, who used his Nobel Prize funds to create an award for young writers.

1981: Walter Abish. HOW GERMAN IS IT?
1982: David Bradley. THE CHANEYSVILLE INCIDENT
1983: Toby Olson. SEAVIEW
1984: John Edgar Wideman. SENT FOR YOU YESTERDAY

1985: Tobias Wolff. THE BARRACKS THIEF
1986: Peter Taylor. THE OLD FOREST AND OTHER TALES
1987: Richard Wiley. SOLDIERS IN HIDING
1988: T. Coraghessan Boyle. WORLD'S END
1989: James Salter. DUSK
1990: E. L. Doctorow. BILLY BATHGATE
1991: John Edgar Wideman. PHILADELPHIA FIRE
1992: Don DeLillo. MAO II
1993: E. Annie Proulx. POSTCARDS
1994: Philip Roth. OPERATION SHYLOCK
1995: David Guterson. SNOW FALLING ON CEDARS
1996: Richard Ford. INDEPENDENCE DAY
1997: Gina Berriault. WOMEN IN THEIR BEDS
1998: Rafi Zabor. THE BEAR COMES HOME
1999: Michael Cunningham. THE HOURS

2000: _____

2001: _____

2002: _____

2003: _____

THE PULITZER PRIZE FOR LITERATURE

Joseph Pulitzer, a publisher of the *New York Globe,* established the Pulitzer Prize through an endowment to Columbia University. Prizes in various fields are given annually. The Literature Award is for fiction in book form by an American author, preferably dealing with American life.

1918: Ernest Poole. HIS FAMILY
1919: Booth Tarkington. THE MAGNIFICENT AMBERSONS
1920: No award
1921: Edith Wharton. THE AGE OF INNOCENCE
1922: Booth Tarkington. ALICE ADAMS
1923: Willa Cather. ONE OF OURS
1924: Margaret Wilson. THE ABLE MCLAUGHLINS
1925: Edna Ferber. SO BIG
1926: Sinclair Lewis. (Prize declined.) ARROWSMITH
1927: Louis Bromfield. EARLY AUTUMN
1928: Thornton Wilder. THE BRIDGES OF SAN LUIS REY
1929: Julia Peterkin. SCARLET SISTER MARY
1930: Oliver La Farge. LAUGHING BOY

1931: Margaret Ayer Barnes. YEARS OF GRACE
1932: Pearl S. Buck. THE GOOD EARTH
1933: T. S. Stribling. THE STORE
1934: Caroline Miller. LAMB IN HIS BOSOM
1935: Josephine Winslow Johnson. NOW IN NOVEMBER
1936: Harold Davis. HONEY IN THE HORN
1937: Margaret Mitchell. GONE WITH THE WIND
1938: John Phillips Marquand. THE LATE GEORGE APLEY
1939: Marjorie Kinnan Rawlings. THE YEARLING
1940: John Steinbeck. THE GRAPES OF WRATH
1941: No award
1942: Ellen Glasgow. IN THIS OUR LIFE
1943: Upton Sinclair. DRAGON'S TEETH
1944: Martin Flavin. JOURNEY IN THE DARK
1945: John Hersey. A BELL FOR ADANO
1946: No award
1947: Robert Penn Warren. ALL THE KING'S MEN
1948: James A. Michener. TALES OF THE SOUTH PACIFIC
1949: James Gould Cozzens. GUARD OF HONOR
1950: A. B. Guthrie. THE WAY WEST
1951: Conrad Richter. THE TOWN
1952: Herman Wouk. THE CAINE MUTINY
1953: Ernest Hemingway. THE OLD MAN AND THE SEA
1954: No award
1955: William Faulkner. A FABLE
1956: MacKinlay Kantor. ANDERSONVILLE
1957: No award
1958: James Agee. A DEATH IN THE FAMILY
1959: Robert Lewis Taylor. THE TRAVELS OF JAIMIE MCPHEETERS
1960: Allen Drury. ADVISE AND CONSENT
1961: Harper Lee. TO KILL A MOCKINGBIRD
1962: Edwin O'Connor. THE EDGE OF SADNESS
1963: William Faulkner. THE REIVERS
1964: No award
1965: Shirley Anne Grau. THE KEEPERS OF THE HOUSE
1966: Katherine Anne Porter. COLLECTED STORIES
1967: Bernard Malamud. THE FIXER
1968: William Styron. THE CONFESSIONS OF NAT TURNER
1969: N. Scott Momaday. HOUSE MADE OF DAWN
1970: Jean Stafford. COLLECTED STORIES
1971: No award
1972: Wallace Stegner. ANGLE OF REPOSE

1973: Eudora Welty. THE OPTIMIST'S DAUGHTER
1974: No award
1975: Michael Shaara. THE KILLER ANGELS
1976: Saul Bellow. HUMBOLDT'S GIFT
1977: No award
1978: James Alan McPherson. ELBOW ROOM
1979: John Cheever. THE STORIES OF JOHN CHEEVER
1980: Norman Mailer. THE EXECUTIONER'S SONG
1981: John Kennedy Toole. A CONFEDERACY OF DUNCES
1982: John Updike. RABBIT IS RICH
1983: Alice Walker. THE COLOR PURPLE
1984: William Kennedy. IRONWEED
1985: Alison Lurie. FOREIGN AFFAIRS
1986: Larry McMurtry. LONESOME DOVE
1987: Peter Taylor. A SUMMONS TO MEMPHIS
1988: Toni Morrison. BELOVED
1989: Anne Tyler. BREATHING LESSONS
1990: Oscar Hijuelos. THE MAMBO KINGS PLAY SONGS OF LOVE
1991: John Updike. RABBIT AT REST
1992: Jane Smiley. A THOUSAND ACRES
1993: Robert Olen Butler. A GOOD SCENT FROM A STRANGE MOUNTAIN
1994: E. Annie Proulx. THE SHIPPING NEWS
1995: Carol Shields. THE STONE DIARIES
1996: Richard Ford. INDEPENDENCE DAY
1997: Steven Millhauser.
MARTIN DRESSLER: THE TALE OF AN AMERICAN DREAMER
1998: Philip Roth. AMERICAN PASTORAL
1999: Michael Cunningham. THE HOURS

2000: _____

2001: _____

2002: _____

2003: _____

THE PULITZER PRIZE FOR DRAMA

The Pulitzer Prize for Drama is for an American play, preferably original and dealing with American life.

1918: Jesse Lynch Williams. WHY MARRY?
1919: No award

1920: Eugene O'Neill. BEYOND THE HORIZON
1921: Zona Gale. MISS LULU BETT
1922: Eugene O'Neill. ANNA CHRISTIE
1923: Owen Davis. ICEBOUND
1924: Hatcher Hughes. HELL-BENT FOR HEAVEN
1925: Sidney Howard. THEY KNEW WHAT THEY WANTED
1926: George Kelly. CRAIG'S WIFE
1927: Paul Green. IN ABRAHAM'S BOSOM
1928: Eugene O'Neill. STRANGE INTERLUDE
1929: Elmer Rice. STREET SCENE
1930: Marc Connelly. THE GREEN PASTURES
1931: Susan Glaspell. ALISON'S HOUSE
1932: George S. Kaufman, Morrie Ryskind, and Ira Gershwin.
OF THEE I SING
1933: Maxwell Anderson. BOTH YOUR HOUSES
1934: Sidney Kingsley. MEN IN WHITE
1935: Zoë Akins. THE OLD MAID
1936: Robert E. Sherwood. IDIOT'S DELIGHT
1937: George S. Kaufman and Moss Hart.
YOU CAN'T TAKE IT WITH YOU
1938: Thornton Wilder. OUR TOWN
1939: Robert E. Sherwood. ABE LINCOLN IN ILLINOIS
1940: William Saroyan. THE TIME OF YOUR LIFE
1941: Robert E. Sherwood. THERE SHALL BE NO NIGHT
1942: No award
1943: Thornton Wilder. THE SKIN OF OUR TEETH
1944: No award
1945: Mary Chase. HARVEY
1946: Russel Crouse and Howard Lindsay. STATE OF THE UNION
1947: No award
1948: Tennessee Williams. A STREETCAR NAMED DESIRE
1949: Arthur Miller. DEATH OF A SALESMAN
1950: Richard Rodgers, Oscar Hammerstein, and Joshua Logan.
SOUTH PACIFIC
1951: No award
1952: Joseph Kramm. THE SHRIKE
1953: William Inge. PICNIC
1954: John Patrick. TEAHOUSE OF THE AUGUST MOON
1955: Tennessee Williams. CAT ON A HOT TIN ROOF
1956: Frances Goodrich and Albert Hackett. THE DIARY OF ANNE FRANK
1957: Eugene O'Neill. LONG DAY'S JOURNEY INTO NIGHT
1958: Ketti Frings. LOOK HOMEWARD, ANGEL

1959: Archibald MacLeish. J.B.
1960: George Abbott, Jerome Weidman, Sheldon Harnick, and Jerry Bock.
FIORELLO
1961: Tad Mosel. ALL THE WAY HOME
1962: Frank Loesser and Abe Burrows.
HOW TO SUCCEED IN BUSINESS WITHOUT REALLY TRYING
1963: No award
1964: No award
1965: Frank D. Gilroy. THE SUBJECT WAS ROSES
1966: No award
1967: Edward Albee. A DELICATE BALANCE
1968: No award
1969: Howard Sackler. THE GREAT WHITE HOPE
1970: Charles Gordone. NO PLACE TO BE SOMEBODY
1971: Paul Zindel. THE EFFECT OF GAMMA RAYS
ON MAN-IN-THE-MOON MARIGOLDS
1972: No award
1973: Jason Miller. THAT CHAMPIONSHIP SEASON
1974: No award
1975: Edward Albee. SEASCAPE
1976: Michael Bennett, James Kirkwood, Nicholas Dante,
Marvin Hamlisch, and Edward Kleban. A CHORUS LINE
1977: Michael Cristofer. THE SHADOW BOX
1978: Donald Coburn. THE GIN GAME
1979: Sam Shepard. BURIED CHILD
1980: Lanford Wilson. TALLEY'S FOLLY
1981: Beth Henley. CRIMES OF THE HEART
1982: Charles Fuller. A SOLDIER'S PLAY
1983: Marsha Norman. 'NIGHT, MOTHER
1984: David Mamet. GLENGARRY GLEN ROSS
1985: Stephen Sondheim and James Lapine.
SUNDAY IN THE PARK WITH GEORGE
1986: No award
1987: August Wilson. FENCES
1988: Alfred Uhry. DRIVING MISS DAISY
1989: Wendy Wasserstein. THE HEIDI CHRONICLES
1990: August Wilson. THE PIANO LESSON
1991: Neil Simon. LOST IN YONKERS
1992: Robert Schenkkan. THE KENTUCKY CYCLE
1993: Tony Kushner. ANGELS IN AMERICA: MILLENNIUM APPROACHES
1994: Edward Albee. THREE TALL WOMEN
1995: Horton Foote. THE YOUNG MAN FROM ATLANTA

1996: Jonathan Larson. RENT
1997: No award
1998: Paula Vogel. HOW I LEARNED TO DRIVE
1999: Margaret Edson. WIT

2000: _____

2001: _____

2002: _____

2003: _____

THE PULITZER PRIZE FOR POETRY

1918: Sara Teasdale. LOVE SONGS
1919 (tie): Carl Sandburg. CORN HUSKERS
Margaret Widdemer. OLD ROAD TO PARADISE
1920: No award
1921: No award
1922: Edwin Arlington Robinson. COLLECTED POEMS
1923: Edna St. Vincent Millay. THE BALLAD OF THE HARP-WEAVER;
A FEW FIGS FROM THISTLES; EIGHT SONNETS IN AMERICAN POETRY, 1922;
and A MISCELLANY
1924: Robert Frost. NEW HAMPSHIRE:
A POEM WITH NOTES AND GRACE NOTES
1925: Edwin Arlington Robinson. THE MAN WHO DIED TWICE
1926: Amy Lowell. WHAT'S O'CLOCK
1927: Leonora Speyer. FIDDLER'S FAREWELL
1928: Edwin Arlington Robinson. TRISTRAM
1929: Stephen Vincent Benét. JOHN BROWN'S BODY
1930: Conrad Aiken. SELECTED POEMS
1931: Robert Frost. COLLECTED POEMS
1932: George Dillon. THE FLOWERING STONE
1933: Archibald MacLeish. CONQUISTADOR
1934: Richard Hillyer. COLLECTED VERSE
1935: Audrey Wurdemann. BRIGHT AMBUSH
1936: Robert P. Tristram Coffin. STRANGE HOLINESS
1937: Robert Frost. A FURTHER RANGE
1938: Marya Zaturenska. COLD MORNING SKY
1939: John Gould Fletcher. SELECTED POEMS
1940: Mark Van Doren. COLLECTED POEMS
1941: Leonard Bacon. SUNDERLAND CAPTURE

1942: William Rose Benét. THE DUST WHICH IS GOD
1943: Robert Frost. A WITNESS TREE
1944: Stephen Vincent Benét. WESTERN STAR
1945: Karl Shapiro. V-LETTER AND OTHER POEMS
1946: No award
1947: Robert Lowell. LORD WEARY'S CASTLE
1948: W. H. Auden. THE AGE OF ANXIETY
1949: Peter Viereck. TERROR AND DECORUM
1950: Gwendolyn Brooks. ANNIE ALLEN
1951: Carl Sandburg. COMPLETE POEMS
1952: Marianne Moore. COLLECTED POEMS
1953: Archibald MacLeish. COLLECTED POEMS
1954: Theodore Roethke. THE WAKING
1955: Wallace Stevens. COLLECTED POEMS
1956: Elizabeth Bishop. POEMS, NORTH AND SOUTH
1957: Richard Wilbur. THINGS OF THIS WORLD
1958: Robert Penn Warren. PROMISES: POEMS 1954–1956
1959: Stanley Kunitz. SELECTED POEMS 1928–1958
1960: W. D. Snodgrass. HEART'S NEEDLE
1961: Phyllis McGinley.
TIMES THREE: SELECTED VERSE FROM THREE DECADES
1962: Alan Dugan. POEMS
1963: William Carlos Williams. PICTURES FROM BREUGHEL
1964: Louis Simpson. AT THE END OF THE OPEN ROAD
1965: John Berryman. 77 DREAM SONGS
1966: Richard Eberhart. SELECTED POEMS
1967: Anne Sexton. LIVE OR DIE
1968: Anthony Hecht. THE HARD HOURS
1969: George Oppen. OF BEING NUMEROUS
1970: Richard Howard. UNTITLED SUBJECTS
1971: William S. Merwin. THE CARRIER OF LADDERS
1972: James Wright. COLLECTED POEMS
1973: Maxine Winokur Kumin. UP COUNTRY
1974: Robert Lowell. THE DOLPHIN
1975: Gary Snyder. TURTLE ISLAND
1976: John Ashbery. SELF-PORTRAIT IN A CONVEX MIRROR
1977: James Merrill. DIVINE COMEDIES
1978: Howard Nemerov. COLLECTED POEMS
1979: Robert Penn Warren. NOW AND THEN: POEMS 1976–1978
1980: Donald Justice. SELECTED POEMS
1981: James Schuyler. THE MORNING OF THE POEM
1982: Sylvia Plath. THE COLLECTED POEMS

1983: Galway Kinnell. SELECTED POEMS
1984: Mary Oliver. AMERICAN PRIMITIVE
1985: Carolyn Kizer. YIN
1986: Henry Taylor. THE FLYING CHANGE
1987: Rita Dove. THOMAS AND BEULAH
1988: William Meredith. PARTIAL ACCOUNT: NEW AND SELECTED POEMS
1989: Richard Wilbur. NEW AND COLLECTED POEMS
1990: Charles Simic. THE WORLD DOESN'T END
1991: Mona Van Duyn. NEAR CHANGES
1992: James Tate. SELECTED POEMS
1993: Louise Glück. THE WILD IRIS
1994: Yusef Komunyakaa. NEON VERNACULAR
1995: Philip Levine. THE SIMPLE TRUTH
1996: Jorie Graham. THE DREAM OF THE UNIFIED FIELD
1997: Lisel Mueller. ALIVE TOGETHER: NEW AND SELECTED POEMS
1998: Charles Wright. BLACK ZODIAC
1999: Mark Strand. BLIZZARD OF ONE

2000: _____

2001: _____

2002: _____

2003: _____

High Spots in Literature

Some collectors center their collecting on titles that have been selected by a notable writer or bibliographer who has chosen what he or she thinks are the best books ever published in a particular genre. The dates on the following lists are the year the particular book was first published.

ANTHONY BURGESS'S NINETY-NINE NOVELS

Author Anthony Burgess lists his choices of the best ninety-nine novels published in English from 1939 to 1984. He opens his introduction with: "1984 has arrived, but Orwell's glum prophecy has not been fulfilled. Some of us half-feared that, on the morning of January 1, we would wake with our seasonal hangovers to see Ingsoc posters on the walls, the helicopters of the Thought Police hovering, and our television sets looking at us."

1939: Henry Green. PARTY GOING
1939: Aldous Huxley. AFTER MANY A SUMMER

1939: James Joyce. FINNEGANS WAKE
1939: Flann O'Brian. AT SWIM—TWO BIRDS
1940: Graham Greene. THE POWER AND THE GLORY
1940: Ernest Hemingway. FOR WHOM THE BELL TOLLS
1940: C. P. Snow. STRANGERS AND BROTHERS
1941: Rex Warner. THE AERODROME
1944: Joyce Cary. THE HORSE'S MOUTH
1944: Somerset Maugham. THE RAZOR'S EDGE
1945: Evelyn Waugh. BRIDESHEAD REVISITED
1946: Mervyn Peake. TITUS GROAN
1947: Saul Bellow. THE VICTIM
1947: Malcolm Lowry. UNDER THE VOLCANO
1948: Graham Greene. THE HEART OF THE MATTER
1948: Aldous Huxley. APE AND ESSENCE
1948: Norman Mailer. THE NAKED AND THE DEAD
1948: Nevil Shute. NO HIGHWAY
1949: Elizabeth Bowen. THE HEAT OF THE DAY
1949: George Orwell. NINETEEN EIGHTY-FOUR
1949: William Sansom. THE BODY
1950: William Cooper. SCENES FROM PROVINCIAL LIFE
1950: Budd Schulberg. THE DISENCHANTED
1951: Anthony Powell. A DANCE TO THE MUSIC OF TIME
1951: J. D. Salinger. THE CATCHER IN THE RYE
1951–69: Henry Williamson. A CHRONICLE OF ANCIENT SUNLIGHT
1951: Herman Wouk. THE CAINE MUTINY
1952: Ralph Ellison. INVISIBLE MAN
1952: Ernest Hemingway. THE OLD MAN AND THE SEA
1952: Mary McCarthy. THE GROVES OF ACADEME
1952: Flannery O'Connor. WISE BLOOD
1952–61: Evelyn Waugh. SWORD OF HONOUR
1953: Raymond Chandler. THE LONG GOODBYE
1954: Kingsley Amis. LUCKY JIM
1957: John Braine. ROOM AT THE TOP
1957–60: Lawrence Durrell. THE ALEXANDRIA QUARTET
1957–60: Colin MacInnes. THE LONDON NOVELS
1957: Bernard Malamud. THE ASSISTANT
1958: Iris Murdoch. THE BELL
1958: Alan Sillitoe. SATURDAY NIGHT AND SUNDAY MORNING
1958: T. H. White. THE ONCE AND FUTURE KING
1959: William Faulkner. THE MANSION
1959: Ian Fleming. GOLDFINGER
1960: L. P. Hartley. FACIAL JUSTICE

1960–65: Olivia Manning. THE BALKANS TRILOGY
1961: Ivy Compton-Burnett. THE MIGHTY AND THEIR FALL
1961: Joseph Heller. CATCH-22
1961: Richard Hughes. THE FOX IN THE ATTIC
1961: Patrick White. RIDERS IN THE CHARIOT
1961: Angus Wilson. THE OLD MEN AT THE ZOO
1962: James Baldwin. ANOTHER COUNTRY
1962: Pamela Hansford Johnson. AN ERROR OF JUDGEMENT
1962: Aldous Huxley. ISLAND
1962: Doris Lessing. THE GOLDEN NOTEBOOK
1962: Vladimir Nabokov. PALE FIRE
1963: Muriel Spark. THE GIRLS OF SLENDER MEANS
1964: William Golding. THE SPIRE
1964: Wilson Harris. HEARTLAND
1964: Christopher Isherwood. A SINGLE MAN
1964: Vladimir Nabokov. THE DEFENCE
1964: Angus Wilson. LATE CALL
1965: John O'Hara. THE LOCKWOOD CONCERN
1965: Muriel Spark. THE MANDELBAUM GATE
1966: Chinua Achebe. A MAN OF THE PEOPLE
1966: Kingsley Amis. THE ANTI-DEATH LEAGUE
1966: John Barth. GILES GOAT-BOY
1966: Nadine Gordimer. THE LATE BOURGEOIS WORLD
1966: Walker Percy. THE LAST GENTLEMEN
1967: R. K. Narayan. THE VENDOR OF SWEETS
1968: J. B. Priestley. THE IMAGE MEN
1968: Mordecai Richler. COCKSURE
1968: Keith Roberts. PAVANE
1969: John Fowles. THE FRENCH LIEUTENANT'S WOMAN
1969: Philip Roth. PORTNOY'S COMPLAINT
1970: Len Deighton. BOMBER
1973: Michael Frayn. SWEET DREAMS
1973: Thomas Pynchon. GRAVITY'S RAINBOW
1975: Saul Bellow. HUMBOLDT'S GIFT
1975: Malcolm Bradbury. THE HISTORY MAN
1976: Brian Moore. THE DOCTOR'S WIFE
1976: Robert Nye. FALSTAFF
1977: Erica Jong. HOW TO SAVE YOUR OWN LIFE
1977: James Plunkett. FAREWELL COMPANIONS
1977: Paul Scott. STAYING ON
1978: John Updike. THE COUP
1979: J. G. Ballard. THE UNLIMITED DREAM COMPANY

1979: Bernard Malamud. DUBIN'S LIVES
1979: V. S. Naipaul. A BEND IN THE RIVER
1979: William Styron. SOPHIE'S CHOICE
1980: Brian Aldiss. LIFE IN THE WEST
1980: Russell Hoban. RIDDLEY WALKER
1980: David Lodge. HOW FAR CAN YOU GO?
1980: John Kennedy Toole. A CONFEDERACY OF DUNCES
1981: Alasdair Gray. LANARK
1981: Paul Theroux. THE MOSQUITO COAST
1981: Gore Vidal. CREATION
1982: Robertson Davies. THE REBEL ANGELS
1983: Norman Mailer. ANCIENT EVENINGS

CYRIL CONNOLLY'S *THE MODERN MOVEMENT*
One Hundred Key Books from England, France, and America
1880–1950

Cyril Connolly defined the Modern Movement as "a revolt against the bourgeois in France, the Victorians in England, the puritanism and materialism of America" and has chosen as his "Key" books those that reflected this spirit.

1881: Henry James. PORTRAIT OF A LADY
1881: Gustave Flaubert. BOUVARD ET PÉCUCHET
1883: Villiers de L'Isle-Adam. CONTES CRUELS
1884: Joris Karl Huysmans. À REBOURS
1887: Charles Baudelaire. OEUVRES POSTHUMES
1886: Arthur Rimbaud. LES ILLUMINATIONS
1887: Stéphane Mallarmé. LES POÉSIES
1885: Guy de Maupassant. BEL AMI
1887–96: Edmond and Jules de Goncourt. JOURNAL
1891: Joris Karl Huymans. LÀ-BAS
1896: Alfred Jarry. UBU ROI
1899: Henry James. THE AWKWARD AGE
1902: André Gide. L'IMMORALISTE
1902: Joseph Conrad. YOUTH: A NARRATIVE, AND TWO OTHER STORIES
1907: Joseph Conrad. THE SECRET AGENT
1903: Henry James. THE AMBASSADORS
1906: George Moore. MEMOIRS OF MY DEAD LIFE
1907: J. M. Synge. THE PLAYBOY OF THE WESTERN WORLD
1907: E. M. Forster. THE LONGEST JOURNEY
1911: Norman Douglas. SIREN LAND
1913: D. H. Lawrence. SONS AND LOVERS

1913: Guillaume Apollinaire. ALCOOLS; POÈMES, 1898–1913
1913: Marcel Proust. DU CÔTÉ DE CHEZ SWANN
1914: William Butler Yeats. RESPONSIBILITIES
1914: Thomas Hardy. SATIRES OF CIRCUMSTANCE
1915: Ford Madox Ford. THE GOOD SOLDIER
1916: Ezra Pound. LUSTRA
1917: James Joyce. PORTRAIT OF THE ARTIST AS A YOUNG MAN
1917: Norman Douglas. SOUTH WIND
1917: T. S. Eliot. PRUFROCK AND OTHER OBSERVATIONS
1917: Paul Valéry. LA JEUNE PARQUE
1918: Percy Wyndham Lewis. TARR
1918: Guillaume Apollinaire. CALLIGRAMMES
1918: Gerard Manley Hopkins. POEMS
1918: Arthur Waley. A HUNDRED AND SEVENTY CHINESE POEMS
1918: Giles Lytton Strachey. EMINENT VICTORIANS
1920: Wilfred Owen. POEMS
1921: D. H. Lawrence. SEA AND SARDINIA
1921: Aldous Huxley. CROME YELLOW
1922: Katherine Mansfield. THE GARDEN PARTY AND OTHER STORIES
1922: William Butler Yeats. LATER POEMS
1922: James Joyce. ULYSSES
1923: Raymond Radiguet. LE DIABLE AU CORPS
1923: Ronald Firbank. THE FLOWER BENEATH THE FOOT
1923: Wallace Stevens. HARMONIUM
1923: E. E. Cummings. TULIPS AND CHIMNEYS
1924: E. M. Forster. A PASSAGE TO INDIA
1925: F. Scott Fitzgerald. THE GREAT GATSBY
1924: Ernest Hemingway. IN OUR TIME
1925: Ezra Pound. A DRAFT OF XVI CANTOS
1926: Ernest Hemingway. THE SUN ALSO RISES
1926: André Gide. SI LE GRAIN NE MEURT
1926: William Somerset Maugham. THE CASUARINA TREE
1927: Virginia Woolf. TO THE LIGHTHOUSE
1928: André Breton. NADJA
1928: William Butler Yeats. THE TOWER
1928: D. H. Lawrence. LADY CHATTERLEY'S LOVER
1928: Evelyn Waugh. DECLINE AND FALL
1928: Edith Sitwell. COLLECTED POEMS
1929: Henry Green. LIVING
1929: Ernest Hemingway. A FAREWELL TO ARMS
1929: Robert Graves. GOODBYE TO ALL THAT
1929: Jean Cocteau. LES ENFANTS TERRIBLES

1929: Ivy Compton-Burnett. BROTHERS AND SISTERS
1930: Hart Crane. THE BRIDGE
1930: T. S. Eliot. ASH WEDNESDAY
1931: Antoine de Saint-Exupéry. VOL DE NUIT
1931: William Faulkner. SANCTUARY
1931: Virginia Woolf. THE WAVES
1931: Edmund Wilson. AXEL'S CASTLE
1932: T. S. Eliot. SELECTED ESSAYS
1932: W. H. Auden. THE ORATORS
1932: Louis-Ferdinand Céline. VOYAGE AU BOUT DE LA NUIT
1932: Aldous Huxley. BRAVE NEW WORLD
1933: Nathanael West. MISS LONELYHEARTS
1933: André Malraux. LA CONDITION HUMAINE
1934: Dylan Thomas. EIGHTEEN POEMS
1934: F. Scott Fitzgerald. TENDER IS THE NIGHT
1934: Henry James. THE ART OF THE NOVEL
1935: Marianne Moore. SELECTED POEMS
1936–39: Henry de Montherlant. LES JEUNES FILLES
1936: Henri Michaux. VOYAGE EN GRANDE GARABAGNE
1938: Jean-Paul Sartre. LA NAUSÉE
1939: Louis MacNeice. AUTUMN JOURNAL
1939: Christopher Isherwood. GOODBYE TO BERLIN
1939: James Joyce. FINNEGANS WAKE
1940: Graham Greene. THE POWER AND THE GLORY
1940: Arthur Koestler. DARKNESS AT NOON
1940: W. H. Auden. ANOTHER TIME
1942: Stephen Spender. RUINS AND VISIONS
1942: Albert Camus. L'ÉTRANGER
1944: T. S. Eliot. FOUR QUARTETS
1945: George Orwell. ANIMAL FARM
1946: Dylan Thomas. DEATHS AND ENTRANCES
1946–51: William Carlos Williams. PATERSON 1, 2, 3, 4
1947: Albert Camus. LA PESTE
1948: John Betjeman. SELECTED POEMS
1948: Ezra Pound. PISAN CANTOS
1949: George Orwell. NINETEEN EIGHTY-FOUR

HAYCRAFT-QUEEN CORNERSTONES, 1748–1948

Howard Haycraft was a historian of the detective story and chose the books he believed formed cornerstones in detective fiction. Mystery writer Ellery Queen then added those titles he thought should also be included. We have put the date in bold type if the title was placed on the list originally by Haycraft.

1748: Voltaire. ZADIG

1828–29: François Eugène Vidocq. MÉMOIRES DE VIDOCQ

1845: Edgar Allan Poe. TALES

1852–53: Charles Dickens. BLEAK HOUSE

1856: "Waters" (William Russell).
RECOLLECTIONS OF A DETECTIVE POLICE-OFFICER

1860: Wilkie Collins. THE WOMAN IN WHITE

1862: Victor Hugo. LES MISÉRABLES

1866: Feodor Dostoevsky. CRIME AND PUNISHMENT

1866: Émile Gaboriau. L'AFFAIRE LEROUGE

1867: Émile Gaboriau. LE DOSSIER NO 113

1868: Émile Gaboriau. LE CRIME D'ORCIVAL

1868: Wilkie Collins. THE MOONSTONE

1869: Émile Gaboriau. MONSIEUR LECOQ

1870: Charles Dickens. THE MYSTERY OF EDWIN DROOD

1872: (Harlan Page Halsey.) OLD SLEUTH, THE DETECTIVE

1874: Allan Pinkerton. THE EXPRESSMAN AND THE DETECTIVE

1878: Anna Katharine Green. THE LEAVENWORTH CASE

1882: Robert Louis Stevenson. NEW ARABIAN NIGHTS

1886: Robert Louis Stevenson. STRANGE CASE OF DR JEKYLL AND MR HYDE

1887: Fergus W. Hume. THE MYSTERY OF A HANSOM CAB

1887: A. Conan Doyle. A STUDY IN SCARLET

1890: A. Conan Doyle. THE SIGN OF FOUR

1892: A. Conan Doyle. THE ADVENTURES OF SHERLOCK HOLMES

1892: Israel Zangwill. THE BIG BOW MYSTERY

1894: Mark Twain. THE TRAGEDY OF PUDD'NHEAD WILSON

1894: Arthur Morrison. MARTIN HEWITT, INVESTIGATOR

1894: A. Conan Doyle. THE MEMOIRS OF SHERLOCK HOLMES

1895: M. P. Shiel. PRINCE ZALESKI

1897: Bram Stoker. DRACULA

1899: E. W. Hornung. THE AMATEUR CRACKSMAN

1902: A. Conan Doyle. THE HOUND OF THE BASKERVILLES

1903: (Erskine Childers.) THE RIDDLE OF THE SANDS

1905: A. Conan Doyle. THE RETURN OF SHERLOCK HOLMES

1906: Godfrey R. Benson. TRACKS IN THE SNOW

1906: Robert Barr. THE TRIUMPHS OF EUGÈNE VALMONT

1907: Jacques Furtrelle. THE THINKING MACHINE

1907: Maurice Leblanc. ARSÈNE LUPIN, GENTLEMAN-CAMBRIOLEUR

1907: Gaston Leroux. LE MYSTÈRE DE LA CHAMBRE JAUNE

1907: R. Austin Freeman. THE RED THUMB MARK

1908: Mary Roberts Rinehart. THE CIRCULAR STAIRCASE

1908: O. Henry. THE GENTLE GRAFTER

1908: G. K. Chesterton. THE MAN WHO WAS THURSDAY
1908–9: Gaston Leroux. LE PARFUM DE LA DAME EN NOIR
1909: R. Austin Freeman. JOHN THORNDYKE'S CASES
1909: Cleveland Moffett. THROUGH THE WALL
1909: Baroness Orczy. THE OLD MAN IN THE CORNER
1909: Carolyn Wells. THE CLUE
1910: Maurice Leblanc. "813"
1910: A. E. W. Mason. AT THE VILLA ROSE
1910: William MacHarg and Edwin Balmer.
THE ACHIEVEMENTS OF LUTHER TRANT
1911: R. Austin Freeman. THE EYE OF OSIRIS
1911: G. K. Chesterton. THE INNOCENCE OF FATHER BROWN
1912: R. Austin Freeman. THE SINGING BONE
1912: Arthur B. Reeve. THE SILENT BULLET
1913: Mrs. Belloc Lowndes. THE LODGER
1913: Sax Rohmer. THE MYSTERY OF DR FU-MANCHU
1913: E. C. Bentley. TRENT'S LAST CASE
1914: Ernest Bramah. MAX CARRADOS
1914: Louis Joseph Vance. THE LONE WOLF
1915: A. Conan Doyle. THE VALLEY OF FEAR
1915: John Buchan. THE THIRTY-NINE STEPS
1916: Thomas Burke. LIMEHOUSE NIGHTS
1917: A. Conan Doyle. HIS LAST BOW
1918: Melville Davisson Post. UNCLE ABNER
1918: J. S. Fletcher. THE MIDDLE TEMPLE MURDER
1920: Agatha Christie. THE MYSTERIOUS AFFAIR AT STYLES
1920: Freeman Wills Crofts. THE CASK
1920: H. C. Bailey. CALL MR FORTUNE
1920: "Sapper" (Cyril McNeile). BULL-DOG DRUMMOND
1920: Arthur Train. TUTT AND MR. TUTT
1921: Eden Phillpotts. THE GREY ROOM
1922: Maurice Leblanc. LES HUITS COUPS DE L'HORLOGE
1922: A. A. Milne. THE RED HOUSE MYSTERY
1923: G. D. H. Cole. THE BROOKLYN MURDERS
1923: Dorothy Sayers. WHOSE BODY?
1924: A. E. W. Mason. THE HOUSE OF THE ARROW
1924: Freeman Wills Crofts. INSPECTOR FRENCH'S GREATEST CASE
1924: Philip MacDonald. THE RASP
1925: Edgar Wallace. THE MIND OF MR. J. G. REEDER
1925: John Rhode. THE PADDINGTON MYSTERY
1925: Earl Derr Biggers. THE HOUSE WITHOUT A KEY
1925: Theodore Dreiser. AN AMERICAN TRAGEDY

1925: Liam O'Flaherty. THE INFORMER
1925: Ronald A. Knox. THE VIADUCT MURDER
1926: Agatha Christie. THE MURDER OF ROGER ACKROYD
1926: S. S. Van Dine. THE BENSON MURDER CASE
(Or alternate: THE "CANARY" MURDER CASE, 1927)
1926: C. S. Forester. PAYMENT DEFERRED
1927: A. Conan Doyle. THE CASE-BOOK OF SHERLOCK HOLMES
1927: S. S. Van Dine (Alternate. See 1926.)
1927: Frances Noyes Hart. THE BELLAMY TRIAL
1928: John Rhode. THE MURDERS IN PRAED STREET
1928: W. Somerset Maugham. ASHENDEN
1929: Anthony Berkeley. THE POISONED CHOCOLATES CASE
1929: Ellery Queen. THE ROMAN HAT MYSTERY
1929: Rufus King. MURDER BY THE CLOCK
1929: W. R. Burnett. LITTLE CAESAR
1929: T. S. Stribling. CLUES OF THE CARIBBEES
1929: Harvey J. O'Higgins. DETECTIVE DUFF UNRAVELS IT
1929: Migeon G. Eberhart. THE PATIENT IN ROOM 18
1930: Dorothy Sayers and Robert Eustace. THE DOCUMENTS IN THE CASE
1930: Frederick Irving Anders. BOOK OF MURDER
1930: Dashiell Hammett. THE MALTESE FALCON
1930: David Frome. THE HAMMERSMITH MURDERS
1931: Dashiell Hammett. THE GLASS KEY
1931: Stuart Palmer. THE PENGUIN POOL MURDER
1931: Francis Beeding. DEATH WALKS IN EASTREPPS
1931: Glen Trevor (James Hilton). MURDER AT SCHOOL
1931: Damon Runyon. GUYS AND DOLLS
1931: Phoebe Atwood Taylor. THE CAPE COD MYSTERY
1932: H. C. Bailey. THE RED CASTLE
1932: Francis Iles. BEFORE THE FACT
1932: Barnaby Ross. THE TRAGEDY OF X
1932: Barnaby Ross. THE TRAGEDY OF Y
1932: R. A. J. Walling. THE FATAL FIVE MINUTES
1932: Clemence Dane and Helen Simpson. RE-ENTER SIR JOHN
1933: Erle Stanley Gardner. THE CASE OF THE VELVET CLAWS
1933: Erle Stanley Gardner. THE CASE OF THE SULKY GIRL
1934: Dorothy Sayers. THE NINE TAILORS
1934: Margery Allingham. DEATH OF A GHOST
1934: James M. Cain. THE POSTMAN ALWAYS RINGS TWICE
1934: Rex Stout. FER-DE-LANCE
1935: Rex Stout. THE LEAGUE OF FRIGHTENED MEN
1935: Richard Hull. THE MURDER OF MY AUNT

1935: John P. Marquand. NO HERO
1937: Anthony Berkeley. TRIAL AND ERROR
1938: Philip MacDonald. THE NURSEMAID WHO DISAPPEARED
1938: John Dickson Carr. THE CROOKED HINGE
1938: John Dickson Carr. THE JUDAS WINDOW
1938: Nicholas Blake. THE BEAST MUST DIE
1938: Michael Innes. LAMENT FOR A MAKER
1938: Clayton Rawson. DEATH FROM A TOP HAT
1938: Graham Greene. BRIGHTON ROCK
1938: Daphne Du Maurier. REBECCA
1938: Mabel Seeley. THE LISTENING HOUSE
1939: Ngaio Marsh. OVERTURE TO DEATH
1939: Eric Ambler. A COFFIN FOR DIMITRIOS
1939: Raymond Chandler. THE BIG SLEEP
1939: Georges Simenon. THE PATIENCE OF MAIGRET
1940: Raymond Chandler. FAREWELL, MY LOVELY
1940: Raymond Postgate. VERDICT OF TWELVE
1940: Frances and Richard Lockridge. THE NORTHS MEET MURDER
1940: Dorothy B. Hughes. THE SO BLUE MARBLE
(Or alternate: IN A LONELY PLACE, 1947)
1940: Cornell Woolrich. THE BRIDE WORE BLACK
1940: Manning Coles. DRINK TO YESTERDAY
1941: Manning Coles. A TOAST TO TOMORROW
1941: H. F. Heard. A TASTE FOR HONEY
1941: Craig Rice. TRIAL BY FURY
(Or alternate: HOME SWEET HOMICIDE, 1944)
1942: Ellery Queen. CALAMITY TOWN
1942: William Irish. PHANTOM LADY
1942: H. H. Holmes. ROCKET TO THE MORGUE
1942: James Gould Cozzens. THE JUST AND THE UNJUST
1944: Dashiell Hammett. THE ADVENTURES OF SAM SPADE
1944: Hilda Lawrence. BLOOD UPON THE SNOW
1944: Craig Rice (Alternate. See 1941.)
1946: Helen Eustis. THE HORIZONTAL MAN
1946: Charlotte Armstrong. THE UNSUSPECTED
1946: Lillian de la Torre. DR. SAM: JOHNSON, DETECTOR
1946: Edmund Crispin. THE MOVING TOYSHOP
(Or alternate: LOVE LIES BLEEDING, 1948)
1947: Dorothy B. Hughes (Alternate. See 1940.)
1947: Edgar Lustgarten. ONE MORE UNFORTUNATE
1947: Roy Vickers. THE DEPARTMENT OF DEAD ENDS
1948: Edmund Crispin (Alternate. See 1946.)

1948: Josephine Tey. THE FRANCHISE AFFAIR
1948: William Faulkner. INTRUDER IN THE DUST

MERLE JOHNSON'S *HIGH SPOTS OF AMERICAN LITERATURE*
In 1929, Merle Johnson defined "high spots" as being "those literary landmarks that rise above mediocrity."

1819: Washington Irving. THE SKETCH BOOK OF GEOFFREY CRAYON, GENT.
(7 volumes)
1821: William Cullen Bryant. POEMS
1826: James Fenimore Cooper. THE LAST OF THE MOHICANS
1837: Nathaniel Hawthorne. TWICE-TOLD TALES
1840: Richard Henry Dana, Jr. TWO YEARS BEFORE THE MAST
1841: Ralph Waldo Emerson. ESSAYS
1844: Clement C. Moore. POEMS
1845: Edgar A. Poe. TALES
1845: Edgar A. Poe. THE RAVEN AND OTHER POEMS
1847: Henry Wadsworth Longfellow. EVANGELINE, A TALE OF ACADIE
1848: James Russell Lowell. THE BIGLOW PAPERS
1849: Henry D. Thoreau.
A WEEK ON THE CONCORD AND MERRIMACK RIVERS
1850: Nathaniel Hawthorne. THE SCARLET LETTER
1850: Ik. Marvel. REVERIES OF A BACHELOR: OR A BOOK OF THE HEART
1851: Herman Melville. MOBY-DICK; OR, THE WHALE
1852: Harriet Beecher Stowe. UNCLE TOM'S CABIN
1854: Henry D. Thoreau. WALDEN; OR, LIFE IN THE WOODS
1855: Henry Wadsworth Longfellow. THE SONG OF HIAWATHA
1855: Walt Whitman. LEAVES OF GRASS
1856: George William Curtis. PRUE AND I
1857: William Allen Butler. NOTHING TO WEAR: AN EPISODE OF CITY LIFE
1858: Oliver Wendell Holmes. THE AUTOCRAT OF THE BREAKFAST-TABLE
1861: Oliver Wendell Holmes. ELSIE VENNER: A ROMANCE OF DESTINY
1865: Edward Everett Hale. THE MAN WITHOUT A COUNTRY
1866: John Greenleaf Whittier. SNOW-BOUND
1868–69: Louisa May Alcott. LITTLE WOMEN (2 volumes)
1868: Charles Godfrey Leland. HANS BREITMANN'S PARTY
1870: Thomas Bailey Aldrich. THE STORY OF A BAD BOY
1870: Bret Harte. THE LUCK OF ROARING CAMP
1871: Louisa May Alcott. LITTLE MEN
1871: John Burroughs. WAKE-ROBIN
1871: Edward Eggleston. THE HOOSIER SCHOOL-MASTER
1871: Bret Harte. POEMS

1871: John Hay. JIM BLUDSO OF THE PRAIRIE BELL, AND LITTLE BREECHES
1871: Joaquin Miller. SONGS OF THE SIERRAS
1873: Will Carleton. FARM BALLADS
1873: Lew Wallace. THE FAIR GOD; OR, THE LAST OF THE 'TZINS
1876: Mark Twain. THE ADVENTURES OF TOM SAWYER
1879: George W. Cable. OLD CREOLE DAYS
1879: Henry James. DAISY MILLER
1880: Lew Wallace. BEN-HUR: A TALE OF THE CHRIST
1881: Joel Chandler Harris. UNCLE REMUS HIS SONGS AND HIS SAYINGS
1883: Edward Eggleston. THE HOOSIER SCHOOL-BOY
1883: James Whitcomb Riley. THE OLD SWIMMIN'-HOLE
1884: Helen Hunt Jackson. RAMONA. A STORY
1884: Frank R. Stockton. THE LADY, OR THE TIGER?
1885: Mark Twain. ADVENTURES OF HUCKLEBERRY FINN
1885: William Dean Howells. THE RISE OF SILAS LAPHAM
1886: Frances Hodgson Burnett. LITTLE LORD FAUNTLEROY
1886: Frank R. Stockton.
THE CASTING AWAY OF MRS. LECKS AND MRS. ALESHINE
1887: Lafcadio Hearn. SOME CHINESE GHOSTS
1887: Thomas Nelson Page. IN OLE VIRGINIA
1888: Edward Bellamy. LOOKING BACKWARD 2000–1887
1888: Frank R. Stockton. THE DUSANTES
1889: Eugene Field. A LITTLE BOOK OF WESTERN VERSE
1889: Eugene Field. A LITTLE BOOK OF PROFITABLE TALES
1890: Harold Frederic. IN THE VALLEY
1890: Lafcadio Hearn. TWO YEARS IN THE FRENCH WEST INDIES
1890: William Dean Howells. A BOY'S TOWN
1890: Thomas A. Janvier. THE AZTEC TREASURE-HOUSE
1891: James Lane Allen. FLUTE AND VIOLIN AND OTHER KENTUCKY TALES
1891: Ambrose Bierce. TALES OF SOLDIERS AND CIVILIANS
1891: Henry Cuyler Bunner. "SHORT SIXES"
1891: Hamlin Garland. MAIN-TRAVELLED ROADS
1891: F. Hopkinson Smith. COLONEL CARTER OF CARTERSVILLE
1892: Howard Pyle. MEN OF IRON
1893: Edwin Markham. THE MAN WITH THE HOE
1894: Paul Leicester Ford. THE HONORABLE PETER STIRLING
AND WHAT PEOPLE THOUGHT OF HIM
1894: Mark Twain. THE TRAGEDY OF PUDD'NHEAD WILSON
AND THE COMEDY THOSE EXTRAORDINARY TWINS
1895: James Lane Allen. A KENTUCKY CARDINAL
1895: Gelett Burgess. THE PURPLE COW
1895: Stephen Crane. THE RED BADGE OF COURAGE

1896: James Lane Allen. AFTERMATH

1896: Mary Mapes Dodge. HANS BRINKER; OR, THE SILVER SKATES

1896: Harold Frederic. THE DAMNATION OF THERON WARE

1897: Alfred Henry Lewis. WOLFVILLE

1897: S. Weir Mitchell, M.D. HUGH WYNNE FREE QUAKER . . .

1897: Henry Van Dyke. THE FIRST CHRISTMAS-TREE

1898: Finley Peter Dunn. MR. DOOLEY IN PEACE AND WAR

1898: Ernest Seton Thompson. WILD ANIMALS I HAVE KNOWN

1898: Edward Noyes Westcott. DAVID HARUM: A STORY OF AMERICAN LIFE

1899: Stephen Crane. WAR IS KIND

1899: Margaret Deland. OLD CHESTER TALES

1899: Elbert Hubbard. A MESSAGE TO GARCIA

1899: Frank Norris. McTEAGUE: A STORY OF SAN FRANCISCO

1899: Morgan Robertson. WHERE ANGELS FEAR TO TREAD

1899: Booth Tarkington. THE GENTLEMAN FROM INDIANA

1899: William Allen White. THE COURT OF BOYVILLE

1900: George Ade. FABLES IN SLANG

1900: Theodore Dreiser. SISTER CARRIE

1900: Mary Johnston. TO HAVE AND TO HOLD

1900: Booth Tarkington. MONSIEUR BEAUCAIRE

1901: Henry Van Dyke. THE RULING PASSION

1902: Owen Wister. THE VIRGINIAN

1903: Jack London. THE CALL OF THE WILD

1903: Frank Norris.

THE EPIC OF THE WHEAT │ THE PIT │ A STORY OF CHICAGO

1904: Henry James. THE GOLDEN BOWL

1904: Charles G. D. Roberts. THE WATCHERS OF THE TRAILS

1906: Gelett Burgess. ARE YOU A BROMIDE?

1906: Ellis Parker Butler. PIGS IS PIGS

1906: O. Henry. THE FOUR MILLION

1906: Frederic Remington. THE WAY OF AN INDIAN

1906: Upton Sinclair. THE JUNGLE

1906: William Allen White. IN OUR TOWN

1907: Jack London. BEFORE ADAM

1908: John Fox, Jr. THE TRAIL OF THE LONESOME PINE

1911: Theodore Dreiser. JENNIE GERHARDT

1911: Edith Wharton. ETHAN FROME

1913: Jack London. JOHN BARLEYCORN

1913: Stewart Edward White. GOLD

1913: Harry Leon Wilson. BUNKER BEAN

1914: Emily Dickinson. THE SINGLE HOUND POEMS FOR A LIFETIME

1914: Robert Frost. NORTH OF BOSTON

1914: Joyce Kilmer. TREES AND OTHER POEMS
1914: Booth Tarkington. PENROD
1915: Edgar Lee Masters. SPOON RIVER ANTHOLOGY
1915: Stewart Edward White. THE GRAY DAWN
1915: Woodrow Wilson. WHEN A MAN COMES TO HIMSELF
1916: Amy Lowell. MEN, WOMEN AND GHOSTS
1916: William McFee. CASUALS OF THE SEA: THE VOYAGE OF A SOUL
1916: Alan Seeger. POEMS
1916: Booth Tarkington. SEVENTEEN
1917: Joseph Hergesheimer. THE THREE BLACK PENNYS
1917: Edna St. Vincent Millay. RENASCENCE AND OTHER POEMS
1917: David Graham Phillips. SUSAN LENOX: HER FALL AND RISE
1918: William Beebe. JUNGLE PEACE
1918: Willa Cather. MY ÁNTONIA
1919: Sherwood Anderson. WINESBURG, OHIO
1919: James Branch Cabell. JURGEN: A COMEDY OF JUSTICE
1920: Sinclair Lewis. MAIN STREET
1920: Carl Sandburg. SMOKE AND STEEL
1920: Stewart Edward White. THE ROSE DAWN
1921: Sherwood Anderson. THE TRIUMPH OF THE EGG
1921: John Dos Passos. THREE SOLDIERS
1921: Hendrik Van Loon. THE STORY OF MANKIND
1922: Hamlin Garland. A PIONEER MOTHER
1922: Emerson Hough. THE COVERED WAGON
1922: Sinclair Lewis. BABBITT
1923: Joseph Hergesheimer. THE PRESBYTERIAN CHILD
1924: Sherwood Anderson. A STORY TELLER'S STORY
1925: Theodore Dreiser. AN AMERICAN TRAGEDY

JACOB BLANCK'S *PETER PARLEY TO PENROD*

This is noted bibliographer Jacob Blanck's selection of the best-loved American juvenile books. In the preface to *Peter Parley to Penrod*, he writes: "Since bookcollecting is a sentimental manifestion what truer type of bookcollecting than the gathering together of the books read as a child and affectionately recalled? Certainly there is no period of man's reading life more often remembered than the first wondering years and the discovery of the strange new worlds that are the printed page."

1827: Peter Parley. THE TALES OF PETER PARLEY
1834?: (Jacob Abbott.) ROLLO: LEARNING TO TALK
1851: Elizabeth Wetherell. THE WIDE, WIDE WORLD
1852: Nathaniel Hawthorne. A WONDER-BOOK FOR GIRLS AND BOYS

1852: Elizabeth Wetherwell. QUEECHY
1852: F. R. Goulding. YOUNG MAROONERS
1853: Nathaniel Hawthorne. TANGLEWOOD TALES, FOR GIRLS AND BOYS
1854: (Maria Susanna Cummins.) THE LAMPLIGHTER
1855: Oliver Optic. THE BOAT CLUB
1855: Thomas Bulfinch. THE AGE OF FABLE
1859: Thomas Bulfinch. THE AGE OF CHIVALRY
1860: Edward S. Ellis. SETH JONES
1861: (Jane Andrews.) THE SEVEN LITTLE SISTERS WHO LIVE
ON THE ROUND BALL THAT FLOATS IN THE AIR
1863: (Adeline D. T. Whitney.) FAITH GARTNEY'S GIRLHOOD
1864: J. T. Trowbridge. CUDJO'S CAVE
1864: Sophie Mae. LITTLE PRUDY
1865: Pansy (Isabella MacDonald Alden). HELEN LESTER
1865: Sophie May. DOTTY DIMPLE
1865: (Edward Everett Hale.) THE MAN WITHOUT A COUNTRY
1866: M. E. Dodge. HANS BRINKER
1867: Martha Farquharson. ELSIE DINSMORE
1867: Harry Castlemon. FRANK ON THE LOWER MISSISSIPPI
1868: Paul Du Chaillu. STORIES OF THE GORILLA COUNTRY
1968: Horatio Alger, Jr. RAGGED DICK
1868: Louisa M. Alcott. LITTLE WOMEN
1869: Rev. Elijah Kellogg. LION BEN OF ELM ISLAND
1870: Frank R. Stockton. TING A LING
1870: Louisa M. Alcott. AN OLD FASHIONED GIRL
1870: Thomas Bailey Aldrich. THE STORY OF A BAD BOY
1871: Louisa M. Alcott. LITTLE MEN
1871: Horatio Alger, Jr. TATTERED TOM
1871: J. T. Trowbridge. JACK HAZARD AND HIS FORTUNES
1873: Susan Coolidge. WHAT KATY DID
1974: C. A. Stephens. THE YOUNG MOOSE HUNTERS
1875: (Horace E. Scudder.)
DOINGS OF THE BODLEY FAMILY IN TOWN AND COUNTRY
1876: Mark Twain. THE ADVENTURES OF TOM SAWYER
1876: (John Habberton.) HELEN'S BABIES
1877: Charles Carleton Coffin. THE BOYS OF '76
1877: Noah Brooks. THE BOY EMIGRANTS
1880: Hezekiah Butterworth. ZIGZAG JOURNEYS IN EUROPE
1880: Lucretia P. Hale. THE PETERKIN PAPERS
1880: Thomas W. Knox. THE BOY TRAVELLERS IN THE FAR EAST
1880: Margaret Sidney. FIVE LITTLE PEPPERS AND HOW THEY GREW
1881: Joel Chandler Harris. UNCLE REMUS

1881: Rev. E. E. Hale and Miss Susan Hale. A FAMILY FLIGHT THROUGH
FRANCE, GERMANY, NORWAY AND SWITZERLAND
1881: James Otis. TOBY TYLER
1881: Rossiter Johnson. PHAETON ROGERS
1881: Frank R. Stockton. THE FLOATING PRINCE
1882: D. C. Beard. THE AMERICAN BOYS HANDY BOOK
1882: James Baldwin. THE STORY OF SIEGFRIED
1882: Louise-Clarke Pyrnelle. DIDDIE, DUMPS, AND TOT
1882: Mark Twain. THE PRINCE AND THE PAUPER
1883: George W. Peck. PECK'S BAD BOY AND HIS PA
1883: Lizzie W. Champney. THREE VASSAR GIRLS ABROAD
1833: Edward Eggleston. THE HOOSIER SCHOOL-BOY
1883: Howard Pyle. THE MERRY ADVENTURES OF ROBIN HOOD
OF GREAT RENOWN, IN NOTTINGHAMSHIRE
1885: Mark Twain. ADVENTURES OF HUCKLEBERRY FINN
1886: Charles E. Carryl. DAVY AND THE GOBLIN
1886: Jane Andrews.
TEN BOYS WHO LIVED ON THE ROAD FROM LONG AGO TO NOW
1886: Frances Hodgson Burnett. LITTLE LORD FAUNTLEROY
1886: Amelia E. Barr. THE BOW OF ORANGE RIBBON
1887: Kirk Munroe. THE FLAMINGO FEATHER
1886: Palmer Cox. THE BROWNIES
1887: James Baldwin. A STORY OF THE GOLDEN AGE
1887: Kate Douglas Wiggin. THE BIRDS' CHRISTMAS CAROL
1888: Robert Grant. JACK HALL
1888: Frances Hodgson Burnett. EDITHA'S BURGLAR
1888: Thomas Nelson Page. TWO LITTLE CONFEDERATES
1888: Frances Courtenay Baylor. JUAN AND JUANITA
1888: Howard Pyle. OTTO OF THE SILVER HAND
1890: W. D. Howells. A BOY'S TOWN
1890: Sarah Orne Jewett. BETTY LEICESTER
1891: Laura E. Richards. CAPTAIN JANUARY
1891: William O. Stoddard. LITTLE SMOKE
1892: Charles E. Carryl. THE ADMIRAL'S CARAVAN
1893: James Otis. JENNY WREN'S BOARDING-HOUSE
1894: Captain Charles King. CADET DAYS
1894: Everett T. Tomlinson. SEARCH FOR ANDREW FIELD
1894: Marshall Saunders. BEAUTIFUL JOE
1894: Kirk Munroe. THE FUR-SEAL'S TOOTH
1896: Annie Fellows-Johnson. THE LITTLE COLONEL
1897: John Bennett. MASTER SKYLARK
1898: Albert Bigelow Paine. THE HOLLOW TREE

1898: Ernest Seton Thompson. WILD ANIMALS I HAVE KNOWN
1899: Ralph Henry Barbour. THE HALF-BACK
1899: William Allen White. THE COURT OF BOYVILLE
1900: Gelett Burgess. GOOPS AND HOW TO BE THEM
1900: L. Frank Baum. THE WONDERFUL WIZARD OF OZ
1901: Alice Caldwell Hegan. MRS. WIGGS OF THE CABBAGE PATCH
1901: Josephine Diebitsch Peary. THE SNOW BABY
1902: John Bennett. BARNABY LEE
1902: W. D. Howells. THE FLIGHT OF PONY BAKER
1902: Henry A. Shute. THE REAL DIARY OF A REAL BOY
1903: Jack London. THE CALL OF THE WILD
1903: Kate Douglas Wiggin. REBECCA OF SUNNYBROOK FARM
1906: Jack London. WHITE FANG
1908: L. M. Montgomery. ANNE OF GREEN GABLES
1908: Peter Newell. THE HOLE BOOK
1908: Emerson Hough. THE YOUNG ALASKANS
1909: Frances Boyd Calhoun. MISS MINERVA AND
WILLIAM GREEN HILL
1910: Owen Johnson. THE VARMINT
1911: Owen Johnson. THE TENNESSEE SHAD
1912: Jean Webster. DADDY-LONG-LEGS
1913: Eleanor H. Porter. POLLYANNA
1914: Booth Tarkington. PENROD
1914: Edgar Rice Burroughs. TARZAN OF THE APES
1916: Booth Tarkington. PENROD AND SAM
1917: Dorothy Canfield. UNDERSTOOD BETSY
1920: Hugh Lofting. THE STORY OF DOCTOR DOLITTLE
1922: Carl Sandburg. ROOTABAGA STORIES
1922: Steward Edward White. DANIEL BOONE WILDERNESS SCOUT
1923: Charles Boardman Hawes. THE DARK FRIGATE
1926: Will James. SMOKY THE COWHORSE

QUEEN'S QUORUM

Mystery writer Ellery Queen (a collaboration of Frederic Dannay and Manfred B. Lee) won five annual Edgars, including the Grand Master award in 1960. Queen originally selected what he considered the 106 most important books published in the detective-crime field in 1948 and later added 19 other titles.

1845: Edgar Allan Poe. TALES
1856: "Waters." RECOLLECTIONS OF A DETECTIVE POLICE-OFFICER
1859: Wilkie Collins. THE QUEEN OF HEARTS

1860: Charles Dickens. HUNTED DOWN
1861: "Anonyma's." THE EXPERIENCES OF A LADY DETECTIVE
1862: Thomas Bailey. OUT OF HIS HEAD
1867: Mark Twain. THE CELEBRATED JUMPING FROG OF CALAVERAS COUNTY
1876: Emile Gaboriau. THE LITTLE OLD MAN OF BATIGNOLLES
1878: James M'Govan. BROUGHT TO BAY
1881: "A New York Detective." DETECTIVE SKETCHES
1882: Robert Louis Stevenson. NEW ARABIAN NIGHTS
1884: Frank R. Stockton. THE LADY, OR THE TIGER?
1888: Eden Phillpotts. MY ADVENTURE IN FLYING SCOTSMAN
1888: Dick Donovan. THE MAN-HUNTER
1892: Israel Zangwill. THE BIG BOW MYSTERY
1892: A. Conan Doyle. THE ADVENTURES OF SHERLOCK HOLMES
1894: L. T. Meade and Dr. Clifford Halifax.
STORIES FROM THE DIARY OF A DOCTOR
1894: Arthur Morrison. MARTIN HEWITT, INVESTIGATOR
1895: M. P. Shiel. PRINCE ZALESKI
1896: Melville Davisson Post. THE STRANGE SCHEMES OF RANDOLPH MASON
1897: Grant Allen. AN AFRICAN MILLIONAIRE
1897: George R. Sims. DORCAS DENE, DETECTIVE
1898: M. McDonnell Bodkin. PAUL BECK, THE RULE OF THUMB DETECTIVE
1898: Rodriquest Ottolengui. FINAL PROOF
1899: Nicholas Carter. THE DETECTIVE'S PRETTY NEIGHBOR
1899: L. T. Meade and Robert Eustace. THE BROTHERHOOD OF KINGS
1900: Herbert Cadett. THE ADVENTURES OF A JOURNALIST
1901: Richard Harding Davis. IN THE FOG
1902: Clifford Ashdown. THE ADVENTURES OF ROMNEY PRINGLE
1902: Bret Harte. CONDENSED NOVELS
1903: Percival Pollard. LINGO DAN
1905: B. Fletcher Robinson. THE CHRONICLES OF ADDINGTON PEACE
1905: Arnold Bennett. THE LOOT OF CITIES
1906: Robert Barr. THE TRIUMPHS OF EUGENE VALMONT
1906: Alfred Henry Lewis. CONFESSIONS OF A DETECTIVE
1907: Maurice Leblanc. THE EXPLOITS OF ARSENE LUPIN
1907: Jacques Futrelle. THE THINKING MACHINE
1908: George Randolph Chester. GET-RICH-QUICK WALLINGFORD
1908: O. Henry. THE GENTLE GRAFTER
1909: Baroness Orczy. THE OLD MAN IN THE CORNER
1909: R. Austin Freeman. JOHN THORNDYKE'S CASES
1909: J. S. Fletcher. THE ADVENTURES OF ARCHER DAWE (SLEUTH-HOUND)
1910: Balduin Groller. DETECTIVE DAGOBERT'S DEEDS AND ADVENTURES
1910: T. W. Hanshew. THE MAN OF THE FORTY FACES

1910: William MacHarg and Edwin Balmer.
THE ACHIEVEMENTS OF LUTHER TRANT
1911: G. K. Chesterton. THE INNOCENCE OF FATHER BROWN
1911: Samuel Hopkins Adams. AVERAGE JONES
1912: Arthur B. Reeve. THE SILENT BULLET
1912: [Gelett Burgess]. THE MASTER OF MYSTERIES
1912: Victor L. Whitechurch. THRILLING STORIES OF THE RAILWAY
1912: R. Austin Freeman. THE SINGING BONE
1913: William Hope Hodgson. CARNACKI THE GHOST-FINDER
1913: Anna Katharine Green. MASTERPIECES OF MYSTERY
1913: Hesketh Prichard. NOVEMBER JOE
1914: Ernest Bramah. MAX CARRODOS
1914: Arthur Sherburne Hardy. DIANE AND HER FRIENDS
1916: Thomas Burke. LIMEHOUSE NIGHTS
1917: A. E. W. Mason. THE FOUR CORNERS OF THE WORLD
1918: Melville Davisson Post. UNCLE ABNER
1918: Ellis Parker Butler. PHILO GUBB
1919: John Russell. THE RED MARK
1920: William Le Queux. MYSTERIES OF A GREAT CITY
1920: Sax Rohmer. THE DREAM-DETECTIVE
1920: J. Storer Clouston. CARRINGTON'S CASES
1920: Vincent Starrett. THE UNIQUE HAMLET
1920: Arthur Train. TUTT AND MR. TUTT
1920: H. C. Bailey. CALL MR. FORTUNE
1922: Maurice Leblanc. THE EIGHT STROKES OF THE CLOCK
1923: Octavus Roy Cohen. JIM HANVEY, DETECTIVE
1924: Agatha Christie. POIROT INVESTIGATES
1925: Edgar Wallace. THE MIND OF MR. J. G. REEDER
1926: Louis Golding. LUIGI OF CATANZARO
(Or see alternate 1936 listing.)
1927: Anthony Wynne. SINNERS GO SECRETLY
1927: Susan Glaspell. A JURY OF HER PEERS
1928: Dorothy L. Sayers. LORD PETER VIEWS THE BODY
1928: G. D. H. and M. I. Cole. SUPERINTENDENT WILSON'S HOLIDAY
1928: W. Somerset Maugham. ASHENDEN
1929: Percival Wilde. ROGUES IN CLOVER
1929: T. S. Stribling. CLUES OF THE CARIBBEES
1929: Harvey J. O'Higgins. DETECTIVE DUFF UNRAVELS IT
1930: Frederick Irving Anderson. BOOK OF MURDER
1931: F. Tennyson Jesse. THE SOLANGE STORIES
1931: Damon Runyon. GUYS AND DOLLS
1932: Georges Simenon. THE THIRTEEN CULPRITS

1933: Leslie Charteris. THE BRIGHTER BUCCANEER
1933: Henry Wade. POLICEMAN'S LOT
1934: Mignon G. Eberhart. THE CASES OF SUSAN DARE
1934: Irvin S. Cobb. FAITH, HOPE AND CHARITY
1934: Ellery Queen. THE ADVENTURES OF ELLERY QUEEN
1936: C. Daly King. THE CURIOUS MR. TARRANT
1936: Louis Golding. PALE BLUE NIGHTGOWN
(Alternate. See 1926.)
1938: E. C. Bentley. TRENT INTERVENES
1939: Margery Allingham. MR. CAMPION AND OTHERS
1940: Carter Dickson. THE DEPARTMENT OF QUEER COMPLAINTS
1940: William MacHarg. THE AFFAIRS OF O'MALLEY
1942: H. Bustos Domecq. SIX PROBLEMS FOR DON ISIDRO PARODI
1944: William Irish. AFTER-DINNER STORY
1944: Dashiell Hammett. THE ADVENTURES OF SAM SPADE
1944: Raymond Chandler. FIVE MURDERERS
1946: Lillian de la Torre. DR. SAM: JOHNSON, DETECTOR
1946: Rafael Sabatini. TURBULENT TALES
1946: Antonio Helú. THE COMPULSION TO MURDER
1947: Stuart Palmer. THE RIDDLES OF HILDEGARDE WITHERS
1947: Roy Vicker. THE DEPARTMENT OF DEAD ENDS
1949: William Faulkner. KNIGHT'S GAMBIT
1950: Lawrence G. Blochman. DIAGNOSIS: HOMICIDE
1951: John Collier. FANCIES AND GOODNIGHTS
1952: Philip MacDonald. SOMETHING TO HIDE
1952: Lord Dunsany. THE LITTLE TALES OF SMETHERS
1953: Edmund Crispin. BEWARE OF THE TRAINS
1953: Roald Dahl. SOMEONE LIKE YOU
1954: Michael Innes. APPLEBY TALKING
1956: Stanley Ellin. MYSTERY STORIES
1956: Evan Hunter. THE JUNGLE KIDS
1957: Charlotte Armstrong. THE ALBATROSS
1958: Craig Rice. THE NAME IS MALONE
1958: Rufus King. MALICE IN WONDERLAND
1959: Georges Simenon. THE SHORT CASES OF INSPECTOR MAIGRET
1961: Patrick Quentin. THE ORDEAL OF MRS. SNOW
1963: Stuart Palmer and Craig Rice. PEOPLE VS. WITHERS & MALONE
1965: Helen McCloy. SURPRISE, SURPRISE!
1966: Robert L. Fish. THE INCREDIBLE SCHLOCK HOMES
1967: Miriam Allen Deford. THE THEME IS MURDER
1967: Michael Gilbert. GAME WITHOUT RULES
1967: Harry Kemelman. THE NINE MILE WALK

Sources for Books

BOOK COLLECTING requires on-the-job training, particularly in the pricing area. The best way to get a feel for prices in the old days (last year) was to visit a number of shops and obtain as many catalogs as possible. Now we have the Internet to surf and look for prices for the books on the Net (more below). The Net is a help, because the ability to visit shops may not be practical if you don't travel much, although you will find that book collecting and travel go very well together, providing a good excuse to take short trips to towns within a few hundred miles or so. And it should be noted that although the Net is a great resource, there is no substitute for actually looking at the books themselves. Traveling allows you visit the tourist attractions, hotels, and restaurants, but also you will now have the pleasure of looking over the stock of the bookstores in town.

Once you have decided what to collect and have a feel for prices, you need to spend some money. There is nothing like spending money to sharpen your wits and force you to take the whole business a little more seriously.

The Internet

First we must explain what we mean by the Internet in relation to the collector. The Internet and the World Wide Web allow booksellers to establish a home page where they can display their entire stock to the book-buying public. These home pages are reached by typing in the web address of the business. Ours, for instance, is www.qb.com. If you come to our site, you can look at our books alphabetically under Literature, which includes fiction, poetry, children's books, illustrated, etc.; or Mystery, which includes detective, nautical, westerns, science fiction, etc. There are also detailed write-ups on the books we publish, our books published by Putnam, and our computer programs for dealers and collectors. And the information is all available, worldwide, twenty-four hours a day.

But the real bonus for the collector is the other way dealers display their stock on the Net. This is to list all of their books on one of the data search services, which are also available twenty-four hours a day. There are four primary servers that put the collector in touch with booksellers. They are ABAA.org (discussed below), Advance Book Exchange (ABEBooks.com), Bibliocity.com, and Bibliofind.com.

Many dealers display their stock on more than one service, and some display on all of the services because there does appear to be a slightly different customer base with each service. There are a few other search services, and one that searches most of the other sites, which can be reached at mxbf.com, but the latter shows only a limited number of the books from each site, so you should look at the main sites as well, particularly if you are searching for an uncommon book.

The listings you will see on the screen will look like catalog entries, with author, title, place, date, description, and price.

Our association, the Antiquarian Booksellers Association of America (ABAA), has a site where only the books for sale by members of the ABAA are displayed (ABAA.org). The ABAA is the largest association of antiquarian booksellers in the world and is affiliated with similar associations in many other countries through the International League of Antiquarian Booksellers (ILAB). The ABAA has a code of ethics, and the members guarantee the books and manuscripts they sell to be as described. Collectors should always check the ABAA site (ABAA.org) before buying. If price and condition are similar, we would suggest buying from a dealer you have dealt with before and trust or an ABAA dealer.

As you can see from the above, the Internet has become a major vehicle for searching for and selling books. It has broadened access to books by offering an instant marketplace of available books. Not that these books were not available before the Net. They were, but most were not visible to the customers. The latest estimate of books being offered by just one of the many book search engines on the Internet is somewhere around 20 million books, and the people who operate that site estimate that they are adding 250 new "dealers" and 600,000 new books a month.

As more and more books are offered for sale daily on the Internet, the true availability for individual titles becomes known. Prices in this marketplace are established by supply and demand. Lower-priced and medium-priced books are more plentiful than before, and therefore the market is pushing the prices of these books lower. Conversely, the true scarcity of many titles is also being shown by their absence on the Net. Specialty dealers who have always scoured the country for books, participated in book fairs across the nation, put out want lists, and received quotes from around the world have always known when a book is extremely hard to find. But now it is becoming more obvious to everyone involved in the book-collecting community that these titles are really scarce or rare. Hard-to-find books are not on the Net, or if they are, they are not on for long, and thus the prices for truly scarce items are being pushed up.

For years, books were priced by a variety of methods that included the frequency that the dealer had seen or handled a particular title, how fast a book sold, how many times it had appeared at auction, and how other dealers priced the same or similar books in their catalogs.

Now instead of knowing only what is available at local bookstores, from book catalogs you receive, or from quotes you have requested from individual book dealers, you can also go online, where millions of books are being offered at varying prices. Sound good? It is, but there is a problem. A major problem. Many of the books being offered at these low prices, and listed as first editions in wonderful condition, are not. In many cases you don't know the person offering the book and must send your check in advance. When you receive the book it sometimes isn't as described. It isn't a first edition and the condition doesn't even come close to being what you expected. You notify the individual or dealer that you are sending it back for refund, and sometimes the return is refused and you are stuck with a book that you don't want. But like all things, it works both ways. Sometimes you make a great buy at a great price.

Previously, most "book scouts" worked from dealers' want lists and catalogs, or price guides, to scout books and sell them to dealers. The scouts didn't know the private customers and had no way of reaching them. Catalogs are expensive. Our small catalogs (no envelopes, 32 to 64 pages) cost $3,000 to $4,000 for printing and postage. This type of expense was too high a hurdle for book scouts, so they were happy to sell their books to specialist dealers at 40 to 50 cents on the dollar. Similarly, starting and small dealers did not have the money to put out catalogs and were happy to sell at lower than presumed retail prices. And many large general bookstore owners didn't have the time or energy to put out catalogs, so they would also price their stock at less than what they thought was full retail, particularly anything outside their field. They didn't expect collectors to find their store on a regular basis and were happy to price for the traveling specialist dealers.

Now, because of the Internet, the scouts and small and starting dealers can also offer their books to the collectors on line for subscriber fees of only $25 to $40 a month.

In addition, book collectors who accumulated duplicates and would normally have traded or sold these copies back to a dealer may now decide to put them on the Net.

Parents, aunts, or uncles die, and they pass on their book collections, sometimes to family members who know nothing about the books they have inherited but they are computer-literate and do know they don't want them, so they put them up on the Net to make a little money. The good books sell immediately, the lesser copies may sell eventually.

So the collector must understand that the books listed on the Net represent the stock of

1 Dealers who operate open stores and spend anywhere from $3,000 to $6,000 to print and mail small catalogs; and from $6,000 to $15,000 for a large or color catalog; attend book fairs throughout the country, spending anywhere from $2,000 to $6,000 for each fair and in some cases more, to sell books, but more important to meet old and new customers.

2 Book scouts who buy titles relatively inexpensively and need quick turnover to keep going. They have no interest in stocking books or for the most part in getting full retail price.

3 Starting small book dealers or part-time dealers operating from their home.

4 General bookstores who depend on walk-in sales and always have priced many of their books under the market in order to appeal to the traveling specialist dealers who constituted a significant portion of their sales.

5 Book collectors who are selling their duplicates at, or below, the prices they paid, which may have been years ago.

6 Anyone who has inherited or accumulated a number of books and decided to sell them.

Except for the first category above, none of the these "dealers" would have had their "stock" available to the general book collecting marketplace before the Internet.

However, we want to stress again the importance of condition and what a large component it is of price for collected books. And make sure condition is taken into account when collectors are making purchase decisions on the Net.

As an example of the price differences among copies of the same title, we offer the following. We have a copy of Faulkner's *Absalom, Absalom!* without the dustwrapper. It's a nice copy with the pages and cover clean. Not fine, but certainly very good. It's priced $60. We also have another copy. In this case, the book is about the same but it's in a worn but complete dustwrapper with some minor chipping. It's priced at $350. We had another copy we sold recently, much nicer, in a bright dustwrapper, and priced at $1,500. Recently a collector we know called to tell us about a copy he had just bought. It was beautiful, almost new. We asked how much he had to spring for it. "Well," he said, "the dealer wanted $4,000, but I got him down to $3,000."

From $60 to $3,000! Same book? No. Same title. All first printings of the first edition, but markedly different condition.

Speaking of Faulkner: We were looking on the Net for a copy of his first book, *The Marble Faun* (1924), a $10,000 to $20,000 book. We found two copies under the listing, neither the first publication but both instead the first combined publication of *The Marble Faun* and *A Green Bough* (1965), a book we think is worth perhaps $75 to $100 in fine condition. The two copies were priced at $1,775 and $2,000. We hope no one buys them at these prices.

These are a few examples of what to be careful about on the Net. When we enter a book into inventory, we spend more time on the description than we do on typing in the rest of the information. In many cases we spend much more time. This is because the condition is the most important part of the entry from the collector's viewpoint. On the Net many of the "dealers" use abbreviations to describe their books. G = good, vg = very good, f = fine, n = near. The first refers to the book and the second to the dustwrapper. So we have g/g = a book in good condition and a dustwrapper in good condition. For example, listings for individual books will state "g/vg," "f/f," "vg/vg-," and our favorite, "f-/nf+." These obviously have meaning to the people that entered them, but they mean little to anyone else. The most common description is "f/f." We have attempted to buy a number of books so described. Unfortunately, many times the books are not "f/f" but are book-club editions, or books with half the dustwrapper spine gone, or books that have mysteriously developed huge dampstains. Don't get us wrong—we ourselves have made mistakes and misdescribed our books, or, more commonly, had a book in stock for years and found when we went to pull it for shipping that the condition has disintegrated from all of the handling over the years. This is always very embarrassing. The point is that after you find a book on the Net, call or e-mail and obtain a specific, detailed description of the book before you buy it, and always check the ABAA.org site before making a final decision.

We know the books that are being exposed to view now on the Net always existed before the Net. Most of these books would have found their way into the trade and on to the final consumer, the collector, eventually. But now we have what may have been a two-year or three-year supply being compressed and shown at once. It is obvious that the 500-plus copies of Stephen King's *It* on the Net would take a long time to absorb and probably never will be absorbed. But we dealers were all aware that the first printings of most of the later books by Stephen King and Tom Clancy were published in quantities of a million or more, and if we handled them at all we priced them at the original price of $20 or $25. Now these books and many others which are common are being offered for $5 and up.

On the other hand, write down the titles of ten books you have spent years looking for and look them up on the Net. See how many are there. We'd wager that you would find very few.

We recently spoke to a collector who had looked on the Net a few months ago and found ten copies of a book he had been looking for. He decided to wait to get a copy, because he had others to buy, and with ten copies he assumed he could get the book later. When he went back, they were all gone!

So, the question is, how long will it take to absorb many of the scarcer books that have shown up in quantity on the Net? We can't answer that question, because we know the answer will be different for each title. Some will take a long time, even if only three are available, because we know that in many cases the customers for a title are scarcer than the book.

We also know, from conducting the research for the current prices for the authors' first books in this book, that there may be five copies of a first edition of a certain title on the net. All described as vg/vg or f/f, which all turn out to be in less, many times much less, than collectible condition.

Another thing we know for sure is that the number of books listed on the Net and the number of people starting to use the Net are increasing every day, and it will be a few years before the rate of increase slows down and all of us will really find out what the true impact of the Internet on book collecting has been.

Catalogs

Catalogs can be obtained for the asking, at least initially. There is a list of dealers who issue catalogs in Appendix B. A complete list of all of the members of the Antiquarian Booksellers Association of America (ABAA) can be obtained free by requesting a copy of the ABAA Membership Directory from ABAA, 20 West 44th Street, New York, NY 10036-6604 (212-944-8291; fax: 944-8293). ABAA members offer a broad choice of antiquarian material in all areas of the printed and written word.

The vast majority of dealers do not charge for their catalogs and will usually send you the current catalog and perhaps one or two more. There are many standard abbreviations and terms used in these catalogs, and we have tried to cover many of them in the Glossary. If you don't purchase anything from their catalogs, the dealers will drop you from their mailing lists on the assumption that you just wanted the catalogs for pricing information or that you are not really interested in the type of books they stock. If you are interested in their books but just do not find anything in the first two catalogs, you should ask if you can send them a list of exactly what you are looking for so they can quote you specific titles as they arrive. Keeping your name on mailing lists is very simple—just buy books. We have people who have asked for our catalogs every two years since we started in business and have never bought a book from us. The cost of preparing, printing, and mailing catalogs is such that few dealers can afford to keep someone on their mailing list who doesn't buy from them. After all, that is the reason the catalogs were prepared—to sell books.

General Used-Book Stores and Sales

There are a great number of sources for books. There are garage sales; school, charity, library, and church book sales; antique stores; and general used-book stores. Most of these are not particularly interested in either keeping up with current prices or trying to sell for the going market price. But you should keep in mind that these are also the places where you can occasionally get stung the worst as a beginner, because there are always a few books that the owners or operators have heard are worth $100 and so they have priced their copy at $100 even though the condition is such that a specialist in the field might be embarrassed to ask more than $25.

There are many dealers around the world, and with pricing being somewhat subjective and collecting interests varying from one geographical location to another, there are always certain authors or subjects that bring premium prices in one region while attracting little interest elsewhere. If you are in a store that doesn't catalog, there is a good chance that the books that don't sell well in that area will be priced much lower than the market price.

Specialist Dealers

The next group is the specialist dealers. These dealers may specialize in just one field or a number of collecting interests, but they don't consider themselves general book dealers, and except for the occasional volume, they will not stock books in other fields. Many have favorite authors or books that they insist on pricing above the market, and authors and books they dislike and price below the market. Then there are the books a dealer has never seen before and therefore assumes are extremely scarce and worth more than the market would indicate, and the books everyone else seems to believe are scarce but that they know are not scarce because they have had five copies in the past two years, and thus they price the book lower than the market would indicate. But on 95 to 99 percent of the stock, they're all pricing in the same range, plus or minus 20 percent.

There are a few dealers who claim (and fewer still who are right) that the condition of any book they carry is so superior to any other available copy that the collector should not mind paying two or three times the going market price for their copy. In these cases the collector should be very satisfied that the book received is in fact in very fine condition and worth the price; otherwise, if the collector finds another copy in similar or better condition at a significantly lower price in the future, she or he will be disappointed not only in the copy but also in the dealer from whom it was purchased.

Auctions

For the book collector there are a number of auction houses that handle books. Swann Galleries in New York City is probably the most active auction house as far as number of books is concerned, because Swann has weekly sales. There are other houses, such as Christie's and Sotheby's, that have important book sales during the year that usually don't include lots that would sell for a less than $500 to $1,000. Christie's is also auctioning less "pricey" books at their Christie's East location. There are a number of other houses that have monthly or quarterly sales. A few of these houses are listed in Appendix C.

Of course the Internet has also begun to have an impact on auctions. The website eBay.com auctions everything under the sun, including books. It can be very addictive and time-consuming, but there are bargains to be purchased. But as mentioned above in the Internet discussion, condition is a problem. Some heavy buyers on eBay have told me they have to return at least a third of the items as misdescribed.

Auction prices tend to vary widely. Many of the books at auction will sell for half the market price, particularly the cheaper books, while sales of books from a major collection will often garner prices for many lots far in excess of the market prices.

Recently eBay purchased Butterfield & Butterfield, an older established auction house; and Southeby's made an arrangement with Amazon.com.

Such transactions may lead to the segretation of better books into a few Internet sites so that buyers will be able to view them more easily.

There also are auction houses in many cities, and occasionally their auctions handle estate sales containing books. These auctions are advertised in local papers, and it's possible to find some real bargains.

Knowledgeable Buying

IN ORDER to become a knowledgeable buyer, you should be aware of issue points, bibliographies in your field, and available pricing information.

We believe strongly that one of the major drawbacks for a beginning book collector is the difficulty of finding out what is available by an author, how to identify the editions, and what is a reasonable price range for individual books. The following will provide some information on these subjects.

First Issue or State, and "Points"

In the case of a number of books, particularly those published before 1900, one can differentiate between the first and later printings only by being aware of the changes made between printings. These changes can be in the text, the type used, the number of pages, the dates in the ads, or the type of binding (cloth, leather, boards, wrappers). In some cases the authors may have wished to make changes in the text themselves, or the publishers may have run out of a certain color cloth for the covers and switched to another color. These differences are known as the "points." The most common points are typographical errors that are discovered and corrected between printings or even midway through the first printing.

When these changes occur, the points indicate the first issue or first state of the printing. The Glossary (at the end of this section) includes a discussion of these terms, but it is worthwhile to quote P. H. Muir's *Book-Collecting as a Hobby,* where the difference between issues and states is summarized as follows:

An "issue" is caused by some change . . . after some copies have already been circulated, [while] a "state" is caused by a . . . change before any copies of the book have been circulated.

In the following list of first books any points associated with a book will be mentioned. The difference in value between issues or states can be great. For instance, the first issue of Dylan Thomas's *18 Poems* (1934) has a flat spine, a leaf between the half title page and the title page, and the front edge roughly trimmed; the second issue (1936) has a rounded spine, leaf (ads) added, and front edge cut evenly. The difference in value between the first and second issue of that book is $2,000 ($3,000 for the first issue and $1,000 for the second).

Bibliographies

The first-edition collector and dealer must know the points connected with the books that they collect or deal in. These points are contained in reference books known as bibliographies. General bibliographies cover many authors or a wide field such as Americana or black literature. One of the most famous is Jacob Blanck's *Bibliography of American Literature* (BAL), which was finally completed with Volume 9 in 1991. BAL is the best single source for bibliographic information on authors who published before 1920. In addition to these general bibliographies, there are specific bibliographies on individual authors. These include books written by or about the author, and in many cases also list the author's appearances in magazines and anthologies, or as contributor of an introduction or preface. The Selected Bibliography (Appendix D) at the end of this book is our start on compiling a bibliography of bibliographies.

We would caution the buyer of a bibliography to attempt to examine a copy of the book before purchasing it. As dealers, we maintain a large reference library of individual-author bibliographies, and we must say that we're surprised at the number of bibliographies that, although extensive and expensive, do not assist one in identifying first editions.

In spite of the foregoing comments, we feel strongly that collectors and dealers should buy bibliographies relevant to their collections or specialties even if they are deficient in describing the first editions. We say this because we have noticed that as the "A" items (primary works) for an author continue to appreciate, there is an increased interest in the other items—for example, magazine appearances (which usually precede book appearances) and books edited by, translated by, or with contributions by the author, such as anthology appearances (which are in many cases the first book appearance of the work). And most of these bibliographies do contain relatively complete information on these secondary items.

The standard-setter in modern bibliography, in our opinion, is Donald Gallup. In his book *On Contemporary Bibliography*, Mr. Gallup states:

It is the bibliographer's first duty to make his bibliography useful. . . .

And what exactly should be his job: His function as I see it may be summarized under three principal headings:

First, to establish the canon of the author's printed work;

Second, to identify and describe first and important later editions of the books, in their variants, states, and issues, with their various bindings and dust jackets, explaining their significance where it is not readily apparent, and accounting, if possible, for any unusual aspects; and

Third, to establish for at least each major book the exact date of publication, date of composition (where this differs substantially), number of copies printed, and price at which the book sold when it was first published. He may, and doubtless will, do other things, but these seem to me to be the essentials.

There are books that are entitled "Checklists" which do not include precise information on how to identify the first printing, but these are not misleading, for they are billed as "Checklists" and not as "Bibliographies." But what do you do when you've bought a "Bibliography" and find that the bibliographer has not bothered to mention the existence of limited editions or how to identify the first editions?

The foregoing complaint has been made so often that we decided that rather than complain (or in addition to complaining), we would do something positive, so we started to publish a series of *Author Price Guides* (APGs), which we try to make as bibliographically correct as possible.

The APGs include:

- A facsimile of the author's signature.
- A brief biographical sketch.
- A separate listing for each issue of each book or pamphlet by the author. In other words, for each title there are separate listings for a limited lettered edition, a numbered edition, first American edition, and first British editions, if applicable.
- Each individual listing includes the title, publisher, place of publication, date of publication, number of copies (if known), exact information for identifying the first printing, retail price estimates for the book with and without a dustwrapper, and a reference to the source of the bibliographical information.

An author's "A" items—that is, the books, pamphlets, and broadsides attributed to the author (147 titles and almost 300 items in the case of Robert Graves)—will be expanded over the years to include important "B" items. Proof copies will be included as seen or reported, but only if color or some other means of differentiating them is known, for we assume almost all books are preceded by proofs.

Given the nature of bibliographic research and volatility of prices, each APG is updated as necessary, and as it does not seem reasonable to require the purchaser to pay full price for updates, the original purchasers of an individual APG are charged full price only the first time they purchase that APG; extra copies and subsequent updates are made available at half price.

The APGs have proved useful as accurate, current, and reasonably priced bibliographical checklists, which include relatively accurate retail price estimates. The APGs will, of course, be improved over the years as collectors, librarians, and dealers contribute new or revised information, which will be incorporated in updates.

A list of the APGs is available from Author Price Guides, 1137 Sugarloaf Mountain Road, Dickerson, MD 20842.

General sources for bibliographic information include:

First Printings of American Authors (FPAA), edited by Matthew G. Bruccoli, C. E. Frazer Clark, Jr., et al. Detroit: Gale Research (1977–79). These five volumes cover about 360 authors, both U.S. and English editions, with title page and first edition identification for all U.S. editions, and fifty of the author's English editions (title, publisher, and dates for English editions of the other 310 authors).

A Bibliographical Introduction to Seventy-five Modern American Authors, by Gary M. Lepper. Berkeley: Serendipity Books (1976). Includes first-edition identification for the U.S. editions of the 75 novelists and poets (unless a title was first published elsewhere, in which case the foreign edition is included).

Science Fiction and Fantasy Authors: A Bibliography of First Printings of Their Fiction, edited by L. W. Currey. (Boston: G. K. Hall, 1979.) It covers 216 authors' works, including first-edition identification. The book is excellent for all science-fiction and fantasy titles (further checking will be required to obtain titles outside these fields).

Bibliography of American Literature (BAL), compiled by Jacob Blanck (volumes 1–6) and edited and completed by Virginia L. Smyers and Michael Winship (volume 7), and by Michael Winship alone (volumes 8 and 9). (New Haven and London: Yale University Press, 1955–1991). It covers 281 authors, from Henry Adams through Elinor Wylie, with full bibliographical details, and extends to the early part of this century. In print and at most libraries.

A general source for title, publisher, and date, by author, would be the series Contemporary Authors (over one hundred volumes; in most public libraries); and the series of reference works published by St. Martin's Press including *Twentieth-Century:*

> *Children's Writers*
> *Crime and Mystery Writers*
> *Romance and Gothic Writers*
> *Science Fiction Writers*
> *Western Writers.*

Reprint Publishers and Book Clubs

There are certain publishers that normally only reprint books originally published by others. The most common are Grosset & Dunlap, A. L. Burt, Blakison, Hurst, Modern Library, Sun Dial, Triangle, and World's Tower Books (although the latter did publish two of Raymond Chandler's first editions). These reprints are not particularly valuable unless a new introduction is included in the edition, although some of the very early scarce titles by very popular authors are sought by collectors if they are in fine condition in dustwrappers, principally because the dustwrappers on these reprints duplicated the front cover and spine of the original trade first editions.

We understand there have been over eight hundred book clubs in the United States during this century. Many of these, we assume, sent their members regular trade editions of a book. In the case of book clubs that printed their own editions, there is normally no problem identifying them if the book has a dustwrapper, as the front flap of the dustwrapper will state that it is a book club edition and will not have a price on the flap.

If the book is by a publisher that states "First Edition" or "First Printing" on the verso of the title page, the lack of this statement will make it easily identifiable as other than a first edition. Book-of-the-Month Club (BoMC) editions, from 1947, printed books using the original publishers' plates, and they look exactly like the publisher's edition and frequently state "First Edition/Printing." Until the last decade or so, these BoMC editions were also easy to identify without the dustwrapper, as they contained a small mark on the lower right corner of the rear cover. (For books from before 1947 it is difficult to differentiate the BoMC edition from the true first edition.) The mark was a small black circle in earlier books, or in more recent years, merely a circular or square depression (blindstamp) in the lower right-hand corner of the back cover. At some point in the last decade or so, the BoMC stopped putting these marks on the back cover and started using a short series of letters and numbers printed so that it runs along the hinge or gutter on the last page (or one of the last pages) of the book. You may have to open the book almost flat to see it. Recently they have stopped differentiating at all, except that there is no price on the dustwrapper. We're trying to find differences in bindings or dustwrappers, and if there are any, we note them in our Author Price Guides; this is obviously going to become a problem in identification.

The Literary Guild book-club editions also state "First Edition," but they are easy to identify as the spine and title page indicate "Literary Guild."

If a book-club edition does not have a dustwrapper and is not a Book-of-the-Month Club edition, it may still be identified by the binding and paper, which will be of poorer quality than a normal publisher's edition. The most difficult book-club editions to identify are, in our opinion, those originally published by New Directions and Viking.

Pricing

How are rare or scarce items priced? Not easily.

There was a comedian in the 1950s named Brother Dave Gardner. When someone would say, "Let's do that again," Brother Dave would say, "You can't do anything again. You can do something similar." Well, if a book or manuscript is truly rare or unique, you won't be able to find anything exactly comparable to base your price on, so you have to find something similar.

In order to provide a complete picture of the process of pricing, we must consult all the sources, though some of these may not be helpful in many cases. It is relatively easy to arrive at a price, or at least, a price range, for most collected books, because copies are bought and sold fairly regularly throughout the year. It does, however, become much more difficult to arrive at a price as one explores the pricing of a unique item, such as a great association copy of a book, a unique manuscript, or even a perfect copy of a relatively common book.

The prices paid by dealers and, in turn, the prices they set on the books or manuscripts they sell are a product of the individual dealers' sense of the real market price based on their own knowledge and readings of the auction records and other dealers' catalogs and price guides.

To show how a price is set for a modern first edition, let's look, for example, at Larry McMurtry's *Lonesome Dove* (New York: Simon & Schuster, 1985), a title published in a relatively large first printing of 42,000 copies at the publication price of $18.95. A nice copy started out on the market, in 1985, at $25. It sold easily. The price moved to $40, then $50, $75, $100, $125, $150, and finally to $175. We had continued to sell the book at $150, but at $175 we had no orders. Now this is a snapshot of a period of a few years. We eventually sold the $175 copy and now the book sells for more, but the point is that the marketplace set the price. The dealers, of course, couldn't continue buying *Lonesome Dove* at $10 or $15, but paid more for each successive copy as the scouts or other sellers demanded a higher price at the wholesale level—which, of course, dictated a higher price at the retail level.

The foregoing is a relatively common process in the marketplace and is easy to understand; however, there is a tendency in some cases in recent years to jump straight to the higher value. In other words, a book which was in high demand, such as Tom Clancy's *The Hunt for Red October,* moved from $50 to $100 to $650 to $750 almost overnight. A dealer (or dealers) decided the book was truly scarce and would sell at the higher level. In this case they appear to have been right, even though the first printing was 30,000 copies, of which 15,000 went to libraries. The book continues to sell at the higher level. Whether it will continue to sell at this level in future years is anyone's guess. But now let's consider the uncorrected proof of *The Hunt for Red October.* The proof in paper wrappers had a proof dustwrapper, which was different from the dustwrapper used on the first edition. A copy in dustwrapper was offered for $3,500. A Clancy collector who wanted the proof but was not willing to pay more than $2,000 had asked us to find him one. Eventually, we purchased the copy that had been priced at $3,500 at a lower price and sold it to our collector for $1,850. This is not to say that the $3,500 price was too high. We have heard of only three copies being offered on the market, so it is a rare item. We don't know what the others sold for, but we believe the price we sold our copy for influenced the asking price of the other two copies.

So it is clear the buyers—the market—really set the prices in these three examples. In the last example, the seller could have held out for the $3,500, and perhaps our customer would have eventually paid it, or someone else might have bought it for $3,500. We'll never know.

There are three types of published value guides that are used to determine prices.

1. PRICE GUIDES BASED ON DEALER CATALOG ENTRIES

The most common price guides are those that report the prices asked for books in dealer catalogs. The oldest and largest of these is the *Bookman's Price Index,* which is published twice a year and has over 50 volumes (and does include a section on association copies). There are others, including Zempel and Verkler's *Book Prices Used and Rare;* the series edited by Michael Cole under the title *International Rare Book Prices;* and many others that are general or specific, such as Shelly and Richard Morrison's annual price guides to *Western Americana* and *Texiana.*

These, and the Internet sites previously discussed, are the most useful sources for finding relatively common collected books. Occasionally, one may be lucky and find an item very close to the one being priced or being offered. Although it is not certain whether an item actually sold for the price asked (more on that below), if one finds multiple entries by different dealers year after year it can be assumed the prices are in the ballpark.

The problems with these guides are that:

a. It is not at all certain that a book sold for the price asked, and it may not always be possible to verify a sale with the dealer.

b. The price may be so out-of-date that a sale isn't relevant to today's market, and the market for certain types of books and manuscripts changes very rapidly.

c. These guides report only on books that have appeared on the market; rare books either do not show up often or, more realistically, are sold without ever being cataloged.

So it is recommended that you start with one of these guides because it is possible something similar has been cataloged recently; but keep in mind that they may not prove useful in every case.

2. AUCTION RECORDS

In the United States, the *American Book Prices Current* is published annually (with index volumes published every four years). The last twenty-five years are also available on a CD-ROM. There are similar publications in Europe and elsewhere. The chances of finding a price for a comparable rare book, association copy, or manuscript in the auction records would be greater than in the dealer catalog price guides, but the prices for the same title in the auction records will vary greatly, which may reflect the condition of each book, or, more probably, who bid that day. It should be understood that many dealers buy books for stock at auctions; therefore, many auction prices may represent wholesale rather than retail prices. In some cases, auction prices may represent forced sales and low prices, while in other cases, when the auction has received high visibility, prices paid may be significantly higher than retail. An example of a highly inflated auction price was that of Henry James's *The Ambassadors,* which sold for $5,000, yet at the same time a buyer could have found five or more copies in comparable condition on dealers' shelves for $500 to $750.

Auction prices, therefore, require the knowledge of a dealer, rare-book librarian, or collector of the particular author to be interpreted properly.

Another point worth mentioning is that since index volumes and annual volumes provide little or no description of condition, when using the auction records it is best to check the index first, then go back to the annual volumes, and then to the actual auction catalog (if it is available) for a complete description.

The problems with auction records are similar to price-guide problems in that they can report only what is put at auction; the prices, therefore, may be out of date. Their advantage over price guides based on dealer catalog entries is that you know the auction prices were actually paid. Remember, auction houses charge a premium to the buyer and seller, so find out if the price included the premium(s).

3. PRICE GUIDES PREPARED BY INDIVIDUALS

These are price guides that express the opinions (informed, we hope) of the compilers of the guides. The prices are based on their experience buying and selling books, as well as their interpretation of auction prices and other dealer catalog prices.

The most commonly used guides at present are (and, obviously, we are not at all biased) this book and our *Collected Books: The Guide to Values* (Putnam, 1998), which lists estimated prices for about 20,000 books.

The Author Price Guides, which we also compile, include all the American and English first editions by a particular author, with points for identification of the first edition and values. One of the reasons for the popularity of these guides is that they contain bibliographical information useful in determining if a particular book in hand is a first edition (or a first state or issue within the first edition).

There are similar works, such as Joseph Connolly's *Modern First Editions* and Tom Broadfoot's *Civil War Books: A Priced Checklist with Advice.* These books represent the authors' opinions of what they would price a copy of the individual book at if they were cataloging it the day the guide was prepared.

The problem with these guides is that the prices are only as good as the knowledge of the authors. The tendency is to price relatively common books high and scarce or rare books low. This is reasonable: common books are cataloged often and the expense of cataloging makes it difficult to price a book at under $25. Also, if the book was published at $25, it is hard to value it at, say $5, which, in fact, is the price you might find it at your local used book store or on the Net. On the other hand, if one is attempting to price a fine copy of Faulkner's *Soldier's Pay* in a dust jacket, and no copy in this condition has been on the market for ten years—at least none that the author is aware of—what price do you put in the guide? You list a price based on the last price you can find, perhaps ten years old, tempered by the prices that you know a few inferior copies have brought on the market in recent years. This may or may not be a reasonable estimate, but the odds are that it will be low, particularly if there is a pent-up demand for the book.

A standard comment on price guides is that they are out-of-date as soon as they are published; actually, we don't find this to be true. Most collected books tend to stay at a certain level for a year or two, and most prices do not become really out of date for three or four years. The comment relates mostly to the current "hot" authors or books that many have heard so much about and for which they find the price guides very low compared with current prices. Did anyone foresee Cormac McCarthy's *The Orchard Keeper* becoming a $3,000 book before *All the Pretty Horses* was published? Was it obvious in 1990 that Hemingway's *For Whom the Bell Tolls* and *The Old Man and the Sea* would be selling for $750 to $1,000 or more in 2000?

No one could have known *The Orchard Keeper* would reach such price heights. Of course, $3,000 is a catalog price and will eventually appear in a price guide; we will have to ask if it actually sold at that figure (although it probably did). As to Hemingway, if one had been astute enough in 1990 to realize that after the October 1987 stock market crash the prices of "high spots" of collected books would rise faster than those of other collected books, you might have foreseen that *For Whom the Bell Tolls* and *The Old Man and the Sea* would go up from about $100 to $150 in 1990 to $1,000 or more in 2000, while *Across the River and into the Trees* would only go up from $100 to $200 or $250. Incidentally, the prices of other post-1930 Hemingway titles have followed the latter trend.

"High spots" are hot, and if you are trying to price a beautiful copy of one that hasn't appeared in dealer catalogs or at auction in years, you will not find any help anywhere, because there are new price records set whenever one appears, and most of these sales are not recorded.

As a final note on price guides and auction records, it should be said that users of these reference works have their own ways of interpreting the prices. A number of people have told us that they always use our guides: some use half our values; some use three-quarters of them; some double our prices; and some believe that our prices are for very good copies and that prices for fine copies would be double and mint copies would be triple.

A local bookstore owner who buys our guides told us he got a copy of a certain book, and if it hadn't been for our guides, he would have priced it at $10. As it was, he found the book listed in our guide for $150 and priced it at $60. We bought it.

For auction records, one can usually assume that the retail price for a comparable copy of a book would be 50 to 100 percent above the auction price; as mentioned above, however, there are many instances where this rule of thumb is way off the mark.

OTHER CONSIDERATIONS

Cost

Obviously, the seller's cost for a book will influence the price that he or she asks for it. This is often a factor when dealers handle unusual if not unique books, and can cause concern on the part of a buyer when a book priced at $x appears in another dealer's catalog or is offered to the buyer at $2x or $3x. In this case, the buyer knows the dealer's cost and may believe the "profit" is too high, but it must be realized that the dealer bought the book because he or she believed the first dealer underpriced it. The price may be "high," but time will tell if it is too high. One of our esteemed colleagues, whenever asked if a book is really worth the price he has placed on it, always responds, "Not yet." This means a sale must legitimize the price. If no sale occurs, the dealer can maintain the price or lower it, although the dealer may decide to withdraw the book from the market for a period; or raise the price, which occasionally results in a sale. The antiquarian book field is a marketplace, and the law of supply and demand applies.

Consignor's desired price

It is not uncommon for an unusual or unique book to be on consignment with a dealer. In this case, the price asked may simply be the price the consignor has set plus a nominal profit for the dealer. The dealer may believe the price is high but know that the consignor will not sell the book for less; therefore, the price is firm.

We recall a case in which a library that had a comprehensive collection of an author's works, including manuscripts and letters, was offered an important collection of the author's letters for a high five-figure amount. The librarian believed that the price was too high. The dealer had the letters on consignment. Eventually the letters were purchased by another university at the same price. Again, if there had been no other buyer for the letters, the price might have been lowered or the letters taken off the market.

Individual dealer "experience"

Often a book becomes more attractive and thus more valuable following a change of ownership. If dealer A has a book that dealer B is interested in, dealer B will often exclaim about the high price, how common the book is, the obvious defects that make it only a marginally collectible book, and so on. But having gotten dealer A's price as low as he can and having purchased the book, dealer B becomes transfixed with the beauty and rarity of the volume. A price is not set immediately, as time is needed for dealer B to absorb the aura of the volume and determine a "fair" price for this now "priceless" tome.

We remember a very knowledgeable dealer seeing a second edition, albeit the first illustrated edition, of a very famous book. He told the dealer who owned it that it was nicely bound but only a second edition, after all, and perhaps worth no more than $300. The other dealer, who had not priced the book yet, listened to the sage advice of the first dealer and priced it at $750. The first dealer bought the book immediately and returned to his shop. After some deliberation, he priced it at $1,250. A third dealer came in and asked how anyone could price a second edition of this book at over $1,000! After much discussion, the third dealer bought the book. This dealer went to some lengths to check on previous prices and found nothing useful in any of the price guides available. He then checked all the major libraries in the United States, England, and France, and he discovered that none of them had a copy of the book. He then priced the book at $10,000, and ultimately sold it at a figure approaching this amount. As a footnote, the second dealer proclaimed that the third dealer and his customer were both fools.

Another story about how dealers' prices are set that might also prove educational: A dealer on a trip spied a book he believed was truly rare. The book was priced at $17,500 and was included in a catalog that had just been mailed by the shop. The dealer asked for and received a dealer discount and left the shop with the book. He was aware that the local university did not have a copy of the book and decided to offer the book to the librarian at $24,000. The librarian, however, had just received the catalog from the shop where the book had been purchased, realized that this was the same copy offered in the catalog at $17,500, and mentioned that she had seen this book for $17,500. The dealer responded that he had bought the book and believed it was much scarcer than the catalog price would indicate and had therefore repriced it $24,000, which he believed was a much more realistic price. The librarian told him that she thought $17,500 was a fair price and that she would be willing to pay that amount. The dealer replied that he owned the book now and believed his price was fair, and left. He then went home and did more research. He learned that the Library of Congress did not have a copy and decided that the book was even scarcer than he had originally thought. He made an appointment with the rare-book librarian at the Library of Congress, and at their meeting he offered him the book for $28,000. The LC librarian had also seen the catalog, and he stated that the price was much too high, implying that the dealer was price-gouging. No sale was made. Although the dealer was upset that the librarian believed the book was overpriced, he was becoming more convinced that it was indeed scarcer than he had thought. He offered it to a midwestern university en route to California the following week for $34,000, and promptly sold it at that price.

We must admit we're not sure that all the details of these stories are accurate, but we know that similar scenarios have been played out before and will be played out again.

Most dealers do not want to sell a customer a book at a high price when another copy may turn up on the market at a much lower price within a few years. When a dealer is pricing a unique book, however, there is no possibility that another copy will come on the market. The problem then is, what is comparable? If it is a great association copy inscribed by Ernest Hemingway, what prices have other Hemingway association copies brought? If it is a manuscript by a prominent author, what prices have other manuscripts by that author brought? If none has been sold, what prices have the manuscripts of authors with comparable reputations sold for? There is usually some comparison that can be made, but many times these comparisons are tenuous.

Another approach is to have an independent appraisal of the book, but this may present a problem if the appraisal is either very high or very low. We were once asked to reappraise a collection, because the owners of the collection refused to sell the material at the original appraised value. We made our own appraisal of the material and honestly thought the original appraisal had been ludicrously low. The owner and the university were able to agree on a price, probably somewhere between the two appraisals, although we were never told the final result. It must be added, though, that there are different kinds of, and reasons for, appraisals—for tax or estate purposes, to help the owner know what to ask for the collection if she or he were to sell or otherwise dispose of it, to inform a potential buyer of the value of an item or a collection, and so on. It would seem reasonable when contemplating the purchase of an expensive collection or item to have one, or perhaps even two, independent appraisals of the value to assure the prospective buyer that the price is within reason.

The truly rare or unique item, if demand is high, can be priced as high as the seller wants, but the seller must find a buyer in order to legitimize the price. Even the fact that a book sells for a certain amount does not necessarily mean another copy will also sell for the same amount. The first book may have found the only buyer in the marketplace willing to pay that much. Also, a high price on one copy may bring other copies into the market, thus increasing the supply and lowering the price. The market is constantly changing, with new hypermodern authors coming into fashion and record prices being set every week, or so it seems. All the materials and expertise available should be used in making a purchasing decision.

Condition Isn't Everything—It's the Only Thing

Vince Lombardi was talking about winning, but book collectors could well rephrase his famous quote. The condition of a first edition or any collectible book is the major determinant of its value. The retail prices estimated herein for an author's first book are for very good to fine copies (in dustwrappers after 1920). There is no doubt that certain collectors might pay two or perhaps even three times this amount for an absolutely mint copy of a book.

First-edition collectors are by nature very hard to please. They would like each of their first editions to look new, and they will pay for such copies. The reverse is also true—a book in poor condition is very difficult to sell. Books valued at $100 in fine condition are practically valueless in very poor condition. If the book is rare, it will of course have some value whatever its condition, but only a fraction of what it would be worth if it were a fine to mint copy.

One thing that should be remembered, in spite of the Lombardi restatement, is that lesser copies (unless they are really dogs) will probably increase in value at the same rate as fine copies, except that the starting base is significantly lower.

Unless one is a book collector, dealer, or book scout, it is difficult to understand how to describe the condition of a book. Even within this group there can be wide differences of opinion, which only confirms the fact that condition descriptions are somewhat subjective.

Many people believe that if a book is twenty or thirty years old, it is in very good condition if the covers are still attached, and if the book is one hundred years old, one should not downgrade it just because the covers are no longer attached ("What do you expect, it's one hundred years old!"). We're sympathetic with their confusion, but we're not interested in buying their books.

The following general gradings are used by book dealers:

MINT: As new, unread.
FINE: Close to new, showing slight signs of age but without any defects.
VERY GOOD: A used book that shows some sign of wear but still has no defects.
GOOD: A book that shows normal wear and aging, still complete and with no major defects.

FAIR: A worn and used copy, probably with cover tears and other defects.

READING COPY: A poor copy with text complete but not much else.

As a guide to condition we have included pictures of the book and dust-wrapper of Charles Fort's first book, *The Outcast Manufacturers,* which was published in 1909, to show what an ninety-year-old book can look like.

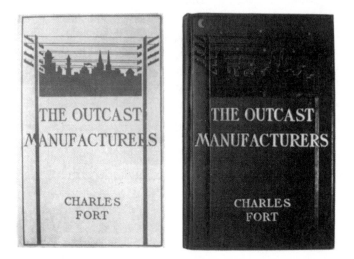

We were called by a family who had been left a copy of Thomas Paine's famous pamphlet published in January of 1776, in which he appealed to the common man to declare his independence. This is a rare and fragile item, having been handed out in the streets during winter, and few have survived intact. Needless to say, we were very excited about the possibility of acquiring this pamphlet. Sad to say, the copy was missing the very last page, on which there was a half page of text. We advised the family to consign it to an auction house. It fetched $8,500 at auction, and later sold with a facsimile page and some cover restoration for about $20,000. Had it been complete, it would probably have sold for $75,000 to $100,00 at the time.

Dustwrappers, or Dust Jackets

The dust jacket, or dustwrapper, that covers a book is a valuable part of a first edition. On recently published books, it is difficult to sell a first edition without a dustwrapper to a collector. On books twenty years old or older, the average increase in value added by the dustwrapper would be close to 400 percent, providing the dustwrapper is in fine condition. This rule would also apply to inexpensive books in the $5 to $40 range, although it would be hard to sell a book in this range without a dustwrapper to a collector at all. But the percent range is fairly consistent on books valued above $40 without a dustwrapper. There are, of course, exceptions to this rule, the most obvious being the value added by the presence of a dustwrapper on the books of Hemingway, Faulkner, or Fitzgerald. It is not unusual for these authors' books to sell for five to ten or even twenty-five times more with a fine dustwrapper than without one. In fact, very good to fine copies of Faulkner's *Soldiers' Pay* and Fitzgerald's *The Great Gatsby* have been sold at twenty to twenty-five times the unjacketed price.

The condition of the dustwrapper is just as important, and perhaps as difficult to describe, as the condition of the book. If a catalog entry does not specifically state that a book is in a dustwrapper, one must assume it is not.

A few examples of dustwrappers illustrating reasonably good condition:

Autographed Books

Author's autographs in a book may be considered in various categories, including signed limited editions, signed trade editions, and association copies.

Signed trade editions are copies of the regular trade first edition signed by the author, with or without an inscription. If the original recipient of the book is not well known or of general interest, some collectors prefer the author's signature without the inscription. These signed books will usually sell for at least twice as much as an unsigned copy, but the real determinant of price will be the value of the author's signature. Some authors are very generous in signing their books; as a result, their signatures may be worth only $10 or $15, representing the price difference between a signed and an unsigned copy of a first edition, or the price of a signed later printing. On the other hand, some authors very rarely sign a book, and their signatures alone may be worth $50 or more; again, this would establish a price. Further, some authors are very free with their signatures but very rarely inscribe copies of their books, and therefore inscribed copies, even if the recipient is unknown, will command a premium.

Association copies are books that include a signed inscription from the author to another famous personality or someone important within the framework of the particular author's life and work. These will be valued more highly than the normal signed first edition, depending on the importance of the recipient involved.

Association copy of a first book. Dedication from Malcolm Lowry to Sylvia Beach, owner of Shakespeare and Company, Paris (reduced).

Glossary

The following is a partial list of terms used in book collecting. The most complete list is contained in John Carter's *ABC for Book Collectors* (see Selected Bibliography).

A.B.A.	Antiquarian Booksellers' Association; the English equivalent of our association (next entry): also the American Bookseller's Association, primarily publishers and sellers of new books.
A.B.A.A.	Antiquarian Booksellers' Association of America.
A.B.P.C.	*American Book Prices Current* (see "Price Guides").
advance copy	A copy for booksellers and reviewers, either bound in paperwraps or a copy of the trade edition with a review slip laid in.

A.L.S.	Autographed letter signed, all in the author's hand.
A.M.S.	Autographed manuscript signed, all in the author's hand.
antiquarian books	A loose term implying collectible books rather than used books. Refers to old, rare, and/or scarce, and usually to books published before 1900.
as issued	Used to emphasize original condition or to highlight something unusual, such as recent books without dustwrappers.
association copy	A manuscript, document, book, etc. that may have belonged to the author, or, more normally, that the author gave to another person with whom he or she was associated. The book contains some tangible identifying evidence, such as inscriptions, signatures, bookplates, letters, or photographs laid in or tipped in.
as usual	A favorite term to describe defects that probably occur only on copies of the book the particular dealer handles, such as "lacks endpapers, as usual," or "lacks title page, as usual."
backstrip	The spine of the book.
B.A.L.	*Bibliography of American Literature* (See "Knowledgeable Buying: Bibliographies").
bastard title	See *front matter* and *half title*.
biblio-	Prefix from the Greek: signifying or pertaining to books.
biblioclast	A destroyer of books.
bibliognost	Someone having a deep knowledge of books.
biblioklept	A stealer of books.
bibliomaniac	Many book dealers and certain collectors.
bibliophile	A lover of books.
bibliophobe	A fear of books (sometimes extended to hate).
bibliopole	The people behind the booths at the book fairs.
binding	The cover of the book.

blindstamp	An impression in the binding of a book that is not colored, as in the Book-of-the-Month Club blindstamp on the back cover.
blurb	A comment from a review (often by another author praising the particular book) printed on the dustwrapper or covers of a proof copy, or on a wraparound band.
boards	The front and back covers of the book are the boards. This term is also used to describe books that have boards covered in paper rather than cloth or leather.
book sizes	The following are approximate heights, in inches:

double elephant folio: 50
atlas folio: 25
elephant folio: 23
F = folio: 15
Q = quarto, 4to: 12
O = octavo, 8vo: 9 3/4
D = duodecimo, 12mo: 7 3/4
S = sixteenmo, 16mo: 6 3/4
T = twentyfourmo, 24mo: 5 3/4
    thirtytwomo, 32mo: 5
    fortyeightmo, 48mo: 4
    sixtyfourmo, 64mo: 3

breaker	A person who breaks up books to sell the plates individually, or the book itself when the covers are so bad that it either has to be rebound or broken up.
broadside	A single sheet printed on one side only.
buckram	A coarse linen binding cloth.
cancel	A cancel is literally any printed matter change to any part of a book, but most commonly it refers to one or more pages that are substituted for existing pages in a book that has already been bound. In other words, an error is found; a new, corrected page is printed (a cancel, or cancel leaf); and the original page is cut out of the book, leaving a stub upon which the cancel page is glued.

chipped	Usually used to describe the fact that small pieces on the edge of the paper dustwrapper have been torn off (chipped away).
cloth	Refers to the binding of the book, when the boards are covered in cloth.
collate	At one time it really meant to compare one copy of a book with another to see if it was the same. Even without another copy, one can determine whether the book was complete by knowing how books are made. In modern times, many bibliographies furnish enough physical information to determine whether the book is complete and the correct edition. *Collate* also means to check each page and plate to assure that the book is complete, which is not a bad idea even on modern books.
colophon	Derived from the Greek, it means "finishing touch." It was on the last page and provided facts about the production, author, title, date, etc. The title page has superseded the colophon as an information source. In modern books, *colophon page* is used to refer to the page in limited editions that lists the type of paper, printer, number of copies, and author's signature.
contemporary	Refers to bindings and hand-colored plates (generally of the period when the book was published) and author inscription (dated the year of publication, preferably near the publication date).
covers	The binding of the book, most particularly the front and back panels of the book.
covers bound-in	The original cloth covers, usually including the spine, bound into the book when a new binding is made. Normally they are mounted as pages at the end of the book. Also refers to the covers of books originally issued in boards or paperwraps, but in these cases the covers are usually bound in their proper positions.
cut edges	Edges trimmed by machine, which applies to most modern books, as opposed to leaving the page edges roughly cut (see *uncut*).
C.W.O.	Check or cash with order.

deckled edge	Rough, irregular edges that are usually found on handmade paper but can be produced in machine-made paper.
dedication copy	A copy of a book with the author's presentation inscription to the person or persons to whom the book was dedicated.
dos-à-dos	Two separate books bound together so that each cover represents the cover for a different title. The Ace paperbacks of many science-fiction books were issued this way, as was William Burroughs's first book, *Junkie,* written under the pseudonym "William Lee."
dummy	A mock-up of the book, used by salesmen in the late nineteenth and early twentieth century to show prospective buyers what the book would look like. It usually had a title page, 10 or 20 pages of text, and then blank pages to fill out the rest of the binding.
dustwrapper	The paper cover, either printed or pictorial, that is issued with the book. Also referred to as a dust jacket or dust cover. Abbreviated *dw.*
edition	Actually, an edition will stand until changed. There may be twenty printings of an edition before a change in the text is made that is significant enough to require a notation that it is a second edition. For the collector, though, the *first edition* is the first printing—or first impression—which means the whole number of books ordered by the publisher to be printed from the same set of type and issued at the same time.
else fine	Usually follows a long list of defects. One of our local book scouts, Ralph Hirschtritt, usually refers to his copies as *ex-mint,* which is certainly descriptive.
endpapers	When a book is bound, the binder adds a double leaf, half of which is pasted down to the inside covers, leaving the other half to form the endpapers, or first and last leaves of the book.
ephemera	Perishable productions never meant to last. Pamphlets, broadsides, photographs, advertisements, in fact almost anything not classified elsewhere.

errata	A printed page or slip of paper, tipped in or laid in, that lists all the mistakes and misprints found after binding.
first and second printing before publication	This indicates the publisher was successful in promoting the book and had more orders before the actual publication date than the first printing quantity would cover; therefore, a second printing was ordered. *Not* a first edition.
first edition	The total number of copies produced in the first impression or printing of a book. Abbreviated *1st ed.* In reality the first edition may have many printings, but only the first printing is considered the first edition as far as collectors are concerned.
first separate edition	First printing in book form of something previously published with other matter. Usually stories or poems that appeared in magazines, anthologies, or collections of the same author's works. For first separate appearance, see *offprint*.
first thus	Means not a first edition, but something is new. It may be revised, have a new introduction by the author or someone else, be the first publication in paperback form, or be the first by another publisher.
fly leaf	The blank page following the endpaper, but often used to describe the endpaper itself.
fly title	See *half title*.
folio	Has several meanings: (a) a leaf numbered on the front; (b) the numeral itself; and (c) a folio-sized book. See *book sizes*.
follow the flag	A term that means that if one collects American authors, precedence would be given to American editions, even if the chronological first edition was published in England. The practice today seems to be either to collect both editions of all titles, or if a few titles were printed on the "wrong" side of the Atlantic, to collect the true first of that title or both editions of that title.
fore-edge painting	The front page edges of the book are bent back to expose a greater area and a watercolor painting is ap-

plied to this surface. After completion, the book is closed and the painting cannot be seen.

foxing Discoloration spots on the pages or page edges, usually brown or yellow, resulting from chemical reaction of certain properties in the paper to the atmosphere.

F.P.A.A. *First Printings of American Authors* (see "Knowledgeable Buying: Bibliographies").

frontispiece An illustration at the front of the book, normally across from the title page. Also referred to as the *frontis.*

front matter The pages preceding the text of a book. *The Bookman's Glossary* gives the following order:

bastard title or fly title
frontispiece
title page
copyright page
dedication
preface or foreword
table of contents
list of illustrations
introduction
acknowledgments
half title

Usually each of these begins on a right-hand page except the frontispiece, which faces the title page, and the copyright page, which is on the reverse, or verso, of the title page.

galley proofs Early proof copies of a book on long strips of paper usually containing two or three pages of text per strip. Normally, only a few copies are pulled in order for the author and/or editor(s) to make changes and catch typographical errors. They are also referred to as galleys or loose galleys. They precede the bound uncorrected proofs and advance reading copies. Recently many publishers have changed to galley proofs of the sheets made on copiers, which presents a problem to book dealers and collectors because these sheets are so easily duplicated.

gathering	A group of leaves formed after the printed sheet has been folded to the size of the book for sewing or gluing into the binding. Also called a *signature, section,* or *quire.*
gilt edges	The page edges have been trimmed smooth and gilt, or gold, has been applied. The abbreviation *g.e.* means gilt edges; *a.e.g.* means all edges gilt; *g.t.* means gilt top; *t.e.g.* means top edge gilt.
glassine	A transparent paper dustwrapper, which some people put a high value on but which is certainly unattractive and ill-fitting with age.
half cloth	Paper-covered boards with the spine bound in cloth.
half leather	The spine is bound in leather and the balance in cloth or paper. Also referred to as *three-quarter leather* when the corners are also bound, but the latter designation was supposed to imply that a good portion of the covers were bound in leather, not just the corners. Also called *half-bound, half binding.*
half title	A page preceding the text containing only the title of the book. There are usually two of these, one before the title page and one after the title page. The former was called a *bastard* or *fly title,* but in recent years booksellers do not seem to differentiate. At present, many publishers call them the first half-title and the second half-title.
hinge	The junctions where the front and back covers meet the spine. John Carter differentiated the inner and outer junctions as *hinges* and *joints,* respectively. Book dealers refer to hinges as being weak or starting, which can mean anything from the paper making up the pastedown and the endpaper is starting to split at the hinge to the cover actually starting to come off. If the copy is also described as *tight* or *still tight,* it could be assumed the break in the paper hasn't yet weakened the binding.
holograph	Means entirely in the handwriting of the author. Usually used for notes, marginal comments, and particularly manuscripts, as the term *autograph* is used for letters entirely in the author's hand (see *A.L.S.*).

hypermodern	Collected first editions published within the last ten years or so. Most were published so recently there is no track record on the author or the book.
impression	The copies of an edition printed at one time. The first impression is the first edition in collector's parlance.
imprint	Originally it meant the person or firm responsible for the actual production of the book. More recently it has been used to refer to the publisher (and place and date) as it appears at the foot of the title page, but it can also be used to refer to the printer's name or the publisher's name on the spine.
incunabula	A Latin word for "things in the cradle." It is used to refer to books printed from movable type before 1501. *Incunable,* or *incunabulum,* is used as the singular, with *incunables,* or *incunabula,* as an alternative plural.
inscribed copy	A copy inscribed by the author for a particular person, not merely autographed by the author. It is often difficult to differentiate between inscribed copies and presentation copies, and for the most part the terms seem to be used interchangeably.
integral	Refers to a leaf when it is part of a gathering or signature, rather than a cancel, or tipped-in, leaf.
interleaved	When blank leaves alternate with the printed leaves a book is said to be interleaved.
issue	*Issues* and *states* of the first impression seem to be used interchangeably, and the differences are at times confusing. An issue occurs when alterations, additions, or excisions are made after all the copies are printed and the book has been published or has gone on sale. The most obvious examples would be books where a number of sets of sheets are run off, but the sheets are bound at different times and in many cases by different publishers. Books such as John Steinbeck's *Cup of Gold* and Dylan Thomas's *18 Poems* (see entries in "First-Book List") exist in more than one issue. States, on the other hand, occur when changes are made during printing, or at least before publication or sale, so that variant copies go on sale at the same time.

So if the publisher finds an error and inserts a cancel page before the first impression is distributed (of course, some copies have gone out to reviewers), we have two states. But some people will call them issues, and in the overall scheme of things this mistake will not be fatal.

jacket

The printed or unprinted cover, usually paper, placed around the bound book. Sometimes called *dust jacket (dj)*, *dustwrapper (dw)*, *dust cover* or *book jacket*.

Japan(ese) vellum

A rather stiff paper with a very smooth glossy surface not unlike vellum. *Japon* is used to refer to French- and British-made imitations, and American imitations are sometimes called *Japon vellum*.

joints

The exterior hinges of books, which are rarely referred to these days, because if they're bad you can just say that the covers are off and you'll be close enough.

juveniles

Children's books.

juvenilia

Works written when the author was a child.

label

Printed paper, cloth, or leather slips glued to the spine or front cover of a book.

laid in

A photo, errata stip, autograph, letter, or review slip laid in the book, not attached to it.

laid paper

Paper that, when held up to the light, shows fine parallel lines (wiremarks) and crosslines (chain marks), produced naturally by the wires of the mold in handmade papers. It can also be simulated by a pattern on the first roller in machine-made paper.

large-paper edition

Produced using the same type as the regular edition but printed on larger paper, resulting in larger margins.

leaf

A piece of paper comprising one page on the front (recto, obverse) and another on the back (verso, reverse).

levant

A loose-grained morocco leather used on fine bindings.

limited edition	An edition that is limited to a stated number of copies and is usually numbered (or lettered) and signed by the author and/or illustrator. It is not necessarily a first edition. Limited editions are normally issued in a different binding than the trade edition and in a slipcase, sometimes referred to as a box (although it really isn't).

Limited editions should be produced in small numbers to be meaningful. Five hundred copies or less is usually more than enough for all but the most popular of authors. One hundred to 200 copies is more realistic for many collected authors, as many collectors are satisfied with trade editions or simply do not have the money for the higher-priced editions.

To have much meaning, the edition must have the total limitation noted in the book; otherwise, one must assume the limitation is very large, particularly if the publisher will not reveal the total on the request of a collector. There have been a number of "limited editions" of more than 100,000 copies. |
marbling	The process of decorating sheets of paper or cloth or the edges of books with a variety of colors in a pattern that has the appearance of marble.
modern firsts	A category that seems to include all authors whose first editions were published in this century. The term has been used since the 1920s. At present it is not very descriptive. "Twentieth-century first-editions" is a much better term to define the stock of most "modern" first-edition dealers.
no date	A catalog entry stating "no date" (abbreviated *n-d*) indicates that the date of publication is not included on the title page, copyright page, or anywhere else in the book. In many instances, if a dealer knows the date of publication the dealer will state: "no date" and then supply the date in either brackets or parentheses.
no place	Similar treatment as in *no date*. Abbreviated as *n-p* or *n-pl.*
no publisher	Similar treatment as in *no date*. Abbreviated as *n-publ.*

obverse The front of a leaf; the right-hand page of an open book. More commonly called the *recto*.

offprint A separate printing of a section of a larger publication, generally of composite authorship, in periodicals or books. Offprints are made from the same typesetting and occasionally are given their own pagination. They normally have a separate paper cover and sometimes a special title page. They are of interest because they represent the first separate appearance of the work, although they are not really a first separate edition.

offset Normally describes the transfer of ink from a printed page or an engraving to the opposite page. Also used as an abbreviation for photo-offset lithography.

out of print Means the publisher no longer has copies that may be ordered. If the publisher plans on reprinting the book, it will merely be out of stock.

out of series Refers to overruns or extra copies of limited editions. This is normal as a hedge against defective copies, and in order to have a few copies for the author's and publisher's use and to send out for review. These copies are not numbered, but occasionally state "out of series." They are normally not signed by the author and even if signed are not usually as attractive to the collector as the numbered copies.

page One side of a leaf.

pamphlet A small separate work issued in paperwraps.

paperback Refers primarily to books in paperwraps published since the 1930s, although it can describe any book with a paper cover.

paper boards As used today, this means stiff cardboard covered in paper; otherwise, there should be a fuller description in the catalog.

parts Refers to part issues or the practice of publishing novels in separate monthly installments in magazine format, particularly in the nineteenth century. Most avidly sought are the Dickens novels in parts with all the advertisements in the "proper" order.

pastedown	That half of the endpaper that lines the inner side of the cover.
perfect binding	Used in most mass-market paperback books and magazines that have too many pages to be stapled. The leaves are glued together on one side rather than stitched and covered. Many hardbound books are actually bound this way these days.
pictorial	Describes a book with a picture on the cover; a *printed cover* implies lettering only.
pirated edition	An edition published without the consent of the author or copyright owner. The ones we most often see are the Taiwan piracies.
plates	Whole-page illustrations printed separately from the text. Illustrations printed in the text pages are called *cuts.*
points	Misprints, corrections, advertisements, cloth color, etc. used to distinguish states, issues, impressions/printings, or editions of one book. Catalogers seem to fall into various categories: those who assume the reader doesn't know anything; those who assume the reader knows everything; and those who assume the reader knows what the cataloger knew before that particular catalog was prepared (why repeat something in catalog 59 that you already covered in detail in catalog 23?).
presentation copy	Assumes the author meant to inscribe the copy for the recipient and actually gave or sent the copy to the recipient, as opposed to inscribing the book for someone the author didn't know, at his or her request. Obviously a difficult call to make in many instances.
price-clipped	Refers to the fact that the price has been clipped from the corner of the dustwrapper flap.
printed cover	Used to describe a dustwrapper or paper cover that is only lettered (without any picture). Most commonly used currently to describe the covers of uncorrected proof copies, e.g., "white printed wraps" (white cover printed in black).
printing	An alternative word for *impression.*

private press	One whose owners or operators print what they like, rather than what a publisher pays them to print. The interest is in fine books. The print runs are small, and although the books are sold to the public directly through subscription, or occasionally through a publisher's organization, the motivation is more to make a fine book than to make a profit. Some examples would include the Baskerville, Daniel, Kelmscott, Ashendene, Cuala, and Golden Cockerel presses.
privately printed	Refers to a book that is not published for sale and is distributed by other than the normal commercial channels.
proofs	These precede the published book. The normal sequence would be galley proof (described above), uncorrected bound (in paperwraps) proof, and advance reading copy bound in paperwraps. The latter is not as common a form as the first two because publishers prefer to send out early copies of clothbound trade editions for review.
provenance	A record of the previous ownership of a particular copy of a book.
publication date	The date the book is to be put on sale, allowing time for distribution to stores and reviewers after the actual printing is complete.
rare	Implies the book is extremely scarce, perhaps only turning up once every ten years or so.
rebacked	Means the binding has been given a new spine, or backstrip.
recased	Means the book was loose or out of its covers and it has been resewn or glued back in, usually with new endpapers.
recto	The front of a leaf, the right-hand page of an open book. Also called the *obverse*.
rejointed	Means the book has been repaired preserving the original covers, including the spine. The repair is always either "almost imperceptible" or "skillfully accomplished."

remainder marks	In many cases the publisher will mark the bottom edges of books sold as remainders with a stamp, a black marker, or spray paint, which speckles the bottom.
remainders	Books that publishers have decided not to stock any longer. The remainder of the stock is sold to a wholesaler, who resells the books to bookstores to sell to the public significantly below the original price. You can find these books for $.99 to $4.98 at most new-book stores. Some very expensive first editions were on remainder shelves at one time. This definition has to be qualified somewhat, however, because occasionally a publisher will remainder a part of his stock while retaining the title on his list at full retail price.
reverse	The back of a leaf or the page on the left of an open book. More commonly called the *verso*.
signatures	The letters or numerals printed in the margin of the first leaf of each gathering. The term is also used to refer to the gathering or section itself.
slipcase	A cardboard case usually covered in paper, cloth, or leather that holds a book with only the spine exposed.
state	See *issue*.
stub	A narrow strip of paper left after most of a leaf has been cut away.
sunned	Means the covers have been bleached or faded by sunlight.
thousands	A few publishers in the nineteenth century added a notice on the title page stating—for instance, "Eighth Thousand"—to indicate a later printing, although they did not state second printing, third printing, etc. These are not first editions.
three-decker	A book in three volumes, almost exclusively used to describe Victorian novels of the late nineteenth century.
tipped in	Means the plate, autograph, letter, photo, etc. is actually attached to the book.

top edge gilt	See *gilt edges.*
trade edition	The regularly published edition. The term is used to differentiate it from a limited signed edition of the same book.
uncut	Means the edges have not been trimmed smooth by a machine. The edges are rough. It is not the same as *unopened.*
unopened	The leaves of the book are still joined at the folds, not slit apart.
unsophisticated	Pure, genuine, unrestored, and if a book is so described, it can mean trouble as far as condition is concerned.
variant	A book that differs in one or more features from others of the same impression, but a positive sequence has not been established. If the sequence were known, it would be a particular state or issue.
vellum	A thin sheet of specially prepared skin of calf, lamb, or kid used for writing or printing, or for the cover.
verso	The left page of an open book. The back of a leaf. Also called the *reverse.*
waterstained	Discoloration and perhaps actual shrinking of the leaves or binding.
working copy	You should receive most of the leaves.
wrap-around band	The band of printed paper the length of the dust-wrapper of a book. Wraparound bands contain favorable reviews or a notation that a book has won a prize, and are put around some copies of books. Obviously fragile, they are of interest to collectors.
wrappers	The printed or unprinted cover of a pamphlet or book bound in paper.
yapped	Refers to the edges of the cover of a book bound in paper or another soft material. These yapped edges are not flush with the pages but extend beyond the edges of the book and are fragile by nature.

Some Suggestions

THE FOLLOWING COMMENTS may be of some help. They are basically our own feelings and may not be shared by others, but here they are for what they are worth.

Building a Collection

If you have decided to collect a number of currently popular authors whose books are not particularly scarce, you would start with the Internet servers mentioned previously. But the advent of the Net makes it even more important to send a want list of the books (including the minimum condition you will accept) to a limited number of specialist dealers. The reason for this is that without the want list, the dealer will probably put the book you want in a catalog or on the Net and it may be sold before you get notice. You will receive a variety of quotes and can choose among them. If you do buy books on the first round, you should send a revised list, perhaps every month, to the dealers who responded so they will not waste their time searching for books you have already bought, and to remind them that you are still actively searching for certain titles.

If your budget only allows for a few books a month, it would probably be wise to limit the want lists to a few dealers, explain your budget limitations, and limit the number of books on the list. In other words, if you have decided to spend $100 a month on your collection and most of the books you want are in the $25-to-$50 range, you will be buying only two to four books a month, and there is no sense in obtaining quotes from dealers on hundreds of books. Also, it will be hard to convince a dealer who quoted you once to do it again if you didn't buy anything from the initial quotes. Alternatively, if you have found a dealer you believe has been fair with you and whom you trust, give him your complete want list, explain your budget limitation, and ask him to buy for you. The dealer can work with you to build your collection. Make it clear that either the dealer will be the only one buying for you, or that you will also be buying from other sources and you will keep your want list updated regularly so that dealers can also keep current with your collection.

If you are interested in only a few authors who have produced a large body of work and have a number of scarce and expensive books in their canon, it seems to us advisable to limit the number of dealers searching for the books. If your job is such that you are tied up most of the day and evening, the correspondence and telephone calls from twenty dealers can get on your nerves and spoil some of your enjoyment in building your collection. Also there is always the possibility that if an expensive item comes up at auction, the dealers might bid against one another to buy it for eventual sale to you at a higher price than you might otherwise have paid.

Caring for Books

Most dealers in scarce or rare books have taken up the practice of protecting the covers of books without dustwrappers by making a cover for the book out of a sheet of acetate and protecting books with dust jackets by covering them with plain acetate or an acetate cover that is backed with acid-free paper. The latter are made by Bro-Dart, and other companies. We have taken to using the covers without backing made by Demco (although they are probably available from others), as many collectors want to see the back of the dust jacket to assure themselves that no repairs have been made or it is not dampstained. Your dealer should be able to order some for you or tell you where you can buy them in your area.

From the viewpoint of the dealer, acetate covers improve the appearance of books, but more important, they protect the books and dustwrappers while they are on the dealer's shelves. The original dustwrappers are an expensive part of the book, and it is easy to tear their edges just by taking the book off the shelf; therefore, it is only reasonable to go to the expense of putting on covers. There are dealers who do not like the idea or looks of the covers, a view I respect, but it is depressing to see a $200 copy of a book turn into a $50 copy after it has been handled by fifty or a hundred people over a few months.

The collector who takes books home may not feel the need to keep the covers on the books, and if the books are not handled much and you don't like their appearance, then we do not see any reason to keep them on. The covers do provide a measure of protection, but they do age over time and probably should be changed after a number of years.

The best protection for a book is a specially made box, but these are labor-intensive and expensive, in the $75-to-$150 range, and are hardly worth the cost to protect a $50 book.

If boxes are not within your budget or cost effective, I would recommend glass-front bookcases as a good investment for your more valuable books.

The most important thing is to keep the books in a relatively clean environment at consistent temperature and humidity levels. This can be accomplished with air conditioning, a dehumidifier, and perhaps an air cleaner.

It is also important to watch the little things, like leaving a book out on a table where a visitor might set a glass on it or something could be spilled nearby and spread to the cover before the book could be picked up; shelving books too tightly so that the top edges are torn when a book is removed; leaving acid-content paper such as newsprint stored in the books, which will darken the pages; or putting thick sheaves of paper in the book, which can loosen the bindings.

Books are fragile, but the worst-made of them have resided in attics for decades without serious damage. So worry more about dampness than dryness; avoid direct sunlight, which can fade the covers badly; and don't put stickers or gummed labels directly on the covers or even on the acetate protectors. They will discolor the books or dust jackets and, if exposed to light while on the acetate protectors can cause discoloration on the dust jacket. The latter is mentioned because we've seen a number of book collections marked with different-colored labels. Try to resist the urge to write your name in your books and only lay in acid-free bookplates, even if signed by the author, instead of gluing them in if you are planning to one day sell your books.

We once had a gentleman call and ask if he could bring in for an offer some signed copies of an author who is quite collectible, and when he arrived we were stunned to see that not only had he written his name (in a large bold signature) above the author's signature but had written that the book was a first edition in ballpoint pen and then *stapled* the dustwrapper (all the way through the boards) to keep anyone from removing it!

Insurance and Appraisals

As far as insurance is concerned, we understand that most homeowner policies have a limit on collectibles and you may have to purchase a special rider to the policy to cover your books. If the books are covered under your basic insurance policy or a rider is required, your company will normally require an appraisal for its files. The easiest and least expensive way to obtain an appraisal is to type an itemized list of your books, or at least the ones that have a value over $25. Include the author, title, publisher, place, date, edition, and very brief description, and leave room on the right margin for the dealer to add the appraisal prices. After you have this list, visit a book dealer and ask the dealer what the charge would be to appraise the books on the list. The dealer will have to visit your home to actually look at the books, but the cost will be significantly lower if the dealer does not have to take the time to make up a list in order to do the appraisal. The dealer can type in the values on your list and provide a cover sheet with the appraisal total. If you have a thousand books and only a hundred of them have a value over $25, just list the hundred books and then add a miscellaneous category for hardbacks and paperbacks, so that these can be included. Many people do not feel the lesser books are worth the trouble, but if you have eight hundred hardback books with an average value of $10 each, it would be nice to get the $8,000 if there were ever a fire in your house.

Additionally, we would like to note that there are vast differences between insurance companies when it comes to books. We had a collector with a million-dollar collection who kept all the valuable books in a bank deposit vault and was being charged $7,000 to $8,000 a year in premiums. At the same time we had another collector with a million-dollar collection stored in a house he hadn't lived in for a few years and he was paying $750 a year. And just recently a collector with perhaps a hundred-thousand-dollar collection told us his insurance company wouldn't insure them at any price. Check around.

Credit

Most specialist dealers accept Visa, MasterCard, and/or American Express. If they do not take credit cards and the amount of the purchase is relatively large, dealers will usually allow you thirty days to pay and may arrange longer time payments if necessary. If this is the first time you have dealt with the dealer, he or she will probably want to hold the book until the balance is paid.

Terms may be preferable to charging even if the dealer does accept credit cards, as the dealer is charged anywhere from 3 percent to 5 percent by the card company and many times an expensive book will not have a large margin and 5 percent could equal 25 to 50 percent of the profit.

Bargaining

Bargaining with a dealer is not unheard of, and if a book has been on the shelf for a year or so, the dealer might be willing to accept an offer of something less than the marked price. But the collector should be careful, because dealers have different attitudes about this and some will never discount. You should ask the dealer very straightforwardly and politely if an offer on a specific title would be acceptable. One must understand that most banks have little confidence in books as collateral, and so all the books on the dealers' shelves have probably been paid for. The nature of the business is to wait for the right buyer to come along, even if this takes over a year in some cases (although 10 to 20 years is not unheard of).

One must be aware that some dealers seem to price many of their books much higher than other dealers in the same field, and of course because of this they can offer significant discounts. This is confusing to the beginning collector, who may become used to a dealer automatically giving discounts of 10, 20, or 30 percent or more, and then assume another dealer will do the same, but instead finds the other dealer is absolutely incensed when asked for a discount.

There is also a danger in continual bargaining if you are a serious collector, because if a scarce book you have wanted for years comes into the store and the dealer has other customers for the book, you can rest assured that you will not be offered the book first if you have established a pattern of bargaining in the past.

We have cataloged for over thirty years, had an open shop for ten years, and visited hundreds of other shops, and it is our feeling that an antiquarian bookstore is a great negative-cash-flow business. Many, but by no means all, of the owners are getting along on a relatively low income, particularly if you compute it on an hourly basis. This is not a complaint, as the vast majority of the owners are perfectly aware that they could be doing something else but do not have any desire to work in another field.

There are reciprocal discounts within the trade, because dealers purchase much of their inventory from other dealers. There are no warehouses stocking inscribed copies of Fitzgerald's books, and if you have a customer for one, your best chance of finding it is on the shelves of another dealer. You, as a collector, do not offer the dealer the long-range opportunities to buy salable inventory, and therefore there is no compelling reason to give you a discount, which seems to come as a shock to certain collectors, fortunately a minority. A few years ago at a book fair we watched a prominent collector whom we have known for years negotiate a dealer down to a 30 percent discount on a book that was fairly priced. A sad scene. The collector probably made $500,000 to $1,000,000 a year, the dealer, probably $30,000 to $40,000 maximum.

Selling Your Books

The antiquarian book field represents a true marketplace. A book is worth what someone will pay for it. Prices can vary widely for the same book during the same year. When you sell a book to a dealer, the value of the book will depend on what the dealer believes to be a reasonable resale value in his particular market. If the book is scarce or rare and the dealer has a ready market for it, the dealer may be willing to pay close to the retail value of the book. If the dealer has no immediate market for the book, but is confident that it will sell within a few months, he will probably offer about 30 to 50 percent of the retail value. If he is uncertain of selling the book within the year, he may be willing to pay only 10 to 20 percent of the value or not be interested at all.

The best market for a collector is another collector. If another collector is not available, one might investigate the possibility of selling them to a dealer, trading to a dealer for credit, putting the books at auction (including eBay or Amazon.com), or listing them on one of the book services discussed elsewhere.

Using This Guide

IN MOST CASES, in our opinion, an author's first book puts an upper limit on the value of his or her books. This is why the value of the first book can often be used as a rough guide to estimating the prices of later books. If a current catalog price or auction record is available, it could, of course, be more reliable. But if such records are not available and you find two books by the same author, one published in 1930 and one in 1940, the one published in 1930 will normally be valued higher, and it will be important to know whether the author's first book was published in 1900 or 1929. This rule applies to unsigned trade editions only (often a signed and limited edition of a later book will be valued more highly than the first or earlier book). There are exceptions—for example, when a first or early book had a large printing or when a later book is much scarcer and/or acclaimed as an "important" book with lasting literary value.

The entries are composed of: author, title, place of publication, date of publication, and only that additional information needed to identify the issue, the state or edition, and the value.

All entries are first editions (first printings) unless otherwise stated. "Trade" is used to indicate the first general edition available for public sale after a limited edition has been issued; usually the same sheets are used for both the limited and trade editions.

If the author's name does not appear on the title page, the entry will start with the title. If the author used a pseudonym, the pseudonym will appear first and the entry will include the author's name in parentheses.

A plus sign after the title indicates "and Other Stories" or "and Other Poems."

. . .

If the place of publication or date does not appear on the title page but does appear somewhere in the book, this information will be in parentheses. This is *particularly significant,* because the presence of a date on the title page may be the only way to differentiate between first and later printings. If information is known but does not appear in the book it will be in brackets.

Important: The section on First Edition Identification by publisher (Appendix E) is applicable to each entry unless otherwise stated.

A First Book

Our definition of a first book is any single-title publication containing more than one page, regardless of size or format, that is bound, stapled, or laid in covers. We do not consider broadsides to be books, and thus have not included James Joyce's first publication, *Et Tu, Healy,* published in 1891 or 1892, as his first book.

We do consider as first books those that represent a collaboration with one other author, although in the first-book list we also include the author's first separate book, because we suspect many collectors may not consider collaborations as valid first books.

Also included are books edited and translated by an author if they preceded the first book written by the author. We do not consider these to be first books but assume some collectors may consider them as the first, as these books are the first to include the author's name on the title page.

In many cases we have included the author's second book. Normally in these cases the first was written anonymously, written under a pseudonym, or is so rare as to be unobtainable—or we just felt like it.

It should be understood that in many cases we have never seen these books and have merely listed first books and values as we have come upon them in dealer or auction catalogs. This means that there are many authors not covered, because we have not encountered listings of their first books and do not feel comfortable listing a price.

Our definition of a first book is necessary in order to understand our selection in the first-book list. There is no real agreement among collectors on what constitutes a first book, and this is probably just as well, because it means the collector must buy three or four titles by certain authors to cover all bets.

Note: Persons interested in offering books listed within this book for sale to book dealers must understand that the prices included here represent the estimated retail price one might expect to pay to a book dealer to purchase a particular book when the book is in the condition noted below. Lesser copies are worth less. Exceptional copies of notable rarities are worth more. Book dealers are classic examples of small independent businesses, and they cannot be expected to pay the estimated value for copies of books listed here. The percentage of value one can expect in sale to a dealer will vary, but one should not anticipate more than 40 to 50 percent of estimated value for other than prime items from a dealer. One alternative to consider is acceptance in trade of books the dealer owns; the percentage of return will probably come closer to 60 percent or more, depending on what you are offering and what you wish to swap for. Most dealers are also not interested in accepting several lower-value books in exchange for higher-value books. Understand further that even though you may own books listed in this volume, that is no guarantee that a dealer will automatically be interested in buying or trading for them. Most dealers specialize in particular areas and are not interested in less-than-prime titles outside their fields. On the other hand, most responsible dealers would be glad to suggest dealers in other fields for books that he or she has no interest in purchasing; this is usually done as a courtesy and not as a payable service.

Estimated Values

The dollar values shown are our estimates of the retail value of the book in very good to fine condition, with a dustwrapper for those published in 1920 and after. Estimated values of books published between 1850 and 1920 are for very good to fine copies without dustwrappers but in original bindings. Therefore, if you have a book published prior to 1920 with a complete dustwrapper, the value would be higher than the value shown. Estimates for books before 1850 are for rebound copies unless otherwise stated. The estimated values are believed to be accurate, plus or minus 20 percent. This may seem to be a very wide range, but it is not unusual to see the same book in different dealer catalogs or at auction with that wide a range (or even wider) within the same year. If you prefer, you can consider the range to represent the difference in condition between a very good copy and a fine copy of the individual book. It is also not unusual for an absolutely mint copy of a book to bring twice the price of a very good to fine copy. On the other hand, copies with even minor defects might sell for as little as 50 percent of the values shown, worn and chipped copies (books and/or dustwrappers) might only be worth 25 to 30 percent of the values shown, and books without dustwrappers (after 1920) would normally sell for 15 to 25 percent of the values shown.

The value listed for any particular title should be considered only as a guide. In some cases the books are truly rare, and the fact that we have estimated a price based on a catalog or auction entry that may have been a few years old does not mean this price is accurate. As many dealers will tell you when you have found a book on their shelves for $200 that is listed in a pricing guide for $100, *"Go buy it from them."*

Condition

1980 to 2000: These are really "modern" first editions. Ninety-nine percent of these books are fiction or poetry. Because they have been published so recently, the prices listed herein would be for very fine copies in **DUSTWRAPPERS** (unless in wraps or a limited edition in slipcase) with *NO DEFECTS,* including such minor things as price-clipped dustwrappers, former owners' names written in, bookplates, remainder marks on bottom page edges, or closed tears (no tape repairs) in the dustwrappers—even though there may be no actual loss of paper on the dustwrappers.

1950 to 1980: These books are a little older, but still copies must be in **ORIGINAL DUSTWRAPPERS** (unless in wraps or a limited edition in slipcase) with no major defects. These books do not have to look as new as the foregoing (1970–90). Also, the price-clipped dustwrapper and closed tears would be more acceptable, but the book has to be fine with the dustwrapper showing only minor wear, fading, or soiling. The absence of the dustwrapper decreases the estimated price of fiction or poetry titles by about 75 percent of the value shown. For nonfiction titles, the absence of the dustwrapper probably decreases the estimated price shown by 20 percent.

1920 to 1950: The book must be very good to fine with only minimal (if any) soiling, **IN A DUSTWRAPPER** (unless in wraps or a limited edition in slipcase) that is clean with only minimal soiling or fading and only a few small chips (⅛ inch or less) and closed tears. Again, as in the above grouping, the absence of a dustwrapper on fiction or poetry titles would greatly reduce the value of the first edition (75 percent on fiction and 20 percent on nonfiction).

1880 to 1919: The book must be clean and bright with no loss or tears on the edges. The estimated prices are for copies without dustwrappers. It should be noted that books published in multiple volumes (usually three volumes, but also two- and four-volume editions) are rare, and prices here are for very good copies in matching condition. Fine to very fine copies would probably bring much more.

1850 to 1879: The book is good to very good with minor edge wear or loss but still tight and clean. If the title is nonfiction, particularly with maps or plates, the condition of the maps or plates is more important than the condition of the binding. The comment above on multiple-volume editions also applies here.

1849 and prior: The book would be rebound (probably within 20 or 30 years of publication) unless otherwise stated, in a clean binding. Copies in early or "contemporary" bindings usually command more than books newly rebound. If the book in question is fiction, poetry, or an extremely important nonfiction work, the original binding would greatly increase the value above the estimated prices shown herein. However, if the title is a nonfiction work, especially with maps and plates, the original or contemporary binding increases the value—but only by a small percentage, perhaps 10 to 20 percent. It is the condition and color (if applicable) of the plates and maps that would determine the value.

The First-Book List

ALL BOOKS LISTED HEREIN ARE
FIRST EDITIONS/FIRST PRINTINGS
OF THE INDIVIDUAL TITLES.

The three columns of prices
represent retail estimates for the titles
in 1986, 1995, and 2000, respectively.

The section on *First-Edition Identification*
by publisher (Appendix E)
is applicable to each entry
unless otherwise stated.

	1986	1995	2000

A

	1986	1995	2000
A., T.B. (Thomas Bailey Aldrich) THE BELLS . . . Boston/New York, 1855	150	250	750
Abbe, George. VOICES IN THE SQUARE. New York, 1938. (Edited his brother's work in 1936.)	—	75	75
Abbey, Edward. JONATHAN TROY. New York (1954)	175	1,250	3,000

	1986	1995	2000
Abbott, Anthony (Charles Fulton Oursler). ABOUT THE MURDER OF GERALDINE FOSTER. New York (1930). Author's first mystery	75	250	350
Abbott, Berenice. CHANGING NEW YORK. New York, 1939. Two states of blue cloth, priority unknown	—	400	600
Abbott, Edward Abbott. *See* A SQUARE			
Abbott, John S(tevens) C(abot). THE MOTHER AT HOME. Boston, 1833. Blue cloth spine, tan boards	—	—	250
Abbott, Lee K. THE HEART NEVER FITS . . . Cedar Falls, 1986	—	—	125
Abdullah, Achmed. THE RED STAIN. New York, 1915	—	60	75
Abe, Kobo. THE WOMAN IN THE DUNES. New York, 1964. (First U.S. edition)	—	100	125
London, 1965	—	—	40

	1986	1995	2000
Abel, Lionel. SOME POEMS OF RIMBAUD. New York (1939). Wraps. (Translated by L. Abel)	60	75	75
Abercrombie, Lascelles. INTERLUDES AND POEMS. 1908	75	75	75
Abish, Walter. DUEL SITE. New York, 1970. Wraps. (300 copies)	75	175	200
Ableman, Paul. I HEAR VOICES. Paris [1958]	40	60	40
Abrahams, Peter. A BLACKMAN SPEAKS OF FREEDOM. Durban, 1938	150	250	350
DARK TESTAMENT. London, 1942	125	200	250
Abrahams, William. INTERVAL IN CAROLINA. New York, 1945	30	40	40
Abse, Dannie. AFTER EVERY GREEN THING. London, 1949	60	75	100
ACELDAMA: A PLACE TO BURY STRANGERS IN. (Aleister Crowley.) London, 1898. Wraps	500	750	1,000
Achebe, Chinua. THINGS FALL APART. London, 1958	75	200	250
New York, 1958	35	125	150
Ackerly, J. R. THE PRISONERS OF WAR. London, 1925	125	200	400
Wraps	—	—	175
(Preceded by POEMS BY FOUR AUTHORS. London, 1923)			
Ackroyd, Peter. OUCH. London, 1971. Wraps. Entire issue of *The Curiously Strong*	—	—	250
LONDON LICKPENNY. London, 1973. Wraps. (26 signed and lettered copies)	—	50	250
Wraps. (474 copies)	—	—	60
Acorn, Milton. IN LOVE AND ANGER. Montreal, 1956	—	—	1,000
Acton, Eliza. POEMS. Ipswich, 1826	—	—	500
Acton, Harold. AQUARIUM. London, 1923. Plain tissue dust-wrapper	200	400	600
Adair, Gilbert. HOLLYWOOD'S VIETNAM. London, 1981	—	—	60
Adam, Helen (Douglas). THE ELFIN PEDLAR: 7 TALES TOLD BY PIXIE POOL. London, 1923	100	175	200
Adamic, Louis. ROBINSON JEFFERS: A PORTRAIT. Seattle, 1929. Wraps	75	75	100
Adams, Alice. CARELESS LOVE. (New York, 1966)	350	350	350
THE FALL OF DAISY DUKE. London, 1967. (New title)	—	250	250

	1986	1995	2000
Adams, Andy. THE LOG OF A COWBOY. Boston, 1903. First issue has map at page 28 not in list of illustrations	125	250	300
Adams, Ansel. TAOS PUEBLO. San Francisco: Grabhorn Press, 1930. Written with Mary Austin. (108 copies)	12K	20K	30K
Boston, 1977. 950 signed (by Adams) and numbered copies	—	750	1,500
Adams, Charles Francis. RAILROAD LEGISLATION. Boston, 1868. Wraps	75	150	150
Adams, Douglas. THE HITCHHIKER'S GUIDE TO THE GALAXY. London, 1979	30	100	125
New York (1980)	25	60	60
Adams, Edward C. L. CONGAREE SKETCHES . . . Chapel Hill, 1927. 200 signed and numbered copies	75	225	300
Trade edition	—	100	125
Adams, Franklin P. IN CUPID'S COURT. Evanston, 1902	—	100	125
TOBOGGANING ON PARNASSUS. Garden City, 1911	—	75	100
Adams, Frederick Upham. PRESIDENT JOHN SMITH. Chicago, 1897	50	75	150
Adams, Hannah. AN ALPHABETICAL COMPENDIUM . . . Boston, 1784	—	2,500	1,000
Adams, Harold. MURDER. New York (1981). Ace Charter 54706. Wraps	—	—	50
Adams, Henry (Brooks). CIVIL SERVICE REFORM. Boston, 1869. Wraps	1,000	1,500	2,000
CHAPTERS OF ERIE +. Boston, 1871. Written with Charles F. Adams	—	200	300
Adams, Herbert. THE SECRET OF BOGEY HOUSE. London, 1924	50	200	600
Adams, James Truslow. MEMORIALS OF OLD BRIDGEHAMPTON. 1916	75	150	200
Adams, Jane. THE GREENWAY. London (1995). Author's first mystery	—	—	200
Adams, John Quincy. LETTERS OF SILESIA. London, 1804	—	—	250
Adams, Léonie. THOSE NOT ELECT. New York, 1925. 10 signed copies on Ingres paper. In plain gray boards	—	750	600
Trade edition	200	250	250
Adams, Ramon F. COWBOY LINGO. Boston, 1936	150	200	250

	1986	1995	2000
Adams, Richard. WATERSHIP DOWN. London, 1972	600	1,000	1,500
New York, 1972	40	75	125
London, 1976. 250 signed and numbered copies bound in morocco. In slipcase. Illustrated by John Lawrence	—	1,000	1,750
Adams, William Taylor. *See* Warren T. Ashton			
Addams, Charles. DRAWN AND QUARTERED. New York (1942)	75	275	350
Ade, George. STORIES OF THE STREETS AND OF THE TOWNS. Chicago, 1894 (Offprint from *Chicago Record*)	—	—	1,250
CIRCUS DAY. Chicago (1896)	300	600	750
ARTIE, A STORY OF . . . Chicago, 1896	60	75	100
Adeler, Max (Charles Heber Clark). OUT OF THE HURLEY-BURLY. Phildelphia, 1874. (Also first book illustrated by A. B. Frost)	75	200	200
Adler, Edward. NOTES FROM A DARK STREET. New York, 1962	20	30	30
ADVENTURES OF A YOUNGER SON. (Edward John Trelawny.) London, 1831. 3 volumes	250	350	350
ADVENTURES OF HARRY FRANCO (THE). (Charles Frederick Briggs.) New York, 1839. 2 volumes	150	350	350
ADVENTURES OF RODERICK RANDOM (THE). (Written by Tobias Smollett.) London, 1748. 2 volumes	750	1,000	750
ADVENTURES OF TIMOTHY PEACOCK . . . (THE). (Daniel Pierce Thompson.) Middlebury, 1835	400	750	750
A. E. (George Russell). *See* E., A.			
Agate, James. L. OF C. (Lines of Communication). London, 1917	100	100	125
Agee, James. PERMIT ME VOYAGE. New Hampshire, 1934	600	600	750
AGNES DE CASTRO. (By Catherine Trotter Cockburn.) London, 1696	—	750	750
Ai (Florence Ogawa). CRUELTY. Boston, 1973	35	75	100
Aickman, Robert. WE ARE FOR THE DARK. London 1951. Written with Elizabeth Jane Howard	—	—	750
Aiken, Conrad (Potter). EARTH TRIUMPHANT. New York, 1914	200	200	250
Aiken, Joan (Delano). ALL YOU'VE EVER WANTED. London, 1953	—	—	75

	1986	1995	2000
THE SILENCE OF HERONDALE. Garden City, 1964	—	—	35
London, 1965. Author's first mystery	—	—	35

Aikin, Anna Laetitia. *See* POEMS

Ainsworth, William Harrison. *See* SIR JOHN CHIVERTON

	1986	1995	2000
Akins, Zoe. INTERPRETATIONS. London, 1912	50	125	125
Aksyonov, Vassily. IT'S TIME, MY LOVE, IT'S TIME. Nashville, 1970. First U.S. edition	—	—	40
ALARIC AT ROME. (Matthew Arnold.) A Prize Poem Recited at Rugby School. 12 pages in wraps. Rugby, England, 1840	5,000	7,500	10K
Albee, Edward. THE ZOO STORY AND THE SANDBOX. (New York, 1960.) Wraps	150	150	175
THE ZOO STORY, THE DEATH OF BESSIE SMITH, THE SANDBOX. New York, 1960. Dustwrapper price: $2.75 (First hardback)	125	175	200
Wraps	—	—	40
London (1962)	100	100	125

Albert, Marvin. *See* Albert Conroy

	1986	1995	2000
Albert, Neil. JANUARY CORPSE. New York, 1991	—	75	200
Alcott, Amos Bronson. OBSERVATIONS ON THE PRINCIPLES AND METHODS OF INFANT INSTRUCTION. Boston, 1830. Privately printed. Wraps	850	1,000	1,000
TABLETS. Boston, 1868. Brown cloth	—	—	175
Alcott, Louisa May. FLOWER FABLES. Boston, 1855. In gift binding	250	600	3,500
In regular binding	125	250	1,500
ALCUIN: A DIALOGUE. (Charles B. Brown.) New York, 1798	300	2,500	5,000
Aldington, Richard. IMAGES. (London, 1915.) Wraps	250	450	250
Boston, 1916. Wraps	75	150	150
Aldiss, Brian W(ilson). THE BRIGHTFOUNT DIARIES. London (1955)	75	150	200
SPACE, TIME AND NATHANIEL. London (1957). First science fiction	—	350	300

Aldrich, Thomas Bailey. *See* A., T.B.

	1986	1995	2000
Aldridge, James. SIGNED WITH THEIR HONOUR. London, 1942	30	50	50
Boston, 1942	25	30	25

	1986	1995	2000
Aldridge, John W. AFTER THE LOST GENERATION. New York (1951)	—	30	40
Alexie, Sherman. THE BUSINESS OF FANCY DANCING. New York, 1992 (Hardcover, 100 copies)	—	—	1,000
Wraps	—	—	200
Alger, Horatio, Jr. BERTHA'S CHRISTMAS VISION. Boston, 1856	850	2,000	2,500
Alegría, Ciro. BROAD AND ALIEN IS THE WORLD. New York, 1940. First English translation	—	100	100
Algren, Nelson. SOMEBODY IN BOOTS. New York (1935). Issued in rust cloth	250	1,000	1,500
Smooth tan cloth, remainder binding	—	—	1,250
Ali, Ahmed. TWILIGHT IN DELHI. London, 1940 (Previous privately printed books in Urdu.)	60	75	100
Allbeury, Ted. A CHOICE OF ENEMIES. New York, 1972	—	125	175
London (1973)	40	125	150
Allegrotto, Michael. DEATH ON THE ROCKS. New York, 1987	—	50	50
Allen, Gracie. HOW TO BECOME PRESIDENT. New York (1940)	75	150	200
Allen, (Charles) Grant. PHYSIOLOGICAL AESTHETICS. London, 1877	—	250	250
BABYLON. London, 1885	50	100	150
Allen, James Lane. FLUTE AND VIOLIN AND OTHER KENTUCKY TALES. New York, 1891			
First issue: sheets bulk 1⅛	40	100	60
Second issue: sheets bulk ¹⁵⁄₁₆	—	75	40
Also variant ¹¹⁄₁₆	—	75	40
Allen, Phoebe. GILMORY. London, 1876. 3 volumes	—	250	250
Allen, William Hervey. BALLADS OF THE BORDER. (El Paso) 1916. Wraps. (Name misspelled "Hervy" on copyright page)	600	750	750
WAMPUM AND OLD GOLD. New Hampshire, 1921. Stiff wraps	75	175	125
Allen, Woody (Allen Stewart Konigsberg). DON'T DRINK THE WATER. French. New York, 1967. Wraps	40	100	100
Random House. NY (1967)	60	300	400
Allen Press. THE TRAIL OF BEAUTY. San Francisco, 1940. First book of the press by Harris Stearns Allen. 100 signed copies	—	—	1,000
Allende, Isabel. THE HOUSE OF THE SPIRITS. New York, 1985	—	125	150

	1986	1995	2000
Alling, Kenneth Slade. CORE OF FIRE. New York (1939). Wraps	—	75	75
New York, 1940. Cloth	—	40	40
Allingham, Margery (Louise). BLACKKER CHIEF DICK. London (1923)	250	850	1,000
Garden City, 1923	200	750	750
Allingham, William. POEMS. London, 1850	—	300	450
Allison, Dorothy. THE WOMEN WHO HATE ME. Brooklyn, 1983. Wraps	—	100	500
THE WOMEN WHO HATE ME: POETRY 1980–1990. Ithaca, 1991. Expanded version. Cloth	—	—	50
Wraps	—	—	50
Allott, Kenneth. POEMS. London: Hogarth Press, 1938	60	125	100
Allsop, Kenneth. ADVENTURES LIT THEIR STAR. London, 1949	—	40	50
Allston, Washington. THE SYLPHS OF THE SEASONS +. Boston, 1813	—	300	350
Alpert, Hollis. THE SUMMER LOVERS. New York, 1958	25	40	40
Alpha and Omega. (Oliver St. John Gogarty.) BLIGHT, THE TRAGEDY OF DUBLIN. Dublin, 1917	200	300	350
Alta. FREEDOM'S IN SIGHT. (Berkeley), 1969. Wraps	—	50	75
Revised, 1970. Wraps	—	25	35
Alther, Lisa. KINFLICKS. New York, 1976	20	35	60
London, 1976	—	—	40
Altsheler, Joseph Alexander. THE HIDDEN MINE. New York, 1896	—	250	350
Alvarez, A. (POEMS). Oxford, 1952. Wraps. FANTASY POETS #15	75	125	125
Alvarez, Julia. HOMECOMING. New York, 1984	—	125	350
Amadi, Elechi. THE CONCUBINE. London (1966)	—	100	75
Amado, Jorge. THE VIOLENT LAND. New York, 1945. (First English translation)	40	125	150
Ambler, Eric. THE DARK FRONTIER. London, 1936	1,500	4,500	3,500
Amis, Kingsley (William). BRIGHT NOVEMBER. London (1947)	300	600	1,500
LUCKY JIM. London, 1953	—	1,500	1,500
Garden City, 1954	—	300	500

	1986	1995	2000
Amis, Martin. THE RACHEL PAPERS. London, 1973	40	450	750
New York, 1974	—	150	250
Ammons, A(rchie) R(andolph). OMMATEUM, WITH DOXOLOGY. Philadelphia (1955). 300 copies, 200 destroyed	800	1,250	2,000
EXPRESSIONS OF SEA LEVEL. Columbus, 1964	—	—	250
Anaya, Rudolfo A. BLESS ME, ULTIMA. (Berkeley), 1972. Cloth	—	—	850
Wraps	—	60	125
Anderson, Alston. LOVER MAN. London, (1959). (Robert Graves introduction)	30	75	75
Garden City, 1959. (Robert Graves introduction)		60	60
Anderson, Forrest. SEA PIECES +. New York, 1935. (155 copies)	125	150	175
Anderson, Frederick Irving. ADVENTURES OF THE INFALLIBLE GODAHL. New York (1914)	200	250	1,500
Anderson, J. R. L. RECKONING ON ICE. London, 1971	—	—	125
Anderson, J(ohn) Redwood. THE MUSIC OF DEATH. Clifton, England, 1904. Wraps	75	125	200
Anderson, Kent. SYMPATHY FOR THE DEVIL. Garden City, 1987	—	50	175
Anderson, Laurie. THE PACKAGE. Indianapolis (1971)	—	—	350
Anderson, Lindsay. MAKING A FILM. London, 1952	—	75	75
Anderson, Maxwell. YOU WHO HAVE DREAMS. New York, 1925. (1,000 copies printed) 25 signed and numbered copies. Issued without dustwrapper	300	300	300
975 numbered copies	60	75	75
(Four collaborations in 1924/25.)			
Anderson, Patrick. A TENT FOR APRIL. Montreal, 1945. Stiff wraps and dustwrapper. First regularly published book, preceded by two published items in his teens	100	350	250
Anderson, Poul. VAULT OF THE AGES. Philadelphia (1952). Blue binding with black lettering or white lettering.	50	200	200
Anderson, Sherwood. WINDY McPHERSON'S SON. New York, 1916. First issue: blue binding with black letters	250	500	500
Anderson, Thomas. YOUR OWN BELOVED SONS. New York, 1956	—	35	50
Andreae, Christine. TRAIL OF MURDER. New York (1992).	—	—	100
Andrews, Jane. THE SEVEN LITTLE SISTERS . . . Boston, 1861	100	125	250

	1986	1995	2000
Andrews, Raymond. APPALACHEE RED. New York, 1978	40	100	75
Andrews, William Loring. A CHOICE COLLECTION OF BOOKS FROM THE ALDINE PRESSES. New York, 1885. Wraps. (50 copies)	400	500	500
Angell, Roger. THE STONE ARBOR +. Boston (1960). (Edward Gorey dustwrapper)	40	50	60
Angelo, Valenti. THE BOOK OF ESTHER. New York, 1935. First book of his Golden Cross Press. 135 signed copies illustrated by Angelo.	—	—	300
NINO. New York, 1938	75	125	75
Angelou, Maya. I KNOW WHY THE CAGED BIRD SINGS. New York (1969). First issue: text bulks ¹⁵⁄₁₆, top stained magenta	35	200	300
Angulo, Jaime De. THE "TRIAL" OF FERRER . . . New York, 1911. Wraps	—	—	300
ANONYMOUS (Michael Fraenkel). Paris (1930). Wraps. (First Carrefour Editions book. Written with Walter Lowenfels)	150	300	300
Ansa, Tina McElroy. BABY OF THE FAMILY. San Diego, 1989.	—	—	125
Ansen, Alan. THE OLD RELIGION. New York, 1959. (300 copies.) Wraps	—	75	75
Anshaw, Carol. AQUAMARINE. Boston, 1992	—	—	40
Anstey, Christopher. *See* THE NEW BATH GUIDE	—	—	100
Anstey, F. (Thomas Anstey Guthrie.) VICE VERSA. London, 1882	75	100	350
Anthony, Peter (Peter and Anthony Shaffer). THE WOMEN IN THE WARDROBE. London (1951)	—	100	175
Anthony, C. L. (Dodie Smith). AUTUMN CROCUS. London, 1931	—	—	100
Anthony, Piers. (P. A. Dillingham Jacob.) CHTHON. New York (1967). Wraps	—	25	35
London, 1970	—	125	75
Antin, David. MARTIN BUBER'S TALES OF ANGELS, SPIRITS AND DEMONS. New York, 1958. Translated by Antin and Jerome Rothenberg. Wraps	60	125	125
DEFINITIONS. (New York, 1967.) Spiral-bound stiff wraps (300 copies)	60	75	75
Antin, Mary. FROM PLOTZK TO BOSTON. Boston, 1899. Cloth Wraps	250 150	300 250	350 250

	1986	1995	2000
Antoninus, Brother. *See* William Everson			
Apes, William. THE EXPERIENCE OF WILLIAM APES . . . New York, 1829	—	1,500	1,750
Appel, Benjamin. BRAIN GUY. New York, 1934	—	200	200
Apple, Max. INTRODUCING THE ORANGING OF AMERICA. (New York, 1973.) Wraps	75	75	100
THE ORANGING OF AMERICA +. New York, 1976	30	50	60
Appleton (Publisher). CRUMBS FROM THE MASTER'S TABLE. New York, 1831. By W. Mason. (First book of press)	100	200	200
Archer, Jeffrey. NOT A PENNY MORE, NOT A PENNY LESS. London, 1976	—	150	250
New York, 1976	—	75	100
ARCHITEC-TONICS . . . New York, 1914. (Includes first book illustrations by Rockwell Kent)	75	250	250
Ard, William. THE PERFECT FRAME. New York, 1951.	—	75	75
Arden, John Serjeant. MUSGRAVE DANCE. London, 1960	35	35	50
Ardizzone, Edward (Jeffrey Irving). IN A GLASS DARKLY. By J. Sheridan Le Fanu. London, 1929. (First book illustrated by Ardizzone)	125	250	250
LITTLE TIM AND THE BRAVE SEA CAPTAIN. London, 1936	—	300	450
Arenas, Reinaldo. HALLUCINATIONS. New York, 1971. (First English translation)	—	125	125
Arensberg, Ann. SISTER WOLF. New York, 1980	20	40	35
Arensberg, Walter Conrad. POEMS. Boston/New York, 1914	60	75	125
Arion Press. PICTURE/POEMS . . . San Francisco, 1975. By Andrew Hoyem. (First book of press)	75	125	125
Arkham House. THE OUTSIDER +. By H. P. Lovecraft. Sauk City, 1939. (Note: There is a reprint dustwrapper not as clear as original.)	900	2,500	3,500
Arlen, Michael. THE LONDON VENTURE. London (1920). (Copies with "1919" reportedly printed later)	125	250	300
New York (1920)	50	150	200
Arlen, Michael J. LIVING ROOM WAR. New York (1969)	—	—	45
Armitage, Merle. THE ARISTOCRACY OF ART. Los Angeles, 1929. Wraps. 500 copies	75	125	150

	1986	1995	2000
Armour, Richard. YOURS FOR THE ASKING. Boston (1942). Preceded by his 1935 doctoral dissertation	35	40	50
Armstrong, Margaret. WESTERN WILD FLOWERS. New York/London 1915. Written with J. J. Thornburg	—	—	500
Armstrong, Martin. EXODUS +. London, 1912	50	100	175
Arno, Peter. WHOOPS, DEARIE! (New York, 1927)	75	125	150
Arnold, Matthew. *See* ALARIC AT ROME			
CROMWELL . . . Oxford, 1843. Wraps	1,000	1,500	1,750
Arnow, Harriette (Louisa Simpson). *See* Harriette Simpson			
HUNTER'S HORN. New York (1949). Second book, first under real name. (First edition stated)	50	125	150
Arthur, T(imothy) S(hay). *See* INSUBORDINATION			
Asbury, Herbert. UP FROM METHODISM. New York, 1926	90	125	125
Ashbery, John (Lawrence). TURANDOT +. New York, 1953. Wraps. (300 copies)	750	1,000	1,250
SOME TREES. New Hampshire, 1956	150	250	500
(Note: preceded by THE HEROS. Living Theatre. New York, 1952.) Mimeographed legal sheets in folder			
Ashdown, Clifford (R. Austin Freeman). THE ADVENTURES OF ROMNEY PRINGLE. London, 1902. Written with J. J. Pitcairn	1,000	1,250	3,000
Asher, Don. THE PIANO SPORT. New York, 1966	25	35	45
Ashton, Warren T. (William Taylor Adams.) HATCHIE, THE GUARDIAN SLAVE. Boston, 1853	75	650	750
Asimov, Isaac. PEBBLE IN THE SKY. New York, 1950	150	750	750
I, ROBOT. New York, 1950	350	1,000	1,250
Wraps	—	—	150
Asprin, Robert Lynn. THE COLD CASH WAR. New York (1977)	—	60	60
Asquith, Cynthia. THE GHOST BOOK . . . London (1926). (Edited by Asquith)	350	600	750
New York, 1927	—	—	500
Astrachan, Sam. AN END TO DYING. New York (1956)	35	40	40
London (1958)	35	35	35

	1986	1995	2000
Athas, Daphne. THE WEATHER OF THE HEART. New York (1947)	40	60	60
Atherton, Gertrude. *See* Frank Lin			
HERMIA SUYDAM. New York (1889). Wraps. Second book, first under own name	40	100	250
Atkinson, Justin Brooks. SKYLINE PROMENADES. New York, 1925. 50 numbered copies in bluish-gray cloth	100	175	200
1,950 numbered copies in blue cloth and patterned boards	75	125	125
Atlee, Philip. THE INHERITORS. NewYork, 1940	125	125	125
Attansio, A. A. RADIX. New York, 1981. Hardback	—	200	400
Wraps	—	30	35
Attaway, William. LET ME BREATHE THUNDER. New York, 1939	150	300	400
Atterley, Joseph (George Tucket). A VOYAGE TO THE MOON. New York, 1827	500	750	1,000
Attoe, David. LION AT THE DOOR. Boston (1989)	—	50	45
Atwood, Margaret (Eleanor). DOUBLE PERSEPHONE. Toronto, 1961. Wraps	1,200	2,500	3,000
THE ANIMALS IN THE COUNTRY. Toronto, 1968	—	—	350
Boston (1968)	—	—	125
Wraps	—	—	35

HOMEWARD ❧
SONGS BY ❧❧❧
THE WAY. A. E.

DUBLIN. WHALEY ❧❧❧
46 DAWSON CHAMBERS 46
MDCCCXCIV. PRICE 1/6 ❧❧❧

POEMS

BY

W. H. AUDEN

LONDON
FABER & FABER
24 RUSSELL SQUARE

	1986	1995	2000
THE EDIBLE WOMAN. Toronto (1969)	200	500	600
(London, 1969)	—	400	450
Boston (1969)	60	300	350

Note: Between 1961 and 1969 Atwood published 8 titles in limited editions. We included EDIBLE WOMAN here, as we have shown it as her first regular publication for years (in error, of course).

Aubrey-Fletcher, Henry Lancelot. *See* Henry Wade

Auchincloss, Louis (Stanton). *See* Andrew Lee

	1986	1995	2000
THE INJUSTICE COLLECTORS. Boston, 1950. Second book, first under own name	75	175	200
Auden, W(ystan) H(ugh). POEMS. (Hampstead, England, 1928.) Wraps. 12 copies recorded	10K	25K	25K
POEMS. London (1930). Stiff wraps in dustwrapper	350	750	1,000
POEMS. New York (1934)	125	300	350
Audubon, John James. THE BIRDS OF AMERICA FROM ORIGINAL DRAWINGS. London, 1827–38. 87 parts or 4 double elephant folios containing 435 plates (no text)	750K	3M	5M
First octavo edition. New York/Philadelphia, 1840–44. 7 volumes	—	30K	40K
New York, 1860, second edition of large folio	—	—	175K
New York (1870–71). 8 octavo volumes	—	17.5K	20K
New York/Amsterdam, 1971–72. 36 paper portfolios in 6 wooden files. Also bound in 4 volumes. 250 copies	—	—	30K
Auel, Jean M. THE CLAN OF THE CAVE BEAR. New York (1980)	50	100	125
Auletta, Ken. THE STREETS WERE PAVED WITH GOLD. New York (1979)	—	—	50
Auslander, Joseph. SUNRISE TRUMPETS. New York, 1924	35	40	50

Austen, Jane. *See* SENSE AND SENSIBILITY

	1986	1995	2000
Auster, Paul. FITS AND STARTS. (Salisbury [UK] 1973). Poems by Jacques Dupin, translated by Auster. 100 copies signed by both and with an original signed lithograph by Alexander Calder as frontispiece	—	—	1,750
UNEARTH. (Weston, Conn., 1974.) Wraps	—	250	250

(Previous translation of anthology, stapled sheets)

	1986	1995	2000
Austin, Jane Goodwin. FAIRY DREAMS . . . Boston (1859)	60	75	150

	1986	1995	2000
Austin, Mary (Hunter). THE LAND OF LITTLE RAIN. Boston, 1903	200	350	500
Boston, 1950. (Photographs by Ansel Adams)	—	150	200
AUTHORSHIP OF THE IMPRECATORY PSALMS. (Thomas Bulfinch.) Boston (1852). Wraps	300	450	450
AUTOBIOGRAPHY OF AN EX-COLOURED MAN. (James W. Johnson.) Boston, 1912	350	1,500	2,500
Avedon, Richard. OBSERVATIONS. New York, 1959. Glassine dustwrapper. Issued in slipcase. Text by Truman Capote	—	400	450
Awahsoose the Bear (Rowland Evans Robinson). FOREST AND STREAM FABLES. New York (1886). Wraps	200	750	850
Axelrod, George. BEGGAR'S CHOICE. New York, 1947	75	150	250
Aydy, Catherine (Emma Tennant). THE COLOUR OF RAIN. London, 1964	—	250	300
Ayrton, Michael. GILLES DE RAIS. By Cecil Gray. London (1945). First book illustrated by Ayrton. Stiff wraps and dustwrapper. (200 signed and numbered copies)	250	350	450

B

	1986	1995	2000
B., J. K. (John Kendrick Bangs.) THE LORGNETTE. New York (1886)	300	450	500
B., H. M. (Max Beerbohm.) CARMEN BECCERIENSE . . . (Surrey), 1890. 4 pages. Latin with notes in English. 2 known copies	5,000	5,000	7,500

	1986	1995	2000
B., M. (Maurice Baring.) DAMOZEL BLANCHE. (Eton, 1891.) Wraps	—	150	200
Babel, Isaac. RED CAVALRY. New York, 1929	—	750	750
Baber, Asa. THE LAND OF A MILLION ELEPHANTS. New York, 1970	—	—	100
Babitz, Eve. EVE'S HOLLYWOOD. New York, 1974	—	40	40
Babson, Marion. COVER-UP. London, 1971	—	—	75
Baca, Jimmy Santiago. JIMMY SANTIAGO BACA. [Santa Barbara, 1978.] Wraps	—	—	100
Bach, Richard. STRANGER TO THE GROUND. New York (1963)	35	75	100
Bacheller, Irving. THE MASTER OF SILENCE. New York, 1892	75	100	100
Bacon, Delia S(alter). TALES OF THE PURITANS. New Hampshire, 1831	—	200	200
Bacon, Josephine Dodge. SMITH COLLEGE STORIES. New York, 1900	40	60	75
Bacon, Leonard. THE BALLAD OF BLONAY . . . Vevy, 1906. Wraps	250	300	300
Bacon, Peggy. THE TRUE PHILOSOPHER +. Boston, 1919	60	175	75
Bagnold, Enid. A DIARY WITHOUT DATES. London, 1918	35	75	75
Bahr, Howard. THE BLACK FLOWER. Baltimore (1997)	—	—	125
Bahr, Jerome. ALL GOOD AMERICANS. New York, 1937. (Hemingway introduction.) Blue cloth (yellow cloth, also with Scribners "A" on copyright page, published in 1939)	150	200	250
Bailey, H(enry). C(hristopher). MY LADY OF ORANGE. London, 1901	35	60	75
Bailey, Paul. AT THE JERUSALEM. London, 1967	—	50	75
Bainbridge, Beryl. A WEEKEND WITH CLAUDE. (London) 1967	40	125	125
Baird, Thomas. TRIUMPHAL ENTRY. New York (1962)	40	40	35
Baker, Asa (Davis Dresser). MUM'S THE WORD FOR MURDER. New York, 1938	75	300	500
Baker, Carlos H. SHADOWS IN THE STONE. Hanover, 1930. 125 signed and numbered copies. Wraps	125	200	200

	1986	1995	2000
Baker, Dorothy. YOUNG MAN WITH A HORN. (Boston) 1938	50	150	250
London, 1938	—	—	150
Baker, Elliott. A FINE MADNESS. New York (1964)	50	75	100
London (1964)	30	50	75
Baker, Howard. ORANGE VALLEY. New York (1931)	—	—	750
Baker, John. POET IN THE GUTTER. London, 1995	—	—	40
New York, 1996	—	—	25
Baker, Nicholson. THE MEZZANINE. New York (1988)	—	125	125
London (1988)	—	35	40
Baker, Richard. DEATH STOPS THE MANUSCRIPT. New York, 1936	—	—	125
Baker, Russell. WASHINGTON CITY ON THE POTOMAC. New York (1958). Text by Baker	—	—	75
AN AMERICAN IN WASHINGTON. New York, 1961	—	35	40
Balchin, Nigel. *See* Mark Spade			
Baldwin, James (Arthur). GO TELL IT ON THE MOUNTAIN. New York (1953)	400	2,000	3,000
London, 1954	100	300	400
Baldwin, Joseph G. REMARKS OF MR. BALDWIN . . . No place, no date [House of Representatives, Montgomery, Alabama, 1843–44]. 16-page pamphlet (speech favoring resolution to rescind . . .)	—	350	750
THE FLUSH TIMES OF ALABAMA AND MISSISSIPPI. New York, 1853	200	300	400
Baldwin, Michael. THE SILENT MIRROR. London (1951)	40	75	75
Ball, John. IN THE HEAT OF THE NIGHT. New York, 1965	—	150	350
Ballantine, Sheila. NORMA JEAN THE TERMITE QUEEN. New York, 1975	30	40	40
Ballantyne, Robert Michael. HUDSON'S BAY . . . Privately printed, Edinburgh, 1848	1,000	2,500	2,500
Edinburgh/London, 1848	350	400	400
Ballard, J(ames) G(raham). THE WIND FROM NOWHERE. New York, 1962. Wraps	—	100	125
THE DROWNED WORLD. London, 1962. First issue: red boards	—	1,500	1,250
New York (1962)	—	50	150

	1986	1995	2000
THE DROWNED WORLD and THE WIND FROM NOWHERE. Garden City, 1965. First combined	—	—	125
Ballou, Jenny. SPANISH PRELUDE. Boston, 1937	30	40	75
Balliett, Whitney. THE SOUND OF SURPRISE. New York, 1959	125	125	150
London, 1960	75	75	100
Ballinger, John. THE WILLIAMSBURG FORGERIES. New York, 1989	—	40	50
Bambara, Toni Cade. GORILLA, MY LOVE. New York (1972) (Edited two books previously.)	40	125	125
Bancroft, George. PROSPECTUS OF A SCHOOL . . . (Cambridge, 1823.) Written with J. C. Coggswell. Wraps	350	200	250
POEMS. Cambridge, 1823	100	200	300
Bancroft, Irving. THE MASTER OF SILENCE. New York, 1892	125	125	125
Bangs, John Kendrick. *See* J.K.B.			
ROGER CAMERDEN. New York, 1887. Wraps	125	250	350
Banks, Iain. THE WASP FACTORY. London (1984)	—	75	250
Boston, 1984	—	50	75
Banks, Lynne Reid. THE L-SHAPED ROOM. London, 1960	—	60	75
Banks, Russell. WAITING TO FREEZE. Northwood Narrows, 1969. Wraps (Previous poems with two other poets.)	—	125	200
Bannerman, Helen. THE STORY OF LITTLE BLACK SAMBO. London, 1899. Pale-green cloth stamped in green with ruled borders and vertical stripes. Issued with the "Dumpy Books for Children No. 4."	—	6K	10K
New York, 1890	—	2,500	3,000
Bannister, Don. SAM CHARD. London, 1979	—	35	30
Bantcock, Nick. GRIFFIN & SABINE. San Francisco (1991). Dustwrapper price clipped and $16.95 on back panel	—	200	125
Banville, John. LONG LANKIN. London, 1970	—	250	500
Banyan Press. *See* Gil Orlovitz			
Barbellion, W.N.P. (Bruce Frederick Cummings.) THE JOURNAL OF A DISAPPOINTED MAN. London, 1919.	100	100	100
New York, 1919	75	75	75

	1986	1995	2000
Barfield, Owen. DANCER, UGLINESS AND WASTE. (London, no date [circa 1922–24].) Wraps	—	200	350
HISTORY IN ENGLISH WORDS. London, 1926. (8 pages of advertisements)	75	125	250
Barich, Bill. LAUGHING IN THE HILLS. New York, 1980	—	35	25
Baring, Maurice. *See* M. B.			
Barker, A(udrey) L(illian). INNOCENTS. London, 1947	60	75	200
New York, 1948	—	—	75
Barker, Clive. THE BOOKS OF BLOOD. London, 1984/1985. Wraps. Volumes 1 through 6	—	200	300
London (1985/1986). Cloth. 6 volumes. 200 signed and numbered copies	—	750	950
London (1985/1986) Cloth. 6 volumes	—	250	300
Barker, Eric (Wilson). THE PLANETARY HEART. Mill Valley, 1942	90	100	100
Barker, George (Granville). CATALOG OF EMOTIONS. (London) 1932. Wraps	—	300	400
ALANNA AUTUMNAL. London, 1933	125	250	300
Barker, Pat. UNION STREET. London (1982)	—	—	250
New York (1983)	—	—	100
Barker, Shirley. THE DARK HILLS UNDER. New Haven, 1933	50	50	40
Barlow, William. THE NAVIGATORS SUPPLY. London, 1597	—	9K	12.5K
Barnard, Robert. DEATH OF AN OLD GOAT. London, 1974	—	125	350
New York (1977)	—	75	125
Barnes, Arthur K. INTERPLANETARY HUNTER. New York (1956)	20	40	40
Barnes, Djuna. THE BOOK OF REPULSIVE WOMEN. (New York, 1915.) Wraps	400	750	1,000
New York (1948). 1,000 copies. Wraps	—	100`	100
Barnes, Julian. METROLAND. London (1980)	50	300	250
New York, 1981	—	150	150
See also Dan Kavanagh			
Barnes, Linda. BLOOD WILL HAVE BLOOD. (New York, 1982.) Wraps	—	—	60
Barney, Natalie C(lifford). QUELQUES PORTRAITS. Paris, 1900	300	450	450
Barnsley, Alan. THE FROG PRINCE +. Aldington, 1952. Wraps	60	75	75

	1986	1995	2000
Barnum, Phineas Taylor. THE LIFE OF P. T. BARNUM. New York, 1855	150	150	200
Baron, Alexander. FROM THE CITY, FROM THE PLOUGH. London, 1948	60	60	75
Barr, Nevada. BITTERSWEET. New York (1984)	—	175	450
TRACK OF THE CAT. New York (1993). Author's first mystery	—	—	250
Barr, Robert. *See* Luke Sharp			
Barre, Richard. THE INNOCENTS. New York (1995)	—	—	35
Barrett, Andrea. LUCID STARS. (New York, 1988.) Wraps	—	—	50
Barrett, Clifton Waller. BLUEPRINT FOR A BASIC . . . (New York), 1944. Mimeographed sheets	60	75	100
Barrett, E. B. (Elizabeth Barrett Browning). THE BATTLE OF MARATHON. London, 1820	12K	40K	60K
Barrie, James M. BETTER DEAD. London, 1888. Wraps.	400	1,000	1,250
Barstow, Stan(ley). A KIND OF LOVING. London (1960).	40	40	40
Barth, John (Simmons). THE FLOATING OPERA. New York (1956)	300	450	500
Garden City, 1967. Revised edition	—	—	100
London (1968). Revised edition	40	75	100
Barthelme, Donald. TWO STORIES FROM DR. CALIGARI. (Boston) 1964. Unbound sheets in box. (Promotional item)	—	500	650
COME BACK, DR. CALIGARI. Boston (1964)	150	200	250
London (1966)	75	75	150
Barthelme, Fredrick. RANGOON. New York, 1970. Cloth	60	150	175
Wraps	25	50	75
Barthes, Roland. WRITING DEGREE ZERO. London, 1967	—	100	150
New York, 1968	—	75	75
Bartlett, John. A BOOK OF HYMNS FOR YOUNG PERSONS. Cambridge, 1854	100	150	175
Also see A COLLECTION OF FAMILIAR QUOTATIONS			
Barton, Bruce. MORE POWER TO YOU. New York, 1917	25	35	35
Bartram, William. TRAVELS THROUGH NORTH & SOUTH CAROLINA. Philadelphia, 1791	8,000	7,500	7,500
London, 1792	4,500	3,000	3,000

	1986	1995	2000
Barzun, Jacques Martin. SAMPLINGS AND CHRONICLES. (Edited by J.M.B.) New York, 1927. (500 copies)	100	125	150
Basbanes, Nicholas A. A GENTLE MADNESS. New York (1995)	—	—	100
Bass, Rick. THE DEER PASTURE. College Station, Texas (1985)	—	100	175
Basso, Hamilton. RELICS AND ANGELS. New York, 1929	75	125	175
Batchelor, John Calvin. THE FURTHER ADVENTURES OF HALEY'S COMET. New York, 1980. Cloth	—	175	200
Wraps	—	35	50
Bateman, Colin. DIVORCING JACK. London (1995). Wraps	—	—	75
New York (1995). First hardback	—	—	35
Bates, H. E. THE LAST BREAD. London (1926). Wraps	150	350	200
Bates, Ralph. SIERRA. London, 1933	60	125	100
Baum, L(yman) Frank. THE BOOK OF HAMBURGS. Hartford, 1886	1,500	2,500	4,500
MOTHER GOOSE IN PROSE. Chicago (1897). (First Maxfield Parrish illustrations.) First issue: gatherings of 8 and 4 leaves at end concluding on p. (268)	300	1,200	4,000
Bausch, Richard. REAL PRESENCE. New York (1980)	—	50	75
Bausch, Robert. ON THE WAY HOME. New York (1982)	—	40	40
Bawden, Nina. WHO CALLS THE TUNE. London, 1953	—	75	100
EYES OF GREEN. New York, 1953. New title	—	—	75
Bax, Clifford. TWENTY CHINESE POEMS. Hampstead, 1910	75	125	125
Baxt, George. A QUEER KIND OF DEATH. New York (1966)	—	—	75
Baxter, Charles. CHAMELEON. New York, 1970. Wraps	—	—	300
Baxter, Glen. DRAWINGS. New York, 1974. Wraps	—	75	75
Baxter, Richard. POETICAL FRAGMENTS. London, 1821.	150	150	150
Bayley, Nicola. NICOLA BAYLEY'S BOOK OF NURSERY RHYMES. London, 1975	—	100	100
New York, 1977	—	—	50
Bayliss, John. THE WHITE KNIGHT +. London, 1944.	40	40	50

Beach, Abel. *See* AN EARLY PIONEER

	1986	1995	2000
Beach, Joseph Warren. SONNETS OF THE HEAD AND HEART. Boston, 1903	50	75	75
Beach, Rex (Ellingwood). PARDNERS. New York, 1905.	60	75	100
Beagle, Peter S. A FINE AND PRIVATE PLACE. New York, 1960	75	200	200
(London, 1960)	—	75	100
Beals, Carleton. *See* Walker Evans			
Bear, Greg. HEGIRA. New York (1979). Wraps	—	50	40
London (1988). First hardback	—	—	35
Beard, Charles Austin. THE OFFICE OF THE JUSTICE . . . New York, 1904. Wraps	75	200	200
Beard, James. HORS D'OEUVRE AND CANAPÉS. New York (1940)	125	200	125
Beasley, Gertrude. MY FIRST THIRTY YEARS . . . (Paris, 1925.) Wraps	400	600	600
Beaton, Cecil. THE TWILIGHT OF THE NYMPHS. London, 1928. 1,200 copies. Book by Pierre Louys, illustrations by Beaton	100	125	125
THE BOOK OF BEAUTY. London (1930)	250	300	450
Beaton, George (Gerald Brenan). JACK ROBINSON. London (1933)	75	400	400
New York, 1934	—	300	300
Beattie, Ann. CHILLY SCENES OF WINTER. Garden City, 1976	75	100	100
DISTORTIONS. Garden City, 1976. (Published simultaneously)	75	125	125
Beaumont, Charles (Charles Nutt). THE HUNGER +. New York (1957)	75	150	275
Beaumont Press. TIDES. Written by John Drinkwater. (London), 1917. 20 signed copies on vellum	—	1,500	1,750
250 copies.	75	200	250
Beauvoir, Simone de. THE BLOOD OF OTHERS. London, 1948	—	75	125
New York, 1948	—	—	50
Becke, Louis. BY REEF AND PALM. London, 1894. Cloth	—	100	250
Wraps	75	75	125
Becker, Stephen. THE SEASON OF THE STRANGER. New York (1951)	50	75	75
Beckett, Samuel (Barclay). WHOROSCOPE. Paris: Hours Press, 1930. Stapled wraps. 100 signed copies	2,250	3,000	5,000
200 unsigned copies	1,000	1,500	2,000

	1986	1995	2000
PROUST. London, 1931	300	350	350
Paris, 1931. Wraps	300	400	450
New York (1957). 250 signed and numbered copies. Issued without dustwrapper	200	500	500
Beckford, William. *See* BIOGRAPHICAL MEMOIRS . . .			
Beckham, Barry. MY MAIN MOTHER. New York (1969)	—	75	100
(London, 1970)	—	—	60
Bedford, Martyn. ACTS OF REVISION. London (1996)	—	—	50
Bedford, Sybille. THE SUDDEN VIEW. London, 1953	—	100	125
New York, 1953	—	75	100
Bedichek, Roy. ADVENTURES WITH A TEXAS NATURALIST. Garden City, 1947	100	150	125
Beebe, Lucius. FALLEN STARS. Cambridge, 1921. Wraps. 50 copies	—	150	150
Boston, 1921	100	100	100
Beebe, (Charles) William. TWO BIRD-LOVERS IN MEXICO. Boston, 1905. First issue: Charles M. Beebe on cover	1,500	1,750	1,750
Second issue: C. William Beebe on cover	250	350	300
Third issue: gold sky background lacking	125	150	150
Fourth issue: lacks pictorial design, just lettered	60	75	100
Beecher, Harriet Elizabeth. PRIMARY GEOGRAPHY FOR CHILDREN . . . Cincinnati, 1833. (Written with Catherine Beecher)	—	2,500	3,000
PRIZE TALE: A NEW ENGLAND SKETCH. Lowell, Massachusetts, 1834	500	1,000	1,250
Beechwood, Mary. MEMPHIS JACKSON'S SON. Boston, 1956	—	125	75
Beeding, Francis. (John Leslie Palmer and Hilary Saunders.) THE SEVEN SLEEPERS. London, 1925	60	100	200
Beer, Patricia. LOSS OF THE MAGYAR. London, 1959. Issued in glassine dustwrapper	50	75	50
Beer, Thomas. THE FAIR REWARDS. New York, 1922	150	150	200
Beerbohm, Max. THE WORKS OF MAX BEERBOHM. New York, 1896. 1,000 copies, 400 pulped	225	350	450
London, 1896	150	250	350
Beeton, Isabella. THE BOOK OF HOUSEHOLD MANAGEMENT. London, 1861. 2 volumes. First issue: "18 Bouverie St." on woodcut title page	500	1,000	2,500
Begley, Louis. WARTIME LIES. New York, 1991	—	75	175

with sincere regards to Mr. and Mrs. Bull from

TWO BIRD-LOVERS IN MEXICO

BY

C. WILLIAM BEEBE

Curator of Ornithology of the New York Zoölogical Park and Life Member of the New York Zoölogical Society; Member of the American Ornithologists' Union

C. William Beebe.

ILLUSTRATED WITH PHOTOGRAPHS
FROM LIFE TAKEN BY THE AUTHOR

Mary Blair Beebe

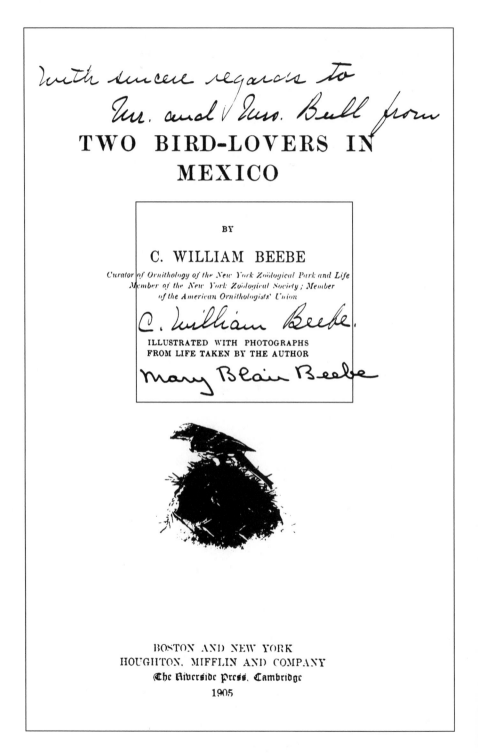

BOSTON AND NEW YORK
HOUGHTON, MIFFLIN AND COMPANY
The Riverside Press, Cambridge
1905

	1986	1995	2000
Behan, Brendan. THE QUARE FELLOW. London, 1956	150	200	200
New York (1956). Boards. 100 numbered copies. Issued without dustwrapper	100	150	250
Wraps	25	35	35
Behm, Marc. THE QUEEN OF THE NIGHT. Boston, 1977	—	60	50
Behn, Aphra. POEMS UPON SEVERAL OCCASIONS. London, 1684	—	—	1,000
Behn, Noel. THE KREMLIN LETTER. New York (1966).	35	100	100
Behrman, Samuel Nathaniel. BEDSIDE MANNER. New York, 1924. Written with J. K. Nicholson. Wraps	50	250	250
THE SECOND MAN. New York, 1927. Stiff wraps in dustwrapper	100	200	200
London, 1928 (Another collaboration, 1926.)	75	125	150
Beinhart, Larry. NO ONE RIDES FOR FREE. New York, 1986	—	50	75
Belitt, Ben. THE FIVE FOLD MESH. New York, 1938	60	60	60
Belknap, Jeremy. *See* THE FORESTERS . . .			
Bell, Acton (Ann Brontë). *See* Ellis Bell			
Bell, Christine. SAINT. Englewood (1985)	—	—	50
Bell, Clive. ART. London, 1914	75	200	250
New York (1914). English sheets	—	150	200
Bell, Currer. (Charlotte Brontë.) JANE EYRE. London, 1847. 3 volumes. First issue: Bell as editor. 36-page catalog in volume 1, dated June and October	6K	15K	45K
London, 1847. Second with Bell as author	—	—	2,000
New York, 1848. Wraps	—	3,000	3,000
Bell, Currer, Ellis, and Acton. (Charlotte, Emily, and Ann Brontë.) POEMS. London, 1846. (Published by Aylott and Jones)	7.5K	25K	40K
Philadelphia, 1848	—	2,000	2,500
London, 1846. (Published by Smith, Elder in 1848)	750	2,000	2,500
Bell, Dewitt. RAVENSWOOD +. Hanover, 1963. (250 copies)	50	75	75
Bell, Ellis. (Emily Brontë.) WUTHERING HEIGHTS. London, 1847. 2 volumes. (1,000 copies.) and AGNES GREY by Acton Bell (Ann Brontë). (1,000 copies.) 3 volumes in total	8K	50K	60K
New York, 1848. Two volumes in wraps	—	—	3,500
Bell, Josephine. (Doris Bell and Collier Ball.) MURDER IN HOSPITAL. London, 1937	50	100	200
Bell, Julian. CHAFFINCHES. Cambridge, 1929. Wraps	75	150	150

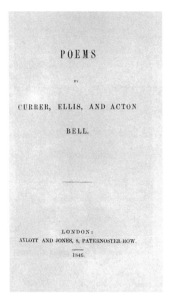

	1986	1995	2000
Bell, Madison Smartt. THE WASHINGTON SQUARE ENSEMBLE. New York, 1983	35	125	150
(London, 1983)	—	75	100
Bell, Marvin. TWO POEMS. Iowa City, 1965. Issued without dustwrapper	—	350	350
Bell, Quentin. ON HUMAN FINERY. London: Hogarth Press, 1947	40	100	150
Bell, Robert. THE BUTTERFLY TREE. Philadelphia (1959)	35	40	60
Bellah, James Warner. SKETCH BOOK OF A CADET FROM GAS-CONY. New York, 1923	75	125	150
Bellamy, Edward. *See* SIX TO ONE			
Belli, Melvin M. BELLI LOOKS AT LIFE AND LAW IN JAPAN. Indi-anapolis (1960). Written with Danny Jones	30	75	50
Belloc, Hilaire. VERSES AND SONNETS. London, 1896	400	600	750
Bellow, Saul. DANGLING MAN. New York (1944)	600	1,500	3,000
London, 1946	250	300	450
Bemelmans, Ludwig. HANSI. New York, 1934	250	400	750
Benchley, Nathaniel. SIDE STREET. New York, 1950	35	60	50

	1986	1995	2000
Benchley, Robert C. OF ALL THINGS. New York, 1921. With and without advertisements at end, priority unknown	300	750	1,000
London, 1922	150	350	400
Benedict, Pinckney. TOWN SMOKES. Princeton (1987). Wraps	—	75	60
Benedikt, Michael. SERENADE IN SIX PIECES. Huntington, 1958. Wraps	—	—	125
CHANGES. Detroit (1961). Wraps	—	—	60
Benét, Laura. FAIRY BREAD. New York, 1921	50	150	200
Benét, Stephen Vincent. FIVE MEN AND POMPEY. Boston, 1915. First issue in purple wraps (trial)	350	250	250
Second issue: brown wraps. (Also noted in a white dust-wrapper)	75	125	100
Benét, William Rose. MERCHANTS FROM CATHAY. New York, 1913	35	75	50
Benford, Gregory. DEEPER THAN THE DARKNESS. New York (1970). Wraps	—	30	35
THE STARS IN SHROUD. New York, 1978. New title, revised, of first book	—	40	35
Bennett, E. A(rnold). A MAN FROM THE NORTH. London, 1898	250	400	400
Bennett, Emerson. THE BRIGAND . . . New York, 1842. Wraps	400	400	450
Bennett, Hal. A WILDERNESS OF VINES. Garden City, 1966	40	150	175
Bensko, John. GREEN SOLDIERS. New Hampshire (1981)	—	25	30
Wraps	—	—	20
Benson, Arthur Christopher. *See* Christopher Carr			
WILLIAM LAUD, ARCHBISHOP OF CANTERBURY. London, 1887. (Second book, first under own name)	100	250	350
Benson, E(dward) F(redric). DODO. London, 1893. 2 volumes	100	350	600
Benson, Mildred. RUTH FIELDING AND HER GREAT SCENARIO. New York, 1927. (Better known for Nancy Drew)	—	—	350
Benson, R. H. THE LIGHT INVISIBLE. London, 1903	60	60	75
Benson, Sally. PEOPLE ARE FASCINATING. New York (1936)	—	60	75
Benson, Stella. I POSE. London, 1915	—	75	75
New York, 1916	—	50	50
Bentley, E(dmund) C(lerihew). *See* E. Clerihew			

	1986	1995	2000
TRENT'S LAST CASE. London (1913)	125	250	250
THE WOMAN IN BLACK. New York, 1913. (New title)	—	75	200
Bentley, Eric Russell. A CENTURY OF HERO WORSHIP. Philadelphia/New York (1944)	40	40	50
Benton, Thomas Hart. EUROPE AFTER 8:15. New York, 1914. (First illustrated. Written by Mencken, Nathan, and W. H. Wright.) First issue: cloth stamped in blue	100	200	300
Second issue: cloth stamped in gold	75	150	200
Berendt, John. MIDNIGHT IN THE GARDEN OF GOOD AND EVIL. New York (1994)	—	40	200
New York, 1995. 2,500 signed and numbered copies. In slipcase	—	—	150
Beresford, J(ohn) D(avys). THE HAMPDENSHIRE WONDER. London, 1911	—	350	350
Beresford-Howe, Constance. THE UNREASONING HEART. New York, 1946	—	50	75
Bereton, Ford (Samuel Rutherford Crockett). DOLCE COR . . . London, 1886	—	250	250
Berge, Carol. THE VULNERABLE ISLAND. Cleveland, 1964. Wraps. (105 copies)	50	100	125
Berger, John. A PAINTER OF OUR TIME. London, 1958	75	125	250
New York, 1959	—	75	125
Berger, Thomas (Louis). CRAZY IN BERLIN. New York (1958). Dustwrapper without Dial Prize notice	75	250	300
With the Dial Prize Winner notice	—	—	200
London, 1965	—	—	100
Bergman, Andrew. WE'RE IN THE MONEY. New York, 1971	—	—	75
THE BIG KISS-OFF OF 1944. New York (1974)	35	60	60
Berkeley, Anthony. *See* THE LAYTON COURT MYSTERY			
Berkman, Alexander. PRISON MEMOIRS OF AN ANARCHIST. New York, 1912	75	100	75
Berkson, Bill. SATURDAY NIGHT POEMS. New York, 1961. Wraps. (300 copies.)	60	125	100
Berlin, Lucia. A MANUAL FOR CLEANING LADIES. No place, 1977. Wraps in envelope	—	75	75
Berne, Eric. THE MIND IN ACTION. New York, 1947	50	75	25

	1986	1995	2000
Berne, Suzanne. A CRIME IN THE NEIGHBORHOOD. Chapel Hill, 1997	—	—	60
Bernhard, Thomas. GARGOYLES. New York, 1970. (First U.S. publication)	—	125	100
Bernstein, Aline. THREE BLUE SUITS. New York, 1933. 600 signed copies. Issued in slipcase	100	125	150
Bernstein, Jane. DEPARTURES. New York (1979)	—	35	25
Bernstein, Jeremy. THE ANALYTICAL ENGINE . . . New York (1964)	—	—	40
Berriault, Gina. THE DESCENT. New York, 1960	30	50	75
(London, 1961)	—	—	60
Berrigan, Daniel. TIME WITHOUT NUMBERS. New York, 1957	50	50	35
Berrigan, Ted (Edmund J.). THE SONNETS. (New York), 1964. (300 copies.) Stapled mimeographed sheets with a back wrapper	60	100	1,000
Grove Press. New York (1964). Wraps (Preceded by at least 2 privately printed pamphlets.)	25	35	60
Berry, Don. TRASK. New York, 1960	30	40	30
Berry, Francis. GOSPEL OF FIRE. London, 1933	60	60	75

	1986	1995	2000
Berry, Wendell (Erdman). NATHAN COLTER. Boston, 1960	200	300	350
San Francisco, 1985. Revised. 26 signed and lettered copies	—	200	250
Berryman, John. *See* FIVE YOUNG AMERICAN POETS			
POEMS. Norfolk (1942). Boards. (500 copies)	250	400	450
Wraps. (1,500 copies)	75	125	· 125
Berton, Pierre. THE ROYAL FAMILY. Toronto, 1954	—	150	150
Bessie, Alvah Cecil. DWELL IN THE WILDERNESS. New York (1935)	100	250	300
London, 1936 (Previous translations.)	—	150	250
Bester, Alfred. THE DEMOLISHED MAN. Chicago (1953). Unknown quantity signed	250	400	450
Unsigned	150	300	350
London (1953)	60	100	100
Betjeman, John. MOUNT ZION, OR IN TOUCH WITH . . . London (1931). Issued without dustwrapper. First issue: blue and gold pattern cover	450	750	1,000
Second issue: striped paper cover	350	500	600
Betts, Doris. THE GENTLE INSURRECTION +. New York, 1954.	100	175	175

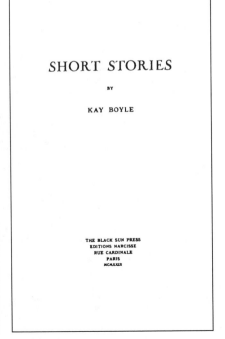

	1986	1995	2000
Beveridge, Albert Jeremiah. THE RUSSIAN ADVANCE. New York, 1903	50	125	35
Beynon, John. (John Beynon Harris.) THE SECRET PEOPLE. London (1935)	400	600	650
Second issue: in green binding with black lettering; dust-wrapper priced "2/6" (probably published in 1936)	—	250	350
Bezzerides, A. I. LONG HAUL. New York (1938)	40	75	300
Bianco, Margery (Williams). THE LITTLE WOODEN DOLL. New York, 1925. (First under this name)	—	75	250
Also see Margery Williams			
Bidart, Frank. GOLDEN STATE. New York (1973)	—	—	100
Wraps	—	—	35
Bierce, Ambrose (Gwinnett). *See* Dod Grile			
Biggers, Earl Derr. IF YOU'RE ONLY HUMAN. 1912	100	350	350
SEVEN KEYS TO BALDPATE. Indianapolis (1913)	75	200	200
Binding, Tim. IN THE KINGDOM OF THE AIR. London, 1993	—	—	60
New York, 1994	—	—	45
Bingham, Sallie. AFTER SUCH KNOWLEDGE. Boston, 1960	40	60	75
Binns, Archie. LIGHTSHIP. New York (1934)	60	75	50
Binstock, R. C. THE LIGHT OF HOME. New York, 1992	—	—	75
Binyon, Laurence. PERSEPHONE. London, 1890. Wraps. (Newdigate Prize)	300	400	500
LYRIC POEMS. London, 1894	150	250	250
POEMS. Oxford, 1895. (200 copies.) Wraps	125	200	250
BIOGRAPHICAL MEMOIRS OF EXTRAORDINARY PAINTERS. (By William Beckford.) London, 1780	—	1,000	1,000
Bion and Moschos. (Robert Lovell and Robert Southey.) POEMS. Bristol, 1794	400	1,500	2,000
Bird, Bessie Calhoun. AIRS FROM THE WOOD WINDS. Philadelphia (1935). (Only book.) 25 signed and numbered copies	150	750	750
300 signed and numbered copies	50	300	300
Bird, Gloria. FULL MOON ON THE RESERVATION. New York (1993). Wraps	—	—	50
Bird, Isabella. *See* THE ENGLISHWOMAN IN AMERICA			

	1986	1995	2000
Bird, Robert Montgomery. *See* CALAVAR			
Bird, William. A PRACTICAL GUIDE TO FRENCH WINE. Paris, no date [1922?]. Wraps	150	200	250
Bird & Bull Press. A COLLECTION OF RECEIPTS . . . Philadelphia, 1958. (First book of press of Henry Morris.) Wraps. 100 numbered copies	1,250	2,000	2,500
Birdsell, Sandra. NIGHT TRAVELLERS. Winnipeg, 1982. Wraps	—	50	40
Birmingham, Stephen. YOUNG MR. KEEFE. Boston, 1958	35	40	35
Birney, (Alfred) Earle. *See* E. Robertson			
DAVID +. Toronto, 1942. (500 copies)	—	200	200
Biro, Val. BUMBY'S HOLIDAY. London, 1943	—	150	150
Birrell, Augustine. *See* OBITER DICTA			
Bishop, Elizabeth. NORTH AND SOUTH. Boston, 1946. (1,000 copies)	350	600	750
Bishop, John Peale. GREEN FRUIT. Boston, 1917	150	300	200
Bishop, Zealia. THE CURSE OF YIG. South Carolina, 1953	75	175	175
Bissell, Richard. A STRETCH ON THE RIVER. Boston, 1950	40	50	50
Bissoondath, Neil. DIGGING UP THE MOUNTAINS. Toronto, 1985	—	100	100
London, 1986	—	50	60
(New York, 1986)	—	—	40
Black, Campbell. ASSASSINS AND VICTIMS. (London, 1969)	—	—	125
Black, E. L. (Sir John Ellerman.) WHY DO THEY LIKE IT . . . (Dijon, 1927.) Wraps	200	300	300
Black, (Harvey) MacKnight. MACHINERY. New York, 1929	75	75	75
Black Manikin Press. *See* Ralph Cheever Dunning			
Black, Mansell. (Elleston Trevor.) SINISTER CARGO. London, 1951	100	150	250
Black Sparrow Press. NOT MEANING NOT TO SEE. By Bernard A. Forrest. (Los Angeles, 1967.) (75 signed copies)	150	250	250
Blackburn, John. A SCENT OF NEW-MOWN HAY. London, 1958	—	—	200
New York, 1958	—	—	35

	1986	1995	2000
Blackburn, Paul. PROENSA. (Majorca) 1953. (Translation.) Wraps	225	225	275
THE DISSOLVING FABRIC. (Majorca) 1955. Wraps	175	300	350
Blackmore, Richard Doddridge. *See* Melanter			
Blackmur, R(ichard) P(almer). T. S. ELIOT. (Cambridge), 1929. Wraps	100	200	250
DIRTYHANDS OR THE TRUE BORN CENSOR. Cambridge (England) 1930. (Offprint from *Hound and Horn*.) Wraps	150	150	200
Blackwell, Elizabeth. THE LAWS OF LIFE. New York, 1852	—	—	7,500
Blackwood, Algernon. THE EMPTY HOUSE +. London, 1906	200	250	750
New York, 1917	75	100	350
Blackwood, Caroline. FOR ALL THAT I FOUND THERE. London, 1973	35	40	35
Blaikie, John Arthur. *See* Edmund Gosse			
Blaise, Clark. A NORTH AMERICAN EDUCATION. Garden City, 1973	—	50	75
Bland, Eleanor Taylor. DEAD TIME. New York (1992)	—	—	75
Blanding, Don. LEAVES FROM A GRASS-HOUSE. (Honolulu, 1923.) Wraps	50	100	200
Blasco, Vicente Ibáñez. THE BLOOD OF THE ARENA. Chicago, 1911	—	—	75
Blatty, William. ULYSSES AND THE CYCLOPS. (Los Angeles, 1956.) Pictorial boards issued without dustwrapper. Written with James J. Cullen	—	150	150
WHICH WAY TO MECCA, JACK? New York, 1960	35	40	35
Blake, Nicholas. (C. Day-Lewis pseudonym.) A QUESTION OF PROOF. London, 1935. (First under this name)	300	500	850
Blau, Ernest E. THE QUEEN'S FALCON. Philadelphia, 1947	—	—	50
Blauner, Peter. SLOW MOTION RIOT. New York (1991)	—	—	40
Blaylock, James P. THE ELFIN SHIP. New York (1982). Wraps	—	25	30
Blechman, Burt. HOW MUCH? New York (1961)	40	40	40
Blesh, Rudi. THIS IS JAZZ. San Francisco (1943). Wraps	150	100	100
London, 1943. Wraps	—	75	75

	1986	1995	2000
Blish, James (Benjamin). JACK OF EAGLES. New York (1952)	100	150	100
London (1973)	—	—	35
Bloch, Robert. SEA KISSED. (London, 1945.) Wraps. First issue: 39 pages. "Printed in Great Britain" on p. 39	250	750	750
Second issue: 36 pages. "Printed in Eire" on p. 36	200	600	450
THE OPENER OF THE WAY. Sauk City, 1945. (2,000 copies)	150	500	400
Block, Herbert. THE HERBLOCK BOOK. Boston, 1952	35	30	35
Block, Lawrence. MONA. New York (1961). Wraps (Note: This is the first in bibliography, but we've seen books by William Ard and Lesley Evans cataloged as the first.)	—	—	125
Blondal, Patricia. A CANDLE TO LIGHT THE SUN. (Toronto, 1960)	—	60	60
Bloom, Amy. COME TO ME. (New York, 1993)	—	—	75
Blount, Roy, Jr. ABOUT THREE BRICKS SHY OF A LOAD. Boston, 1974	—	—	35
Blum, Etta. POEMS. New York, 1937	40	50	50
Blunden, E(dmund) C(harles). POEMS 1913 AND 1914. (Horsham, 1914.) Wraps. (100 copies)	300	850	1,000
Blunt, Wilfred Scawen. *See* PROTEUS SONNETS AND SONGS			
Bly, Robert (Elwood). *See* Hans Hvass			
THE LION'S TAIL AND EYES. Madison, 1962. (Written with J. Wright and W. Duffy) (Previous translation in 1960 and a broadside in 1961.)	100	175	175
SILENCE IN THE SNOWY FIELDS. Middleton (1962). Cloth	125	150	150
Wraps	50	50	50
Blyton, Enid (Mary). CHILD WHISPERS. London, 1922	—	100	100
Bodenheim, Maxwell. MINNA AND MYSELF. New York, 1918. First issue: "Master-Posner" for "Master-Poisoner" p. (67). (Written with Ben Hecht. This was also his first book.)	75	75	75
Bodine, A. Aubrey. MY MARYLAND. Baltimore, 1952	—	50	50
Bodkin, M(atthais) McDonald. WHITE MAGIC. London, 1897	150	150	200
PAUL BECK: THE RULE OF THUMB DETECTIVE. London, 1898	500	500	750
Bodley Booklets #1. THE HAPPY HYPOCRITE: A FAIRY TALE. By	200	200	250

	1986	1995	2000
Max Beerbohm. New York/London, 1897. First issue: period on cover, colophon dated December 1896			
Bogan, Louise. BODY OF THIS DEATH. New York, 1923	250	600	350
Bogarous, Edgar. VARIOUS JANGLING KEYS. New Haven, 1953	—	—	60
Bogdanovich, Peter. THE CINEMA OF ORSON WELLES. New York (1961). Wraps	—	—	150
Bogner, Norman. IN SPELLS NO LONGER BOUND. London (1961)	40	40	50
Bogosian, Eric. IN THE DARK. New York, 1983. Wraps	—	—	75
Bok, Edward W(illiam). THE YOUNG MAN IN BUSINESS. Philadelphia, 1894. Wraps	100	100	125
Boles, Robert. THE PEOPLE ONE KNOWS. Boston, 1964	30	60	75
Bolitho, William. LEVIATHAN. London, 1923	30	75	75
New York, 1924	—	—	60
Böll, Heinrich. ACQUAINTED WITH THE NIGHT. New York (1954). First book in English	—	—	50
London (1955)	—	—	40
Bolt, Robert (Oxton). FLOWERING CHERRY. London (1958) (First play, *A Man for All Seasons,* not published until 1961.)	50	100	75
Bolton, George G. A SPECIALIST IN CRIME. London, 1904. (Only book)	150	150	125
Bolton, Isabel. (Mary Britton Miller.) DO I WAKE OR SLEEP. New York, 1946	—	—	75
Bombal, Maria-Luisa. HOUSE OF MIST. New York (1947). Rewritten by author in English	—	60	100
Bond, (Thomas) Michael. BEAR CALLED PADDINGTON. London, 1958	—	250	300
Boston, 1960	—	175	200
Bond, Nelson (Slade). MR. MERGENTHWIRKER'S LOBBLIES +. New York, 1946	60	75	100
Bonfiglioli, Kyril. DON'T POINT THAT THING AT ME. London (1972)	—	—	100
Bonner, Cindy. LILY. Chapel Hill, 1992	—	—	35
Bonner, Marjorie. THE SHAPES THAT CREEP. New York, 1946	—	—	125

	1986	1995	2000
Bontemps, Arna (Wendall). GOD SENDS SUNDAY. New York, 1931	175	950	1,500
Booth, Evangeline Cory. LOVE IS ALL. New York (1908)	50	75	75
Booth, Philip. LETTER FROM A DISTANT LAND: POEMS. New York, 1957	35	75	50
Booth, General William. IN DARKEST ENGLAND AND THE WAY OUT. London (1890). First issue: last line of dedication in smaller type than preceding line	—	250	175
New York, 1890	—	—	150
Borges, Jorge Luis. FICCIONES. London (1962). First English translation	—	250	400
New York (1962)	—	125	300
New York: Limited Editions Club (1984)	—	—	500
Borrow, George (Henry). *See* CELEBRATED TRIALS			
Boswell, Robert. DANCING AT THE MOVIES. Iowa City (1986). (1,500 copies)	—	125	125
Boswell, Thomas. HOW LIFE IMITATES THE WORLD SERIES. Garden City, 1972	—	40	60
Bosworth, Sheila. ALMOST INNOCENT. New York (1984)	—	—	25
Bottoms, David. JAMMING WITH THE BAND AT THE VFW. (Austell, Georgia, 1978.) Wraps	—	60	60
SHOOTING RATS AT THE BIBB COUNTY DUMP. (New York, 1980)	—	50	30
Bottrall, Ronald. THE LOOSENING +. Cambridge, 1931. Issued in tissue dustwrapper	50	75	125
Boucher, Anthony. (William Anthony Parker White.) THE CASE OF THE SEVEN OF CALVARY. New York, 1937	150	450	650
Boulle, Pierre. THE BRIDGE OVER THE RIVER KWAI. (First translation in English.) London, 1954	100	175	200
New York, 1954	50	100	125
Bourdain, Anthony. BONE IN THE THROAT. New York, 1995	—	—	25
Bourdillon, Francis W. AMONG THE FLOWERS +. London, 1878	75	125	200
Bourjaily, Vance (Nye). THE END OF MY LIFE. New York, 1947	75	100	75
Bourke-White, Margaret. EYES ON RUSSIA. New York, 1931	300	400	450
Bourne, Randolph S(illiman). YOUTH AND LIFE. Boston, 1913	125	200	300

	1986	1995	2000
Bova, Ben. STAR CONQUERORS. Philadelphia (1959)	150	200	250
Bowden, Charles. KILLING THE HIDDEN WATERS. Austin (1977)	—	—	300
Bowen, Catherine Drinker. A HISTORY OF LEHIGH UNIVERSITY. (Bethlehem, Pennsylvania), 1924	—	200	200
Bowen, Elizabeth. ENCOUNTERS. London, 1923	750	1,000	1,250
Bowen, Marjorie. (Gabrielle M. V. Long.) THE VIPER OF MILAN. London, 1906	100	125	75
Bowen, Peter. YELLOWSTONE KELLY . . . Ottawa, 1987	—	—	125
Bowering, George. STICKS AND STONES. Vancouver [1962]. Wraps	—	—	2,000
Bowers, Dorothy. POSTSCRIPT TO POISON. London (1938)	—	—	300
Bowers, Edgar. THE FORM OF LOSS. Denver, 1956	—	150	250
Bowles, Jane. TWO SERIOUS LADIES. New York (1943)	400	750	750
London, 1965	75	100	100
Bowles, Paul (Frederick). TWO POEMS. (New York, 1934.) Wraps	600	4,000	4,500
THE SHELTERING SKY. London (1949)	250	1,000	1,500
(New York, 1949)	150	750	750

	1986	1995	2000
Bowman, David. LET THE DOG DRIVE. New York (1992)	—	175	200
Boyd, Blanche. NERVES. Plainfield, Vermont (1973). Wraps	—	35	25
Boyd, James. DRUMS. New York, 1925	200	350	350
New York (1928). Illustrated by N. C. Wyeth. 525 signed	125	750	1,250
and numbered copies			
Trade edition	—	75	250
Boyd, Thomas. THROUGH THE WHEAT. New York, 1923	125	150	300
Boyd, William. A GOOD MAN IN AFRICA. London, 1981.	75	750	750
New York (1982)	30	75	100
Boyer, Richard L. THE GIANT RAT OF SUMATRA. New York	—	60	35
(1976). Wraps			
London, 1977	—	—	350
Boyle, Jack. BOSTON BLACKIE. New York (1919).	100	450	450
Boyle, Kay. SHORT STORIES. Paris, 1929. Wraps in tied folder.	1,000	1,250	1,500
15 signed and numbered copies			
150 numbered copies	350	600	600
WEDDING DAY +. New York (1930). (New title.) (Two	75	300	350
spine variants noted: "KAY | BOYLE | WEDDING | DAY | & |			
OTHER | STORIES" and "SHORT | STORIES | KAY | BOYLE"—			
otherwise the same—priority unknown)			
London, 1932	—	200	250
Also see Gladys Palmer Brook			
Boyle, Patrick. LIKE ANY OTHER MAN. London, 1966	40	60	60
Boyle, T. Coraghessan. DESCENT OF MAN. Boston (1979).	40	350	500
2,500 copies			
London, 1980	—	150	250
Boyle, Thomas. THE COLD STOVE LEAGUE. Chicago, 1983	—	50	25
BOZ (Charles Dickens). *See* SKETCHES BY "BOZ"			
Brackenridge, H(ugh) H(enry). *See* A POEM ON THE RISING			
GLORY . . .			
Brackett, Leigh. NO GOOD FROM A CORPSE. New York (1944)	—	—	600
Bradbury, Malcolm (Stanley). EATING PEOPLE IS WRONG. London, 1959	50	125	100
New York, 1960	—	60	60
Bradbury, Ray (Douglas). DARK CARNIVAL. Sauk City, 1947	500	850	1,000
London (1948)	250	350	350

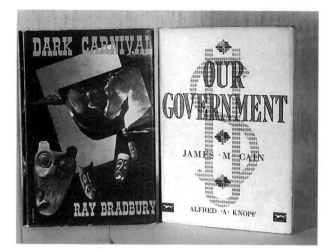

	1986	1995	2000
Bradby, Anne. (Anne Ridler.) SHAKESPEARE CRITICISM 1919–1935. London, 1936	100	125	50
Braddon, Mary Elizabeth. GARIBALDI +. London, 1861	400	750	1,000
LADY AUDLEY'S SECRET. London, 1862. 3 volumes	400	1,000	1,250
Bradfield, Scott. THE SECRET LIFE OF HOUSES. London (1988)	—	60	60
DREAM OF THE WOLF. New York, 1990. New title	—	—	50
Bradford, Gamaliel. TYPES OF AMERICAN CHARACTER. New York, 1895	50	150	100
Bradford, Richard. RED SKY AT MORNING. Philadelphia (1968)	40	50	60
Bradford, Roark. OL' MAN ADAM AND HIS CHILLUN. New York, 1928	75	125	125
Bradley, David. SOUTH STREET. New York, 1975	75	200	250
Bradley, Edward. COLLEGE LIFE. Oxford, 1849/1850. (6 parts in 5)	600	750	750
Bradley, Marion Zimmer. THE DOOR THROUGH SPACE. New York (1961). Wraps Privately printed books in 1960 and 1961.	—	25	25
Bradshaw, Gillian. HAWK OF MAY. New York (1980)	—	—	35
Bradstreet, Anne. *See* THE TENTH MUSE . . .			
Bragdon, Claude F. THE GOLDEN PERSON IN THE HEART. Gouverner, New York, 1898. 350 numbered copies	75	75	50

	1986	1995	2000
Braine, John (Gerard). ROOM AT THE TOP. London, 1957	100	200	250
Boston, 1957	25	60	60
Braithwaite, E. R. TO SIR, WITH LOVE. Englewood Cliffs (1959)	35	100	100
London, 1959	—	75	75
Braithwaite, William Stanley. LYRICS OF LIFE AND LOVE. Boston, 1904. (500 copies)	150	300	400
Bramah, Ernest (Ernest Bramah Smith). ENGLISH FARMING . . . London, 1894. Stiff wraps	150	200	250
Brammer, William. THE GAY PLACE. Boston, 1961. First issue: rear dustwrapper flap has name of designer	100	250	300
Second issue: rear dustwrapper flap has name of designer covered by design	60	150	150
Third issue: rear dustwrapper flap has name of designer removed	40	100	100
Branch, Anna Hempstead. THE HEART OF THE ROAD +. Boston, 1901	40	40	40
Brand, Christianna. (Mary Christianna Lewis.) DEATH IN HIGH HEELS. London, 1941	60	150	200
New York, 1954	—	—	40
Brand, Max. *See* Frederick Faust			
THE UNTAMED. New York, 1919. Author's first western, and first using this name	75	175	300
Brand, Millen. THE OUTWARD ROOM. New York, 1937. First issue: pictorial dustwrapper, Sinclair Lewis blurb	30	30	30
Second issue: printed dustwrapper, Lewis, Dreiser, and Hurst blurbs	15	15	15
Brandeis, Louis D. OTHER PEOPLE'S MONEY. New York (1914)	—	300	300
Brandt, Bill. THE ENGLISH AT HOME. London (1936). Issued in glassine dustwrapper	—	450	450
New York, 1936. Issued in tissue dustwrapper	—	350	350
Brashler, William. THE BINGO LONG TRAVELING . . . New York (1973)	30	100	100
Brasil, Angela. A TERRIBLE TOMBOY. London, 1904	—	300	300
Brassai. PARIS DE NUIT. Paris, 1933. Text by Paul Morand. Spiral-bound, stiff wraps	—	850	1,500
New York, 1987	—	—	125
Bratby, John. BREAKDOWN. Cleveland (1960)	—	60	60

	1986	1995	2000
Braun, Lilian Jackson. THE CAT WHO COULD READ BACKWARDS. New York, 1966	—	150	200
Brautigan, Richard. THE RETURN OF THE RIVERS. (San Francisco, 1958.) Wraps	1,000	1,500	2,000
Braverman, Katherine. DROPPING IN. Los Angeles, 1973	50	75	75
Brecht, Bertolt. A PENNY FOR THE POOR. New York, 1938. First English translation (partially by Christopher Isherwood)	—	200	300
Bremster, Ray. POEMS OF MADNESS. (New York) 1965. Wraps. (Ginsberg introduction)	30	50	60
Brenan, Gerald. *See* George Beaton			
Brennan, Joseph Payne. HEART OF EARTH. Prairie City (1949)	125	200	150
NINE HORRORS AND A DREAM. Sauk City, 1958.	90	200	150
Brenton, Howard. REVENGE. London, 1970. Wraps	—	75	75
(Previous private printing.)			
Breslin, Jimmy. *See* Jimmy Demaret			
SUNNY JIM . . . FITZSIMMONS. Garden City, 1962	40	60	75
Breton, André. YOUNG CHERRY TREES SECURED AGAINST HARES. New York, 1946	—	150	200
Brett, Simon. (Anthony Lee.) CAST, IN ORDER OF DISAPPEARANCE. London, 1975	40	75	125
New York (1976)	25	35	75
Brewster, Ralph H. THE GOOD BEARDS OF ATHOS. London: Hogarth, 1935	100	150	150
Breytenbach, Breyten. SINKING SHIP BLUES. Oakville, Ontario, 1977. Wraps	—	100	125
Bridges, Robert. POEMS. London, 1873. (Suppressed by author in 1878)	400	400	750
Bridie, James. SOME TALK OF ALEXANDER. London, 1926. Purple cloth with gilt lettering	100	100	100
Briggs, Charles Frederick. *See* THE ADVENTURES OF HARRY FRANCO			
Briggs, K(atherine) M(ary). THE LEGEND OF MAIDEN-HAIR. London, 1915	—	200	200

	1986	1995	2000
Brigham, Besmilr. AGONY DANCES: DEATH OF A DANCING DOLL. Portland, 1969. Wraps. (450 copies)	—	—	100
Brilliant, Ashley. I MAY NOT BE TOTALLY PERFECT, BUT . . . Santa Barbara (1979). Cloth. Issued without dustwrapper. (1,000 copies)	—	150	150
Wraps	—	30	30
Brink, André (Philippus). THE AMBASSADOR. (Cape Town), 1964. First English translation	—	60	125
FILE ON A DIPLOMAT. London, 1967. (New title)	—	40	75
Brinnin, John Malcolm. THE GARDEN IS POLITICAL. New York, 1942	50	50	35
Brisbane, Albert. SOCIAL DESTINY OF MAN . . . Philadelphia, 1840	300	500	500
Briscoe, Connie. SISTERS AND LOVERS. New York (1994)	—	—	75
Brissman, Barry. SWING LOW. New York (1972)	25	35	35
Bristow, Gwen. THE INVISIBLE HOST. New York, 1930. Written with Bruce Manning	50	75	75
Brite, Poppy Z. LOST SOULS. New York, 1992	—	—	50
Brittain, Vera M. VERSES OF A V. A. D. London, 1918	75	150	150
Brodeur, Paul (Adrian). THE SICK FOX. Boston (1963)	35	35	40
Brodkey, Harold. FIRST LOVE & OTHER SORROWS. New York (1957)	100	200	250
London, 1958	—	100	125
Bromell, Henry. THE SLIGHTEST DISTANCE. Boston, 1974	25	25	30
Bromfield, Louis. THE GREEN BAY TREE. New York, 1924	250	300	350
Bromige, David (Mansfield). THE GATHERING BUFFALO. (New York) 1965. Wraps. (350 copies)	50	75	75
Bronk, William. LIGHT AND DARK. (Ashland), 1956. Wraps	150	150	200
Bronowski, Jacob. THE POET'S DEFENCE. Cambridge, 1919. First issue: red cloth lettered in gilt	50	100	100
Brontë Ann, Charlotte, and Emily. *See* Acton, Currer, and Ellis Bell			
Brook, Gladys Palmer. RELATIONS & COMPLICATIONS . . . London (1929). Ghostwritten by Kay Boyle	—	350	450

	1986	1995	2000
Brooke, Jocelyn. SIX POEMS. Oxford, 1928. Wraps	300	300	350
DECEMBER SPRING. London, 1946	75	100	125
Brooke, Rupert. THE PYRAMIDS. Rugby, 1904. Wraps	6K	10K	15K
THE BASTILLE. A. J. Lawrence. Rugby, 1905. Wraps	4K	6K	8K
George E. Over. Rugby, 1905 (1920). Wraps	200	250	750
POEMS. London, 1911. (First commercial publication.) Issued without dustwrapper. (500 copies)	200	600	750
Brookner, Anita. J.A. DOMINIQUE INGRES 1780–1867. London, 1965. Large wraps	—	—	125
WATTEAU. London, 1968	—	150	125
THE DEBUT. New York, 1981. (New title)	25	75	35
A START IN LIFE. London (1981). (First novel) (Three translations 1960–63.)	—	150	150
Brooks, Cleanth. THE RELATIONS OF THE ALABAMA-GEORGIA DIALECT . . . Baton Rouge, 1935. Issued without dustwrapper	200	125	100
Brooks, Gwendolyn. SONG AFTER SUNSET. 1936. (one known copy)	3,000	5,000	5,000
A STREET IN BRONZEVILLE. New York, 1945	250	400	600

"THE BASTILLE."

A PRIZE POEM

RECITED IN RUGBY SCHOOL, JUNE 24, 1905.

RUGBY:
A. J. LAWRENCE, PRINTER TO THE SCHOOL.
1905.

	1986	1995	2000
Brooks, Jeremy. THE WATER CARNIVAL. London, 1957	50	50	50
Brooks, Richard. THE BRICK FOXHOLE. New York (1945)	50	75	100
Brooks, Terry. THE SWORD OF SHANNARA. New York (1977)	—	—	150
Brooks, Van Wyck. *See* VERSES BY TWO UNDERGRADUATES			
THE WINE OF PURITANS. Boston, 1908	75	100	100
Brophy, Brigid. THE CROWN PRINCESS. London, 1953	50	60	75
Brossard, Chandler. WHO WALK IN DARKNESS. (New York, 1952.) Cloth	75	125	125
Wraps	—	40	40
London (1952)	60	75	75
BROTHERS (THE): A TALE OF THE FRONDE. (Henry William Herbert.) New York, 1835. 2 volumes. First issue: brown cloth. In original cloth	150	450	450
Broughton, James (Richard). SONGS FOR CERTAIN CHILDREN. San Francisco, 1947	350	350	350
THE PLAYGROUND . . . (San Francisco), 1949.	60	60	50
Broumas, Olga. BEGINNING WITH O. New Haven, 1977	—	75	125
Broun, Heywood. WHEREIN THE CRITIC DEFENDS THE EDITOR . . . (New York, 1917.) Wraps. An offprint from *The New York Tribune*	—	—	250
A.E.F.: WITH GENERAL PERSHING . . . New York, 1918	—	150	150
Brown, Alice. *See* STRATFORD-BY-THE-SEA			
Brown, Cecil. THE LIFE & LOVES OF MR. JIVEASS NIGGER. New York, 1969	30	75	60
London (1970)	—	—	40
Brown, Charles Brockton. *See* ALCUIN . . . *Also see* WIELAND . . .			
Brown, Christy. MY LEFT FOOT. London, 1954	—	200	250
New York (1955)	—	—	100
Brown, Claude. MANCHILD IN THE PROMISED LAND. New York (1965)	30	100	150
London (1966)	5	60	100
Brown, Dee. BURY MY HEART AT WOUNDED KNEE. New York, 1970	—	—	200
Brown, Frank Landon. TRUMBULL PARK. Chicago (1959)	40	60	60

	1986	1995	2000
Brown, Fredric. THE FABULOUS CLIPJOINT. New York, 1947	200	500	750
Brown, George Douglas. *See* Kennedy King			
THE HOUSE WITH THE GREEN SHUTTERS. London, 1901	50	75	100
Brown, George MacKay. LET'S SEE THE ORKNEY ISLAND. Port William, no date [1948]. Wraps	—	125	150
Brown, H. Rap. DIE NIGGER DIE! New York, 1969	40	100	75
Brown, Harry. THE END OF A DECADE. Norfolk (1940). Boards in dustwrapper	35	35	35
Wraps	15	15	15
Brown, Larry. FACING THE MUSIC. Chapel Hill, 1988	—	100	200
Brown, Lloyd (Lewis). IRON CITY. New York, 1951. Cloth	75	75	75
Wraps	40	40	40
Brown, Norman O. HERMES THE THIEF. (Madison, Wisconsin) 1947	—	100	150
Brown, Oliver Madox. GABRIEL DENVER. London, 1873	—	1,200	1,500
Brown, Rita Mae. THE HAND THAT CRADLES THE ROCK. New York, 1971	40	100	100
Brown, Robert Carlton. (Bob.) THE REMARKABLE ADVENTURES OF CHRISTOPHER POE. Chicago, 1913	—	100	100
Brown, Rosellen. SOME DEATHS IN THE DELTA. University of Massachusetts Press (1970). Cloth	30	75	75
Wraps	15	25	35
Brown, Sterling A. SOUTHERN ROAD. New York (1932)	750	1,000	1,500
Brown, Wesley. TRAGIC MAGIC. New York (1978)	20	40	40
Brown, William Hill. *See* THE POWER OF SYMPATHY			
Brown, William W. THE NARRATIVE OF WILLIAM W. BROWN FUGITIVE SLAVE. Boston, 1847	—	1,250	1,500
Brown, Zenith Jones. *See* David Frome			
Browne, Howard. WARRIOR OF THE DAWN. Chicago (1943)	75	100	100
Browning, E(lizabeth) B(arrett). *See* E. B. Barrett			
Browning, Robert. *See* PAULINE: A FRAGMENT OF A CONFESSION			
PARACELSUS. London, 1835	1,000	1,000	1,000

	1986	1995	2000
Brownjohn, Alan (Charles). TRAVELERS ALONE. Liverpool, 1954. Wraps	75	75	75
Brownlow, William G(annaway). HELPS TO THE STUDY OF PRESBYTERIANISM . . . Knoxville, 1834	—	—	350
Brownmiller, Susan. SHIRLEY CHISHOLM. Garden City (1970)	—	50	35
Brownson, Orestes Augustes. AN ADDRESS, ON THE FIFTY-FIFTH . . . Ithaca, 1831. Wraps	300	300	350
Brownstein, Michael. BEHIND THE WHEEL. C Press (1967). (200 copies) Wraps. 6 signed and lettered copies	150	200	250
10 signed and numbered copies	125	150	175
184 unsigned copies	50	50	60
Bruce, Lenny. HOW TO TALK DIRTY . . . (Chicago, 1965)	—	100	75
Bruce, Leo. (Rupert Croft-Cooke). RELEASE THE LIONS. London, 1933. Author's first mystery	75	450	750
Bruchac, Joseph. INDIAN MOUNTAIN +. Ithaca (1971). Wraps	—	—	125
Brunner, John. *See* Gill Hunt			
Brunton, Mary. *See* SELF-CONTROL			
Bryan, C. D. P. S. WILKINSON. New York (1965)	—	40	25
Bryant, Arthur. RUPERT BUXTON. Cambridge, 1926	—	100	100
Bryant, Edward. AMONG THE DEAD. New York (1973)	15	75	75
Bryant, William Cullen. *See* EMBARGO			
THE EMBARGO . . . Boston, 1809. (Second edition.) First issue: wraps	750	1,000	1,500
Second issue: wraps stitched	500	750	750
POEMS. Cambridge, 1821. First collection of poetry.	—	—	1,500
Bryher. *See* Annie Winifred Ellerman			
Buber, Martin. I AND THOU. Edinburgh, 1937. Wraps	—	—	250
Buchan, John. ESSAYS AND APOTHEGMS OF FRANCIS BACON. London (1894). Edited by Buchan	175	400	350
SIR QUIXOTE OF THE MOORS. London, 1895. Assumed first issue: title running down spine	250	600	600
Variant spine reading "Sir/Quixote"	—	—	400
New York, 1895.	125	300	300
Buck, Howard. THE TEMPERING. New Hampshire, 1919. Wraps. (First title in Yale series of Younger Poets)	40	75	75

	1986	1995	2000
Buck, Pearl. EAST WIND, WEST WIND. New York (1930)	300	400	400
London, 1931	—	—	250
Buckler, Ernest. THE MOUNTAIN AND THE VALLEY. New York, 1952	75	200	300
Buckley, Christopher. 6 POEMS. (Fresno), 1975	—	60	75
Buckley, William F. GOD AND MAN AT YALE. Chicago, 1951	75	125	125
Budrys, Algis. FALSE NIGHT. New York (1954). Wraps	—	50	35
Buechner, (Carl) Frederick. THIS IS A CHAPTER FROM A LONG DAY'S DYING . . . New York (1949). Wraps	175	175	175
A LONG DAY'S DYING. New York, 1950	50	75	75
Bukowski, Charles. FLOWER, FIST AND BESTIAL WAIL. (Eureka, California, 1959.) Wraps	350	1,000	1,250
(Two previous broadsides in 1956 and 1950)			
Bulfinch, Thomas. *See* AUTHORSHIP			
Bullen, Frank T. THE CRUISE OF THE "CACHALOT." London, 1898	200	300	300
New York, 1899	75	150	150
Bullett, Gerald (William). DREAMS O' MINE. London, 1915	—	100	100
THE PROGRESS OF KAY. London, 1916	60	75	75
Bullins, Ed. HOW DO YOU DO . . . Mill Valley (1967). Wraps	30	60	60
Bull-us, Hector. (James K. Paulding.) THE DIVERTING HISTORY OF JOHN BULL . . . New York, 1812	600	600	600
Bulwer-Lytton, Edward George. ISMAEL: AN ORIENTAL TALE. London, 1820	350	450	450
FALKLAND. London, 1827. Author's first novel	—	850	850
New York, 1930	—	—	100
Bulwer-Lytton, Edward Robert. *See* CLYTEMNESTRA			
Bumpus, Jerry. ANACONDA. Western Springs (1967). Issued without dustwrapper	30	40	25
Bunin, Ivan. THE GENTLEMAN FROM SAN FRANCISCO. Boston, 1918. (Published with Andreyev's LAZARUS)	75	100	100
Richmond: Hogarth Press, 1922	175	175	175
Bunner, H(enry) C(uyler). A WOMAN OF HONOR. Boston, 1883	60	100	200

	1986	1995	2000
(Previous pamphlets and collaborations)			
Bunting, Basil. REDIMICULUM MATELLARUM. Milan, 1930	2,000	3,500	4,000
Burdette, Robert J(ones). THE RISE AND FALL OF THE MUS-TACHE +. Burlington, Iowa, 1877	50	75	75
Burford, William. MAN NOW. Dallas, 1954	75	75	60
Burgess, Anthony. (John Anthony Burgess Wilson). TIME FOR A TIGER. London, 1956	350	750	750
Burgess, (Frank) Gelett. THE PURPLE COW. (San Francisco, 1895.) First issue: printed on both sides of paper	200	400	500
Second issue: printed on one side only	75	125	125
Burke, James. FLEE SEVEN WAYS. London, 1963	30	40	75
Burke, James Lee. HALF OF PARADISE. Boston, 1965	—	1,250	2,250
Burke, Kenneth (Duva). THE WHITE OXEN +. New York, 1924	200	350	350
Burke, Leda. (David Garnett.) DOPE-DARLING. London, 1919. (Second book)	125	200	200
Burke, Thomas. VERSES. (Guilford, 1906.) Wraps. (25 copies)	1,000	1,000	1,000
NIGHTS IN TOWN. London, 1915	100	125	150
Burland, Brian. ST. NICHOLAS & THE TUB. New York (1964). Written with Joseph Low	—	75	75
Burley, W. J. A TASTE OF POWER. London, 1966	—	—	300
Burnett, Frances Hodgson. THAT LASS O' LOWRIE'S. New York, 1877. First issue: illustrator's name on title page	100	150	150
Second issue: illustrator's name not on title page	—	75	75
Burnett, Whit. THE MAKER OF SIGNS. New York, 1934	60	75	60
Burnett, W(illiam) R(iley). LITTLE CAESAR. New York, 1929	500	750	1,000
Burnham, David. THIS OUR EXILE. New York, 1931	40	50	60
Burns, John Horne. THE GALLERY. New York (1947).	75	100	175
Burns, Olive Ann. COLD SASSY TREE. New York (1984)	—	75	100
London (1988)	—	—	40
Burns, Rex. THE ALVAREZ JOURNAL. New York (1975)	—	75	40

	1986	1995	2000
Burns, Robert. POEMS, CHIEFLY IN THE SCOTTISH DIALECT. Kilmarnock Edition. 1786	6K	15K	25K
Edinburgh, 1787. First issue: "skinking" p. 263	500	1,250	2,000
Second issue: "stinking" p. 263	250	600	1,000
London, 1787	—	400	750
Philadelphia, 1788	—	750	1,250
Burns, Ron. ROMAN NIGHTS. New York (1991)	—	—	150
Burnshaw, Stanley. POEMS. Pittsburgh, 1927	200	200	200
Burroughs, Edgar Rice. TARZAN OF THE APES. McClurg. Chicago, 1914. First issue: printer's name on copyright page in Old English letters. (A copy in dustwrapper sold for $37,500 at auction in 1998.)	1,000	2,000	3,500
A. L. Burt. New York (1914)	—	150	200
London (1917). Ads dated Autumn	300	750	750
Burroughs, John. NOTES ON WALT WHITMAN AS POET AND PERSON . . . New York, 1867. First issue: leaves trimmed to 6⅞″ cloth and wraps	200	1,250	1,250
Second issue: leaves trimmed to 7¼″	75	750	750
WAKE-ROBIN. New York, 1871	—	300	350
Burroughs, William (Seward). *See* William Lee			
NAKED LUNCH. Paris, 1959. Wraps and dustwrapper. (Green border on title page. "Francs : 1500" on back cover of book)	250	1,000	2,000
New York (1962). (3,500 copies)	50	300	500
London (1964)	—	125	250
Burroughs, William, Jr. SPEED. New York, 1970. Cloth	—	75	100
Wraps	—	—	40
Burroway, Janet. DESCENT AGAIN. London, 1960	30	35	40
Burt, (Maxwell) Struthers. THE MAN FROM WHERE. Philadelphia, 1904. Pictorial wraps	—	150	200
IN THE HIGH HILLS. Boston, 1914	50	60	60
Burton, Miles. (Cecil John Charles Street). THE HARDWAY DIAMONDS MYSTERY. London, 1930	—	—	350
New York, 1930	—	—	75
Burton, Sir Richard F(rancis). GOA, AND THE BLUE MOUNTAINS . . . London, 1851. First issue: light-fawn cloth, 5″ x 8⅛″	750	3,500	3,500
Second issue: light-blue cloth, 4¾″ x 8″	400	2,000	2,000

	1986	1995	2000
Burton, Robert. THE ANATOMY OF MELANCHOLY. Oxford, 1621. With conclusion (omitted in later editions)	—	25K	35K
Oxford, 1624. Second edition, revised	—	—	3,000
Philadelphia, 1836. First American edition. 2 volumes	—	—	1,000
Busch, Frederick. I WANTED A YEAR WITHOUT FALL. London (1971)	60	100	100
Buss, Kate. JEVONS BLOCK. Boston, 1917	50	60	40
Butler, Ellis Parker. *See* PIGS IS PIGS			
PIGS IS PIGS. New York, 1906. (Second edition)	30	60	75
Butler, Frances Anne (Kemble). POEMS. Philadelphia, 1844	150	150	150
Butler, Gwendolyn. RECEIPT FOR MURDER. London, 1956	—	—	150
Butler, Jack. WEST OF HOLLYWOOD. Little Rock (1980). Cloth	—	175	175
Wraps	—	35	35
Butler, Octavia E. PATTERNMASTER. Garden City, 1976	—	150	300
Butler, Robert Olen. THE ALLEYS OF EDEN. New York (1981)	—	200	200
Butler, Samuel. A FIRST YEAR IN CANTERBURY SETTLEMENT. London, 1863. First issue: 32 pages of advertisements; light-brown endpapers	400	400	600
Butler, William. THE EXPERIMENT. London (1961)	75	75	75
Butor, Michael. A CHANGE OF HEART. New York (1958). First English translation	—	60	75
Butts, Mary (Francis). SPEED THE PLOW +. London (1923)	500	500	500
Byatt, A. S. SHADOW OF A SUN. London, 1964	60	200	350
New York (1964)	—	—	200
Byles, Mather. A POEM ON THE DEATH OF HIS LATE MAJESTY KING GEORGE. (Boston, 1727)	1,000	1,000	1,000
Bynner, Edwin Lasseter. *See* NIMPORT			
Bynner, (Harold) Witter. AN ODE TO HARVARD +. Boston, 1907. (Issued in three different bindings)	50	75	75
Byrd, Max. CALIFORNIA THRILLER. New York: Bantam (1981), Number 14508-8. Wraps	—	—	30
London (1984). First hardback	—	—	35
Byrd, Richard. SKYWARD. New York, 1928. 500 signed copies. Boxed	150	350	400
First trade edition	35	75	100

	1986	1995	2000
Byrne, (Brian Oswald) Donn. STORIES WITHOUT WOMEN. New York, 1915	75	125	100
Byron, George Gordon Lord. FUGITIVE PIECES. London, 1806. 3 known copies	—	75K	75K
London, 1886. (100 copies)	—	750	1,000
Byron, Robert. EUROPE IN THE LOOKING GLASS . . . London, 1926	300	650	750

C

	1986	1995	2000
Cabell, James Branch. THE EAGLE'S SHADOW. New York, 1904. First issue: dedication to "M.L.P.B."	100	150	150
Second issue: dedication to "Martha Louise Branch"	50	75	75
New York, 1923. Revised edition	30	75	75
Cable, George Washington. OLD CREOLE DAYS. New York, 1879. First issue: no advertisements in back	150	300	300
Second issue: advertisements in back	75	150	150
Cabral, Olga. CITIES AND DESERTS. New York (1959). Boards	—	—	100
Wraps	—	—	50
Cabrera Infante, Guillermo. THREE TRAPPED TIGERS. New York (1971)	—	150	125
Cadigan, Pat. MIND PLAYERS. London, 1988. First hardback	—	40	40
Cahan, Abraham. YEKL . . . New York, 1896	150	250	350
Cain, George. BLUESCHILD BABY. New York (1970)	50	50	30
Cain, James M(allahan). 79TH DIVISION HEADQUARTERS TROOP: A RECORD. Written with Gilbert Malcolm. No place or date [circa 1919]	—	750	750
OUR GOVERNMENT. New York, 1930	250	500	500
THE POSTMAN ALWAYS RINGS TWICE. New York, 1934	750	1,250	3,500
London, 1934	—	—	600
Cain, Paul (George Sims). FAST ONE. Garden City, 1933	400	750	4,500
CALAVAR . . . (Robert Montgomery Bird.) Philadelphia, 1834. 2 volumes	400	500	500
Calder, Alexander. ANIMAL SKETCHING. New York (1926)	350	450	350
Caldwell, Erskine. THE BASTARD. New York (1929). (1,100 copies in total edition) 200 signed copies (6 page prospectus preceded)	400	750	900
900 unsigned copies	175	250	200

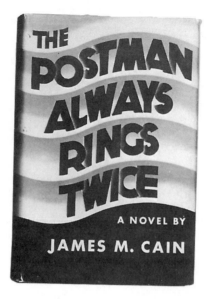

	1986	1995	2000
Caldwell, James. PRINGLE +. Denver (1948). Wraps. (400 copies)	40	75	75
Caldwell, Taylor. DYNASTY OF DEATH. New York, 1938	50	75	125
London, 1939	—	—	100
Calisher, Hortense. IN THE ABSENCE OF ANGELS. Boston, 1951	75	100	125
London, 1953	60	75	100
Calkins, Clinch. POEMS. New York, 1928	40	50	50
Callaghan, Morley (Edward). STRANGE FUGITIVE. New York, 1928	200	500	350
Calvert, George Henry. ILLUSTRATIONS OF PHRENOLOGY. Baltimore, 1832. (Edited by Calvert)	100	175	175
Calvin, Ross. SKY DETERMINES . . . New York, 1934	100	150	150
Calvino, Italo. THE PATH TO THE NEST OF SPIDERS. Boston (1957). First English translation	75	125	500
Camberg, Muriel (Muriel Spark). OUT OF A BOOK. Leith [1933?]	300	1,250	1,250
Cambor, Kathleen. THE BOOK OF MERCY. New York, 1966	—	—	35
Cameron, Norman. THE WINTER HOUSE +. London, 1935	60	75	75
Cameron, Peter. ONE WAY OR ANOTHER. New York (1986)	—	—	75
Middlesex, 1986	—	—	25

	1986	1995	2000
Campbell, Alice. JUGGERNAUT. London, no date [1928].	—	125	150
New York, 1929	—	—	100
Campbell, Bebe Moore. SUCCESSFUL WOMEN, ANGRY MEN. New York (1986)	—	75	125
Campbell, George. FIRST POEMS. Kingston, Jamaica, 1945. Green boards	—	—	500
Campbell, J. Ramsey. THE INHABITANT OF THE LAKE . . . Sauk City, 1964. (2,000 copies)	75	150	150
Campbell, John W., Jr. THE ATOMIC STORY. New York (1947)	75	150	75
THE MIGHTIEST MACHINE. Providence (1947)	75	200	200
Campbell, Joseph. A SKELETON KEY TO FINNEGANS WAKE. Written with Henry Morton Robinson. New York (1944)	—	—	150
London, 1947	—	—	60
Campbell, R. Wright. THE SPY WHO SAT AND WAITED. New York (1975)	—	—	60
Campbell, Roy. THE FLAMING TERRAPIN. London (1924)	150	200	150
New York, 1924	75	100	125
Campbell, Walter S. *See* Stanley Vestal			
Campbell, Will. BROTHER TO A DRAGONFLY. New York, 1977. Cloth	25	35	60
Wraps	—	—	20
Camus, Albert. THE OUTSIDER. London (1946). (Cyril Connolly introduction)	125	350	450
THE STRANGER. (New title.) New York, 1946. (Does not include Connolly introduction)	75	250	350
Cane, Melville. JANUARY GARDEN. New York (1926)	35	35	25
Canetti, Elias. THE TOWER OF BABEL. New York, 1946	—	125	75
Canin, Ethan. EMPEROR OF THE AIR. Boston, 1988	—	75	75
Cannell, Dorothy. THE THIN WOMAN . . . New York, 1984	—	—	300
Canning, Victor. MR. FINCHLEY DISCOVERS HIS ENGLAND. London, 1934	—	60	75
THE CHASM. London, 1947. (First mystery)	35	75	100
Cantor, Jay. THE SPACE BETWEEN. Baltimore (1981)	—	75	75

	1986	1995	2000
Cantwell, Robert. LAUGH AND LIE DOWN. New York, 1931. First issue: in pictorial dustwrapper	—	500	600
Second issue: in printed dustwrapper with reviews	75	250	300
Canty, Kevin. A STRANGER IN THIS WORLD. Garden City, 1994	—	—	40
Capa, Robert. DEATH IN THE MAKING. New York (1938)	150	350	500
Cape, Judith. (P. K. Page.) THE SUN AND THE MOON. New York, 1944	—	—	350
Capek, Karl. THE MAKROPOULOS SECRET. London, 1922. (First English translation)	200	300	350
Boston, 1925	125	200	150
Capote, Truman. OTHER VOICES, OTHER ROOMS. New York (1948)	150	300	500
London, 1948	100	200	200
Caputo, Philip. A RUMOR OF WAR. New York (1977)	—	100	100
Card, Orson Scott. HOT SLEEP. New York (1979). Wraps	—	—	100
SONGMASTER. New York (1980). Third book, first hardback	—	—	100
Carey, Peter. THE FAT MAN IN HISTORY. St. Lucia, 1974	—	200	250
New York (1980)	—	50	125
London, 1980	—	—	100
Carleton, William M. FAX: A CAMPAIGN POEM. Chicago, 1868. Wraps	750	750	750
Carlile, Clancy. AS I WAS YOUNG AND EASY. New York, 1958	25	30	40
Carlson, Ron. BETRAYED BY F. SCOTT FITZGERALD. New York (1977)	—	—	50
Carlyle, Thomas. *See* THE LIFE OF FRIEDRICH SCHILLER			
Carmen, Bliss (Bliss Carman). LOW TIDE ON GRAND PRE. Toronto (1889/1890?). 13 pages. (Name misspelled.) Wraps	2,500	4,500	4,500
New York, 1893. Cloth	400	500	500
London, 1893	200	250	500
Carmer, Carl. FRENCH TOWN. New Orleans (1928). (500 copies) Stiff wraps. (Previous textbook collaboration and edited books)	100	150	150
Carnevali, Emanuel. A HURRIED MAN. (Paris, 1925.) Wraps. (300 copies)	150	300	300
Carpenter, Don. HARD RAIN FALLING. New York (1966)	35	50	75
London (1966)	30	35	35

	1986	1995	2000
Carpenter, Edward. NARCISSUS +. London, 1873	200	250	400
Carpentier, Alejo. THE LOST STEPS. London, 1956. First book in English	—	125	135
New York, 1956	—	100	75
Carr, Caleb. CASING THE PROMISED LAND. New York, 1980	—	—	175
Carr, Christopher. (A. C. Benson.) MEMOIRS OF ARTHUR HAMILTON. London, 1886	100	200	200
Carr, John Dickson. IT WALKS BY NIGHT. New York, 1930	750	1,750	3,500
Carrefour Press. *See* ANONYMOUS			
Carrier, Constance. THE MIDDLE VOICE. Denver (1955)	40	75	40
Carroll, James. MADONNA RED. Boston (1976). Author's first novel	20	40	50
Carroll, Jim. ORGANIC TRAINS. No place [New York], no date [1968]. Mimeographed sheets in stapled wraps	125	175	450
Carroll, Jonathan. THE LAND OF LAUGHS. New York (1980)	—	175	200
Carroll, Lewis. (Charles Lutwidge Dodgson.) RULES FOR COURT CIRCULAR. No place (January, 1860). 4-page leaflet. 3 items listed under Dodgson in 1860, but this would seem to precede them	—	—	1,000
Carroll, Paul. THE POEM IN ITS SKIN. Chicago (1968)	30	50	50
(Carroll edited the *Dahlberg Reader* in 1966.)			
Carruth, (Fred) Hayden. THE ADVENTURES OF JONES. New York, 1894. Pictorial tan cloth	—	—	175
Carruth, Hayden. THE CROW AND THE HEART. New York, 1959. Wraps	40	75	75
Carryl, Charles E. THE RIVER SYNDICATE. New York, 1899	40	75	100
Carryl, Guy Wetmore. FABLES FOR THE FRIVOLOUS. New York, 1898	50	75	100
(Previous pamphlets.)			
Carson, Claran. THE INSULAR CATS. (Belfast, 1973.) Wraps	—	—	150
Carson, Rachel. UNDER THE SEA WIND. New York, 1941	150	350	450
Carter, Angela. UNICORN. Leeds, 1966	150	400	450
SHADOW DANCE. London, 1966	60	250	350

	1986	1995	2000
HONEYBUZZARD. New York (1966). (New title)	40	75	100
Carter (Asa Forrest). *See* GEORGE AND LURLEEN WALLACE			
Carter, Forrest. THE REBEL OUTLAW: JOSEY WALES. (Gannt, Alabama, 1973)	—	450	1,000
GONE TO TEXAS. (New York, 1975.) (New title)	—	150	300
Carter, Hodding. CIVILIAN DEFENSE . . . New York (1942). (Written with Col Dupuy)	50	100	100
LOWER MISSISSIPPI. New York (1942)	50	75	75
Carter, Lin. SANDALWOOD AND JADE. St. Petersburg, 1951. Wraps	—	35	35
Carter, Ross S. THOSE DEVILS IN BAGGY PANTS. New York (1951)	40	60	100
Cartier-Bresson, Henri. PHOTOGRAPHS OF HENRI CARTIER-BRESSON. MoMA, New York, 1947.			
Cloth in dustwrapper	—	—	250
Wraps	—	—	125
BEAUTIFUL JAIPUR. Jaipur (1948)	—	—	750
Cartland, Barbara. JIG-SAW. London (1925)	300	400	400
Caruso, Enrico. CARICATURES. New York, 1908. Folio	—	250	1,500
Caruthers, William Alexander. *See* A Virginian			
THE KENTUCKIAN IN NEW YORK. New York, 1834. 2 volumes	300	450	450
Carver, Raymond. NEAR KLAMATH. Sacramento, 1968. Wraps (3 offprints precede.)	500	2,000	2,500
WINTER INSOMNIA. (Santa Cruz, 1970) (1,000 copies) Wraps. Noted in green and yellow and also green and white (but less often)	125	175	250
Cary, Arthur (Joyce). VERSE. Edinburgh, 1908. (Joyce Cary's first book.) *Also see next entry*	2,500	3,500	3,500
Cary, (Arthur) Joyce. AISSA SAVED. London, 1932	400	600	750
Case, David. THE CELL . . . New York (1969)	—	75	150
Casey, Frank. TALES OF A WAYWARD INN. New York, 1938	—	—	150
Casey, John. AN AMERICAN ROMANCE. New York, 1977	20	100	125

	1986	1995	2000
Casey, Michael. OBSCENITIES. New Haven, 1972. Cloth in dustwrapper	75	100	100
Wraps	—	35	25
Caskoden, Edwin. (Charles Major.) WHEN KNIGHTHOOD WAS IN FLOWER . . . Indianapolis, 1898	—	100	75
Cassady, Neal. THE FIRST THIRD. San Francisco, 1971. Wraps	—	50	75
Cassidy, Carolyn. HEART BEAT. Berkeley, 1976. 150 signed and numbered copies	75	200	150
Cassidy, John. A STATION IN THE DELTA. New York (1979)	25	40	40
Cassill, R(onald) V(erlin). THE EAGLE ON THE COIN. New York (1950)	30	60	40
Casson, Stanley. MURDER BY BURIAL. New York, 1938	—	—	150
Castaneda, Carlos. THE TEACHINGS OF DON JUAN. Berkeley, 1968	90	250	450
London, 1971	—	—	100
Castle, John. (Arthur Hailey and John Castle.) FLIGHT INTO DANGER. London, 1958	100	150	200
Castlemon, H(arry) C. (Charles Austin Fosdick.) FRANK, THE YOUNG NATURALIST. Cincinnati, 1865	150	350	350
Castro, Fidel. HISTORY WILL ABSOLVE ME. (New York, 1961.) Cloth. (First English translation)	—	—	100
Wraps	—	—	50
Cather, Willa Silbert. APRIL TWILIGHTS. Boston, 1903. Issued without dustwrapper	850	2,000	2,500
New York, 1923. Revised edition. 450 signed numbered copies in slipcase	—	—	750
Trade edition	—	—	250
London, 1924	—	—	400
Cato, Nancy. THE DARKENED WINDOW. Sydney, 1950	—	75	125
Caudwell, Sarah. THUS WAS ADONIS MURDERED. London, (1981)	—	250	250
New York, 1981	—	50	75
Caunitz, William J. ONE POLICE PLAZA. New York, 1984	30	40	40
London, 1984	—	—	20
Causley, Charles. FAREWELL AGGIE WESTON. Aldington, 1951. Wraps	—	75	75
Caute, David. AT FEVER PITCH. London, 1959	40	60	60
New York, 1961	—	—	30

APRIL TWILIGHTS

POEMS BY

Willa Sibert Cather

ART I ET V ERI- TATI

Boston: Richard G. Badger

The Gorham Press: 1903

	1986	1995	2000
Cawein, Madison Julius. BLOOMS OF THE BERRY. Louisville, 1887. (500 copies)	75	125	125
Cecil, Henry. FULL CIRCLE. London, 1948	—	125	150
CELEBRATED TRIALS AND REMARKABLE CASES. (Written by Geo. Barrow.) London, 1825. 6 volumes	500	500	500
Céline, Louis Ferdinand. JOURNEY TO THE END OF THE NIGHT. London, 1934	—	300	350
Boston, 1934	50	100	200
Centaur Press. SONG OF THE BROAD AX. By Walt Whitman. Philadelphia, 1924	100	200	200
Cervantes, Lorna Dee. EMPLUMADA. Pittsburgh (1981). Cloth	—	—	125
Wraps	—	—	20
Chabon, Michael. THE MYSTERIES OF PITTSBURGH. New York (1988)	—	40	50
London (1988)	—	—	35
Chaez, Denise. THE LAST OF THE MENU GIRLS. New York (1986). Wraps	—	—	100
Chambers, Robert W(illiam). IN THE QUARTER. Chicago, 1893	150	600	750
Chandler, Raymond. THE BIG SLEEP. New York, 1939	1,750	9.5K	12.5K
London, 1939	—	2,500	2,500
San Francisco, 1986. (425 copies.) Issued without dust-wrapper	—	450	500
Channing, William Ellery. (1780–1841.) THE DUTIES OF CHIL-DREN. Boston, 1807. Wraps	250	500	500
Channing, William Ellery. (1818–1901.) POEMS. Boston, 1843	75	125	125
Chant, Joy. RED MOON AND BLACK MOUNTAIN. London, 1970	—	150	125
New York, 1976	—	—	25
Chaplin, Sid. THE LEAPING LAD +. London, 1946	60	60	75
Chapman, Arthur. OUT WHERE THE WEST BEGINS. Boston, 1917	25	75	35
Chapman, John Jay. *See* THE TWO PHILOSOPHERS			
EMERSON AND OTHER ESSAYS. New York, 1898	50	75	50
Chappell, Fred. RENAISSANCE PAPERS 1962: SHAKESPEARE'S CORIOLANUS . . . No place, no date [1962]. Wraps	—	100	125

	1986	1995	2000
IT IS TIME, LORD. New York, 1963	100	175	200
London, 1965	—	125	125
Chappell, George S. COLONIAL ARCHITECTURE IN VERMONT. New York, 1918. Wraps	50	175	250
Char, Rene. HYPNOS WALKING. New York (1956). First English translation	—	75	75
CHARLES AUCHESTER. (Elizabeth Sara Sheppard.) London, 1853. 3 volumes	300	500	500
Charles, Kate. A DRINK OF DEADLY WINE. London (1991)	—	75	75
Charteris, Hugo. A SHARE OF THE WORLD. London, 1953	50	60	60
Charteris, Leslie. (Charles Bowyer Lin). X ESQUIRE. London, 1927	300	1,250	3,500
Charyn, Jerome. ONCE UPON A DROSHKY. New York (1964)	40	40	75
Chase, James Hadley. NO ORCHIDS FOR MISS BLANDISH. London, 1939	—	—	1,500
(New York, 1942)	—	—	1,000
Chase, Joan. DURING THE REIGN OF THE QUEEN OF PERSIA. New York (1983)	—	35	40
Chatwin, Bruce. IN PATAGONIA. London, 1977. Map endpapers	125	600	1,000
Plain white endpapers	—	—	750
New York (1978)	—	—	200
Chavez, Fray Angelico. CLOTHED WITH THE SUN. Santa Fe, 1939	—	75	100
Chayefsky, Paddy. TELEVISION PLAYS. New York, 1955	35	60	60
Cheever, John. THE WAY SOME PEOPLE LIVE. New York (1943)	75	500	1,250
Cheever, Susan. LOOKING FOR WORK. New York (1979)	15	30	30
London, 1979	15	20	20
Chehak, Susan Taylor. THE STORY OF ANNIE D. Boston, 1989	—	—	40
Cheney, Brainard. LIGHTWOOD. Boston, 1939	—	60	75
Chesbro, George. SHADOW OF A BROKEN MAN. New York, 1977	—	75	75
London, 1981	—	—	40

	1986	1995	2000
Chesnutt, Charles W(addell). THE CONJURE WOMAN. Boston, 1899. 150 large-paper copies	1,000	1,250	1,500
Trade edition	250	500	600
Chester, Alfred. HERE BE DRAGONS. Paris, 1955. Wraps. 125 deluxe copies (25 for presentation)	125	300	450
1,000 regular copies. Card covers. In dustwrapper and glassine	75	150	150
Chester, George Randolph. GET-RICH-QUICK WALLINGFORD. New York, 1908	75	100	100
Chesterton, Cecil. GLADSTONIAN GHOSTS. London (1905)	60	100	100
Chesterton, G(ilbert) K(eith). GREYBEARDS AT PLAY. London, 1900	250	500	750
Chestnut, Robert (Clarence L. Cooper, Jr.). THE SYNDICATE. Chicago (1960). Wraps	75	125	100
Child, Lee. KILLING FLOOR. New York (1997)	—	—	75
London (1997)	—	—	50
Child, Lydia Marie. *See* HOBOMOK			
Childers, Erskin. THE RIDDLE OF THE SANDS. London, 1903	—	—	4,000
Childress, Alice. LIKE ONE OF THE FAMILY. Brooklyn (1956). 100 numbered copies. Issued without dustwrapper in slipcase	—	200	200
Trade	100	125	125
Childress, Mark. A WORLD MADE OF FIRE. New York, 1984	—	60	100
London, 1985	—	—	35
Chin, Frank. THE CHICKENCOOP CHINAMAN | THE YEAR OF THE DRAGON. Seattle (1981).	—	—	75
CHINESE POEMS. (Arthur Waley.) London, 1916. Wraps. (About 50 copies)	1,500	4,500	4,500
Chivers, Thomas Holley. THE PATH OF SORROW. Franklin (Tennessee), 1832	850	1,000	1,000
Chomsky, Noam. SYNTACTIC STRUCTURES. (The Hague) 1957. Wraps	—	300	500
Chopin, Kate. AT FAULT. St. Louis, 1890. Wraps	—	3,000	3,000
Chopping, Richard. THE FLY. London (1965)	—	—	100
New York, 1965	—	75	50

	1986	1995	2000
Christie, Agatha (Mary Clarissa). MYSTERIOUS AFFAIR AT STYLES. New York, 1920. (Priced with dustwrapper)	—	15K	15K
Without dustwrapper	—	—	3,500
Toronto, 1920. Printed in U.S. with an integral title page, so we assume it preceded the British edition	—	—	7,500
Without dustwrapper	—	—	1,500
London, 1921. With dustwrapper	—	—	12,500
Without dustwrapper	—	—	2,500
Chubb, Ralph. MANHOOD. Curridge, 1924. (200 copies) 45 copies on handmade paper	—	500	500
Regular edition. (200 copies?) Wraps	125	250	250
Chubb, Thomas Caldecott. THE WHITE GOD +. New Haven, 1920. Stiff wraps	35	60	60
Church, Peggy Pond. FAMILIAR JOURNEY. Sante Fe, 1936	—	—	90
Churchill, Caryl. OWNERS. London, 1973. Cloth	—	75	100
Wraps	—	15	35
Churchill, Winston. (American author.) THE CELEBRITY. New York, 1898	35	75	100
Churchill, Sir Winston S. THE STORY OF MALAKAND FIELD FORCE. London, 1898. No errata slip	1,000	4,000	6,000
Errata slip tipped in immediately preceding first folding map	—	—	5,000
Colonial Library (for distribution in India and the British Colonies). The front cover and spine have "1897" but actually distributed after the London edition	—	—	2,500
Churton, Henry (Albion W. Tourgee). TOINETTE. New York, 1874. (First novel)	100	200	200
Chute, Carolyn. THE BEANS OF EGYPT, MAINE. New York, 1985	60	300	400
THE BEANS. London, 1985. Dustwrapper back panel blank	—	100	100
With blurbs on back panel	—	—	60
Ciardi, John (Anthony). HOMEWARD TO AMERICA. New York, 1940	75	125	150
Cicellis, Kay. THE EASY WAY. London, 1950. (Sackville-West introduction)	35	60	60
New York (1950)	35	40	45
Cioran, E. M. THE TEMPTATION TO EXIST. Chicago, 1968	—	150	75
CITY LIGHTS. *See* L. Ferlinghetti			
Clair, Maxine. COPING WITH GRAVITY POEMS. (Washington, D.C., 1988.) Wraps	—	—	60

	1986	1995	2000
Clampitt, Amy. MULTITUDES, MULTITUDES. New York (1973). Wraps	90	250	350
Clancy, Tom. THE HUNT FOR RED OCTOBER. Annapolis (1984)	150	650	650
Clare, John. POEMS DESCRIPTIVE OF RURAL LIFE . . . London, 1820	—	—	1,750
Clark, Charles E. PRINCE AND BOATSWAIN. Greenfield, Massachusetts (1915). (Edited and three chapters by Marquand and J. M. Morgan.) Issued without dustwrapper	175	200	200
Clark, Dick. YOUR HAPPIEST YEARS. (New York, 1959)	—	30	30
Clark, Eleanor. THE BITTER BOX. Garden City, 1946	75	100	100
London, 1947	—	—	50
Clark, Emily. INNOCENCE ABROAD. New York, 1931	—	60	60
Clark, John(son). PEPPER SONG OF A GOAT. Ibadan (1961)	—	50	50
Clark, L(ewis) Garlord. KNICK-KNACKS FROM AN EDITOR'S TABLE. New York, 1852	—	—	175
Clark, Larry. TULSA (PHOTOGRAPHS). (New York, 1971.) Stiff wraps	—	—	600
Cloth. (1,000 copies)	—	—	800
Clark, Mary Higgins. ASPIRE TO HEAVEN . . . New York, 1969	—	125	400
WHERE ARE THE CHILDREN? New York, 1975. (First mystery)	—	100	250
Clark, Tom. TO GIVE A PAINLESS LIGHT. 1963. Typescript carbon (3 copies)	500	1,000	1,000
THE SAND BURG. London (1966). Wraps. 60 signed and numbered copies	75	250	300
Trade. (440 copies)	35	100	75
AIRPLANES. (Essex, England) 1966. Wraps. 4 signed and numbered copies	150	500	500
Trade	40	100	75
(Priority in 1966 uncertain.)			
Clark, Walter Van Tilburg. CHRISTMAS COMES TO HJALSEN. (Reno, 1930.) Wraps	350	750	750
TEN WOMEN IN GALE'S HOUSE. Boston (1932)	—	600	650
Clarke, Arthur C(harles). INTERPLANETARY FLIGHT. London, 1950	30	450	750
New York (1951)	—	60	500

	1986	1995	2000
Clarke, Austin. THE VENGEANCE OF FIONN. Dublin, 1917	100	150	350
Clarke, Austin C. THE SURVIVORS OF THE CROSSING. Toronto, 1964	60	125	125
Clarke, Richard. FEVER AND THE COLD EYE. Toronto (1966). Cloth. (50 copies)	—	—	100
Wraps. (200 copies)	—	—	50
CLASS POEM. (James Russell Lowell.) (Cambridge) 1838. In original wraps	600	1,500	1,500
Claude. (Claude Durrell.) MRS. O'. London (1957). (Lawrence Durrell's third wife)	40	75	60
Clavell, James. KING RAT. Boston (1962)	150	450	600
London (1963)	100	125	200
Cleaver, Eldridge. SOUL ON ICE. New York (1968). (2,500 copies)	25	75	200
London, 1969	25	50	75
Cleeves, Ann. A BIRD IN THE HAND. London, 1986	—	60	50
Clemens, Samuel Langhorne. *See* Mark Twain			
Clement, Hal (Harry C. Stubbs). NEEDLE. Garden City, 1950	75	250	200
London, 1961	—	—	75
Clemons, Walter. THE POISON TREE +. Boston, 1959	60	60	60
London, 1959	—	50	50
Clerihew, E. (E. C. Bentley.) BIOGRAPHY FOR BEGINNERS. London (1905). Illustrated by G. K. Chesterton. Wraps	250	500	350
Boards with cloth spine	—	—	400
Clifford, Francis. HONOUR THE SHRINE. London, 1953	—	—	125
Clifton, Lucille. GOOD TIMES. New York (1969)	—	100	125
Clifton, Mark. THEY'D RATHER BE RIGHT. New York (1957) (Written with Frank Riley)	60	60	60
CLOCKMAKER (THE). (Thomas Chandler Haliburton.) Halifax, 1836	750	750	750
Philadelphia, 1839–40. 3 volumes	—	—	275
Clough, A(rthur) H(ugh). A CONSIDERATION OF OBJECTS. Oxford, 1847	500	500	500
(2 previous pamphlets at Rugby.)			
Clouston, J(oseph) Storer. THE LUNATIC AT LARGE. London, 1899	50	75	75

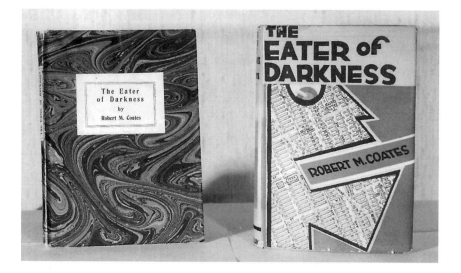

	1986	1995	2000
CLYTEMNESTRA . . . (Edward Robert Bulwer Lytton.) London, 1855	350	500	500
Coates, Robert M(yron). THE EATER OF DARKNESS. (Paris, 1926.) Wraps	450	500	500
New York, 1929	350	350	750
Cobb, Humphrey. PATHS OF GLORY. New York, 1935. (Only book)	50	125	150
London (1935)	50	75	75
Cobb, Irvin Shrewsbury. BACK HOME. New York (1912). First issue: "Plimpton Press" on copyright page and publisher's name in 3 lines on spine	60	75	75
Coblentz, Stanton A(rthur). THE THINKER +. New York, 1923	—	125	125
THE WONDER STICK. New York, 1929	75	75	75
Cockburn, Catherine Trotter. *See* AGNES DE CASTRO			
Cockton, Henry. THE LIFE AND ADVENTURES OF VALENTINE VOX . . . London (1840)	—	300	300
Codrescu, Andrei. LICENSE TO CARRY A GUN. Chicago (1970)	25	50	100
Cody, Liza. DUPE. London (1980)	—	—	500
Coestler, A. (Arthur Koestler.) *See* Dr. A. Costler			
Coetzee, J(ohn) M(ichael). DUSKLANDS. Johannesburg, 1974	125	500	350
New York (1985). Wraps	—	75	75

	1986	1995	2000
Coffey, Brian. POEMS. Dublin, 1930. (Written with Denis Devlin.) Wraps	200	200	200
THREE POEMS. Paris, 1933. (250 copies) Wraps	175	175	275
Coffin, Robert Peter Tristram. CHRISTCHURCH. New York, 1924	75	125	125
Cohen, Arthur A. MARTIN BUBER. London (1957)	—	125	125
THE CARPENTER YEARS. (New York, 1967)	35	60	75
Cohen, Leonard (Norman). LET US COMPARE MYTHOLOGIES. Montreal (1956)	450	2,000	1,500
Cohen, Lester. SWEEPINGS. New York, 1926	—	75	75
Cohen, Marvin. THE SELF-DEVOTED FRIEND. New York, 1967	25	40	30
Cohen, Octavus Roy. THE OTHER WOMAN. New York, 1917. (Written with J. U. Giesy)	60	100	100
THE CRIMSON ALIBI. New York, 1919	60	100	100
Coker, Elizabeth Boatwright. DAUGHTER OF STRANGERS. New York, 1950	—	75	75
Cole, G(eorge) D(ouglas) H(oward). THE BROOKLYN MURDERS. London, 1923	350	350	1,000
Cole, Henri. THE MARBLE QUEEN. New York, 1986	—	—	50
Cole, Peter. RIFT. New York, 1986. 135 signed and numbered copies	—	—	150
Cole, Tom. AN END TO CHIVALRY. Boston (1965)	25	35	40
Coleman, Elliott. THE POEMS OF ... New York (1936)	—	—	35
Coleman, Wanda. ART IN THE COURT OF THE BLUE FAG. Santa Barbara, 1977. Wraps	15	25	25
MAD DOG BLACK LADY. Santa Barbara, 1979. 26 signed and lettered copies	60	125	175
200 signed and numbered copies	25	60	75
Coleridge, Hartley. POEMS. Volume 1 [all published]. Leeds, 1833. Errata slip at end	250	350	450
POEMS, SONGS AND SONNETS. Leeds (1833). (New title). Second issue. Cancel title page	—	—	350
Coleridge, Samuel Taylor. THE FALL OF ROBESPIERRE. London, 1794	500	1,750	10K

	1986	1995	2000
Coles, Manning. (Cyril Henry Coles and Adelaide Manning.) DRINK TO YESTERDAY. London (1940)	600	750	750
New York, 1941	—	200	150
Colette. (Sidonie Gabrielle.) THE VAGRANT. London, 1912	60	350	450
COLLECTION OF FAMILIAR QUOTATIONS (A) (John Bartlett.) Cambridge, 1855. First issue: brown cloth	250	650	750
Collier, John. HIS MONKEY WIFE. London, 1930	350	450	600
New York, 1931	200	300	300
Collins, Jackie. THE WORLD IS FULL OF MARRIED MEN. Cleveland, 1968	—	—	35
Collins, Michael. (Dennis Lynds.) ACT OF FEAR. New York (1967)	30	75	75
Collins, Wilkie. MEMOIRS OF THE LIFE OF WILLIAM COLLINS. London, 1848. 2 volumes	450	1,250	1,500
Colony, Horatio. A BROOK OF LEAVES. Boston, 1955	35	40	40
Colter, Cyrus. THE BEACH UMBRELLA. Iowa City (1970)	25	75	150
Chicago (1970)	—	—	30
Colton, James. (Joseph Hansen.) LOST ON TWILIGHT ROAD. Fresno (1964). Wraps	50	200	200
Colum, Mary. FROM THESE ROOTS. London, 1935	50	75	75
New York, 1937	—	—	30
Colum, Padraic. THE LAND. Dublin, 1905	75	100	150
Colwin, Laurie. PASSION AND AFFECT. New York, 1974. (14 stories)	40	75	100
DANGEROUS FRENCH MISTRESS. London (1975). New title. (10 stories)	30	50	50
Combs, Tram. PILGRIM TERRACE . . . San German, Puerto Rico, 1957. Wraps and dustwrapper	40	50	75
Comfort, Alex(ander). THE SILVER RIVER. London, 1937	75	100	100
Comfort, Will Levington. TROOPER TALES. New York (1899)	—	75	50
COMPLEAT ANGLER . . . , THE. (Izaak Walton.) London, 1653	7.5K	30K	50K
London/Edinburgh/Philadelphia, 1837. 2 volumes	—	1,000	1,250
New York, 1847. States "First American Edition"	—	600	750
Compton, D(avid) G(uy). THE QUALITY OF MERCY (London, 1965.) His first science-fiction title	—	—	150

	1986	1995	2000
Compton-Burnett, Ivy. DOLORES. London, 1911. (Written with her brother.) (1,055 copies)	400	750	1,000
PASTORS AND MASTERS. London, 1925	250	350	300
Conaway, James. THE BIG EASY. Boston, 1970	—	50	100
London, 1971	—	—	100
Condon, Richard (Thomas). THE OLDEST CONFESSION. New York (1958)	30	60	60
London, 1959	—	—	30
CONFESSIONS OF AN ENGLISH OPIUM-EATER. (Thomas De Quincey.) London, 1822			
(Advertisement leaf at end)	750	1,250	2,000
(Without advertisement leaf)	500	1,000	1,500
CONFESSIONS OF HARRY LORREQUER (THE). (Charles Lever.) Dublin (1839)	250	400	250
Congdon, A. Kirby. IRON ARK. (New York, 1962.) Wraps. (500 copies)	30	50	50
Conley, Robert J. BACK TO MALACHI. Garden City, 1986	—	60	75
Connell, Evan S(helby). THE ANATOMY LESSON +. New York, 1957	60	125	200
London (1958)	40	75	100
Connelly, Marc(us). DULCY. New York, 1921. (Written with George S. Kaufman)	125	500	600
Connett, Eugene V. *See* DERRYDALE PRESS			
Connington, J. J. (Alfred Walter Stewart.) NORDENHOLT'S MILLION. London, 1923	—	—	750
DEATH AT SWAYTHLING COURT. London, 1926. First mystery Wrote a number of books on chemistry under his own name from 1907 to 1922.	—	—	750
Connolly, Cyril. THE ROCK POOL. Paris, 1936.			
Wraps	350	500	600
New York, 1936	150	250	350
London, 1947. (New postscript)	50	75	100
Connolly, James B(rendan). JEB HUTTON. New York, 1902	100	150	150
Connolly, Michael. THE BLACK ECHO. Boston, 1992	—	40	75
Connor, Tony. WITH LOVE SOMEHOW. London, 1962	—	—	45
Conquest, (George) Robert (Acworth). POEMS. London, 1955	50	75	75

	1986	1995	2000
CONQUEST (THE) . . . By A Negro Pioneer. (Oscar Micheaux.) Lincoln, Nebraska, 1913	125	750	2,000
Conrad, Barnaby. THE INNOCENT VILLA. New York (1948)	40	50	50
Conrad, Joseph. (Theodor Jósef Konrad Korzeniowski.) ALMAYER'S FOLLY. London, 1895. First issue: "e" missing in "generosity"; "of" omitted in penultimate line p. 110	1,000	2,000	2,000
New York, 1895. (650 copies)	600	750	1,500
Conroy, Albert. (Marvin Albert.) THE ROAD'S END. New York, 1952. Wraps	—	100	100
Conroy, Frank. STOP-TIME. New York (1967)	40	75	100
London (1968)	30	40	50
Conroy, Jack (John Weley). THE DISINHERITED. (New York, 1933.) First issue: pictorial dustwrapper	150	250	250
Second issue: printed dustwrapper	—	125	150
London (1934)	—	—	200
(Previously coedited three books.)			
Conroy, Pat. THE BOO. Verona (1970). (2,000 copies)	150	2,500	3,500
Atlanta, 1988. 20 signed and lettered copies	—	600	1,000
250 signed and numbered copies	—	300	300
THE WATER IS WIDE. Boston, 1972	75	500	800
CONSIDERATIONS ON SOME RECENT SOCIAL THEORIES. (Charles Eliot Norton.) Boston, 1853	125	175	175
Constantine, K. C. (pseudonym of Carl Kosak.) THE ROCKS-BURG RAILROAD MURDERS. New York, 1972. First issue: no reviews on back of dustwrapper	150	300	300
Second issue: reviews on back of dustwrapper	100	200	200
Constantine, Storm. THE ENCHANTMENTS OF FLESH AND SPIRIT . . . (London, 1987)	—	—	50
Cook, Kenneth. WAKE IN FRIGHT. London, 1961	—	50	75
New York, 1962	—	—	35
Cook, Robin. THE CRUST AND ITS UPPERS. London, 1962	—	50	250
Cook, Thomas H. BLOOD INNOCENTS. New York, 1980. Wraps	—	60	60
Cooke, John Esten. *See* LEATHER STOCKING AND SILK			
Cooke, Rose. *See* Rose Terry			
Coolbrith, Ina Donna. A PERFECT DAY +. San Francisco, 1881. Folio issue	150	250	250
Regular issue	60	100	100

	1986	1995	2000
Coolidge, Calvin. ADDRESS DELIVERED BY . . . July 4, 1916. Boston, 1916. Wraps	—	350	450
Coolidge, Dane. HIDDEN WATER . . . Chicago, 1910	75	75	75
Coonts, Stephen. FLIGHT OF THE INTRUDER. Annapolis, 1986	—	60	60
Cooper, Alvin Carlos. STROKE OF MIDNIGHT. Nashville, 1949. Wraps	—	—	100
Cooper, Clarence. *See* Robert Chestnut			
THE SCENE. New York (1960)	25	50	125
London (1960)	—	—	50
Cooper, J(oan) California. A PIECE OF MINE. Navarro (1984). Wraps	—	75	75
Cooper, James Fenimore. *See* PRECAUTION			
Cooper, Madison. SIRONIA, TEXAS. Boston, 1952. 2 volumes. (350 copies with signed page—only seen with second printing of first volume)	200	200	200
Regular edition	60	75	75
Cooper, Natasha. FESTERING LILIES. London, 1990	—	—	50
Cooper, Susan. MANDRAKE. (London, 1964)	—	—	250
Cooper, Susan Rogers. THE MAN IN THE GREEN CHEVY. New York, 1988	—	350	600
Cooper, William. *See* H(arry) S(ummerfield) Hoff			
Coover, Robert. THE ORIGIN OF THE BRUNISTS. New York (1966)	125	200	175
London (1967)	—	75	60
(Previous translation published in Guatemala in 1965.)			
Cope, Wendy. ACROSS THE CITY. London, 1980. Wraps. 30 signed and numbered copies	—	200	400
150 copies. Wraps	—	100	125
Coppard, A(lfred) E(dgar). ADAM & EVE & PINCH ME. Waltham, 1921. (Also first Golden Cockerel Press.) First issue: white buckram. (160 copies)	300	400	350
Second issue: salmon boards. (340 copies)	150	200	150
New York (1922). (350 copies)	100	125	100
Corby, Herbert. HAMPDENS GOING OVER. London, 1945	30	75	75
Corle, Edwin. MOJAVE. New York, 1934	100	200	250
Corley, Donald. THE HAUNTED JESTER. New York, 1931	—	—	50

	1986	1995	2000
Corley, Edwin. FIVE PLAYS FOR TWO MEN. (No place) 1951. Wraps. (Written with Claude Hubbard)	75	100	100
Corman, Avery. OH, GOD! New York (1971)	—	50	60
Corman, Cid (Sidney). SUBLUNA. (Dorchester, Mass., 1944.) Wraps. (400 copies)	75	150	150
Corn, Alfred. ALL ROADS AT ONCE. New York (1976)	—	35	35
Cornford, Frances. *See* F.C.D.			
POEMS. Hampstead (1910)	150	300	150
Cornford, John. A MEMOIR. London, 1938. Posthumously published. Edited by Pat Sloan	75	75	75
Cornish, Sam. GENERATIONS. Boston (1971)	—	—	45
Cornwell, Bernard. SHARPE'S EAGLE. London, 1981	—	250	350
New York, 1981	—	75	75
Cornwell, Patricia. A TIME FOR REMEMBERING . . . San Francisco (1983)	—	250	400
POSTMORTEM. New York, 1990	—	500	1,000
(London, 1990)	—	200	350
Correll & Gosden. SAM 'N' HENRY. Chicago (1926). Cloth	—	350	350
Wraps	—	150	150
Corrington, John William. WHERE WE ARE. Washington, 1962. Wraps. (225 copies)	—	100	100
Corso, (Nunzio) Gregory. THE VESTAL LADY ON BRATTLE +. Cambridge, 1955. Wraps. (500 copies)	200	200	350
Cortázar, Julio. THE WINNERS. New York (1965)	35	75	100
London, 1965	—	60	75
Corvo, Baron (Frederick William Rolfe). *See* TARCISSUS . . .			
STORIES TOTO TOLD ME. London, 1898. Wraps	400	850	850
Corwin, Norman. THEY FLY THROUGH THE AIR WITH THE GREATEST OF EASE. Weston, Vermont (1939)	—	100	100
Cossery, Albert. MEN GOD FORGOT. Cairo (1944). Wraps. First English translation	125	125	125
(Berkeley) 1946. Issued without dustwrapper	50	50	65
Costler, Dr. A. (Arthur Koestler.) ENCYCLOPEDIA OF SEXUAL KNOWLEDGE. London (1934)	250	450	450

	1986	1995	2000
THE PRACTICE OF SEX. London (1936). "Coester" on title page	200	350	350
Cotton, John. GOD'S PROMISE . . . London, 1630	750	750	750
Coulette, Henri. THE WAR OF THE SECRET AGENTS +. New York (1966)	20	30	40
Coupland, Douglas. GENERATION "X." Toronto, 1991. Wraps	—	150	150
New York, 1991. Wraps	—	—	35
Cournos, John. A DILEMMA . . . Philadelphia, 1910. Translation of Leonid Andrei Yeff's book by Cournos	75	100	100
THE MASK. London, 1919	100	150	150
Coward, (Sir) Noel (Pierce). I'LL LEAVE IT TO YOU. London, 1920. Wraps. (French Acting Edition No. 2496)	300	450	500
Cowen, William Joyce. MAN WITH FOUR LIVES. New York (1934)	50	50	50
Cowley, Malcolm. RACINE. Paris, 1923. (150 to 200 copies but most burned per author.) Wraps	3,500	3,500	2,500
ON BOARD THE MORNING STAR. Written by P. MacOrlan, translated by Cowley. New York, 1924	200	250	250
BLUE JUNIATA. New York (1929)	300	400	450
Cox, A(nthony) B(erkeley). *See* THE LAYTON COURT MYSTERY			
Cox, Palmer. SQUIBS OF CALIFORNIA. Hartford, 1874	75	300	350
Coxe, George Harman. MURDER WITH PICTURES. New York, 1935	250	300	450
Coxe, Louis O(sbourne). UNIFORM OF FLESH. Princeton, 1947. Mimeographed sheets in stiff wraps (with R. H. Chapman)	100	150	200
THE SEA FARING +. New York (1947)	50	50	50
Coyle, Kathleen. PICADILLY. London, 1923	200	300	350
New York (1923)	—	100	150
Cozzens, Frederick Swarthout. *See* Richard Haywarde			
Cozzens, James Gould. CONFUSION. Boston, 1924. (2,000 copies) First issue: gray-green cloth, top edge red	500	750	750
Crace, Jim. CONTINENT. London (1986)	—	60	75
New York (1987)	—	30	35

	1986	1995	2000
Crackanthorpe, Hubert. WRECKAGE. London, 1893. 16 pages of advertisements dated Oct. 1892	75	200	225
Cradock, Mrs. Henry. JOSEPHINE AND HER DOLLS. London, 1916	—	250	350
Craig, Edward Gordon. HENRY IRVING/ELLEN TERRY, ETC./ A BOOK OF PORTRAITS. (Chicago, 1899.) 100 (estimated) special paper copies. Bound in yellow buckram	—	—	500
Craig, Strete. IF ALL ELSE FAILS. New York, 1980	—	—	75
Craik, Dinah Marie Mulock. *See* THE OGILVIES			
Crais, Robert. THE MONKEY'S RAINCOAT. New York (1987). Wraps. Bantam 26336	—	75	150
London, 1989	—	60	300
Cranch, Christopher Pearse. A POEM DELIVERED IN THE FIRST CONGREGATION CHURCH . . . Boston, 1840. Wraps	200	350	350
Crane, Hart. WHITE BUILDINGS. (New York) 1926. (500 copies in total.) First issue: Allen Tate's name incorrectly spelled on title page as "Allan"	2,500	3,500	3,500
Second issue: tipped-in title page with corrected spelling	1,250	1,750	1,750
Paris, 1930. Wraps and dustwrapper. (200 copies)	600	750	750
Crane, Nathalia. THE JANITOR'S BOY +. New York, 1924. (500 signed copies)	75	100	125
London, 1925	—	—	35
Crane, Stephen. *See* Johnston Smith			
BLACK RIDERS +. Boston, 1895. 50 copies on Japan vellum in white vellum or full green levant	1,000	2,000	3,500
Trade edition. (500 copies)	300	750	750
(No place) 1905	—	150	150
MAGGIE. New York, 1896. First issue: title page in old English type	200	750	750
Second issue: title page in Roman type	125	350	350
London, 1896	200	500	500
Cranston, Alan. THE KILLING OF PEACE. New York, 1945 (Preceded by a translation of *Mein Kampf.*)	30	60	60
Crapsey, Adelaide. VERSE. Rochester, New York, 1915	75	125	125
Crawford, F(rancis) Marion. OUR SILVER . . . New York, 1881. Wraps	300	350	350
MR. ISAACS. New York, 1883	40	75	250

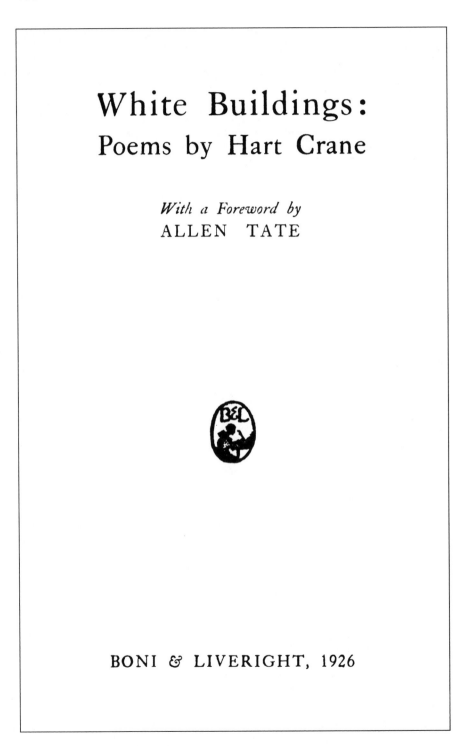

White Buildings:
Poems by Hart Crane

With a Foreword by
ALLEN TATE

BONI & LIVERIGHT, 1926

	1986	1995	2000
Crawford, Isabella Vallancy. OLD SPOOKSES' PASS. No place [Toronto] (1884). 1,000 sheets in 3 bindings. First issue [1884]: Gray card covers. (Approximately 50 copies sold)	—	—	1,500
Second issue [1884]: green card covers. New title page	—	—	1,250
Third issue [1898]: blue cloth	—	—	1,250
Crawford, Lucy. THE HISTORY OF THE WHITE MOUNTAINS . . . White Hills, 1846	125	250	600
Crawford, Max. WALTZ ACROSS TEXAS. New York (1975)	25	50	50
Crawford, Stanley. GASCOYNE. New York (1966)	40	75	50
London, 1966	—	50	30
Creagh, Patrick. A ROW OF PHARAOHS. London (1962)	—	—	45
Creasey, John. SEVEN TIMES SEVEN. London, 1932	250	450	500
Creekmore, Hubert. PERSONAL SUN. Prairie City, 1940. Wraps	50	50	50
Creeley, Robert (White). LE FOU, POEMS. Columbus, 1952. Wraps. (500 copies)	500	750	650
Crevecoeur, Michael Guillaume Jean de. *See* LETTERS			
Crews, Harry. THE GOSPEL SINGER. New York, 1968	200	750	900
Crews, Judson. PSALMS FOR A LATE SEASON. New Orleans, 1942	—	—	100
Creyton, Paul (John Townsend Trowbridge). PAUL CREYTON'S GREAT ROMANCE! KATE THE ACCOMPLICE . . . Boston (1849). Wraps	1,500	2,000	2,000
Crichton, (John) Michael. *See* Jeffrey Hudson, John Lange			
Cripps, Arthur Shearly. LYRE EVANGELISTICA. Oxford/ London, 1909	60	150	150
Crisp, Quentin. COLOUR IN DISPLAY. London, 1938	100	200	200
Crispin, Edmund (Robert Bruce Montgomery). THE CASE OF THE GILDED FLY. London, 1944	150	200	350
OBSEQUIES AT OXFORD. Philadelphia (1945). (New title)	75	125	200
Croaker, Charles. THE VALE OF OBSCURITY . . . Chichester, 1830	—	—	175
Croaker, Croaker & Co. & Croaker, Jr. (Joseph Rodman Drake & Fitz-Green Halleck.) POEMS. New York, 1819	750	750	500
Crockett, S(amuel) R(utherford). *See* Ford Bereton			
THE STICKIT MINISTER . . . London, 1893	50	100	150

	1986	1995	2000
Croft-Cooke, Rupert. SONGS OF A SUSSEX TRAMP. Steyning, 1922. 600 numbered copies	100	175	175
Also see Leo Bruce			
Crofts, Freeman Wills. THE CASK. London (1920). 2 pages of advertisements at back and "Spring List, 1920"	1,500	3,000	5,000
Crompton, Richmal. JUST WILLIAM. London, 1922	—	450	450
Cronin, A(rchibald) J(oseph). DUST INHALATION BY HEMATITE MINERS. (London) 1926. Wraps. Offprint	300	300	300
INVESTIGATIONS IN FIRST-AID ORGANIZATION . . . London, 1927. Wraps	250	250	250
HATTER'S CASTLE. London, 1931	125	150	300
Crosby, Caresse. CROSSES OF GOLD. Paris, 1925. (100 copies)	750	1,500	1,500
Exeter (England), 1925. Wraps	150	300	300
Crosby, Henry Grew (Harry). ANTHOLOGY. (Paris, 1924.) Wraps (or perhaps bound in half leather; seems most are)	750	2,250	2,250
Cross, Amanda (Carolyn G. Heilbrun). THE GARNETT FAMILY. New York, 1961	—	125	125
IN THE LAST ANALYSIS. New York (1964)	75	150	150
Crothers, Rachel. CRISS CROSS. New York, 1904. Wraps	—	150	175
Crothers, Samuel McChord. MISS MUFFET'S CHRISTMAS PARTY . . . St. Paul, 1891. Wraps	250	250	350
Crouch, Stanley. AIN'T NO AMBULANCES FOR NO NIGGUHS TONIGHT. New York, 1972	—	—	75
Crowder, Henry. HENRY MUSIC. Paris, 1930. 100 signed and numbered copies. Issued in tissue dustwrapper	2,500	5,000	5,000
Crowe, Cameron. FAST TIMES AT RIDGEMONT HIGH. New York, 1981	—	—	100
Crowley, (Edward Alexander) Aleister. *See* ACELDAMA			
Crowley, John. THE DEEP. New York (1975)	100	200	200
(London, 1977)	—	125	125
Crowley, Mart. THE BOYS IN THE BAND. New York (1968)	40	60	100
Wraps	—	—	30
Crumley, James. ONE TO COUNT CADENCE. New York, 1969	150	350	350
THE WRONG CASE. New York, 1975	—	400	600

	1986	1995	2000
Crump, Paul. BURN, KILLER, BURN. Chicago (1962)	25	35	75
Cruz, Victor Hernandez. PAPO GOT HIS GUN! New York, 1966. Wraps. (260 copies)	—	100	125
Cullen, Countee. COLOR. New York, 1925	250	300	1,000
Cummings, Bruce Frederick. *See* W. N. P. Barbellion			
Cummings, E(dward) E(stlin). THE ENORMOUS ROOM. New York (1922). First issue: word not blacked out p. 219 last line	600	1,000	3,000
Second issue: word blacked out p. 219	400	750	750
London (1928)	200	350	350
Cummings, Ray(mond King). THE GIRL IN THE GOLDEN ATOM. London (1922)	350	750	1,000
New York, 1923	—	—	600
Cummington Press. FIVE CUMMINGTON POETS. Cummington, Massachusetts, 1939. 300 Copies. Wraps	250	250	250
Cummins, Maria S. *See* THE LAMPLIGHTER			
Cunard, Nancy. OUTLAWS. London, 1921. (Assume issued without dustwrapper)	600	300	375
Cuney, Waring. PUZZLES. Utrecht, 1960. (175 copies in slipcase)	250	250	250
Cunningham, A(lbert) B(enjamin). MURDER AT DEER LICK. New York, 1939	200	300	300

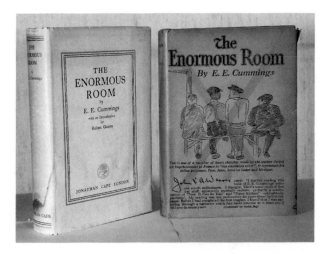

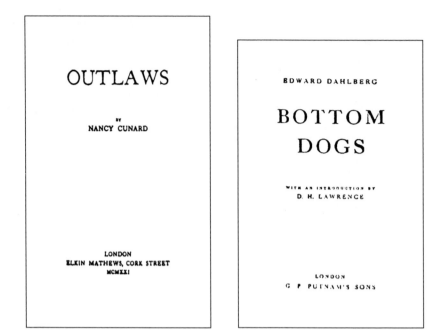

OUTLAWS

BY
NANCY CUNARD

LONDON
ELKIN MATHEWS, CORK STREET
MCMXXI

EDWARD DAHLBERG

BOTTOM
DOGS

WITH AN INTRODUCTION BY
D. H. LAWRENCE

LONDON
G P PUTNAM'S SONS

	1986	1995	2000
Cunningham, J(ames) V(incent). THE HELMSMAN. San Francisco, 1942. (300 copies in total.) Cloth	600	750	850
Wraps. First issue: beige wallpaper (floral design)	250	400	400
Second issue: plain green wraps (over boards) (Preceded by mimeographed syllabus.)	—	300	300
Cunningham, Michael. GOLDEN STATES. New York, 1984	—	—	150
Cunningham-Graham, R. B. ECONOMIC EVOLUTION. Leatham, 1891	—	125	125
NOTES ON THE DISTRICT OF MENTEITH. London, 1895. Wraps	150	150	150
Cuppy, William J(acob). MAROON TALES. Chicago, 1910	35	35	35
Curly, Daniel. THAT MARRIAGE BED . . . Boston (1957)	25	25	25
Curley, Thomas. IT'S A WISE CHILD. New York (1960)	40	40	60
London (1961)	—	—	40
Curran, Dale. A HOUSE ON A STREET. New York (1934)	40	40	40
Curtis, George William. *See* NILES NOTE OF A HOWADJI			
Curtis, Jack. GREEN AGAIN. (Mexico City, 1951.) Wraps. 500 numbered copies	40	75	40

	1986	1995	2000
Curwood, James Oliver. THE COURAGE OF CAPTAIN PLUM. Indianapolis (1908)	50	150	150
Cushing, Harvey. THE PITUITARY BODY AND ITS DISORDERS. Philadelphia (1912)	—	750	650
Cushman, Dan. MONTANA, HERE I BE. New York, 1950. Wraps	—	—	40
Cussler, Clive. THE MEDITERRANEAN CAPER. New York (1973). Wraps	—	—	200
ICEBERG. New York (1975). (2,500 copies)	—	125	2,000
Custance, Olive. OPALS. London, 1897	150	150	250
Custer, Elizabeth B. BOOTS AND SADDLES. New York, 1885	—	—	200
Later printing (same date). Adds portrait and map	—	—	150

D

	1986	1995	2000
D., F.C. (Frances Crofts Darwin Cornford.) THE HOLTBURY IDYLL. No place or date [circa 1908]	1,500	1,750	2,000
D., H. (Hilda Doolittle.) CHORUSES FROM IPHIGENEIA IN AULIS. London, 1916	250	350	450
Cleveland, 1916. Wraps. 40 numbered copies	1,250	1,500	2,000
SEA GARDEN. London, 1916. Laid green paper over boards.	—	—	850
Red paper wrappers (with flaps) over cardboard	350	500	500
Boston, 1916. (English sheets)	200	300	300
Dabbs, James McBride. THERE IS A LAD HERE. (Louisville, 1943?)	50	75	150
WHEN JUSTICE AND EXPEDIENCY MEET (Columbia, 1947.) Wraps	25	40	75
Dabydeen, David. SLAVE SONG. London, 1984	—	75	75
Dahl, Roald. THE GREMLINS. New York (1943)	300	500	750
London (1944)	250	450	600
OVER TO YOU . . . New York (1946)	100	300	250
London, 1946	100	300	300
Dahlberg, Edward. BOTTOM DOGS. London (1929). (520 copies)	250	250	250
New York (1930)	150	150	150
Daiches, David. THE PLACE OF MEANING IN POETRY. London, 1935	50	75	75
Daly, Elizabeth. UNEXPECTED NIGHT. New York, 1940	60	75	100

	1986	1995	2000
Daly, Thomas Augustine. CANZONI. Philadelphia, 1906. First issue: "feety" on p. 17	50	50	75
Daly, Victor. NOT ONLY WAR. Boston (1932)	—	—	150
D'Amato, Barbara. HARDBALL. New York (1990)	—	—	40
Dana, James Dwight. A SYSTEM OF MINEROLOGY. New Haven, 1837	—	—	3,500
New York, 1844. Second edition	—	—	750
New York, 1850. Third edition	—	—	500
New York, 1854. Fourth edition	—	—	350
Dana, Richard H(enry), Sr. POEMS. Boston, 1827. (Several pamphlets preceded)	175	200	200
Dana, Richard Henry. *See* TWO YEARS BEFORE THE MAST			
TWO YEARS BEFORE THE MAST. Boston, 1869. First under his name. With new preface and added chapter	—	250	450
Dane, Clemence (Winifred Ashton). A REGIMENT OF WOMEN. London, 1917	35	75	75
Daniels, Jonathan. DEVIL TRENDS. Chapel Hill, 1922	—	100	150
CLASH OF ANGELS. New York, 1930	—	60	100
Dannay, Frederic. *See* Ellery Queen			
Danticat, Edwidge. BREATH, EYES, MEMORY. New York (1994).	—	—	75
Darrow, Clarence (Seward). REALISM IN LITERATURE AND ART. Chicago (1899). Wraps. First edition stated	—	300	300
A PERSIAN PEARL . . . Erie Aurora, New York, 1899	—	600	600
Darwin, Charles. . . . EXTRACTS FROM LETTERS ADDRESSED TO PROF HENSLOW . . . Cambridge (1835). In original wraps	—	10K	15K
JOURNAL OF RESEARCHES . . . London, 1839. With two folding maps	1,250	4,500	6,000
Davenport, Guy (Mattison). THE INTELLIGENCE OF LOUIS AGASSIZ. Boston (1963). Edited and introduction by Davenport. (400 copies)	125	150	150
CARMINA ARCHILOCHI. Berkeley/Los Angeles, 1964. Cloth	—	250	250
Wraps	—	75	75
Davidman, Joy. LETTER TO A COMRADE. New Hampshire, 1938	75	100	100
Davidson, Diane Mott. CATERING TO NOBODY. New York (1990)	—	—	250

	1986	1995	2000
Davidson, Donald. AN OUTLAND PIPER. Boston, 1924	200	300	300
Davidson, John. DIABOLUS AMANS. Glasgow, 1885	500	750	750
Davidson, Lionel. NIGHT OF WENCESLAS. London, 1960	100	100	125
Davie, Donald (Alfred). PURITY OF DICTION IN ENGLISH VERSE. London, 1952	75	125	125
(POEMS) FANTASY POETS. Oxford, 1954. Cloth	150	450	450
Wraps	50	250	250
Davies, Hugh Sykes. PETRON. London, 1935	75	100	100
Davies, Linda. NEST OF VIPERS. London (1994)	—	—	50
Davies, Rhys. THE SONG OF SONGS +. London (1927). Wraps. (1,000 copies in total.) 100 signed copies	150	200	200
900 unsigned copies	40	40	40
Davies, W(illiam) H. THE SOUL'S DESTROYER +. (London, 1905.) Wraps	600	600	750
Davies, William. SONGS OF A WAYFARER. London, 1869	50	75	100
Davies, W. Robertson. SHAKESPEARE'S BOY ACTORS. London (1939)	500	1,500	2,000
Daviot, Gordon (Elizabeth MacKintosh). THE MAN IN THE QUEUE. London, 1929	200	300	400
New York, 1929	125	200	250
Davis, Angela. IF THEY COME IN THE MORNING. New York, 1971	40	60	75
Davis, Burke. WHISPER MY NAME. New York, 1949	60	125	125
Davis, Dorothy Salisbury. THE JUDAS CAT. New York, 1949	25	75	125
Davis, George. COMING HOME. New York (1971)	—	—	100
Davis, H(arold) L(enoir). HONEY IN THE HORN. New York, 1935	50	175	450
Davis, Lindsey. SILVER PIGS. London, 1989	—	—	1,000
New York, 1989	—	75	75
Davis, Norbert. THE MOUSE IN THE MOUNTAIN. New York, 1943	—	—	450
Davis, Patrick A. THE GENERAL. New York (1998)	—	—	35
Davis, Rebecca Harding. MARGRET HOWTH. Boston, 1862	50	75	100

	1986	1995	2000
Davis, Richard Harding. ADVENTURES OF MY FRESHMAN. Bethlehem (Pennsylvania) (1883). Wraps About 10 copies known.	600	1,500	2,500
GALLEGHER +. New York, 1891. First issue: no advertisement for "Famous Women . . ." in back. Wraps	200	300	400
Cloth	75	150	200
London, 1891	75	125	150
Davis, Tech. TERROR AT COMPASS LAKE. Garden City, 1935	—	75	100
Davis, Terry. VISION QUEST. New York, 1979	—	50	50
Davison, Peter. THE BREAKING OF DAY +. New Haven, 1964	—	45	45
Davy, Sir Humphry. RESEARCHES, CHEMICAL AND PHILOSOPHICAL . . . London, 1800	—	6,000	7,500
Dawkins, Cecil. THE QUIET ENEMY. London, 1963	—	75	75
New York, 1963	—	50	50
Dawson, Fielding. A SIMPLE WISH FOR A SINCERE . . . Black Mountain (1949). Wraps	250	350	350
6 STORIES OF THE LOVE OF LIFE. Black Mountain (1949). Wraps	225	250	250
Day, Clarence (Shepard). DECENNIAL RECORD OF THE CLASS OF 1896. New York, 1907	75	75	75
THE '96 HALF-WAY BOOK. New York, 1915	35	50	50
THIS SIMIAN WORLD. New York, 1920	150	200	200
London (1921)	25	125	150
Day, Dianne. THE STRANGE FILES OF FREEMONT JONES. New York (1995). First mystery	—	—	200
Day, John (Publisher). THE MUSIC FROM BEHIND THE MOON. New York, 1926. By James Branch Cabell. (Boxed)	30	75	75
Day-Lewis, C(ecil). BEECHEN VIGIL +. London (1925). Wraps. (At least one copy in cloth)	350	450	600
Also see Nicholas Blake			
Dayan, Yael. NEW FACE IN THE MIRROR. London (1959)	—	40	50
Deal, Borden. WALK THROUGH THE VALLEY. New York, 1956	—	—	175
Dean, Capt. Harry. *See* Sterling North			
Deane, Seamus. WHILE JEWELS ROT. Belfast (1967). White wraps	—	—	300

	1986	1995	2000
DeAssis, Machado. EPITAPH OF A SMALL WINNER. New York (1952). First English translation	—	—	75
London, 1953	—	75	60
DeBeauvoir, Simon E. THE BLOOD OF OTHERS. London, 1948. (First English translation)	75	100	125
New York, 1948	35	50	60
DeBernières, Louis. THE WAR OF DON EMMANUEL'S NETHER PARTS. London, 1990 (2,500 copies)	—	100	200
New York (1991)	—	—	60
DeCamp, L(yon) Sprague. LEST DARKNESS FALL. New York, 1941. First science fiction	—	—	200
London (1955)	—	—	125
DeCasseres, Benjamin. THE SHADOW EATER. New York, 1915. (Boni.) 150 signed copies	75	75	100
650 unsigned copies	50	50	50
New York, 1917. (Wilmarth)	25	25	35
DeCasseres, Walter. THE SUBLIME BOY. New York, 1926. Deluxe. (100 copies)	75	75	100
Regular	40	40	40
Deck, John. ONE MORNING FOR PLEASURE. New York (1968)	30	40	40
Deeping, Warwick. UTHER AND IGRAINE. London, 1903	75	100	100
New York, 1903	50	75	75

	1986	1995	2000
DeForest, John W(illiam). HISTORY OF THE INDIANS OF CON-NECTICUT . . . Hartford, 1851. First issue: p. vii misnumbered "iiv"	150	250	250
Dehn, Paul. THE DAY'S ALARM. London (1949)	35	50	60
Deighton, Len. THE IPCRESS FILE. London (1962). First issue: no reviews on front dustwrapper flap	150	600	750
New York, 1963	75	250	350
DeJong, David Cornel. BELLY FULLA STRAW. New York, 1936	35	35	35
De La Mare, Walter. *See* Walter Ramal			
HENRY BROCKEN. London, 1904. First issue: without top edges gilt	75	150	150
DeLand, Margaret. THE OLD GARDEN +. Boston, 1886	100	150	200
Delaney, Shelagh. A TASTE OF HONEY. New York (1959). 50 numbered copies. Wraps	100	150	200
Wraps	—	—	35
Delany, Samuel R(ay). THE JEWELS OF APTOR. New York (1962). Wraps. Bound dos-à-dos with a James White novel	40	40	40
London, 1968. First hardcover	—	75	100
De La Roche, Mazo. EXPLORERS OF THE DAWN. New York, 1922	—	125	125
Delbanco, Nicholas. THE MARTLET'S TALE. Philadelphia (1966)	50	75	60
London, 1966	—	60	50
DeLillo, Don. AMERICANA. Boston, 1971	60	300	350
Dell, Floyd. WOMEN AS WORLD BUILDERS. Chicago, 1913. (A few hundred copies, according to author)	150	150	175
Deloria, Vine, Jr. CUSTER DIED FOR YOUR SINS. New York, 1969	—	—	150
Del Rey, Lester. ". . . AND SOME WERE HUMAN." Philadelphia, 1948. (Hand-lettered title page)	75	150	50
Philadelphia, 1949	50	60	35
Del Vecchio, John M. THE 13TH VALLEY (CHAPTER 26). New York (1981). Wraps	60	75	75
THE 13TH VALLEY. New York, 1982	25	50	50
Delving, Michael (Jay Williams). THE STOLEN ORACLE. New York, 1943	—	75	100

	1986	1995	2000
SMILING THE BOY FELL DEAD. New York, 1967. First mystery	30	50	100
Demaret, Jimmy. MY PARTNER BEN HOGAN. New York (1954). (Ghostwritten by Jimmy Breslin)	50	60	100
DeMarinis, Rick. A LOVELY MONSTER. New York, 1975	—	60	60
Demby, William. BEETLECREEK. New York, 1950. (Preceded by publication of this book in Italian in Milan)	60	150	150
DeMille, Nelson. BY THE RIVERS OF BABYLON. New York, 1978. First hardback	—	—	150
DeMorgan, William Frend. JOSEPH VANCE . . . London, 1906	75	75	50
Denby, Edwin. SECOND HURRICANE. Boston (1938). Wraps. (Lyrics from play)	—	300	500
IN PUBLIC, IN PRIVATE. Prairie City (1948). First issue: blue cloth	300	450	600
Second issue: gray cloth	175	350	500
Dennie, Joseph. THE LAY PREACHER . . . Walpole, New Hampshire, 1796	—	600	600
Philadelphia, 1817. (Different content)	—	450	450
Dennis, Patrick. AUNTIE MAME. New York (1955)	—	125	200
Dentinger, Jane. MURDER ON CUE. Garden City, 1983	—	50	30
Depons, F. A VOYAGE TO THE EASTERN PART OF TERRA FIRMA . . . New York, 1806. 3 volumes	—	—	750
TRAVELS IN SOUTH AMERICA . . . London, 1807. 2 volumes	—	350	450
De Quincey, Thomas. *See* CONFESSIONS OF AN ENGLISH OPIUM-EATER			
Derleth, August. TO REMEMBER. Vermont, 1931. Wraps. (129-page pamphlet)	300	600	750
MURDER STALKS THE WAKELY FAMILY. New York, 1934	200	600	750
DEATH STALKS THE WAKELY FAMILY. London, 1937	125	350	500
Derrydale Press. MAGIC HOURS. By Eugene V. Connett. New York, 1927. (100 copies) (First book of press)	7.5K	9K	10K
DERRY, DERRY DOWN. (Edward Lear.) London (1846). Wraps. (175 copies) (First book for children)	2K	5K	7.5K

	1986	1995	2000
Desani, G(ovindas) V(ishnoodes). ALL ABOUT MR. H. HATTERR. London: Aldor (1948)	—	—	600
ALL ABOUT HATTERR. London: Saturn (1949)	40	75	350
New York (1951)	—	—	250
London (1970). Revised edition	—	—	125
DESCENDANT, THE. (Ellen Glasgow.) New York, 1897. First issue: author's name not on spine. New York imprint only. Last advertisement is *Tom Sawyer Abroad*	100	300	300
DESPERATE REMEDIES. (Thomas Hardy.) London, 1871. 3 volumes. (500 copies.)	3K	12.5K	17.5K
New York, 1874. ("author's edition.") Yellow cloth	250	500	750
DeTeran, Lisa St. Aubin. THE STREAK. London, 1980. One of 50 signed copies in wraps	—	—	250
KEEPERS OF THE HOUSE. London (1982)	60	150	200
Deutsch, Babette. BANNERS. New York (1919)	50	75	75
Devlin, Denis. INTERCESSIONS: POEMS. London (1937). (300 copies) Previous collaboration	40	75	100
De Voto, Bernard. THE CROOKED MILE. New York, 1924	75	125	125
De Vries, Peter. BUT WHO WAKES THE BUGLER? Boston, 1940	200	450	450
Dew, Robb Foreman. DALE LOVES SOPHIE TO DEATH. New York, 1981	25	40	30
Dewdney, Christopher. GOLDER'S GREEN. (Toronto) 1971	—	650	850
Dewey, John. PSYCHOLOGY. New York, 1887	350	500	350
Dewey, Thomas B. HUE AND CRY. New York, 1944. First mystery	—	75	75
Dexter, Colin. LAST BUS TO WOODSTOCK. London (1975)	—	750	1,500
(New York, 1975.) English sheets	—	350	750
Dexter, Pete. GOD'S POCKET. New York (1983)	—	100	125
London (1985)	—	—	50
DIARY OF SECTION VIII AMERICAN AMBULANCE FIELD SERVICE. (William Seabrook.) (Boston) 1917	75	75	35
Dibdin, Michael. THE LAST SHERLOCK HOLMES STORY. London, 1978	—	125	350
New York (1978)	—	—	50
Dibdin, T(homas) F(rognall). POEMS. London, 1797. (500 copies)	500	500	500

	1986	1995	2000
Dick, Philip K(indred). SOLAR LOTTERY. New York (1955). Wraps. (Ace Double novel D-103)	—	100	100
WORLD OF CHANCE. London (1956). First hardback edition of SOLAR LOTTERY under new title	—	—	1,250
Boston, 1976. First U. S. hardback edition of SOLAR LOTTERY, issued without dustwrapper	—	—	150
A HANDFUL OF DARKNESS. London, 1955. First issue: blue boards lettered in silver	600	750	1,500
Second issue: orange boards lettered in black	400	500	1,000
Both issues have been seen with later dustwrapper with WORLD OF CHANCE on back panel.			
Dick, R. A. (Josephine A. Lincoln.) THE GHOST AND MRS. MUIR. Chicago/New York (1945)	50	200	250
Dickens, Charles. *See* SKETCHES BY "BOZ"			
Dickens, Monica. ONE PAIR OF HANDS. New York, 1939	60	100	125
Dickey, James (Lafayette). DROWNING WITH OTHERS.			
Middleton, Connecticut, 1962. Cloth	150	250	300
Wraps	100	125	75
(Preceded by INTO THE STONE with two other poets.)			
Dickey, William. OF THE FESTIVITY. New Haven, 1959	40	40	75
Dickinson, Charles. WALTZ IN MARATHON. New York, 1983	—	35	35
Dickinson, Emily. POEMS. Boston, 1890. (500 copies)	1,000	4,500	7,500
More in original tissue and slipcase.			
London, 1891. (480 copies)	500	2,000	3,000
Dickinson, G. Lowes. FROM KING TO KING. London, 1891	—	75	75
Dickinson, Patric. THE SEVEN DAYS OF JERICHO. London (1944). Wraps	30	40	75
Dickinson, Peter. THE WEATHERMONGER. London, 1968. (Children's book)	75	100	125
Boston, 1969	—	—	35
SKIN DEEP. London (1968). First mystery	—	75	200
THE GLASS-SIDED ANTS' NEST. New York, 1968. New title	—	—	50
Didion, Joan. RUN RIVER. New York (1963)	75	125	200
London: Cape (1964)	—	75	100
Di Donato, Pietra. CHRIST IN CONCRETE. Esquire Publ. Chicago (1937). Pictorial boards in glassine dustwrapper	60	75	75
Indianapolis (1939). (Expanded.) Signed tipped-in leaf	40	50	60
Trade edition	20	25	35

	1986	1995	2000
Diehl, William. SHARKEY'S MACHINE. New York (1978)	—	—	60
Dillard, Annie. TICKETS FOR A PRAYER WHEEL. Columbia (Missouri) (1974)	60	400	500
Dillon, George. BOY IN THE WIND. New York, 1927	50	60	60
Diment, Adam. THE DOLLY DOLLY SPY. London, 1967	50	75	100
New York, 1967	—	—	35
Dinesen, Isak (Karen Blixen). SEVEN GOTHIC TALES. New York, 1934. 1,010 numbered copies in slipcase. Leather	250	400	500
Black cloth	150	250	300
Trade edition	100	150	200
London, 1934. Rex Whistler dustwrapper	150	400	500
Di Palma, Ray. MAX. (Iowa City) 1969. Wraps	—	150	150
DiPrima, Diane. THIS KIND OF BIRD FLIES BACKWARD. (New York, 1958.) Wraps	40	60	125
Disch, Thomas M. THE GENOCIDES. (New York (1965). Wraps	—	50	50
London, 1967	—	750	750
Boston, 1976. First U.S. hardback edition	—	—	60
Disney, Doris Miles. A COMPOUND FOR DEATH. Garden City, 1943	30	40	100
Disney, Walter E. MICKEY MOUSE BOOK. New York (1930). Wraps with green background (or white background) without illustrated strip on back cover (priority uncertain, although white is less common). Must include activity page	—	7,500	6,000
DISSERTATION ON THE HISTORY . . . OF THE BIBLE . . . , A. (Timothy Dwight.) New Hampshire, 1772	250	250	350
Dixon, Stephen. NO RELIEF. Ann Arbor (1976). Stiff wraps	25	30	30
Dixon, Thomas, Jr. THE LEOPARD'S SPOT . . . New York, 1902. Presentation issue signed	90	125	150
Regular edition unsigned	30	30	50
Dobbs, Michael. HOUSE OF CARDS. London, 1989	—	—	100
Dobie, James Frank. A VAQUERO OF THE BRUSH COUNTRY. Dallas, 1929. First issue: "Rio Grande River" on map on endpaper	300	500	500
Second issue: with "Rio Grande"	—	300	300
Dobree, Bonamy. RESTORATION COMEDY 1660–1720. Oxford, 1924	125	125	75
Dobson, Austin. VIGNETTES IN RHYME . . . London, 1873	125	200	350
Pamphlet preceded.			

	1986	1995	2000
Dobyns, Stephen. CONCURRING BEASTS. New York, 1972	—	50	100
A MAN OF LITTLE EVILS. New York (1973). First mystery	—	—	75
Doctorow, E(dgar) L(awrence). WELCOME TO HARD TIMES. New York, 1960	150	450	500
BAD MAN FROM BODIE. London, 1961. (New title)	125	300	350
Dodd, E. R. THIRTY-TWO POEMS. London, 1929. Wraps	—	60	60
Dodd, Susan. NO EARTHLY NOTION. New York, 1986	—	40	50
Dodge, David. DEATH AND TAXES. New York, 1941	75	75	100
Dodge, Jim. FUP. (Berkeley, 1983.) Wraps	—	75	125
New York (1984)	—	—	15
Dodge, M. E. (Mary Mapes Dodge.) THE IRVINGTON STORIES. New York, 1865	125	125	250
Dodge, Mary Abigail. *See* Gail Hamilton			
Dodson, Owen. POWERFUL LONG LADDER. New York, 1946	75	300	250
Doerr, Harriet. STONES FOR IBARRA. New York, 1984	—	100	150
London (1985)	—	—	50
Doig, Ivan. A HISTORY OF THE PACIFIC NORTHWEST FOREST . . . (Portland, 1977). Stapled wraps	—	—	250
THIS HOUSE OF SKY. New York, 1978	—	100	125
Donaldson, D. J. CAJUN NIGHTS. New York, 1988. Author's first mystery	—	40	200
Donleavy, J. P. THE GINGER MAN. Paris (1955). Wraps. "Francs: 1.500" on rear cover	350	600	600
London, 1956	100	175	250
Paris, 1958. Cloth. First issue: original dustwrapper flaps	100	500	600
Second issue: dustwrapper flaps glued on	50	125	150
New York (1958)	50	100	150
Donne, John. PSEUDO-MARTYR . . . London, 1610	5K	6K	10K
Donnell, David. POEMS. Thornhill, Ontario, 1961. Tan velvet wraps	—	—	150
Donnelly, I(gnatius). THE MOURNER'S VISION. Philadelphia, 1850. Gray boards	—	250	300
ATLANTIS . . . New York, 1882 (Pamphlets preceded)	150	150	200

	1986	1995	2000
Donoso, José. CORONATION. London, 1965	—	150	150
New York, 1965. (First publication in English)	—	100	60
Donovan, Dick. (Joyce E. Muddock.) THE MAN HUNTER. London, 1888	250	350	350
Dooley, Roger B. LESS THAN THE ANGELS. Milwaukee (1946)	—	75	75
Dooley, Thomas A. DELIVER US FROM EVIL. New York, 1956	—	75	75
Dooling, Richard. CRITICAL CARE. New York (1992)	—	—	25
Doolittle, Hilda. *See* H. D.			
Doolittle, Jerome. THE BOMBING OFFICER. New York (1982)	—	50	35
Dorfman, Ariel. MISSING. London, 1974. Wraps. First book in English	—	—	75
Dorn, Ed(ward Merton). WHAT I SEE IN THE MAXIMUS POEMS. (Ventura, California) 1960. Wraps	150	175	200
Dorr, Nell. IN A BLUE MOON. New York, 1939. Issued without dustwrapper in slipcase	—	125	150
Dorris, Michael. NATIVE AMERICANS, 500 YEARS LATER. New York (1975). Photos by Joseph C. Farber	—	—	100
A YELLOW RAFT IN BLUE WATER. New York, 1987	—	40	75
(London, 1988)	—	—	75
Dos Passos, John (Roderigo). ONE MAN'S INITIATION–1917. London (1920). (750 copies bound for English edition). First issue with "flat" obliterated, p. 35:32	600	750	1,000
Second issue with "flat" lettering perfect	—	—	600
New York, 1922. (500 copies from English sheets.) First issue	500	600	750
Second issue	—	—	500
Dostoevsky, F. CRIME AND PUNISHMENT. London, 1886	—	—	2,000
Douglas, Ellen. (Josephine Haxton.) A FAMILY'S AFFAIRS. Boston, 1962	100	200	150
London (1963)	50	100	100
Douglas, Keith. ALAMEIN TO ZEM ZEM. London, 1946	100	250	250
Douglas, Lord Alfred. POEMS. Paris, 1896. Wraps. 20 on Hollande paper	450	450	750
Trade edition	150	150	450
(Previous translation.)			
Douglas, Norman. *See* Normyx			

	1986	1995	2000
Douglass, Frederick. NARRATIVE OF THE LIFE OF FREDERICK DOUGLASS AN AMERICAN SLAVE WRITTEN BY HIMSELF. Boston, 1845	—	1,250	1,500
THE NARRATIVE OF FREDERICK DOUGLASS . . . Wortley (England) 1846	—	—	1,250
Douskey, Franz. INDECENT EXPOSURE. New Hampshire, 1976. Wraps	30	30	35
Dove, Rita. TEN POEMS. Lisbon, Iowa, 1977	—	250	1,250
Doves Press. DE VITA ET MORIBUS . . . By C. Tacitus. London, 1900. 5 vellum copies	3K	4.5K	6K
Regular edition. (225 copies)	850	850	1,000
Dowden, Edward. MR. TENNYSON AND MR. BROWNING. (London) 1863		250	350
POEMS. London, 1867	—	—	200
Dowdy, Andrew. NEVER TAKE A SHORT PRICE. New York (1972)	25	35	35
Dowell, Coleman. THE GRASS DIES. London (1968)	75	125	100
ONE OF THE CHILDREN IS CRYING. New York, 1968. (New title)	40	100	35
Dowson, Ernest. THE DILEMMAS. London, 1895	—	—	200
VERSES. London, 1896. (30 large-paper copies in imitation vellum)	1,500	3,500	4.5K
Trade edition. (300 copies)	200	600	1,000
Doyle, Arthur Conan. A STUDY IN SCARLET. London, 1888. Wraps. First issue: "younger" spelled correctly in Preface	15K	100K	125K
Second issue: "youuger" for "younger" in Preface	10K	15K	20K
Philadelphia, 1890. Wraps	2,500	3,000	7,500
Cloth	1,500	2,000	5,000
London, 1891. Second edition	—	—	350
Doyle, Roddy. THE COMMITMENTS. Dublin, 1987. Wraps	—	250	250
Drabble, Margaret. A SUMMER BIRD-CAGE. London, 1963	150	150	250
New York, 1964	75	75	150
Drago, Harry Sinclair. SUZANNA . . . New York (1922)	—	—	125
Drake, Joseph Rodman. *See* Croaker			
THE CULPRIT FAY. New York, 1835	125	125	125
New York: Grolier Club, 1923. One of 300 copies	—	—	175

	1986	1995	2000
Drake, Leah Bodine. A HORNBOOK FOR WITCHES. Sauk City, 1950	750	1,500	1,500
Drant, R. Palasco (Art Young). HELL UP TO DATE. Chicago (1982). Pictorial boards without dustwrapper	—	200	200
DREAM DROPS . . . BY A DREAMER. (Amy Lowell.) Boston (1887). Cloth with white linen spine. (99 copies)	2,500	3,000	3,000
Wrappers. (151 copies)	1,500	2,250	2,250
Dreiser, Theodore. SISTER CARRIE. New York, 1900. (About 1,000 copies)	800	3,500	6,000
London, 1901	250	1,000	1,500
New York, 1907	—	250	350
Drexler, Rosalyn. I AM THE BEAUTIFUL STRANGER. New York (1965)	35	40	40
Drinkwater, John. POEMS. Birmingham, England, 1903	150	300	350
Drury, Allen. ADVISE AND CONSENT. Garden City, 1959	—	—	150
London (1960)	—	—	75
Dubie, Norman. THE HORSEHAIR SOFA. (Plainfield, 1969)	—	—	1,000
DuBois, W(illiam) E(dward) B(urghardt). SUPPRESSION OF THE AMERICAN SLAVE TRADE. New York, 1896	750	1,000	2,000
DuBois, William. THE CASE OF THE DEADLY DIARY. Boston, 1940	—	—	250
Dubus, Andre. THE LIEUTENANT. New York, 1967	50	250	300
Duer, Alice (Later Miller). POEMS. New York, 1896. (Written with Caroline Duer)	30	60	125
Duffy, Bruce. THE WORLD AS I FOUND IT. New York, 1987	—	40	50
Duffy, Maureen. THAT'S HOW IT WAS. London (1962)	—	—	75
Dufresne, John. THE WAY THAT WATER ENTERS STONE. New York (1991)	—	—	150
Dugan, Alan. GENERAL PROTHALAMION IN POPULOUS TIMES. (New York, 1961.) Broadside. (100 copies)	90	150	200
POEMS. New York, 1961. Cloth	50	75	60
Wraps	20	20	20
Duggan, Alfred. KNIGHT WITHOUT ARMOUR. London, 1950	60	75	75
Dujardin, Edouard. WE'LL TO THE WOODS NO MORE. New York, 1938. (First English translation)	75	100	150

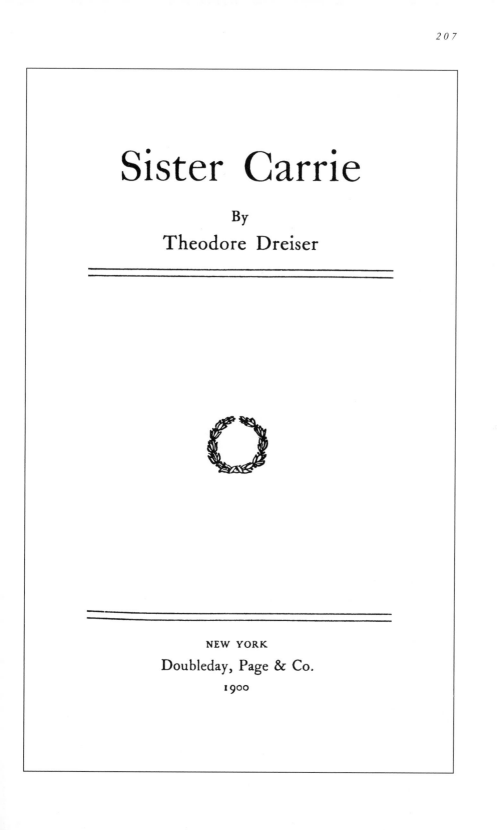

Sister Carrie

By
Theodore Dreiser

NEW YORK
Doubleday, Page & Co.
1900

	1986	1995	2000
Duke, Osbourne. SIDEMAN. New York (1956)	40	60	100
Dulles, Allen (Welsh). GERMANY'S UNDERGROUND. New York, 1947	40	60	75
DuMaurier, Daphne. THE LOVING SPIRIT. London, 1931	100	300	400
DuMaurier, George. SIR GAWAINE HYS PENANCE: A LEGEND OF CAMELOT. (London) 1866. Wraps	—	1,000	1,000
PETER IBBETSON. New York, 1892	100	100	100
London, 1892. 2 volumes	150	150	150
Dunant, Sarah. SNOW STORMS IN A HOT CLIMATE. London (1988)	—	—	100
Dunas, Jeff. CAPTURED WOMEN. New York, 1981.	—	—	75
Dunbar, Paul (Laurence). OAK AND IVY. Dayton, Ohio, 1893. (500 copies)	125	350	6,000
Duncan, David James. THE RIVER WHY. San Francisco (1983)	—	—	150
Duncan, Robert (Edward). HEAVENLY CITY, EARTHLY CITY. (Berkeley) 1947. Green cloth. (100 signed copies)	750	1,500	2,000
White pictorial boards in dustwrapper. (250 copies)	500	1,000	1,000
Duncan, Ronald (Frederick). THE COMPLETE PACIFIST. London (1937). Wraps	75	100	100
Duncan, Sara Jeanette. A SOCIAL DEPARTURE. New York, 1890	50	75	50
Dunn, Douglas. TERRY STREET. London, 1969	—	50	100
Dunn, Katherine. ATTIC. New York, 1970	—	250	250
(London, 1970)	—	—	100
Dunn, Nell. UP THE JUNCTION. London, 1963	40	40	40
Philadelphia, 1966	30	30	30
Dunne, Finley Peter. *See* MR. DOOLEY IN PEACE AND WAR			
Dunne, John Gregory. DELANO . . . New York (1967)	25	75	75
Dunnett, Dorothy. THE GAME OF KINGS. London, 1961	—	250	350
New York (1961)	—	—	250
Dunning, John. THE HOLLAND SUGGESTIONS. Indianapolis, 1975	—	200	1,000
Dunning, Ralph Cheever. ROCOCO. Paris: Black Manikin Press, 1926. First book of this press	200	200	150
Dunphy, Jack. JOHN FURY. New York (1946)	40	60	75

	1986	1995	2000
Dunsany, Lord (Edward J.M.D.P.). THE GODS OF PEGANA. London, 1905. First issue: drummer blindstamped on front cover	150	300	450
Second issue: without blindstamp	100	200	250
Durant, Will. PHILOSOPHY AND THE SOCIAL PROBLEM. New York, 1917	50	75	100
Duras, Marguerite. THE SEA WALL. New York, 1952	—	—	75
Durham, Marilyn. THE MAN WHO LOVED CAT DANCING. New York (1972)	25	40	50
Durrell, Claude. *See* CLAUDE			
Durrell, Gerald. THE OVERLOADED ARK. London (1953)	75	125	125
New York, 1953	30	75	75
Durrell, Lawrence (George). QUAINT FRAGMENT. (London) 1931. Blue wraps or red boards. (Fewer than 10 copies)	12K	35K	40K
TEN POEMS. London, 1932. (12 signed copies)	4K	15K	20K
Wraps	2K	5K	6K
THE PIED PIPER OF LOVERS. London, 1935. (First novel)	2K	3.5K	4K
(Four other items from 1932–35.)			
Dutton, Geoffrey. NIGHT FLIGHT AND SUNRISE. Adelaide, 1944	—	75	100

Quaint   Fragment

BY

LAWRENCE DURRELL

The
CECIL PRESS
1931

	1986	1995	2000
Dwight, Theodore. AN ORATION, SPOKEN BEFORE THE SOCIETY OF THE CINCINNATI. New Haven, 1792	125	200	250
Dwight, Timothy. *See* A DISSERTATION . . .			
Dworkin, Andrea. CHILD. Crete, 1966	—	—	200
Dwyer, K. R. (Dean R. Koontz.) CHASE. New York, 1972. (First hardback)	—	250	250
Dwyer-Jones, Alice. PRICE OF INHERITANCE. London (1963)	50	50	50
Dyja, Thomas. PLAY FOR A KINGDOM. New York (1977)	—	—	60
Dykeman, Wilma. THE FRENCH BROAD. New York (1955)	50	50	50
Dylan, Bob. TARANTULA. New York, 1966	—	75	60
Dyment, Clifford. FIRST DAY. London, 1935	40	75	75

E

	1986	1995	2000
E., A. (George W. Russell.) HOMEWARD: SONGS BY THE WAY. Oxford, 1894. Wraps	250	450	450
(Preceded by Theosophical Society pamphlet.)			
Earley, Tony. HERE WE ARE IN PARADISE. Boston, 1994	—	—	50
EARLY PIONEER, AN. (Abel Beach.) Buffalo, 1895. 600 numbered copies	40	75	100
Eastlake, William (Derry). GO IN BEAUTY. New York (1956) London, 1957	125 75	300 100	400 150
Eastman, Max. THE ENJOYMENT OF POETRY. New York, 1913 London, 1913	— —	150 100	35 25
Eaton, Charles Edward. THE BRIGHT PLAIN. Chapel Hill, 1942	—	60	75
Eberhart, Mignon G(ood). THE PATIENT IN ROOM 18. Garden City, 1929	150	250	350
Eberhart, Richard. A BRAVERY OF EARTH. London (1930) New York (1930). (English sheets)	250 150	300 200	300 200
Eckert, Allan W. THE GREAT AUK. Boston/Toronto (1963)	50	50	50
Eco, Umberto. THE PICTURE HISTORY OF INVENTIONS. London, 1962 New York, 1963	— —	150 —	200 150

	1986	1995	2000
Economou, George. THE GEORGIC. London, 1968. Wraps. 50 signed and numbered copies	75	75	75
250 signed and numbered copies	35	35	35
Eddings, David. HIGH HUNT. New York, 1973	—	50	100
Eddington, Arthur Stanley. STELLAR MOVEMENTS . . . London, 1914	125	150	200
Eddison, E(ric) R(ucker). POEMS, LETTERS AND MEMORIES OF PHILIP SIDNEY NAIRN. London, 1916. (109 pages. Introduction by Eddison.) Issued without dustwrapper	150	250	250
THE WORM OUROBOROS. London (1922). First issue: no blindstamped windmill on rear cover	250	450	600
Second issue: with windmill	200	350	450
New York, 1926	150	150	300
Eddy, Mary (Morse) Baker. *See* Mary Baker Glover			
Edel, Leon. HENRY JAMES: LES ANNÉES DRAMATIQUES. Paris, 1931. Wraps. (300 copies)	—	100	200
Edgar, Patrick Nisbett. THE AMERICAN RACE-TURF REGISTER . . . New York, 1833. Volume 1 (all published)	750	750	1,000
Edgerton, Clyde. RANEY. Chapel Hill (1985)	—	350	400
Edman, Irwin. HUMAN TRAITS . . . New York, 1919. Wraps	100	125	100
New York, 1920. Cloth	50	75	75
Edmonds, Walter D(umaux). ROME HAUL. Boston, 1929 Presentation edition, one of 1,001 copies	—	—	450
Trade edition	200	300	350
Edson, Russell. APPEARANCES. Stamford, 1961. Wraps	50	60	100
Edwards, Dorothy. RHAPSODY. Wishart. London, 1927	60	60	125
Edwards, Junius. IF WE MUST DIE. Garden City, 1963	—	100	100
Edwards, Page. THE MULES THAT ANGELS RIDE. Chicago, 1972	35	50	25
Edwards, S. W. GO NOW IN DARKNESS. Chicago, 1964. Wraps in dustwrapper	35	35	35
Egan, Jennifer. EMERALD CITY. London (1993)	—	—	75
New York, 1996	—	—	25
Egerton, George (Mary Chavelita Dunne [later Bright]). KEYNOTES. London, 1893. Green cloth	100	100	150
Eggleston, Edward. NORTHWESTERN SANITARY FAIR . . . No place, no date [1865?]. (4-page appeal for funds)	—	750	750

	1986	1995	2000
THE MANUAL: A PRACTICAL GUIDE TO SUNDAY-SCHOOLWORK. Chicago, 1869. First issue: with "A. Zeese" imprint on copyright page	150	300	300
MR. BLAKE'S WALKINGSTICK. Chicago, 1870. Wraps (One previous anonymous pamphlet.)	200	200	200
Ehle, John. MOVE OVER, MOUNTAIN. New York, 1957	—	175	200
Ehrlich, Max. THE BIG EYE. Garden City, 1949. First stated	60	75	50
Eigner, Larry (Lawrence Joel). POEMS. Canton, Mass., 1941. Wraps. (25 copies)	2,000	2,000	2,000
FROM THE SUSTAINING AIR. Mallorca, 1953. (250 copies) Wraps	300	400	400
Eiseley, Loren. THE IMMENSE JOURNEY. New York (1957)	75	150	200
Eisenhower, D(wight). GUILDHALL ADDRESS IN LONDON . . . [London] Overbrook Press, 1945. Wraps. 750 copies	—	—	250
Eliot, George (Mary Ann Evans). *See* David Friedrich Strauss			
SCENES OF CLERICAL LIFE. London, 1858. 2 volumes in original cloth	750	7,500	17,500
New York, 1858. Wraps	—	—	1,250
Also see Marian Evans			
Eliot, Henry Ward, Jr. HARVARD CELEBRITIES. Cambridge (1901). (T.S.'s father)	—	75	100
Eliot, T(homas) S(tearns). PRUFROCK +. London, 1917. (500 copies). Wraps	2K	6K	10K
Elkin Mathews, Publisher. *See* Richard LeGallienne			
Elkin, Stanley (Lawrence). BOSWELL. New York (1964)	100	100	150
Elkins, Aaron. FELLOWSHIP OF FEAR. New York, 1982	—	350	1,000
Ellenbogen, George. WINDS OF UNREASON. Montreal (1957)	50	50	50
Ellerman, Annie Winifred. REGION OF LUTANY +. London, 1914. Wraps	750	750	750
Ellerman, Sir John. *See* E. L. Black			
Ellet, Mrs. E(lizabeth). POEMS. Phildelphia, 1835. (Previous translation)	125	175	200
Ellin, Stanley. DREADFUL SUMMIT. New York, 1948	75	125	200
London (1958)	—	—	50

	1986	1995	2000
Elliott, Bob, and Ray Goulding. BOB AND RAY'S STORY OF LINDA LOVELY AND THE FLEEBUS. New York, 1960	—	75	75
Elliott, George P(aul). PARKTILDEN VILLAGE. Boston (1958)	50	50	50
Elliott, Janice. CAVE WITH ECHOES. London, 1962	35	35	35
Elliott, Sumner Locke. CAREFUL, HE MIGHT HEAR YOU. New York, 1963. Author's name on spine of dustwrapper in red or black (variant)	30	75	75

(A number of his plays were produced in Sydney before he emigrated, but we believe none was published before this.)

	1986	1995	2000
Elliott, William. ADDRESS TO THE PEOPLE OF ST. HELENA PARISH. Charleston, 1832. Wraps	150	350	350
Ellis, A. E. THE RACK. London, 1958	50	40	50
New York, 1958	—	—	40
Ellis, Alice Thomas. THE SIN EATER. London, 1977	—	60	125
Ellis, Bret Easton. LESS THAN ZERO. New York (1985)	—	50	75
Ellis, Havelock. THE NEW SPIRIT. London, 1890	100	200	250
Ellis, Ron. EARS OF THE CITY. (London, 1998)	—	—	50
Ellison, Harlan (Jay). THE DEADLY STREETS. New York (1958). Wraps	60	125	175
RUMBLE. New York, 1958 (Note: priority in 1958 uncertain.)	—	150	150
Ellison, James Whitfield. I'M OWEN HARRISON HARDING. New York, 1955	20	25	25
Ellison, Jerome. THE PRISONER ATE A HEARTY BREAKFAST. New York (1939)	—	—	75
Ellison, Ralph. THE INVISIBLE MAN. New York (1952)	200	1,000	1,500
London, 1953	100	250	500
Ellroy, James. BROWN'S REQUIEM. (New York, 1981.) Wraps	—	100	125
London (1984). First hardback	—	75	450
Ellson, Hal. DUKE. New York, 1949	40	75	100
Ellsworth, Robert. CHINESE FURNITURE. New York, 1971. Folio	—	400	750
Elman, Richard M. A COAT FOR THE TSAR. University of Texas Press (1958)	—	—	100

	1986	1995	2000
Elmslie, Kenward. PAVILIONS. New York, 1961. Wraps. (300 copies)	—	100	150
Ely, David. (David Ely Lilienthal). TROT. New York (1963)	25	25	40
EMBARGO (THE), OR SKETCHES OF THE TIMES . . . (William Cullen Bryant.) Boston, 1808. 12 pages in self-wraps with cover title	4,000	8,500	10K
Emerson, Ralph Waldo. LETTER FROM THE REV R. W. EMERSON TO . . . Boston (1832). Wraps	—	20K	25K
A HISTORICAL DISCOURSE . . . Concord, 1835	250	400	1,000
Also see NATURE			
Emmons, Richard. THE FREDONIAD. Boston, 1827. 4 volumes	200	200	250
Empson, William. LETTER IV. London, 1929	—	250	350
POEMS. London, 1935	125	175	250
Emshwiller, Carol. JOY IN OUR CAUSE. New York (1974)	—	40	40
Ende, Michael. THE NEVER ENDING STORY. New York (1983)	—	—	50
Endore, S. Guy. CASANOVA: HIS KNOWN AND UNKNOWN LIFE. New York (1929)	40	50	50
London (1930)	40	50	50

	1986	1995	2000
Engel, Howard. THE SUICIDE MURDERS. Toronto, 1980	—	100	75
England, George Allan. UNDERNEATH THE BOUGH. New York (1903)	—	200	350
Engle, Marian. NO CLOUDS OF GLORY. Toronto, 1968	—	100	125
Engle, Paul (Hamilton). WORN EARTH. New Haven, 1932	125	125	150
(Coedited anthology in 1931.)			
Engleman, Paul. DEAD IN CENTER FIELD. New York (1983). Wraps.	—	—	30
ENGLISHWOMAN IN AMERICA, (THE). (Isabella Bird.) London, 1856	—	—	450
Ennis, John. NIGHT ON HIBERNIA. (Dublin, 1976)	—	—	100
ENQUIRY INTO THE PRESENT STATE OF POLITE LEARNING IN EUROPE, AN. (Oliver Goldsmith's first original work.) London, 1759	—	1,000	1,000
Enright, D. J. SEASON TICKET. Alexandria, Egypt, 1948. Wraps	—	250	250
Enslin, Theodore (Vernon). THE WORK PROPOSED. (Ashland, Massachusetts) 1958. Limited to 250 copies. Stiff wraps	175	175	125
Ephron, Nora. AND NOW . . . HERE'S JOHNNY. (New York, 1968). Wraps	—	—	25
WALLFLOWER AT THE ORGY. New York, 1970	—	35	35
Epstein, Seymour. PILLAR OF SALT. New York (1960)	60	75	50
Erdman, Paul E. THE BILLION DOLLAR SURE THING. New York, 1974	—	40	30
Erdrich, Louise. JACKLIGHT. New York (1984). Wraps	100	200	200
LOVE MEDICINE. New York (1984) (London, 1985)	— —	175 —	175 100
Erickson, Steve. DAYS BETWEEN STATIONS. New York (1985)	—	50	75
Ertz, Susan. MADAME CLAIRE. London, 1923	75	125	125
Eshleman, Clayton. MEXICO & NORTH. (New York/San Francisco, 1961). Wraps. 26 lettered copies	75	250	300
Regular edition	40	75	75
Esquivel, Laura. LIKE WATER FOR CHOCOLATE. New York, 1992.	—	—	125

	1986	1995	2000
Esteven, John. THE DOOR OF DEATH. New York (1928)	—	—	150
Estleman, Loren D. THE OKLAHOMA PUNK. Canoga Park, 1976. Wraps	—	—	250
Etchison, Dennis. THE DARK COUNTRY. (Santa Cruz, 1982). One of 100 signed (on label) of 1,000 copies	—	—	450
One of 900 copies	—	—	150
EUPHRANOR, A DIALOGUE ON YOUTH. (Edward FitzGerald.) London, 1851	300	750	600
Evanovich, Janet. ONE FOR THE MONEY. New York, 1994	—	—	100
London (1994). Wraps	—	—	35
(Previous romance novels.)			
Evans, Donald. DISCORDS. Philadelphia, 1912	100	100	150
Evans, E. Everett. MAN OF MANY MINDS. Reading (1953). 300 signed and numbered copies	60	100	100
Trade edition. First issue: blue cloth	25	40	40
Second issue: boards	15	25	30
Evans, John. ANDREWS' HARVEST. New York, 1933	75	75	100
Evans, John (Howard Browne). HALO IN BLOOD. Indianapolis (1946). (First under this name)	—	100	250
Evans, Margiad. COUNTRY DANCE. London, 1932	75	100	150
Evans, Marian (George Eliot). THE ESSENCE OF CHRISTIANITY. London, 1854. First issue: black cloth with "Marian Evans" on spine	1,000	2,000	2,500
Second issue: purple cloth with "George Eliot" on spine (Evans' translation of Ludwig Feuerbach's book. The only use of her real name.)	750	1,500	1,750
Evans, Max. SOUTHWEST WIND. San Antonio, 1958	—	50	125
Evans, Nathaniel. POEMS ON SEVERAL OCCASIONS . . . Philadelphia, 1772	—	—	200
Evans, Nicholas. THE HORSE WHISPERER. London, 1995	—	—	100
New York, 1995	—	—	50
Evans, Oliver. YOUNG MAN WITH A SCREWDRIVER. Lincoln (1950)	—	—	75
Evans, Walker. THE CRIME OF CUBA. Philadelphia (1933). Book by Carlton Beals. First book appearance of Evans's photos	150	400	450
AMERICAN PHOTOGRAPHS. New York (1939)	—	400	600

	1986	1995	2000
Everett, Edward. A DEFENCE OF CHRISTIANITY. Boston, 1814	100	200	250
Everson, William (Oliver). (Brother Antoninus.) THESE ARE THE RAVENS. San Leandro, California, 1935. Wraps	400	500	500
Ewart, Gavin. POEMS AND SONGS. London (1939)	150	250	200
Ewing, Max. TWENTY-SIX SONNETS FROM THE PARONOMASIAN . . . (New York, 1924.) Wraps	50	50	125
Exley, Frederick. A FAN'S NOTES. New York (1968)	50	150	200
London (1970)	50	75	100

F

	1986	1995	2000
F., M. T. (Katherine Anne Porter.) MY CHINESE MARRIAGE. New York, 1921. Ghostwritten by Porter for Mie Taim Franking	400	1,250	1,250
Without dustwrapper	—	—	100
Faber, Geoffrey. INTERFLOW . . . London, 1915	—	—	150
Fabes, Gilbert. THE AUTOBIOGRAPHY OF A BOOK. London (1926)	75	150	125
Fainlight, Harry. SUSSICRAN. (London, 1965.) Wraps. 50 signed copies	75	100	100
100 unsigned copies	35	50	50
Fair, Ronald L. MANY THOUSAND GONE. New York (1965)	60	125	100
London (1965)	—	—	75
FAIR DEATH, A. (Sir Henry Newbolt.) London (1881). Wraps	100	125	150
Fairless, Michael. (Margaret Fairless Barber.) THE GATHERING OF BROTHER HILARIUS. London, 1901	50	125	125
New York, 1901	—	—	100
Fairman, Henry Clay. THE THIRD WORLD . . . Atlanta, 1895	200	350	450
New York, 1896	100	125	200
Falkner, J. Meade. THE LOST STRADIVARIUS. London, 1895. First issue has ads dated 10/95	75	75	600
Falkner, W(illiam) C(lark). THE WHITE ROSE OF MEMPHIS. New York, 1881	—	125	350
Fallaci, Oriana. THE USELESS SEX. New York, 1964 (First published in Italy in 1961.)	—	75	35
Fallon, Peter. AMONG THE WALLS. (Dublin, 1971). Wraps	—	—	150
FANNY. (Fitz-Greene Halleck.) New York, 1819. Gray wraps	300	400	1,500
Rebound	—	—	500

	1986	1995	2000
FANSHAWE: A TALE. (Nathaniel Hawthorne.) Boston, 1828	12K	30K	35K
Fante, John. WAIT UNTIL SPRING, BANDINI. New York (1938)	125	300	750
Santa Barbara, 1983. 26 signed and lettered copies	—	—	500
200 signed and numbered copies	—	—	250
Fariña, Richard. BEEN DOWN SO LONG IT LOOKS LIKE UP TO ME. New York (1966)	50	200	200
Farjeon, Eleanor. PAN-WORSHIP. London, 1908	60	100	150
Farmer, Philip José. THE GREEN ODYSSEY. New York (1957). Cloth	850	1,250	1,500
Wraps	30	60	40
Farnol, (John) Jeffery. MY LADY CAPRICE. London, 1907	35	35	35
Farrar, John Chapman. DREAMS OF BOYHOOD . . . No place, 1914. Wraps	—	75	75
Farrell, Henry. WHAT EVER HAPPENED TO BABY JANE? New York (1960)	35	100	125
London (1960)	—	—	75
Farrell, J. G. A MAN FROM ELSEWHERE. London, 1963	125	175	250
Farrell, James T(homas). YOUNG LONIGAN. New York, 1932. Brown cloth	250	750	1,000
(Reissued in 1935 in blue cloth; Introduction, dated 1935, by F. Thrasher inserted; title page still dated 1932)	100	350	350
Farren, Julian. THE TRAIN FROM PITTSBURGH. New York, 1948	25	25	25
Farris, John. HARRISON HIGH . . . New York (1959)	—	—	75
Fast, Howard (Melvin). TWO VALLEYS. New York, 1933	250	600	600
Fats, Minnesota. THE BANKSHOT +. Cleveland (1966). Written with Tom Fox	—	75	50
Faulkner, Fritz. WINDLESS SKY. London, 1936	—	125	150
Faulkner, John. MEN WORKING. New York (1941)	60	75	100
Faulkner, William. THE MARBLE FAUN. Boston (1924)	15K	20K	25K
SOLDIERS' PAY. New York, 1926	6K	15K	20K
London, 1930	750	1,250	1,750
Fauset, Jessie Redmon. THERE IS CONFUSION. New York, 1924	100	150	2,500
Faust, Frederick. ONE OF CLEOPATRA'S NIGHTS. Berkeley, 1914. 15-page pamphlet	—	—	750

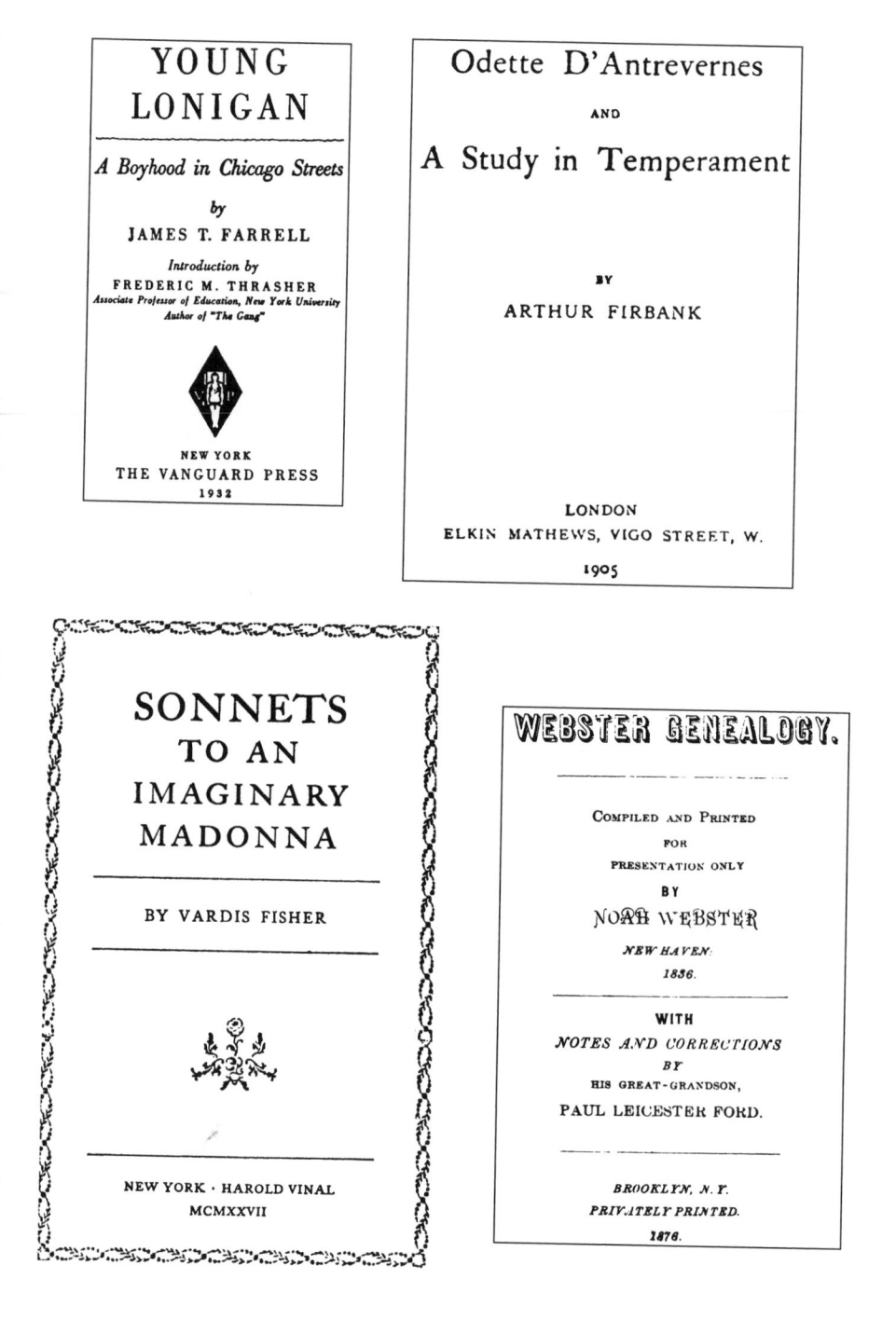

YOUNG
LONIGAN

A Boyhood in Chicago Streets

by
JAMES T. FARRELL

Introduction by
FREDERIC M. THRASHER
Associate Professor of Education, New York University
Author of "The Gang"

NEW YORK
THE VANGUARD PRESS
1932

Odette D'Antrevernes

AND

A Study in Temperament

BY

ARTHUR FIRBANK

LONDON
ELKIN MATHEWS, VIGO STREET, W.

1905

SONNETS
TO AN
IMAGINARY
MADONNA

BY VARDIS FISHER

NEW YORK · HAROLD VINAL
MCMXXVII

WEBSTER GENEALOGY.

COMPILED AND PRINTED
FOR
PRESENTATION ONLY
BY
NOAH WEBSTER
NEW HAVEN:
1836.

WITH
NOTES AND CORRECTIONS
BY
HIS GREAT-GRANDSON,
PAUL LEICESTER FORD.

BROOKLYN, N.Y.
PRIVATELY PRINTED.
1876.

	1986	1995	2000
Also see Max Brand			
Faust, Irvin. ENTERING ANGEL'S WORLD . . . New York, 1963	50	60	60
ROAR LION ROAR +. New York (1964)	40	50	40
Faust, Seymour. THE LOVELY QUARRY. New York, 1958. Wraps	20	25	35
Favil Press. GLEANINGS. By Clifford Bax. Kensington, 1921. (40 copies)	100	200	200
FAVORITE OF NATURE, THE. (Mary Ann Kelty.) London, 1821. 3 volumes	—	400	400
Fearing, Kenneth. ANGEL ARMS. New York, 1929	200	250	250
Feather, Leonard. INSIDE JAZZ (INSIDE BE-BOP). New York (1949). Wraps	125	125	150
Feibleman, James. DEATH OF THE GOD IN MEXICO. New York (1931)	150	200	250
Feibleman, Peter S. A PLACE WITHOUT TWILIGHT. Cleveland (1958)	50	60	75
London (1958)	—	—	50
Feiffer, Jules. SICK, SICK, SICK. New York, 1958	40	50	35
London (1959). First hardback edition	—	—	35
Feikema, Feike. (Frederick Manfred.) THE GOLDEN BOWL. St. Paul, 1944	100	125	75
Feinstein, Elaine. IN A GREEN EYE. (London, 1966.) 30 signed and numbered copies	60	100	200
Wraps	—	—	75
Feinstein, Isidor. *See* I. F. Stone			
Feist, Raymond. MAGICIAN. Garden City, 1982	—	—	350
Feldman, Irving (Mordecai). WORKS AND DAYS +. Boston (1961)	75	75	75
London (1961)	60	60	60
Fenollosa, Ernest Francisco. EAST AND WEST. New York, 1893	—	250	250
Fenton, James. OUR WESTERN FURNITURE. Oxford (1968). Wraps. 200 copies	125	300	500
12 signed and numbered copies	—	850	1,250
Ferber, Edna. DAWN O'HARA. New York (1911)	50	125	125
Ferguson, Helen. (Helen Woods, who also used the name Anna Kavan.) A CHARMED CIRCLE. London (1929)	350	350	450

	1986	1995	2000
Ferlinghetti, Lawrence. PICTURES OF THE GONE WORLD. San Francisco (1955). 25 signed hardbound copies.	500	750	1,000
Wraps. (500 copies) (Price: 65¢) (First City Lights book.)	200	350	450
Fermor, Patrick Leigh. THE TRAVELLER'S TREE. London, 1950 (Preceded by a 1938 translation.)	60	200	250
Ferrell, Anderson. WHERE SHE WAS. New York, 1985	25	25	35
Ferrier, Susan E. MARRIAGE, A NOVEL. Edinburgh/London, 1818. 3 volumes	300	400	400
Ferril, Thomas Hornsby. HIGH PASSAGE. New York, 1926	75	75	100
Ferrini, Vincent. NO SMOKE. Portland, 1941	50	100	100
Fessier, Michael. FULLY DRESSED AND IN HIS RIGHT MIND. New York, 1935	50	50	100
Fetherston, Patrick. DAY OFF. (London, 1955.) Wraps	—	40	40
Fiacc, Patraic. BY THE BLACK STREAM . . . (Dublin, 1969). Wraps in dustwrapper	—	—	75
Ficke, Arthur Davidson (and Thomas Newell Metcalf). THEIR BOOK. (Chicago, 1901.) 50 numbered copies	150	1,000	1,000
FROM THE ISLES. (Surrey) 1907. Wraps	100	400	400
Fiedler, Leslie (Aaron). AN END TO INNOCENCE. Boston (1955)	25	40	40
Field, Ben. THE COCK'S FUNERAL. New York (1937)	40	40	50
Field, Edward. STAND UP, FRIEND, WITH ME. New York (1963)	20	25	35
Field, Eugene. TRIBUNE PRIMER. (Denver, 1881.) Wraps	5,000	7,500	7,500
Brooklyn, 1882	300	400	400
THE MODEL PRIMER. Brooklyn (1882)	—	350	350
Field, Peter. (Laura and Francis Hobson.) OUTLAWS THREE. New York, 1934	250	350	350
DRY GULCH ADAMS. New York, 1934	250	300	300
Field, Rachel Lyman. RISE UP, JENNIE SMITH. New York (1918). Wraps	125	250	250
Fielding, Gabriel. *See* Alan Barnsley			
Fielding, Sarah. THE ADVENTURES OF DAVID SIMPLE. London, 1744. 2 volumes	—	1,000	1,250

	1986	1995	2000
Fields, James T(homas). ANNIVERSARY POEM . . . Boston, 1838. In original wraps	50	125	125
POEMS. Boston, 1849	50	75	175
Fields, w. c. FIELDS FOR PRESIDENT. New York, 1940	—	600	600
FIGHT AT DAME EUROPA'S SCHOOL. Philadelphia, 1871. (First book illustrated by Thomas Nast.) Written anonymously by H. W. Pullen	100	200	150
New York, 1871	—	—	75
Finch, Amanda. BACK TRAIL . . . New York, 1951. Wraps	50	50	50
Findley, Timothy. THE LAST OF THE CRAZY PEOPLE. London, 1967	—	250	250
New York (1967)	—	—	75
Finkel, Donald. SIMEON. New York, 1964	—	75	75
Finlay, Ian H(amilton). THE SEA-BED +. Edinburgh (1958). Wraps in dustwrapper	200	250	750
Finley, Karen. SHOCK TREATMENT. San Francisco (1990). Wraps	—	35	35
Finney, Charles G. THE CIRCUS OF DR. LAO. New York, 1935	175	300	450
Lunenberg: Limited Editions Club, 1982. In slipcase	—	—	150
Newark: Janus Press, 1984. One of 150 copies	—	—	2,500
Finney, Jack. (Walter Braden Finney.) 5 AGAINST THE HOUSE. Garden City, 1954	75	150	500
Finney, Sterling (E. B. White). LESS THAN NOTHING . . . New York (1927). Issued without dustwrapper	250	350	750
Firbank, (Arthur Annesly) Ronald. ODETTE D'ANTRE-VERNES and A STUDY IN TEMPERAMENT. London, 1905. 10 large paper copies on vellum. Signed	1,000	2,500	4,000
Wraps. (500 copies)	250	500	750
FIRE OVER LONDON . . . (William Sansom.) London, 1941. Wraps	—	175	175
FIRST LESSONS IN GRAMMAR . . . (Elizabeth Peabody.) Boston, 1830	150	250	300
Fish, Donald. AIRLINE DETECTIVE. London, 1962. (Ian Fleming introduction)	75	100	100
Fish, Robert L(loyd). THE FUGITIVE. New York, 1962	50	60	125
Fisher, Alfred Young. THE GHOST IN THE UNDERBLOWS. Los Angeles, 1940. (300 copies)	125	125	350

	1986	1995	2000
Fisher, Bud (Harry Conway). THE MUTT AND JEFF CARTOONS. Boston, 1910	100	250	150
Fisher, M(ary) F(rances) K(ennedy). SERVE IT FORTH. New York, 1937	150	500	600
Fisher, Roy. CITY. Worcester, 1961. Wraps	75	100	100
Fisher, Rudolph. THE WALLS OF JERICHO. New York, 1928	—	—	2,500
Fisher, Steve. *See* Lane, Grant			
Fisher, Tibor. UNDER THE FROG. Edinburgh (1992). Wraps (paperback original)	—	—	75
New York (1992). First hardcover edition	—	—	35
Fisher, Vardis. SONNETS TO AN IMAGINARY MADONNA. New York, 1927	150	300	350
Fisher, William. THE WAITERS. Cleveland (1953)	35	100	100
Fiske, John. TOBACCO AND ALCOHOL. New York, 1869	50	300	750
Fitch, Ensign Clarke (Upton Sinclair). SAVED BY THE ENEMY. New York, 1898	200	600	750
Fitch, George. THE BIG STRIKE AT SIWASH. New York, 1909	60	60	30
Fitch, (William) Clyde. THE KNIGHTING OF THE TWINS +. Boston (1891)	150	150	100
Fitts, Dudley. TWO POEMS. No place (1932.) Wraps. (100 signed copies)	125	150	150
FitzGerald, Edward. *See* EUPHRANOR . . .			
Fitzgerald, F(rancis) Scott (Key). THIS SIDE OF PARADISE. New York, 1920. (Published April 1920 and Scribner seal.)	3K	7.5K	12.5K
Third printing has signed "Author's Apology" London (1921)	—	—	3,000
(Four previous musical scores.)	—	—	3,500
Fitzgerald, Robert (Stuart). POEMS. New York (1935)	75	125	125
Fitzgerald, Zelda. SAVE ME THE WALTZ. New York, 1932. (3,010 copies)	600	1,250	2,500
London (1953)	60	125	350
Fitzgibbon, Constantine. THE ARIAN BIRD. London, 1949	50	75	75
FIVE YOUNG AMERICAN POETS. Norfolk (1940). (John Berryman, et al.) (800 copies.) Considered Berryman's first book as the five "books" were combined by publisher. Gray-blue cloth. Also navy-blue cloth variant	200	300	400

	1986	1995	2000
Flaccus, Kimball. IN PRAISE OF MARA. Hanover, 1932. Wraps. (100 copies in total.) 25 signed and numbered copies	—	200	200
75 unsigned copies	100	100	100
AVALANCHE OF APRIL. New York, 1934	50	50	60
Flagg, Fannie. COMING ATTRACTIONS. New York (1981)	—	60	75
Flaherty, Robert. MY ESKIMO FRIENDS. New York, 1924	300	450	450
Flanagan, Mary. BAD GIRLS. London, 1984	—	40	40
Flanner, Hildegarde. YOUNG GIRL. Berkeley (1920). Wraps	—	—	250
THIS MORNING. New York, 1921. Wraps	—	200	175
Flanner, Janet. THE CUBICAL CITY. New York, 1926	350	1,000	1,250
Flecker, James (Elroy). THE BEST MAN EIGHT'S WEEK. Oxford, 1906. Wraps	300	300	350
THE BRIDGE OF FIRE: POEMS. London, 1907. Wraps. First issue: no quote from *Sunday Times*	125	125	200
Fleetwood, Hugh. A PAINTER OF FLOWERS. London, 1972	40	40	40
Fleming, Ian (Lancaster). CASINO ROYALE. London, 1953. Dustwrapper without *Sunday Times* review on front flap	1,250	4,500	10K
Second printing with review	—	—	1,500
New York, 1954	300	1,000	2,500
Fleming, Oliver (Philip and Ronald MacDonald). AMBRO-TOX AND LIMPING DICK. London, 1920	150	300	1,000
Fleming, Peter. BRAZILIAN ADVENTURE. London (1933)	75	125	150
New York, 1934	—	75	75
Flender, Harold. PARIS BLUES. New York (1957)	30	50	75
Fletcher, J(oseph) S(mith). ANDREWLINA. London, 1889	50	75	350
Fletcher, John Gould. FIRE AND WINE. London (1913) (First or second book—there were five published in 1913.)	100	125	150
THE DOMINANT CITY. London, 1913	—	175	200
Flexner, Hortense. CLOUDS AND COBBLESTONES. Boston, 1920	—	60	100
Flint, F. S. IN THE NET OF THE STARS. London, 1909	125	125	125
Flint, Timothy. A SERMON, PREACHED . . . Newburyport, 1808. Wraps	150	300	400

	1986	1995	2000
Flower, Robin. ERIE +. London (1910). Wraps	60	75	125
Flynn, Errol. SHOWDOWN. New York, 1946	—	75	200
Flynn, Robert. NORTH TO YESTERDAY. New York, 1967	40	40	60
Follett, Ken(neth Martin). *See* Symon Myles. *See also* Zachary Stone			
Foote, Horton. HARRISON, TEXAS: EIGHT TELEVISION PLAYS. New York (1956)	60	75	125
THE CHASE. New York (1956). Issued the same day as the foregoing book (Privately printed play(s) precede.)	40	75	150
Foote, John Tintor. BLISTER JONES. Indianapolis (1913)	50	60	40
Foote, Shelby. THE MERCHANT OF BRISTOL. (Greenville, 1947.) Wraps. 260 signed and numbered copies	350	600	750
TOURNAMENT. New York, 1949	75	175	250
Forbes, Bryan. TRUTH LIES SLEEPING. London (1950)	75	75	75
Forbes, Colin. TRAMP IN ARMOUR. London, 1969	—	—	75
New York, 1970	—	—	30
Forbes, Esther. O GENTEEL LADY. Boston, 1926	—	—	75
Forbes, Leslie. BOMBAY ICE. London (1998). Wraps	—	—	125
	—	—	25
New York (1998)	—	—	35
Forché, Carolyn. GATHERING THE TRIBES. New Haven, 1976. Cloth	—	125	350
Wraps	—	35	75
Ford, Charles Henry. THE YOUNG AND THE EVIL. (Written with Parker Tyler.) Paris (1933). (First book for both.) Wraps. 50 numbered copies	400	600	1,000
Trade edition	250	300	500
A PAMPHLET OF SONNETS. Majorca, 1936. (50 copies signed by Ford and Pavel Tchelitchew, the illustrator)	250	450	750
Unsigned	—	250	350
THE GARDEN OF DISORDER +. London (1938). (30 signed copies.) Issued without dustwrapper	250	300	400
460 unsigned copies	100	150	150
Norfolk (1938). English edition in New Directions dust-wrapper	100	150	175

Ford, Ford Madox. *See* Ford Madox Hueffer

	1986	1995	2000
Ford, G. M. WHO IN HELL IS WANDA FUCA? New York (1985)	—	—	100
Ford, Jesse Hill. MOUNTAINS OF GILEAD. Boston, 1961	40	75	75
Ford, Leslie. (Mrs. Zenith Jones Brown.) *See* David Frome			
Ford, Paul Leicester. WEBSTER GENEALOGY . . . NEW HAVEN 1836. Brooklyn, 1876. Notes by Ford. (250 copies) Wraps	150	200	250
THE BEST LAID PLANS. Brooklyn, 1889	50	75	75
Ford, Richard. A PIECE OF MY HEART. New York, 1976	35	200	400
London, 1987	—	75	100
Fordham, Mary Weston. MAGNOLIA LEAVES. Tuskegee (1897). Introduction by Booker T. Washington	100	300	750
Foreman, L. L. DON DESPERADO. New York, 1941	—	—	75
Foreman, Michael. THE PERFECT PRESENT. London, 1967	—	125	125
Forester, C. S. A PAWN AMONG KINGS. London, 1924	750	1,500	3,500
Toronto, 1924	—	—	1,750
FORESTERS, AN AMERICAN TALE, THE. (By Jeremy Belknap.) Boston, 1792. 3 variants, no priority (Preceded by THE HISTORY OF NEW HAMPSHIRE . . . and a number of broadsides.)	—	600	1,000
Forrest, Felix C. (Paul Linebarger.) RIA. New York (1947) (Most books under Cordwainer Smith.)	75	100	125
Forrest, Leon. THERE IS A TREE MORE ANCIENT THAN EDEN. New York (1973)	—	50	75
Forster, E(dward) M(organ). WHERE ANGELS FEAR TO TREAD. Edinburgh, 1905. First issue: title not stated in ads. (1,050 copies)	500	1,750	2,500
Second issue: title in ads	150	1,250	1,500
New York, 1920. In dustwrapper	—	—	350
Forsyth, Frederick. THE BIAFRA STORY. (Middlesex, 1969.) Wraps	75	125	175
THE DAY OF THE JACKAL. London (1971)	75	150	175
New York, 1971	35	75	75
Fort, Charles. THE OUTCAST MANUFACTURERS. New York, 1909. First issue: blue ribbed cloth lettered in gold	150	200	200
Second issue: blue mesh cloth lettered in red	125	150	100
FORTRESS OF SORRENTO, THE. (Mordecai M. Noah.) New York,1808. Wraps	300	750	1,000
Rebound	—	250	350

	1986	1995	2000
Foster, Michael. FORGIVE ADAM . . . New York, 1935	60	60	50
FOUR ELEGIES . . . (John Scott.) London, 1760	—	500	500
Fowler, Earlene. FOOL'S PUZZLE. New York (1994)	—	—	40
Fowler, Gene. TRUMPET IN THE DUST. New York (1930)	—	125	125
Fowles, John. THE COLLECTOR. London, 1963. First issue: dustwrapper flap without reviews	650	750	750
Boston (1963)	100	125	125
Fox, John (William). A CUMBERLAND VENDETTA. New York, 1896. First issue: final entry in contents is "Hell Fer Sartain"	50	200	250
Second issue: final entry is "Hell—Fer-Sartain Creeek"	—	125	150
Fox, Len. GUM LEAVES AND BAMBOO. (New South Wales, 1959)	—	100	100
Fox, Paula. POOR GEORGE. New York (1967)	50	125	100
Fox, William Price. SOUTHERN FRIED. Greenwich (1962). Wraps	35	50	50
Fraenkel, Michael. *See* ANONYMOUS and WERTHER'S . . .			
Frame, Janet. THE LAGOON. Christchurch (1951)	300	450	1,250
OWLS DO CRY. London, 1961	—	100	125
Francis, Dick (Richard Stanley). SPORT OF QUEENS. London, 1957	200	950	1,000
DEAD CERT. London, 1962	450	3,000	7,500
New York (1962)	150	1,000	1,500
New York, 1989. 26 signed and lettered copies in slipcase	—	250	350
100 signed and numbered copies	—	100	150
Francis, Robert. STAND WITH ME HERE. New York, 1936	60	175	175
Francome, John, and MacGregor, James. EAVESDROPPER (London, 1986.)	—	—	50
Frank, Anne. THE DIARY OF ANNE FRANK. Garden City, 1952. First edition stated	—	—	300
Frank, Pat. MR. ADAM. New York, 1946	—	50	50
Frank, Robert. (Photographs.) FROM INCAS TO INDIOS. New York, 1956	—	125	125
London, 1956	—	125	125
Frank, Waldo. THE UNWELCOME MAN. Boston, 1917	125	125	125
Frankau, Gilbert. ETON ECHOES. Eton, 1901. Wraps	100	125	125

	1986	1995	2000
Frankenberg, Lloyd. THE RED KITE. New York (1939). (500 copies)	40	60	60
FRANKENSTEIN. (Mary Wollstonecraft Shelley.) London, 1818. 3 volumes. (Over $100,000 in original boards.)	15K	35K	50K
London, 1831. Third edition with new preface	—	—	6K
Philadelphia, 1833. 2 volumes. First U.S. edition	—	—	5K
New York: Grosset & Dunlap (1931). Photoplay edition	—	—	1,750
Fraser, Antonia. *See* Antonia Pakenham			
Fraser, G. S. THE FATAL LANDSCAPE. (London, 1943.) Wraps	—	125	175
Fraser, George MacDonald. FLASHMAN. London (1969)	60	200	250
New York, 1969	—	125	150
Frayn, Michael. THE DAY OF THE DOG. London, 1962	—	75	75
Frazer, Sir James George. TOTEMISM. Edinburgh, 1887	125	350	400
Frazier, Charles. COLD MOUNTAIN. New York (1997). First state: "looking like a man-woman" on p. 25 line 16	—	—	150
New York, 1997. 500 signed and numbered. Not issued for sale. Issued in slipcase	—	—	750
Frazier, Ian. DATING YOUR MOM. New York (1986)	—	30	30
Frederic, Harold. SETH'S BROTHER'S WIFE. New York, 1887. First issue: copyright 1886 and no ads	150	300	300
Frederick, John T. GREEN BUSH. New York, 1925	—	60	60
Freeling, Nicolas. LOVE IN AMSTERDAM. London, 1962	60	100	250
Freeman, Arthur. IZMIR. (Cambridge, 1959). Wraps	—	75	100
Freeman, Gillian. THE LIBERTY MAN. London, 1955	40	40	40
Freeman, John. TWENTY POEMS. London, 1909. Wraps	60	60	75
Freeman, Mary E. Wilkins. *See* Mary E. Wilkins			
Freeman, R(ichard) Austin. TRAVELS AND LIFE IN ASHANTI AND JAPAN. London, 1898	750	1,250	1,250
Also see Clifford Ashdown			
Freemantle, Brian. GOODBYE TO AN OLD FRIEND. London, 1973	—	—	75
New York (1973)	—	—	60

	1986	1995	2000
French, Albert. BILLY. New York (1993)	—	—	60
French, Nicci. THE MEMORY GAME. London (1997)	—	—	50
Freneau, Philip (Morin). *See* A POEM, ON THE RISING GLORY . . .			
THE AMERICAN VILLAGE. New York, 1772	—	2,000	2,500
Freud, Anna. INTRODUCTION TO THE TECHNIC OF CHILD ANALYSIS. New York, 1928. First English translation	—	—	200
Freud, Sigmund. THE INTERPRETATION OF DREAMS. New York, 1913	150	1,000	1,500
Fried, Erich. THEY FIGHT IN THE DARK. (London, 1944.) Wraps	75	100	100
Friedan, Betty. THE FEMININE MYSTIQUE. New York (1963)	40	125	250
Friedman, Bruce Jay. THE RASCAL'S GUIDE. New York (1958). Wraps. Edited by B.J.F.	—	35	40
STERN. New York, 1962.			
(Previous edited anthology)	50	75	100
Friedman, I. K. THE LUCKY NUMBER. Chicago, 1896	75	100	150
Friedman, Kinky. GREENWICH KILLING TIME. New York, 1986	—	30	75
Friedman, Mickey. HURRICANE SEASON. New York, 1983	—	50	40
Friedman, Sanford. TOTEMPOLE. New York, 1965	—	—	50
Frome, David. (Zenith Jones Brown.) THE MURDER OF AN OLD MAN. London, 1929	75	200	300
Fromm, Erich. ESCAPE FROM FREEDOM. New York, 1941	—	—	200
Frost, A(rthur) B(urdette). STUFF AND NONSENSE. New York (1884). Boards	100	175	150
Also see Max Adeler			
Frost, Robert (Lee). TWILIGHT. (Lawrence, Massachusetts, 1894). 2 known copies	40K	50K	75K
Charlottesville, 1966. Facsimile wraps. 20 copies on hand-made paper	—	350	500
150 copies	—	150	250

	1986	1995	2000
A BOY'S WILL. London, 1913. First issue: brown or bronze cloth with lettering in gilt, edges rough-cut	1,250	5,000	7,500
Vellum-paper boards stamped in red	350	2,500	3,500
Cream linen-paper wraps, stamped in black without border rule; 8-petaled flower ornament	—	1,500	2,500
With 4-petaled flower ornament	—	1,250	1,750
135 signed and numbered copies of above	—	1,750	3,000
New York, 1915. "aind" for "and" in last line on p. 14	350	600	600
Above in dustwrapper	—	—	2,000
"and" corrected on p. 14	—	250	250
Fruchter, Norman. COAT UPON A STICK. (London, 1962)	50	50	50
Fry, Christopher. THE BOY WITH A CART . . . London, 1939. Wraps	75	250	250
New York, 1951	—	—	35
Fry, Roger E. GIOVANNI BELLINI. London, 1899	75	150	150
Frye, Northrop. FEARFUL SYMMETRY: A STUDY OF WILLIAM BLAKE. Princeton, New Jersey, 1947	—	125	125
Fuchs, Daniel. SUMMER IN WILLIAMSBURG. New York (1934)	200	1,250	1,500
London (1935)	125	350	500
FUCK THE SYSTEM. (By Abbie Hoffman.) (New York, 1967.) No publisher. Stapled wraps	75	150	500
Fuentes, Carlos. WHERE THE AIR IS CLEAR. New York (1960)	30	75	125
Fugard, Athol. THE BLOOD KNOT. Johannesburg, 1963. (Issued without dustwrapper)	200	300	300
New York, 1964	—	75	125
Fugard, Sheila. THE CASTAWAYS. Johannesburg, 1972	—	125	125
FULL VINDICATION OF THE MEASURES OF THE CONGRESS . . . , A. (Alexander Hamilton.) New York, 1774	—	4K	10K
Fuller, Henry Black. *See* Stanton Page			
Fuller, John. FAIRGROUND MUSIC. London, 1961	25	25	25
Fuller, R(ichard) Buckminster. NINE CHAINS TO THE MOON. Philadelphia (1938)	150	200	350
Fuller, Roy (Broadbent). POEMS. London (1939)	150	150	150
Fuller, S(arah) M(argaret). CONVERSATIONS WITH GOETHE. Boston, 1839. (Translated by Fuller). In original cloth	500	500	1,500
Rebound	—	—	500
SUMMER ON THE LAKES . . . Boston/New York, 1844	300	300	600
Boston/New York, 1845. Wraps	75	100	750

	1986	1995	2000
Furman, Garrit. RURAL HOURS. No place, 1824. Boards	125	150	150
Fussell, Paul. THEORY OF PROSODY IN EIGHTEENTH-CENTURY ENGLAND. New London, Connecticut, 1954. Wraps	40	75	100
Futrelle, Jacques. THE CHASE OF THE GOLDEN PLATE. New York, 1906	200	200	200
Fyfield, Frances. (Frances Hegarty.) A QUESTION OF GUILT. London, 1988	—	60	60
New York, 1989	—	25	35

G

	1986	1995	2000
Gaddis, Thomas E. BIRDMAN OF ALCATRAZ. New York (1955)	35	75	75
London (1962)	—	50	50
Gaddis, William. THE RECOGNITIONS. New York (1955)	200	500	600
London (1962)	—	150	200
Gág, Wanda. MILLIONS OF CATS. New York, 1928. 250 signed and numbered copies with original engraving. Issued in slipcase	350	1,000	2,500
Trade edition in dustwrapper	125	350	750
Gaines, Charles. STAY HUNGRY. New York, 1972	20	25	50
Gaines, Ernest J. CATHERINE CARMIER. New York, 1964	125	350	750
Gaitskill, Mary. BAD BEHAVIOR. New York, 1988	—	40	50
Gale, Zona. ROMANCE ISLAND. Indianapolis (1906)	50	100	100
Gallagher, Stephen. CHIMERA. New York (1982)	—	—	150
Gallagher, Tess. STEPPING OUTSIDE. Lisbon, Iowa (1974). Cloth	—	750	1,500
Wraps	—	300	600
Gallant, Mavis. THE OTHER PARIS. Boston, 1956	75	125	125
London (1957). (Len Deighton dustwrapper)	—	75	100
Gallico, Paul (William). FAREWELL TO SPORT. New York, 1938	150	200	250
THE ADVENTURES OF HIRAM HOLIDAY. New York, 1939	150	250	250
Gallup, George. SURVEY OF READER INTEREST. No place, 1931. Wraps	—	—	150
Galouye, Daniel F. DARK UNIVERSE. New York (1961). Wraps	—	—	25
London (1962). First hardback	—	—	250
Boston, 1976. First U.S. hardback	—	—	40

Galsworthy, John. *See* John Sinjohn

	1986	1995	2000
Gann, Ernest. ALL-AMERICAN AIRCRAFT. New York, 1941	—	—	150
García, Cristina. DREAMING IN CUBAN. New York, 1992	—	—	40
García Lorca, Federico. BITTER OLEANDER. London, 1935	150	200	250
García Márquez, Gabriel. NO ONE WRITES THE COLONEL +. New York (1968). Dustwrapper with photo by Jerry Bauer	125	600	600
Dustwrapper with photo by Rodrigo Moya	—	—	400
(London, 1971)	—	350	350
Gardiner, John Rolf. GREAT DREAM OF HEAVEN. New York, 1974	—	60	60
Gardner, Erle Stanley. THE CASE OF THE VELVET CLAWS. New York, 1932	1,000	3,500	4,500
Gardner, Isabella (Stewart). BIRTHDAYS FROM THE OCEAN. Cambridge, 1955	35	50	50
Gardner, John (Champlin). THE FORMS OF FICTION. New York, 1962. (Written with Lennis Dunlap.) Issued without dustwrapper	125	150	125
Gardner, John (Edmund). SPIN THE BOTTLE. London (1964)	75	125	150
THE LIQUIDATOR. London, 1964	50	75	100
DRAGON, DRAGON +. No place. (Christmas, 1962.) Mimeographed pages in stiff boards	1,500	1,500	2,000
THE MILLER'S MULE +. No place. 1965. Mimeographed pages in stiff boards	1,000	1,000	1,500
THE COMPLETE WORKS OF THE GAWAIN POET. Chicago (1965). Translated by Gardner	200	300	350
THE RESURRECTION. (New York, 1966)	450	500	500
(Ph.D. dissertation prior to 1962)			
Gardner, Leonard. FAT CITY. New York (1969)	25	50	50
Garfield, Brian. RANGE JUSTICE. New York, 1960	—	75	125
Garland, (Hannibal) Hamlin. UNDER THE WHEEL. Boston, 1890. Wraps	250	500	600
MAIN TRAVELED ROADS. Boston, 1891. Gray printed wraps with "First Thousand" at bottom	100	250	400
Blue or gray cloth with sheets bulking ⅞″	—	—	200
Chicago, 1893. 110 large paper copies	75	250	300

	1986	1995	2000
Garner, Alan. THE WEIRDSTONE OF BRISINGAMEN. London, 1960	—	450	500
New York, 1960	—	—	125
Garner, Claud. WETBACK. New York (1947)	—	—	50
Garnett, David. THE KITCHEN GARDEN . . . London (1909). Wraps. (Translated and adapted by DG from French work of Prof. Gressent)	150	300	300
Also see Leda Burke			
Garnett, Edward. THE PARADOX CLUB. London, 1888	40	150	125
Garnett, Richard. *See* PRIMULA			
Garrett, George (Palmer). KING OF THE MOUNTAIN. New York (1957)	0	75	100
Garrett, (Gordon) Randall. *See* Robert Randall			
Garrigue, Jean. THE EGO AND THE CENTAUR. (Norfolk, 1947)	35	50	50
Garson, Barbara. MACBIRD. Independent Socialist Club. (Berkeley, 1966.) Legal sheets mimeographed and stapled	35	125	125
(Berkeley, 1966.) Wraps		25	35
Garth, Will. LAWLESS GUNS. New York, 1937 (House name attributed to Henry Kuttner.)	—	250	300
Garve, Andrew (Paul Winterton). NO TEARS FOR HILDA. London, 1950	50	75	75
New York, 1950	—	40	40
Gary, Romain. THE COMPANY OF MEN. New York, 1950	50	60	60
Gascoyne, David. ROMAN BALCONY +. London, 1932	750	1,500	1,500
Gash, Jonathan. *See* STREETWALKER			
PONTIFF. (London, 1971)	—	—	1,000
THE JUDAS PAIR. London, 1977. (First mystery)	—	200	600
New York, 1977	—	75	200
Gaskell, Elizabeth C. *See* MARY BARTON . . .			
Gaskell, Jane. STRANGE EVIL. London, 1957	50	60	125
Gass, William H(oward). OMENSETTER'S LUCK. (New York, 1966)	125	200	200
London, 1967	75	100	100
Gasset, José Ortega. *See* Ortega y Gassett, José			

	1986	1995	2000
Gathorne-Hardy, Robert. LACEBURY MANOR. London, 1930	100	100	100
Gault, William Campbell. DON'T CRY FOR ME. New York, 1952	35	100	100
Gavin, Ewart. POEMS AND SONGS. New York, 1939	—	100	100
Gavin, Thomas. KING-KILL. New York, 1977	20	25	35
Gawsworth, John (Fytton Armstrong). *See* Scrannel, Orpheus			
CONFESSION VERSE. London, 1931. 12 numbered copies in boards	—	—	150
One of 250 copies in wraps	—	—	75
Geddes, Virgil. FORTY POEMS. Paris (1926). Wraps	75	125	125
Gee, Maurice. THE BIG SEASON. London, 1962	60	60	60
Geertz, Clifford. THE RELIGION OF JAVA. Glencoe, 1960	—	75	175
Geismar, Maxwell. WRITERS IN CRISIS. Boston, 1942	35	35	35
Gelber, Jack. THE CONNECTION. New York (1960). Wraps	35	40	40
London (1961). Cloth	30	40	40
Geller, Stephen. SHE LET HIM CONTINUE. New York, 1960	—	40	40
Gellhorn, Martha (Ellis). WHAT MAD PURSUIT. New York, 1934	125	200	200
Genet, Jean. OUR LADY OF THE FLOWERS. Paris (1949). (475 copies.) Imitation red or blue morocco, without dustwrapper	150	250	250
GENIUS OF OBLIVION. By a Lady of New Hampshire (Sarah Josepha Hale). Concord, 1823	125	400	400
Gent, Peter. NORTH DALLAS FORTY. New York, 1973	25	40	40
Genthe, Arnold. PICTURES OF OLD CHINATOWN. New York, 1908. (Text by Will Irwin)	125	200	250
New York, 1913	—	350	200
Gentle, Mark S(yminton). LORDS OF THE STARSHIP. London (1971)	—	—	250
Gentle, Mary. A HAWK IN SILVER. London (1977)	—	—	75
GEORGE BALCOMBE. (Nathaniel Beverly Tucker.) New York, 1836. 2 volumes	100	100	100
GEORGE AND LURLEEN WALLACE. (Asa Forest Carter.) (Centre, Alabama, 1967.) Stapled wraps	—	450	600

	1986	1995	2000
George, Elizabeth. A GREAT DELIVERANCE. New York (1988)	—	60	75
London (1989)	—	—	60
George, Henry. OUR LAND AND LAND POLICY . . . San Francisco, 1871. (Map in black and red)	600	1,000	1,250
GEORGIA SCENES, CHARACTERS, INCIDENTS, ETC. . . . (Augustine Baldwin Longstreet.) Augusta 1835	1,500	3,000	3,000
Second edition. New York, 1840. Illustrated	200	350	350
Gerhardi, William (Alexander). FUTILITY. London (1922)	175	200	250
New York (1922)	125	150	200
Gernsback, Hugo. RADIO FOR ALL. Philadelphia, 1922	—	150	300
RALPH 124C41 +. Boston, 1925	600	1,500	2,500
Ghiselin, Brewster. AGAINST THE CIRCLE. New York, 1946. (1,250 copies)	50	75	60
Ghose, Zulfikar. THE LOSS OF INDIA. London (1964)	—	—	150
GHOST IN THE BANK OF ENGLAND, THE. (Eden Phillpotts.) London, 1888	500	1,500	1,750
GIANNI JUNE 23RD–APRIL 30TH 1933. (Iris Origo.) (London) 1933	—	250	250
Gibbings, Robert. IORANA! A TAHITIAN JOURNAL. Boston, 1932. 385 signed and numbered copies	250	350	350
Trade edition in slipcase	125	175	200
London, 1932	100	150	150
Gibbons, Euell. STALKING THE WILD ASPARAGUS. New York (1962)	35	40	60
Gibbons, Kaye. ELLEN FOSTER. Chapel Hill, 1987	—	125	125
London (1988)	—	60	60
Gibbons, Stella. THE MOUNTAIN BEAST +. London, 1930. Wraps	60	75	200
Gibbs, Barbara. THE WELL. Albuquerque (1941). Wraps	150	250	250
Gibbs, Wolcott. BIRD LIFE AT THE POLE. New York, 1931	75	175	100
Gibran, Kahlil. THE MADMAN: HIS PARABLES AND POEMS. New York, 1918	75	125	200
Gibson, Charles Dana. DRAWINGS. New York, 1894	200	250	350
Gibson, Richard. MIRROR FOR MAGISTRATES. London (1958)	—	60	200

	1986	1995	2000
Gibson, Walter B. AFTER DINNER TRICKS. Columbus, Ohio, 1921	—	100	200
Also see Maxwell Grant			
Gibson, W(ilfrid) W(ilson). URLYN THE HARPER +. London, 1902. Wraps	150	200	200
Gibson, William. I LAY IN ZION. New York, 1947. Wraps	35	75	100
A WINTER CROOK. New York, 1948	50	50	40
Gibson, William. NEUROMANCER. New York (1984.) Wraps. (Ace paperback)	—	60	150
London, 1984	—	400	1,000
West Bloomfield, 1986. 375 signed and numbered copies (Origin of the word "cyberpunk")	—	200	450
Gidlow, Elsa. ON A GREY THREAD. Chicago, 1923	50	50	100
Gifford, Barry. KEROUAC'S TOWN . . . Santa Barbara, 1973. Pictorial boards	—	—	100
Wraps	—	—	40
Gifford, Thomas. THE WIND CHILL FACTOR. New York (1975)	—	—	125
Gilb, Dagoberto. WINNERS ON THE PASS LINE. El Paso (1985). Wraps. (No hardbound edition)	—	—	100
Gilbert, Anthony (Lucy Beatrice Malleson) *See* Keith, J. Kilmeny			
THE TRAGEDY AT FREYNE. London, 1927. Third book, first under the name Gilbert	—	—	500
New York, 1927	—	—	350
Gilbert, Jack. VIEWS OF JEOPARDY. New Haven, 1962	—	—	750
Gilbert, Mercedes. AUNT SARA'S WOODEN GOD. Boston (1938)	—	—	750
Gilbert, Michael (Francis). CLOSE QUARTERS. London, 1947	150	250	500
Gilbert, Ruth. LAZARUS +. Wellington, 1949. 65 signed and numbered copies	100	150	200
Gilbert, W(illiam) S(chwenk). A NEW AND ORIGINAL EXTRAVAGANZA ENTITLED DULCAMARA . . . London, 1866. Wraps	750	1,000	1,250
Gilbreth, Frank B(unker). CHEAPER BY THE DOZEN. New York, 1948. (Written with Carey)	25	50	175
Gilchrist, Ellen. THE LAND SURVEYOR'S DAUGHTER. (Fayetteville) 1979. Wraps	75	500	750

	1986	1995	2000
IN THE LAND OF DREAMY DREAMS. Fayetteville, 1981. Cloth	200	850	850
Wraps. (1,000 copies)	75	150	150
(London, 1982)	—	75	50
Gilder, Richard Watson. THE NEW DAY . . . New York, 1876	50	60	250
Gill, Brendan. DEATH IN APRIL +. Windham, Connecticut, 1935. (160 copies)	150	200	300
Gill, Eric. SERVING AT MASS. Sussex, 1916. Wraps	1,200	1,500	1,750
Gilliatt, Penelope. ONE BY ONE. London, 1965	—	75	125
New York, 1965	—	40	60
Gillilan, Strickland W. INCLUDING FINNIGIN. (Philadelphia, 1908)	100	100	50
Gilman, Charlotte Perkins. *See* Charlotte Perkins			
Gilmore, Millen. SWEET MAN. New York (1930)	75	150	250
London (1930)	—	—	150
Gilpin, Laura. THE PUEBLOS: A CAMERA CHRONICLE. New York, 1941	—	175	200
Gingrich, Arnold. CAST DOWN THE LAUREL. (New York, 1935)	25	50	50
Ginsberg, Allen. HOWL: FOR CARL SOLOMON. San Francisco, 1955. Wraps. (50 mimeographed copies)	5K	7.5K	25K
SIESTA IN BALBA AND RETURN. Icy Cape, Alaska, 1956. Wraps. (56 copies)	3,000	5,000	5,000
HOWL +. San Francisco (1956). Wraps. (COVER PRICE: 75¢)	300	450	2,500
HOWL. San Francisco, 1971. 275 signed copies issued without dustwrapper	150	400	1,000
GINX'S BABY: HIS BIRTH AND OTHER MISFORTUNES. (John Edward Jenkins.) London, 1870	250	250	400
Gioia, Dana. DAILY HOROSCOPE. Iowa City (1982). One of 250 copies in wraps	—	—	125
St. Paul: Graywolf Press (1986). 750 copies hardbound	—	—	100
Wraps	—	—	25
Giono, Jean. HILL OF DESTINY. New York, 1929. First English translation	—	60	75
Giorno, John. POEMS. New York, 1967. 50 signed and numbered copies. Wraps. (Cover by Robert Rauschenberg)	75	200	250
Regular edition in wraps	—	—	50

	1986	1995	2000
Giovanni, Nikki. BLACK FEELNG, BLACK TALK. [Wilmington] (1968). Wraps	75	100	300
[New York, 1969]. Pictorial purple wraps	—	—	100
New York: Morrow (1970). Hardbound in dustwrapper	—	—	75
Gissing, George. WORKERS IN THE DAWN. London, 1880. 3 volumes. (Black endpapers)	1,000	7,500	8,500
Givens, John. SONS OF THE PIONEERS. New York (1977)	—	35	35
Gladstone, William (Ewart). THE STATE IN ITS RELATIONS WITH THE CHURCH. London, 1838	300	500	500
Glasgow, Ellen. *See* THE DESCENDENT			
PHASES OF AN INFERIOR PLANET. New York, 1898. With erratum slip	75	175	175
Glaspell, Susan. THE GLORY OF THE CONQUERED. New York (1909)	60	75	100
Glass, Montague (Marsden). POTASH AND PERLMUTTER. Boston (1910)	40	60	60
Glasser, Ronald J. 365 DAYS. New York (1971)	—	60	60
Glassman, Joyce. COME AND JOIN THE DANCE. New York, 1962	—	—	75
GLENARVON. (Lady Caroline Lamb.) London, 1816. 3 volumes	—	500	1,000
Glover, Mary Baker (Eddy). SCIENCE AND HEALTH ... Boston, 1875. (1,000 copies) First issue: errata slip without index. Seen in black, red or purple cloth	1,500	3,000	3,500
Glück, Louise. FIRSTBORN: POEMS. (New York, 1968.) Cloth	75	175	200
Wraps	30	40	50
London, 1969. 50 signed copies	125	200	300
Trade edition. Cloth	—	—	125
Wraps	20	35	40
Godden, Rumer. CHINESE PUZZLE. London (1936)	150	250	300
Godey, John. (Morton Freedgood.) THE GUN & MRS. SMITH. Garden City (1947)	50	125	150
Godfrey, Dave. DEATH GOES BETTER WITH COCA-COLA. Toronto, 1967	—	100	50
Godoy, José F. WHO DID IT? San Francisco, 1883. Wraps	150	150	200
Godwin, Gail. THE PERFECTIONISTS. New York (1970)	75	200	200
Gogarty, Oliver St. John. *See* ALPHA AND OMEGA			

"A book all dog-lovers will delight in"

CHINESE PUZZLE
by
RUMER GODDEN

	1986	1995	2000
Gogol, Nikolai. *See* HOMELIFE IN RUSSIA			
Goines, Donald. DOPEFIEND. Los Angeles (1971). Wraps with title and subtitle above author's name on cover and without blurb "Greatest living ghetto writer . . ."	—	—	100
Gold, H. L. THE OLD DIE RICH +. New York (1955)	30	30	60
Gold, Herbert. BIRTH OF A HERO. New York, 1951	50	60	60
Gold, Ivan. NICKEL MISERIES. New York (1963) London, 1964	25 25	30 30	40 35
Gold, Michael. (Irving Granich.) JOHN BROWN. New York, 1923	150	150	250
Goldberg, Gerald Jay. THE NATIONAL STANDARD. New York (1968)	30	30	40
Goldberg, R(ube). FOOLISH QUESTIONS. Boston (1909)	100	150	200
Golden, Arthur. MEMOIRS OF A GEISHA. New York (1997)	—	—	100
Golden, Harry. ONLY IN AMERICA. Cleveland (1958)	—	—	35
Golden, Marita. MIGRATIONS OF THE HEART. New York (1983)	—	—	40
Golden Cockerel Press. *See* A. E. COPPARD			
GOLD-HUNTER'S ADVENTURE . . . , THE. (William Henry Thomes.) Boston, 1864	250	250	500
Golding, Louis. SORROW OF WAR. London (1919)	25	35	75
Golding, W(illiam) G(erald). POEMS. London, 1934. Wraps	3,500	4,000	4,000
LORD OF THE FLIES. London (1954). Red cloth Also a trial binding in blue cloth New York (1955)	1,000 — 175	2,000 2,000 750	5,000 5,000 1,000
Goldman, Emma. ANARCHISM +. New York, 1910	125	200	200
Goldman, William. TEMPLE OF GOLD. New York, 1957	100	150	200
Goldring, Douglas. A COUNTRY BOY +. London, 1910. Wraps	50	50	50
Goldsmith, Oliver. *See* James Willington *and* AN ENQUIRY INTO . . .			
Gombrowicz, Witold. PORNOGRAFIA. New York (1966). (First English translation)	—	50	40
Gooch, Mrs. (Elizabeth Sara Villa-Real.) AN APPEAL TO THE PUBLIC . . . London, 1788	—	500	600

	1986	1995	2000
Goodis, David. RETREAT FROM OBLIVION. New York, 1939	—	2,000	2,000
Goodman, Allegra. TOTAL IMMERSION. New York (1989)	—	—	150
Goodman, Mitchell. THE END OF IT. New York: Horizon (1961)	—	—	40
Goodman, Paul. TEN LYRIC POEMS. (New York, 1934.) Wraps	200	400	400
Goodrich, Marcus. DELILAH. New York (1941). Only book	25	35	35
Goodrich, Samuel Griswold. *See* Peter Parley			
Goodwin, Stephen. KIN. New York (1975)	25	40	40
Goodwyn, Frank. THE DEVIL IN TEXAS. Dallas, 1936	—	75	75
Goran, Lester. THE PARATROOPER OF MECHANIC AVENUE. Boston, 1960	30	30	25
Gordimer, Nadine. FACE TO FACE. Johannesburg (1949)	400	1,250	1,000
THE SOFT VOICE OF THE SERPENT. New York, 1952	75	300	250
London (1953)	100	150	150
Gordon, Caroline. PENHALLY. New York, 1931	600	1,500	1,500
Gordon, Giles. PICTURES FROM AN EXHIBITION. London, 1970	—	40	40
Gordon, Mary. FINAL PAYMENTS. New York (1978)	25	40	40
London (1978)	—	35	40
Gordon, Mildred. THE LITTLE MAN WHO WASN'T THERE. Garden City, 1946	35	60	60
Gordon, Taylor. BORN TO BE. New York, 1929. (Covarrubias illustrations.) First issue without dedication	75	150	450
With dedication	—	—	300
Gore-Booth, Eva. POEMS. London, 1898	35	35	35
Gores, Joe (Joseph N.). A TIME OF PREDATORS. New York (1969)	100	125	250
Gorey, Edward. THE UNSTRUNG HARP. New York (1953)	125	200	250
GORGEOUS POETRY. (J. B. [Beachcomber] Morton.) London, 1920	60	100	100
Gorman, Herbert S. THE FOOL OF LOVE. New York (1920). Wraps	—	125	125
Gosling, Paula. A RUNNING DUCK. London, 1978	—	60	50

	1986	1995	2000
Goss, Clay. HOMECOOKIN' FIVE PLAYS. Washington, 1974	—	—	40
Gosse, Edmund. MADRIGALS, SONGS AND SONNETS. London, 1870. (Written with John A. Blaikie)	150	600	600
Gottschalk, Laura Riding. THE CLOSE CHAPLET. London, 1926. Issued without dustwrapper	600	750	750
New York (1926). Tissue dustwrapper	450	500	500
ANATOLE FRANCE AT HOME. By Marcel Le Guff. New York, 1926. (Translated by Gottschalk)	200	250	250
Gough, Laurence. GOLDFISH BOWL. London, 1987	—	125	150
Gould, Gerald. LYRICS. London, 1906. Wraps	35	75	75
Gould, John. A CENTURY OF BIRDS FROM THE HIMALAYA MOUNTAINS. London, (1831) 1832. 80 plates. First issue: backgrounds uncolored	—	12K	17.5K
Second issue: backgrounds colored	—	15K	25K
Gould, Wallace. CHILDREN OF THE SUN . . . Boston (1917)	35	50	50
Gover, (John) Robert. THE ONE HUNDRED DOLLAR MISUNDERSTANDING. London, 1961	50	75	125
New York (1962). Presumed first issue dustwrapper with gold lettering	35	50	50
With green lettering	—	—	40
Gowen, Emmett. MOUNTAIN BORN. Indianapolis (1932)	75	75	75
Goyen, (Charles) William. THE HOUSE OF BREATH. New York (1950)	75	125	150
London, 1951	50	75	75
Goytisolo, Juan. THE YOUNG ASSASSINS. New York, 1958	25	40	60
Grady, James. SIX DAYS OF THE CONDOR. New York (1974)	25	75	125
Grafton, C. W. THE RAT BEGAN TO GNAW THE ROPE. New York, 1943	—	60	450
London, 1944	—	—	250
Grafton, Sue. KEZIAH DANE. New York (1967)	—	500	600
London (1968)	—	200	250
"A" IS FOR ALIBI. New York (1982)	—	950	1,250
(London, 1986)	—	300	350
Graham, Caroline. FIRE DANCE. (London, 1982). Wraps	—	—	100
THE KILLINGS AT BADGER'S DRIFT. London (1987). First Inspector Barnaby mystery	—	—	225
(Bethesda, 1988)	—	50	100

	1986	1995	2000
Graham, John. (David Graham Phillips.) THE GREAT GOD SUC-CESS. New York (1901)	60	100	125
Graham, Jorie. HYBRIDS OF PLANTS AND OF GHOSTS. Princeton (1980). Cloth	—	—	500
Wraps	—	60	75
Graham, R. B. Cunninghame. NOTES ON THE DISTRICT OF MENTIETH. London, 1895. Wraps	150	300	250
Graham, Sheilah. GENTLEMAN-CROOK. London, 1933	75	75	125
Graham, Tom. (Sinclair Lewis). HIKE AND THE AERO-PLANE. New York (1912). First issue: "August 1912" on copyright page. (1,000 copies printed)	200	5,000	6,000
Graham, W(illiam) S(ydney). CAGE WITHOUT GRIEVANCE. Glasgow (1942)	75	300	400
Grahame, Kenneth. PAGAN PAPERS. London, 1894. (Title page designed by Aubrey Beardsley. 615 copies)	150	350	300
Grainger, Francis Edward. *See* Headon Hill			
Granger, Bill. THE NOVEMBER MAN. New York (1979). Wraps	—	60	60

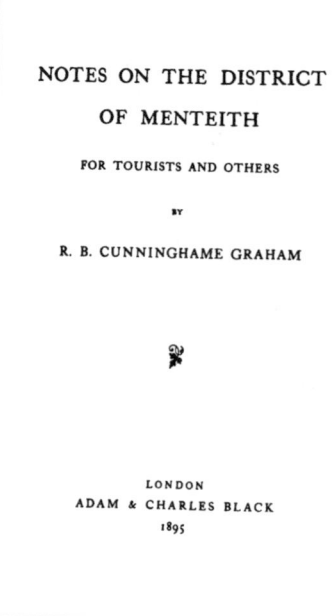

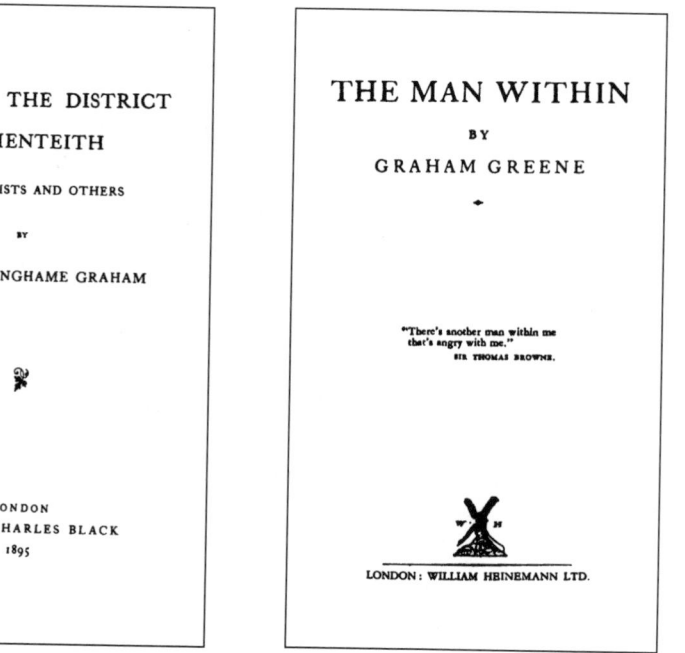

	1986	1995	2000
Grant, Anne. POEMS OF VARIOUS SUBJECTS. Edinburgh, 1803	50	100	150
Grant, J. C. THE ROCK SHOOT. Edinburgh, 1928	35	75	100
Grant, Marie M. ARTISTE. London, 1871. 3 volumes	—	300	350
Grant, Maxwell. (Walter B. Gibson.) THE LIVING SHADOW. New York (1931). (First hardbound of Shadow.) Issued without dustwrapper. (First mystery)	100	250	300
Grass, Günter. THE TIN DRUM. London, 1961	40	75	100
New York (1962)	40	60	75
Grau, Shirley Ann. THE BLACK PRINCE. New York, 1955. Dustwrapper without reviews	60	100	175
With reviews	—	75	100
Graves, Alfred Percival. SONGS OF KILLARNEY. London, 1873	—	125	200
Graves, John. HOME PLACE. Fort Worth, 1958. Wraps. (200 copies)	400	500	500
GOODBYE TO A RIVER. New York, 1960	75	125	150
(Austin) 1989. 500 signed copies. Issued without dustwrapper	—	150	175
Graves, Robert (Ranke). OVER THE BRAZIER. London, 1916. Wraps	1,000	1,250	1,250
London, 1917	—	—	350
London (1920). Second edition with new foreword	400	400	500

OVER THE BRAZIER

BY
ROBERT GRAVES

THE POETRY BOOKSHOP   8ᴰ NET

	1986	1995	2000
Gray, Alasdair. LANARK. Edinburgh, 1981	—	200	600
Edinburgh, 1985. 1,000 signed and numbered copies	—	150	200
New York (1981)	—	—	35
New York, 1985. First U.S. hardbound edition	—	—	35
Gray, Francine du Plessix. DIVINE DISOBEDIENCE. New York, 1970	30	50	50
London (1970)	—	40	40
Gray, John (Henry). SILVER POINTS. London, 1893. (250 numbered copies.) Original cloth designed by Charles Ricketts	450	2,000	2,000
Ordinary issue	—	—	750
Gray, Simon. COLMAIN. London (1963)	50	75	100
Graywolf Press. THE EARTH. Port Townsend, 1974. Wraps. 5 signed copies. (First book of press. A single poem by William Stafford. Sewn into wraps. Only 4 copies exist)	300	1,250	1,500
Greacen, Robert. THE BIRD. Dublin, 1941. (250 copies.) Stiff wraps	150	200	250
Green, Anna K(atherine Rohles). THE LEAVENWORTH CASE. New York, 1878. First issue: "f" missing from "fresh" last line p. 215	1,500	1,500	3,500
Green, Annie. THE SELBYS. New York, 1930	40	50	40
Green, Ben K. HORSE CONFORMATION . . . (Fort Worth, 1963)	125	125	125
Green, George Dawes. THE CAVEMAN'S VALENTINE. New York (1994)	—	—	50
Green, Hannah. (Joanne Greenburg.) I NEVER PROMISED YOU A ROSE GARDEN. New York (1964)	—	75	125
Green, Henry. (Henry Vincent Yorke.) BLINDNESS. London, 1926	1,500	3,000	4,500
New York (1926)	250	1,250	1,500
Green, Julian. AVARICE HOUSE. New York, 1917	30	50	50
Green, Leonard. DREAM COMRADES +. Oxford, 1916	—	125	125
Green, Paul. TRIFLES OF THOUGHT. New York, 1917	50	75	75
Greenan, Russell H. IT HAPPENED IN BOSTON? New York (1968)	30	35	50
Greenaway, Kate. THE QUIVER OF LOVE. (Written with Walter Crane.) (London, 1876)	250	750	1,000

	1986	1995	2000
UNDER THE WINDOW. London (1878). With printer's imprint on back of title page and "End of Contents" p. 14	150	500	350
New York, 1878	—	—	200
Greenberg, Joanne. THE KING'S PERSONS. New York (1963)	40	100	125
London (1963)	35	75	100
Greene, A. C. A PERSONAL COUNTRY. New York, 1969	50	50	40
Greene, Bob. WE DIDN'T HAVE NONE OF THEM FAT FUNKY ANGELS. California (1971)	—	50	50
Greene, Barbara. LAND BENIGHTED. London, 1938	—	175	125
Greene, Graham. BABBLING APRIL. London, 1925	2,500	5,000	5,000
THE MAN WITHIN. London (1929)	1,000	2,500	2,500
Garden City, 1929	300	1,000	1,250
New York: Bantam, 1948. First paperback edition. In dustwrapper	—	—	100
Greenleaf, Stephen. GRAVE ERROR. New York (1979)	30	50	75
Greer, Ben. SLAMMER. New York, 1975	35	50	60
Gregor, Arthur. OCTAVIAN SHOOTING TARGETS. New York (1954)	40	75	75
Gregory, Dick. FROM THE BACK OF THE BUS. New York, 1962. Wraps	—	40	40
Gregory, Horace. CHELSEA ROOMING HOUSE: POEMS. New York, 1930	100	125	150
ROOMING HOUSE. London, 1932. (New title.) Stiff wraps	75	100	100
Gregory, Susanna. A PLAGUE ON BOTH YOUR HOUSES. (London, 1996.) Wraps	—	—	125
Gresham, William Lindsay. NIGHTMARE ALLEY. New York (1946)	50	125	175
Gressent, Professor. *See* DAVID GARNETT			
Grey Owl. THE MEN OF THE LAST FRONTIER. New York, 1932	—	—	200
Grey, Romer. THE CRUISE OF THE "FISHERMAN." New York, 1929	—	300	300
Grey, (P.) Zane. BETTY ZANE. New York (1903). (Issued without dustwrapper)	400	2,000	2,500
New York (1903) with "second edition" on title page	—	—	1,000
London, 1903	—	—	1,500

	1986	1995	2000
Gribble, Leonard R. THE CASE OF THE MARSDEN RUBIES. Garden City, 1930	—	40	50
Grierson, Edward. REPUTATION FOR A SONG. London (1952)	—	—	35
Grieve, C(hristopher) M(urray). ANNALS OF FIVE SENSES. Montrose (Scotland), 1923	350	500	500
Griffin, Howard. CRY CADENCE. New York, 1947	30	100	100
Griffin, John H(oward). THE DEVIL RIDES OUTSIDE. Fort Worth, 1952	75	100	125
London, 1953	60	75	75
Griffin, Jonathan. THE HIDDEN KING. London (1955)	75	75	75
Griffith, D. W. THE RISE AND FALL OF FREE SPEECH IN AMERICA. Los Angeles, 1916	350	350	400
Griffith, (Jones) George. THE ANGEL OF THE REVOLUTION. London, 1893	150	200	200
Grigson, Geoffrey. SEVERAL OBSERVATIONS. London [1939]	75	100	100
Grile, Dod. (Ambrose Bierce). THE FIEND'S DELIGHT. London, no date [1873?]	600	1,250	1,000
New York, 1873. Brown or purple-brown cloth. Without publisher's advertisements	400	750	750
Grimes, Martha. THE MAN WITH A LOAD OF MISCHIEF. Boston (1981)	75	250	350
Grimes, Nikki. GROWIN'. New York (1977)	—	—	40
Grimké, A(ngelina) E(mily). APPEAL TO THE CHRISTIAN WOMEN OF THE SOUTH. (New York, 1836.) Wraps	250	350	600
Grimm, M. M. GERMAN POPULAR STORIES. London, 1823 and 1826. 2 volumes. First in English. First issue: without umlaut in "Märchen" on title page	—	5,000	5,500
In original bindings	—	—	8,500
Grinnell, George B. PAWNEE HERO . . . New York, 1889	150	450	300
Grisham, John. A TIME TO KILL. New York (1989). Dustwrapper price, bar code on back, no mention of *The Firm* on dustwrapper flap. Book-club dustwrapper mentions *The Firm* and has Tarrytown on title page	—	1,750	1,750
New York, 1993. One of 350 signed and numbered copies	—	—	500
London (1993)	—	—	40
Grogan, Emmett. RINGOLEVIO . . . London, 1972	—	60	40
New York (1978)	—	35	25

	1986	1995	2000
Groom, Winston. BETTER TIMES THAN THESE. New York (1978)	—	75	75
Gross, Milt. NIZE BABY. New York (1926)	—	125	150
Gross, Samuel. THE ANATOMY, PHYSIOLOGY AND DISEASES OF THE BONES AND JOINTS. Philadelphia, 1830	—	—	1,250
Grossinger, Richard. THE STARMAKER. (Madison, Wisconsin, 1968.) Wraps	40	40	40
Grossman, Alfred. ACROBAT ADMITS. New York, 1959	30	50	50
Grosz, Georg. TWELVE REPRODUCTIONS . . . Chicago, 1921. Wraps. First U.S. publication	150	600	750
Grubb, Davis. THE NIGHT OF THE HUNTER. (New York, 1953.) 1,000 signed copies	75	200	250
Trade edition	60	150	150
London (1954)	40	100	100
Gruber, Frank. PEACE MARSHALL. New York, 1939	—	150	350
THE FRENCH KEY. New York (1940)	100	125	250
Gruelle, Johnny (Barton). MR. TWEE DEEDLE. New York, 1913	—	250	300
Grumbach, Doris. THE SPOIL OF THE FLOWERS. Garden City, 1962	125	150	150
Guedalla, Philip. IGNIS FATUI . . . Oxford/London, 1911. Wraps	100	100	100
Guest, Barbara. THE LOCATION OF THINGS. New York, 1960. Wraps. (300 copies)	90	100	450
Guest, Edgar Albert. HOME RHYMES. Detroit, 1909	50	50	50
Guest, Judith. ORDINARY PEOPLE. New York, 1976	25	50	50
Guiney, Louise Imogen. SONGS AT THE START. Boston, 1884. BAL notes 5 bindings, priority unknown, but the one in half morocco seems to sell for more	100	125	125
Half morocco (Preceded by two pamphlets and a broadside.)	—	—	200
Guiterman, Arthur. BETEL NUTS. San Francisco (1907)	—	—	75
Gunn, Thom(son William). (POEMS). Fantasy Press. Oxford, 1953. Wraps	500	500	600
FIGHTING TERMS. (Oxford, 1954.) Wraps. First issue: final	400	650	500

	1986	1995	2000
"t" in "thought" omitted on first line of p. 38. Yellow cloth. Issued without dustwrapper			
Second issue: corrected	—	250	200
New York, 1958. Stiff wraps. First issue: without review label attached	50	150	125
Second issue: with review label attached	—	100	75
FIGHTING TERMS: A SELECTION. Berkeley, 1983. 25 copies	—	1,250	1,250
Gunther, John. THE RED PAVILION. New York, 1926	50	150	125
London, 1926	—	100	100
Gurganus, Allan. BREATHING LESSONS. Rocky Mount, 1981. Wraps	—	250	200
OLDEST LIVING CONFEDERATE WIDOW TELLS ALL. New York, 1989	—	60	40
London, 1989	—	50	35
Gurney, Ivor. SEVERN AND SOMME. London, 1917	—	—	250
Gustafson, Ralph. THE GOLDEN CHALICE. London, 1935. Boards in tissue wrap	—	—	350
Guterson, David. THE COUNTRY AHEAD OF US BEHIND. New York (1989)	—	—	300
Guthrie, A(lfred) B(ertram), Jr. MURDERS AT MOON DANCE. New York, 1943	400	600	1,250
Guthrie, Ramon. TROBAR CLUS. Northampton, Massachusetts, 1923. 250 signed copies	75	75	75
Guthrie, Thomas Anstey. *See* F. Anstey			
Guthrie, Woody. BOUND FOR GLORY. New York, 1945	150	300	400
Guy, Rosa. BIRD AT MY WINDOW. Philadelphia, 1966	—	125	175
(London, 1966)	—	75	75
Gysin, Brion. TO MASTER, A LONG GOODNIGHT. New York (1946)	60	100	100

H

	1986	1995	2000
H.D. *See* D., H. (Hilda Doolittle)			
H.H. (Helen Hunt Jackson.) BETHMENDI: A PERSIAN TALE. Boston, 1867. Translated by Doolittle	200	300	300
VERSES. Boston 1870	150	300	300
Habberton, John. HELEN'S BABIES. Boston (1876). Wraps. First issue: measures 1¾6″	150	300	350
London, 1877	—	—	100

	1986	1995	2000
Hacker, Marilyn. THE TERRIBLE CHILDREN. No place. (1967.) Stapled wraps	—	75	250
Haffner, Margaret. A MURDER AT CROWS. London (1992)	—	—	35
Hagedorn, Herman, Jr. THE SILVER BLADE. Berlin, 1907. Wraps	100	175	250
(Previous broadside and collaboration.)			
Hager, Jean. THE GRANDFATHER MEDICINE. New York (1989)	—	—	150
Haggard, H(enry) Rider. CETYWAYO . . . London, 1882. (750 copies)	500	1,500	2,000
Haig-Brown, Roderick. SILVER. London, 1931	—	500	500
Hailey, Arthur. FLIGHT INTO DANGER. London, 1958. (Written with John Castle)	75	150	150
Toronto, 1958. Published simultaneously	—	150	150
THE FINAL DIAGNOSIS. New York, 1959	50	60	60
Hailey, Elizabeth Forsythe. A WOMAN OF INDEPENDENT MEANS. New York (1978)	—	—	75
Haines, John. WINTER NEWS. Middletown (1966)	30	50	100
Haines, William. (William Heyen.) WHAT HAPPENED IN FORT LAUDERDALE. New York (1958). Wraps. (Written with William Taggard)	50	75	50
Halberstam, David. THE NOBLEST ROMAN. Boston, 1961	35	60	125
Haldane, Charlotte. MAN'S WORLD. London, 1926	125	250	250
Haldane, J(ohn) B(urdon) S(anderson). DAEDALUS OR SCIENCE AND THE FUTURE. London, 1924	—	—	150
Haldeman, Charles. THE SUN'S ATTENDANT. London (1963)	25	75	100
London (1964)	—	—	50
Haldeman, Joe (W.). WAR YEAR. New York (1972)	30	100	100
Hale, Edward Everett. *See* MARGARET PERCIVAL IN AMERICA			
Hale, Kathleen. ORLANDO, THE MARMALADE CAT . . . London (1938)	—	300	400
Hale, Nancy. THE YOUNG DIE GOOD. New York, 1932	100	125	150
Hale, Sarah Josepha. *See* THE GENIUS OF OBLIVION			

	1986	1995	2000
Haley, Alex. ROOTS. Garden City (1974). 59-page excerpt from *Reader's Digest* in illustrated wraps	—	100	125
Garden City, 1976. 500 signed and numbered copies in slipcase	150	450	600
Trade edition	35	100	100
London (1977)	—	—	75

Also see Malcolm X

Haley, J. Evetts. THE XIT RANCH OF TEXAS. Chicago, 1929. Issued in tissue dustwrapper	500	500	600

Haliburton, Thomas Chandler. AN HISTORICAL AND STATISTICAL ACCOUNT OF NOVA SCOTIA . . . Halifax, 1825. 2 volumes	—	—	600

See also THE CLOCKMAKER

Hall, Adam. *See* Mansell Black

Hall, Arthur Vine. TABLE MOUNTAIN . . . Capetown (1896)	175	200	200

Hall, Austin. PEOPLE OF THE COMET. (Los Angeles, 1948.) First science fiction	25	35	50

Hall, Baynard Rush. RIGHTEOUSNESS THE SAFE-GUARD . . . (Indianapolis, 1827)	75	75	75

Hall, Donald (Andrew). (POEMS) Fantasy Poets No. 4. Oxford (1952). Wraps	200	250	350
EXILE. Swinford (1952). Wraps (Edited one book previously.)	—	250	300

Hall, Henry. *See* THE TRIBUNE BOOK OF OPEN AIR SPORTS

Hall, J. C. THE SUMMER DANCE +. London, 1951. (First separate work)	60	75	75

Hall, James. LETTERS FROM THE WEST . . . London, 1828 (Two previous pamphlets.)	—	350	400

Hall, James B(yron). NOT BY THE DOOR. New York (1954)	50	75	50

Hall, James Norman. KITCHENER'S MOB. Boston, 1916	50	75	75

Hall, James W. UNDER COVER BY DAYLIGHT. New York, 1987	—	60	60
London (1988)	—	—	40

Hall, Marguerite Radclyffe. 'TWIXT EARTH AND STARS. London, 1906	200	300	600

Hall, O(akley) M. MURDER CITY. New York (1949)	40	75	125
London, 1950	—	75	100

Halleck, Fitz-Greene. *See* CROAKER and FANNY . . .

	1986	1995	2000
Halliday, Brett. (Davis Dresser.) *See* Anthony Scott			
Halper, Albert. PURPLE PUDDING. Chicago, 1927. Linen spine and purple-paper-covered boards. Assume issued without dustwrapper	—	—	500
CHICAGO SIDE-SHOW. New York, 1932. (110 copies) Wraps	200	300	300
UNION SQUARE. New York, 1933	75	75	125
Halpern, Daniel. TRAVELING ON CREDIT. New York (1972)	—	—	75
Hamady, Walter. THE DISILLUSIONED SOLIPSIST. Mt. Horeb, 1954. (60 copies.) (Also first Perishable Press)	2,000	2,500	2,500
Hamburger, Michael. POEMS OF HÖLDERLIN. London, 1943. (Translation and 97-page introduction)	75	75	100
LATER HOGARTH. London, 1945	100	100	100
Hamill, Sam. HEROES OF THE TETON MYTHOS. Denver, 1973. Cloth (10 copies)	—	200	350
Wraps	—	75	75
Hamilton, Alexander. *See* A FULL VINDICATION . . .			
Hamilton, Clive. (C. S. Lewis.) SPIRITS IN BONDAGE. London, 1919	250	450	500
Hamilton, Donald. DATE WITH DARKNESS. New York (1947). Wraps	—	—	50
Hamilton, Edmond. THE METAL GIANTS. Washborn, no date [1932]. Mimeographed pamphlet	—	275	350
THE HORROR ON THE ASTEROID. London, 1936	600	600	600
Hamilton, Gail. (Mary Abigail Dodge). COUNTRY LIVING AND COUNTRY THINKING. Boston, 1862	150	150	350
Hamilton, George R. THE SEARCH FOR LOVELINESS +. London, 1910	60	60	60
Hamilton, Gerald. *See* Patrick Weston			
Hamilton, Jane. THE BOOK OF RUTH. New York (1988).	—	—	250
Hamilton, Nan. KILLER'S RIGHTS. New York (1984)	—	—	25
Hammett, (Samuel) Dashiell. RED HARVEST. New York, 1929. First issue: no review on back panel of dustwrapper	2,000	8,500	10K
Hamner, Earl, Jr. FIFTY ROADS TO TOWN. New York (1953)	35	60	100

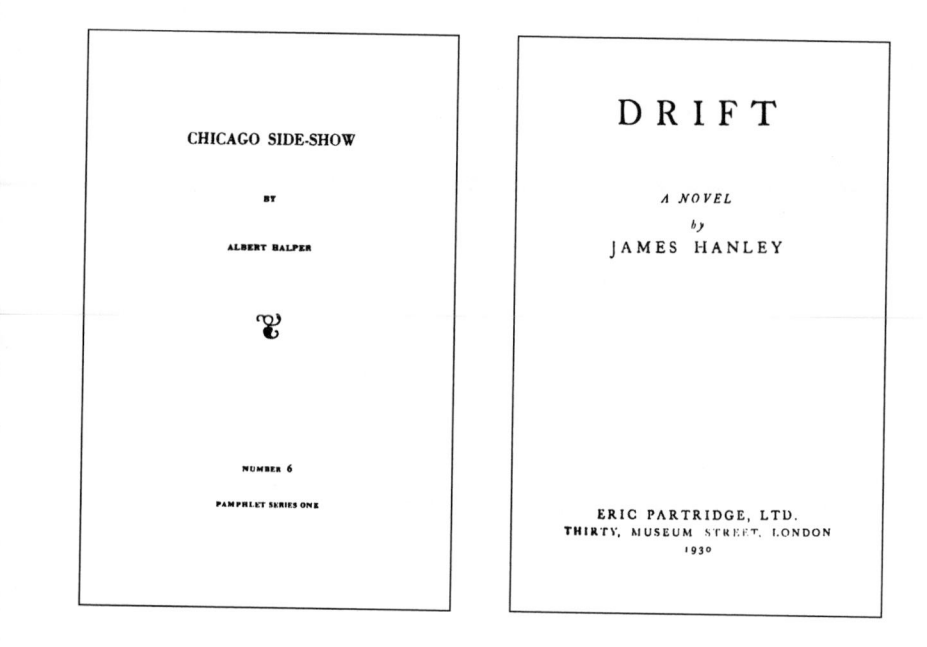

CHICAGO SIDE-SHOW

BY

ALBERT HALPER

NUMBER 6

PAMPHLET SERIES ONE

DRIFT

A NOVEL

by

JAMES HANLEY

ERIC PARTRIDGE, LTD.
THIRTY, MUSEUM STREET, LONDON
1930

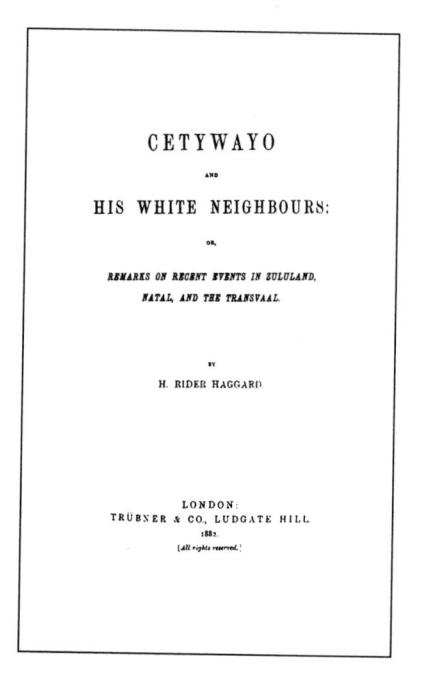

CETYWAYO

AND

HIS WHITE NEIGHBOURS:

OR,

REMARKS ON RECENT EVENTS IN ZULULAND,
NATAL, AND THE TRANSVAAL.

BY

H. RIDER HAGGARD

LONDON:
TRÜBNER & CO, LUDGATE HILL.
1882.
[All rights reserved.]

	1986	1995	2000
Hamsun, Knut. HUNGER. London, 1899. Wraps	—	350	350
Handke, Peter. KASPAR +. New York, 1969. First English translation	—	40	75
Handy, W. C. BLUES: AN ANTHOLOGY. New York, 1926. Edited by Handy	300	500	750
Hanff, Helene. 84 CHARING CROSS ROAD. New York, 1970	—	—	75
London, 1977	—	—	75
Hanley, James. DRIFT. London, 1930. (10 signed copies)	1,000	1,000	1,000
Trade edition. (490 copies)	150	200	300
Hannah, Barry. GERONIMO REX. New York (1972)	100	125	200
Hanrahan, Barbara. THE SCENT OF EUCALYPTUS. London, 1973	—	50	60
Hansberry, Lorraine. A RAISIN IN THE SUN. New York (1959). Wraps	50	75	100
New York (1959). First edition not stated	—	300	350
Hansen, Joseph. *See* James Colton			
FADEOUT. New York, 1970. (First mystery)	—	150	125
Hansen, Ron. DESPERADOES. New York, 1979	—	75	100
Hanson, Kenneth O. 8 POEMS 1958 [wrapper title]. (Portland, 1958.) Sheets laid into printed wrappers with flap	—	—	200
Hanson, Pauline. THE FOREVER YOUNG. Denver (1948). Wraps. (300 copies)	35	40	50
Hardwick, Elizabeth. THE GHOSTLY LOVER. New York (1945)	125	200	300
Hardy, Thomas. *See* DESPERATE REMEDIES			
UNDER THE GREENWOOD TREE. London, 1872. 2 volumes	—	—	10K
Hare, Cyril. (Alfred Alexander Gordon Clark.) TENANT FOR DEATH. London, 1937	60	750	750
Hare, David. SLAG. London (1971). Wraps	40	40	30
Harington, Donald. THE CHERRY PIT. New York (1965)	—	75	75
Harland, Henry. *See* Sidney Luska			
Harland, Marion. (Mary Hawes Terhune.) ALONE. Richmond, 1854	350	350	350
Harman, William. TREASURY HOLIDAY. Middletown (1970)	—	35	50

	1986	1995	2000
Harness, Charles L(eonard). FLIGHT INTO YESTERDAY. New York (1953)	—	—	100
Harper, Frances E(llen) W(atkins). MISCELLANEOUS POEMS. Philadelphia, 1854	—	1,500	3,000
IOLA LEROY, OR SHADOWS UPLIFTED. Philadelphia, 1892. (Later printings had Boston imprint)	300	1,250	2,500
Harper, Michael S(teven). DEAR JOHN, DEAR COLTRANE. Pittsburgh (1970)	—	—	100
Wraps	—	—	35
Harrigan, Stephen. ARKANSAS. New York, 1980	25	30	35
Harrington, Alan. THE REVELATIONS OF DR. MODESTO. New York, 1955	40	50	50
(London, 1957.) Len Deighton dustwrapper	50	75	100
Harrington, William. WHICH THE JUSTICE . . . London (1963)	35	50	75
New York (1963)	—	—	50
Harris, Bertha. CATCHING SARADOVE. New York (1969)	40	75	100
Harris, Frank. ELDER CONKLIN +. New York, 1894	75	75	75
London, 1895	50	50	50
Harris, Joel Chandler. UNCLE REMUS: HIS SONGS AND SAYINGS. New York, 1881. First state/printing: "presumptive" for "presumptuous" last line p. 9 and no mention of this book in ads at back. (Very fine copies have brought up to $4,000 at auction)	350	1,500	2,500
Second state/printing	—	450	600
UNCLE REMUS AND HIS LEGENDS OF THE OLD PLANTATION. London, 1881. (New title)	250	750	1,000
UNCLE REMUS: HIS SONGS AND SAYINGS. New York, 1895. 250 signed and numbered copies	—	2,000	2,500
Trade edition	—	—	200
Harris, M. Virginia. WEDDIN' TRIMMIN'S. New York (1949)	—	200	200
Harris, Mark. TRUMPET THE WORLD. New York (1946)	50	100	100
Harris, Robert. SELLING HITLER. London, 1986	—	—	30
FATHERLAND. London (1992)	—	—	350
Harris, Thomas. BLACK SUNDAY. New York (1975)	—	175	200
London, 1975	—	75	75

Harris, Timothy.

	1986	1995	2000
KRONSKI/McSMASH. London, 1969	—	75	75
New York, 1969	35	60	60
Harris, Will. THE BAY PSALM BOOK MURDER. New York, 1983	—	100	175
Harris, William J. HEY FELLA WOULD YOU MIND . . . Ithaca (1974). Issued without dustwrapper	—	40	75
Wraps	—	—	40
Harris, Wilson. PALACE OF THE PEACOCK. London (1960)	60	125	200
Harrison, Jamie. THE EDGE OF THE CRAZIES. New York (1995)	—	—	50
Harrison, Jim. (James Thomas.) PLAIN SONG. New York (1965). Cloth	125	400	500
Wraps	—	75	100
Harrison, Kathryn. THICKER THAN WATER. New York (1991)	—	—	50
Harrison, Michael. WEEP FOR LYCIDAS. London, 1934	—	125	125
Harrison, T(ony). EARTHWORKS. Leeds, 1964. Wraps	—	125	100
Harrison, Tom. LETTER TO OXFORD. (1933.) Wraps	40	75	75
Harrison, William. THE THEOLOGIAN. New York (1965)	40	40	40
Harriss, Will. THE BAY PSALM BOOK MURDER. New York, 1963	—	100	125
Hart, Joseph C. *See* MIRIAM COFFIN			
Hart, Josephine. DAMAGE. London (1991)	—	75	75
New York, 1991	—	25	30
Hart, William S. and Mary. PINTO BEN +. New York (1919)	25	30	35
Harte, (Francis) Bret. *See* OUTCROPPINGS			
CONDENSED NOVELS +. New York, 1867. First book	250	500	500
THE LOST GALLEON. San Francisco, 1867. First verse	300	600	600
Hartland, Michael. DOWN AMONG THE DEAD MEN. London, 1983	—	—	60
Hartley, L(eslie) P(oles). NIGHT FEARS +. London, 1924	200	400	1,500
Hartley, Marsden. ADVENTURE IN THE ARTS. New York (1921)	—	1,250	750
TWENTY-FIVE POEMS. (Paris, 1923.) Wraps	400	750	1,000
Hartnett, Michael. ANATOMY OF A CLICHÉ. (Dublin, 1968). Wraps	—	—	100

	1986	1995	2000
Hartwell, Mary. A WOMAN IN ARMOUR. New York, 1875	—	275	300
Harvey, John. LONELY HEARTS. London (1989)	—	—	200
New York (1989)	—	—	60
Harwood, Lee. TITLE ILLEGIBLE. London, 1965. Mimeographed stapled sheets	75	100	100
Hasford, Gustav. THE SHORT TIMERS. New York (1979)	50	125	200
London (1985)	—	—	125
THE HASHEESH EATER. (Fitz-Hugh Ludlow.) New York, 1857	200	500	400
Hass, Robert. FIELD GUIDE. New Haven, 1973	35	40	750
Wraps	—	—	50
Hassall, Christopher. POEMS OF TWO YEARS. London, 1935. Wraps	—	75	75
Hassler, Jon. FOUR MILES TO PINECONE. New York, 1977	—	150	300
STAGGERFORD. New York, 1977. (First novel)	40	125	250
Hathaway, Katharine. THE LITTLE LOCKSMITH. New York, 1943	—	40	30
Hauser, Marianne. DARK DOMINION. New York (1947)	40	40	40
Hautman, Pete. *See* Peter Murray			
DRAWING DEAD. New York, 1993. (First mystery) (34 children's books 1992–94.)	—	50	50
Hawker, Robert Stephen. *See* Reuben			
Hawkes, J(ohn) C(lendinnin) B(urne). FIASCO HALL. Cambridge, 1943. Wraps. (100 copies—60 destroyed)	750	1,500	1,250
THE CANNIBAL. Norfolk (1949). Gray cloth (Second printing is in rust cloth but no statement of later printing except on dustwrapper.)	—	250	250
Hawley, Cameron. EXECUTIVE SUITE. Boston (1952)	—	—	75
Hawthorne, Julian. BRESSANT. New York, 1873	100	150	150
Hawthorne, Nathaniel. *See* FANSHAWE			
TWICE-TOLD TALES . . . Boston, 1837	1,500	5,000	5,000
Hay, Helen. SOME VERSES. Chicago, 1898	—	75	75
Hay, John. JIM BLUDSO OF THE PRAIRIE BELLE. Boston, 1871. Orange wraps	100	150	150

	1986	1995	2000
(Previous pamphlets.)			
Hayakawa, S. J. LANGUAGE IN THOUGHT AND ACTION. Madison, 1939. Blue flexible wraps	150	250	350
Haycox, E. FREE GRASS. New York, 1929	—	—	350
Hayden, Robert E. HEART-SHAPE IN THE DUST. Detroit, 1940	—	—	450
Hayes, Joseph. AND CAME THE SPRING. New York (1942). Wraps. (Written with M. Hayes)	50	125	125
DESPERATE HOURS. New York, 1954. First mystery	—	—	75
Haymon, S. T. DEATH AND THE PREGNANT VIRGIN. London (1980). Author's first mystery	—	—	75
Hayne, Paul H(amilton). POEMS. 1855	—	350	350
Haynes, David. RIGHT BY MY SIDE. New Rivers Press, 1993. (2,500 copies) Wraps	—	—	125
Hays, H. R. STRANGE CITY. Boston (1929)	—	100	100
Hayter, Sparkle. WHAT'S A GIRL GOTTA DO? New York: Soho, 1994.	—	—	60
Haywarde, Richard. (Frederick Swarthout Cozzens.) PRISMATICS. New York, 1853	150	250	250
Haywood, Gar Anthony. FEAR OF THE DARK. New York, 1988	—	75	175
Hazel, Robert. THE LOST YEAR. Cleveland (1953)	—	—	40
POEMS 1951–1961. Morehead (1961)	30	50	50
Hazlitt, W. Carew. THE HISTORY OF THE VENETIAN REPUBLIC . . . London, 1860. 4 volumes	100	150	400
Hazo, Samuel. DISCOVERY +. New York (1959). Wraps	25	40	40
Hazzard, Shirley. CLIFFS OF FALL +. London, 1963	60	200	200
New York, 1963	—	125	75
Healy, Dermot. BANISHED MISFORTUNE +. London, 1982	—	50	75
Healy, Jeremiah. BLUNT DARTS. New York (1984)	—	250	350
Heaney, Seamus. ELEVEN POEMS. Belfast (1965). First issue: cream wraps, laid paper, cover device in red-violet sun	600	1,750	1,750
Second issue: white wraps, wove paper, cover device in black purple	300	750	750
Third issue: gray paper in stiff green wraps	150	350	450

	1986	1995	2000
DEATH OF A NATURALIST. London (1966)	350	400	600
New York, 1966. (English sheets)	250	300	400
Hearn, Lafcadio. ONE OF CLEOPATRA'S NIGHTS. By T. Gautier. New York, 1882. Translated by Hearn. First issue: publisher's name in capitals on spine	200	1,000	750
STRAY LEAVES FROM STRANGE LITERATURE. Boston, 1884. First issue: has J.R. & O. on spine	250	650	850
Hearne, John. VOICES UNDER THE WINDOW. London (1955)	—	100	100
Hearon, Shelby. AT HOME AFTER 1840 . . . Austin, 1966. 100 signed and numbered copies. (Text by Hearon, drawings by Peggy Goldstein)	125	200	200
Regular edition. (1,000 copies)	60	60	75
Heath-Stubbs, John. WOUNDED THAMMUZ. London, 1942. Thin paper boards in dustwrapper	—	60	60
Hecht, Anthony (Evan). A SUMMONING OF STONES. New York (1954)	100	150	200
Hecht, Ben. *See* Maxwell Bodenheim			
THE HERO OF SANTA MARIA. New York (1920). Wraps. (Written with Frank Shay)	200	200	200
ERIK DORN. New York, 1921. First issue: yellow lettering on cover	125	300	300
Hecht, Daniel. SKULL SESSION. (New York, 1998.)	—	—	30
Heck, Peter J. DEATH ON THE MISSISSIPPI. New York (1995)	—	—	75
Hedge, Frederic Henry. A SERMON PREACHED . . . Boston, 1834. Wraps	100	150	150
Hedley, Leslie Woolf. THE EDGE OF INSANITY. Los Angeles, 1949. Wraps	60	100	100
Hegen, Alice Caldwell. MRS. WIGGS OF THE CABBAGE PATCH. New York, 1901. Gold sky on front cover	40	125	175
Heggen, Thomas. MISTER ROBERTS. Boston, 1946	50	100	200
London, 1948	50	75	100
Hegi, Ursula. INTRUSIONS. New York, 1981	—	—	125
Heinemann, Larry. CLOSE QUARTERS. New York (1977)	25	100	100
Heinlein, Robert (Anson). THE DISCOVERY OF THE FUTURE. New York: Novacious Press, 1941. (200 copies.) Wraps	—	2,000	1,750

	1986	1995	2000
ROCKET SHIP GALILEO. New York (1947)	300	1,000	1,000
Heller, Joseph. CATCH-22. New York, 1961. (Dustwrapper price $5.95)	350	1,250	2,000
London (1962). First issue: dustwrapper with blurb about book on back	100	200	300
Second issue: dustwrapper with blurbs by other authors	—	150	150
Hellman, Lillian. THE CHILDREN'S HOUR. New York, 1934	250	650	650
London (1962). Wraps and dustwrapper	75	200	250
Helprin, Mark. A DOVE OF THE EAST +. New York, 1975	40	100	125
London, 1976	—	75	75
Helps, Sir Arthur. *See* THOUGHTS IN THE CLOISTER			
Hemans, Felicia Dorothea. POEMS. London, 1808	200	250	250
Hemingway, Ernest. THREE STORIES AND TEN POEMS. (Paris, 1923.) (300 copies.) Wraps	5K	20K	25K
IN OUR TIME. Paris, 1924. (170 copies)	4K	17.5K	25K
New York, 1925	1,000	3,500	7,500
London, 1926	500	1,500	3,000
New York, 1930	300	500	1,000
Hemingway, Leicester. THE SOUND OF THE TRUMPET. New York (1953)	35	60	60
Hemley, Cecil. SEAS AND SEASONS. New York (1951). Wraps	—	100	100
Hempel, Amy. REASONS TO LIVE. New York (1985)	—	50	75
Henderson, David. FELIX OF THE SILENT FOREST. New York, 1967. One of 25 hardbound signed copies	—	—	300
Wraps	—	—	40
Henderson, Elliot Blaine. PLANTATION ECHOES. Columbus, 1904	125	200	300
Henderson, George Wylie. OLLIE MISS. New York, 1935	75	150	350
London (1935)	—	—	250
Henderson, William McCranor. STARK RAVING ELVIS. New York (1984)	—	35	35
Henderson, Zenna. PILGRIMAGE. Garden City, 1961	—	350	350
London, 1962	—	—	75
Henley, Beth. AM I BLUE. (New York, 1982.) Wraps	40	75	75
Henley, William Ernest. A BOOK OF VERSES. London, 1888. 20	—	—	850

	1986	1995	2000
signed and numbered copies, large-paper issue, printed on Japan vellum			
75 copies in white tissue dustwrapper	600	600	600
Trade edition. Stiff wraps	100	200	200
Henri, Adrian. TONIGHT AT NOON. London (1968). 26 signed and lettered copies	60	60	60
100 signed and numbered copies	30	30	30
Henry, Arthur. NICHOLAS BLOOD, CANDIDATE. New York (1890)	75	100	50
Henry, O. (Wm. Sidney—later Sydney—Porter.) CABBAGES AND KINGS. New York, 1904. First issue: McClure, Phillips & Co. on spine	150	350	350
Henry, Sue. MURDER ON THE IDITAROD TRAIL. New York, 1991	—	75	200
Henry, Will. (Henry Wilson Allen.) NO SURVIVORS. New York, 1950	—	200	350
Henty, G(eorge) A(lfred). A SEARCH FOR A SECRET. London, 1867. 3 volumes	3,000	4,500	6,000
Herbert, Sir A(lfred) P(atrick). POOR POEMS AND ROTTEN RHYMES. Winchester, England, 1910. Wraps	175	300	300
Herbert, Frank (Patrick). SURVIVAL AND THE ATOM. (Santa Rosa, 1950.) Wraps. An offprint	400	500	500
THE DRAGON IN THE SEA. Garden City, 1956	—	350	400
London, 1960	—	—	125
Herbert, Henry William. *See* THE BROTHERS . . .			
Herbert, James. THE RATS. (London, 1974)	—	450	450
Herbst, Josephine. NOTHING IS SACRED. New York, 1928	125	150	175
Herford, Oliver. ARTFUL ANTICKS. New York, 1888	125	150	50
Hergesheimer, Joseph. THE LAY ANTHONY. New York, 1914	75	100	100
Herlihy, James Leo. BLUE DENIM. New York, 1958. (Written with Wm. Noble)	40	75	60
THE SLEEP OF BABY FILBERTSON. New York, 1959	50	75	50
London, 1959	30	40	30
Herr, Michael. DISPATCHES. New York, 1977	75	100	150
London (1978)	—	35	60
Herriot, James. ALL CREATURES GREAT AND SMALL. New York (1972)	30	75	75

	1986	1995	2000
Herrmann, John. WHAT HAPPENS. (Paris, 1926.) Wraps	150	200	500
Herron, Stella Wynne. BOWERY PARADE +. New York (1936). Glassine dustwrapper	50	60	40
Hersey, John (Richard). MEN ON BATAAN. New York, 1942	125	200	250
Hertzog, Carl. *See* Owen P. White			
Hess, Joan. STRANGLED PROSE. New York, 1986	—	75	100
Hesse, Hermann. DEMIAN. New York, 1923. (First English translation)	300	500	1,000
Hewitt, John. CONACRE. No place, 1943	—	—	500
Hewlett, Maurice. EARTHWORK OUT OF TUSCANY. London, 1895. (500 copies)	125	125	100
Heyen, William. *See* William Haines			
DEPTH OF FIELD. Baton Rouge, 1970	25	35	50
Heyer, Georgette (Mrs. George Ronald Rougier). THE BLACK MOTH. Boston, 1921	100	200`	400
Heyward, DuBose. CAROLINA CHANSONS. New York, 1922. (Written with H. Allen)	100	175	175
SKYLINES AND HORIZONS. New York, 1924	100	150	150
Heyward, Jane Screven. WILD ROSES +. New York Washington, 1905	—	150	150
Hiaasen, Carl. *See* Neil Schulman			
POWDER BURN. New York, 1981. (Written with William D. Montalbano)	—	250	500
TOURIST SEASON. New York, 1986. (First solely authored title) (Two ghostwritten books precede.)	—	125	300
Hickmott, Allerton Cushman. FABRIC OF DREAMS. (Hartford, 1925.) 11 copies on Kelmscott	200	200	200
100 copies	100	100	100
Higgins, Aidan. FELO DE SE. London, 1960	—	—	40
Higgins, Brian. THE ONLY NEED. London, 1980	—	50	50
Higgins, Colin. HAROLD AND MAUDE. Philadelphia (1971)	30	60	60

	1986	1995	2000
Higgins, Dick. WHAT ARE LEGENDS? (Calais, Maine, 1960). Wraps	25	75	75
Higgins, F. R. SALT AIR. Dublin, 1923	—	100	125
Higgins, George V(incent). THE FRIENDS OF EDDIE COYLE. New York, 1972. First issue: green cloth (priority assumed)	35	60	60
Second issue: blue cloth	25	40	40
London (1972)	35	40	40
Highsmith (Mary) Patricia (Ploughman). STRANGERS ON A TRAIN. New York, 1950	350	750	2,000
London, 1950	300	600	1,250
Highwater, Jamake. *See* J. Marks			
Hijuelos, Oscar. OUR HOUSE IN THE LAST WORLD. New York (1983)	—	100	175
Hildreth, Richard. *See* THE SLAVE			
Hill, Geoffrey. (POEMS). The Fantasy Poets—Number Eleven. Swinford, 1952. Wraps	—	500	500
FOR THE UNFALLEN. London, 1959	—	300	300
Hill, Headon. (Francis Edward Grainger.) CLUES FROM A DETECTIVE'S CAMERA. London, 1893	50	125	300
Hill, Reginald. A CLUBBABLE WOMAN. London, 1970	—	200	750
Hill, Susan. THE ENCLOSURE. London, 1961	50	75	75
Hillerman, Tony. THE BLESSING WAY. New York (1970). States "First Edition" and has "70 71 . . . 3 2 1" on last blank page	—	1,250	1,500
(London, 1970)	—	500	500
New York, 1989. 26 signed and lettered copies	—	300	300
100 signed and numbered copies	—	150	150
Hillyer, Robert S(illman). SONNETS +. Cambridge, 1917	50	125	75
Hilton, James. CATHERINE HERSELF. London (1920)	400	1,000	1,250
London, 1935. Second edition with new preface	—	—	300
Himes, Chester (Bomar). IF HE HOLLERS LET HIM GO. Garden City, 1945	150	400	750
(London, 1947)	—	200	300
HIND AND THE PANTHER TRANSVERS'D . . . , THE. (By Matthew Prior.) London, 1687	—	400	400
Hine, Daryl. FIVE POEMS. Toronto (1955). Wraps	150	450	350

	1986	1995	2000
Hinton, S. E. THE OUTSIDERS. New York (1967)	75	200	200
Also in pictorial binding without dustwrapper	—	100	125
Hirsch, Edward. FOR THE SLEEPWALKER. New York, 1981. Cloth	—	75	100
Wraps	—	—	35
Hirsch, Sidney. THE FIRE REGAINED. New York, 1913. Considered the first "Fugitive Book"	150	150	150
Hirschman, Jack. FRAGMENTS. (New York, 1952.) (Privately published.) Wraps	250	250	300
A CORRESPONDENCE OF AMERICANS. Bloomington, 1960. Issued with glassine dustwrapper	60	75	75
HISTORY OF A SIX WEEKS' TOUR THROUGH A PART OF FRANCE . . . (Mary W. and Percy B. Shelley.) London, 1817	1,500	2,000	2,500
Hjortsberg, William. ALP. New York (1969)	50	75	75
London (1970)	35	60	35
Hoag, Jonathan E. THE POETICAL WORKS OF . . . New York, 1923. Anonymously edited by H. P. Lovecraft, who also contributed the Preface and six poems	—	300	400
Hoagland, Edward. CAT MAN. Boston, 1956	60	100	200
Hoagland, Kathleen. FIDDLER IN THE SKY. New York (1944)	35	60	60
Hoban, Russell (Conwell). WHAT DOES IT DO . . . New York, 1959	—	175	250
HOBOMOK . . . (Lydia Marie Child.) Boston, 1824	400	750	1,000
Hobson, Laura Z. *See* Field, Peter			
A DOG OF HIS OWN. New York, 1941	150	200	250
Hochman, Sandra. VOYAGE HOME. (Paris, 1960.) Wraps	50	75	50
Hocking, Mary. THE WINTER CITY. London, 1961	—	60	60
Hodges, George W. SWAMP ANGEL. New York, 1958	—	75	150
Hodgson, Ralph. THE LAST BLACKBIRD +. London, 1907. First issue: top edges gilt, edges uncut	75	100	100
New York, 1907	50	50	50
Hodgson, William Hope. THE BOATS OF THE "GLEN CARRIG." London, 1907	500	850	1,000
THE HOUSE ON THE BORDERLAND. London, 1908	450	1,250	2,000
Sauk City, 1946	250	400	450

	1986	1995	2000
Høeg, Peter. SMILLA'S SENSE OF SNOW. New York (1993)	—	—	25
Hoff, H(arry) S(ommerfield). TRINA. London, 1934	75	75	75
Hoffenstein, Samuel. LIFE SINGS A SONG. New York, 1916	—	125	100
Hoffer, Eric. THE TRUE BELIEVER. New York (1951)	20	50	50
Hoffman, Abbie. *See* FUCK THE SYSTEM			
Hoffman, Alice. PROPERTY OF. New York (1977)	—	100	125
London, 1978	—	50	75
Hoffman, Charles Fenno. *See* A WINTER IN THE WEST			
Hoffman, Daniel (Gerard). PAUL BUNYAN . . . Philadelphia, 1952	40	75	100
AN ARMADA OF THIRTY WHALES. New York, 1954. (789 copies.)	35	75	100
Hogan, Linda. MEAN SPIRIT. New York (1990). First mystery. Two volumes of poetry preceded	—	—	50
Hogarth Press. TWO STORIES. By V. and L. Woolf. Richmond (England) 1917. Wraps. (150 copies)	5K	7.5K	15K
Hogg, James. SCOTTISH PASTORALS . . . Edinburgh, 1801	500	750	1,000
Holcombe, W(illiam) H(enry). A MYSTERY OF NEW ORLEANS. Philadelphia, 1890	60	200	300
Holdstock, Robert. EYE AMONG THE BLIND. London (1976)	—	50	35
Garden City, 1977	—	—	25

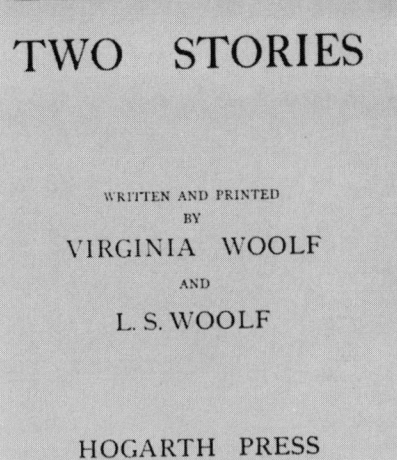

PUBLICATION NO. 1.

TWO STORIES

WRITTEN AND PRINTED
BY
VIRGINIA WOOLF
AND
L. S. WOOLF

HOGARTH PRESS
RICHMOND
1917

	1986	1995	2000
Hollander, John. A CRACKLING OF THORNS. New Haven, 1958. (Foreword by Auden)	50	75	75
Hollinghurst, Alan. CONFIDENTIAL CHATS WITH BOYS. Oxford, 1982. Wraps	—	125	200
Hollo, Anselm (Paul Alexis). SATEIDEN VALILLA. Helsinki, 1956	100	150	200
ST. TEXT AND FINNPOEMS. Birmingham (England), 1961	125	75	100
Holman, Sheri. A STOLEN TONGUE. New York (1977)	—	—	40
Holme, Constance. CRUMP FOLK GOING HOME. London, 1913	—	50	75
Holmes, John A. ALONG THE ROW +. (Medford) 1929. Wraps. 500 copies	—	150	150
Holmes, John Clellon. GO. New York, 1952	300	750	750
THE BEAT BOYS. London (1959). New title. Wraps	—	75	75
Holmes, Mary J(ane). TEMPEST AND SUNSHINE . . . New York, 1854. First issue: advertisement for "new copy-right works . . ."	50	250	250
Holmes, Justice Oliver Wendell. THE COMMON LAW. Boston, 1881. First issue: green cloth. Reading "John Wilson . . ."	300	1,750	2,000
Second issue: russet cloth. Reading "University Press"	—	1,500	1,750
Third issue: russet cloth. Reading "S. J. Park Hill & Co."	—	1,500	1,250

	1986	1995	2000
Holmes, Oliver Wendell. POEMS. Boston, 1836. (With Boston imprint only)	250	400	500
Boston/New York, 1836	—	—	200
London, 1846	—	250	250
Holst, Spencer. 25 STORIES. No place, no date. Wraps	—	—	200
THIRTEEN ESSAYS. New York (1960). Wraps	60	60	100
Holt, Tom. POEMS. London, 1973	—	100	35
Holtby, Winifred. ANDERBY WOLD. London, 1923	75	125	200
HOME LIFE IN RUSSIA. (Nikolai Gogol.) London, 1854. 2 volumes	750	1,250	2,000
Homes, A. M. JACK. New York (1989)	—	—	125
Honig, Edwin. GARCÍA LORCA. Norfolk (1944)	40	50	50
London (1945)	35	40	40
Hood, Mary. HOW FAR SHE WENT. Athens, Georgia (1984)	—	50	125
Hook, James. *See* PEN OWEN			
Hook, Sidney. THE METAPHYSICS OF PRAGMATISM. Chicago/London, 1927	—	300	250
Hooker, Richard. (H. Richard Hornberger.) M.A.S.H. New York, 1968	60	350	500
Hoover, Herbert C. THE KAIPING COAL MINES AND COAL FIELD, CHIHLE PROVINCE, NORTH CHINA. No publisher, no place. Stapled offprint(?), 9 pages of text and seven (7) unnumbered color plates	—	1,000	1,250
PRINCIPLES OF MINING. New York, 1909. (Written with Lou Henry Hoover)	150	350	300
Hope, Anthony. (Anthony Hope Hawkins.) THE MAN OF MARK. London, 1890	—	—	400
Hope, Bob. THEY GOT ME COVERED. Hollywood, 1941. Cloth	—	—	100
Wraps	35	40	40
Hopkins, Gerard Manley. POEMS. London (1918). Red cloth	400	2,000	2,000
Blue-paper-covered boards	—	—	1,000
Horan, Robert. A BEGINNING. New Hampshire, 1948. (1,014 copies)	50	75	100
Horgan, Paul. VILLANELLE OF EVENING. No place, 1926. Wraps. (200 copies)	1,000	1,250	1,250

	1986	1995	2000
LAMB OF GOD. Roswell, 1927. Wraps. (60 copies)	1,500	1,500	1,500
MEN OF ARMS. Philadelphia (1931). (Juvenile.) (500 copies.) Boards	600	1,000	1,000
THE FAULT OF ANGELS. New York (1933)	125	150	100
Hornby, Nick. FEVER PITCH. London, 1992	—	—	750
Hornsby, Wendy. NO HARM. New York (1987)	—	—	35
Hornung, E(rnest) W(illiam). UNDER TWO SKIES. London, 1892	50	75	100
Horwood, William. DUNCTON WOOD. London, 1980	—	75	60
New York (1980)	—	—	40
Hoskins, Katherine. A PENETENTIAL PRIMER. Cummington, 1945. (350 copies.) Wraps	60	60	60
Hospital, Janette Turner. THE IVORY SWING. (Toronto, 1982.)	—	100	100
London, 1983	—	—	50
Houdini, Harry (Erich Weiss). THE RIGHT WAY TO DO WRONG. Boston, 1906. Wraps	150	350	1,500
Hough, Emerson. THE SINGING MOUSE STORIES. New York, 1895. (Cover by Will Bradley)	150	200	125
Hough, Lindy. THE VIBRATING SERPENT. Madison (1968)	30	40	75
Houghton, Claude. (C. H. Oldfield.) THE PHANTOM HOST +. London, 1917. Wraps	50	50	75
Hoult, Norah. POOR WOMEN! London, 1928. 960 copies for sale	60	60	100
Hours Press. PERONNIK THE FOOL. Written by George Moore. Chapelle-Reanville, 1928. (200 signed copies.) (2 previous pamphlets published for the authors)	200	250	450
Household, Geoffrey. (Edward West.) THE TERROR OF VILLE DONGA. London (1936)	150	300	500
THE SPANISH CAVE. Boston, 1936. (New title)	—	200	250
THE THIRD HOUR. London, 1937	75	150	250
Boston, 1938	60	125	200
Housman, A. E. A SHROPSHIRE LAD. London, 1896. (350 copies.) "Shropshire" on label 33 mm wide	1,500	1,500	2,500
New York, 1897. (150 copies)	750	1,000	2,000

	1986	1995	2000
Housman, Clemence. THE WERE-WOLF. London/Chicago, 1896	125	200	250
Housman, Laurence. A FARM IN FAIRYLAND. London, 1894. 50 large-paper copies	200	1,000	1,000
Regular issue	—	—	250
Houston, James. THE WHITE DAWN. New York, 1971	—	40	25
Houston, Pam. COWBOYS ARE MY WEAKNESS. New York (1992). Tipped-in title page	—	125	200
Title page bound in London (1993)	—	—	150
	—	—	50
Hovenden, Robert M. EPHEMERIDES . . . London, 1844	100	125	125
Hovey, Richard. POEMS. Washington, D.C., 1880. Cloth	500	1,000	1,000
Wraps	250	750	750
Howard, Brian. GOD SAVE THE KING. Paris: Hours Press, (1930). (150 copies)	250	400	350
Howard, Elizabeth Jane. THE BEAUTIFUL VISIT. London (1950)	75	100	100
Howard, H. R. (Editor.) THE HISTORY OF VIRGIL A. STEWART. New York, 1836	250	300	350
Howard, (James) H. W. BOND AND FREE. Harrisburg, 1886. Portrait of author as frontispiece. Omitted from later editions	300	750	1,000
Howard, Maureen. NOT A WORD ABOUT NIGHTINGALES. London, 1960	—	125	100
New York (1962)	35	60	50
Howard, Richard. THE VOYEUR. Written by A. Robbe-Grillet. New York, 1958. Translated by Howard. Wraps	25	50	60
QUANTITIES. Middletown (1962). Wraps (6 previous translations.)	25	35	40
Howard, Robert E. A GENT FROM BEAR CREEK. London (1937). (Most destroyed)	3,500	6,000	7,500
West Kingston, 1965. (732 copies)	—	150	125
SKULL FACE AND OTHERS. Sauk City, 1946	—	600	650
Howe, E(dgar) W(atson). THE STORY OF A COUNTRY TOWN. Atchison, Kansas, 1882. First issue: no lettering on spine base and "D. Caldwell, manufacturer, Atchison Kan" rubber-stamped inside cover	100	150	150
Howe, Irving. THE U.A.W. AND WALTER REUTHER. New York (1949). Written with B. J. Widick	—	60	40

	1986	**1995**	**2000**
SHERWOOD ANDERSON. (New York, 1951)	35	40	50
Howe, Julia Ward. *See* PASSION FLOWERS			
Howe, Mark A(nthony) DeWolfe. RARI NANTES . . . Boston, 1893. (80 copies.) Wraps	150	150	350
Howells, William Dean. *See* POEMS OF TWO FRIENDS			
LIVES AND SPEECHES OF ABRAHAM LINCOLN AND HANNI-BAL HAMLIN. Columbus, 1860. (Written with J. L. Hayes.) Wraps. First issue: pp. [95–96] blank	300	400	500
Second issue: p. [96] has engraving	—	200	350
VENETIAN LIFE . . . London (1866)	500	500	500
New York, 1866. (English sheets)	400	400	400
Cambridge, 1892. 2 volumes in vellum. (250 copies)	—	250	250
Boston, 1842. 2 volumes	—	100	150
Cambridge, 1907. 2 volumes. 550 signed and numbered copies	—	350	400
Howes, Barbara. THE UNDERSEA FARMER. Pawlet: Banyon Press, 1948. (250 copies)	100	150	100
Hoyem, Andrew. THE WAKE. San Francisco, 1963. 35 deluxe copies	100	250	250
Wraps. (750 copies)	30	40	40
Hoyningen-Huene, George. AFRICAN MIRAGE. New York, 1938	150	200	250
Hoyt, Richard. DECOYS. New York (1980)	—	30	50
Hubbard, L(afayette) Ron. BUCKSKIN BRIGADES. New York, 1937	1,500	2,500	3,500
Hudson, Jeffrey. (Michael Crichton.) A CASE OF NEED. New York/Cleveland (1968). Crichton's first hardbound book	—	—	750
London (1968)	—	—	250
Hudson, W. H. THE PURPLE LAND THAT ENGLAND LOST. London, 1885. 2 volumes. First issue: October advertisements in second volume	1,500	1,000	1,500
Hueffer, Ford Madox (Ford). THE BROWN OWL. London, 1892. (Actually 1891)	600	750	750
New York, 1891	—	—	500
Hughart, Barry. BRIDGE OF BIRDS . . . New York, 1984	—	35	50
Hughes, Daniel. WAKING IN A TREE. New York (1963)	25	30	50

	1986	1995	2000
Hughes, Dorothy B(elle Flannagan). DARK CERTAINTY. New Haven, 1931	—	200	300
THE SO BLUE MARBLE. New York (1940). (First mystery)	175	350	1,000
Hughes, Glenn. SOULS +. San Francisco, 1917	60	60	60
Hughes, Glyn. THE STANEDGE BULL +. London, 1966	—	60	75
Hughes, Hatcher. HELL-BENT FOR HEAVEN. New York, 1924. (Pulitzer Prize winner)	75	175	200
Hughes, Langston. THE WEARY BLUES. New York, 1926. First issue: dustwrapper without blurb to *Fine Clothes to the Jew*	600	3,500	7,500
Second issue: dustwrapper with blurb to *Fine Clothes to the Jew*	—	1,500	2,000
Hughes, Richard. (Arthur Warren.) GIPSY-NIGHT +. Berkshire (1922). (750 copies)	150	200	200
Chicago, 1922. 63 signed copies	150	300	300
Hughes, Rupert. THE LAKERIM ATHLETIC CLUB. New York, 1898	75	600	450
Hughes, Ted. THE HAWK IN THE RAIN. London (1957). (Preceded New York edition by five days)	150	200	200
New York (1957)	150	200	200
Hughes, Thomas. *See* TOM BROWN'S SCHOOL DAYS			
Hugo, Richard F. POEMS. (Portland, 1959.) Wraps	100	450	500
A RUN OF JACKS. Minnesota (1961)	75	250	30
Hugo, Victor. HANS OF ICELAND. London, 1825	—	500	1,000
Huie, William Bradford. MUD ON THE STARS. New York (1942)	50	100	125
Hull, Richard. THE MURDER OF MY AUNT. New York (1935)	—	—	500
Hulme, Kathryn. HOW'S THE ROAD. Philadelphia, 1928. 30 copies	100	100	200
ARAB INTERLUDE. Philadelphia, 1930	60	60	125
Hulme, Keri. THE BONE PEOPLE. Baton Rouge (1985). (2,500 copies)	30	60	150
Hulme, T. E. AN INTRODUCTION TO METAPHYSICS. New York (1912)	—	300	300
London, 1913. Translation and introduction by Hulme of Henri Bergson's work	100	250	250
Hume, Cyril. WIFE OF THE CENTAUR. New York (1923)	125	175	175

	1986	1995	2000
Hume, David. *See* A TREATISE OF HUMAN NATURE			
Hume, Fergus. THE MYSTERY OF THE HANSON CAB. Melbourne, 1886. (4 known copies)	1,000	3,000	5,000
London (1887). Wraps	500	750	1,500
Humphrey, William. THE LAST HUSBAND +. New York, 1953	150	150	200
London, 1953	100	100	125
Humphreys, Josephine. DREAMS OF SLEEP. New York (1984)	—	—	50
London (1985)	—	—	30
Humphries, Rolfe. A LITTLE ANTHOLOGY OF VERY SHORT POEMS . . . (Chicago, 1922.) Edited by Humphries	50	100	100
EUROPA +. New York, 1928. (350 copies)	75	150	150
Huncke, Herbert. HUNCKE'S JOURNAL. New York, 1965. Wraps	30	60	60
Huneker, James G(ibbons). MEZZOTINTS IN MODERN MUSIC. New York, 1899	100	150	75
Hunt, E. Howard. EAST OF FAREWELL. New York, 1942. Signed tipped-in page	75	125	150
Regular edition	40	60	75
Hunt, Gill (John Brunner). GALACTIC STORM. London (1952). Wraps	100	125	125
Hunt, (Leigh) J. H. L. JUVENILIA: OR, COLLECTION OF POEMS. London, 1801	750	750	1,000
Hunt, Violet. THE MAIDEN'S PROGRESS. London, 1894	250	300	300
New York, 1894	200	250	250
Hunter, Dard. *See* RIP VAN WINKLE			
OLD PAPERMAKING. (Chillicothe) 1923. 200 signed copies	—	3,000	4,500
Hunter, Evan. FIND THE FEATHERED SERPENT. Philadelphia (1952)	50	150	250
Hunter, Jessie Prichard. BLOOD MUSIC. New York (1993)	—	—	25
Hunter, Kristen. GOD BLESS THE CHILD. New York (1964)	75	100	150
London (1965)	—	—	100
Hunter, Stephen. THE MASTER SNIPER. New York, 1980	—	40	300
Huntley, Lydia. (Lydia Huntley Sigourney.) MORAL PIECES . . . Hartford, 1815	150	200	200

	1986	1995	2000
Hurston, Zora Neale. JONAH'S GOURD VINE. Philadelphia, 1934	400	3,500	5,000
London, 1934	—	—	2,000
Hutchins, Maude (Phelps). DIAGRAMMATICS. New York (1932). (Written with M. J. Adler.) First issue: 7⅛″ x 9³⁄₁₆″. October, 1932. (250 copies)	100	100	100
Second issue: 9 ¼″ x 12 ¼″. December 1932. (250 copies.) Boxed	75	75	75
GEORGIANA (New York, 1948)	35	35	40
Hutton, Laurence. PLAYS AND PLAYERS. New York, 1875	75	100	125
Huxley, Aldous. THE BURNING WHEEL. Oxford, 1916. Wraps	750	1,000	1,000
Huxley, Elspeth. MURDER AT GOVERNMENT HOUSE. London, 1937	75	250	250
New York, 1937	—	175	150
Huxley, Julian. HOLYROOD: THE NEWDIGATE POEM. Oxford, 1908	—	150	200
THE INDIVIDUAL IN THE ANIMAL KINGDOM. Cambridge, 1912	75	200	250
Hvass, Hans. ILLUSTRATED BOOK ABOUT REPTILES . . . Grosset & Dunlap. New York (1960). (Robert Bly translation)	—	250	250
Hyde, Anthony. THE RED FOX. London (1985)	—	—	25
Hyman, Mac. NO TIME FOR SERGEANTS. New York (1954)	35	60	100
Hyman, Stanley Edgar. THE ARMED VISION. New York, 1948	40	125	100

I

Ibáñez, Vicente Blasco. *See* Blasco Ibáñez, Vicente			
Ignatow, David. POEMS. Prairie City, Illinois (1948). Wraps	300	500	500
Imbs, Bravig. EDEN: EXIT THIS WAY +. Paris, 1926. Wraps	150	200	200
INCIDENTAL NUMBERS. (Elinor Wylie.) London, 1912. (65 copies)	5,000	5,000	5,000
INEZ: A TALE OF THE ALAMO. (Written by Augusta Jane Evans Wilson.) New York, 1855	150	350	350
Infante, Guillermo Cabrera. *See* Cabrera Infante, Guillermo			
Ingalls, Rachel. THEFT. London, 1970	—	150	100

	1986	1995	2000
THEFT and THE MAN WHO WAS LEFT BEHIND. New York, 1970	—	100	50
Inge, William. COME BACK, LITTLE SHEBA. New York (1950). First printing stated	60	200	300
Ingersoll, Robert G. AN ORATION DELIVERED . . . AT ROUSE'S HALL, PEORIA, ILL. . . . Peoria, 1869. Wraps. (First published work)	100	150	150
Ingraham, Joseph Holt. *See* THE SOUTH-WEST			
Inman, Col. Henry. STORIES OF THE OLD SANTE FE TRAIL. Kansas City, 1881	150	250	250
Innes, Michael. (John Innes MacIntosh Stewart.) DEATH AT THE PRESIDENT'S LODGING. London, 1936	400	1,000	1,500
SEVEN SUSPECTS. New York, 1936. New title	150	350	750
INSUBORDINATION . . . (Written by T. S. Arthur.) New York, 1841	300	300	350
Invincible, Ned (Edward Smyth Jones). THE ROSE THAT BLOOMETH IN MY HEART. [Louisville] (1908)	200	300	300
Iremonger, Valentin. RESERVATIONS. London, 1950. (750 copies)	—	75	75
Iris, Scharmel. LYRICS OF A LAD. Chicago, 1914	75	75	100
Iron, Ralph (Olive Schreiner). THE STORY OF AN AFRICAN FARM. London, 1883. 2 volumes	750	1,000	1,250
Irvine, Robert R. BAPTISM FOR THE DEAD. New York, 1988.	—	—	50
Irving, John. SETTING FREE THE BEARS. New York (1968)	250	750	1,000
Irving, Washington. *See* F. Depons, Launcelot Langstaff, and Diedrich Knickerbocker			
Irwin, Russell. POEMS. New York, 1888	—	—	125
Irwin, Wallace. THE LOVE SONNETS OF A HOODLUM. Paul Elder. San Francisco, 1901. Wraps	20	50	60
Second edition. San Francisco: Elder & Shepard, 1902	—	50	50
Isaacs, Susan. COMPROMISING POSITIONS. New York, 1978	—	40	40
Isherwood, Christopher. ALL THE CONSPIRATORS. London, 1928	1,000	1,750	3,500
London, 1957. (Adds new introduction)	—	75	125

	1986	1995	2000
Ishiguro, Kazuo. A PALE VIEW OF THE HILLS. (London, 1982)	—	1,000	1,500
New York (1982). White or green endpapers, priority unknown	—	200	300
ITALIAN SKETCH BOOK, THE. By an American. (Henry T. Tuckerman.) Philadelphia, 1835	125	200	300
Ives, Charles. ESSAYS BEFORE A SONATA. New York, 1920. Issued without dustwrapper?	300	1,250	1,250
Izzi, Eugene. THE TAKE. New York, 1987	—	40	40

J

	1986	1995	2000
Jackson, Charles. THE LOST WEEKEND. New York (1944)	60	150	300
London, 1945	—	100	100
Jackson, Daniel, Jr. *See* Isaac Mitchell	—	200	300
Jackson, Jon A. THE DIEHARD. New York (1977)	—	—	100
London (1978)			
Jackson, Shirley. THE ROAD THROUGH THE WALL. New York, 1948	125	350	600
Jacobi, Carl. REVELATIONS IN BLACK. Sauk City, 1947	60	125	125
London (1974)	—	—	50
Jacobs, Jane. THE DEATH AND LIFE OF GREAT AMERICAN CITIES. New York (1961)	—	—	75
Jacobs, W. W. MANY CARGOES. London, 1896	125	150	150
Jacobsen, Josephine. LET EACH MAN REMEMBER. Dallas (1940)	100	500	500
Jacobson, Dan. THE TRAP. New York (1955)	25	35	35
Jaeger, Doris U. (Doris Ullman.) FACULTY OF THE COLLEGE OF PHYSICIANS & SURGEONS. New York, 1919	—	500	750
Jaffe, Jody. A HORSE OF A DIFFERENT KILLER. New York (1995)	—	—	40
Jaffe, Rona. THE BEST OF EVERYTHING. New York (1958)	—	60	60
London (1959)	—	—	35
Jaffe, Sherril. YOUNG LUST & OTHERS. Santa Barbara, 1973. Wraps	15	25	25
SCARS MAKE YOUR BODY MORE INTERESTING. Santa Barbara, 1974. 26 signed and numbered copies in acetate dustwrapper	60	100	125
200 signed and numbered copies in acetate dustwrapper	25	40	50

	1986	1995	2000
Jahnn, Hans Henry. THE SHIP. New York (1961). (First English translation)	—	40	35
Jakes, John (William). THE TEXANS RIDE NORTH . . . Philadelphia (1952)	30	175	125
James, C(yril) L(ionel) R(obert). THE LIFE OF CAPTAIN CIPRIANI. Nelson (England), 1932. Wraps	175	175	250
James, Henry, Jr. A PASSIONATE PILGRIM +. Boston, 1875. First issue: J. R. Osgood & Co. on spine	850	2,000	2,000
Second issue: Houghton Osgood & Co	400	750	750
Third issue: Houghton, Mifflin & Co	300	400	400
James, M(ontague) R(hodes). GHOST STORIES OF AN ANTIQUARY. London, 1904. 16-page catalog dated Nov. 1904 inserted at rear	200	1,750	3,000
New York, 1905	—	—	750
James, Norah C. SLEEVELESS ERRAND. London: Scholartis Press, 1929. Banned in England	—	—	750
Paris, 1929 First book published by J. Kahane. 50 signed copies	400	400	400
450 unsigned copies	100	125	125
James, P(hyllis) D(orothy). COVER HER FACE. London, 1962	300	1,250	3,000
New York (1966)	75	450	500
James, Will(iam Roderick). COWBOYS NORTH AND SOUTH. New York, 1924	150	600	600
James, William. THE LITERARY REMAINS OF THE LATE HENRY JAMES. Boston, 1885. (edited and introduction by W.J.)	—	350	400
PRINCIPLES OF PSYCHOLOGY. New York, 1890. Two volumes. First issue with "Psychology" hyphenated in the ads opposite the title pages in both volumes	750	750	1,750
Second issue, with "Psychology" hyphenated	—	—	1,000
Jameson, (M.) Storm. THE POT BOILS. London, 1919	75	100	75
Janeway, Elizabeth. THE WALSH GIRLS. Garden City, 1943	30	60	60
Janowitz, Tama. AMERICAN DAD. New York (1981)	—	50	40
Janvier, Thomas Allbone. COLOR STUDIES. New York, 1885. (1,000 copies)	125	150	200
Jarrell, Randall. BLOOD FOR A STRANGER. New York (1942)	350	500	450
Also see FIVE YOUNG AMERICAN POETS			
Jeffers, (John) Robinson. FLAGONS & APPLES. Los Angeles, 1912. (500 copies)	750	1,500	1,500

	1986	1995	2000
CALIFORNIANS. New York, 1916. First commercial book. Advance review with perforated stamp on title page	175	300	450
Without perforated stamp	—	—	350
Jefferson, Beatrice. SMALL TOWN MURDER. New York, 1941	—	35	50
Jefferson, Thomas. *See* A Native			
NOTES ON THE STATE OF VIRGINIA. London, 1787. With folding map and table	2.5K	7.5K	15K
Philadelphia, 1788 (Preceded by 1782 [actually 1785] Paris edition.)	—	3,000	3,500
Jen, Gish. TYPICAL AMERICAN. Boston, 1991	—	40	40
Jenkins, Dan. SPORTS ILLUSTRATED'S BEST 18 GOLF HOLES IN AMERICA. New York, 1966	—	75	40
Jenkins, John Edward. *See* GINX'S BABY			
Jennings, Elizabeth. (POEMS.) Fantasy Poets No. 1. (Swinford, 1953.) Wraps	75	150	150
A WAY OF LOOKING. London, 1955	50	50	75
Jennings, Humphrey. POEMS. New York, 1951. 100 numbered copies. Wraps	—	150	175
Jepson, Edgar (Alfred). THE DICTATOR'S DAUGHTER. London, 1902	75	75	100
Jerome, Jerome K. ON STAGE AND OFF. London, 1885	200	300	350
THE IDLE THOUGHTS OF AN IDLE FELLOW. London 1886	150	200	250
Jerrold, Douglas William. MEN OF CHARACTER. London, 1838. 3 volumes	—	350	350
Jessup, Richard. THE CUNNING AND THE HAUNTED. New York (1954). Wraps	—	40	40
THE CINCINNATI KID. Boston (1963)	30	60	75
Jewel, Bishop John. *See* TRUE COPIES . . .			
Jewett, Sarah Orne. DEEPHAVEN. Boston, 1877.			
First issue: "was" vs. "so" on p. 65:16	200	500	750
Second issue: "so" vs. "was"	75	250	300
Cambridge, 1894. 250 large-paper copies	—	250	250
Jhabvala, R(uth) Prawer. TO WHOM SHE WILL. London (1955)	125	250	250
AMRITA. New York, 1956. (New Title)	—	125	125

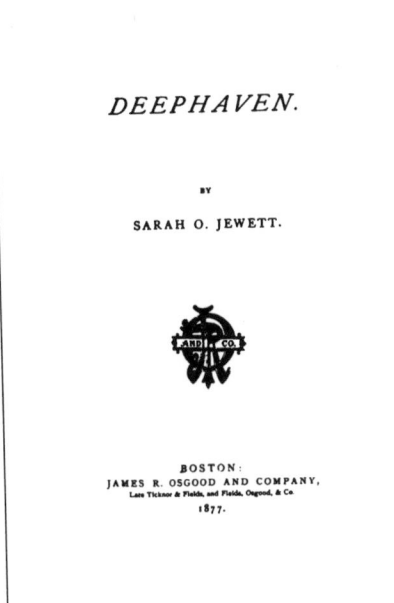

	1986	1995	2000
Johns, Orrick. ASPHALT +. New York, 1917. Reportedly the boards precede the cloth issue	60	100	50
Johns, Veronica Parker. HUSH, GABRIEL! New York (1940).	—	—	150
Johns, W(illiam) E(arl). THE CAMELS ARE COMING. London, 1932	—	200	200
Johnson, B. S. TRAVELLING PEOPLE. (London, 1963)	150	250	250
Johnson, Benj. F. (James Whitcomb Riley.) THE OLD SWIMMING HOLE +. Indianapolis, 1883. Wraps	600	600	1,000
(Facsimile in 1909 lacks "W" in "Williams" on p. 41)	25	50	60
Johnson, Charles R(ichard). BLACK HUMOR. Chicago, 1970. Wraps	—	200	100
FAITH AND THE GOOD THING. New York (1974). First novel	—	150	250
Johnson, Denis. THE MAN AMONG THE SEALS. Iowa City (1969). Issued without dustwrapper. 260 Copies	—	350	600
Johnson, Diane. FAIR GAME. New York, 1965	60	75	60

	1986	1995	2000
Johnson, Dorothy M. BEULAH BUNNY TELLS ALL. New York, 1942.	—	—	200
MISS BUNNY INTERVENES. London, 1948	—	50	200
Johnson, E. Pauline. THE WHITE WAMPUM. London, 1895	—	350	400
Johnson, James Weldon. *See* THE AUTOBIOGRAPHY OF AN EX-COLOURED MAN			
New York, 1927. Second printing, first under his name	—	—	500
Johnson, Josephine (Winslow). NOW IN NOVEMBER. New York, 1934	40	60	100
Johnson, Joyce. *See* Glassman, Joyce			
Johnson, Lionel. SIR WALTER RALEIGH IN THE TOWER. (Chester) 1885. Wraps	—	6,000	6,000
THE ART OF THOMAS HARDY. London, 1894. (150 copies)	500	650	650
Trade edition	150	200	150
POEMS. London/Boston, 1895. 25 signed and numbered copies	1,000	6,000	5,000
Trade edition. (750 copies)	750	350	450
Johnson, Martin. THROUGH THE SOUTH SEAS. New York, 1913	—	250	250
Johnson, Merle (DeVore). A BIBLIOGRAPHY OF MARK TWAIN. New York, 1910. (500 copies)	150	200	250
Johnson, Pamela Hansford. SYMPHONY FOR FULL ORCHESTRA. London, 1934. Cloth	—	250	250
Wraps	125	125	125
Johnson, Ronald. A LINE OF POETRY, A ROW OF TREES. Highlands, 1964. 50 signed and numbered copies	200	350	350
Stiff wraps. (500 copies)	75	75	100
Johnson, Samuel. *See* Mr. LeGrande			
Johnson, Uwe. SPECULATIONS ABOUT JAKOB. New York (1963)	25	35	35
London (1963)	—	—	25
Johnston, Jill. MARMALADE ME. New York, 1971. Wraps	—	40	25
Johnston, Mary. PRISONER OF HOPE. Boston, 1898	50	75	75
Johnston, Paul. BODY POLITIC. (London, 1977.)	—	—	125
Jolas, Eugene. RHYTHMUS, Volume 2. Peoria, 1924. Wraps. Entire issue devoted to Jolas	—	125	150
CINEMA: POEMS. New York, 1926	200	300	300

	1986	1995	2000
Jolly, Andrew. LIE DOWN IN ME. New York (1970)	50	50	40
Jolly, Elizabeth. PALOMINO. Victoria (1980)	—	—	100
London (1980). Reportedly issued simultaneously	—	—	75
Jones, Brian. POEMS. London, 1966. Wraps	—	40	40
Jones, D. G. FROST ON THE SUN. Toronto, 1957. Wraps in dust-wrapper	—	150	175
Jones, David (Michael). IN PARENTHESIS. London (1937)	500	850	850
London (1961). 70 signed and numbered copies. (Jones and Eliot)	900	2,500	2,500
New York (1961). First issue: Eliot introduction not listed on contents page	75	100	75
Second issue: Eliot introduction listed	35	60	60
Jones, Douglas C. THE TREATY OF MEDICINE LODGE. Norman, Okla., 1966	—	75	100
Jones, Edward Smyth. *See* Ned Invincible			
THE SYLVAN CABIN +. Boston, 1911	50	75	100
San Francisco, 1915. Wraps. (First separate edition)	150	75	75
Jones, Gayl. CORREGIDORA. New York (1975)	40	75	125
Jones, Glyn. THE BLUE BED +. London (1937)	50	75	100
New York, 1938	—	—	50
Jones, Gwyn. RICHARD SAVAGE. London, 1935	60	75	125
New York, 1935	—	—	100
Jones, Howard Mumford. A LITTLE BOOK OF LOCAL VERSE. La Crosse, 1915. Wraps	60	75	75
Jones, James. FROM HERE TO ETERNITY. New York, 1951. Presentation edition with signed and numbered tipped-in page. (About 1,500 copies)	225	300	600
Regular trade edition	125	175	250
London, 1952	75	100	100
Jones, James Athearn. *See* Matthew Murgatroyd			
Jones, Joshua Henry. BY SANCTION OF LAW. Boston, 1924. (Two books of poetry precede)	75	75	250
Jones, (Everett) Leroi. (Imamu Amiri Baraka.) CUBA LIBRE. New York, 1961. Wraps	200	250	350
PREFACE TO A TWENTY VOLUME SUICIDE NOTE. New York (1961). Wraps. First issue: ads in bold caps	35	100	100
Second issue: ads not in bold caps (3 intervening broadsides.)	25	40	35

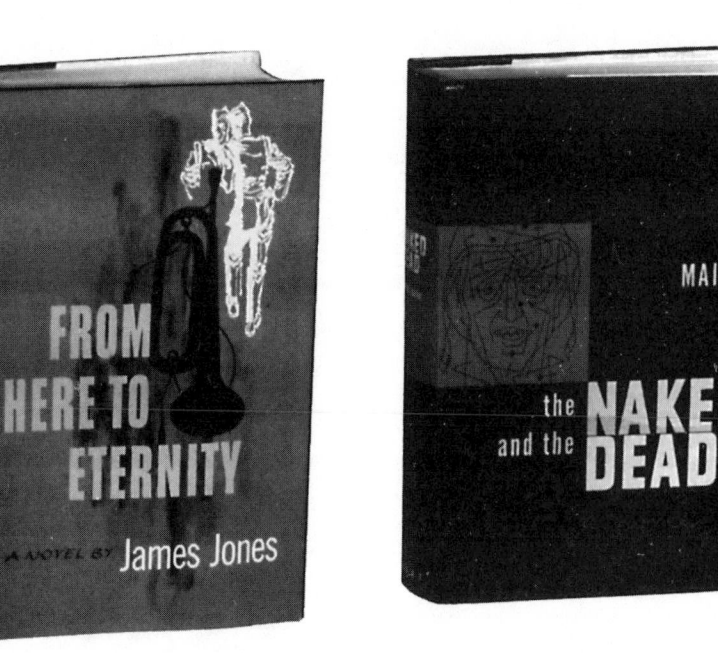

	1986	1995	2000
Jones, Madison Percy. THE INNOCENT. New York (1957)	60	75	75
Jones, Nettie. FISH TALES. New York (1983)	—	25	40
Jones, Thom. PUGILIST AT REST. Boston, 1993	—	50	50
Jong, Erica. FRUITS AND VEGETABLES. New York (1971). Cloth	35	75	75
Wraps	15	25	25
Jonson, Ben(jamin). EVERY MAN OUT OF HIS HUMOUR. London, 1600	2,500	5,000	5,000
Jordan, Neil. NIGHT IN TUNISIA. Dublin (1976). Wraps	—	250	300
London, 1979	—	100	100
New York (1980)	—	60	40
Jordon, June. WHO LOOK AT ME. New York, 1969	30	40	40
Joseph, Clifton. METROPOLITAN BLUES. (Toronto, 1983.) 500 Copies in wraps	—	40	30
Joseph, Jenny. THE UNLOOKED FOR SEASON. London, 1960	—	75	75
Josephson, Matthew. GALIMATHIAS. New York (1923). Stiff wraps. (250 numbered copies)	125	200	250
Joss, John. SIERRA. (Los Altos, 1977)	—	100	100
New York (1978)	—	—	35

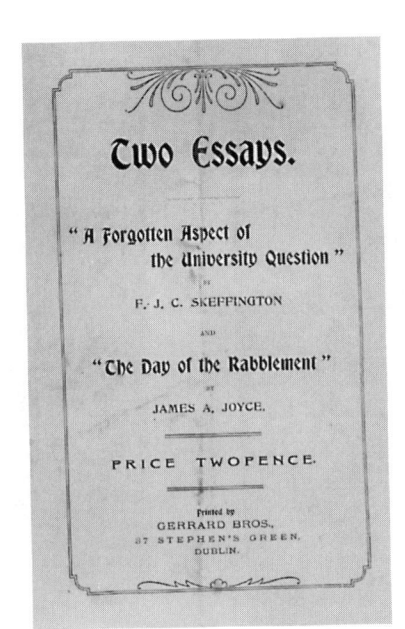

	1986	1995	2000
JOURNAL OF A FEW MONTHS' RESIDENCE IN PORTUGAL . . . London, 1847. 2 volumes. (Dorothy Wordsworth Quillinan)	—	750	1,000
Joyce, James. TWO ESSAYS. Dublin (1901). Wraps. (Written with F. J. C. Skeffington.) (Contains "Day of the Rabblement")	5K	10K	10K
THE HOLY OFFICE. (Pola, 1904 or 1905.) Broadside	8K	12K	12.5K
CHAMBER MUSIC. London, 1907. First issue: thick laid endpapers with horizontal chain lines. Poems in signature C are well centered	6,000	7,500	7,500
Second issue: thick wove endpapers, signature C is poorly centered	1,250	2,500	4,000
Third issue: thin wove transparent endpapers, signature C is poorly centered	1,250	2,500	3,000
London, 1918. Wraps. "Second Edition"	250	400	750
Boston (1918). Unauthorized edition. Issued in tissue dustwrapper	200	250	250
New York, 1918. (Assumed no dustwrapper)	200	200	300
London, 1923. Egoist Press. (107 copies)	200	600	750
Jonathan Cape (1927). (393 copies)	100	450	450
Judah, Samuel B(enjamin) H(erbert). THE MOUNTAIN TORRENT . . . New York, 1820	200	350	350
Just, Ward. TO WHAT END. Boston, 1968	30	60	75
Juster, Norton. THE PHANTOM TOLLBOOTH. New York, 1961.	—	—	200

	1986	1995	2000
Justice, Donald. THE OLD BACHELOR +. Miami, 1951. Wraps. (240 copies)	250	600	600
THE SUMMER ANNIVERSARIES. Middletown, Conn. (1960). Cloth	50	100	100
Wraps	20	30	30

K

	1986	1995	2000
K., R.A. (Ronald Knox.) SIGNA SEVERA. Eton College, 1906. Wraps	250	350	400
Kael, Pauline. I LOST IT AT THE MOVIES. Boston (1965)	40	60	75
London (1996)	—	50	60
Kafka, Franz. THE CASTLE. London, 1930. (First English translation)	250	1,250	2,000
New York, 1930	150	500	850
Kahane, Jack. TWO PLAYS. Manchester (England), 1912. Wraps	150	300	500
Kahn, E. J., Jr. THE ARMY LIFE. New York, 1942	—	75	50
Kahn, Roger. INSIDE BIG LEAGUE BASEBALL. New York, 1962	—	150	200
Kakonis, Tom. MICHIGAN ROLL. New York (1988)	—	—	50
Kaler, James Otis. *See* James Otis			
Kallman, Chester. ELEGY. New York (1951). Wraps. (500 copies)	50	75	50
Kaltenborn, H. V. KALTENBORN EDITS THE NEWS. New York (1937). (Ghostwritten by Mary McCarthy.) Cloth in dustwrapper	125	200	200
Wraps in dustwrapper	50	100	125
Kaminsky, Stuart M. DON SIEGEL: DIRECTOR. New York (1974). Wraps	—	40	75
BULLET FOR A STAR. New York, 1977. First mystery	—	—	50
London, 1981			
Kandel, Lenore. A PASSING DRAGON. (Studio City, Calif. 1959.) Wraps	30	75	100
Kanin, Garson. BORN YESTERDAY. New York, 1946	50	150	100
Kanon, Joseph. LOS ALAMOS. New York (1997)	—	—	50
Kantor, MacKinlay. DIVERSAY. New York, 1928. Also first book by Coward McCann. First issue: no reviews on dustwrapper	125	200	300

	1986	1995	2000
Karlins, Marvin. THE LAST MAN IS OUT. New York, 1969	—	—	100
Karp, David. THE BIG FEELING. New York (1952). Wraps	35	35	35
ONE. New York (1953). (First hardback, sixth book)	35	50	50
Karp, Ivan. DOOBIE DOO. Garden City (1965). Warhol and Lichtenstein dustwrapper	30	100	125
Katz, Steve. THE LESTRIAD. Leece, 1962. (300 copies.) Wraps	100	125	125
Katzenbach, John. IN THE HEAT OF THE SUMMER. New York, 1982	—	—	50
London, 1982	—	—	25
Kaufman, George S. DULCY. New York (1921). Written with Marc Connelly	200	600	500
Kavan, Anna (Helen Woods). *See* Helen Ferguson			
Kavanagh, Dan. (Julian Barnes.) DUFFY. London (1980). (Second book, first mystery)	40	200	200
Kavanagh, P. J. ONE AND ONE. London, 1959	—	—	75
Kavanagh, Patrick. D'OLIER MUSIC CO'S FAMOUS SONGS. Dublin, 1930. Wraps	—	750	750
PLOUGHMAN. London, 1936. Wraps	75	1,000	750
Kay, Terry. THE YEAR THE LIGHTS CAME ON. Boston, 1976	—	—	100
Kaye, Philip B. TAFFY. New York, 1950	75	100	125
Kaye-Smith, Sheila. THE TRAMPING METHODIST. London, 1908	125	150	175
Kazan, Elia. AMERICA AMERICA. New York (1962)	30	40	50
Kazantzakis, Nikos. ZORBA THE GREEK. London (1952). (First English translation)	150	250	350
New York, 1953	—	—	200
Kazin, Alfred. ON NATIVE GROUND. New York (1942)	75	125	200
London (1943)	50	75	100
Keating, H. R. F. DEATH AND THE VISITING FIREMAN. London, 1959	40	125	250
New York, 1973	—	30	50
Keats, John. POEMS. London, 1817	8K	10K	12.5K
Keeble, John. CRAB CANYON. New York, 1971	—	—	75
Keene, Carolyn. THE SECRET OF THE OLD CLOCK. New York,	—	1,250	1,750

	1986	1995	2000
1930. (By Mildred Benson.) First issue: dustwrapper with Nancy Drews 1 through 3 advertised; book has ad for first 8 Hardy Boys			
Second issue: dustwrapper advertises first 4 Nancy Drews and book advertises 9 hardbacks	—	600	1,000
KEEP COOL. (John Neal.) Baltimore, 1817. 2 volumes	300	500	500
Kees, Weldon. THE LAST MAN. San Francisco, 1943. Boards without dustwrapper. (300 copies)	75	200	750
Keillor, Garrison. G.K. THE DJ. New York, 1977. Stapled wraps	—	—	125
HAPPY TO BE HERE. New York, 1982	30	75	75
Keith, J. Kilmeny (Lucy Beatrice Malleson a.k.a. Anthony Gilbert). THE MAN WHO WAS LONDON. London, 1925	—	—	450
Keller, David H(enry). THE THOUGHT PROJECTOR. New York (1930). Wraps. First science fiction	60	150	150
Keller, Helen. THE STORY OF MY LIFE. Boston, 1904	—	—	100
Kellerman, Faye. THE RITUAL BATH. New York, 1986	—	40	100
London, 1987	—	—	50
Kellerman, Jonathan. WHEN THE BOUGH BREAKS. New York, 1985	—	150	175
(Two nonfiction titles precede.)			
Kelley, Edith Summers. WEEDS. New York (1923)	125	250	400
London, 1924	100	200	250
Kelley, Emma Dunham. MEGDA. Boston, 1891	—	600	750
Kelley, William Melvin. A DIFFERENT DRUMMER. Garden City, 1962	75	150	200
Kellogg, Majorie. TELL ME THAT YOU LOVE ME, JUNIE MOON. New York, 1968	30	30	30
Kelly, Robert. ARMED DESCENT. (New York, 1961.) Stiff wraps	50	75	100
Kelly, Susan. THE GEMINI MAN. New York, 1985	—	75	75
Kelly, Walt. POGO. New York (1951). Wraps. 5 variants, priority unknown	50	60	75
Kelty, Mary Ann. *See* THE FAVOURITE OF NATURE			
Kemble, Frances Ann. FRANCIS THE FIRST. London, 1832. Wraps	—	200	300

	1986	1995	2000
Kemelman, Harry. FRIDAY THE RABBI SLEPT LATE. New York (1964). Price of $3.95 and bulking 1″ thick	35	75	100
Kemp, Arnold. EAT OF ME, I AM THE SAVIOR. New York, 1972	—	40	40
Kenan, Randall. A VISITATION OF SPIRITS. New York (1989)	—	60	50
Keneally, Thomas. THE PLACE AT WHITTON. London (1964)	100	350	450
New York (1965)	—	—	300
Kennan, George. TENT LIFE IN SIBERIA. New York, 1870	100	125	150
Kennan, George F. AMERICAN DIPLOMACY 1900–1950. Chicago (1951)	40	50	60
Kennedy, Edward. THE FRUITFUL BOUGH. Privately printed, 1965. (Tribute to father collected by E.M.K.)	100	250	350
DECISIONS FOR A DECADE. New York, 1968	40	50	30
Kennedy, John F(itzgerald). WHY ENGLAND SLEPT. New York, 1940	400	750	850
London (1940)	150	200	250
Kennedy, John Pendleton. *See* Mephistopheles. *Also see* SWALLOW BARN			
Kennedy, Margaret. THE CONSTANT NYMPH. Garden City, 1925	—	—	100
Kennedy, Mark. THE PECKING ORDER. New York (1953)	30	75	75
Kennedy, Raymond. MY FATHER'S ORCHARD. Boston, 1963	30	40	40
Kennedy, Robert. THE ENEMY WITHIN. New York (1960)	40	100	150
Kennedy, Thomas. POEMS. Washington, 1816	100	150	150
Kennedy, William. THE INK TRUCK. New York, 1969	175	450	450
London, 1970	—	—	100
Kennedy, X. J. (Joseph Charles Kennedy.) NUDE DESCENDING A STAIRCASE. Garden City (1961)	50	60	75
Kenner, Hugh. PARADOX IN CHESTERTON. New York, 1947	—	125	150
London, 1948	125	100	125
Kenney, Susan. GARDEN OF MALICE. New York (1983)	—	—	40
Kenny, Maurice. DEAD LETTERS SENT +. San Francisco (1958). Wraps in dustwrapper	—	50	50
Kent, Rockwell. *See* ARCHITEC-TONICS			

	1986	1995	2000
THE SEVEN AGES OF MAN. New York, 1918. First collected illustrations	150	250	400
WILDERNESS . . . New York, 1920. First issue: cover in gray	250	400	600
Second issue: cover in tan	150	300	500
Los Angeles (1970). 1,500 signed copies in slipcase	—	150	250
Kernahan, (John) Coulson. A BOOK OF STRANGE SINS. London, 1893	40	50	100
Kerouac, John (Jack). (Jean-Louis.) THE TOWN AND THE CITY. New York (1950)	300	600	850
London, 1951	200	250	500
Kerr, Jean. OUR HEARTS WERE YOUNG AND GAY. Chicago (1946)	—	75	75
Kerr, Philip. MARCH VIOLETS. London, 1989	—	100	250
New York (1989)	—	—	40
Kerrigan, Anthony. LEAR IN THE TROPIC OF PARIS. Barcelona, 1953. Wraps. (100 copies)	60	75	75
Kersh, Gerald. JEWS WITHOUT JEHOVAH. London, 1934	125	200	250
Kesey, Ken (Elton). ONE FLEW OVER THE CUCKOO'S NEST. New York, 1962	300	1,500	3,000
London, 1962. Changes made to text: Red Cross nurse replaced by "Public Relations," who is a man, and all physical descriptions altered	75	300	400
Keyes, Daniel. FLOWERS FOR ALGERNON. New York (1966). First novel	—	—	600
London, 1966	—	—	300
Keyes, Frances Parkinson. THE OLD GRAY HOMESTEAD. New York, 1919	—	60	75
Keyes, Sidney. THE IRON LAUREL. London, 1942. Stiff wraps and dustwrapper	40	75	100
Keynes, John Maynard. INDIAN CURRENCY AND FINANCE. London, 1913	—	—	1,500
Kidder, Tracy. THE ROAD TO YUBA CITY. Garden City, 1974	—	150	175
Kiefer, Warren. THE LINGALA CODE. New York, 1972	—	60	75
Kiely, Benedict. COUNTIES OF CONTENTION. Cork, 1945	75	100	125
Kienzle, William. ROSARY MURDERS. New York, 1979	—	50	40
Kijewski, Karen. KATWALK. New York, 1989	—	175	350

	1986	1995	2000
Killens, John O. YOUNGBLOOD. New York, 1954	75	150	200
Kilmer, Aline. CANDLES THAT BURN. New York (1919)	30	50	50
Kilmer, (Alfred) Joyce. SUMMER OF LOVE. New York, 1911. Baker & Taylor at foot of spine. Issued in glassine dustwrapper	250	350	350
Kincaid, Jamaica. AT THE BOTTOM OF THE RIVER. New York (1983)	35	100	150
King, Alan. ANYBODY WHO OWNS HIS OWN HOME DESERVES IT. New York, 1962	—	40	30
King, Alexander. MINE ENEMY GROWS OLDER. New York (1958). In two dustwrappers	—	75	60
King, Florence. SOUTHERN LADIES AND GENTLEMEN. New York (1975)	—	75	50
King, Francis. TO THE DARK TOWER. (London) 1946	100	150	150
King, Grace (Elizabeth). MONSIEUR MOTTE. New York, 1888	75	125	125
King, John. LECTURES UPON IONAS. Oxford, 1597	—	600	600
King, Kennedy. (George Douglas Brown.) LOVE AND A SWORD. London, 1899	—	100	75
King, Larry L. THE ONE-EYED MAN. New York (1966)	50	75	60
King, Laurie R. A GRAVE TALENT. New York, 1993	—	—	600
London, 1995	—	—	75
King, Martin Luther, Jr. STRIDE TOWARD FREEDOM. New York, 1958	100	250	250
London, 1959	50	150	250
King, Ross. DOMINO. (London, 1995.)	—	—	75
King, Rufus (Frederick). NORTH STAR, A DOG OF THE CANADIAN NORTHWEST. New York, 1925	—	125	125
MYSTERY DELUXE. New York (1927). First mystery	35	75	250
King, Stephen. CARRIE. Garden City, 1974	175	750	1,000
London, 1974	—	600	900
Kingsley, Charles. THE SAINT'S TRAGEDY ... London, 1848	200	600	250
Kingsley, Henry. THE RECOLLECTIONS OF GEOFFREY HAMLYN. Cambridge, 1859. 3 volumes	300	300	500
Boston, 1859	—	—	150

	1986	1995	2000
Kingsmill, Hugh. *See* Hugh Lunn			
Kingsolver, Barbara. THE BEAN TREES. New York (1988)	—	175	350
London, 1989	—	—	75
Kingston, Maxine Hong. THE WOMAN WARRIOR. New York, 1976	50	100	150
London, 1977	—	75	75
Kinnell, Galway. BITTER VICTORY. (Written by Rene Hardy, translated by G.K.) Garden City, 1956	125	200	150
WHAT A KINGDOM IT WAS. Boston, 1960	125	150	150
Kinsella, Thomas. THE STARLIT EYE. Dublin, 1952	100	250	600
Kinsella, W(illiam) P(atrick). DANCE ME OUTSIDE. (Ottawa, 1997.) Cloth	250	1,250	1,000
Wraps. (No differentiation among a number of printings)	40	50	150
Boston, 1986	—	75	35
Kipling, Rudyard. SCHOOLBOY LYRICS. Lahore, 1881. Wraps. (50 copies.) White presumed to precede brown	12K	17.5K	22.5K
DEPARTMENTAL DITTIES +. Lahore, 1886. Wraps	—	2,000	5,000
Kirkup, James (Falconer). INDICATIONS. London, 1942. Written with J. Ormond and J. Bayliss. Stiff wraps	125	150	150
COSMIC SHAPE. London (1946). 500 numbered copies. (Written with Ross Nichols)	75	100	125
THE DROWNED SAILOR +. London, 1947	60	100	40
Kirkwood, Jim (James). THERE MUST BE A PONY. Boston (1960)	40	50	50
Kirn, Walter. MY HARD BARGAIN. New York, 1990	—	—	25
Kirsch, Robert R. IN THE WRONG RAIN. Boston (1959)	40	40	40
Kirst, Hans Helmut. THE REVOLT OF GUNNAR ASHE. Boston (1955)	40	75	75
Kirstein, Lincoln. FLESH IS HEIR. New York, 1932	75	150	200
Kisner, James. NERO'S VICE. New York (1981)	—	—	30
Kissinger, Henry A. A WORLD RESTORED ... Boston, 1957	75	100	75
Kitchin, C(lifford) H(enry) B(enn). CURTAINS. Oxford, 1919. Wraps	75	300	100
Kiteley, Brian. STILL LIFE WITH INSECTS. New York, 1989.	—	—	35

	1986	1995	2000
Kittredge, William. THE VAN GOGH FIELD +. Columbia, Missouri, 1978. Issued without dustwrapper	—	300	450
Kizer, Carolyn. POEMS. Portland (1959). Wraps	100	300	300
THE UNGRATEFUL GARDEN. Bloomington (1961). Cloth	75	125	125
Wraps	20	30	30
Kjelgaard, Jim. FOREST PATROL. New York, 1948	—	75	75
Klane, Robert. THE HORSE IS DEAD. New York, 1968. First edition stated	50	100	125
Klein, A. M. HATH NOT A JEW. New York, 1940. Issued without dustwrapper	—	500	500
Klein, Ted. THE CEREMONIES. New York, 1984	—	40	35
Klein, William. NEW YORK. LIFE IS GOOD ... London (1956). Including small guidebook attached with ribbon	—	1,250	1,250
Kline, Otis Adelbert. THE PLANET OF PERIL. Chicago, 1929	—	—	600
Kneale, Higel. TOMATO CAIN +. London, 1949	40	40	40
Knickerbocker, Diedrich. (Washington Irving.) A HISTORY OF NEW YORK FROM THE BEGINNING OF THE WORLD ... New York, 1809. 2 volumes with 268 pages in volume 1	1,000	1,250	1,500
New York, 1812. 2 volumes. With alterations	—	—	300
Knight, Alanna. ENTER SECOND MURDERER. London (1988). (First of the Inspector Faro series)	—	—	30
Knight, Clifford (Reynolds). *See* Reynolds Knight			
THE AFFAIR OF THE SCARLET CLUB. New York, 1937. (Second book, first mystery)	—	250	400
Knight, Eric. INVITATION TO LIFE. New York (1934)	—	—	250
LASSIE COME HOME. Philadelphia (1940)	—	350	600
London (1941)	—	200	450
Knight, Reynolds. TOMMY OF THE VOICES. Chicago, 1918	—	75	75
Also see Clifford Knight			
Knister, Raymond. WHITE NARCISSUS. Toronto, 1929. First issue in green cloth with labels	—	—	350
Knowles, John. A SEPARATE PEACE. London, 1959	400	750	1,500
New York, 1950. First issue: pictorial dustwrapper	150	500	750
Second issue: printed dustwrapper	75	150	200

	1986	1995	2000
Knowlton, Charles. ELEMENTS OF MODERN MATERIALISM . . . Adams, Mass., 1829	750	600	450
Knox, Ronald A(rbuthnott). *See* K., R. A.			
Kober, Arthur. THUNDER OVER THE BRONX. New York, 1935	35	50	150
Kobo, Abe. WOMAN IN THE DUNES. New York, 1964	—	125	150
Koch, Kenneth. POEMS. (With Nell Blaine's PRINTS.) New York, 1953. Stiff wraps. (300 copies)	400	1,000	1,250
Koestler, Arthur. *See* A. Costler			
SPANISH TESTAMENT. London, 1937. Cloth	250	300	350
Wraps. (Left Book Club)	75	75	75
Kohler, Vince. RAINY NORTH WOODS. New York (1990)	—	—	25
Kohler, Wolfgang. THE MENTALITY OF APES. New York, 1925	100	150	75
Komroff, Manuel. THE GRACE OF LAMBS. New York, 1925	—	—	60
Koontz, Dean R(ay). STAR QUEST. New York (1968). Wraps. Paperback original. (Bound with DOOM OF THE GREEN PLANET by Emil Petaja) *Also see* K. R. Dwyer	—	75	35
Korda, Michael. MALE CHAUVINISM! HOW IT WORKS. New York (1973)	40	50	25
Kornbluth, C. M. TAKE OFF. Garden City, 1952	—	—	100
Kosinski, Jerzy (Nikodem). *See* Joseph Novak			
THE PAINTED BIRD. Boston, 1965. (Third book, first under his name.) First issue: extraneous line top of p. 270	200	300	400
London, 1966	—	—	150
Kotzwinkle, William. THE FIREMAN. New York, 1969	75	250	350
Kovacs, Ernie. ZOOMAR. New York, 1957	35	60	75
Kovic, Ron. BORN ON THE FOURTH OF JULY. New York, 1976	—	75	90
Kramer, Jane. OFF WASHINGTON SQUARE. New York (1963)	—	40	25
Kramer, Larry. FAGGOTS. New York, 1978	—	—	25
Kramm, Joseph. THE SHRIKE. New York (1952)	—	75	75
Kreymborg, Alfred. LOVE AND LIFE +. New York (1908). (500 copies)	75	100	100

	1986	1995	2000
Krich, John. CHICAGO IS. Venice (1976). 170 copies. Issued with dustwrapper	—	—	150
Krim, Seymour. VIEWS OF A NEARSIGHTED CANNONEER. New York (1961). Wraps	20	30	40
Krist, Gary. THE GARDEN STATE. San Diego, 1988	—	—	30
Kroll, Harry Harrison. THE MOUNTAIN SINGER. New York, 1928	—	—	250
THE CABIN IN THE COTTON. New York, 1931. 250 signed and numbered copies	—	—	200
Trade edition	35	75	100
Kromer, Tom. WAITING FOR NOTHING. New York, 1935	125	250	250
Kronenberger, Louis. THE GRAND MANNER. New York, 1929	40	100	75
London, 1929	—	—	40
Krutch, Joseph Wood. COMEDY AND CONSCIENCE . . . New York, 1924. Wraps	100	200	100
Kuhn, Thomas S. THE COPERNICAN REVOLUTION. Cambridge, 1957	—	100	100
Kumin, Maxine W. SEBASTIAN AND THE DRAGON. New York, 1960	50	100	100
HALFWAY. New York (1961)	50	60	60
Kundera, Milan. THE JOKE. London, 1969	—	150	300
New York (1969)	100	125	125
Kunitz, Stanley (Jasspon). INTELLECTUAL THINGS. Garden City, 1930	125	150	300
Kupferberg, Tuli. SELECTED FRUITS AND NUTS. New York (1959). Wraps	—	100	125
Kurz, Ron. LETHAL GAS. New York, 1974	—	50	50
Kuttner, Henry. *See* Will Garth. *Also see* Lewis Padgett			
Kuzma, Greg. SOMETHING AT LEAST VISIBLE. Lansin, 1969. Wraps	—	—	50
Kyd, Thomas. (Alfred Bennett Harbage.) BLOOD IS A BEGGAR. Philadelphia/New York (1946)	35	50	50
Kyger, Joanne. THE TAPESTRY AND THE WEB. San Francisco, 1965. 27 signed and numbered copies	125	125	150
Trade. (1,000 copies.) Cloth	50	50	40
Wraps	15	15	15

	1986	1995	2000
L			
L., E.V. (Edward Verrall Lucas.) SPARKS FROM A FLINT. London, 1890	60	100	150
L., W. (Walter Lowenfels.) EPISODES AND EPISTLES. New York, 1925	125	200	300
Lady of Philadelphia. *See* SEVENTY FIVE RECIPES . . .			
La Farge, Christopher. HOXIE SELLS HIS ACRES. New York, 1934	25	100	100
La Farge, Oliver (Hazard Perry). LAUGHING BOY. Boston, 1929. (Previous collaboration)	75	250	400
Lafferty, R. A. PAST MASTER. New York (1968). Wraps	—	40	35
London, 1968	—	125	100
La Flesche, Francis. THE MIDDLE FIVE. Boston, 1900	—	—	250
La France, Marston. MIAMI MURDER-GO-ROUND. Cleveland (1951).	—	—	125
Laing, Alexander. FOOL'S ERRAND. New York, 1928	—	100	100
Laing, Dilys. ANOTHER ENGLAND. New York, 1941	—	35	35
Lamantia, Philip. EROTIC POEMS. (Berkeley) 1946	200	300	400
Lamar, Mirabeu B. VERSE MEMORIALS. New York, 1857	1,500	2,000	2,000
Lamb, Lady Caroline. *See* GLENARVON			
Lamb, Charles. POEMS. London, 1797. (Published with POEMS by S. T. Coleridge. Second edition)	—	1,000	1,000
A TALE OF ROSAMUND GRAY . . . Birmingham, 1798. (First separate book. Rare with Birmingham on title page)	—	2,500	4,000
London, 1798	—	—	1,000
Lamb, Wally. SHE'S COME UNDONE. New York, 1992	—	—	50
Lambert, Gavin. THE SLIDE AREA. London, 1959	—	—	150
New York, 1959	—	75	100
Lamkin, Speed. TIGER IN THE GARDEN. Boston, 1950	40	40	60
Lamming, George (Eric). IN THE CASTLE OF MY SKIN. London (1953)	50	100	150
New York (1953)	—	75	50
L'Amour, Louis. SMOKE FROM THIS ALTAR. Oklahoma City (1939). First issue: Orange cloth	150	750	1,000
Second issue: Green cloth	—	600	750

	1986	1995	2000
LAMPLIGHTER, THE. (Maria S. Cummins.) Boston, 1854. (Noted in black (BAL), green or blue cloths)	—	1,000	1,000
Lampman, Archibald. AMONG THE MILLET. Ottawa, 1888. First issue: double rule above & below title on spine. In rose cloth	175	250	250
Lampson, M. Robbins (Robin). ON REACHING SIXTEEN. Geyserville, 1916. String-tied wraps	—	100	100
Lamson, David. WE WHO ARE ABOUT TO DIE. New York, 1935	50	50	50
Lanchester, John. THE DEBT TO PLEASURE. London (1996). First issue: MacMillan on dustwrapper, title, and copyright page	—	—	300
Second issue: Picador on dustwrapper, title, and copyright page	—	—	75
New York, 1996	—	—	25
Landesman, Peter. THE RAVEN. Dallas (1995)	—	—	60
Landor, Walter Savage. GEBIR: A POEM. London, 1798. In original wraps	—	3,000	2,500
Rebound	—	—	1,250
Landreth, Marsha. THE HOLIDAY MURDERS. New York, 1992	—	—	60
Lane, Grant (Steve Fisher). SPEND THE NIGHT. New York, 1935	—	—	750
Lane, Margaret. FAITH, HOPE, NO CHARITY. London, 1935	—	50	75
Lane, Pinkie Gordon. WIND THOUGHTS. Fort Smith (1972). Wraps	—	50	75
Lang, Andrew. BALLADS AND LYRICS OF OLD FRANCE +. London, 1872	60	300	250
Lang, V(iolet) R(anney). THE PITCH. New York, 1962. (Edward Gorey illustrations.) Wraps	60	100	125
Lange, Dorothea. AN AMERICAN EXODUS . . . New York, 1939. Written with Paul S. Taylor	—	300	750
Lange, John. (Michael Crichton.) ODDS ON. New York, 1966. Wraps	30	125	200
Langer, Susanne K. PHILOSOPHY IN A NEW KEY. Cambridge, 1942	—	250	150
Langstaff, Launcelot. (Washington Irving, William Irving, and J. K. Paulding.) SALMAGUNDI . . . New York, 1807/8. 20 parts. Bound without wraps (complex, check BAL)	2,500	2,500	2,500
Langton, Jane. THE MAJESTY OF GRACE. New York, 1961	—	—	125

	1986	1995	2000
THE TRANSCENDENTAL MURDER. New York, 1964. Third book, first mystery	—	250	300
Lanham, Edwin. SAILORS DON'T CARE. Paris, 1929. 10 signed and numbered copies	—	650	1,000
Wraps. (500 copies)	400	400	600
New York, 1930	125	150	200
Lanier, Sidney. TIGER-LILIES. New York, 1867. First issue: title page on stub	100	500	500
Lanier, Virginia. DEATH IN BLOODHOUND RED. Sarasota (1995). First-state dustwrapper has "Athony" vs. "Anthony" on dustwrapper	—	—	450
Lansdale, Joe R. ACT OF LOVE. New York (1981). Wraps	—	—	35
London, 1989	—	—	60
New York, 1992. One of 750 signed and numbered copies	—	—	50
Larcom, Lucy. SIMILITUDES. Boston, 1854	75	125	200
Lardner, Ring(old Wilmer.) ZANZIBAR. Niles, Mich. (1903). Wraps	—	6,000	6,000
MARCH SIXTH THE HOMECOMING. (Chicago, 1914). First edition not stated. Issued without dustwrapper	—	5,000	5,000
HONEYMOON. New York: McClure, 1915. Wraps	—	—	3,500
BIB BALLADS. Chicago (1915). (500 copies) (More if in orignal box)	125	350	250
Lardner, Ring W., Jr. THE YOUNG IMMIGRUNTS. Indianapolis (1920). With a preface by the father (who must have written the book, since the son was only four years old)	150	350	250
JUNE MOON. New York, 1930. Written with George S. Kaufman. (Junior is now fourteen years old.)	—	150	250
THE ECSTASY OF OWEN MUIR. New York, 1954	—	—	50
London, 1954	—	—	75
Larkin, Philip. THE NORTH SHIP. London (1945). Black cloth. Published at 6s	600	2,500	3,500
Second edition: dark-red buckram [1965]. Published at 21s	—	200	250
Third edition. Faber. London (1966)	—	100	125
Larner, Jeremy. DRIVE, HE SAID. New York (1964). First issue: wraps	15	15	25
Second issue: hardback	25	25	35
London, 1965	—	—	35

	1986	1995	2000
Larsen, Nella. QUICKSAND. New York, 1928	—	—	2,500
Lasdun, James. THE SILVER AGE. London (1985)	—	—	40
LaSpina, Greye. INVADERS FROM THE DARK. Sauk City, 1960	—	100	125
Lathen, Emma. (Mary Jane Latsis and Martha Henissart.) BANKING ON DEATH. New York, 1961	200	400	400
London, 1961	—	—	200
Latimer, Jonathan (Wyatt). MURDER IN THE MADHOUSE. Garden City, 1935	200	400	750
Latimer, Margery. WE ARE INCREDIBLE. New York (1928)	175	250	300
Lattimore, Richard (Alexander). HANOVER POEMS. New York, 1927. Written with A. K. Laing	60	75	75
Lattimore, Steve. CIRCUMNAVIGATION. Boston, 1997	—	—	25
Laughlin, Clarence John. NEW ORLEANS AND ITS LIVING PAST. Boston, 1941. Text by David L. Cohen. 1,030 signed copies (in glassine dustwrapper) in slipcase	—	600	750
Laughlin, James. THE RIVER. Norfolk, 1938. Wraps	150	150	200
SOME NATURAL THINGS. Norfolk, 1945	75	100	100
Laurence, Margaret. A TREE FOR POVERTY. Nairobi, 1954. (Somali anthology edited by Laurence.) Wraps	150	1,250	1,500
THIS SIDE OF JORDAN. Toronto, 1960	150	300	300
Wraps	—	—	75
New York (1960)	35	100	125
London (1960)	—	—	100
Laurents, Arthur. HOME OF THE BRAVE. New York (1946)	20	75	125
Lauterbach, Ann. BOOK ONE. New York, 1975. Oblong mimeographed stapled sheets in green wraps. One of 100 signed numbered copies	—	—	350
MANY TIMES, BUT THEN. Austin, 1979	—	—	150
Laver, James. CERVANTES . . . Oxford (1921). Wraps	50	125	150
Lavin, Mary. TALES FROM BECTIVE BRIDGE. Boston, 1942. (999 copies)	125	350	350
London, 1943	125	250	250

	1986	1995	2000
Lawrence, D(avid) H(erbert). THE WHITE PEACOCK. New York, 1911. (Copyright 1910)	7,000	7,500	7,500
New York, 1911. (Copyright 1911.) (Precedes English edition by one day)	2,500	2,000	2,000
London, 1911. First issue: publisher's windmill device on back cover; pp. 227–30 tipped in	750	1,250	1,250
Second issue: pp. 227–30 integral	400	500	500
Lawrence, Hilda. BLOOD UPON THE SNOW. New York, 1944	—	50	100
Lawrence, T(homas) E(dward). (T. E. Shaw.) CARCHEMISH. London, 1914. (Written with C. L. Woolley)	500	850	1,500
THE WILDERNESS OF ZIN. (London, 1915.) (Written with C. L. Woolley)	300	500	1,000
SEVEN PILLARS OF WISDOM. (London) 1926. Inscribed "complete" and signed "T.E.S." (170 of 211 copies)	12K	40K	50K
London (1935). (750 copies)	750	1,500	2,000
New York, 1935. (750 copies)	600	1,500	2,000
Lawson, Henry. SHORT STORIES IN VERSE AND PROSE. Sydney, 1894. Wraps	—	850	1,500
Lawton, John. BLACK OUT. London, 1995. Author's first mystery	—	—	300
Lax, Robert. THE CIRCUS OF THE SUN. (New York, 1960.) Cloth. 500 signed and numbered copies	—	150	125
Wraps	—	50	50
Laye, Camara. THE DARK CHILD. New York, 1954	—	—	75
LAYTON COURT MYSTERY (THE). By "?" (Anthony Berkeley, pseudonym of A. B. Cox.) London, 1925	400	1,250	5,000
Layton, Irving. HERE AND NOW. Montreal, 1945. Wraps	500	1,500	1,750
Lazarus, Emma. POEMS AND TRANSLATIONS. New York, 1866	50	300	300
Lea, Homer. THE VERMILLION PENCIL. New York, 1908	60	75	100
Lea, Tom. RANDADO. (El Paso, Texas, 1941.) Stiff wraps. 100 signed copies. Wraps	3,500	3,500	3,500
Cloth (bound later)	—	2,250	2,250
Leacock, Stephen (Butler). ELEMENTS OF POLITICAL SCIENCE. Boston, 1906	100	150	200
LITERARY LAPSES +. Montreal, 1910	150	200	200
Leaf, (Wilbur) Munro. *See* Mun			
ROBERT FRANCIS WEATHERBEE. New York, 1935	—	—	125

	1986	1995	2000
Lear, Edward. VIEWS IN ROME AND ITS ENVIRONS. London, 1841. Folio	2K	4K	5K
A BOOK OF NONSENSE. (London), 1846. 2 volumes *Also see* DERRY, DERRY DOWN	—	12.5K	15K
LEATHER STOCKING AND SILK. (John Esten Cooke.) New York, 1854	200	300	300
LEAVES OF GRASS. (Walt Whitman.) Brooklyn, 1855. First issue: marbled endpapers, frontispiece on plain paper, no press notices	7.5K	35K	50K
Second issue: yellow endpapers, frontispiece on plain India paper, 8 pages of notices	2.5K	15K	25K
Second edition. Brooklyn, 1856. 384 pages.	—	—	15K
Leavis, F. R. MASS CIVILIZATION AND MINORITY CULTURE. Cambridge, 1930. Wraps	50	75	75
Leavitt, David. FAMILY DANCING. New York, 1984	60	75	125
London, 1985	—	75	100
LeBlanc, Maurice (Marie Emile). THE EXPLOITS OF ARSENE LUPIN. New York, 1907	50	250	250
LeCain, Errol. KING ARTHUR'S SWORD. London, 1968	—	50	75
LeCarré, John. (David John Moore Cornwell.) CALL FOR THE DEAD. London, 1960	1,250	3,500	10K
New York, 1962. (White dustwrapper)	200	1,000	3,000
Le Clezio, M. M. G. THE INTERROGATION. London, 1964	25	35	60
New York, 1964	—	—	50
Le Doux, Louis Vernon. SONGS FROM THE SILENT LAND. New York, 1964	—	75	75
Lee, Andrea. RUSSIAN JOURNAL. New York (1981)	—	50	50
Lee, Andrew. (Louis Auchincloss.) THE INDIFFERENT CHILDREN. New York (1947)	150	400	200
Lee, Dennis. THE KINGDOM OF ABSENCE. Toronto (1967). 300 numbered copies. Wraps. Publisher's name spelled incorrectly on title page	125	200	125
Lee, George W. BEALE STREET: WHERE THE BLUES BEGAN. New York, 1934	—	300	500
Lee, Gus. CHINA BOY. New York (1991)	—	40	40
Lee, Gypsy Rose. (Rose Louise Hovick.) THE G-STRING MURDERS. New York, 1941. (Ghostwritten by Georgiana Ann Randolph a.k.a. Craig Rice)	125	175	175

	1986	1995	2000
Lee, Harper. TO KILL A MOCKINGBIRD. Philadelphia (1960). First issue: dustwrapper photo of author by Truman Capote. "First Edition" stated	250	2,500	7,500
London, 1960	75	300	750
Lee, Laurie. THE SUN MY MONUMENT. London, 1944	75	75	100
Garden City, 1947	25	40	50
Lee, Manfred Bennington. *See* Ellery Queen			
Lee, Spike. SPIKE LEE'S GOTTA HAVE IT. New York, 1987. Wraps	—	35	35
Lee, William. (William Burroughs.) JUNKIE. (Ace Double-book.) New York (1953). Wraps	175	450	750
London (1957). Wraps	—	150	250
London (1973). First hardback	—	150	250
LeFanu, Joseph Sheridan. THE COCK AND ANCHOR. Dublin, 1845. 3 volumes	350	2,000	2,500
Leffland, Ella. MRS. MUNCK. Boston, 1970	—	75	75
LeGallienne, Richard. MY LADIES' SONNETS. (Liverpool, England) 1887. (250 signed copies)	300	500	500
Trade edition	100	250	250
VOLUMES IN FOLIO. London, 1889. (Also first book published by Elkin Mathews.) 53 large-paper copies	250	300	300
250 regular copies (Three privately printed books or leaflets preceded.)	100	150	150
Legman, G(ershon). ORAGENITALISM. New York, 1940	—	400	650
LOVE & DEATH. (New York) 1949. Red cloth	150	250	250
Wraps	—	50	75
LeGrande, Mr. A VOYAGE TO ABYSSINIA BY FATHER JEROME LOBO. London, 1735. (Translated by Samuel Johnson)	1,500	1,500	1,750
Le Guin, Ursula. ROCANNON'S WORLD. New York (1966). Wraps. Bound dos-à-dos with a novel by A. Davidson	60	50	50
New York, 1975. First hardback. Issued without dustwrapper	—	75	100
Lehane, Dennis. A DRINK BEFORE THE WAR. New York, 1994	—	—	60
Lehmann, John. A GARDEN REVISITED. London, 1931. (400 copies) (1928 broadsheets preceded.)	125	175	200
Lehmann, Rosamond (Nina). DUSTY ANSWER. London, 1927	125	125	300
New York, 1927	—	—	50

	1986	1995	2000
Lehrer, Warren. VERSATIONS . . . Mattapoisett, 1980. 150 signed and numbered copies	—	200	250
Leib, Franklin Allen. FIRE ARROW. Novato (1988)	—	—	40
Leiber, Fritz (Reuter), Jr. NIGHT'S BLACK AGENTS. Sauk City, 1947	125	250	250
London, 1975	—	75	75
Leigh-Fermor, Patrick. THE TRAVELLER'S TREE. London, 1950	50	125	250
New York (1950)	—	—	75
Leland, Charles (Godfrey). MEISTER KARL'S SKETCH BOOK. Philadelphia, 1855	100	300	300
Leland, Jeremy. A RIVER DECREES. London, 1969	—	50	60
LeMay, Alan. PAINTED PONIES. New York (1927)	100	200	300
Lembke, Janet. RIVER TIME. (New York, 1989)	—	—	25
Lengel, Frances. (Alexander Trocchi.) THE CARNAL DAYS OF HELEN SEFERIS. Paris, 1954. Wraps	175	175	200
L'Engle, Madeleine. THE SMALL RAIN. New York (1945)	—	150	300
Lennon, John. IN HIS OWN WRITE. London, 1964. Issued without dustwrapper	60	75	75
New York, 1964	—	—	30
Leon, Donna. DEATH AT LA FENICE. (London, 1992)	—	—	75
New York, 1992	—	—	50
Leonard, Elmore. THE BOUNTY HUNTERS. Houghton Mifflin. Boston, 1954	300	1,750	3,500
Ballantine. New York, 1954. Wraps	75	150	200
Leonard, George. SHOULDER THE SKY. New York (1959)	30	30	30
Leonard, John. THE NAKED MARTINI. New York (1964)	35	60	60
(London, 1965)	—	—	40
Leonard, William Ellery. BYRON AND BYRONISM IN AMERICA. Boston, 1905. Wraps	—	150	75
SONNETS AND POEMS. Boston, 1906	75	75	100
Leopold, Aldo. REPORT ON A GAME SURVEY OF THE NORTH CENTRAL STATES. Madison, 1931. Wraps	—	—	125
A SAND COUNTY ALMANAC. New York, 1949	—	500	500
Lerman, Rhoda. CALL ME ISHTAR. Garden City, 1973	—	30	25

	1986	1995	2000
Leroux, Gaston. THE MYSTERY OF THE YELLOW ROOM. London, 1908	50	100	250
New York, 1908	—	—	125
Lesley, Craig. WINTER KILL. Boston, 1984	—	75	125
Leslie, David Stuart. THE DEVIL BOAT. London, 1956	—	50	75
Leslie, Eliza. *See* SEVENTY-FIVE RECEIPES . . .			
Leslie, (Sir John Randolph) Shane. SONGS OF ARIEL. Dublin, 1908	100	200	200
Lessing, Doris (May). THE GRASS IS SINGING. London (1950)	150	300	450
New York, 1950	75	200	200
Lester, Julius. TO BE A SLAVE. New York, 1968	35	100	150
Lesy, Michael. WISCONSIN DEATH TRIP. New York (1973)	—	—	125
London, 1973	—	—	100
Lethem, Jonathan. GUN, WITH OCCASIONAL MUSIC. New York (1994).	—	—	75
LETTERS FROM AN AMERICAN FARMER. (Michel Crevecoeur.) London, 1782. (2 folding maps)	—	2,500	3,000
Dublin, 1782. Wraps. (2 folding maps)	1,000	2,000	2,500
Lever, Charles. *See* THE CONFESSIONS OF HARRY LORREQUER			
Levertoff, Denise (Levertov). THE DOUBLE IMAGE. London, 1946	175	200	225
Levi, Peter (Chad Tiger). EARTHLY PARADISE. (Privately printed, 1958)	100	200	200
THE GRAVEL PONDS. London, 1960	75	75	75
Levi, Primo. IF THIS IS A MAN. New York, 1959. (First English translation)	—	200	200
Levin, Bernard. THE PENDULUM YEARS. London, 1970	—	35	35
Levin, Harry. THE BROKEN COLUMN . . . Cambridge (Mass.), 1931	75	75	75
Levin, Ira. A KISS BEFORE DYING. New York, 1953. Issued without endpapers	35	125	400
London, 1954	—	—	50
Levin, Meyer. REPORTER. New York (1929). (Withdrawn by publisher)	75	100	100
Levine, Norman. MYSSIUM. Toronto, 1948	—	300	300

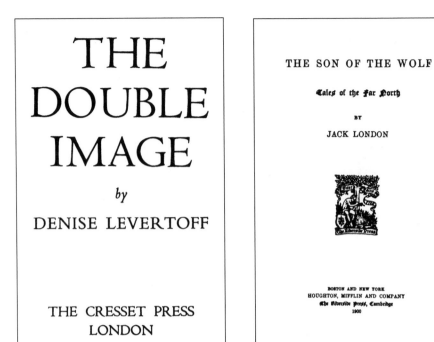

THE
DOUBLE
IMAGE

by

DENISE LEVERTOFF

THE CRESSET PRESS
LONDON

THE SON OF THE WOLF

𝕮𝖆𝖑𝖊𝖘 of 𝖙𝖍𝖊 𝕱𝖆𝖗 𝕹𝖔𝖗𝖙𝖍

BY

JACK LONDON

BOSTON AND NEW YORK
HOUGHTON, MIFFLIN AND COMPANY
𝕿𝖍𝖊 𝕽𝖎𝖛𝖊𝖗𝖘𝖎𝖉𝖊 𝕻𝖗𝖊𝖘𝖘, 𝕮𝖆𝖒𝖇𝖗𝖎𝖉𝖌𝖊
1900

	1986	1995	2000
THE ANGLED ROAD. London, 1952. (First novel)	—	—	100
Toronto, 1952. (British sheets)	—	150	150
Levine, Paul. TO SPEAK FOR THE DEAD. New York, 1990	—	35	40
Levine, Philip. ON THE EDGE. Iowa City (1963). 220 numbered copies. Issued without dustwrapper	250	750	1,500
Levy, Andrea. EVERY LIGHT IN THE HOUSE BURNIN'. Headline, 1994	—	—	40
Lewin, Michael Z. HOW TO BEAT COLLEGE TEXTS. New York, 1970	—	40	40
ASK THE RIGHT QUESTIONS. New York (1971)	—	75	450
London, 1972	—	—	150
Lewis, Alfred Henry. WOLFVILLE. New York (1897). First issue: "Moore" in perfect type p. 19:18	100	150	125
Lewis, Alun. RAIDERS' DAWN +. London, 1942	—	100	100
Lewis, C. S. *See* Clive Hamilton			
Lewis, David. END AND BEGINNING. Johannesburg, 1945. Wraps. 50 signed and numbered copies	75	125	150
450 unsigned	25	40	50

	1986	1995	2000
Lewis, Ethelreda. THE HARP. New York (1925)	75	75	150
Lewis, Grace Hegger. HALF A LOAF. New York (1931). (Sinclair's wife)	60	75	150
Lewis, Heather. HOUSE RULES. New York, 1994	—	—	25
Lewis, Janet. THE INDIANS IN THE WOODS. (Bonn, Germany, 1922.) Wraps	400	500	500
Lewis, Matthew Gregory. THE MONK. London, 1796. 3 volumes	750	3,500	3,500
Lewis, Norman. SEA AND SAND. London, 1938	—	200	300
Lewis, (Harry) Sinclair. *See* Tom Graham			
OUR MR. WRENN. New York, 1914. First under own name	75	200	250
Lewis, Wyndham. TIMON OF ATHENS. (London, 1913.) 16 plates in large portfolio	2,000	6,000	6,000
THE IDEAL GIANT. London (1917). (200 copies) Self-wraps string-tied into cloth-backed pictorial board folder	600	2,000	2,000
TARR. New York, 1918. Red cloth	250	500	500
Blue cloth	150	300	325
London, 1918	100	300	200
Lezama Lima, José. PARADISO. New York, 1968	—	75	75
Lhomond, M. ELEMENT OF FRENCH GRAMMAR. *See* Henry Wadsworth Longfellow			
Lieber, Joel. HOW THE FISHES LIVE. New York, 1967	30	30	30
Lieberman, M. M. MAGGOT AND WORM. West Branch, 1969. (300 numbered copies)	40	75	75
Liebling, A. J. THEY ALL SANG . . . New York, 1934	125	350	350
BACK WHERE I CAME FROM . . . New York (1938)	200	500	600
LIFE OF FRIEDRICH SCHILLER (THE). (Thomas Carlyle.) London, 1825	850	250	450
Lifshin, Lyn (Diane). WHY IS THE HOUSE DISSOLVING? San Francisco, 1968. Wraps	40	40	30
Lightman, Alan. TIME TRAVEL AND PAPA JOE'S PIPE . . . New York, 1984	—	—	75
Lima, Frank. INVENTORY. (New York, 1964.) Wraps. (300 copies)	40	40	125

	1986	1995	2000
Lin, Frank. (Gertrude Franklin Atherton.) WHAT DREAMS MAY COME. Chicago (1888).			
Wraps	300	750	750
Cloth	150	350	350
London, 1889	50	100	250
Lincoln, Joseph (Crosby). CAPE COD BALLADS. Trenton, New Jersey, 1902	125	150	200
Lincoln, Victoria. THE SWAN ISLAND MURDERS. New York (1930)	—	—	60
Lindbergh, Anne Morrow. NORTH TO THE ORIENT. New York, 1935	35	75	200
Lindbergh, Charles A. WE. New York, 1927. 1,100 signed and numbered copies, boxed. 100 for presentation. Numbered M1 to M100.	—	3,000	3,500
1,000 numbered copies. numbered 1–1,000	800	2,000	2,500
Trade edition. First issue: red buckram with top edges gilt. Dustwrapper priced $2.50. First words on front flap "They called me "Lucky" . . .	100	400	500
Second issue: blue cloth (priority assumed). Top edge yellow	—	250	300
(Later dustwrapper without price and first words "In this publisher's . . .")			
Lindsay, David. A VOYAGE TO ARCTURUS. London (1920). Red cloth. First issue has an 8-page catalog at rear	1,000	2,000	2,500
Later binding in dustwrapper	—	—	2,000
Lindsay, Jack. FAUNS AND LADIES. Sydney, 1923. 210 signed and numbered copies. First woodcut signed in full by Norman Lindsay, two following initialed	500	750	2,000
Trade edition	—	—	750
Lindsay, Norman. NORMAN LINDSAY'S BOOK NUMBER ONE. Sydney, 1912. Wraps	—	250	300
(Usually with NUMBERS TWO and THREE.)			
Lindsay, (Nicholas) Vachel. THE TREE OF LAUGHING BELLS. (New York, 1905.) Wraps	2,000	2,500	2,500
A MEMORIAL OF LINCOLN . . . (Springfield, Illinois, 1908/1909)	500	750	1,000
THE TRAMP'S EXCUSE +. (Springfield, Illinois, 1909.) Wraps	1,500	1,500	1,500
GENERAL WM BOOTH ENTERS INTO HEAVEN +. New York, 1913	75	100	100
Linebarger, Paul. (Myron Anthony.) GOSPEL OF SUN CHUNG SHAN. Paris, 1932. Edited with introduction and comments by Linebarger	—	250	150

	1986	1995	2000
THE POLITICAL DOCTRINE OF SUN YAT-SEN. Baltimore, 1937 *Also see* Felix C. Forrest. (Best known as Cordwainer Smith)	—	—	100
LINES ON LEAVING THE BEDFORD STREET SCHOOLHOUSE. (George Santayana.) (Boston, 1880.) 4 pages. Wraps	750	750	750
Linington, Elizabeth. THE PROUD MAN. New York, 1955 *Also see* Dell Shannon	—	—	60
Lion & Unicorn Press. PREFACE TO THE MANUALE TI-POGRAFICO OF 1818. London (1953). 60 Copies	100	150	150
Lippard, George. ADRIAN, THE NEOPHYTE . . . Philadelphia, 1843. Wraps	75	75	75
Lippman, Walter. A PREFACE TO POLITICS. New York, 1913 (Previous translations.)	50	75	100
Lipsky, Eleazar. THE KISS OF DEATH. New York, 1947. Wraps	—	—	25
Lish, Gordon. DEAR MR. CAPOTE. New York (1983). First novel	—	—	40
Little, Loyd. PARTHIAN SHOT. New York (1975).	—	—	75
Litvinoff, Emanuel. CONSCRIPTS. London, 1941. Wraps	75	75	75
Lively, Penelope. ASTERCOTE. London, 1970	—	150	75
Livesay, Dorothy. GREEN PITCHER. Toronto, 1928. Wraps. (200 copies)	—	750	1,250
Livingstone, David. *See* NARRATIVE . . .			
Llewellyn, Richard. (Richard David Vivian Llewellyn Lloyd.) HOW GREEN WAS MY VALLEY. London (1939). 200 signed and numbered copies in slipcase	250	400	500
Trade	100	125	200
New York, 1940	75	75	75
Llosa, Mario Vargas. THE TIME OF THE HERO. New York, 1966	—	60	75
London (1967)	—	60	60
Locke, David Ross. *See* Petroleum V. Nasby			
Locker, Frederick. LONDON LYRICS. London, 1857	250	300	375
Lockridge, Richard. MR. AND MRS. NORTH. New York, 1936	75	350	350
Lockridge, Richard and Frances. THE NORTHS MEET MURDER. New York, 1940	150	450	750

	1986	1995	2000
Lockridge, Ross. RAINTREE COUNTY. Boston, 1948	75	125	175
London (1949)	50	100	100
Lodge, David. THE PICTUREGOERS. London, 1960	275	350	300
Lodge, George Cabot. THE SONG OF THE WAVE. New York, 1898	50	75	125
Loeb, Harold (Albert). DOODAB. New York, 1925	125	125	150
Loewinsohn, Ron(ald William). WATERMELONS. New York, 1959. Wraps. (1,000 copies)	35	40	50
Lofting, Hugh. THE STORY OF DOCTOR DOOLITTLE. New York, 1920	200	1,250	1,250
Lofts, Norah. I MET A GYPSY. New York, 1935. 250 numbered copies in dustwrapper and slipcase	40	75	75
Logan, John. CYCLE FOR MOTHER CABRINI. New York (1955). 30 signed and numbered copies with signed wood block	200	250	250
250 signed and numbered copies	125	125	125
Hardcover copy of trade edition for review	—	75	75
Trade. Wraps	30	40	50
Logue, Christopher. WAND AND QUADRANT. Paris, 1953. Wraps. 300 signed and numbered copies	125	150	250
300 unnumbered copies	75	75	125
London, Jack (John Griffith). THE SON OF THE WOLF. Boston/New York, 1900. Three trial bindings are known (no priority):			
Binding A: rough grass-green V cloth, stamped in silver			
Binding B: greenish-black V cloth, stamped in silver			
Binding C: white buckram stamped in red only			
Any of the above bindings	—	—	3,500
Wraps. 19 copies (possibly for review)	—	—	7,500
First trade edition. Gray cloth stamped in silver. Pagination (i–viii); no blank leaf following p. (252); collation: 1(4), 2–22(6)	500	1,500	1,500
Second printing. Gray cloth stamped in silver. Pagination: (i–vi) blank leaf following p. (252). Identifiable only by its collation (the first 6 gatherings have 8 leaves, and then all but the last have 6 leaves)	—	—	600
Long, David. EARLY RETURNS. Jawbone Press, 1981. (1,000 copies) Tall wraps	—	—	125
Long, Frank Belnap. A MAN FROM GENOA +. Athol, 1926	750	850	1,000
Long, Haniel. POEMS. New York, 1920	500	500	250
Longfellow, Henry Wadsworth. ELEMENTS OF FRENCH GRAM-	250	250	350

	1986	1995	2000
MAR. By M. Lhomond. Portland, 1830. (HWL translated anonymously)			
FRENCH EXERCISES. By M. Lhomond. Portland, 1830. (HWL translated)	250	250	350
EXERCISES AND ELEMENTS . . . Bound as 1 volume in 1830. (Represents first book to bear HWL's name)	350	350	450
Also see OUTRE-MER			
Longfellow, Samuel. THE WORD PREACHED . . . New York, 1853. Wraps	75	75	75
Longley, Michael. TEN POEMS. Belfast (1965). White wraps	—	—	250
Second issue in green wraps	—	—	100
Longstreet, Augustus Baldwin. AN ORATION . . . (Augusta, 1831.) Wraps	3,500	3,500	3,500
Rebound	—	2,000	2,000
Also see GEORGIA SCENES . . .			
Loos, Anita. HOW TO WRITE PHOTOPLAYS. New York, 1920. Written with W. J. Emerson	200	400	400
BREAKING INTO THE MOVIES. New York (1921). Written with W. J. Emerson	200	350	350
GENTLEMEN PREFER BLONDES. New York, 1925. First issue: incorrect spelling on Contents page, Chapter 4 "Divine" for "Devine"	175	350	600
Lopez, Barry. DESERT NOTES. Kansas City (1976)	—	250	250
Lopez-Medina, Sylvia. CANTORA. Albuquerque (1992)	—	—	30
Lorca, Federico. BITTER OLEANDER. London, 1935	150	650	750
Lorde, Audre. THE FIRST CITIES. New York (1968). Wraps	20	100	150
Lothrop, Harriet. (Mulford Stone.) *See* Margaret Sidney			
LOVE EPISTLES OF ARISTAENETUS, THE. (Richard Sheridan, co-translator.) London, 1771	600	1,250	1,250
Lovecraft, H. P. *See* Jonathan E. Hoag			
LOOKING BACKWARD . . . (Cover title.) Haverhill, Mass. [1920]. Wraps. 40 copies	—	—	3,500

	1986	1995	2000
THE SHUNNED HOUSE. Athol, Mass., 1928. (Bound by Paul Cook, about 8 copies)	3K	10K	10K
Unbound folded signatures. (Derleth sold about 50 sets. The rest were used on Arkham House edition)	1,500	2,500	3,000
Various bindings of sheets between 1928 and 1963. Issued without dustwrapper	1,500	2,500	3,000
Arkham House. Sauk City, Wisc., 1963. (100 copies) in plain brown dustwrapper. (At least 4 pamphlets/offprints precede.)	1,250	4,500	5,000

Lovell, Robert. *See* Robert Southey

Lovesey, Peter. WOBBLE TO DEATH. London (1970)	40	200	300
New York (1970)	—	100	150

Lovesey, Phil. DEATH DUTIES. (London, 1998)	—	—	25

Lowell, Amy. *See* DREAM DROPS BY A DREAMER

A DOME OF MANY-COLORED GLASS. Boston, 1912	300	400	400

Lowell, James Russell. *See* CLASS POEM

A YEAR'S LIFE. Boston, 1841. (With or without errata)	225	300	250

Lowell, Robert. THE LAND OF UNLIKENESS. (Cunningham, Mass.) 1944. 26 signed and numbered copies	7,500	7,500	6,500
224 copies	3,000	3,000	2,500
LORD WEARY'S CASTLE. New York (1946)	300	300	400

Lowenfels, Walter. *See* W.L.

Lowndes, Marie Belloc. THE PHILOSOPHY OF THE MARQUISE. London, 1899	75	75	100

Lowry, Beverly. COME BACK, LOLLY RAY. Garden City, 1977	—	100	75

Lowry, Malcolm. ULTRAMARINE. London, 1933	5,000	6,500	7,500
Revised Edition. Philadelphia, 1962	75	150	200
London (1963)	50	100	125
Toronto (1963)	50	100	75

Lowry, Robert. MURDER PIE. Cincinnati, 1939. Wraps	—	150	250
TRIP TO BLOOMIN' MOON. Cincinnati, 1939. Wraps (Priority uncertain.)	—	150	150

Lowther, Pat. THIS DIFFICULT FLOWERING. Vancouver, 1968. Wraps	—	40	40

Loy, Mina. SONGS TO JOANNES. New York, 1917. Wraps. (April issue of *Others* magazine)	300	300	300

	1986	1995	2000
LUNAR BAEDECKER. (Paris, 1923.) Wraps	750	750	1,500
Lubschez, Ben Judah. MANHATTAN . . . New York, 1927 (Preceded by a textbook in 1926.)	—	400	400
Lucas, E. V. *See* E.V.L.			
Lucie-Smith, (John) Edward (McKenzie). (POEMS). Fantasy Press. Oxford, 1954. Wraps	125	125	125
Ludlow, Fitz-Hugh. *See* THE HASHEESH EATER			
Ludlum, Robert. THE SCARLATTI INHERITANCE. New York (1971). Printed acetate dustwrapper	75	250	250
London (1971)	60	125	125
New York, 1990. 26 signed and lettered copies	—	150	175
100 signed and numbered copies	—	75	100
Luhan, Mabel Dodge. LORENZO IN TAOS. New York, 1932	200	300	300
London, 1933	—	—	150
Lumley, Brian. THE CALLER OF THE BLACK. Sauk City, 1971	—	50	125
Lumpkin, Grace. TO MAKE MY BREAD. New York (1932)	75	75	75
Lunn, Hugh. (Hugh Kingsmill.) THE WILL TO LOVE. London, 1919	50	75	75
Lurie, Alison. V. R. LANG. Munich (1959). (300 copies) Wraps. (Edward Gorey cover)	175	250	250
LOVE AND FRIENDSHIP. London, 1962	—	—	125
New York, 1962	—	—	100
Luska, Sidney. (Henry Harland.) AS IT IS WRITTEN. New York (1885)	150	150	150
Lustgarten, Edgar (Marcus). A CASE TO ANSWER. London, 1947	35	75	100
(New title) ONE MORE UNFORTUNATE. New York, 1947	25	50	75
Lyall, Gavin. THE WRONG SIDE OF THE SKY. New York, 1961	35	50	125
Lynn, Elizabeth A. WATCH TOWER. New York (1979)	—	—	45
Lyon, Harris Merton. SARDONICS: SIXTEEN SKETCHES. New York, 1909	125	150	150
Lyons, Arthur. THE SECOND COMING: SATANISM IN AMERICA. New York (1970)	50	200	200
THE DEAD ARE DISCREET. New York (1974)	—	300	250
London, 1977	—	—	100

	1986	1995	2000
Lyons, Danny. THE BIKERIDERS. New York (1968). Wraps	—	—	600
Lytle, Andrew (Nelson). BEDFORD FORREST AND HIS CRITTER COMPANY. New York, 1931. Minton Balch	350	600	650
New York (1931). Putnam	125	200	250
Lytton, David. THE GODDAM WHITE MAN. London, 1960	30	40	75
New York, 1961	—	—	30
Lytton, Edward Robert Bulwer. *See* Bulwer-Lytton, Edward Robert. *Also see* CLYTEMNESTRA			

M

	1986	1995	2000
M., E. H. W. (E. H. W. Meyerstein.) THE DOOR. Oxford/London, 1911. Wraps	40	40	60
Maas, Willard. FIRE TESTAMENT. New York, 1935. Wraps. 135 signed and numbered copies	75	100	125
Mabie, Hamilton Wright. NORSE STORIES RETOLD . . . Boston, 1882	75	125	150
MacArthur, Charles G. (Private.) A BUG'S-EYE VIEW OF THE WAR. No place, 1919	—	125	200
MacArthur, Douglas. MILITARY DEMOLITIONS. (Fort Leavenworth, 1909)	—	600	600
Macauley, Robie. THE DISGUISES OF LOVE. New York (1952)	—	75	35
Macaulay, Rose. ABBOTS VERNEY. London, 1906	100	100	150
Macaulay, Thomas Babington. POMPEII, a poem . . . (Cambridge, 1819)	250	350	400
MacBeth, George. A FORM OF WORDS. Oxford, 1954. (150 copies)	125	150	275
MacCaig, Norman. FAR CRY. London, 1943. Wraps	—	100	125
MacCarthy, Desmond. THE COURT THEATRE 1904–1907. London, 1907	100	150	150
MacDiarmid, Hugh. SANGSCHAW. Edinburgh, 1925	—	350	350
MacDonagh, Donagh. TWENTY POEMS. Dublin, 1934. Wraps. (Written with Niall Sheridan)	—	200	200
VETERANS +. Cvala Press. Dublin, 1941. (270 copies)	250	250	300
MacDonald, George. WITHIN AND WITHOUT +. London, 1855	300	3,500	3,500
New York, 1872	—	350	350

	1986	1995	2000
MacDonald, Gregory. RUNNING SCARED. New York (1964)	—	60	100
FLETCH. Indianapolis (1974). First mystery	—	—	75
MacDonald, John D(ann). THE BRASS CUPCAKE. New York, 1950. Wraps	50	75	200
London, 1974. First hardback	—	100	300
WINE OF THE DREAMER. New York (1951). First U.S. hardback	—	—	300
MacDonald, Marianne. DEATH'S AUTOGRAPH. London (1996)	—	—	450
New York (1997)	—	—	40
MacDonald, Philip. *See* Oliver Fleming			
MacDonald, Ross. *See* Kenneth Millar			
MacDonald, William Colt. RESTLESS GUNS. New York, 1929	—	—	300
MacEwan, Gwendolyn. SELAH. Toronto, 1961	—	1,200	1,200
MacFall, Haldane. THE WOOINGS OF JEZEBEL PETTYFER. London, 1898. First issue, picture of Jezebel on front cover	150	300	250

THE WOOINGS OF
JEZEBEL PETTYFER

Being the personal history of **Jehu
Sennacherib Dyle**, commonly called
Masheen Dyle ; together with an
account of certain things that chanced
in the **House of the Sorcerer** ;
here set down

by
HALDANE MACFALL

LONDON
GRANT RICHARDS
9 HENRIETTA STREET, COVENT GARDEN, W.C.
1898

LIZA
OF LAMBETH

BY
William Somerset Maugham

LONDON
T. FISHER UNWIN
Paternoster Square
1897

	1986	1995	2000
THE HOUSE OF THE SORCERER. Boston, 1900. (New title)	100	175	175
MacGrath, Harold. ARMS AND THE WOMAN. New York, 1899	40	40	40
THE PUPPET CROWN. Indianapolis, 1901	—	30	30
MacHarg, William (Briggs). THE ACHIEVEMENTS OF LUTHER TRANT. Boston (1910). (Written with E. Balmer)	100	150	150
Machen, Arthur. ELEUSINIA. Hereford, 1881. Wraps. (One known copy) *Also see* Leolinus Siluriensis	10K	15K	15K
MacInnes, Colin. TO THE VICTOR THE SPOILS. London (1950)	100	175	175
MacInnes, Helen. ABOVE SUSPICION. Boston, 1941 (Two previous translations.)	50	75	100
MacKay, Sheena. TODDLER ON THE RUN . . . London, 1964	—	125	175
MacKaye, Percy (Wallace). SPINNING SONG. New York, 1894	—	—	200
JOHNNY CRIMSON. Boston, 1895. Wraps. (50 copies)	300	350	375
Trade edition	—	150	150
MacKenzie, (Montague) Compton. POEMS. Oxford, 1907. Wraps	150	250	150
MacLaine, Christopher. THE CRAZY BIRD. (San Francisco) 1951. Boards. 100 numbered copies	75	75	150
MacLane, Mary. THE STORY OF MARY MACLANE BY HERSELF. Chicago, 1902	50	100	50
MacLaren, Ross J. THE STUFF TO GIVE THE TROOPS. London, 1944	75	75	150
MacLaverty, Bernard. SECRETS +. Belfast, 1977	—	100	150
MacLean, Alistair. H.M.S. ULYSSES. London, 1955	40	75	100
Garden City, 1956	—	50	50
MacLean, Norman. A RIVER RUNS THROUGH IT. Chicago (1976)	75	1,250	1,500
Chicago (1983). 500 signed and numbered copies	—	750	1,000
West Hatfield (1989). 200 signed and numbered copies. Issued without dustwrapper	—	750	1,000
London, 1990	—	50	60
MacLeish, Archibald. CLASS POEM. (New Haven) 1915. (4-page leaflet)	2,500	2,500	2,500
SONGS FOR A SUMMER DAY. (New Haven) 1915. Wraps	500	500	500

	1986	1995	2000
TOWER OF IVORY. New Haven, 1917. (750 copies)	150	150	200
MacLennan, Hugh. OXYRHYNEHUS: AN ECONOMIC & SOCIAL STUDY. Princeton, 1935. First book under this name	—	1,200	750
MacLeod, Charlotte. MYSTERY OF THE WHITE KNIGHT. New York (1964)	—	—	250
MacLeod, Fiona. (William Sharp.) PHARAIS. Derby, 1894. (75 signed and numbered copies)	200	200	250
MacLeod, Joseph (Todd Gordon). BEAUTY AND THE BEAST. London, 1927	75	75	100
New York, 1928	—	—	75
THE ECLIPTIC. London, 1930. Wraps	50	50	50
MacLeod, Norman. HORIZONS OF DEATH. New York, 1934. Wraps. 100 signed and numbered copies	125	250	250
263 numbered copies	50	150	150
MacLow, Jackson. THE PRONOUNS. (Bronx, 1964.) Stapled mimeographed sheets	—	60	60
MacNamara, Brinsley. THE VALLEY OF THE SQUINTING WINDOWS. Dublin, 1918	75	125	150
New York, 1920	—	—	75
MacNeice, (Frederick) Louis. BLIND FIREWORKS. London, 1929	400	1,000	750
MacPherson, Jay. NINETEEN POEMS. Mallorca, 1952. Wraps	—	650	650
MacSweeney, Barry. THE BOY FROM THE GREEN CABERET . . . Sussex, 1967. (100 copies)	40	60	100
London (1968)	—	—	30
New York (1969)	—	—	25
Madden, David. THE BEAUTIFUL GREED. New York (1961)	50	75	50
Madge, Charles. THE DISAPPEARING CASTLE. London (1937)	40	40	35
Magee, David. JAM TOMORROW. Boston, 1941	60	100	100
Magoon, Carey. I SMELL THE DEVIL. New York, 1943	—	—	125
Magowan, Robin. IN THE WASH. Mallorca, 1958. Wraps	35	75	75
Mahan, A(lfred). T(hayer). THE NAVY IN THE CIVIL WAR. New York, 1883	125	350	350
THE GULF AND INLAND WATERS. New York, 1883	—	—	250
Mahon, Derek. TWELVE POEMS. Belfast, no date [1965]. Wraps	—	600	600

	1986	1995	2000
Mailer, Norman. THE NAKED AND THE DEAD. New York (1948)	250	750	1,000
London (1949). (240 copies)	400	600	750
London, 1949. Trade	150	150	200
Preceded by THE FOUNDATION (Privately printed mimeographed sheets.)			
Mainwaring, Daniel. (Geoffrey Homes.) ONE AGAINST THE EARTH. New York, 1933	—	300	750
Mais, Roger. THE HILLS WERE JOYFUL TOGETHER. London (1953)	—	—	60
Maitland, Barry. THE MARX SISTERS. London, 1994	—	—	300
Maitland, Margaret. (Margaret Oliphant.) PASSAGES IN THE LIFE OF . . . London, 1849. 3 volumes	350	450	450
Major, Charles. *See* Edwin Caskoden			
Major, Clarence. THE FIRES THAT BURN IN HEAVEN. [Chicago, circa 1954.] Wraps. 2 copies known	—	—	2,500
ALL-NIGHT VISITORS. New York (1969)	—	—	125
Malamud, Bernard. THE NATURAL. New York (1952). Red, blue, or gray cloth (priority uncertain; 2 review copies have been seen in gray, but author's copy was blue)	250	1,250	3,000
London, 1963. (Glossary added)	75	300	500
Malanga, Gerard. 3 POEMS FOR BENEDETTA BARZINI. (New York, 1967.) Wraps. (500 copies)	75	75	100
Malcolm X. THE AUTOBIOGRAPHY OF MALCOLM X. New York (1965). (Written with Alex Haley)	75	850	1,000
Malcolm, John. A BACK ROOM IN SOMERS TOWN. London (1984).	—	—	300
New York (1985)	—	—	25
Mallea, Eduardo. THE BAY OF SILENCE. New York, 1944. First book in English. Blue cloth	—	75	75
Orange cloth	—	—	35
Malone, Michael. PAINTING THE ROSES RED. New York, 1974	—	125	125
Malouf, David. BICYCLE AND OTHER POEMS. St. Lucia (1970). Wraps	—	300	450
THE YEAR OF THE FOX +. New York, 1979. (New Title)	—	75	125
Malraux, André. THE CONQUERORS. London, 1929	75	300	300

	1986	1995	2000
Maltz, Albert. PEACE ON EARTH. French. New York, 1934. Wraps. Written with George Sklar	—	125	150
BLACK PIT. New York, 1935. (First solely authored book)	100	175	125
London 1965	60	60	60
Mamet, David. AMERICAN BUFFALO. New York: Samuel French (1977). Wraps	40	75	250
New York: Grove Press (1977). Wraps	—	—	200
New York: Grove Press (1978). Cloth	50	150	500
San Francisco, 1992. 400 signed and numbered copies	—	350	450
Man, Henry. MR. BENTLEY, THE RURAL PHILOSOPHER. London, 1775	—	—	2,000
Manchester, William. DISTURBER OF THE PEACE. New York (1951)	40	75	75
THE SAGE OF BALTIMORE. London (1952). (New Title)	35	60	75
Mandel, Eli. FUSELI POEMS. Toronto (1960). 250 Copies. Wraps	—	300	300
Mandel, George. FLEE THE ANGRY STRANGERS. Indianapolis (1952)	—	—	125
Manfred, Frederick (Feikema). See Feike Feikema			
Manhood, H. A. NIGHTSEED. London, 1928	50	60	100
Mann, E. B. THE MAN FROM TEXAS. New York, 1931	—	—	250
Mann, Horace. LECTURES ON EDUCATION. Boston, 1845 (Preceded by a number of pamphlets.)	300	300	250
Mann, Jessica. A CHARITABLE END. London (1971)	—	—	75
Mann, Thomas. ROYAL HIGHNESS. New York, 1916. (First English translation)	75	200	250
Mannes, Marya. MESSAGE FROM A STRANGER. London, 1948	25	25	50
New York, 1948	—	—	25
Manning, Frederic. THE VIGIL OF BRUNHILD. London, 1907	75	125	150
Manning, Olivia. THE WIND CHANGES. London, 1937	—	150	200
New York, 1938	—	—	100
Mano, D. Keith. BISHOP'S PROGRESS. Boston, 1968	40	60	60
Mansfield, Katherine. IN A GERMAN PENSION. London (1911). (500 copies)	500	1,500	2,000
Maracle, Lee. I AM WOMAN. (North Vancouver, 1988)	—	—	35

	1986	1995	2000
March, Joseph Moncure. THE SET-UP. New York, 1928 (275 copies)	60	75	100
March, William. (Wm Edw. March Campbell.) COMPANY M. New York, 1933. Issued in clear dustwrapper with printed paper flaps	300	300	450
Marcus, Frank. THE KILLING OF SISTER GEORGE. London, 1965	60	60	50
MARGARET PERCIVAL IN AMERICA. (Edward Everett Hale.) Boston, 1850	100	175	200
Marius, Richard. THE COMING OF RAIN. New York, 1969	—	60	35
Marjoram, J. (Ralph H. Mottram.) REPOSE +. London, 1907. Wraps	125	125	125
Markfield, Wallace (Arthur). TO AN EARLY GRAVE. New York, 1964	40	50	40
Markham, Beryl. WEST WITH THE NIGHT. Boston, 1942	—	500	750
London (1943)	—	350	450
Markham, (Charles) Edwin. THE MAN WITH THE HOE. Appeared as supplement to *San Francisco Examiner.* 4 pages	250	350	400
San Francisco, 1899. Wraps	125	250	250
New York, 1899. First issue: "fruitless" p. 35:5	75	75	100
Marks, J. (Jamake Highwater.) ROCK & OTHER FOUR LETTER WORDS. New York, 1968. Wraps	—	60	60
Markson, David. EPITAPH FOR A TRAMP. (New York, 1959.) Wraps (Edited two books previously as Mark Merrill.)	20	35	50
Markus, Julia. LA MORA. Washington (1976). Wraps. (1,000 copies)	25	30	50
Marlowe, Derek. A DANDY IN ASPIC. London, 1966	—	75	75
New York (1966)	25	40	50
Maron, Margaret. DEATH OF A BUTTERFLY. Garden City, 1984. Author's first hardcover	—	—	100
Marquand, John Philips. *See* Charles E. Clark			
THE UNSPEAKABLE GENTLEMEN. New York, 1922. First issue: Scribners seal on copyright page	150	300	350
Second issue: Scribners seal on copyright page. Note to ABA members signed by Marquand tipped in. Gray buckram spine and dark-gray boards with ABA label on front	—	75	100
Márquez, Gabriel García. *See* García Márquez, Gabriel			

	1986	1995	2000
Marquis, Don(ald Robert Perry.) DANNY'S OWN STORY. Garden City, 1912	75	75	75
Marryat, Frederick. A CODE OF SIGNALS FOR USE OF VESSELS . . . London, 1818	250	250	350
THE NAVAL OFFICER . . . London, 1829. 3 volumes	300	350	450
Mars-Jones, Adam. LANTERN LECTURE. London, 1981	—	50	75
Marsh, (Dame Edith) Ngaio. A MAN LAY DEAD. London (1934.)	200	500	750
Marsh, Patrick. BREAKDOWN. New York, 1953	25	25	25
Marsh, Willard. WEEK WITH NO FRIDAY. New York (1965)	40	40	25
Marshall, Paule. BROWN GIRL, BROWNSTONES. New York, 1959	150	600	750
Marshall, William. YELLOWTHREAD STREET. London (1975)	—	—	175
New York (1976)	—	—	30
Marston, Philip. SONG TIDE +. London, 1871	100	250	250
Martin, Carl R. GO YOUR STATIONS, GIRL. San Francisco (1991). 250 signed and numbered copies.	—	—	75
Wraps (500 copies)	—	—	25
Martin, George V(ictor). FOR OUR VINES HAVE TENDER GRAPES. New York (1940)	—	50	125
Martin, J. Wallis. A LIKENESS IN STONE. (London, 1997)	—	—	450
Martin, Peter. THE LANDSMAN. Boston (1952)	—	50	50
Martin, Steve. CRUEL SHOES. Los Angeles, 1977. Issued without dustwrapper. 750 numbered copies	40	50	150
Trade edition	—	—	35
Martin, Valerie. LOVE. Amherst, 1977. Wraps	—	—	100
Marvel, Ik. (Donald Grant Mitchell.) FRESH GLEANINGS . . . New York, 1847. 2 volumes. Wraps	100	125	150
1 volume. Cloth	—	50	60
Marx, Groucho. BEDS. New York, 1930. (Has publisher's colophon on copyright page)	125	650	750
Marx, Harpo. HARPO SPEAKS. New York, 1961	—	100	100

	1986	1995	2000
Marx, Karl. CAPITAL: A CRITICAL ANALYSIS . . . Humboldt. New York (1886)	—	—	4,500
London, 1887. 2 volumes. Red cloth	—	3,000	4,500
London, 1887. 1 volume	—	—	2,500
Appleton. New York, 1889. Mustard-yellow cloth	—	2,000	2,500
MARY BARTON: A TALE OF MANCHESTER LIFE. (Elizabeth C. Gaskell.) London, 1848. 2 volumes in original mulberry-colored cloth	500	1,250	6,000
Masefield, John. SALT WATER BALLADS. London, 1902. First issue: "Grant Richards" on title page	500	600	750
Second issue: "Elkin Mathews" on title page	350	350	350
Maso, Carole. GHOST DANCE. San Francisco, 1986	—	—	25
Mason, A(lfred) E(dward) W(oodley). BLANCHE DE MALETROIT. London, 1894. (Adapted from Robert Louis Stevenson's work)	40	100	125
A ROMANCE OF THE WASTEDALE. London (1895)	75	150	175
Mason, Bobbie Ann. NABOKOV'S GARDEN. Ann Arbor (1974). (Precedes THE GIRL SLEUTH, although dustwrapper implies otherwise.) Cloth	100	250	250
Wraps	—	75	75
Mason, (Francis) Van Wyck. SEEDS OF MURDER. New York, 1930	—	300	500
Massey, T. Gerald. VOICE OF FREEDOM AND LYRICS OF LOVE. London, 1851	125	250	250
Massie, Alan. CHANGE AND DECAY IN ALL AROUND I SEE. London, 1978	—	60	60
Masson, David I. THE CALTRAPS OF TIME. London (1968)	—	150	150
Masters, Anthony. A POCKETFUL OF RYE. London, 1964	35	40	40
Masters, Edgar Lee. A BOOK OF VERSES. Chicago, 1898	200	750	1,000
Masters, John. COMPLEAT INDIAN ANGLER. London, 1938	100	200	450
NIGHTRUNNERS OF BENGAL. New York, 1951	50	75	75
Mather, Increase. THE MYSTERY OF ISRAEL'S SALVATION. (London) 1669	3,000	6,000	7,500
Matheson, Richard. SOMEONE IS BLEEDING. New York (1953). Wraps	100	150	200
BORN OF MAN AND WOMAN. Philadelphia, 1954. (First hardback, third book)	150	400	400

	1986	1995	2000
Mathews, Elkin, Publisher. *See* Richard LeGallienne			
Mathews, Harry. THE CONVERSIONS. New York (1962)	60	75	125
London (1962)	—	—	75
Mathews, Jack. (John Harold Matthews, Jr.) BITTER KNOWL-EDGE. New York (1964)	35	40	50
Mathews, John Joseph. WAH'KON-TAH . . . Norman, 1932	—	—	50
Matthews, T. S. TO THE GALLOWS I MUST GO. New York, 1931	—	100	75
Matthews, William. BROKEN SYLLABLES. Aurora (1969)	—	—	125
Matthiessen, Peter. RACE ROCK. New York (1954)	100	300	300
London, 1954	100	175	175
Maugham, Robin. THE 1946 MS. London, 1943	125	150	150
Maugham, W(illiam) Somerset. LIZA OF LAMBETH. London, 1897. First issue: Brackets around "All Rights Reserved" on copyright page. (2,000 copies)	600	1,250	1,250
Second issue	—	750	750
London, 1947. 1,000 signed and numbered copies	—	300	300
Mauldin, Bill (William Henry). STAR SPANGLED BANTER. San Antonio, Texas, 1941. Wraps	125	200	200
Maurois, André. THE SILENCE OF COLONEL BRAMBLE. London, 1919	40	60	60
New York, 1920. In dustwrapper	150	150	200
Also see Penguin Books			
Maxwell, Gavin. HARPOON AT A VENTURE. London, 1952	60	60	60
Maxwell, Gilbert. LOOK TO THE LIGHTNING. New York, 1933	50	75	50
Maxwell, William. BRIGHT CENTER OF HEAVEN. New York, 1934	250	750	1,250
Toronto, 1937	—	—	350
London, 1937	—	—	350
May, Elaine. A MATTER OF POSITION. New York, 1962. Mimeographed sheets in folder	—	175	200
NOT ENOUGH ROPE. New York (1964). Wraps	—	75	75
Mayer, Tom. BUBBLE GUM AND KIPLING. New York, 1964	35	75	50
Mayfield, Julian. THE HIT. New York (1957)	40	75	60
Mayhall, Jane. COUSIN TO HUMAN. New York (1960)	—	60	75

	1986	1995	2000
Mayne, William. FOLLOW THE FOOTPRINTS. London, 1953	—	150	150
Mayo, E(dward) L(eslie). THE DIVER. Minneapolis (1947)	50	50	50
Mayo, W(illiam) S(tarbuck). KALOOLAH ... New York, 1849	—	—	200
Mayor, Archer. OPEN SEASON. New York (1988)	—	—	150
London (1989)	—	—	100
McAlmon, Robert. EXPLORATIONS. London, 1921. Issued without dustwrapper	750	1,000	1,000
McCaffrey, Anne. RESTOREE. New York (1967). Wraps	—	35	25
London (1968)	—	150	200
McCaig, Norman. FAR CRY. (London, 1943.) Wraps	75	100	75
McCammon, Robert R. BAAL. New York (1978). Wraps	—	50	35
New York, 1979	—	—	500
Bath, 1985	—	400	400
McCann, Colum. FISHING THE SLOE-BACK RIBER. London (1994).	—	—	200
McCarry, Charles. CITIZEN NADER. New York, 1972	40	100	50
THE MIERNICK DOSSIER. New York (1973)	50	100	125
McCarthy, Cormac. THE ORCHARD KEEPER. New York (1965)	75	2,000	3,000
(London, 1966)	50	1,000	1,000

McCarthy, Mary (Therese). *See* H. V. Kaltenborn

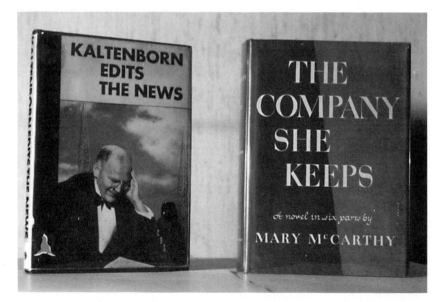

	1986	1995	2000
THE COMPANY SHE KEEPS. (New York) 1942	125	150	100
London, 1943	75	75	60
McClanahan, Ed. THE NATURAL MAN. New York, 1983	20	30	35
McClendon, Lise. THE BLUEJAY SHAMAN. New York (1994).	—	—	30
McClure, James. THE STEAM PIG. London, 1971	30	150	250
New York (1971)	25	75	75
McClure, Michael. PASSAGE. Big Sur, 1956. Stiff wraps (200 copies)	450	500	600
McCluskey, John. LOOK WHAT THEY DONE TO MY SONG. New York, 1974	—	75	50
McCord, David. (Thompson Watson.) ODDLY ENOUGH. Cambridge, 1926	40	75	75
McCord, Howard. PRECISE FRAGMENTS. Dublin, 1963. Wraps. (250 copies)	40	75	100
McCorkle, Jill. THE CHEERLEADER. (Chapel Hill, 1984)	—	150	125
JULY 7TH. (Chapel Hill, 1984.) (Published simultaneously)	—	150	125
McCourt, Frank. ANGELA'S ASHES. New York (1996).	—	—	350
McCourt, James. MAWRDEW CZGOWCHWZ. New York (1975)	—	50	60
McCoy, Horace. THEY SHOOT HORSES, DON'T THEY. New York, 1935	300	450	750
London, 1935	—	—	300
McCracken, Elizabeth. HERE'S YOUR HAT WHAT'S YOUR HURRY. Turtle Bay, 1993.	—	—	75
McCrum, Robert. IN THE SECRET STATE. London, 1980	—	50	30
McCrum, Sharyn. SICK OF SHADOWS. New York (1984). Wraps	—	40	75
McCullers, (Lula) Carson. THE HEART IS A LONELY HUNTER. Boston, 1940	350	750	1,750
London, 1943	200	250	250
McCullough, Colleen. TIM. New York (1974)	50	125	125
McCutcheon, George Barr. GRAUSTARK. Chicago, 1901. First issue: "Noble" for "Lorry" p. 150:6	75	100	100
McDermott, Alice. A BIGAMIST'S DAUGHTER. New York (1982)	—	75	175
McDonald, Gregory. RUNNING SCARED. New York (1964)	—	—	100

	1986	1995	2000
McEldowney, Eugene. A KIND OF HOMECOMING. London (1994).	—	—	50
McElroy, Joseph. A SMUGGLER'S BIBLE. New York (1966)	150	250	250
London (1968)	—	—	100
McEwan, Ian. FIRST LOVE, LAST RITES. London (1975)	75	350	400
New York (1975)	25	75	125
McFadden, Roy. SWORDS AND PLOUGHSHARES. London (1943)	—	100	100
McFarland, Dennis. THE MUSIC ROOM. Boston, 1990	—	60	40
McFee, William. (Morley Dunshon.) LETTERS FROM AN OCEAN TRAMP. London, 1908. First issue: "Cassell & Co." on spine	125	200	200
McGahern, John. THE BARRACKS. London, 1963	—	500	500
New York, 1964	—	100	100
McGinley, Patrick. BOGMAIL. London, 1978	40	75	100
New York, 1981. First issue: Priced $9.95. Joan Kahn comment on back	—	50	50
Second issue: Priced $10.95. Review on back	—	35	35
McGinley, Phyllis. ON THE CONTRARY. New York, 1934	100	150	200
McGivern, William P(eter). BUT DEATH RUNS FASTER. New York, 1948	35	75	125
McGovan, James. (William C. Honeyman.) BROUGHT TO BAY. Edinburgh, 1878	100	200	250
McGrath, Patrick. BLOOD AND WATER AND OTHER TALES. New York, 1988	—	50	75
McGreevy, Thomas. INTRODUCTION TO . . . DA VINCI. London, 1929. 875 numbered copies. McGreevy's translation of Valéry's work	75	100	100
THOMAS STEARNS ELIOT. London, 1931	60	75	75
McGuane, Thomas. THE SPORTING CLUB. New York (1968)	75	200	250
(London, 1969)	60	100	125
McHale, Tom. PRINCIPATO. New York (1970)	25	40	40
McIlvanney, William. REMEDY IS NONE. London (1966)	—	150	150
McInerney, Jay. BRIGHT LIGHTS, BIG CITY. New York (1984). Wraps	35	50	40
London, 1985. First Hardback	50	100	75
McKay, Claude. SONGS OF JAMAICA. Kingston, Jamaica, 1912. Stiff wraps	1,500	3,000	2,000

	1986	1995	2000
SPRING IN NEW HAMPSHIRE +. London (1920). Wraps. (Third book)	400	1,500	1,500
McKendrick, Jamie. THE SIROCCO ROOM. Oxford (1991). Pictorial wraps	—	—	100
McKenna, Richard. THE SAND PEBBLES. New York (1962)	25	125	100
McKenna, Stephen. THE RELUCTANT LOVER. London, 1913	100	200	40
McKillip, Patricia A. THE HOUSE ON PARCHMENT STREET. New York, 1973	—	—	250
McKinley, Georgia. THE MIGHTY DISTANCE. Boston, 1965	40	40	40
McKnight, Reginald. MUSTAPHIA'S ECLIPSE. Pittsburgh (1988)	—	50	75
McKuen, Rod. AND AUTUMN CAME. New York (1954)	90	150	100
McLaverty, Michael. LOST FIELDS. London, 1942	35	60	75
New York, 1941	—	—	40
McLuhan, (Herbert) Marshall. FOOTPRINTS IN THE SANDS OF CRIME. 1946. *Sewanee Review* offprint. Stapled wraps	—	1,000	1,000
THE MECHANICAL BRIDE. New York (1951). Reprinted in "Limited Edition" according to dustwrapper but book itself does not indicate. (Differences between first edition and "Limited Edition": $4.50 vs. $12.50; white endpaper vs. yellow; and white cover lettering vs. gold.) [1973]	75	175	200
London, 1967	—	50	50
McMahon, Thomas. PRINCIPLES OF AMERICAN NUCLEAR CHEMISTRY: A NOVEL. Boston (1970)	—	60	60
McManus, Kay. RAVEN +. Leeds (1966)	25	60	75
LISTEN AND I'LL TALK. (London, 1969)	25	40	50
McMillan, Terry. MAMA. Boston, 1987	—	300	300
London, 1987	—	—	100
McMurtrie, Douglas C(rawford). THE DISABLED SOLDIER. New York, 1919. In dustwrapper	40	300	300
Without dustwrapper	—	—	100
(Previous pamphlets.)			
McMurtry, Larry (Jeff). HORSEMAN, PASS BY. New York (1961)	500	1,750	1,750
McNally, T. M. LOW FLYING AIRCRAFT. Athens (1991)	—	—	40
McNamee, Eoin. THE LAST OF DEEDS. Dublin, 1989	—	—	200

	1986	1995	2000
THE LAST OF DEED AND LOVE IN HISTORY. London (1992). Wraps	—	—	60
New York (1996)	—	—	30
McNeile, H(erman) C(yril). (Sapper.) THE LIEUTENANT AND OTHERS. London, 1915	100	150	100
McNichols, Charles L. CRAZY WEATHER. New York, 1943	—	150	150
McNickle, D'arcy. THE SURROUNDED. New York (1936)	—	—	2,000
McNulty, John. THIRD AVENUE, NEW YORK. Boston, 1946	—	75	60
McPhee, John. A SENSE OF WHERE YOU ARE. New York (1965)	150	500	750
New York (1978). New preface. Cloth	—	—	100
Wraps	—	—	35
McPherson, James A. HUE AND CRY. Boston (1969)	40	250	250
(London, 1969)	—	125	125
McPherson, Sandra. ELEGIES FOR THE HOT SEASON. Bloomington (1970)	—	75	75
McPherson, William. TESTING THE CURRENT. New York (1984)	25	35	25
McTaggart, John. STUDIES IN THE HEGELIAN DIALECTIC. Cambridge, 1896	—	150	175
Meacham, Ellis K. THE EAST INDIAMAN. Boston (1968)	—	50	50
Mead, Harold. THE BRIGHT PHOENIX. (New York, 1956.) Cloth	75	75	50
Wraps	15	15	15
Mead, Margaret. COMING OF AGE IN SAMOA. New York, 1928	—	250	250
London (1929)	—	—	200
Meadows, Catherine. HENBANE. London, 1934	—	—	125
Meagher, Maude. WHITE JADE. Boston, 1930	50	75	100
Meek, M. R. D. WITH FLOWERS THAT FELL. London (1983)	—	—	150
Mehta, Ved. FACE TO FACE. Boston (1957)	—	50	50
Melanter. (R. D. Blackmore.) POEMS. London, 1854	600	750	1,000
Meltzer, David. POEMS. (San Francisco, 1957.) (Written with Donald Schenker.) 25 signed copies. Cloth	150	250	250
5 signed copies. Cloth. Blood-stained copies	250	400	450
Wraps. (470 copies)	75	75	125
(San Francisco, 1957.) Without Schenker's work. Wraps	—	—	150

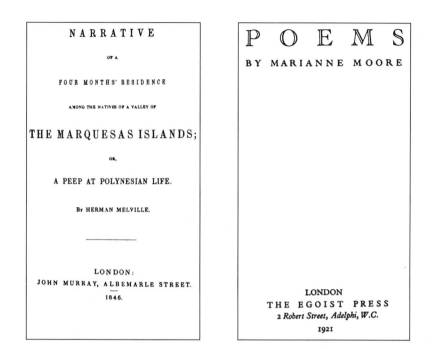

	1986	1995	2000
RAGAS. San Francisco, 1959. Wraps. (1,500 copies)	30	50	60
Melville, Herman. NARRATIVE OF A FOUR MONTH . . . London, 1846. First issue: "Pomarea" on p. 19:l. 2 volumes in original wraps	5K	15K	15K
1 volume. In original red cloth	2,000	3,000	3,500
Second issue: "Pomare" on p. 19:1	1,000	1,500	1,750
TYPEE: A PEEP AT POLYNESIAN LIFE. New York, 1846. 2 volumes in wraps	3,000	8,500	10K
1 volume: blue or brown cloth	1,500	2,500	4,500
Melville, Pauline. SHAPE SHIFTER. London (1990)	—	—	75
Menaker, Daniel. FRIENDS AND RELATIVES. Garden City, 1966	—	—	100
Mencken, H(enry) L(ouis). VENTURES INTO VERSE. Baltimore, 1903. Two issues, bound in boards	4,000	7,500	10K
Wraps. (100 Copies in total)	4,000	5,000	5,000
GEORGE BERNARD SHAW. Boston, 1903. (noted at 7¾" tall and 7⅞" priority unknown)	175	350	300
Mendelson, Jane. I WAS AMELIA EARHART. New York (1996)	—	—	40
Menen, (Salvator) Aubrey. THE PREVALENCE OF WITCHES. London, 1947	50	50	100
New York, 1948	—	—	40

	1986	1995	2000
Mephistopheles. (John Pendleton Kennedy.) A REVIEW OF MR. CAMBRELENG'S REPORT . . . Baltimore, 1830. Wraps	—	—	200
Meredith, George. POEMS. London (1851). Half title and errata at end	750	1,500	1,500
Meredith, William (Morris). LOVE LETTERS FROM AN IMPOSSIBLE LAND. New Hampshire, 1944	125	150	200
Merriam, Eve. FAMILY CIRCLE. New Haven, 1946	25	50	50
Merril, Judith. SHADOW ON THE HEARTH. Garden City, 1950	25	60	35
Merrill, James (Ingram). JIM'S BOOK. Privately printed. New York, 1942	3,500	4,000	5,000
THE BLACK SWAN +. Athens, 1946. Wraps. (100 copies)	1,500	3,000	4,500
FIRST POEMS. New York, 1951. (990 copies) (First regularly published book)	175	200	350
Merritt, A(braham). THE MOON POOL. New York (1919). Cloth. First issue: no ad on p. (434). Sheets bulk 3.2 cm	75	250	200
Merton, Thomas. THIRTY POEMS. Norfolk (1944). Boards	150	350	400
Wraps	60	125	150
Mertz, Barbara. TEMPLES, TOMBS AND HIEROGLYPHS. New York (1964). (aka Elizabeth Peters.)	—	—	150
Merwin, W(illiam) S(tanley). A MASK FOR JANUS. New Hampshire, 1952	300	350	500
Metalious, Grace. PEYTON PLACE. New York, 1956	—	125	125
Metcalf, John. THE SMOKING LEG. London, 1925	100	250	250
Metcalf, John. THE LADY WHO SOLD FURNITURE. Toronto, 1970. In black cloth	—	75	75
In gray boards	—	—	40
Metcalf, Paul. WILL WEST. Asheville, 1956. Wraps. (500 copies)	75	125	175
Mew, Charlotte. THE FARMER'S BRIDE. London, 1916. Wraps	125	150	150
London, 1921	—	50	75
Mewshaw, Michael. MAN IN MOTION. New York (1970)	30	50	50
Meyer, Nicholas. TARGET PRACTICE. New York (1974)	60	75	35
Meyer, Thomas. THE BANG BOOK. Jargon. No place, 1971. Cloth in acetate dustwrapper	30	35	20
Wraps in acetate dustwrapper			

	1986	1995	2000
Meyerstein, Edward Henry W. *See* E.H.W.M.			
Meynell, Alice. *See* A. C. Thompson			
Mezey, Robert. THE WANDERING JEW. Mt. Vernon, 1960. Wraps. 350 Copies (Previous collected appearance in 1957.)	60	125	150
Michaels, Anne. THE WEIGHT OF ORANGES. Toronto, 1985. Wraps	—	—	350
Michaels, Barbara. (Barbara Louise Gross Mertz.)			
THE MASTER OF BLACK TOWER. New York, 1966 London, 1967.	—	200	200
Also see Barbara Mertz	—	100	100
Michaels, Leonard. GOING PLACES. New York (1969)	—	40	30
Micheaux, Oscar (or Micheaud). *See* THE CONQUEST			
Micheline, Jack. RIVER OF RED WINE +. New York (1958). Wraps	40	75	100
Michener, James A(lbert). TALES OF THE SOUTH PACIFIC. New York, 1947	225	1,250	2,500
New York, 1950. 1,500 signed copies. Special ABA edition without dustwrapper	100	350	450
London, 1951	—	350	750
(One previous nonfiction collaboration.) THE UNIT IN THE SOCIAL STUDIES. Cambridge (1940). Wraps. (Written with Harold M. Long)	500	600	750
Middleton, Arthur. (Edward J. O'Brien.) FORGOTTEN THRESHOLD. New York (1914)	75	75	100
Middleton, Christopher. POEMS. London (1944)	75	100	100
Middleton, Richard. THE GHOST SHIP +. London, 1912	100	100	200
New York, 1926. One of 300 Copies	—	—	125
Middleton, Stanley. A SHORT ANSWER. London, 1958	60	60	60
Midwood, Barton. BODKIN. New York (1967)	25	40	35
Milburn, George. OKLAHOMA TOWN. New York (1931)	—	125	175
Miles, Josephine. LINES AT THE INTERSECTION. New York, 1939	50	100	75
Miles, Keith. BULLET HOLE. (London, 1986.) Author's first golfing mystery	—	—	35
New York, 1987	—	—	25

	1986	1995	2000
Miles, Richard. THAT COLD DAY IN THE PARK. New York (1965).	—	—	35
Millar, Kenneth. (Ross MacDonald.) DARK TUNNEL. New York, 1944	2,000	4,000	4,000
Millar, Margaret. (Mrs. Kenneth Millar.) THE INVISIBLE WORM. Garden City, 1941	250	300	350
Millay, Edna St. Vincent. RENASCENCE +. New York, 1917. 15 signed copies on Japanese vellum	4,000	7,500	7,500
First edition: Glaslan watermark paper. (2 blank leaves precede half title)	125	250	300
Third edition: not on Glaslan watermark paper. (no blank leaves) (Previous Vassar material.)	50	100	125
Millen, Gilmore. SWEET MAN. New York, 1930	100	250	350
London (1930)	—	—	150
Miller, Alice. *See* Alice Duer			
Miller, Andrew. INGENIOUS PAIN. (London, 1997.)	—	—	50
Miller, Arthur. SITUATION NORMAL . . . New York (1944)	150	250	300
Miller, Caroline. LAMB IN HIS BOSOM. New York, 1933. (Only book—Pulitzer)	100	150	200
Miller, Geoffrey. THE BLACK GLOVE. New York, 1981	—	35	30
Miller, Heather Ross. THE EDGE OF THE WOODS. New York, 1964	50	75	60

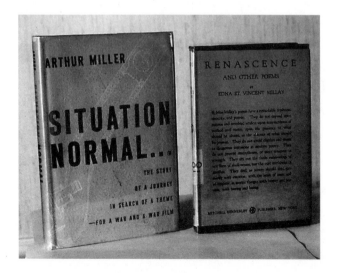

	1986	1995	2000
Miller, Henry (Valentine). TROPIC OF CANCER. Paris (1934). Decorated wraps. First issue: has "First published September 1934" on copyright page and a wraparound band	3K	7.5K	12.5K
Second issue: without notice	750	1,500	2,000
New York, 1940. First (printed) American edition, issued without dustwrapper	—	—	350
New York (1961). First authorized American edition. Patterned boards and cloth spine. One of 100 signed copies, issued without dustwrapper	—	—	2,500
Trade edition in dustwrapper	—	—	100
THE COSMOLOGICAL EYE. Norfolk, 1939. (First U.S. publication.) First issue: eye on cover, dustwrapper price $2.50	125	250	500
Miller, Jason. STONE STEP. (Stoneridge, 1969.) 300 Copies	—	—	125
Miller, Joaquin. (Cincinnatus Hiner Miller.) *See* SPECIMENS			
Miller, Max. I COVER THE WATERFRONT. New York (1932)	—	150	75
Miller, Merle. ISLAND 49. New York (1945)	35	40	50
Miller, Patrick. THE NATURAL MAN. London, 1924	100	125	150
New York, 1924	—	—	75
Miller, Sue. THE GOOD MOTHER. New York (1986)	—	40	35
Miller, Vassar. ADAM'S FOOTPRINT. New Orleans, 1956. Printed wrapper of stiff wraps	60	75	150
Miller, Walter (M., Jr.) A CANTICLE FOR LEIBOWITZ. Philadelphia/New York (1960)	400	1,000	850
London (1960)	150	350	350
Miller, Warren. THE SLEEP OF REASON. London, 1956	100	100	100
New York, 1960. Wraps. (New introduction)	—	40	40
Also see Amanda Vail			
Millhauser, Steven. EDWIN MULLHOUSE. New York, 1972	—	60	150
London (1979)	—	—	75
Mills, James. PANIC IN NEEDLE PARK. New York (1966)	35	50	75
Milne, A(lan) A(lexander). LOVERS IN LONDON. London, 1905	100	500	600
Milosz, Czeslaw. THE CAPTIVE MIND. London, 1953	—	60	200
New York, 1953	—	—	150
Milton, Ernest. TO KISS THE CROCODILE. New York, 1928	50	125	75
Mingus, Charlie. BENEATH THE UNDERDOG. New York, 1977	—	75	50
Minot, Stephen. CHILL OF DUSK. Garden City, 1964	35	75	50

	1986	1995	2000
Minot, Susan. MONKEYS. New York (1986)	—	50	50
MIRIAM COFFIN: OR, THE WHALE FISHERMAN. (Joseph C. Hart.) New York/Philadelphia, 1834. 2 volumes	250	400	500
London, 1834. 3 volumes	—	—	1,000
Mishima, Yukio. (Hiraoka Kimitake.) THE SOUND OF WAVES. New York, 1956. (First English translation)	50	75	100
MR. DOOLEY IN PEACE AND WAR. (Finley Peter Dunne.) Boston, 1898	50	75	75
Mistry, Robhinton. TALES FROM FIOZSHA BRAG. Toronto (1987). Wraps	—	100	125
SWIMMING LESSONS +. Boston, 1989. New title. First state with an integral title/copyright page that bears the wrong copyright date (1989 instead of 1987)	—	—	75
Second state with corrected, tipped-in title page	—	—	35
Mitchell, Adrian. (POEMS.) FANTASY POETS NO. 24. London, 1954. Wraps	40	40	40
Mitchell, Donald G(rant). THE DIGNITY OF LEARNING. New York, 1841. Wraps bound in *Also see* Ik Marvel	200	250	250
Mitchell, Gladys. SPEED DEATH. New York, 1929	—	200	250
Mitchell, Isaac. THE ASYLUM: OR, ALONSO AND MELISSA. Poughkeepsie, 1811. 2 volumes. (Many later editions credited to Daniel Jackson, Jr.)	500	1,000	1,000
Mitchell, Joseph. MY EARS ARE BENT. New York (1938)	40	150	600
Mitchell, Julian. IMAGINARY TOYS. London, 1961	40	40	40
Mitchell, Margaret. GONE WITH THE WIND. New York, 1936. "May 1936" on copyright page and ad for this book in second column on back of dustwrapper	850	4,000	7,500
In second-issue dustwrapper with this book at top of the ad in left column	—	—	1,500
Mitchell, S(ilas) Weir. *See* E.W.S.			
THE WONDERFUL STORIES OF . . . Philadelphia, 1867. (170 large-paper copies)	750	1,000	1,250
Trade (A number of biological and natural science pamphlets preceded.)	200	300	450
Mitchell, Stewart. POEMS. New York, 1921	75	150	150

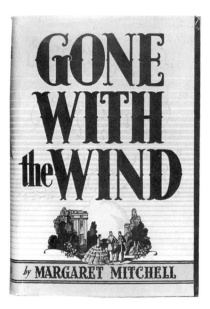

	1986	1995	2000
Mitchell, W. O. WHO HAS SEEN THE WIND. Toronto, 1947	—	500	500
Boston, 1947	40	60	300
Mitford, Mary Russell. POEMS. London, 1810. First issue: leaf of "alterations"	400	1,000	1,500
Mitford, Nancy. HIGHLAND FLING. London, 1931	125	175	250
Mittelholzer, Edgar (Austin). CREOLE CHIPS. British Guiana, 1937	125	250	300
CORENTYNE THUNDER. London, 1941	100	200	250
Mo, Timothy. THE MONKEY KING. (London, 1978)	35	250	200
MODERN PAINTERS . . . (John Ruskin.) London, 1843	—	1,750	1,750
Moffett, Cleveland (Langston). THROUGH THE WALL. New York, 1909	100	125	450
Mojtabai, A. G. MUNDOME. New York (1974)	—	—	40
Molloy, Robert. PRIDE'S WAY. New York, 1945	40	40	40
Momaday, N(atachee) Scott. THE COMPLETE POEMS OF FREDERICK GODDARD TUCKERMAN. New York, 1965. (Edited by Momaday)	50	125	150
THE JOURNEY OF TAI-ME. Santa Barbara (1968). (100 copies) Boxed	500	2,000	2,500

	1986	1995	2000
HOUSE MADE OF DAWN. New York (1968)	—	—	300
Monahan, James. FAR FROM THE LAND +. London, 1944	—	150	75
Monette, Paul. THE CARPENTER AT THE ASYLUM. Boston (1975)	—	—	50
Monk, Maria. AWFUL DISCLOSURES . . . New York, 1836. In original cloth	400	250	250
Monro, Harold. POEMS. London, 1906. Wraps	—	100	100
Monroe, Harriet. VALERIA +. Chicago, 1891. Subscribers' edition. (300 copies)	200	200	250
Chicago, 1892. Regular edition	75	75	100
Montague, C(harles) E(dward). A HIND LET LOOSE. London (1910). (150 copies)	150	350	350
Trade edition	75	150	150
Montague, John. FORMS OF EXILE. Oxford (1958). Wraps (Preceded by POEMS on mimeographed sheets, about 1955.)	75	150	200
Montalbano, William D. *See* Carl Hiaasen			
Montecino, Marcel. CROSS KILLER. New York, 1988	—	100	60
Montessori, Maria. THE MONTESSORI METHOD. New York, 1912	—	—	350
Montgomery, L(ucy) M(aud). ANNE OF GREEN GABLES. Boston, 1908. Beige, green, or brown cloth, no priority	175	5,000	6,000
Montgomery, Marion. THE WANDERING OF DESIRE. New York, 1962	40	60	60
Moody, Rick. GARDEN STATE. Wainscott (1992).	—	—	200
Moody, William Vaughn. THE MASQUE OF JUDGEMENT. Boston, 1900. Boards. (150 copies)	150	100	100
Regular edition	50	50	50
Moon, William Least Heat. (William Trogdon.) BLUE HIGHWAY. Boston (1982)	40	90	100
Mooney, Ted. EASY TRAVEL TO OTHER PLANETS. New York (1981)	—	25	30
London, 1981	—	—	20
Moorcock, Michael. *See* Desmond Reid			
THE STEALER OF SOULS. London (1963). First issue: orange boards	75	150	200
Second issue: green boards	60	100	150

	1986	1995	2000
Moore, Brian. WREATH FOR A REDHEAD. Toronto, 1951. Harlequin romance. Wraps	200	300	750
SAILOR'S LEAVE. New York (1953). New title. Wraps	—	250	250
JUDITH HEARNE. (London, 1955.) (First hardback)	125	300	1,000
THE LONELY PASSION OF JUDITH HEARNE. Boston, 1955. (First U.S. hardback)	100	150	300
Moore, Catherine Lucile. *See* Lewis Padgett			
Moore, Clement C(larke). *See* OBSERVATIONS UPON CERTAIN PASSAGES . . . *Also see* A NEW TRANSLATION . . .			
Moore, Edward (Edwin Muir). WE MODERNS +. London (1918)	200	200	200
Moore, George. FLOWERS OF PASSION. London, 1878. Black cloth. With copyright and errata slip	250	500	500
Moore, Julia A. THE SENTIMENTAL SONG BOOK. Grand Rapids, 1876. Wraps. 52 pages (later 66)	—	500	500
Moore, Lorrie. SELF-HELP. New York, 1985.	—	—	200
London (1985)	—	—	125
Moore, Marianne. POEMS. London, 1921. Wraps	500	750	900
Moore, Merrill. THE NOISE THAT TIME MAKES . . . New York (1929)	125	125	125
Moore, Susanna. MY OLD SWEETHEART. Boston, 1982	—	35	150
Moore, Thomas. ODES OF ANACREON. London, 1800. (Translation and notes)	250	400	400
Moore, T(homas) Sturge. TWO POEMS. London, 1893. Privately printed	—	250	250
THE VINEDRESSER +. London, 1899 (Previous privately printed pamphlet preceded.)	100	150	100
Moraes, Dom. GREEN IS THE GRASS. London, 1951	—	200	200
Morand, Paul. OPEN ALL NIGHT. London, 1923. (First English Translation)	—	—	75
New York, 1923	40	75	50
Moravia, Alberto. (Alberto Pincherle.) THE INDIFFERENT ONES. New York (1932)	75	150	150

	1986	1995	2000
Morecamp, Arthur. (Thomas Pilgrim.) THE LIVE BOYS . . . Boston (1878)	200	300	750
Morgan, Berry. PURSUIT. Boston, 1966	—	75	100
London, 1967	—	50	75
Morgan, Charles (Langbridge). THE GUNROOM. London, 1919. Blue-grained or blue-ribbed cloth—priority uncertain	75	150	300
Morgan, Seth. HOMEBOY. New York, 1990. (Note: proof copies seen with title as DEAD MAN WALKING)	—	75	75
Morgan, Thomas Hunt. THE DEVELOPMENT OF THE FROG'S EGG. New York, 1897 (Student pamphlet preceded.)	—	400	500
Morison, Samuel Eliot. HARRISON GRAY OTIS. Boston, 1913. 2 volumes	150	250	300
Morley, Christopher (Darlington). THE EIGHTH SIN. Oxford/London, 1912. Wraps. (250 copies)	1,000	1,500	1,250
PARNASSUS ON WHEELS. Garden City, 1917. First issue: space between "y" and "e" p. 4:8	150	150	200
Morley, John David. PICTURES FROM THE WATER TRADE. London (1985)	—	60	75
Morrell, David. FIRST BLOOD. New York (1972)	40	125	125
London (1972)	35	75	75
Morris, Bradford. PASSING FROM THE PROVINCES. No place [Santa Barbara], 1981. (76 copies.) Wraps	—	—	75
Morris, James (later Jan). COAST TO COAST. London, 1956	—	175	175
AS I SAW THE U.S.A. (New York, 1956.) (New Title)	—	125	125
Morris, Julian. (Morris West.) MOON IN MY POCKET. Sydney (1948)	100	150	150
Morris, Lewis. *See* SONGS OF TWO WORLDS			
Morris, Mary. VANISHING ANIMALS +. Boston (1979)	—	—	40
Morris, William. THE DEFENSE OF GUENEVERE +. London, 1858. 10 Copies on vellum	—	10K	10K
Trade. (300 copies)	600	600	1,000
Morris, Willie. NORTH TOWARD HOME. Boston, 1967	50	60	100
Morris, Wright. MY UNCLE DUDLEY. New York (1942)	1,000	1,000	1,000

	1986	1995	2000
Morrison, Arthur. THE SHADOWS AROUND US . . . London, 1891	250	250	350
MARTIN HEWITT, INVESTIGATOR. London, 1894. (Third book, first mystery)	1,000	1,000	1,000
Morrison, James Douglas (Jim). THE LORDS. Los Angeles, 1969. 100 Copies	100	850	2,500
THE NEW CREATURES. Los Angeles, 1969. 100 Copies	—	750	1,000
THE LORDS AND THE NEW CREATURES. New York (1970)	—	175	200
Morrison, Theodore. THE SERPENT IN THE CLOUD. Boston, 1931	40	60	60
Morrison, Toni. THE BLUEST EYE. New York (1970)	300	1,750	2,500
London, 1979	40	200	600
Morrow, James. THE WINE OF VIOLENCE. New York, 1981	—	—	100
Morse, L. A. THE FLESH EATERS. New York, 1979	—	75	75
Morse, Samuel French. TWO POEMS. Windward Press, 1934. 35 signed and numbered copies	—	—	300
THE YELLOW LILIES. Hanover, 1935. 85 signed and numbered copies	—	250	250
TIME OF YEAR. (Cummington), 1943. (275 copies)	75	100	100
Mortimer, John. CHARADE. London (1947)	—	250	250
Morton, David. SHIPS IN HARBOR. New York, 1921	60	75	75
Morton, J. B. *See* GORGEOUS POETRY			
Morton, Sarah Wentworth. OUABI: OR THE VIRTUES OF NATURE. Boston, 1790	100	500	500
MORTON OF MORTON'S HOPE . . . (John Lothrop Motley.) London, 1839. 2 volumes	300	400	450
MORTON'S HOPE . . . (John Lothrop Motley.) New York, 1839. 2 volumes	250	350	250
Mosel, Tad. JINXED. French. No date [circa 1949]. Wraps	—	75	75
OTHER PEOPLES HOUSES. New York, 1956	—	75	50
Moseley, Margaret. BONITA FAYE. Dallas (1996). (1,000 copies)	—	—	150
Moses, Robert. THE CIVIL SERVICE OF GREAT BRITAIN. New York, 1914. Wraps	50	100	250

	1986	1995	2000
Mosley, Walter. DEVIL IN A BLUE DRESS. New York, 1990	—	75	125
Moss, Howard. THE WOUND AND THE WEATHER. New York (1946)	75	100	125
Moss, Stanley. THE WRONG ANGEL. New York (1966)	—	30	50
Motion, Andrew. GOODNESTONE. (London, 1972.) Wraps	—	75	150
Motley, John Lothrop. *See* MORTON OF . . . *Also see* MORTON'S HOPE			
Motley, Willard. KNOCK ON ANY DOOR. New York (1947)	50	100	100
London, 1948	—	—	50
Mottram, Ralph Hale. *See* J. Marjoram			
MOUNSEER NONTONGPAW: A NEW VERSION. (Mary W. Shelley.) London, 1808. Original wraps	5,000	7,500	10K
Rebound	—	2,500	2,500
Mowat, Farley. PEOPLE OF THE DEER. Boston, 1952. Blue-green cloth	75	125	150
Mowry, Jess. RATS IN THE TREES. Santa Barbara, 1990. Wraps	—	50	50
Moyes, Patricia. DEAD MEN DON'T SKI. London, 1959	—	75	225
Moynahan, Julian. SISTERS AND BROTHERS. New York (1960)	25	35	40
Muir, Edwin. *See* Edward Moore			
WE MODERNS. New York, 1920. Includes Mencken introduction	150	250	150
Muir, Emily. SMALL POTATOES. New York, 1940	35	50	50
Muir, John. THE MOUNTAINS OF CALIFORNIA. New York, 1894. (Page "1" so numbered)	250	750	750
Second issue	—	600	600
London, 1894	—	500	500
(Previous offprints and edited books.)			
Mukherjee, Bharati. THE TIGER'S DAUGHTER. Boston, 1972	—	75	125
London, 1973	—	—	125
Muldoon, Paul. KNOWING MY PLACE. (Belfast, 1971)	—	—	400
Mulford, Clarence Edward. BAR-20. (Hopalong Cassidy.) New York, 1907. First issue: "Blazing Star" in list of illustrations	125	350	450
Second issue: without "Blazing Star" in list	60	250	300
Muller, Marcia. EDWIN OF THE IRON SHOES. New York (1977)	—	125	125

	1986	1995	2000
Mulligan, John. SHOPPING CART SOLDIERS. Curbstone Press, 1997	—	—	30
Mulock, Dinah. *See* THE OGILVIES			
Mumey, Nolie. A STUDY OF RARE BOOKS. Denver, 1930. (1,000 signed copies)	150	175	225
Mumford, Lewis. THE STORY OF UTOPIAS. New York (1922)	200	400	400
Mun (Munro Leaf). LO, THE POOR INDIAN. New York, 1934	—	—	125
Mundy, Talbot. (William Lancaster Gribbon.) RUNG HO! New York, 1914	100	250	175
Mungo, Raymond. FAMOUS LONG AGO. Boston (1970)	—	—	75
Munro, Alice. DANCE OF THE HAPPY SHADES. (Toronto, 1968.) (Award sticker applied later)	125	300	600
(New York, 1973)	—	150	150
Munro, H(ector) H(ugh). (Saki.) THE RISE OF THE RUSSIAN EMPIRE. London, 1900 *Also see* Saki	200	300	300
Munro, Neil. THE LOST PIBROCK +. Edinburgh, 1896	75	125	125
Munroe, Kirk. WAKULLA +. New York, 1886	50	60	60
Munson, Douglas Anne. EL NIÑO. New York, 1990	—	40	25
Munson, Gorham. WALDO FRANK A STUDY. New York (1923). (Stieglitz frontispiece photo.) 500 numbered copies (Frontispiece normally silvered on edges, worth more clean.)	300	500	600
Murdoch, (Jean) Iris. SARTRE: ROMANTIC RATIONALIST. Cambridge (1953)	150	300	300
New York, 1953	—	200	125
Murgatroyd, Captain Matthew. (James Athearn Jones.) THE REFUGEE. New York, 1823. 2 volumes	400	400	400
Murphy, Audie. TO HELL AND BACK. New York (1949)	60	75	100
Murphy, Dennis. THE SERGEANT. New York, 1958	—	35	35
Murphy, Dervla. FULL TILT. London, 1965	—	50	75
Murphy, Richard. THE ARCHAEOLOGY OF LOVE. Dublin, 1955	—	125	175
Murray, Albert. THE OMNI-AMERICANS . . . New York (1970)	40	75	100
Murray, M(argaret) A. EGYPTIAN POEMS. London (1920)	75	75	75

	1986	1995	2000
Murray, Pauli. ALL FOR MR. DAVIS. (Written with Murray Kempton.) New York, no date [1942]. Wraps	—	—	350
PROUD SHOES. New York (1956).	60	150	200
Murray, Peter. YOU CAN JUGGLE. (Plymouth, Mass.) 1992. Issued without dustwrapper	—	35	35
Murray, William. THE FUGITIVE ROMANS. New York (1955)	—	100	100
Murry, John Middleton. FYODOR DOSTOEVSKY. London, 1916	—	100	75
Musgrave, Susan. SONGS OF THE SEA-WITCH. Vancouver, 1970	—	150	150
Myers, John Myers. THE HARP AND THE BLADE. New York, 1941	—	150	150
Myles, Simon. (Ken Follett.) THE BIG BLACK. London, 1974	75	150	200
Myrer, Anton. EVIL UNDER THE SUN. New York, 1951	35	60	75

N

	1986	1995	2000
Nabb, Magdalen. DEATH OF AN ENGLISHMAN. London (1981). New York (1982)	—	—	150
	—	—	35
Nabokoff (Nabokov), Vladimir. LAUGHTER IN THE DARK. Indianapolis (1938). (First U.S. edition. Revised version of CAMERA OBSCURA translated by Nabokov) Green cloth is said to be first issue; also noted in red, brown, and orange cloths	400	1,250	1,500
In variant color cloths	—	—	1,250
See next entry			

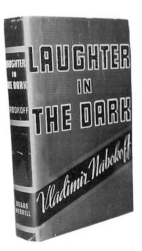

	1986	1995	2000
Nabokoff-Sirin (Nabokov), Vladimir. CAMERA OBSCURA. London (1936). (First book translated into English)	1,500	15K	25K
Without dustwrapper	—	—	2,500

Nabokov, Vladimir. *See two entries above*

	1986	1995	2000
Naipaul, Shiva. FIREFLIES. London, 1970. Cloth	75	150	200
Wraps	—	50	50
New York, 1971	35	75	75
Naipaul, V(idiadhar) S. THE MYSTIC MASSEUR. (London, 1957)	250	400	600
New York (1959)	75	200	200
Narayan, R. J. SWAMI AND FRIENDS. London, 1935	—	150	500
(East Lansing) 1953	—	100	75
Nardi, Marci. POEMS. Denver (1956)	50	50	50
NARRATIVE OF DR. LIVINGSTON'S DISCOVERIES IN CENTRAL AFRICA. (David Livingstone.) London, 1857	400	750	1,000
Nasby, Petroleum V. (David Ross Locke.) THE NASBY PAPERS. Indianapolis, 1864. Wraps. First issue: "Indianapolic" front cover	150	350	350
Second issue: spelled correctly	100	250	250
Nash, Ogden. THE CRICKET OF CARADOR. Garden City, 1925. (Written with J. Alger)	250	600	750
HARD LINES. New York, 1931	250	250	250
(London, 1932)	150	150	150

Nast, Thomas. *See* THE FIGHT AT DAME EUROPA'S SCHOOL

	1986	1995	2000
Nathan, George Jean. THE ETERNAL MYSTERY. New York, 1913	60	75	75
Nathan, Robert (Gruntal). PETER KINDRED. New York, 1919	60	150	150
Native, A. (Thomas Jefferson). A SUMMARY VIEW OF THE RIGHTS OF BRITISH AMERICA . . . Williamsburg (1774)	25K	250K	300K
Philadelphia, 1774	10K	30K	40K
London, 1774	—	—	30K
Also see Jefferson, Thomas			
NATURE. (Ralph Waldo Emerson.) Boston, 1836. First issue: page 94 numbered 92. In original cloth	750	2,500	3,500
Rebound	—	—	1,500
Second issue: page 94 correctly numbered. In original cloth	350	1,250	2,500
Rebound	—	—	750
Naumoff, Lawrence. THE NIGHT OF THE WEEPING WOMEN. New York (1988)	—	—	40

	1986	1995	2000
Nava, Michael. THE LITTLE DEATH. Boston (1986). Wraps. "$6.94" and "June 30, 1988" on last page	—	—	50
Naylor, Gloria. THE WOMEN OF BREWSTER PLACE. New York, 1982	50	400	500
London, 1983	—	—	150
Neagoe, Peter. STORM. Paris, 1932. Published by New Review. Wraps. (1 copy noted in cloth. Preceded Obelisk edition)	150	200	250
Neal, John. *See* KEEP COOL			
Neel, Janet. DEATH'S BRIGHT ANGEL. London (1988)	—	—	250
New York (1989)	—	—	30
Neely, Barbara. BLANCHE ON THE LAM. New York, 1992	—	125	200
Negro Pioneer, A. *See* THE CONQUEST			
Neihardt, John G(neisenau). THE DIVINE ENCHANTMENT +. New York, 1900. (Supposedly the author burned most copies)	650	750	1,000
Neilsen, Kay. IN POWDER AND CRINOLINE. Fairy tales retold by Sir Arthur Quiller-Couch. London (1913). Neilsen's first book	—	—	1,500
Neilson, Francis. MANABOZO. London, 1899	—	100	100
Neilson, (J.) Shaw. OLD GRANNY SULLIVAN. Sydney, 1916	—	—	400
HEART OF SPRING. Sydney, 1919 (Two previous pamphlets.)	—	60	200
Nelson, Charles. THE BOY WHO PICKED THE BULLETS. New York, 1981	—	—	50
Nelson, Kent. THE STRAIGHT MAN. (Berkeley, 1978.) Wraps	—	—	50
Nemerov, Howard. THE IMAGE AND THE LAW. (New York, 1947)	100	100	150
Nesbit, E(dith). LAYS AND LEGENDS. London, 1886 (Preceded by edited anthology SPRING SONGS AND SKETCHES.)	200	300	250
Neugeboren, Jay. BIG MAN. Boston, 1966	35	50	50
Neville, Katherine. THE EIGHT. New York, 1989.	—	—	40
NEW BATH GUIDE, OR, MEMOIRS . . . , THE. (Christopher Anstey.) London, 1766	100	300	300
(New Directions.) PIANOS OF SYMPATHY. Norfolk, 1936.	300	300	250

	1986	1995	2000
Wraps. Written by Montague O'Reilly. First book of the press. First issue: blue wraps			
Second issue: red wraps	—	200	200
NEW DIRECTIONS IN PROSE AND POETRY. Norfolk, 1936. (First in series.) Yellow boards. Issued without dustwrapper	200	300	300
Wraps	100	150	200
NEW TRANSLATION WITH NOTES OF THE THIRD SATIRE OF JUVE-NAL. (Clement Moore and John Duer.) New York, 1806. First issue: "additional errata" leaf	250	500	750
Newbolt, Sir Henry. *See* A FAIR DEATH			
Newby, Eric. THE LAST GRAIN RACE. London, 1956	50	100	75
Newby, P(ercy) H(oward). A JOURNEY TO THE INTERIOR. London, 1945	60	75	125
Newell, Audrey. WHO KILLED CAVELOTTI? New York (1930)	—	—	150
Newell, Peter. *See* TOPSYS AND TURVEYS			
Newhouse, Edward. YOU CAN'T SLEEP HERE. New York (1934)	100	250	500
Newlove, John. GRAVE SIRS. Vancouver, 1962. Stiff wraps. First issue in stiff black smooth wraps	200	250	750
Second issue in black, grainy stiff wraps	—	—	350
Newman, Frances. THE SHORT STORY'S MUTATIONS. New York, 1924. (Noted in pink or gray dustwrapper)	250	350	250
Newman, J. Ed. THE GIANT RAT OF SUMATRA. Roanoke, 1973. Wraps in dustwrapper. About 100 Copies marked second printing	—	—	250
Newton, A(lfred) Edward. THE AMENITIES OF BOOK COLLECT-ING. Boston, 1918. First issue: without index; p. 268:3 has "Piccadilly," in dustwrapper with printing on spine only	60	125	500
Second issue: has index and printing also on front of dustwrapper	25	75	300
Ng, Fae Myene. BONE. New York, 1993	—	35	35
Nichols, Beverley. PRELUDE. London, 1929	—	300	300
Nichols, John. THE STERILE CUCKOO. New York (1965)	50	125	200
London (1965)	—	—	100
Nichols, Robert. INVOCATION . . . London, 1915. First issue: blue wraps	75	150	200
Second issue: green wraps	—	100	150
Third issue: white cloth with black lettering	—	75	100

	1986	1995	2000
Nicholson, Meredith. SHORT FLIGHTS. Indianapolis, 1891	125	125	125
Nicholson, Norman. FIVE RIVERS. (London, 1944)	60	75	50
Nicolson, Harold. PAUL VERLAINE. London (1921)	250	350	350
Boston, 1921	—	—	200
SWEET WATERS. London, 1921	—	350	300
Niedecker, Lorine. NEW GOOSE. Prairie City (1946)	800	1,250	2,000
Nightingale, Florence. NOTES ON NURSING. London (1859). Ads dated 1860. Lacking translation-rights notice below imprint. Wraps or cloth	—	—	750
London (1859). With translation notice	—	—	600
London (1860)	—	—	350
New York, 1860	—	250	500
Boston, 1860	—	—	350
NILE NOTES OF A HOWADJI. (George William Curtis.) New York, 1851. Wraps	200	200	250
Cloth	100	100	150
NIMPORT. (Edwin Lasseter Bynner.) Boston, 1877	—	175	175
Nims, John Frederick. THE IRON PASTORAL. New York (1947)	35	60	40
Nin, Anaïs. D. H. LAWRENCE: AN UNPROFESSIONAL STUDY. Paris, 1932. 550 numbered copies	250	450	500
London, 1961	20	50	100
(Denver, 1964)	—	—	35
Nissenson, Hugh. A PILE OF STONES. New York (1965)	60	75	50
Niven, Larry. (Laurence Vancott.) WORLD OF PTAVVS. New York (1966). Wraps	—	35	35
(London, 1968)	—	200	250
Nixon, Richard. THE CHALLENGES WE FACE. New York (1960)	75	125	150
Noah, Mordecai Manuel. *See* THE FORTRESS . . .			
Noguchi, Yone. SEEN & UNSEEN. San Francisco, 1896	75	300	300
Nonesuch Press. GENESIS. London, 1924. 12 woodcuts by Paul Nash. First Nonesuch book. 375 Copies in orange dustwrapper	—	1,250	1,500
Noon, Jeff. VURT. London (1993). Wraps	—	—	40
Nordan, Lewis. WELCOME TO THE ARROW CATCHER FAIR. Baton Rouge, 1983	—	—	750
Wraps	—	—	50

THE STORY OF THE IRISH CITIZEN ARMY

By P. O CATHASAIGH

The first account that has been given of the formation of the Irish Citizen Army during the Dublin strike of 1913-14, and the part played by it in the subsequent history of Ireland. The author, who was himself a leading figure in the movement, writes with vigour and conviction upon the role of labour in Ireland, and expressing a very definite opinion as to the relations of the workers to the National movement. The book contains original character sketches of Larkin, Connolly, Captain White, and Madame Markiewicz, and some facts bearing on the relations between the Citizen Army and the Volunteers now emerge for the first time.

MAUNSEL & CO., LTD.

ONE SHILLING NET

	1986	1995	2000
Nordhoff, Charles B., and Hall, James N. THE LAFAYETTE FLYING CORPS. Boston, 1920. 2 volumes	600	1,250	2,500
Nordhoff, Charles Bernard. THE FLEDGLING. Boston, 1919	20	75	75
Norman, Charles. TRAGIC BEACHES. New York, 1925. 100 signed copies	100	125	200
Norman, Howard. THE OWL SCATTERER. Boston (1986) (Previous translation.)	—	125	125
Norman, Marc. BIKE RIDING IN LOS ANGELES. New York, 1972	20	50	40
Normyx. (Norman Douglas.) UNPROFESSIONAL TALES. London, 1901. Author's first fiction book. (750 copies printed; 8 sold by author; about 600 copies pulped) (Preceded by a number of pamphlets.)	650	1,000	1,000
Norris, (Benjamin) Frank(lin). YVERNELLE + . Philadelphia, 1892 (actually 1891)	1,000	2,000	2,500
Norris, Gloria. LOOKING FOR BOBBY. New York, 1985	—	35	25
Norris, Hoke. ALL THE KINGDOMS OF EARTH. New York (1956)	—	35	35
Norris, Kathleen. MOTHER A STORY. New York, 1911	60	150	150
Norse, Harold. THE UNDERSEA MOUNTAIN. Denver, 1953	40	75	250

	1986	1995	2000
North, Darian. CRIMINAL SEDUCTION. (New York, 1993)	—	—	25
North, Gil. SERGEANT CLUFF STANDS FIRM. London, 1960	—	—	30
North, Sterling. THE PEDRO GORINO. Boston, 1929. (Written with Capt. Harry Dean)	125	150	100
TIGER. Chicago, 1933	—	125	150
PLOWING ON SUNDAY. New York, 1934	75	75	75
Northamptonshire Peasant *See* John Clare			
Norton, André. (Alice Mary Norton.) THE PRINCE COMMANDS . . . New York, 1934	600	750	1,500
Norton, Charles Eliot. *See* CONSIDERATIONS . . .			
Norton, Mary. THE MAGIC BED-KNOB . . . New York, 1943	—	250	250
Nott, Kathleen. MILE END. London: Hogarth, 1938	75	150	150
Nourse, Alan Edward. TROUBLE ON TITAN. Philadelphia (1954)	40	150	250
Nova, Craig. TURKEY HASH. New York (1972)	35	60	75
Novak, Joseph. (Jerzy Kosinski.) THE FUTURE IS OURS, COMRADE. Garden City, 1960	250	250	250
Noyes, Alfred. THE LOOM OF YEARS. London, 1902	50	50	50
Noyes, John H(umphrey). THE BEREAN . . . Putney, 1847	200	300	500
Nunn, Kem. TAPPING THE SOURCE. New York (1984)	—	40	100
Nutt, Howard. SPECIAL LAUGHTER . . . Prairie City (1940)	125	125	75
Nuttin, Wallace. WINDSOR CHAIRS. Sauges (1917)	—	—	75
Nye, Edgar Wilson. A HOWL IN ROME. Chicago (1880). Wraps	100	150	200
BILL NYE AND BOOMERANG . . . Chicago, 1881	75	125	150
Nye, Hermes. FORTUNE IS A WOMAN. (New York, 1958.) Wraps	30	30	40
Nye, Nelson. PISTOLS FOR HIRE. New York (1941)	—	125	150
Nye, Robert. JUVENILIA 1. (Northwood, Middlesex, 1961.) 25 signed and numbered copies	75	100	75

	1986	1995	2000

O

	1986	1995	2000
Oakes, Philip. UNLUCKY JONAH. Reading, 1954	—	75	75
Oates, Joyce Carol. BY THE NORTH GATE. New York (1963)	100	300	350
Obelisk Press. SLEEVELESS ERRAND. Paris, 1930. (Written by Norah C. James. First book of press)	100	100	100
OBITER DICTA. (Augustine Birrell.) London, 1884	50	75	100
O'Brian, Patrick. THE LAST POOL. London, 1950	—	600	1,500
O'Brien, Dan. EMINENT DOMAIN. Iowa City (1987)	—	50	100
O'Brien, Edna. THE COUNTRY GIRLS. London, 1960	50	150	150
New York, 1960	—	—	75
O'Brien, Edward J. THE FLOWING OF THE TIDE. New York, 1910	50	100	100
O'Brien, Fitzjames. A GENTLEMAN FROM IRELAND. New York [1858]. Wraps	—	350	350
O'Brien, Flann. (Brian O'Nolan.) AT SWIM-TWO-BIRDS. London (1939). First issue: black cloth	2,000	4,500	5,000
Second issue: gray-green cloth. (Issued in 1941 or 1942)	800	3,500	4,000
New York (1939 stated but actually published in 1951)	100	175	200
O'Brien, John. LEAVING LAS VEGAS. Wichita (1990)	—	—	250
O'Brien, Kate. DISTINGUISHED VILLA. London, 1926	125	250	350
O'Brien, Tim. IF I DIE IN A COMBAT ZONE. New York (1973)	250	1,000	2,000
London (1973)	50	200	300
OBSERVATION UPON CERTAIN PASSAGES IN MR. JEFFERSON'S "NOTES ON VIRGINIA." (Clement C. Moore possible author.) New York, 1804. Wraps	300	500	750
O'Casey, Sean. *See next entry*			
O'Cathasaigh, P. (Sean O'Casey.) THE STORY OF THE IRISH ARMY. Dublin, 1919. Wraps. First issue: gray wraps	100	300	350
Second issue: tan wraps	75	150	175
(Preceded by previous pamphlets.)			
O'Connell, Carol. MALLORY'S ORACLE. London (1994).	—	—	60
New York (1994)	—	—	30
O'Connor, Edwin. THE ORACLE. New York (1951)	25	60	60
O'Connor, (Mary) Flannery. WISE BLOOD. New York (1952)	650	1,750	2,500
London (1955)	250	350	500

	1986	1995	2000
O'Connor, Frank. (Michael O'Donovan.) GUESTS OF THE NA-TION. London, 1931	250	750	750
New York, 1931	—	—	300
O'Connor, Jack. CONQUEST. New York, 1930	125	200	250
O'Connor, Philip F. OLD MORALS, SMALL CONTINENTS . . . Iowa City (1971)	25	60	40
O'Connor, Robert. BUFFALO SOLDIERS. New York (1993)	—	—	125
Odets, Clifford. THREE PLAYS. New York: Covici-Friede (1935)	60	250	300
Second issue: Random House	—	125	125
O'Donnell, Lillian. DEATH ON THE GRASS. New York (1960)	—	—	150
O'Donnell, Peter. MODESTY BLAISE. (London, 1965)	75	75	150
New York, 1965	35	40	75
O'Duffy, Eimhar. A LAY OF THE LIFFEY +. Dublin, 1918. Wraps	60	100	125
Oe, Kenzaburo. A PERSONAL MATTER. New York (1968). First English translation	—	—	150
London (1969)	—	—	75
O'Faolain, Julia. WE MIGHT SEE SIGHTS. London (1968)	60	75	60
O'Faolain, Sean. MIDSUMMER NIGHT MADNESS +. London (1932)	250	300	300
New York, 1932	125	150	150
Offord, Carl Ruthaven. THE WHITE FACE. New York (1943)	100	150	150
Offutt, Chris. KENTUCKY STRAIGHT. New York (1992)	—	—	100
O'Flaherty, Liam. THY NEIGHBOR'S WIFE. London (1923)	175	250	300
Ogawa, Florence. *See* AI			
OGILVIES, THE. (By Dinah Maria Mulock [Mrs. Craik].) London, 1849. 3 volumes	300	500	500
O'Gorman, Ned. (Edward Charles O'Gorman) THE NIGHT OF THE HAMMER. New York, 1959	20	40	40
O'Hanlon, Redmond. JOSEPH CONRAD AND CHARLES DARWIN. Edinburgh (1984)	—	—	200
O'Hara, Frank. (Francis Russell.) A CITY WINTER +. New York, 1951. (Larry Rivers illustrations.) 20 signed copies. Cloth	1.5K	7.5K	15K
130 numbered copies. Wraps	500	1,000	2,000

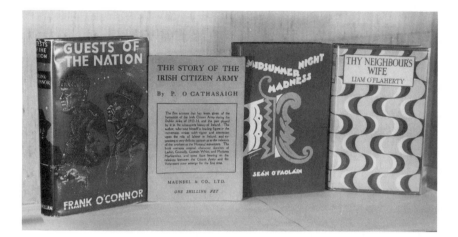

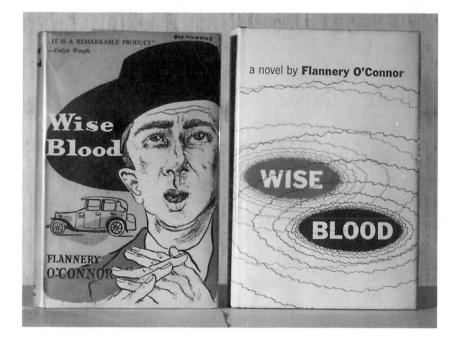

	1986	1995	2000
O'Hara, John. APPOINTMENT IN SAMARRA. New York (1934). First issue: back panel of dustwrapper has ads for "Recent Fiction"	600	3,500	3,500
London (1935) (Preceded by REMINISCENCES: FROM "KUNGSHOLM" written anonymously for Swedish American Line)	250	500	750
Okri, Ben. FLOWERS AND SHADOWS. London (1980). Wraps	—	—	250
OLD LIBRARIAN'S ALMANACK, THE. (Edmund L. Pearson.) Woodstock, Vermont, 1909	75	100	100
Oliphant, Margaret. *See* Margaret Maitland			
Oliver, Chad. MISTS OF DAWN. Philadelphia (1952)	30	60	200
London, 1954	—	—	150
SHADOWS IN THE SUN. New York: Ballantine (1954). Second book, first science fiction	—	—	450
Wraps	—	—	35
Oliver, Mary. NO VOYAGE +. London (1963)	—	300	350
Boston, 1965. Cloth	60	100	250
Wraps	—	—	100
Oliver, Steve. MOODY GETS THE BLUES. Seattle (1996)	—	—	35
Ollivant, Alfred. BOB, SON OF BATTLE. New York, 1898	75	300	200
Olmstead, Robert. RIVER DOGS. New York (1987). Wraps	—	—	35
Olsen, Tillie. TELL ME A RIDDLE. Philadelphia, 1961. Cloth	150	400	450
Wraps	—	—	50
London, 1964	30	50	100
New York, 1978. 100 signed, numbered copies. Issued without dustwrapper in slipcase	—	200	200
Olson, Charles. *See* SPANISH SPEAKING . . .			
CALL ME ISHMAEL. New York (1947)	250	350	350
New York (1958). 100 numbered copies	—	200	250
Wraps	—	—	25
London, 1967	50	75	75
Olson, Elder. THING OF SORROW. New York, 1934	25	60	50
Olympia Press. AMOROUS EXPLOITS OF A YOUNG RAKEHELL. Paris, 1953. (R. Seaver's translation of APOLLINAIRE.) First book of press.) Wraps	50	125	150
O'Marie, Sister Carol Anne. A NOVENA FOR MURDER. New York (1984)	—	—	35
O'Nan, Stewart. IN THE WALLED CITY. Pittsburgh (1993)	—	—	150

	1986	1995	2000
SNOW ANGELS. New York (1994).	—	—	75
Ondaatje, Michael. THE DAINTY MONSTERS. Toronto, 1967. 500 numbered copies	200	1,500	1,500
O'Neill, Eugene G(ladstone). THIRST +. Boston (1914). (1,000 copies)	250	400	400
O'Neill, Frank. AGENTS OF SYMPATHY. New York (1985)	—	—	40
O'Neill, Rose Cecil. THE LOVES OF EDWY. Boston, 1904	40	100	175
Onetti, Juan Carlos. THE SHIPYARD. New York, 1968. First English translation	—	100	175
Onions, Oliver. THE COMPLEAT BACHELOR. London, 1900	60	75	100
Oppen, George. DISCRETE SERIES . . . New York, 1934	300	500	1,000
Oppenheim, E(dward) Phillips. EXPIATION. London, 1887	50	200	300
Oppenheimer, Joel (Lester). FOUR POEMS TO SPRING. (Black Mountain, 1951.) Wraps	250	750	1,500
THE DANCER. Highlands, N.C., 1952. (Jargon 2)	500	1,500	2,500

Optic, Oliver. *See* William Taylor Adams

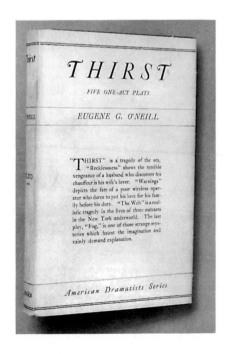

	1986	1995	2000
Orage, A. R. *See* (A) PLEA FOR SCOTLAND			
FRIEDRICH NIETZSCHE . . . London, 1906	50	100	125
Chicago, 1911. (English sheets)	—	75	100
Orcutt, William Dana. ROBERT CAVALIER. Chicago, 1904	60	125	125
Orczy, Baroness (Emmuska). THE EMPEROR'S CANDLESTICKS. London, 1899	150	250	600
New York, 1908	—	—	200
O'Reilly, John Boyle. SONGS FROM THE SOUTHERN SEAS . . . Boston, 1873	—	—	150
O'Reilly, Montage. *See* New Directions			
Orenstein, Frank. MURDER ON MADISON AVENUE. New York (1983)	—	—	40
Origo, Iris. *See* GIANNI JUNE 23RD . . .			
Orlovitz, Gil. CONCERNING MAN. New York: Banyan Press, 1947. 350 numbered copies. (Also first of press)	75	100	150
Ortega y Gasset, José. THE REVOLT OF THE MASSES. London (1932)	125	300	350
New York (1932)	75	150	200
Ortiz, Simon J. GOING FOR THE RAIN. New York (1976)	—	—	150
Orton, Joe. ENTERTAINING MR. SLOANE. London (1964)	75	125	175
Orwell, George. (Eric Arthur Blair.) DOWN AND OUT IN PARIS AND LONDON. London, 1933	3,000	4,000	4,000
New York, 1933	850	1,750	1,750
Osborn, John Jay, Jr. THE PAPER CHASE. Boston, 1971	35	125	150
Osborn, Laughton. *See* SIXTY YEARS . . .			
Osborn, Paul. THE VINEGAR TREE. New York (1931)	—	75	60
Osborne, John. LOOK BACK IN ANGER. London, 1957. Wraps. (Evans Bros. edition preceded Faber edition)	100	200	250
Faber and Faber London, 1957	—	—	150
New York, 1957	40	60	100
O'Shaughnessy, Arthur W. E. AN EPIC OF WOMEN +. London, 1870. First issue: pictorial title precedes title	200	200	250
O'Sheel, Shaemus. THE BLOSSOMY BOUGH. New York, 1911	35	100	125

	1986	1995	2000
Ostenso, Martha. A FAR LAND. New York, 1924. 25 signed and lettered copies	—	250	250
125 signed and numbered copies	50	100	100
Ostroff, Anthony. IMPERATIVES. New York (1962)	25	50	25
O'Sullivan, Seumas. (James Sullivan Starkey.) THE TWILIGHT PEOPLE. Dublin, 1905. Wraps	125	200	200
Otis, James. (Otis Kaler.) TOBY TYLER OR TEN WEEKS WITH A CIRCUS. New York, 1881. First issue: title and illustration on spine centered	150	350	350
Ottley, Roi. NEW WORLD A-COMING. Boston, 1943	—	—	75
Otto, Whitney. HOW TO MAKE AN AMERICAN QUILT. New York (1991)	—	—	50
OUR NIG; OR, SKETCHES FROM THE LIFE OF A FREE BLACK . . . (Harriet E. Wilson.) Boston, 1859	—	10K	10K
Oursler, Fulton. BEHOLD THE DREAMER! New York (1924) *Also see* Anthony Abbott	—	125	125
OUTCROPPINGS . . . (Edited anonymously by Bret Harte.) San Francisco/New York, 1866. Various cloth colors	250	350	350
OUTRE-MER: A PILGRIMAGE BEYOND THE SEA. No. I . . . (Henry Wadsworth Longfellow.) Boston, 1833–34. Volume 1: wraps. Binding A: five-line quotation; imprint in two lines; no publisher's name. (Blanck notes that there are a number of variant wrappered and cloth bindings.) Volume 2: printed blue wraps. (Blanck notes a number of variant bindings with variant binding A being in brown paper boards with brown muslin spine lettered in gold)	1,500	1,500	3,000
New York, 1835. 2 volumes in original cloth (Five Spanish translations between French grammars and this)	—	750	750
Owen, Howard. LITTLE JOHN. Sag Harbor (1992). Cloth	—	200	200
Wraps	—	50	50
Owen, Mary Alicia (Editor). VOODOO TALES AS TOLD AMONG THE NEGROES . . . New York, 1893	—	350	750
Owen, Robert. A NEW VIEW OF HUMAN SOCIETY . . . London, 1813/14. (4 parts in 1)	1.2K	7.5K	20K
Owen, Robert Dale. MORAL PHYSIOLOGY . . . New York, 1831	750	1,000	1,000
Owen, Wilfred. POEMS. London, 1920	600	1,250	3,000
New York (1921)	350	750	2,000

	1986	1995	2000
Owens, Guy. CAPE FEAR COUNTRY AND OTHER POEMS. (Lake Como, 1958)	—	—	200
Owens, Rochelle. NOT BE ESSENCE THAT CANNOT BE. New York (1961). Wraps	50	50	100
OWL CREEK LETTERS, THE. (William C. Prime.) New York, 1848	125	250	250
Oxenham, Elsie J(eanette) (Dunkerley). GOBLIN ISLAND. London, 1907	—	350	450
Ozick, Cynthia. TRUST. New York (1966)	100	250	500
(London, 1966)	75	100	150

P

	1986	1995	2000
Padgett, Abigail. CHILD OF SILENCE. New York (1993)	—	—	75
Padgett, Lewis. (H. Kuttner and C. L. Moore.) THE BRASS RING. New York, 1946. (Moore's first book)	100	250	300
Padgett, Ron. IN ADVANCE OF THE BROKEN ARM. New York, 1964. Wraps. 200 numbered copies	—	50	250
Page, Dorothy Myra. GATHERING STORM. London, 1932	—	125	150
Page, Marco. FAST COMPANY. New York, 1938	—	—	250
Page, P. K. *See* Judith Cape			
Page, Stanton. (Henry Blake Fuller.) THE CHEVALIER OF PENSIERI-VANI. Boston, 1890. Wraps	200	350	400
Cloth	75	200	200
Page, Thomas Nelson. IN OLE VIRGINIA . . . New York, 1887. First issue: has ads headed "Popular Books . . . OLD CREOLE DAYS . . ."	60	150	175
Paine, Albert Bigelow. GABRIEL: A POEM. (Fort Scott, 1889.) Wraps	—	300	300
Painter, Charlotte. THE FORTUNES OF LAURIE BREAUX. Boston, 1961	40	40	40
Pakenham, Antonia. (Antonia Fraser.) KING ARTHUR AND THE KNIGHTS OF THE ROUND TABLE. London, 1954	—	100	100
Paley, Grace. THE LITTLE DISTURBANCES OF MAN. Garden City, 1959	75	200	300
London, 1960	35	100	100

	1986	1995	2000
Palmer, (Charles) Stuart. THE ACE OF JADES. New York, 1931	300	600	750
THE PENGUIN POOL MURDERS. New York, 1931	250	500	600
Pancake, Breece D'J. THE STORIES OF BREECE . . . Boston (1983)	30	35	40
Pangborn, Edgar. WEST OF THE SUN. New York, 1953	—	125	75
Paretsky, Sara. INDEMNITY ONLY. New York (1982)	—	1,250	1,250
London, 1982	—	350	350
Pargeter, Edith. (Ellis Peters.) HORTENSIUS, FRIEND OF NERO. London (1936). One of 125 signed and numbered copies in glassine dustwrapper	—	—	750
Trade edition.	—	—	600
New York, 1937	—	450	450
Parini, Jay. SINGING IN TIME. St. Andrews (Scotland) (1972). Wraps	—	60	75
Park, Ruth. THE HARP IN THE SOUTH. Sydney, 1948	—	—	125
London (1948)	—	—	100
New York (1987)	—	—	30
Parker, Arthur C. EXCAVATIONS IN AN ERIE INDIAN VILLAGE . . . Albany, 1907. Wraps	—	—	300
Parker, Dorothy. MEN I'M NOT MARRIED TO. Garden City, 1922. (Dos-à-dos)	200	450	750
(Previous collaborations.)			
Parker, Robert B(rown). THE GODWULF MANUSCRIPT. Boston, 1974	150	350	400
Parker, T. Jefferson. LAGUNA HEAT. New York, 1985	—	30	75
Parker, Theodore. THE PREVIOUS QUESTION . . . Boston, 1840. Wraps	100	200	200
Parkinson, C. Northcote. EDWARD PELLEW . . . London (1934)	125	200	250
Parkman, Francis. THE CALIFORNIA AND OREGON TRAIL. New York, 1849. 2 volumes in wraps	8.5K	8.5K	20K
1 volume in original cloth with terminal catalog inserted, not integral and paged either 3–6 or 3–10	1,000	1,500	4,500
Second printing with integral catalog paged 1–6	—	—	2,500
Third printing, as above, and "see page 260" on frontispiece	—	—	1,500
Parks, Gordon. FLASH PHOTOGRAPHY. Grosset & Dunlap. New York (1947). Wraps	—	150	200

	1986	1995	2000
THE LEARNING TREE. New York (1963)	35	100	100
London (1964)	—	—	100
Parks, Tim. TONGUES OF FLAME. New York (1985)	—	35	50
London (1985)	—	—	50
Parley, Peter. (S. G. Goodrich.) THE TALES OF PETER PARLEY ABOUT AMERICA. Boston, 1827. In original boards and red leather spine	3.5K	7.5K	10K
Rebound	—	—	5K
Parrish, Anne. A POCKETFUL OF POSES. New York (1923)	75	175	200
Parrish, Maxfield. *See* L. Frank Baum			
Parsons, Louella. HOW TO WRITE FOR THE MOVIES. Chicago, 1915	75	100	150
Partch, Virgil. IT'S HOT IN HERE. New York, 1944	—	—	60
Parton, James. THE LIFE OF HORACE GREELEY . . . New York, 1855	75	100	100
PASSAGES FROM THE DIARY OF A LATE PHYSICIAN. (Samuel Warren.) New York, 1831. (Pirated)	350	350	350
London, 1832. 2 volumes	150	150	200
PASSION FLOWERS. (Julia Ward Howe.) Boston, 1854	125	350	350
Pastan, Linda. A PERFECT CIRCLE OF SUN. Chicago (1971)	40	60	75
Patchen, Kenneth. BEFORE THE BRAVE. New York (1936)	250	300	350
Pater, Walter. STUDIES IN THE HISTORY OF THE RENAISSANCE. London, 1873	75	200	300
Patmore, Coventry. POEMS. London, 1844	750	600	500
Paton, Alan (Stewart). MEDITATION FOR A YOUNG BOY CONFIRMED. London, 1944	200	750	1,000
CRY THE BELOVED COUNTRY. London, 1948	100	300	350
New York, 1948	50	250	300
Patrick, Chann. THE HOUSE OF RETROGRESSION. New York (1932).	—	—	400
Patrick, Q. (Richard Wilson Webb et al.) COTTAGE SINISTER. London, 1931	100	500	750
THE GRINDLE NIGHTMARE. New York, 1935	—	—	1,000

	1986	1995	2000
Patrick, Vincent. THE POPE OF GREENWICH VILLAGE. New York, 1979	—	25	30
Patterson, Harry. SAD WIND FROM THE SEA. London, 1959	—	100	125
Patterson, James. THE THOMAS BERRYMAN NUMBER. Boston, 1976	—	—	250
London (1977)	—	—	125
Patterson, Richard North. THE LASKO TANGENT. New York, 1979	—	50	250
Patton, George S., Jr. *See* SABER EXERCISE			
Pauker, John. YOKED BY VIOLENCE. Denver, 1949	75	75	60
Paul, Eliot. INDELIBLE, A STORY OF LOVE . . . Boston, 1922	200	600	600
Paul, Louis. THE PUMPKIN COACH. New York, 1935	25	40	40
Paulding, J(ames) K(irke). *See* Launcelot Langstaff. *Also see* Hector Bull-us			
PAULINE: A FRAGMENT OF A CONFESSION. (Robert Browning.) London, 1833 *Also see* Robert Browning	25K	40K	50K
PAUSE! London, 1910. (By Arthur Henry Sarsfield Ward, a.k.a. Sax Rohmer)	200	600	1,000
Pavey, L. A. MR. LINE. London, 1931	40	75	75
New York, 1931	—	—	50
Payne, David. CONFESSIONS OF A TAOIST ON WALL STREET. Boston, 1984	—	60	40
Payton, Lew. DID ADAM SIN? Los Angeles (1937). Wraps	50	100	100
Peabody, Elizabeth Palmer. *See* FIRST LESSONS . . .			
Peake, Mervyn. CAPTAIN SLAUGHTERBOARD DROPS ANCHOR. London, 1939	2,000	2,500	3,500
London, 1945	250	300	350
SHAPES AND SOUNDS. London, 1941	—	350	350
Pearce, Donn. COOL HAND LUKE. New York (1965)	50	100	250
London, 1965	—	60	125

	1986	1995	2000
Pears, Iain. THE RAPHAEL AFFAIR. London, 1990	—	60	75
New York (1990)	—	—	40
Pearson, Edmund L. *See* THE OLD LIBRARIAN'S ALMANACK			
Pearson, T. R. A SHORT HISTORY OF A SMALL PLACE. New York, 1985	—	75	75
Peattie, Donald Culross. BLOWN LEAVES. (Chicago) 1916. Wraps	1,000	1,000	1,000
Peck, George (Wilbur). ADVENTURES OF ONE TERRENCE McGRANT . . . New York, 1871	150	300	300
PECK'S BAD BOY AND HIS PA. Chicago, 1883. Cloth	250	400	350
Wraps	—	300	400
Pedrazas, Allan. THE HARRY CHRONICLES. New York (1985)	—	—	35
Pelecanos, George P. A FIRING OFFENSE. New York, 1992	—	—	175
Pelican Books. THE INTELLIGENT WOMAN'S GUIDE TO SOCIALISM. By G. B. Shaw. London, 1937. 2 volumes. Wraps in dustwrapper. (First book of this imprint)	50	150	200
Pelieu, Claude. AUTOMATIC PILOT. New York/San Francisco (1964). Wraps	35	60	75
Pemberton, Sir Max. DIARY OF A SCOUNDREL. London, 1891	50	300	600
JEWEL MYSTERIES I HAVE KNOWN . . . London, 1894	100	250	500
PEN OWEN. (James Hook.) Edinburgh, 1822. 3 volumes	—	350	350
Pendleton, Tom. THE IRON ORCHARD. New York (1966)	40	40	75
Penguin Books. ARIEL. By André Maurois. London, 1935. Wraps in dustwrapper	—	300	350
Penn, Irving. MOMENTS PRESERVED. New York, 1960. Issued in dustwrapper and slipcase	—	500	600
Pennington, Patience. (Elizabeth Pringle.) A WOMAN RICE PLANTER. New York, 1913	60	100	100
Pentecost, Hugh. (Judson Pentecost Philips.) CANCELLED IN RED. New York, 1939	40	150	200
PENTLAND RISING, THE. (Robert Louis Stevenson.) Edinburgh, 1866. Wraps	1,750	3,000	4,500

	1986	1995	2000
Perchik, Simon. THE BOMBER MOON. (New York, 1950.) Wraps	50	75	75
Percy, Walker. SYMBOL AS NEED. Fordham University. New York (1954). An offprint in stapled wraps	500	1,000	750
THE MOVIEGOER. New York, 1961	600	2,000	2,500
London, 1963	200	600	600
Percy, William Alexander. SAPHO IN LEVKAS +. New York, 1915	75	150	175
Perelman, S(idney) J(oseph). DAWN GINSBURG'S REVENGE. New York (1929). First issue: apple-green binding	600	1,250	1,750
Second issue: silver binding	250	750	1,250
Perez-Reverte, Arturo. THE FLANDERS PANEL. New York (1994)	—	—	30
Perishable Press. *See* Walter Hamady			
Perkins, Charlotte. *See* Charlotte Perkins Stetson			
Perkoff, Stuart Z. THE SUICIDE ROOM. Karlsruhe, 1956. Wraps. (200 copies)	50	175	250
Perles, Alfred. SENTIMENTS LIMITROPHES. Paris, 1935. Wraps	125	150	150
Perrotta, Tom. BAD HAIRCUT. Bridgehampton (1994)	—	—	60
Perry, Anne. THE CATER STREET HANGMAN. New York (1979)	—	—	2,500
Perry, Charles. PORTRAIT OF A YOUNG MAN DROWNING. New York, 1962	40	50	60
Perry, George S. WALLS RISE UP. New York, 1939	60	60	60
Perry, Thomas. THE BUTCHER'S BOY. New York, 1982	100	150	600
Perse, St. J(ohn). (Aléxis St. Léger.) ANABASIS. London, 1930. (Translated by T. S. Eliot.) 350 copies signed by Eliot. Slipcase	500	600	750
Trade. Top edge green. White dustwrapper	150	200	250
New York, 1938	—	—	125
PESSIMUS: A RHAPSODY . . . (Frederick William Orde Ward.) London, 1865	—	200	200
Peterkin, Julia. GREEN THURSDAY. New York, 1924. 2,000 numbered copies	125	200	200

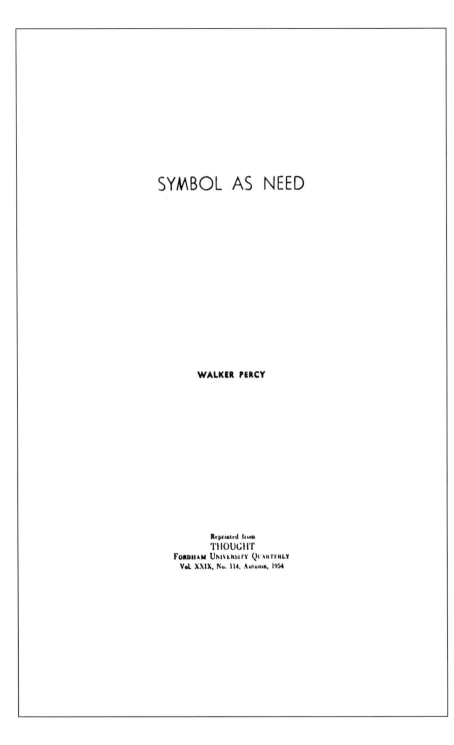

SYMBOL AS NEED

WALKER PERCY

Reprinted from
THOUGHT
FORDHAM UNIVERSITY QUARTERLY
Vol. XXIX, No. 114, Autumn, 1954

	1986	1995	2000
Peters, Curtis Arnoux. *See* Peter Arno			
Peters, Elizabeth. (Barbara Louise Gross Mertz.) THE JACKAL'S HEAD. New York (1968). (First under this name) *Also see* Barbara Michaels and Barbara Mertz	—	200	150
Peters, Ellis. DEATH MASK. London, 1959. (First under this name)	—	500	300
Garden City, 1960 *Also see* Edith Pargeter	—	—	250
Peters, Lenrie. POEMS. Ibadan (1964). Wraps	—	100	100
Petievich, Gerald. MONEY MEN AND ONE-SHOT DEAL. New York, 1981	—	75	75
Petrakis, Harry Mark. LION AT MY HEART. Boston, 1959	60	75	75
London, 1959	40	60	60
Petry, Ann (Lane). THE STREET. Boston, 1946	75	350	400
Pharr, Robert Dean. THE BOOK OF NUMBERS. Garden City, 1969	50	75	125
London (1970)	—	—	60
Philip, Kerr. MARCH VIOLETS. London (1989)	—	—	100
New York (1989)	—	—	35
Phillips, David Graham. *See* John Graham			
Phillips, Jayne Anne. SWEETHEARTS. Carrboro, 1976. 10 copies in boards. Signed	—	750	750
Wraps. (400 copies)	125	200	250
St. Paul, 1978. Wraps. (600 copies) (Preceded by two related broadsides.)	30	75	75
Phillips, Mike. BLOOD RIGHTS. London, 1989	—	50	75
Phillips, Stephen. ORESTES +. London, 1884. Wraps	150	150	150
Phillpotts, Eden. *See* THE GHOST IN THE BANK OF ENGLAND			
MY ADVENTURES IN THE FLYING SCOTSMAN. London, 1888. Stiff wraps. First issue: rainbow-colored cloth	1,000	1,500	1,500
Wraps	—	1,750	1,750
Phoutrides, Aristides. LIGHTS AT DAWN. Boston, 1917	30	50	50
Piatt, John J. *See* POEMS OF TWO FRIENDS			
Pickard, Tom. HIGH ON THE WALLS. London, 1967. 50 signed copies	60	100	60
Trade	20	40	40

	1986	1995	2000
Picthall, Marmaduke. SAID THE FISHERMAN. London, 1903	75	100	100
Piercy, Marge. BREAKING CAMP. Middletown (1968). Cloth	50	125	125
Wraps	15	35	40
Pierpont, John. THE PORTRAIT. Boston, 1812	35	75	75
Pierson, Clara D. AMONG THE MEADOW PEOPLE. New York, 1897	—	—	150
PIGS IS PIGS. (Ellis Parker Butler.) Chicago, 1905. (Author's name on first page of text)	200	400	500
Pike, Albert. PROSE SKETCHES AND POEMS . . . Boston, 1834. In original cloth	1,250	2,000	4,500
Rebound	—	—	2,500
Pilgrim, Thomas. *See* Arthur Morecamp			
Pillin, William. POEMS. Prairie City, 1939. Wraps	40	100	100
Pim, Herbert Moore. THE PESSIMIST. Dublin, 1914	—	125	125
SELECTED POEMS. Dublin, 1917. Wraps	60	60	75
Pinchot, Gifford. BILTMORE FOREST. Chicago, 1893	75	75	100
Pinckney, Darryl. HIGH COTTON. New York (1992)	—	75	50
Pinckney, Josephine. SEA-DRINKING CITIES. New York, 1927. 225 signed and numbered copies	—	300	350
Trade (250 copies)	125	150	200
Pinkerton, Allan. TESTS ON PASSENGER CONDUCTORS. Chicago, 1867. Wraps	200	250	350
Pinsky, Robert. LANDOR'S POETRY. Chicago/London, 1968	—	—	100
Pinter, Harold. THE BIRTHDAY PARTY. London, 1959. (Encore Publications.) Wraps	175	250	300
Piper, H. Beam. MURDER IN THE GUNROOM. New York, 1953	—	—	300
Pirandello, Luigi. THE LATE MATTIA PASCAL. New York (1923). First English translation	—	—	125
Pirsig, Robert M. ZEN AND THE ART OF MOTORCYCLE MAINTE-NANCE. New York (1974)	50	250	250
London (1974)	40	75	100
New York, 1984. 1,000 signed and numbered copies	—	250	250
Pitt-Kethley, Fiona. LONDON. London, 1984. Wraps	—	50	75
Pitter, Ruth. FIRST POEMS. London, 1920. Stiff wraps	75	175	200

	1986	1995	2000
Plaidy, Jean. BEYOND THE BLUE MOUNTAINS. New York (1947)	50	60	50
Plante, David. THE GHOST OF HENRY JAMES. London, 1970. With or without errata	100	200	150
Boston, 1970	50	125	100
Plath, Sylvia. SCULPTOR. Greencourt Review. No place (1959). Wraps. Offprint. (Reportedly 25 copies)	—	1,500	2,000
THE COLOSSUS +. London (1960)	850	850	1,500
New York (1962)	125	200	300
Also see A WINTER SHIP			
Player, Robert. THE INGENIOUS MR. STONE . . . London, 1945	—	100	75
PLEA FOR SCOTLAND, (A). (A. R. Orage.) Glasgow, 1903	—	—	200
Plimpton, George. LETTERS IN TRAINING. No place, 1946	—	300	750
THE RABBIT'S UMBRELLA. New York, 1955	50	150	150
Plomer, William. (Charles Franklyn.) TURBOT WOLFE. London, 1925	200	400	450
Plowman, Max. FIRST POEMS. London, 1913	50	75	10
Plumly, Stanley. IN THE OUTER DARK. Baton Rouge (1970)	—	—	60
Plunket, Robert. MY SEARCH FOR WARREN HARDING. New York, 1983	—	35	35
Plunkett, James. THE EAGLES AND THE TRUMPETS. Dublin, 1954	—	150	200
THE TRUSTING AND THE MAIMED +. New York (1955). New title	35	100	100
Plunkett, Joseph Mary. THE CIRCLE AND THE SWORD. Dublin, 1911. Wraps	200	200	250
Plutzik, Hyam. DEATH AT THE PURPLE RIM. New York, 1941. Privately printed in wraps.	—	—	450
New York: Yale University, 1941.	—	—	350
Poe, Edgar Allan. *See* TAMERLANE			
TAMERLANE +. London, 1884. Vellum. (100 copies)	1,250	2,500	2,500
San Francisco, 1923. 125 numbered copies. 2 volumes. Issued in slipcase	—	1,000	600
No place or date [London, 1931]. 295 numbered copies. Wraps	—	350	450
POEM AND VALEDICTORY ORATION . . . (Edw. R. Sill.) New York, 1861. Wraps	150	150	100

	1986	1995	2000
POEM ON THE RISING GLORY OF AMERICA. (Hugh Henry Brackenridge and Philip Freneau.) Philadelphia, 1772	200	2,500	3,500
POEMS. (Anna Laetitia Alkin.) London, 1773	—	300	300
POEMS. (Siegfried Sassoon.) (London, 1906.) Wraps. (50 copies)	2,500	5,000	5,000
POEMS BY TWO BROTHERS. (Charles Alfred and Frederick Tennyson.) London (1827). Boards. (Alfred's first book)	1,500	7,500	8,500
Rebound	—	3,000	3,500
Wraps. Small-paper copies	750	3,500	4,000
Rebound	—	1,000	1,500
London, 1893. Second edition	—	—	75
New York, 1893. First U.S. edition	—	—	60
POEMS OF TWO FRIENDS. (William Dean Howells and John J. Piatt.) Columbus, Ohio, 1860	800	750	750
Pohl, Frederik. THE SPACE MERCHANTS. New York (1953). (Written with C. M. Kornbluth.) Cloth	100	300	250
Wraps	15	40	35
(Previous edited anthologies)			
ALTERNATING CURRENTS. New York, 1956. Cloth	500	500	500
Wraps	25	35	35
Polite, Carlene Hatcher. THE FLAGELLANTS. New York (1967) (French edition in 1966 preceded.)	25	60	60
Politi, Leo. LITTLE PANCHO. New York, 1938	75	75	300
Pollini, Francis. NIGHT. Paris (1960). Wraps and dustwrapper	50	100	100
London (1960)	—	—	60
Boston, 1961	—	—	50
Pollock, Channing. BEHOLD THE MAN. Washington, 1901	75	100	100
Ponicsan, Darryl. THE LAST DETAIL. New York, 1970	35	75	60
Pool, Marie Louise. A VACATION IN A BUGGY. New York, 1887	50	50	50
Poole, Ernest. KATHERINE BRESHOVSKY ... Chicago, 1905. Pictorial wraps	100	300	300
Pope, Dudley. FLAG 4. London (1954)	—	—	75
RAMAGE. London (1965)	—	—	150

	1986	1995	2000
Porter, Alan. THE SIGNATURE OF PAIN +. London, 1930	—	60	50
New York, 1931	50	75	50
Porter, Eleanor H(odgman). CROSS CURRENTS. Boston, 1907	—	150	150
Porter, Gene (Stratton). THE SONG OF THE CARDINAL. Indi- anapolis (1903) *Also see* THE STRIKE AT SHANE'S	125	250	200
Porter, Joyce. DOVER ONE. London (1964)	—	—	75
New York, 1964	—	—	35
Porter, Katherine Anne. *See* M.T.F.			
OUTLINE OF MEXICAN POPULAR ARTS AND CRAFTS. (Los Angeles) 1922. Wraps	500	2,000	2,500
Porter, Katherine Anne Herwig Shaw. *See* Kathleen Winsor			
Porter, Peter. ONCE BITTEN, TWICE BITTEN. London, 1961	—	75	125
Middlesex, 1961. One of 25 signed numbered copies	—	—	200
Porter, William Sidney. *See* O. Henry			
Porterfield, Nolan. A WAY OF KNOWING. New York (1971)	40	50	30
Portis, Charles. NORWOOD. New York (1966)	40	125	125
Posner, David. AND TOUCH CLEANED EARTH. Trenton, 1940	—	150	175
THE DOUBLE VISION. Paris, 1948. Wraps	75	100	100
Post, Melville Davisson. THE STRANGE SCHEMES OF RANDOLPH MASON. New York, 1896. Wraps	350	500	1,500
Cloth	300	400	1,250
Postgate, Raymond (William). VERDICT OF TWELVE. London (1940)	100	200	250
New York, 1940	40	100	125
Potok, Chaim. THE CHOSEN. New York, 1967	—	75	150
Potter, Beatrix. THE TALE OF PETER RABBIT. London (1901). (Privately printed.) December, 1901. (250 copies)	3K	85K	100K
February, 1902. (200 copies)	2K	15K	25K
October, 1902. First trade. Boards and cloth. First issue: holly leaf end papers; "wept" for "shed" p. 51	750	1,500	7,500
New York, 1995. One of 250 signed by Sendak	—	—	1,000
Potter, Dennis. THE GLITTERING COFFIN. London, 1960	35	100	250

	1986	1995	2000
Pottle, Frederick A. SHELLEY AND BROWNING. Chicago, 1923. 125 numbered copies	—	200	250
Pound, Ezra (Loomis). A LUME SPENTO. (Venice, Italy) 1908. Wraps. (150 copies)	20K	40K	60K
Milan (1958). Stiff gray wraps. One of 2,000 Copies in dustwrapper	—	—	200
(New York, 1965.) In acetate dustwrapper	—	—	75
Powell, Adam Clayton, Jr. MARCHING BLACKS. New York, 1945	40	75	75
Powell, Anthony (Dymoke). BARNARD LETTERS. London, 1928. (Edited)	—	1,000	1,500
AFTERNOON MEN. London, 1931	750	1,750	4,500
New York (1932)	350	1,000	1,750
Powell, Dawn. WHITHER. Boston (1925)	—	—	3,500
Powell, Enoch. FIRST POEMS. Oxford, 1937. Wraps	—	40	40
Powell, Lawrence Clark. AN INTRODUCTION TO ROBINSON JEFFERS. Dijon, 1932. Wraps. (225 copies—85 for presentation)	300	500	500
ROBINSON JEFFERS THE MAN AND HIS WORKS. Los Angeles, 1934. (750 copies)	200	350	350
Powell, Padgett. EDISTO. New York (1984)	20	50	40
THE POWER OF SYMPATHY. Boston, 1789. (By William Hill Brown, originally attributed to Sara Wentworth Morton.) 2 volumes	—	—	10K
Power, Susan. THE GRASS DANCER. New York (1994)	—	—	50
Powers, J(ames) F(arl). PRINCE OF DARKNESS. Garden City, 1947	75	150	125
London, 1948	60	75	75
Powers, Richard. THREE FARMERS ON THEIR WAY TO A DANCE. New York (1985).	—	175	250
London (1988)	—	75	100
Pownall, David. THE RAINING TREE WAR. London, 1974	—	50	60
Powys, John Cowper. CORINTH. (Oxford, 1891.) Wraps. Cover states "English Verse." Powys' name appears at the end of the text	750	750	1,000
ODES +. London, 1896	600	600	750

	1986	1995	2000
Powys, Laurence. AT THE HARLOT'S BURIAL. London, 1930. Wraps	—	50	75
Powys, Llewelyn. CONFESSIONS OF TWO BROTHERS. Rochester, 1916. (Written with J. C. Powys)	50	75	100
THIRTEEN WORTHIES. London, 1923	125	150	150
Powys, Philippa. DRIFTWOOD. London, 1930	125	150	150
Powys, T(heodore) F(rancis). AN INTERPRETATION OF GENESIS. London, 1907. (100 copies)	400	500	600
London, 1929. One of 490 signed copies in slipcase	—	—	250
New York, 1929. First U.S. edition. One of 260 signed copies in glassine wraps and slipcase	—	—	250
THE SOLILOQUY OF A HERMIT. New York, 1916	60	300	350
SOLILOQUIES OF A HERMIT. London, 1918. First issue: light-blue boards	40	75	75
Second issue: dark-blue boards	35	50	50
Prager, Emily. A VISIT FROM THE FOOTBINDER. New York (1982)	—	35	40
Pratchett, Terry. THE CARPET PEOPLE. Gerrards Cross, 1971	—	—	450
Prather, Richard S(cott). CASE OF THE VANISHING BEAUTY. New York (1950). Wraps	20	40	30
Pratt, E. J. *See* RACHEL: A SEA-STORY OF NEWFOUNDLAND			
Pratt, Fletcher. THE HEROIC YEARS . . . 1801–1815. New York, 1934	60	75	75
PRECAUTION: A NOVEL. (James Fenimore Cooper.) New York, 1820. 2 volumes. First issue: errata slip. In original boards	2,000	4,500	5,000
Rebound	—	1,500	1,500
London, 1821. 3 volumes. Rebound	—	1,500	1,500
Prewett, Frank. POEMS. Richmond (England) (1921). Wraps	60	75	400
Price, Anthony. THE LABYRINTH MAKERS. London, 1970	—	—	400
Garden City, 1971	—	—	125
Price, Emerson. INN OF THAT JOURNEY. Caldwell, 1939	40	50	50
Price, Jonathan. (POEMS.) London: The Fantasy Poets, 1954. Wraps	—	—	100

	1986	1995	2000
Price, (Edward) Reynolds. ONE SUNDAY IN LATE JULY. London, 1960. Wraps. (Offprint from *Encounter Magazine*.) Wraps	2,500	2,500	2,500
A LONG AND HAPPY LIFE. New York, 1962. First issue: names on dustwrapper blurbs printed in pale yellowish-green	100	150	175
London, 1962	75	100	125
Price, Richard. THE WANDERERS. Boston, 1974	35	75	75
London, 1975	35	50	50
Priest, Christopher. INDOCTRINAIRE . . . London, 1970	—	125	200
New York (1970)	—	—	30
Priestley, J(ohn) B(oynton). THE CHAPMAN OF RHYMES. London, 1918. Wraps	400	600	750
Prime, William Cowper. *See* THE OWL CREEK LETTERS . . .			
PRIMULA . . . (Richard Garnett.) London, 1858	200	300	350
Prince, F(rank) T(empleton). POEMS. London (1938)	75	75	75
(Norfolk, 1941.) Wraps in dustwrapper	60	60	40
Pringle, Elizabeth Waties Allston. *See* Patience Pennington			
Pringle, Terry. THE PREACHER'S BOY. Chapel Hill, 1988	—	—	30
Prior, Matthew. *See* THE HIND AND THE PANTHER . . .			
Pritchett, V(ictor) S(awdon). MARCHING SPAIN. London, 1928. Cloth	250	350	400
Wraps. (Left Book Club)	75	75	100
Probyn, May. POEMS. London, 1881	—	100	100
Proffitt, Nicholas. GARDENS OF STONE. New York, 1983	—	35	35
Prokosch, Frederick. THREE MYSTERIES. New Hampshire, 1932	250	250	250
THE ASIATICS. New York, 1935. (First novel, tenth book)	75	100	100
London, 1935	75	75	75
Pronzini, Bill. THE STALKER. New York (1971)	—	100	175
Prose, Francine. JUDAH THE PIOUS. New York, 1973	30	60	50
London (1973)	—	40	40

	1986	1995	2000
Proteus. (Wilfred Scawen Blunt.) SONNETS AND SONGS. London, 1875	200	200	150
Proulx, E. Annie. SWEET AND HARD CIDER . . . Charlotte, Vermont. (1980). Glossy wraps	—	—	175
HEART SONGS. New York, 1988. (First fiction)	—	300	750
Prowell, Sandra West. BY EVIL MEANS. New York (1993)	—	—	200
Pryce-Jones, David. OWLS AND SATYRS. London, 1961	—	50	60
Prynne, J. H. FORCE OF CIRCUMSTANCE & OTHER POEMS. London, 1962.	—	—	175
Pudney, John. SPRING ENCOUNTER. London, 1933	50	60	125
Puig, Manuel. BETRAYED BY RITA HAYWORTH. New York, 1971	—	175	150
Purdy, Al. THE ENCHANTED ECHO. Vancouver, 1944	600	600	600
Purdy, James. DON'T CALL ME BY MY RIGHT NAME +. New York, 1956. Wraps (noted in both gray and white variants)	125	250	275
Putnam, Howard Phelps. TRINC. New York (1927)	75	75	75
Putnam, Samuel. EVAPORATION . . . Winchester, 1923. (Written with Mark Turbyfill)	100	200	175
FRANCOIS RABELAIS . . . New York (1929)	50	125	125
Puzo, Mario. THE DARK ARENA. New York (1955)	60	100	150
Pyle, A. M. TROUBLE MAKING TOYS. New York (1985)	—	—	35
Pyle, Ernie. ERNIE PYLE IN ENGLAND. New York (1941)	—	75	75
Pyle, Howard. YANKEE DOODLE. New York, 1881. First illustrated book	500	750	750
THE MERRY ADVENTURES OF ROBIN HOOD. New York, 1883. Leather	—	1,000	1,000
Cloth	400	600	750
London, 1883	300	500	600
Pym, Barbara. SOME TAME GAZELLE. London, 1950	125	300	350
New York, 1983	—	—	35
Pynchon, Thomas. V. Philadelphia (1963)	350	850	1,500
London (1963)	200	250	450

Don't Call Me By My Right Name

AND OTHER STORIES

by James Purdy

WITH ILLUSTRATIONS BY THE AUTHOR

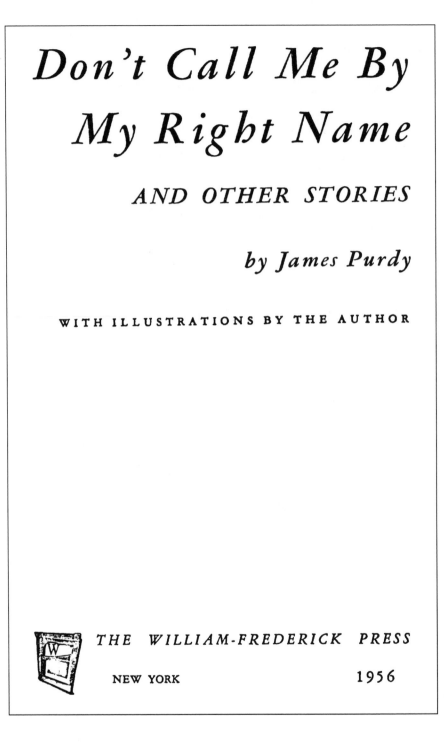

THE WILLIAM-FREDERICK PRESS

NEW YORK   1956

	1986	1995	2000

Q

Q. (Sir Arthur Quiller-Couch.) DEAD MAN'S ROCK. London, 1887 — 250, 400, 450

Q. (Sir Arthur Quiller-Couch.) DEAD MAN'S ROCK. London, 1887	250	400	450
Queen, Ellery. (Frederic Dannay and Manfred B. Lee.) ROMAN HAT MYSTERY. New York, 1929	1,000	3,500	6,000
New York (1974). 250 signed and numbered copies in dustwrapper	—	200	250
Queneau, Raymond. THE SKIN OF DREAMS. New Directions (New York, 1948). Translated by H. J. Kaplan. Wraps. Direction 5.	—	—	150
Quennell, Peter. MASQUES AND POEMS. Berkshire (1922)	125	200	200
Querry, Ron. THE DEATH OF BERNADETTE LEFTHAND. Santa Fe (1993)	—	—	125
Quiller-Couch, Sir Arthur. *See* Q.			
Quillinan, Dorothy Wordsworth. *See* JOURNAL OF A FEW MONTH'S RESIDENCE IN PORTUGAL . . .			
Quine, W.V.O. A SYSTEM OF LOGISTIC. Cambridge, 1934	—	150	350
Quinn, Arthur Hobson. PENNSYLVANIA STORIES. Philadelphia, 1899	75	100	100
Quinn, Seabury (Grandin). ROADS. (New York, 1938.) Wraps. (Reprinted from *Weird Tales*)	150	2,500	2,500
Sauk City: Arkham House, 1948	75	150	150
Quinn, Simon. (Martin Cruz Smith.) THE MIDAS COFFIN. New York, 1975. Wraps	—	—	25

R

R., C.G. (Christina G. Rossetti.) VERSES. London, 1847. Unlettered blue cloth wraps or lettered cloth boards	4,000	6,000	7,500
R., E. (W.W.E. Ross.) LACONICS. Ottawa, 1930	—	1,750	2,500
Raban, Jonathan. THE TECHNIQUE OF MODERN FICTION. London, 1968. Wraps	—	40	50
Rabe, David. THE BASIC TRAINING OF PAVLO HUMMEL and STICKS AND BONES. New York (1973). Cloth	—	60	75
Wraps	—	20	35
RACHEL: A SEA-STORY OF NEWFOUNDLAND. (E. J. Pratt.) New York, 1917. Wraps	—	3,000	3,000

	1986	1995	2000
Radcliffe, Ann (Ward). THE CASTLES OF ATHLIN AND DUN-BAYNE. London, 1789	—	—	5,000
THE MYSTERIES OF UDOLPHO. London, 1794. 4 volumes	500	1,500	3,000
Radiguet, Raymond. THE COUNT'S BALL. New York (1929)	—	200	300
Rago, Henry. THE PHILOSOPHY OF ESTHETIC INDIVIDUALISM. Notre Dame, 1941. Wraps	75	100	100
Raine, Kathleen (Jessie). STONE AND FLOWER, POEMS. (London, 1943)	90	125	175
Raine, William MacLeod. A DAUGHTER OF RAASAY. New York (1902)	150	150	150
Rakosi, Carl. SELECTED POEMS. (New York, 1941.) Wraps	—	150	75
Ramal, Walter. (Walter De La Mare.) SONGS OF CHILDHOOD. London, 1902	400	600	650
London, 1923. 310 signed copies	—	150	200
Rand, Ayn. WE THE LIVING. New York, 1936. States "Published, April, 1936"	1,000	2,500	4,500
London (1936)	750	2,500	3,000
New York, 1959. Revised edition	—	—	250
Randall, Julia. THE SOLSTICE TREE. Baltimore, 1952	50	60	75
Randall, Margaret. GIANT OF TEARS +. New York, 1959. Wraps. 500 numbered copies	—	—	75
Randall, Robert. (Randall Garrett and Robert Silverberg.) THE SHROUDED PLANET. New York, 1957	35	50	50
Random House. CANDIDE. New York, 1928. 1,470 copies signed by Rockwell Kent	150	300	300
Rankin, Ian. THE FLOOD. Edinburgh (1986). Reportedly 800 copies	—	—	500
Ransom, John Crowe. POEMS ABOUT GOD. New York, 1919	500	600	600
Ransom Press. OPEN SHUTTERS. By Oliver Jenkins. Chicago, 1922. (245 copies)	150	125	150
Ransome, Arthur. THE SOULS OF THE STREET +. London, 1904	60	600	600
Raphael, Frederic. OBBLIGATO. London, 1956	50	60	60
Raphaelson, Samson. THE JAZZ SINGER. New York, 1925	—	200	250
Rathbone, Julian. DIAMONDS BID. London, 1967	—	40	50

	1986	1995	2000
Rattigan, Terrence (Mervyn). FRENCH WITHOUT TEARS. London, 1937. Cloth	75	200	200
Wraps	—	75	75
New York, 1938	—	150	150
Raven, Simon. THE FEATHERS OF DEATH. London, (1959)	50	150	150
New York (1960)	—	—	50
Rawlings, Majorie Kinnan. SOUTH MOON UNDER. New York, 1933. (Scribner's "A" on copyright page)	150	750	850
Raworth, Tom. THE RELATION SHIP. (London, 1966.) 50 signed and numbered copies. Wraps	50	125	150
450 copies. Wraps	30	60	50
Rawson, Clayton. DEATH FROM A TOP HAT. New York, 1938	250	350	1,000
Reach, Angus B(ethune). CLEMENT LORIMER . . . London, (1849). With frontispiece and 11 plates	400	500	500
Read, Herbert. SONGS OF CHAOS. London (1915)	200	450	450
NAKED WARRIORS. London, 1919. (First commercially published book)	100	300	300
Read, Piers Paul. GAME IN HEAVEN WITH TUSSY MARX. London, 1966	50	50	75
New York, 1966	25	25	35
Read, Thomas Buchanan. PAUL REDDING . . . Boston, 1845	125	150	150
Reade, Charles. PEG WOFFINGTON. London, 1853	100	200	350
Boston, 1855	—	—	150
Reading, Peter. WATER AND WASTE. Walton-on-Thames, 1970. Wraps	—	150	150
Reamy, Tom. BLIND VOICES. New York, 1978	—	40	50
Reaney, James. THE RED HEART. Toronto, 1949	300	350	350
Reavey, George. FAUST'S METAMORPHOSES . . . Seine (1932). Wraps	100	250	250
Rechy, John. CITY OF THE NIGHT. New York (1963)	30	75	75
London, 1964	—	50	50
Redding, J(ay) Saunders. TO MAKE A POET BLACK. Chapel Hill, 1939	50	350	300
Redgrove, Peter (William). THE COLLECTOR +. London, 1960	40	100	100
Redman, Ben Ray. MASQUERADE. New York, 1923	25	35	60

	1986	1995	2000
Reed, Henry. A MAP OF VERONA +. London (1946)	75	75	200
New York (1947)	—	—	75
Reed, Ishmael. THE FREELANCE PALLBEARERS. Garden City, 1967	60	150	175
Reed, Jeremy. TARGET: PRELIMINARY POEMS. LaHaule, Jersey, 1972. 100 signed and numbered copies. Wraps	—	75	100
Reed, John Silas. DIANA'S DEBUT. Harvard (Cambridge, 1910). Lyrics by Reed. Wraps	—	1,750	1,750
SANGAR, TO LINCOLN STEFFENS. Riverside, Conn., 1913. Wraps. 500 copies. Boxed	100	300	350
THE DAY IN BOHEMIA. New York, 1913. Stiff wraps. 500 copies. In slipcase. (Priority uncertain)	100	300	350
Reed, Kit. MOTHER ISN'T DEAD SHE'S ONLY SLEEPING. New York, 1961	35	50	35
Reese, Lizette Woodworth. A BRANCH OF MAY. Baltimore, 1887	250	300	300
Reeve, Arthur B(enjamin). THE POISONED PEN. New York, 1911	—	—	350
London, 1916	—	—	250
Reeves, James. THE NATURAL NEED. Oeya/London (1935)	125	125	150
Reid, Alastair. TO LIGHTEN MY HOUSE. Scarsdale (1953) (Previous privately printed pamphlet.)	40	60	40
Reid, Desmond. (Michael Moorcock and Jim Cawthorn.) CARIBBEAN CRISIS. London (1962). Wraps	75	175	100
Reid, Forrest. THE KINGDOM OF TWILIGHT. London, 1904	125	350	350
Reid, (Thomas) Mayne. THE WHITE CHIEF . . . London, 1855. 3 volumes	500	600	1,000
Reid, Victor S. NEW DAY. New York, 1949	75	75	60
London, 1950	—	50	50
Reiser, Anton. ALBERT EINSTEIN: A BIOGRAPHICAL PORTRAIT. New York, 1930. (Translated anonymously by Louis Zukofsky)	600	750	750
London (1931)	400	500	500
Reisner, Mary. SHADOWS ON THE WALL. New York, 1943.	—	—	225
Remarque, Erich Maria. ALL QUIET ON THE WESTERN FRONT. London (1929)	125	250	600
Boston, 1929	75	150	150

	1986	1995	2000
Remington, Frederic (Sackrider). PONY TRACKS. New York, 1895. Suede	1,000	1,000	1,000
Cloth	250	450	500
Renault, Mary. (Mary Challans.) PURPOSES OF LOVE. London, 1939	125	300	350
PROMISE OF LOVE. New York, 1940. (New title)	75	175	200
Rendell, Ruth. FROM DOON WITH DEATH. London (1964)	125	1,250	2,500
Garden City, 1965	—	600	750
Renek, Morris. THE BIG HELLO. New York, 1961	30	30	40
Repplier, Agnes. BOOKS AND MEN. Boston, 1888	50	75	100
Reuben. (Robert Stephen Hawker.) TENDRILS. London, 1821	—	—	2,000
Rexroth, Kenneth. IN WHAT HOUR. New York, 1940	200	250	300
Reynolds, Tim. POEMS 1962–4. No place, 1964. 25 signed and numbered copies. Wraps. (8″ x 11″ stapled sheets)	—	150	150
RYOANJI. New York, 1964 (Preceded by a self-published item.)	35	40	40
Reznikoff, Charles. RHYTHMS. Brooklyn (privately printed, 1918). Wraps	1,000	1,750	1,750
Rhode, John. (Major Cecil John Charles Street.) THE STORY OF A GREAT CONSPIRACY. London (1924)	150	300	600
THE WHITE MENACE. New York (1926). New title	100	200	350
Rhodes, Eugene Manlove. GOOD MEN AND TRUE. New York, 1910	100	200	200
Rhodes, W(illiam) H(enry). CAXTON'S BOOK. San Francisco, 1876	250	250	250
RHYMES OF IRONQUILL. (By Eugene Fitch Ware.) Topeka, 1885	75	75	75
Rhys, Ernest. A LONDON ROSE +. London, 1894	75	125	150
Rhys, Jean. LEFT BANK +. New York (1927)	400	500	1,000
London (1927)	—	—	750
Ricci, Nino. LIVES OF THE SAINTS. Dunvegan, Ontario, 1990. Wraps	—	75	100
THE BOOK OF SAINTS. New York, 1991. New title	—	—	50

Rice, Alice (Caldwell) Hegen. *See* Alice Hegen

PONY
TRACKS

*WRITTEN AND
ILLUSTRATED BY*
FREDERIC REMINGTON

NEW YORK
HARPER & BROTHERS PUBLISHERS
FRANKLIN SQUARE
1895

GOODBYE,
COLUMBUS

AND FIVE SHORT STORIES

BY PHILIP ROTH

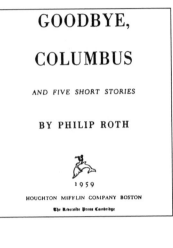

1959
HOUGHTON MIFFLIN COMPANY BOSTON
The Riverside Press Cambridge

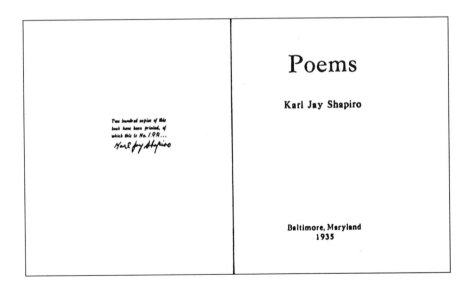

Poems

Karl Jay Shapiro

Two hundred copies of this
book have been printed, of
which this is No. 198...

Karl Jay Shapiro

Baltimore, Maryland
1935

	1986	1995	2000
Rice, Anne. INTERVIEW WITH THE VAMPIRE. New York, 1976	50	750	750
London, 1976	—	350	350
New York, 1992. 1,000 signed copies	—	250	250
Rice, Craig. (Georgiana Ann Randolph.) 8 FACES AT 3. New York, 1939	—	150	250
Rice, Grantland. SOME DAY I'M GOING HOME. Chicago (1914)	—	—	125
Rich, Adrienne Cecile. ARIADNE: A PLAY IN THREE ACTS. (Baltimore) 1939. Wraps	2,000	1,500	3,000
NOT I, BUT DEATH. Baltimore, 1941. Wraps	1,500	1,500	1,500
Green boards	—	—	2,000
A CHANGE OF WORLD. New York, 1951	350	450	750
Richard, Mark. THE ICE AT THE BOTTOM OF THE WORLD. New York, 1989	—	40	50
Richards, David Adams. SMALL HEROICS. Fredericton, (1972). Stiff card wraps	—	125	250
COMING OF WINTER. Ottawa, 1974. (First novel.) Cloth	—	300	350
Wraps	—	—	35
Richards, I. A. THE FOUNDATION OF AESTHETICS. London (1922). Written with C. K. Ogden and James Wood	100	150	150
THE MEANING OF MEANING. New York, 1923. Written with C. K. Ogden	100	150	150
PRINCIPLES OF LITERARY CRITICISM. New York, 1924	100	125	125
London, 1925	75	100	100
Richardson, Dorothy. THE QUAKERS PAST AND PRESENT. London, 1914	—	250	250
GLEANINGS FROM THE WORK OF GEORGE FOX. London, 1914	—	200	200
POINTED ROOFS. London, 1915	150	150	150
New York, 1916	125	125	125
Richardson, O(wen) W(illians). THE ELECTRON THEORY OF MATTER. Cambridge, 1914	—	200	200
Richler, Mordecai. THE ACROBATS. (London, 1954)	200	450	500
New York, 1954. (Less than 1,000 copies)	100	300	350
Richter, Conrad. BROTHERS OF NO KIN +. New York (1924). White dustwrapper	500	600	750
Orange dustwrapper	300	400	500

	1986	1995	2000
Rickword, Edgell. BEHIND THE EYES. London, 1921	30	30	30
Ridge, Lola. THE GHETTO +. New York, 1918	40	75	75
Riding, Laura. *See* Laura Riding Gottschalk			
Ridler, Anne (Barbara). *See* Anne Bradby			
POEMS. London, 1939. (Most destroyed in blitz)	100	125	75
Riley, James Whitcomb. *See* Benj. F. Johnson			
Rilke, Rainer Maria. POEMS. New York, 1918. 500 copies. (First English publication)	125	300	300
Rinehart, Mary Roberts. THE CIRCULAR STAIRCASE. Indianapolis (1908). (September copyright)	75	125	150
Ring, Ray. TELLURIDE SMILE. New York (1988)	—	—	35
RIP VAN WINKLE. (By Washington Irving.) Roycrofters' (East Aurora 1905). Initials and title page by Dard Hunter (his first book contribution)	100	200	250
Rives, Amelia. A BROTHER TO DRAGONS. New York, 1888	75	75	50
Rives, Richard. EMERGENCY. London, 1966	—	50	50
Roark, Garland. WAKE OF THE RED WITCH. Boston, 1946	30	50	50
Robbe-Grillet, Alain. THE VOYEUR. New York (1958). Translated by Richard Howard.	—	—	200
Robbins, Harold. (Harold Ruben.) NEVER LOVE A STRANGER. New York, 1948	30	75	100
Robbins, Tom. GUY ANDERSON. Seattle, 1965. Wraps	—	750	850
ANOTHER ROADSIDE ATTRACTION. Garden City, 1971	150	500	600
London, 1973	—	200	250
Roberson, Ed. WHEN THE KING IS A BOY. Pittsburgh (1970). Cloth	—	50	50
Wraps	—	20	20
Roberts (Charles G. D). ORION AND OTHER POEMS. Philadelphia, 1880	—	—	250
Roberts, B(righam) H(enry). THE LIFE OF JOHN TAYLOR. Salt Lake, 1892	150	175	200
Roberts, Elizabeth Madox. IN THE GREAT STEEP'S GARDEN. (Colorado Springs, 1915.) Wraps	3,500	4,000	5,000

	1986	1995	2000
UNDER THE TREE. New York, 1922	150	350	350
Roberts, Emma. ORIENTAL SCENES . . . Calcutta, 1830	—	—	400
Roberts, Keith. THE FURIES. (London, 1966.)	—	125	600
Roberts, Kenneth L(ewis). PANATELA . . . (Ithaca) 1907. Wraps. (Song book written with R. Berry)	300	600	750
EUROPE'S MORNING AFTER. New York (1921)	200	500	1,000
Roberts, Les. AN INFINITE NUMBER OF MONKEYS. New York (1987)	—	—	25
Roberts, Morley. THE WESTERN AVERNUS . . . London, 1887	150	250	750
Roberts, Robert. THE HOUSE SERVANT'S DIRECTORY . . . Boston/New York, 1827	—	6,500	7,500
New York, 1828. Second edition	—	—	3,500
Roberts, W. Adolphe. THE HAUNTING HAND. New York, 1926	—	—	1,500
Robertson, Ben. TRAVELERS' REST. Clemson, South Carolina (1938)	—	500	500
Robertson, E. (Earle Birney.) CONVERSATIONS WITH TROTSKY. London, 1936	1,500	2,500	3,000
Robeson, Paul. HERE I STAND. New York (1958). Cloth	100	300	300
Wraps	—	150	100
London (1958)	—	150	150
Robinson, Edwin Arlington. THE TORRENT AND THE NIGHT BEFORE. Cambridge, 1896. Wraps	2,000	2,500	2,500
THE CHILDREN OF THE NIGHT. Boston, 1897. 50 Copies. Vellum	1,500	2,000	2,000
500 Copies. Laid paper	400	750	750
Robinson, Linda S. MURDER IN THE PLACE OF ANUBIS. New York, 1994	—	50	125
Robinson, Marilynne. HOUSEKEEPING. New York, 1980	20	60	100
Robinson, Peter. WITH EQUAL EYE. Toronto, 1979. Wraps	—	250	350
GALLOWS VIEW. Markham (Canada), 1987	—	200	250
New York, 1990	—	40	35
Robinson, Rowland Evans. *See* AWAHSOOSE, THE BEAR			
UNCLE 'LISHA'S SHOP. New York, 1887	50	300	75
Robison, Mary. DAYS. New York, 1979	25	75	50

	1986	1995	2000
Rodd, (James) Rennell. SONGS TO THE SOUTH. London, 1881	125	1,000	1,000
Philadelphia, 1882	—	350	350
(Previous 1880 Newdigate prize poem.)			
Rodgers, W. R. AWAKE +. London, 1941	40	40	40
Roditi, Edouard (Herbert). POEMS FOR F. Paris (1935). 200 signed numbered copies in wraps	175	500	250
Rodker, John. POEMS. London (1914). Boards. 50 signed and numbered copies	600	750	950
Wraps	150	250	300
Rodman, Seldon. MORTAL TRIUMPH +. New York (1932)	60	125	125
Roe, Edward Payson. BARRIERS BURNED AWAY. New York, 1872	50	50	50
Roethke, Theodore. OPEN HOUSE. New York, 1941. (1,000 copies)	600	750	750
Rogers, Jane. SEPARATE TRACKS. London (1983)	—	—	40
Rogers, Will(iam Penn Adair). THE COWBOY PHILOSOPHER ON PROHIBITION. New York (1919)	50	150	150
Rogin, Gilbert. THE FENCING MASTER +. New York, 1965	25	40	40
Rohmer, Sax. (Arthur Henry Sarsfield Ward.) THE MYSTERY OF DR. FU-MANCHU. London (1913)	250	500	750
THE INSIDIOUS DR. FU-MANCHU. New York, 1913. (New title)	75	150	750
Rolfe, Frederick William. *See* Baron Corvo			
Rolvaag, O. E. GIANTS IN THE EARTH. New York, 1927	100	175	150
Romanof, Panteleimon. THREE PAIRS OF SILK STOCKINGS. New York, 1931. (First English translation)	—	100	100
Romilly, Gilles and Edmond. OUT OF BOUNDS. London, 1935	—	175	200
Rook, Alan. SONGS FROM A CHERRY TREE. Oxford, 1938. Wraps	50	75	75
Rooke, Leon. LAST ONE HOME SLEEPS IN THE YELLOW BED. Baton Rouge (1968)	25	40	40
ROOKWOOD. (By William Harrison Ainsworth.) London, 1834. 3 volumes	—	600	600
Rooney, Andy. AIR GUNNER. New York (1944). Written with Bud Hutton	40	60	75

	1986	1995	2000
Roosevelt, Eleanor. IT'S UP TO THE WOMEN. New York, 1933. One of 1,000 signed copies, in slipcase	—	—	1,000
Trade edition	75	200	300
Roosevelt, Franklin D. WHITHER BOUND? Boston, 1926	200	600	1,000
Roosevelt, Theodore. THE SUMMER BIRDS OF THE ADIRON- DACKS. (Salem, 1877.) Wraps. (Written with H. D. Minot)	400	1,750	3,000
THE NAVAL WAR OF 1812 . . . New York, 1882	200	750	1,250
Root, E. Merrill. LOST EDEN. New York, 1927	50	50	35
Rorem, Ned. THE PARIS DIARY OF NED ROREM. New York (1966)	—	40	35
Ros, Amanda M'Kittrick. IRENE IDDESLEIGH. Belfast, 1897. With slip of "Printer's errors"	75	150	150
Rose, Wendy. HOPI ROADRUNNER DANCING. Greenfield Center (1973). Wraps	—	—	75
Rosen, R. D. STRIKE THREE YOU'RE DEAD. New York, 1984	—	125	150
Rosenbach, A. S. W. SAMUEL JOHNSON'S PROLOGUE . . . New York, 1902. (100 copies)	350	500	500
30 copies on Japan vellum	—	1,000	1,250
THE UNPUBLISHABLE MEMOIRS. New York, 1917. (First regularly published)	35	125	125
Rosenberg, Harold. TRANCE ABOVE THE STREETS. New York (1942). 80 signed and numbered copies. Issued in glassine dustwrapper	—	300	250
Rosenberg, Isaac. NIGHT AND DAY. (London, 1912.) Wraps	6,000	7,500	7,500
YOUTH. London, 1915. Wraps	600	750	1,250
Rosenberg, Robert. CRIMES OF THE CITY. New York (1991)	—	—	25
Rosenfeld, Isaac. PASSAGE FROM HOME. New York (1946)	60	60	75
Roskolenko, Harry. SEQUENCE ON VIOLENCE. New York (1938)	—	150	200
Ross, Alan. THE DERELICT DAY. London, 1947	60	75	75
Ross, Maggie. THE GASTEROPOD. London (1968)	—	50	35
Ross, W. W. E. *See* E. R.			
Rossetti, Christina. *See* C.G.R.			

	1986	1995	2000
GOBLIN MARKET. London, 1862. (16-page catalog at rear)	400	500	1,500
London, 1893. 160 copies. Illustrated by Laurence Housman	—	750	1,000
London (1933). First Rackham illustrated. One of 10 signed copies with original drawing	—	—	10K
One of 400 signed copies	—	—	1,000
Rossetti, Dante Gabriel. SIR HUGO THE HERON. London, 1843. Wraps	1,500	2,500	2,500
Rossetti, William Michael. THE COMEDY OF DANTE ALIGHIERI PART 1. London, 1865. (Translated by Rossetti)	—	350	450
SWINBURNE'S POEMS & BALLADS. London, 1886	75	250	300
Rossner, Judith. WHAT KIND OF FEET DOES A BEAR HAVE? Indianapolis, 1963	75	200	250
TO THE PRECIPICE. New York (1966)	50	75	75
Rosten, Leo C. THE WASHINGTON CORRESPONDENTS. New York (1937)	—	100	100
Rosten, Norman. RETURN AGAIN, TRAVELLER. New Haven, 1940	40	125	75
Roth, Henry. CALL IT SLEEP. New York, 1934	1,500	2,500	5,000
Paterson, New Jersey, 1960	—	150	200
London, 1963	50	100	200
San Francisco: Arion Press, 1995. One of 300 signed and numbered copies in slipcase	—	—	750
Roth, Philip (Milton). GOODBYE, COLUMBUS +. Boston, 1959	175	600	750
London, 1959. (Title story only)	100	150	200
Roth, Samuel. FIRST OFFERING. New York, 1917. (500 copies)	50	75	50
Rothenberg, Jerome. *See* David Antin entry			
NEW YOUNG GERMAN POETS. San Francisco, 1959. Wraps. (Edited and translated)	35	75	75
WHITE SUN BLACK SUN. (New York, 1960.) Wraps	60	100	100
Rowan, Carl T. SOUTH OF FREEDOM. New York, 1952	40	75	50
Roy, Arundhati. THE GOD OF SMALL THINGS. London (1997)	—	—	125
New York (1997). Advance copy in wraps and slipcase, signed by author	—	—	150
Trade edition	—	—	60

Royall, Anne (Newport). *See* SKETCHES OF HISTORY . . .

	1986	1995	2000
Royce, Josiah. THE RELIGIOUS ASPECT OF PHILOSOPHY. Boston, 1885	—	250	125
Royde-Smith, Naomi. UNA AND THE RED CROSS . . . London, 1905	60	100	250
New York, 1927	—	—	150
Ruark, Robert. GRENADINE ETCHING. New York, 1947	60	100	150
Rubens, Bernice. SET ON EDGE. London, 1960	40	60	75
Rubin, Jerry. DO IT! New York (1970). Cloth	—	—	75
Wraps	—	—	15
Rukeyser, Muriel. THEORY OF FLIGHT. New Haven, 1935	250	300	300
Rule, Jane. THE DESERT OF THE HEART. Toronto, 1964	60	60	150
London, 1964	—	40	100
Rumaker, Michael. EXIT 3 +. New York, 1958	40	75	75
Runyon, Damon. THE TENTS OF TROUBLE. New York (1911). Flex cover	75	250	250
Rush, Norman. WHITES. London, 1986	—	125	100
New York, 1986	—	100	75
Rushdie, Salman. GRIMUS. London, 1975	100	300	450
New York (1979)	35	100	125
Ruskin, John. SALSETTE AND ELEPHANTA . . . Oxford, 1839. In original wraps *Also see* MODERN PAINTERS	600	1,500	2,000
Russ, Joanna. PICNIC ON PARADISE. New York (1968). Wraps	—	25	25
London (1969)	—	100	100
Russell, Alan. NO SIGN OF MURDER. New York (1990)	—	—	60
Russell, Bertrand. GERMAN SOCIAL DEMOCRACY. London, 1896	1,500	2,500	2,500
Russell, Charles (Marion). STUDIES OF WESTERN LIFE. Cascade, Montana (1890)	4,500	6,000	6,000
New York, 1890. First issue: no text on "War"	2,000	2,000	2,000
Second issue: text on "War"	1,750	1,750	1,750
Russell, Eric Frank. SINISTER BARRIER. Surrey (1943)	200	450	450
Reading, 1948. 500 signed and numbered copies	125	200	150
Trade	50	100	75
Russell, George. *See* A.E.			
Russell, Peter. PICNIC TO THE MOON. No place, 1944	100	100	100

	1986	1995	2000
Russell, Sanders. POEMS. Woodstock, 1941	75	75	150
THE CHEMICAL IMAGE. (San Francisco, 1947.) Wraps	50	50	150
Russell, William. *See* Waters			
Russell, William Clark. FRA ANGELO. London, 1865. Wraps	2,500	2,500	2,500
THE HUNCHBACK'S CHARGE. London, 1867. 3 volumes	2,000	2,500	2,500
Russo, Richard. MOHAWK. New York, 1986. Wraps	—	40	35
London, 1987	—	75	75
Rutherford, Ernest. RADIO-ACTIVITY. Cambridge, 1904	—	600	750
Rutledge, Archibald. UNDER THE PINES +. No place, 1906	75	100	150
Ryan, Abram Joseph. FATHER RYAN'S POEMS. Mobile, 1879. Portrait and one illustration	125	200	200
POEMS, PATRIOTIC, RELIGIOUS . . . Baltimore, 1880. Large-paper edition	75	125	125
Ryan, Don. ANGEL'S FLIGHT. New York, 1927	75	75	150
Ryan, Richard. LEDGES. (Oxford, 1970.) Wraps	30	30	50
Ryga, George. SONGS OF MY HANDS +. Edmonton, Alberta, 1956. Wraps	—	200	300

S

	1986	1995	2000
S., E.W. and S.W.M. (Elizabeth W. Stevenson and S. Weir Mitchell.) THE CHILDREN'S HOUR. Philadelphia, 1864	300	600	750
Philadelphia, 1866	—	—	400
S., I. (Isidor Schneider.) DOCTOR TRANSIT. New York, 1925	125	175	175
S., P.B. (Percy Bysshe Shelley.) ZASTROZZI. London, 1810	—	15K	20K
London: Golden Cockerel Press, 1955. One of 60 with extra set of 8 plates, in slipcase	—	—	600
One of 200 in slipcase	—	—	200
S., S.H. (Stephen Spender.) NINE EXPERIMENTS. Oxford, 1928	6K	25K	15K
Sabatini, Rafael. THE TAVERN KNIGHT. London, 1914	60	250	250
Sábato, Ernesto. THE OUTSIDER. New York, 1950	—	250	250
SABER EXERCISES. Washington, D.C.: GPO, 1914. Wraps. (By George S. Patton, Jr.—p. 3 "Prepared by Second Lieutenant . . .")	—	—	600

	1986	1995	2000
Sackler, Howard. WANT MY SHEPHERD: POEMS. New York, 1954	40	125	125
THE GREAT WHITE HOPE. New York, 1968	40	75	75
Sacks, Oliver. AWAKENINGS. London, 1973	—	—	300
Garden City, 1974	—	—	75
Sackville, Lady Margaret. POEMS. London, 1901	—	—	75
Sackville-West, Edward. PIANO QUINTET. London, 1925	75	250	250
New York, 1925. (English sheets)	—	150	150
Sackville-West, V(ictoria Mary). CHATTERTON. Seven Oaks, 1909. Boards	—	7,500	7,500
Wraps	3,500	5,000	6,000
CONSTANTINOPLE. London, 1915. Wraps	450	500	500
Sadler, Barry. I'M A LUCKY ONE. New York, 1967	—	100	35
Sadler, Michael. (Thomas Harvey.) HYSSOP. London (1915)	60	75	75
Sagan, Françoise (pseudonym). BONJOUR TRISTESSE. New York, 1955	35	60	50
London, 1955	—	50	50
Saint-Aubin de Teran, Lisa. THE STREAK. London, 1980. 50 signed and numbered copies. Wraps	—	300	350
KEEPERS OF THE HOUSE. London (1982)	75	150	75
Saint-Exupéry, Antoine de. NIGHT-FLIGHT. Paris, 1932. Wraps	75	300	400
London (1932)	—	250	500
New York (1932)	50	150	250
Saki. (Hector H. Munro.) *See* H. H. Munro			
THE WESTMINSTER ALICE. London, 1902. Wraps. First issue: pale-green wraps	75	350	400
Second issue: darker matte green wraps	—	300	350
Pictorial cloth	200	300	300
Salamanca, J. R. THE LOST COUNTRY. New York, 1958	50	100	125
Salas, Floyd. TATTOO THE WICKED CROSS. New York (1967)	20	25	40
Salinger, J(erome) D(avid). THE CATCHER IN THE RYE. New York (1951). "First Edition" stated	500	3,000	6,000
London, 1951	200	450	600
Sallis, James. A FEW LAST WORDS. New York (1970)	—	—	150

SALMAGUNDI . . . *See* Launcelot Langstaff

Modern Masterpieces in English

Night-Flight

by

Antoine de Saint-Exupéry

Translated by Stuart Gilbert

Crosby Continental Editions
Paris

	1986	1995	2000
Salt, Sydney. THIRTY PIECES. Majorca, 1934. 500 numbered copies. First issue: back panel of dustwrapper without reviews	75	75	100
Salter, James. THE HUNTERS. New York (1956)	50	350	750
Saltus, Edgar Evertson. BALZAC. Boston, 1884	50	100	125
Salzman, Mark. IRON & SILK. New York (1986)	—	125	150
(London, 1987)	—	75	75
Sams, Ferrol. RUN WITH THE HORSEMAN. (Atlanta, 1982)	—	40	40
Sanborn, Franklin Benjamin. EMANCIPATION IN THE WEST INDIES. Concord, 1862. Wraps (Two previous broadsides.)	150	400	600
Sanborn, Pitts. VIE DE BORDEAUX. Philadelphia, 1916. Boards	40	60	60
Sánchez, Ricardo. CANTO Y GRITO MI LIBERACIÓN . . . El Paso (1971).	—	—	50
Sanchez, Thomas. RABBIT BOSS. New York, 1973	25	60	75
London (1974)	—	—	50
Sandburg, Carl. (Charles August.) IN RECKLESS ECSTASY. Galesburg, 1904	6,000	7,500	8,500
INCIDENTALS. Galesburg (1907). Wraps	2,500	3,500	4,500
CHICAGO POEMS. New York, 1916. First issue: ads dated 3/16	150	250	250
Second issue: ads undated	60	100	125

	1986	1995	2000
Sanders, Dori. CLOVER. Chapel Hill, 1990	—	60	60
Sanders, Ed. POEM FROM JAIL. (San Francisco, 1963). Wraps	50	60	40
Sanders, Lawrence. THE ANDERSON TAPES. New York (1970)	40	60	75
Sandford, John. RULES OF PREY. New York (1989)	—	—	75
Sandlin, Tim. SEX AND SUNSETS. New York (1987)	—	40	40
Sandoz, Mari. OLD JULES. Boston, 1935	60	75	75
Sandoz, Paul. LEGEND. Geneva, 1925. Wraps	50	75	60
Sandy, Stephen. CAROMS. Groton, Mass., 1960. Wraps. (70 copies)	60	125	125
Sanford, John. *See* Julian L. Shapiro			
THE OLD MAN'S PLACE. New York, 1935. 25 signed and numbered copies	125	150	200
Unsigned	75	75	100
Sansom, Clive. IN THE MIDST OF DEATH. London, 1940. Wraps	—	—	150
Sansom, William. *See* FIRE OVER LONDON			
FIREMAN FLOWER. London, 1944	125	200	200
New York, no date [1944] (Previous collaboration.)	—	75	75
Santayana, George. *See* LINES ON LEAVING . . .			
SONNETS AND OTHER VERSES. Cambridge/Chicago, 1894. 60 numbered, large-paper copies	400	750	750
Trade. (450 copies)	100	200	250
Santee, Ross. MEN AND HORSES. New York (1926)	150	250	250
Santiago Baca, Jimmy. JIMMY SANTIAGO BACA. No place [Santa Barbara], 1978. An offprint in wraps	—	—	125
Saperstein, Alan. MOM KILLS KIDS AND SELF. New York, 1979	—	35	35
Saroyan, Aram. POEMS. New York, 1963. (Written with J. Caldwell and R. Kolmer)	25	50	40
IN. Eugene, Oregon, 1964	25	50	50
Saroyan, William. THE DARING YOUNG MAN . . . New York, 1934	150	350	350
(Covelo, 1984.) (25 copies) Deluxe edition. Separate suite of woodcuts (handcolored, signed and numbered by artist)	—	—	750
(Covelo, 1984.) (220 copies) Issued in slipcase	—	250	300

	1986	1995	2000
Sarraute, Nathalie. PORTRAIT OF A MAN UNKNOWN. New York, 1958	—	50	50
Sarton, May. ENCOUNTER IN APRIL. Boston, 1937	200	450	450
Sartre, Jean-Paul. NO EXIT AND THE TIME FLIES. London, 1946	—	200	250
New York, 1947	—	—	150
Sassoon, Siegfried. *See* POEMS			
Satterthwait, Walter. COCAINE BLUES. (New York, 1980.) Wraps	—	—	75
WALL OF GLASS. New York, 1987. First hardback, third book	—	150	400
Saunders, James. ALAS, POOR FRED. Scarborough, 1960. 33 pp. Wraps	—	—	60
Savage, D. S. THE AUTUMN WORLD. London (1939).	—	—	50
Savage, Thomas. THE PASS. Garden City, 1944	40	75	100
Savoy, Willard. ALIEN LAND. New York, 1944	50	75	75
Saxe, John Godfrey. PROGRESS: A SATIRICAL POEM. New York, 1846. Boards	100	150	150
Sayers, Dorothy. OP. 1. Oxford, 1916. Wraps. (350 copies)	500	750	750
WHOSE BODY? New York (1923). First issue: without "Inc." after Boni & Liveright on title	1,500	2,500	3,500
London (1923)	1,000	2,000	2,500
Sayles, John. PRIDE OF THE BIMBOS. Boston, 1975	50	125	150
Saylor, Steven. ROMAN BLOOD. New York (1991).	—	—	750
Scarborough, Elizabeth Ann. THE HEALER'S WAR. New York (1988)	—	40	50
Scarfe, Francis. INSCAPES. London (1940)	40	60	75
Schaefer, Jack. SHANE. Boston, 1949	250	1,500	3,000
Boston, 1954. First illustrated edition	—	—	600
London, 1963	40	450	600
Schaeffer, Susan Fromberg. THE WITCH AND THE WEATHER REPORT. New York, 1972. Wraps	—	75	60
Schevill, James. TENSIONS. (Berkeley, 1947)	60	100	100
Schiff, Sydney. CONCESSIONS. London, 1913	50	125	125

	1986	1995	2000
Schine, Cathleen. ALICE IN BED. New York, 1983.	—	—	75
Schlesinger, Arthur M., Jr. ORESTES A. BROWNSON. Boston, 1939	40	75	100
Schlick, Moritz. SPACE AND TIME IN CONTEMPORARY PHYSICS. New York, 1920	—	250	250
Schmidt, Arno. EVENING EDGED IN GOLD. New York, 1980	—	200	200
Schnackenberg, Gjertrud. PORTRAITS AND ELEGIES. Boston (1982)	—	—	100
Schneck, Stephen. THE NIGHT CLERK. New York, 1965	—	75	100
Schneider, Isidor. *See* I.S.			
Schoolcraft, Henry Rowe. A VIEW OF THE LEAD MINES . . . New York, 1819	400	750	1,500
Schoonover, Lawrence. THE BURNISHED BLADE. New York, 1948	35	75	75
Schorer, Mark. A HOUSE TOO OLD. New York (1935)	75	75	75
Schreiner, Olive. *See* Ralph Iron			
Schulberg, Budd. WHAT MAKES SAMMY RUN. New York (1941)	200	750	750
Schulman, Neil. FINALLY . . . I'M A DOCTOR. New York (1976). Ghostwritten by Carl Hiaasen	—	200	200
Schutz, Benjamin M. EMBRACE THE WOLF. New York (1985). Author's first mystery	—	—	30
Schuyler, James (Marcus). SHOPPING AND WAITING. New York, 1953. 6 stapled mimeographed sheets	—	750	750
ALFRED AND GUINEVERE. New York, 1958	50	250	250
Schwartz, Delmore. IN DREAMS BEGIN RESPONSIBILITIES. Norfolk (1938)	200	600	600
Schwartz, Lynne Sharon. ROUGH STRIFE. New York, 1980	20	40	30
Schwerner, Armand. THE LIGHT FALL. (New York, 1963.) Wraps	—	40	40
Scott, Alexander. THE LATEST IN ELEGIES. Glasgow, 1949. 300 numbered copies	60	75	100
Scott, Anthony. (Davis Dresser.) MARDI GRAS MADNESS. New York, 1934	—	300	450

	1986	1995	2000
Scott, Duncan Campbell. THE MAGIC HOUSE +. London, 1893	125	150	200
Scott, Evelyn. PRECIPITATIONS. New York, 1920. First issue: pale gray-green cloth	100	250	250
Second issue: red cloth (priority assumed)	—	200	200
Scott, Joanna. FADING, MY PARMACHEENE BELLE. New York, 1987.	—	—	75
Scott, John. *See* FOUR ELEGIES			
Scott, Michael. *See* TOM CRINGLE'S LOG			
Scott, Paul. "I GERONTIUS." London (1941). Wraps	—	750	1,000
JOHNNIE SAHIB. London, 1952	200	300	300
Scott, Winfield Townley. ELEGY FOR ROBINSON. New York (1936). (100 copies) Wraps	175	200	250
Scrannel, Orpheus (John Gawsworth). AN UNTERRESTRIAL PITY. London, 1931. 50 signed and numbered copies. Wraps	—	—	100
Scully, James. THE MARCHES. New York, 1967 (Edited two previous books 1965/66.)	25	60	50
Scupham, Peter. THE SMALL CONTAINERS. (Cheshire, 1972). One of 60 signed and numbered copies	—	—	150
Seabrook, William. *See* DIARY OF SECTION . . .			
Seale, Bobby. SEIZE THE TIME. New York (1970)	30	60	60
Seale, Doris. BLOOD SALT. Little Rock (1989). Wraps	—	—	40
Searle, Ronald. CO-OPERATION IN A UNIVERSITY TOWN. London (1939). Searle's first illustrated book. Text by W. Henry Brown	100	200	250
FORTY DRAWINGS. Cambridge, 1946	200	300	350
Seaver, Edwin. THE COMPANY. New York, 1930	40	40	250
See, Carolyn. THE REST IS DONE WITH MIRRORS. Boston, 1970	$\frac{—}{60}$	$\frac{75}{75}$	$\frac{75}{75}$
Seeger, Alan. POEMS. New York, 1916			
London, 1917	40	50	60
Segal, Erich. THE BRAGGART SOLDIER . . . New York (1963). Wraps. (Translation of play by Plautus)	30	75	100
ROMAN LAUGHTER. Cambridge, 1968	50	75	100

	1986	1995	2000
Segal, Lore. OTHER PEOPLE'S HOUSES. New York (1964)	—	75	50
London, 1965	—	50	40
Seitz, Don C(arlin). SURFACE JAPAN. London, 1911	60	100	150
ELBA AND ELSEWHERE. London, 1910 (Two previous books.)	—	75	75
Seizen Press. LOVE AS LOVE, DEATH AS DEATH. By Laura Riding. London, 1928	400	500	600
Selby, Hubert. LAST EXIT TO BROOKLYN. New York (1964)	35	125	125
London (1966)	60	75	75
Self, Will. SLUMP. London (1985). Cartoons. Wraps	—	—	75
THE QUANTITY THEORY OF INSANITY. London (1991). Wraps	—	—	75
SELF-CONTROL. (Mary Brunton.) London, 1810. 3 volumes	—	750	750
Seltzer, Charles Alden. THE COUNCIL OF THREE. New York, 1900	60	75	75
Selvon, Samuel. A BRIGHTER SUN. London, 1952	—	50	100
New York, 1953	—	—	75
Sendak, Maurice (Bernard). ATOMICS FOR THE MILLIONS. New York (1947). Text by Eidinoff & Ruchlis. First book illustrations by M.S. (Statement on paper quality on copyright page, omitted in later printings)	250	1,000	1,000
KENNY'S WINDOW. ((New York, 1956.) Dustwrapper priced $2.00. No statement of edition	—	750	1,000
SENSE AND SENSIBILITY. (Jane Austen.) London, 1811. 3 volumes. First issue: ruled lines on half title in volume 1⅖″	12K	12K	25K
Second issue: lines 1⅞″	3K	3.5K	15K
London, 1813. Second edition	—	—	8K
London,1833. Third edition. First one-volume edition	—	—	5K
Philadelphia, 1833. 2 volumes	—	—	2K
Serling, Rod. PATTERNS. New York, 1957	40	75	100
Service, Robert. SONG OF A SOURDOUGH. Toronto, 1907. Brown cloth. "Author's Edition" on title page. 100 Copies according to Service	600	2,500	3,000
Trade edition without "Author's Edition"	—	250	350
Serviss, Garrett P(utnam). ASTRONOMY WITH AN OPERA-GLASS. New York, 1888	—	—	150
THE MOON METAL. New York, 1900. First science fiction, third book	75	150	175

	1986	1995	2000
Seth, Vikram. MAPPINGS. (Saratoga, California, 1980.) 150 signed copies in wraps	—	450	600
FROM HEAVEN LAKE: TRAVELS THROUGH SINKIANG AND TIBET. London (1983)	—	250	250
Seton, Anya. MY THEODOSIA. Boston, 1941	50	75	75
Seton, Ernest Thompson. A LIST OF THE MAMMALS OF MANI-TOBA. Toronto (1886). Wraps	1,500	2,000	3,000
STUDIES IN THE ART OF ANATOMY OF ANIMALS. London, 1896	300	850	850
Settle, Mary Lee. THE LOVE EATERS. London (1954)	200	300	350
New York (1954). (First not stated)	100	200	250
Seuss, Dr. (Theodor Seuss Geisel). AND TO THINK THAT I SAW IT ON MULBERRY STREET. New York, 1937 Pictorial boards in dustwrapper. First edition not stated	250	1,000	1,500
SEVENTY-FIVE RECIPES FOR PASTRIE . . . New York/Boston, 1828. By a Lady of Philadelphia (Eliza Leslie)	—	—	4,000
Sewell, A(nna). BLACK BEAUTY . . . London (1877). First issue: red, green or blue pictorial cloth, horse's head in gilt looking right. (*See* Carter's MORE BINDING VARIANTS for more detail)	1,200	4,000	5,000
Boston (1890). Orange printed wraps	300	750	750
Buff boards	—	—	600
Sexton, Anne. TO BEDLAM AND PART WAY BACK. Boston, 1960	100	250	400
Shaara, Michael. THE BROKEN PLACE. New York (1968)	60	150	250
Shacochis, Bob. EASY IN THE ISLANDS. New York (1985)	—	50	75
Shaffer, Peter. *See* Peter Anthony			
Shakespear, O(livia). LOVE ON A MORTAL LEASE. London, 1894	—	125	125
Shames, Laurence. THE BIG TIME . . . New York, 1986	—	—	60
FLORIDA STRAITS. New York (1992). First mystery	—	—	100
Shange, Ntozake. FOR COLORED GIRLS WHO HAVE CONSIDERED SUICIDE . . . (San Lorenzo, 1976.) Wraps. First issue: name spelled Ntosake; $.95 Cover price	125	250	250
New York (1977)	35	60	75
Shanks, Edward. SONGS. London, 1915. Wraps	100	125	125
Shannon, Dell. (Barbara Elizabeth Linington.) CASE PENDING. New York, 1960. First mystery under this name	50	125	150
London (1960)	—	—	75

	1986	1995	2000
Shapiro, David. JANUARY. New York (1965). First regularly published book (Preceded by three privately printed books.)	35	60	60
Shapiro, Harvey. THE EYE. Denver (1953)	35	40	40
Shapiro, Julian L. (John Sanford.) THE WATER WHEEL. Ithaca (1933)	350	1,000	2,000
Shapiro, Karl (Jay). POEMS. Baltimore, 1935. 200 signed and numbered copies	900	750	500
PERSON PLACE AND THING. (New York, 1942)	75	75	100
Sharp, Luke. (Robert Barr.) FROM WHOSE BOURNE? London, 1893	75	100	125
Sharp, William. THE HUMAN INHERITANCE, THE NEW HOPE, MOTHERHOOD. London, 1882 *Also see* Fiona MacLeod	—	250	250
Sharpe, Tom. RIOTOUS ASSEMBLY. London (1971)	200	250	250
New York, 1973	—	100	100
Shattuck, Roger. THE BANQUET YEARS . . . New York (1958)	40	40	50
Shaw, George Bernard. CASHEL BYRON'S PROFESSION. (London), 1886. Wraps. First issue: 24.8 x 15.4 cm	500	1,500	2,000
Second issue: varied from 22.9 x 14 cm to 23.6 x 14.9 cm	—	1,250	1,500
New York (1886). Seaside Library, white wraps lettered in blue. (Unauthorized)	—	450	500
Chicago, 1901. Pictorial cloth (Two previous pamphlets.)	—	—	200
Shaw, H(enry). THE HISTORY AND ANTIQUITIES OF THE CHAPEL. London, 1829. 19 plates	—	—	750
Shaw, Irwin. BURY THE DEAD. New York (1936)	100	175	250
Shaw, Robert. THE HIDING PLACE. London (1959)	50	60	50
Cleveland/New York (1959)	35	40	40
Shaw, Thomas B(udge). OUTLINES OF ENGLISH LITERATURE . . . St. Petersburg, 1847	—	—	500
Sheckley, Robert E. UNTOUCHED BY HUMAN HANDS. New York (1954). Cloth	75	150	150
Wraps	15	25	25
London (1955)	—	—	100
Sheed, Wilfred. JOSEPH. New York (1958)	60	75	75
Sheldon, Sidney. THE NAKED FACE. New York (1970)	—	75	75

	1986	1995	2000
Shelley, Mary Wollstonecraft. *See* HISTORY OF A SIX . . . *Also see* FRANKENSTEIN			
Shelley, Percy Bysshe. *See* P.B.S.			
Shepard, Odell. A LONELY FLUTE. Boston, 1917. Boards	50	75	100
Shepard, Sam. FIVE PLAYS. Indianapolis (1967)	90	250	250
Wraps	—	—	50
London (1969)	60	100	150
Shepherd, Jean. IN GOD WE TRUST, ALL OTHERS PAY CASH. Garden City, 1966	—	40	100
Sheppard, Elizabeth Sara. *See* CHARLES AUCHESTER			
Sheridan, Richard Brinsley. *See* THE LOVE EPISTLES . . .			
Sherwin, Judith Johnson. URANIUM POEMS. New Haven, 1969	20	25	25
Sherwood, Robert E(mmet). BARNUM WAS RIGHT. Cambridge, 1920. Stiff wraps	—	250	250
THE ROAD TO ROME. New York, 1927	50	75	125
Shiel, M. P. PRINCE ZALESKI. London, 1895. (16-page catalog at rear)	200	850	1,250
Boston, 1895	—	275	450
Shields, Carol. OTHERS. Ottawa, 1972	—	125	350
SMALL CEREMONIES. Toronto, 1976. (First edition)	—	250	350
Shippey, Lee. THE TESTING GROUND. Boston, 1926	—	100	100
WHERE NOTHING EVER HAPPENS. Boston, 1935	—	75	75
Shivers, Louise. HERE TO GET MY BABY OUT OF JAIL. New York (1983)	—	75	60
Shockley, Ann Allen. LOVING HER. Indianapolis (1974)	40	75	75
Sholokhov, Mikhail. AND QUIET FLOWS THE DON. London (1934). (First English translation)	—	150	200
Shorthouse, J. Henry. JOHN INGLESANT. Birmingham (England), 1880. 100 Copies	300	750	750
London, 1881. 2 Volumes	—	—	250
Shove, Fredegond. DREAMS AND JOURNEY. Oxford, 1918. Wraps	—	50	60
Shulman, Irving. THE AMBOY DUKES. New York, 1947	50	125	150

	1986	1995	2000
Shute, Nevil (Norway). MARAZAN. London, 1926	300	500	1,500
Shuttle, Penelope. NOSTALGIA NEUROSIS +. Aylesford, 1968. 26 signed and lettered copies. Issued in glassine dustwrapper	—	150	100
Trade in wraps	—	50	35
ALL THE USUAL HOURS OF SLEEPING. London, 1969	—	50	40
Sibley, Celestine. THE MALIGNANT HEART. Garden City (1958).	—	—	150
Siddons, Anne River. JOHN CHANCELLOR MAKES ME CRY. New York, 1974	—	100	100
Sidney, Margaret. (Harriet Mulford Stone Lothrop.) FIVE LITTLE PEPPERS AND HOW THEY GREW. Boston (1880). First issue: caption p. 231 reads "said Polly"	350	450	500
Sidhwa, Bapsi. THE CROW EATERS. London (1980)	—	—	50
New York (1981)	—	—	30
Sienkiewicz, Henryk. IN VAIN. Boston, 1899	—	100	150
Sigal, Clancy. WEEKEND IN DINLOCK. London, 1960	40	40	40
Boston, 1960	35	35	35
Sigerson, Dora. VERSES. London, 1893	—	125	125
Sigourney, Lydia Huntley. *See* Lydia Huntley			
Silber, Joan. HOUSEHOLD WORDS. New York (1980)	—	40	40
Silkin, Jon. THE PORTRAIT +. Ilfracombe (1950). Wraps	150	250	250
THE PEACEABLE KINGDOM. London, 1954	60	125	125
Silko, Leslie Marmon. LAGUNA WOMAN. Greenfield Center. New York (1974). Wraps	—	500	1,500
CEREMONY. New York (1977). First-issue dustwrapper without reviews of this book on back flap	—	350	350
Second issue with reviews	—	—	175
Sill, Edward Rowland. *See* POEM AND VALEDICTORY ORATION . . .			
THE HERITAGE +. New York 1868	125	125	125
Sillitoe, Alan. CHOPIN'S WINTER IN MAJORCA 1838–1839. Mallorca, 1955. Translated by Sillitoe	—	300	500
WITHOUT BEER OR BREAD. Dulwich Village, 1957. Wraps	350	450	350
SATURDAY NIGHT AND SUNDAY MORNING. London, 1958	100	250	250
New York, 1959	—	—	100

	1986	1995	2000
Silone, Ignazio. FONTAMARA. New York, 1934	—	50	40
Siluriensis, Leolinus. (Arthur Machen.) THE ANATOMY OF TO-BACCO. London (1884). Second book	200	400	400
Silva, Daniel. THE UNLIKELY SPY. London (1996).	—	—	35
Silverberg, Robert. REVOLT ON ALPHA C. New York (1955)	60	200	150
Silverstein, Shel. TAKE TEN. (Tokyo) 1955. Issued without dustwrapper	60	100	100
Simak, Clifford. THE CREATOR. (Los Angeles, 1946.) Wraps	50	100	100
Simenon, Georges. THE DEATH OF MONSIEUR GALLET. New York, 1932. (First English translation)	100	750	1,000
Simic, Charles. WHAT THE GRASS SAYS. Santa Cruz (1967). Wraps. (1,000 copies)	60	75	150
Simmons, Charles. PLOTS THAT SELL TO TOP-PAY MAGAZINES. New York (1952)	—	150	150
POWDERED EGGS. New York, 1964	25	50	75
Simmons, Dan. SONG OF KALI. (New York, 1985)	—	200	200
Simmons, Herbert A. CORNER BOY. Boston, 1957	25	60	100
Simmons, James. BALLAD OF A MARRIAGE. Belfast (1966). Wraps	—	—	100
Simms, William Gilmore. LYRICAL +. Charlestown, 1827	500	850	1,250
Simon, (Marvin) Neil. HEIDI. New York, 1959. Wraps. Written with William Friedburg	75	125	250
COME BLOW YOUR HORN. New York, 1963. ("First Printing" not stated)	60	150	300
Simon, Roger L. THE BIG FIX. San Francisco, 1973. Wraps	—	25	25
Simon, Roger Lichtenberg. HEIR. New York (1968)	25	30	30
Simpson, Dorothy. THE HARBINGERS OF FEAR. London, 1977. (No U.S. edition)	—	—	150
THE NIGHT SHE DIED. London (1981). First Inspector Thanet mystery	—	—	100
New York (1981)	—	—	50
Simpson, Harriette. MOUNTAIN PATH. New York (1936) *Also see* Harriet Arnow	600	750	1,750

	1986	1995	2000
Simpson, Helen. LIGHTNING SKETCHES. Boston, 1918. Wraps	50	50	50
Simpson, Louis. (Aston Marantz.) THE ARRIVISTES. New York (1949). Wraps. (500 copies)	200	250	250
Paris (1950)	175	200	200
Simpson, Mona. ANYWHERE BUT HERE. New York, 1987	—	50	60
Sims, George. THE SWALLOW LOVERS. No place [1941]. Wraps	—	—	75
Sims, George R(obert). THE TERRIBLE DOOR. London (1964)	75	75	75
New York, 1964	—	35	40
Sinclair, Andrew. THE BREAKING OF BUMBO. New York, 1959	40	50	50
London, 1959	35	40	40
Sinclair, April. COFFEE WILL MAKE YOU BLACK. New York, 1994	—	40	40
Sinclair, Clive. BIBLIOSEXUALITY. London, 1973	35	40	50
Sinclair, Upton. *See* Fitch, Ensign Clarke			
Singer, Burns. (James Hyman.) THE GENTLE ENGINEER. Rome, 1952	40	40	50
Singer, I. J. THE SINNER. New York, (1933). (First translation in English)	125	125	150
Singer, Isaac Bashevis. THE FAMILY MOSKAT. New York, 1950. (First translation in English.) First edition stated	100	250	350
Singer, Mark. FUNNY MONEY. New York, 1985	—	25	25
Sinjohn, John. (John Galsworthy.) FROM THE FOUR WINDS. London (1897). (500 copies)	500	750	1,000
SIR JOHN CHIVERTON. (William H. Ainsworth and John P. Aston.) London, 1826	250	300	450
Siringo, Charles Angelo. A TEXAS COWBOY . . . Chicago, 1885. Wraps.	7.5K	12.5K	15K
Black pictorial cloth	—	—	7,500
Chicago: Siringo and Dobson, 1886. Second edition	—	—	1,000
Chicago: Rand McNally, 1886. Wraps	—	—	750
Cloth	—	—	500
New York (1886). Wraps	—	—	300
New York (1950). Illustrated by Tom Lea	—	—	100
Siskind, Aaron. PHOTOGRAPHS. New York, 1959	—	—	300
Sissman, L. E. DYING: AN INTRODUCTION. Boston (1967)	25	25	60

	1986	1995	2000
Sisson, C(harles) H(ubert). AN ASIATIC ROMANCE. London, 1953	40	50	75
Sitwell, Constance. FLOWERS AND ELEPHANTS. London, 1927	—	50	75
Sitwell, Edith. THE MOTHER +. Oxford, 1915. (500 Copies, 200 pulped.) Wraps	500	600	750
Sitwell, Osbert. TWENTIETH CENTURY HARLEQUINADE +. Oxford, 1916. Written with Edith Sitwell. (500 copies) Wraps	200	250	300
THE WINSTONBURG LINE. London, 1919. Pictorial wraps	150	200	250
Sitwell, Sacheverell. THE PEOPLE'S PLACE. Oxford, 1918. Wraps. (400 copies)	150	500	200
SIX TO ONE: A NANTUCKET IDYL. (Edward Bellamy.) New York, 1878. Cloth	300	400	500
Wraps	200	300	350
SIXTY YEARS OF THE LIFE OF JEREMY LEVIS. (Laughton Osborn.) New York, 1831	100	125	125
Sjowall, Maj., and Per Wahloo. ROSEANNA. New York, 1967	—	125	150
SKETCHES BY "BOZ." (Charles Dickens.) London, 1836/7. 3 volumes. (2 volumes dated 1836, 1 volume dated 1837.) In original cloth	3.5K	10K	15K
Rebound	—	—	5K
London, 1837–39. 20 parts in original wraps	10K	30K	35K
SKETCHES OF HISTORY, LIFE AND MANNERS . . . (Anne Royall.) New Haven, 1826	400	750	850
Skinner, M. L. BLACK SWAN. London, 1925 (Previous book with D. H. Lawrence.)	60	75	100
Slade, Michael. HEADHUNTER. London, 1984	—	150	125
New York, 1985	—	—	50
Sladek, John. THE REPRODUCTIVE SYSTEM. London (1968)	—	—	100
MECHASM. New York (1969). New title. Wraps	—	—	25
Slaughter, Carolyn. THE STORY OF THE WEASEL. London, 1976	—	50	75
RELATIONS. New York (1977). New title	—	—	25
SLAVE (THE); OR, THE MEMOIRS OF ARCHY MOORE. (Richard Hildreth.) Boston, 1836. 2 volumes	300	500	600
Slesar, Henry. THE GRAY FLANNEL SHROUD. New York, 1959	—	40	50
Slesinger, Tess. THE UNPOSSESSED. New York, 1934	50	75	175

	1986	1995	2000
Slick, Jonathan. (Ann Sophia Stephens.) HIGH LIFE IN NEW YORK. (New York, 1843.) First separate book. Wraps	150	750	1,000
Sloan, Samuel. THE MODEL ARCHITECT. Philadelphia (1952)	—	—	2,000
Philadelphia, 1860. New edition	—	—	1,000
Smart, Elizabeth. BY GRAND CENTRAL STATION . . . London, 1945	—	350	350
Smiley, Jane. BARN BLIND. New York (1980)	—	350	750
Smith, A. J. M. POETRY OF ROBERT BRIDGES. Montreal, no date [early 1930s]. Wraps	1,200	1,500	1,500
NEWS OF THE PHOENIX +. Toronto, 1943	100	150	75
Smith, Adam. THE THEORY OF MORAL SENTIMENTS. London, 1759	1.K	8.5K	12.5K
Philadelphia, 1817. 2 volumes	—	750	1,000
Smith, Alexander. POEMS. London, 1853. First issue: ads dated November 1852	60	125	75
Smith, C(harles) W(illiam). THIN MEN OF HADDAM. New York, 1973	—	60	75
Smith, Charlie. CANAAN. New York (1984)	—	125	100
London, 1985	—	50	50
Smith, Clark Ashton. THE STARTREADERS +. San Francisco, 1912	125	125	250
Smith, Cordwainer. *See* Paul Linebarger. *Also see* Felix Forrest			
Smith, Dave. BULL ISLAND. Poquoson, Virginia (1970). Wraps	—	600	600
Smith, Dinitia. THE HARD RAIN. New York, 1980	—	—	25
Smith, Dodie (Dorothy Gladys). *See* C. L. Anthony.			
THE HUNDRED AND ONE DALMATIANS. London, 1956. First children's book	—	250	350
New York, 1957	—	150	250
Smith, E. Boyd. MY VILLAGE. New York, 1896	—	125	150
Smith, Edward E. THE SKYLARK OF SPACE. (Providence: Buffalo Book Co., 1946.) (Written with Mrs. Lee Hawkins Garby.) (500 copies)	175	350	350
Providence: Hadley Co., (1947)	50	75	125
Smith, F(rancis) Hopkinson. OLD LINES IN NEW BLACK. Boston, 1885	60	150	200

	1986	1995	2000
Smith, George O. VENUS EQUILATERAL. Philadelphia, 1947	60	75	125
Smith, J. Thorne. BILTMORE OSWALD. New York (1918)	50	75	100
Smith, Johnston. (Stephen Crane.) MAGGIE: A GIRL OF THE STREETS. (New York, 1893.) Wraps (For second edition, see under Stephen Crane.)	7.5K	17.5K	17.5K
Smith, Joseph, Jr. THE BOOK OF MORMON. Palmyra, New York, 1830. In original leather, with 2-page preface and testimonial leaf at end, and without index	5K	10K	40K
Rebound	—	—	30K
Second issue in original leather	—	—	7,500
Second edition: Kirtland, Ohio, 1837	—	6,000	7,500
Third edition: Nauvoo, Illinois, 1840. Original sheep	—	3,500	4,000
Liverpool, 1841. Original calf	—	2,500	3,500
Edinburgh, 1841	—	—	2,500
Smith, Julie. DEATH TURNS A TRICK. New York (1982)	—	150	300
Smith, Kate Douglas (Wiggin). THE STORY OF PATSY . . . San Francisco, 1883. Wraps	500	1,000	1,250
Smith, Kay. FOOTNOTE TO THE LORD'S PRAYER +. (Montreal, 1951.) Stapled wraps	—	—	150
Smith, Ken. ELEVEN POEMS. Leeds, 1964. 13 pp. Wraps	—	100	75
Smith, Lee. THE LAST DAY THE DOGBUSHES BLOOMED. New York, 1968	100	250	450
Smith, Lillian. THESE ARE THINGS TO DO. Clayton, Georgia, 1943	—	150	300
STRANGE FRUIT. New York, 1944	35	100	150
London, 1945	25	75	75
Smith, Logan Pearsall. THE YOUTH OF PARNASSUS +. London, 1895. Blue or red cloth, priority unknown	125	200	250
Smith, Mark. TOYLAND. Boston (1965)	40	40	60
Smith, Martin (Cruz). THE INDIANS WON. New York (1970). Wraps	—	125	150
(London, 1982.) First hardback	—	—	200
GYPSY IN AMBER. New York (1971)	35	200	200
Smith, Michael Marshall. ONLY FORWARD. (New York, 1994.) Wraps	—	—	50
Smith, Murray. THE DEVIL'S JUGGLER. London (1993).	—	—	60

	1986	1995	2000
Smith, Pauline. THE LITTLE KAROO. London, 1925	—	100	200
New York (1925)	—	—	125
Smith, Robert Paul. SO IT DOESN'T WHISTLE. New York (1941)	40	50	50
Smith, Stevie. (Florence Margaret Smith.) NOVEL ON YELLOW PAPER. London (1936)	300	350	750
New York, 1937. First issue: patterned cloth. Dustwrapper price clipped and stamped $2.00. (Priority assumed)	150	200	250
Second issue: blue cloth. Dustwrapper priced $2.50	—	150	175

Note: In the 1995 edition we had assumed $2.50 was first, but copy of a proof in wraps price-clipped with $2.00 stamped on flap and publication date and $2.00 price noted was reported to us, which would indicate $2.00 and patterned cloth is first. The "bibliography," and there is one, almost 200 pages long, gives absolutely no information on the books other than title, publication, and date.

	1986	1995	2000
Smith, T. Dudley. (Elleston Trevor.) OVER THE WALL. London, 1943	150	200	300
INTO THE HAPPY GLADE. London, 1943 (Priority unknown.)	150	200	250
Smith, Wilbur. WHEN THE LION FEEDS. London (1964)	60	100	250
New York (1964)	—	75	150
Smith, William Gardner. LAST OF THE CONQUERERS. New York, 1948	75	100	200
Smith, William Jay. POEMS. Pawlett, Vermont: Banyon Press, 1947. 500 numbered copies in glassine wraps	75	125	125
Smollett, Tobias. *See* THE ADVENTURES OF RODERICK			
Snelling, William J. *See* TALES OF THE NORTHWEST . . .			
Snider, Denton Jacques. CLARENCE. St. Louis, 1872. Wraps	125	125	150
Snodgrass, W(illiam) D(ewitt). HEART'S NEEDLE. New York, 1959. (1,500 copies)	150	200	250
Hessle (England), 1960	100	175	200
Snow, C(harles) P(ercy). DEATH UNDER SAIL. London (1932)	300	750	750
Garden City (1932)	125	200	300
Snow, Charles Wilbert. SONGS OF THE NEUKLUK. Council, Alaska, 1912. Written with Ewen MacLennan	250	350	600
Snyder, Gary (Sherman). RIPRAP. (Ashland, Mass.), 1959. Wraps. (500 copies)	300	400	750
Sohl, Jerry. THE HAPLOIDS. New York, 1952	—	—	40

	1986	1995	2000
Solano, Solita. THE UNCERTAIN FEAST. New York, 1924	40	40	75
Solomita, Stephen. A TWIST OF THE KNIFE. New York (1988)	—	—	40
Solomon, Carl. MISHAPS PERHAPS. (San Francisco, 1966.) Wraps	20	40	50
Solzhenitsyn, Alexander. ONE DAY IN THE LIFE OF IVAN DENISOVICH. Praeger. New York (1963). (First English translation)	50	150	250
Dutton. New York, 1963. Cloth	50	100	150
Wraps	10	25	40
Pall Mall, London, 1963. (Never seen)	—	100	200
Gollancz. London, 1963	—	100	150
Sommer, Scott. NEARING'S GRACE. New York, 1979	25	40	50
Sommerfield, John. THEY DIE YOUNG. London, 1930	50	50	75
SONGS OF TWO WORLDS. London, 1871. (By Lewis Morris)	—	—	75
Sontag, Susan. THE BENEFACTOR. New York (1963)	35	45	60
Soos, Troy. MURDER AT EBBETS FIELD. Kensington (1994)	—	—	75
Sorrentino, Gilbert. THE DARKNESS SURROUNDS US. Highlands, North Carolina, 1960. Wraps	40	75	60
Soto, Gary. THE ELEMENTS OF SAN JOAQUIN. (Pittsburgh, 1977.) 50 signed and numbered copies. In unprinted dustwrapper	50	75	450
Souster, (Holmes) Raymond. WHEN WE WERE YOUNG. Montreal, 1946. Wraps	500	750	1,250
Southern, Terry. FLASH AND FILIGREE. (London, 1958) New York (1958). Dustwrapper priced $3.50. and no mention of *Dr. Strangelove* in blurbs.	100	150	150
Full cloth	50	100	100
Southey, Robert. POEMS . . . Written with Robert Lovell. Bath, 1795	300	1,500	2,500
Boston, 1799	150	750	1,000
SOUTH-WEST, THE. (Joseph Holt Ingraham.) New York, 1835. 2 volumes	400	500	400
Southworth, Emma Dorothy. RETRIBUTION . . . New York, 1849	100	300	300
Spackman, W. M. HEYDAY. New York (1953). Cloth	75	125	150
Wraps	20	35	50

	1986	1995	2000
Spade, Mark. (Nigel Balchin.) HOW TO RUN A BASSOON FACTORY. London, 1934	50	50	50
SPANISH SPEAKING AMERICANS IN THE WAR. (Charles Olson.) Washington (D.C., 1944). Wraps	—	1,500	2,000
Spark, Muriel (Sarah). *See* Muriel Camberg			
REASSESSMENT. London (1948). Written with W. Howard Sergeant. Folded leaf	—	200	350
TRIBUTE TO WORDSWORTH. London (1950). Edited with Derek Stanford	75	150	250
200 numbered copies	—	250	350
CHILD OF LIGHT. Essex (1951)	150	175	250
SPECIMENS. (Joaquin Miller.) (Canyon City, Oregon, 1868.) Wraps. (Preface signed C. H. Miller)	3,000	4,500	5,000
Speicher, John. LOOKING FOR BABY PARADISE. New York (1967)	40	40	60
Spencer, Bernard. AEGEAN ISLAND +. London (1946)	30	60	100
Garden City, 1948	—	—	50
Spencer, Claire. GALLOW'S ORCHARD. London (1930)	35	75	75
New York (1930)	35	50	50
Spencer, Elizabeth. FIRE IN THE MORNING. New York, 1948	200	500	600
London (1953)	—	—	150
Spencer, Herbert. THE PROPER SPHERE OF GOVERNMENT. London, 1843	—	250	350
SOCIAL STATISTICS. London, 1851	150	200	300
Spencer, Scott. LAST NIGHT AT THE BRAIN THIEVES BALL. Boston, 1973	40	100	125
Spencer, Theodore. STUDIES IN METAPHYSICAL POETRY. New York, 1939. Written with Mark Van Doren	60	100	100
THE PARADOX IN THE CIRCLE. Norfolk (1941). Cloth	40	75	75
Wraps	—	—	35
Spender, Stephen (Harold). *See* S.H.S.			
TWENTY POEMS. Oxford (1930). 75 signed copies	750	1,000	1,000
60 unsigned copies	400	750	750
POEMS. London (1933)	175	250	250
New York, 1934	100	175	175

	1986	1995	2000
Speyer, Leonora. HOLY NIGHT. (By Hans Travsil.) New York, 1919. Paraphrased into English by LS. (500 copies) (Cover by Eric Gill)	75	125	200
A CANOPIC JAR. New York (1921)	75	100	100
Spicer, Jack. CORRELATION METHODS OF COMPARING IDOLECTS . . . Offprint of "Language" 1952. Wraps. Written with David W. Reed. (Fewer than 100 copies)	400	1,250	1,250
AFTER LORCA. (San Francisco, 1957.) Wraps. 26 signed copies	300	400	2,500
(474 copies)	125	175	1,250
Spiegelman, Art. MAUS: A SURVIVOR'S TALE. New York (1986). Wraps	—	—	125
Spillane, Mickey. (Frank Morrison Spillane.) I, THE JURY. New York, 1947	200	750	2,500
Springarn, J(oel) E(lias). A HISTORY OF LITERARY CRITICISM . . . New York, 1899	—	200	250
Springs, Elliott White. NOCTURNE MILITAIRE. New York (1927)	200	300	350
Spyri, Johanna. HEIDI. Boston, 1885. 2 volumes in 1	—	—	5,000
Philadelphia, 1922. Illustrated by Jessie Willox Smith	—	—	750
Square, A. (Edward Abbott Abbott.) FLATLAND . . . Boston, 1885	—	150	450
Squire, Ephraim G. *See* WAIKNA			
Squire, Jack Collings. SOCIALISM AND ART. London (1907)	150	175	150
Squires, James. RADCLIFFE CORNAR. Philadelphia (1940). Issued with printed tissue dustwrapper	50	50	50
Stacton, David. AN UNFAMILIAR COUNTRY. (Swinford, 1953.) Wraps (Preceded by a few scholarly offprints.)	225	300	400
Stafford, Jean. BOSTON ADVENTURE. Boston (1944)	50	100	150
London, 1946	—	—	75
Stafford, William E(dgar). DOWN IN MY HEART. Elgin, Illinois (1947)	850	850	1,500
WEST OF YOUR CITY. Los Gatos, l960. Cloth and boards. Issued with plain white dustwrapper with price on rear flap	500	750	1,000
Wraps. Issued with plain white dustwrapper with price on rear flap	300	300	350

	1986	1995	2000
Standish, Robert. THE THREE BAMBOOS. London, 1942	50	50	50
Stanford, Ann. IN NARROW BOUND. Denver (1943). Wraps	125	125	125
Stanford, Don(ald E). NEW ENGLAND EARTH +. San Francisco (1941). Wraps	125	125	100
Stanford, Theodore Anthony. DARK HARVEST. Philadelphia (1936). Issued without dustwrapper	35	35	35
Stanley, Arthur Penrhyn. THE GYPSIES . . . Oxford, 1837	—	150	250
Stanley, Edward. ELMIRA . . . Norwich, 1790	—	400	400
Stapledon, W(illiam) Olaf. LATTER-DAY PSALMS. London, 1914	150	200	200
Starbuck, George. BONE THOUGHTS. New Haven, 1960	25	40	35
Stark, Freya. BAGHDAD SKETCHES. Baghdad, 1932	150	250	750
New York (1938). Including photos, drawings and text not in 1932 edition	—	—	500
Starrett, (Charles) Vincent (Emerson). ARTHUR MACHEN. Chicago, 1918. 250 signed and numbered copies	200	300	250
Stavis, Barrie. THE CHAIN OF COMMAND. New York (1945)	—	50	75
Stead, Christina (Ellen). THE SALZBURG TALES. London (1934)	150	250	400
New York, 1934	100	175	250
Steadman, Ralph. THE JELLY BOOK. London, 1967	—	—	200
New York (1970)	—	—	100
STILL LIFE WITH RASPBERRY . . . London, 1969. 500 were signed	—	—	250
1,500 unsigned copies	—	—	150
(First book illustrations were in Daisy Ashford's *Love & Marriage*. London, 1965.)			
Stearns, Harold. LIBERALISM IN AMERICA. New York (1919)	—	50	100
Stedman, Edmund Clarence. POEMS, LYRICAL AND IDYLLIC. New York, 1860	100	100	100
Steed, Neville. TIN PLATE. London, 1986	—	35	75
Steele, Max. DEBBY. New York, 1950	—	30	40
Stefansson, Vilhjalmur. MY LIFE WITH THE ESKIMO. New York, 1913	175	200	200
London, 1913. (U.S. sheets)	125	150	150
Steffens, (Joseph) Lincoln. THE SHAME OF THE CITIES. New York, 1904	150	200	200

	1986	1995	2000
Stegner, Page. ESCAPE INTO AESTHETICS . . . New York, 1966	25	50	75
London, 1967	—	—	50
Stegner, Wallace (Earle). CLARENCE EDWARD DUTTON: AN APPRAISAL. Salt Lake City (1935?). Wraps	—	600	7,500
REMEMBERING LAUGHTER. Boston, 1937	125	350	450
Steig, Henry. SEND ME DOWN. New York, 1941	35	40	50
Steig, William. MAN ABOUT TOWN. New York, 1932	40	100	100
Stein, Aaron Marc. SPIRALS. New York, 1930	—	300	300
Stein, Gertrude. THREE LIVES. New York, 1909. (700 copies) Issued without dustwrapper	900	1,500	1,750
London, 1915. (300 copies from American sheets)	200	1,000	1,500
Stein, Leo. THE A.B.C. OF AESTHETICS. New York, 1927	—	—	200
Steinbeck, John (Ernst). CUP OF GOLD. McBride. New York, 1929. First issue: top edge stained (although price same for unstained)	3.5K	7.5K	10K
Second issue: Covici-Friede. New York (1936). Remainder sheets. Maroon cloth	400	750	1,250
Blue cloth	125	300	300
London (1937)	1,200	1,250	2,000

THREE LIVES

STORIES OF THE GOOD
ANNA, MELANCTHA AND
THE GENTLE LENA

BY
GERTRUDE STEIN

THE GRAFTON PRESS
NEW YORK   MCMIX

	1986	1995	2000
Steinem, Gloria. THE BEACH BOOK. New York, 1963	40	60	40
Steiner, F(rancis) George. POEMS. (Fantasy Poets #8.) Swinford, 1952. Wraps	100	150	200
Stepanchev, Stephen. THREE PRIESTS IN APRIL. Baltimore, 1956	50	75	75
Stephens, Ann Sophie. *See* Jonathan Slick			
Stephens, James. INSURRECTIONS. Dublin, 1909 (Cataloged in 1998 in first issue dustwrapper with 1/– price and "Maunsel & Co. Ltd." On upper cover for about $300.)	75	100	100
Stephenson, Neal. THE BIG U. New York (1984). Wraps	—	—	300
ZODIAC. New York (1988). Wraps	—	—	35
Steptoe, John. STEVIE. New York (1969)	—	—	100
Sterling, George. THE TESTIMONY OF THE SUNS +. San Francisco, 1903. 650 Copies	100	125	125
San Francisco, 1927. 300 numbered copies with comments by Ambrose Bierce	—	300	300
Stern, Gerald. THE NAMING OF BEASTS AND OTHER POEMS. Omaha, 1973. (100 copies)	—	—	1,500
Stern, James. THE HEARTLESS LAND. London, 1932. (First regularly published)	200	200	250
Stern, Richard G(ustave). GOLK. New York (1960)	25	25	40
London, 1960	—	—	40
Stern, Richard Martin. THE BRIGHT ROAD TO FEAR. New York (1958). First mystery	—	—	100
Stetson, Charlotte Perkins. IN THIS OUR WORLD. London, 1893	—	3,000	5,000
San Francisco, 1895. Wraps	—	1,000	2,000
San Francisco, 1895. Second edition in blue cloth. Adds 46 poems	—	—	450
Stevens, Shane. GO DOWN DEAD. New York, 1966	25	75	200
Stevens, Wallace. HARMONIUM. New York, 1923. First issue: checkered boards. (500 copies)	1,000	3,000	5,000
Second issue: striped boards. (215 copies)	500	1,750	3,000
Blue cloth. (715 copies)	400	1,250	2,000
New York, 1931. Drops 3 poems that were in the first edition and adds 14 new poems. Various bindings	—	500	750

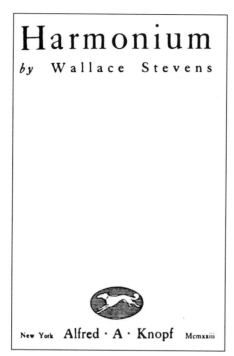

Harmonium
by Wallace Stevens

New York Alfred · A · Knopf Mcmxxiii

	1986	1995	2000
Stevenson, Adlai E. MAJOR CAMPAIGN SPEECHES . . . New York (1953). One of 1,000 signed and numbered copies issued without dustwrapper. In slipcase	75	100	200
Stevenson, Robert Louis. *See* THE PENTLAND RISING			
AN INLAND VOYAGE. London, 1878	400	1,000	1,000
Boston, 1883	—	350	350
Stewart, Donald Ogden. A PARODY OUTLINE OF HISTORY. New York, 1921	35	60	175
Stewart, Fred Mustard. THE MEPHISTO WALTZ. New York (1969)	35	35	40
Stewart, George R., Jr. MODERN METRICAL TECHNIQUE. New York, 1922. Wraps	—	150	150
Stewart, John. THE PLEASURES OF LOVE. London, 1806	—	175	175
Stewart, Mary. MADAM, WILL YOU TALK? London, 1955	60	200	250
New York (1956)	—	—	100
Still, James. HOUNDS ON THE MOUNTAIN. New York, 1937. 50 numbered copies (not for sale)	—	350	350
(750 copies)	150	200	200

	1986	1995	2000
Stockton, Frank R(ichard). TING-A-LING. New York, 1870 (Previous pamphlet.)	250	750	350
Stoddard, Charles Warren. POEMS. San Francisco, 1867. (750 copies)	100	125	200
SOUTH-SEA IDYLS. Boston, 1875	75	100	175
Stoddard, Richard Henry. FOOTPRINTS. New York, 1849. Wraps	1,500	1,500	1,500
Stoker, Bram. ADDRESS . . . DINING HALL . . . TRINITY COLLEGE . . . Dublin, 1872. Wraps	500	1,500	2,000
THE DUTIES OF CLERKS . . . Dublin, 1879. Wraps	400	1,000	1,500
UNDER THE SUNSET. London, 1882	200	450	600
Stone, A. R. A BOOK OF LETTERING. London, 1935	60	150	150
Stone, Chuck. TELL IT LIKE IT IS. New York, 1968	—	—	75
KING STRUT. Indianapolis (1970)	—	40	50
Stone, Eric. IN A HEARTBEAT. (Novato, 1996)	—	—	25
Stone, I. F. (Isador Feinstein.) THE COURT DISPOSES. New York (1937)	75	150	200
Stone, Irving. PAGEANT OF YOUTH. New York, 1933	75	175	250
Stone, Michael. THE LOW END OF NOWHERE. New York (1996).	—	—	35
Stone, Robert. A HALL OF MIRRORS. Boston, 1967	150	500	600
London (1968)	75	250	300
Stone, Zachary. THE MODIGLIANI SCANDAL. London (1976). (First book by Ken Follett using this pseudonym)	—	—	300
Stopes, Marie C(harlotte). THE STUDY OF PLANT LIFE FOR YOUNG PEOPLE. London, 1906	100	100	100
Stoppard, Tom. LORD MALQUIST AND MR. MOON. (London, 1966)	125	200	300
New York, 1968	40	75	100
ROSENCRANTZ AND GUILDENSTERN ARE DEAD. London, 1967	—	—	500
New York, 1967. First edition stated	—	—	250
Wraps	—	—	40
Storey, David (Malcolm). THIS SPORTING LIFE. (London, 1960)	125	300	500
New York, 1960	—	100	125

	1986	1995	2000
Storm, Hans Otto. FULL MEASURE. New York, 1929	50	75	150
Story, Joseph. THE POWER OF SOLITUDE. Boston (1800)	200	300	500
Stout, Rex. (Todhunter.) HOW LIKE A GOD. New York, 1929	350	1,500	1,750
London, 1931	—	750	750
FER-DE-LANCE. New York, 1934. (First mystery)	—	5,000	6,000
London, 1935	—	—	1,500
Stow, Randolph. A HAUNTED LAND. London, 1956	75	75	75
Stowe, Calvin E(llis), translator. JOHN'S HISTORY OF THE HEBREW COMMONWEALTH . . . Andover, 1828.	—	—	200
Stowe, Harriet (Elizabeth) Beecher. *See* Harriet Beecher			
Strachey, G. L(ytton). LANDMARKS IN FRENCH LITERATURE. London (1912). First issue: top edge stained green. 8 pages ads	150	200	250
Strachey, Julia. CHEERFUL WEATHER FOR THE WEDDING. London, 1932	—	—	125
Strachey, Mrs. Richard. NURSERY LYRICS. London, 1893	200	350	450
(Reissued with new title page and binding—"LADY STRACHEY")	100	100	150
Straight, Susan. AQUABOOGIE. Minneapolis, 1990. Wraps	—	—	50
Straley, John. THE WOMAN WHO MARRIED A BEAR. New York (1992)	—	35	40
Strand, Mark. SLEEPING WITH ONE EYE OPEN. Iowa City, 1964. (225 copies)	300	750	1,500
Strand, Paul. PHOTOGRAPHS 1915–1945. New York (1945). Cloth	—	100	250
Wraps	—	50	75
(Previous issues of *Camera Work* were devoted to his work.)			
Strange, Michael. MISCELLANEOUS POEMS. New York, 1916	—	40	40
STRATFORD-BY-THE-SEA. (Alice Brown.) New York, 1844	75	100	200
Straub, Peter. ISHMAEL. (London, 1972.) Wraps. 100 signed and numbered copies. Issued in dustwrapper	200	200	200
Strauss, David Friedrich. (George Eliot.) THE LIFE OF JESUS. London, 1846. 3 volumes in original cloth. Translated by Mary Ann Evans (George Eliot)	750	5,000	5,000
Rebound	—	—	1,500
Strauss, Theodore. NIGHT AT HOGWALLOW. Boston, 1937	35	30	30

	1986	1995	2000
Strawberry Hill Press. ODES. (Thomas Gray.) 1757. With "ILISSUS" on p. 8 and no comma after "swarm" on p. 16. (2,000 copies)	600	1,000	1,000
Streatfield, (Mary) Noel. THE WHICHARTS. London, 1931	—	75	150
BALLET SHOES. London, 1936	—	200	250
Street, Cecil John Charles. *See* John Rhode			
Street, George Edmund. BRICK AND MARBLE IN THE MIDDLE AGES. London, 1855	400	600	750
Street, James H. LOOK AWAY. New York, 1936	50	75	75
Street, Julian (Leonard). MY ENEMY THE MOTOR. New York, 1908	40	75	75
Streeter, Edward. DERE MABLE: LOVE LETTERS OF A ROOKIE. New York (1918). Pictorial boards	25	25	35
STREETWALKER. (Reportedly written anonymously by Jonathan Gash.) London, 1959.	—	—	450
Strete, Craig. THE BLEEDING MAN. New York (1977)	—	—	60
Stribling, T(homas) S(igismund). CRUISE OF THE DRY DOCK. Chicago (1917). (250 Copies published per author)	75	150	150
Strieber, Whitley. THE WOLFEN. New York, 1978	—	—	60
STRIKE AT SHANES, THE. Boston: American Humane Education Society (1893). (Reportedly by Gene Stratton Porter, if so, her first book.) Noted as 6¹⁵⁄₁₆″ tall and 7³⁄₁₆″. Both in brown cloth. We had it for $1,500 in *Collected Books,* but the Internet prices prevail)	—	—	500
Boston: A. Flanaghan (1896). Wraps	—	—	100
Striker, Randy. (Randy Wayne White.) KEY WEST CONNECTION. New York (1981). Wraps (Signet J9567).	—	—	35
Strong, Jonathan. TIKE +. Boston, 1969	25	50	50
London (1969)	—	—	40
Strong, L. A. G. DALLINGTON RHYMES. (200 copies privately printed 1919)	300	400	400
DUBLIN DAYS. Oxford, 1921. Wraps	75	100	125
Strong, Phil. STATE FAIR. New York, 1932. First issue has copyright by publisher	—	150	175
Second issue: copyright by author (handstamped)	—	125	125
Third issue: canceled title/copyright page (copyright by author)	—	75	75

	1986	1995	2000
Strong, Tony. THE POISON TREE. London (1997)	—	—	50
New York (1997)	—	—	40
Stroud, Robert. DISEASES OF CANARIES. Kansas City, 1933. (Birdman of Alcatraz) Issued without dustwrapper	125	150	200
Struther, Jan. (Joyce Maxtone Graham.) BETSINDA DANCES +. Oxford/London, 1931. Wraps	75	75	75
Stuart, Dabney. THE DIVING BELL. New York, 1966	—	50	50
Stuart, H. (Francis Stuart.) WE HAVE KEPT THE FAITH. Dublin, 1923	350	350	350
Stuart, Jesse (Hilton). HARVEST OF YOUTH. Howe, Oklahoma (1930). (20 Copies per author)	2,000	3,000	3,500
MAN WITH A BULL TONGUE PLOW. (New York, 1934)	400	600	600
Stuart, Lyle. THE SECRET LIFE OF WALTER WINCHELL. New York, 1953	—	—	35
Sturgeon, Theodore. IT. Philadelphia, 1948. 29-page excerpt from *Without Sorcery*	500	1,500	1,500
WITHOUT SORCERY. Philadelphia, 1948. 80 signed copies. Red buckram. Issued in slipcase	300	1,750	1,750
Trade edition	125	250	300
Styron, William. LIE DOWN IN DARKNESS. Indianapolis (1951)	150	300	350
London, 1952	—	150	200
Suckow, Ruth. COUNTRY PEOPLE. New York, 1924. (600 copies)	100	125	175
Trade	50	75	100
Sudek, Josef. SUDEK. New York, 1978	—	—	250
Sullivan, Frank. THE LIFE AND TIMES OF MARTHA HEPPLE-TWAITE. New York, 1926	50	125	250
Summers, Hollis (Spurgeon). CITY LIMIT. Boston, 1948	50	75	75
Summers, Montague. ANTINOUS +. London [1907]	—	450	450
Susann, Jacqueline. EVERY NIGHT, JOSEPHINE. New York, 1963	—	—	75
Suthren, Victor. THE BLACK COCKADE. Toronto, 1977	—	50	75
New York (1977)	—	—	60
London (1978)	—	—	50
Svevo, Italo. THE HOAX. London, 1929. First book to be translated into English	—	—	300
New York, 1930	—	—	200

	1986	1995	2000
Swados, Harvey. JEWISH POPULATION STUDIES IN THE U.S. New York, 1949. Wraps. Written with Ben B. Seligman	—	150	150
OUT WENT THE CANDLE. New York, 1955	50	50	60
Swallow, Alan. THE PRACTICE OF POETRY. Albuquerque, 1942. Wraps	—	125	175
XI POEMS. Prairie Press. Muscatine, 1943. 300 numbered copies. Wraps	60	100	150
SWALLOW BARN. (Joseph Pendleton Kennedy.) Philadelphia, 1832. 2 volumes in original half cloth	400	600	1,200
Rebound	—	—	500
(Previous collaboration.)			
Swanwick, Michael. IN THE DRIFT. London, 1989. (First hardback)	—	50	50
Sward, Robert. ADVERTISEMENTS. Chicago, 1958. (368 copies.) Wraps	30	40	75
Swarthout, Glendon. WILLOW RUN. New York, 1943	—	100	150
Sweeney, Matthew. WITHOUT SHORES. (Leicester, 1978.) Wraps	—	—	75
Swenson, May. ANOTHER ANIMAL. New York, 1954	—	75	100
Swift, Graham. THE SWEET SHOP OWNER. (London, 1980)	75	350	350
New York, 1985. Wraps	—	—	35
Swinburne, Algernon Charles. THE QUEEN MOTHER and ROSAMOND. London, 1860. First issue: A. G. Swinburne on spine label	600	2,500	2,500
Second issue: Pickering imprint. "A. C." on label	400	2,000	2,000
Third issue: J. C. Hotten title page	300	500	350
Swingler, Randall. DIFFICULT MORNING. London (1933)	60	60	100
Sykes, Gerald. THE NICE AMERICANS. New York, 1951	35	60	75
Symonds, J(ohn) A(ddington). THE ESCORIAL. Oxford, 1860. Wraps	200	400	500
Symons, A. J. A. EMIN. London, 1928. 300 numbered copies. Issued without dustwrapper	100	150	150
Symons, Arthur. AN INTRODUCTION TO THE STUDY OF BROWNING. London, 1886. Ads dated January 1887. Green cloth (later decorated brown cloth)	100	125	125

	1986	1995	2000
DAYS AND NIGHTS. London, 1889	1,000	1,500	250

DAYS AND NIGHTS. London, 1889
A great example of misreading two auction prices, $1,700 and $2,200, by neglecting to note that both of these copies were inscribed.

Symons, Julian (Gustave). CONFUSIONS ABOUT X. London (1939)	250	250	200
Synge, John M(illington). IN THE SHADOW OF THE GLEN. New York, 1904. Wraps. (50 copies)	1,000	2,000	2,500
THE SHADOW OF THE GLEN AND RIDERS TO THE SEA. London, 1905. Wraps	225	500	600

T

Tabb, John Banister. POEMS. (Baltimore, 1882)	400	400	400
Taggard, Genevieve. WHAT OTHERS HAVE SAID . . . Berkeley (1919). Wraps	150	150	150
FOR EAGER LOVERS. New York, 1922	100	100	100
Taine, John. (Eric Temple Bell.) THE PURPLE SAPPHIRE. New York (1924)	150	450	250
Talbot, William Henry Fox. THE PENCIL OF NATURE. London, 1844–46. In 6 installments in printed wraps. (First commercially published book to use photographic illustrations)	—	250K	250K
New York, 1969	—	—	200
TALES OF THE NORTHWEST . . . (William J. Snelling.) Boston, 1830	—	350	350
Talese, Gay. NEW YORK: A SERENDIPITER'S JOURNEY. New York (1961)	35	50	50
Tallent, Elizabeth. MARRIED MEN AND MAGIC TRICKS . . . (Berkeley, 1982.) Cloth	—	—	100
Wraps	—	—	35
IN CONSTANT FLIGHT. New York, 1983	—	35	35
TAMERLANE. By a Bostonian. (Edgar Allan Poe.) Boston, 1827. Wraps	250K	250K	300K

TAMERLANE. By a Bostonian. (Edgar Allan Poe.) Boston, 1827. Wraps
    Also see Poe

Tan, Amy. THE JOY LUCK CLUB. New York (1989). Noted with a price of $26.50 Canadian and publisher's blurb in box at bottom of rear flap on first, changed on later printings to $24.95 and bottom of front flap	—	300	200
London (1989)	—	100	100

	1986	1995	2000
Tapply, William G. DEATH AT CHARITY'S POINT. New York (1984)	—	150	200
TARCISSUS, THE BOY MARTYR OF ROME . . . (Baron Corvo Frederick Wm. Rolfe.) (Essex, England, 1880.) Wraps	3,000	3,500	4,000
Tarkington, (Newton) Booth. THE GENTLEMAN FROM INDIANA. New York, 1899. First issue: p. 245:12 last word "eye" and p. 245:16 reads "so pretty"	75	150	150
Second issue: p. 245:12 as in first issue; p. 245:16 reads "her heart"	—	100	75
Third issue: p. 245:12 last word "glance"	—	75	50
Tarn, Nathaniel. OLD SAVAGE/YOUNG CITY. London (1964)	50	60	60
Tartt, Donna. THE SECRET HISTORY. New York, 1992	—	40	50
Tate, Allen. (John Orley.) THE GOLDEN MEAN +. (Nashville, 1923.) (Written with R. Wills.) 200 numbered copies	3,500	3,500	2,500
STONEWALL JACKSON. New York, 1928	400	500	600
London (1930)	—	—	400
MR. POPE +. New York, 1928	450	750	750
Tate, James (Vincent). CAGES. Iowa City, 1966. 45 numbered copies. Wraps	250	300	3,000
THE LOST PILOT. New Haven, 1967	100	150	250
Tauber, Peter. THE SUNSHINE SOLDIERS. New York (1971)	25	40	35
Tavel, Ronald. STREET OF STAIRS. New York (1968)	—	50	50
Taylor, Andrew. CAROLINE MINUSCULE. London (1982)	—	—	125
Taylor, (James) Bayard. XIMENA +. Philadelphia, 1844	250	1,000	1,750
Taylor, D. J. GREAT EASTERN LAND. London, 1986.	—	—	50
Taylor, Eleanor Ross. WILDERNESS OF LADIES. New York (1960)	50	75	75
Taylor, Elizabeth. AT MRS. LIPPINCOTE'S. London, 1945	125	200	300
New York (1946)	75	100	100
Taylor, Frederick Winslow. THE PRINCIPLES OF SCIENTIFIC MANAGEMENT . . . New York, 1911. Green cloth, 118 pages	—	1,250	1,000
Red cloth, 144 pages, revised and expanded	—	750	500
Taylor, Margaret. JASPER THE DRUMMIN' BOY. New York, 1947	—	75	60
Taylor, Peter (Hillsman). A LONG FOURTH +. New York (1948)	150	350	500
London (1949)	150	150	200

	1986	1995	2000
Taylor, Philip Meadows. CONFESSIONS OF A THUG. London, 1839. 3 volumes	200	850	850
Taylor, Phoebe Atwood. THE CAPE COD MYSTERY. Indianapolis (1931)	250	750	1,000
Taylor, Robert Lewis. ADRIFT IN A BONEYARD. Garden City, 1947	60	100	100
Teasdale, Sara. SONNETS TO DUSE +. Boston, 1907	200	750	750
Tenn, William. (Philip J. Klass.) OF ALL POSSIBLE WORLDS. New York, 1955	—	200	200
London (1956). (Adds 3 stories not in U.S. edition)	—	75	75
Tennant, Emma. *See* Catherine Aydy			
THE TIME OF THE CRACK. London, 1973	40	100	100
Tennyson, Lord Alfred. *See* POEMS BY TWO BROTHERS			
TIMBUCTOO. (Cambridge Prize poem, 1829.) Wraps	1,250	2,000	2,500
POEMS, CHIEFLY LYRICAL. London, 1830. In original drab or pink paper boards. First issue: p. 91 misnumbered "19"	1,000	1,500	2,500
Second issue: p. 91 correctly numbered	—	1,000	1,250
Tennyson, Frederick. DAYS AND HOURS. London, 1854	100	100	200
TENTH MUSE, LATELY SPRUNG UP IN AMERICA, THE. (Anne Bradstreet.) London, 1650	5K	10K	12.5K
Boston, 1678	—	30K	35K
Terhune, Albert Payson. SYRIA FROM THE SADDLE. New York, 1896	150	200	250
Terkel, Studs. GIANTS OF JAZZ. New York (1957)	75	150	150
Terry, Rose. POEMS. Boston, 1861. Ads dated Dec. 1860	—	75	75
Tessier, Thomas. IN SIGHT OF CHAOS. (London, 1971.) One of 100 signed copies in wraps	—	—	200
Tevis, Walter. THE HUSTLER. (New York, 1959)	75	350	750
London (1960)	40	125	300
Tey, Josephine. *See* Gordon Daviot			
Thackeray, William Makepeace. *See* Theophile Wagstaff			
THE YELLOW PLUSH CORRESPONDENCE. Philadelphia, 1838. Cloth and boards	1,500	1,500	2,000
Green cloth wraps	—	—	2,500

	1986	1995	2000
Thaxter, Celia. POEMS. New York, 1872	100	250	400
Thayer, Caroline Matilda Warren. THE GAMESTERS . . . Boston, 1805	—	—	400
Thayer, Ernest L. CASEY AT THE BAT. New York: Amsterdam Book Co., (1901). Green pictorial wraps printed on rectos only (except copyright on verso of title), marginal illustrations in sepia	—	6,000	6,000
Chicago, 1912. First hardbound	—	—	1,500
Thayer, Lee. THE MYSTERY OF THE THIRTEENTH FLOOR. New York, 1919	25	50	75
(Two juveniles preceded.)			
Theroux, Alexander. THREE WOGS. Boston, 1972. First issue dustwrapper has sepia-toned photograph and back flap text including "Trappist Monastery in Kentucky"	60	200	250
Theroux, Paul. WALDO. Boston, 1967	150	200	250
London, 1968	125	150	200
Thom, Robert. VIATICUM. Columbus, 1949. One of 25 signed copies. Wraps	—	—	100
One of 200 Copies. Wraps	35	35	35
Thoma, Richard. GREEN CHAOS. Seine (1931). Wraps. 100 signed and numbered copies	150	150	150
Thomas, Audrey. TEN GREEN BOTTLES. Indianapolis, 1967	—	150	40
Thomas, Craig. RAT TRAP. London, 1976	—	—	175
Thomas, D(onald) M(ichael). PERSONAL AND POSSESSIVE. London, 1964	350	750	500
TWO VOICES. London, 1968. Cloth. Issued in glassine dustwrapper. 50 signed and numbered copies	250	250	250
Wraps in glassine dustwrapper	75	75	60
New York, 1968. Wraps in glassine dustwrapper	50	50	50
Thomas, Dylan (Marlais). 18 POEMS. London: Sunday Referee & Parton Bookshop, (1934). First issue: flat spine, leaf between half title and title pages, front page roughly trimmed. (250 copies)	2,000	3,000	3,000
Second issue: rounded spine. (1936.) (250 copies)	750	1,000	750
Thomas, Edward. WOODLAND LIFE. London, 1897.			
Red cloth	400	600	600
Blue-green buckram	—	—	450
Smooth green cloth	—	—	300
Thomas, Gwyn. WHERE DID I PUT MY PITY. London, 1946. Stiff wraps and dustwrapper	60	75	75

	1986	1995	2000
Thomas, Hugh. THE WORLD'S GAME. London, 1957	60	60	40
Thomas, Jerry. THE BARTENDER'S GUIDE. New York, 1862	125	175	300
Thomas, John. DRY MARTINI ... New York (1926)	—	100	125
Thomas, Joyce Carol. BITTERSWEET. San Jose (1973)	—	60	75
Thomas, Leslie. THIS TIME NEXT WEEK. London, 1964	40	50	50
Thomas, Lowell. WITH LAWRENCE IN ARABIA. New York, 1924	—	—	150
Thomas, Norman. THE CONSCIENTIOUS OBJECTOR IN AMERICA. New York, 1923	100	150	150
Thomas, Piri. DOWN THESE MEAN STREETS. New York, 1967	35	60	60
Thomas, R(onald) S(tuart). THE STONES OF THE FIELD. Carmarthen, 1946	300	500	500
Thomas, Robert Bailey. THE FARMER'S ALMANAC ... FOR ... 1793. Belknap & Hall. Boston (1793)	—	3,000	4,000
Thomas, Ross. THE COLD WAR SWAP. New York, 1965	200	750	750
THE SPY IN THE VODKA. (London, 1967)	—	—	350
Thomas, Will. GOD IS FOR WHITE FOLKS. New York (1947)	60	125	200
Thomason, John W. FIX BAYONETS. New York, 1926	150	200	250
Thomes, William Henry. *See* THE GOLDHUNTER'S ...			
Thompson, A. C. (Alice Meynell.) PRELUDES. London, 1875. First issue: brown endpapers	75	150	600
Thompson, Daniel Pierce. *See* THE ADVENTURES OF TIMOTHY PEACOCK ...			
THE LAWS OF VERMONT. Montpelier, 1835	250	350	350
Thompson, Dorothy. THE DEPTHS OF PROSPERITY. New York (1925). Written with P. Bottome	150	250	300
Thompson, Dunstan. THE SONG OF TIME. Cambridge (1941). (50 copies) Wraps	100	150	150
Thompson, Earl. A GARDEN OF SAND. New York (1970)	40	40	75
London, 1971	40	40	60
Thompson, Flora. BOG-MYRTLE AND PEAT. London, 1922. Wraps	—	250	350
Thompson, Francis. THE LIFE AND LABORS OF BLESSED JOHN BAPTIST ... London (1891). Green wraps	—	1,500	2,000

	1986	1995	2000
POEMS. London, 1893. 12 signed copies	1,000	4,500	4,500
(500 copies) First issue: ads dated October	300	350	400
Thompson, Hunter S. HELL'S ANGELS. New York (1967)	90	400	650
London, 1967.	—	—	200
Thompson, Jim (James Myers). NOW AND ON EARTH. New York, 1942	—	3,500	4,500
Thompson, Lawrence. THE NAVY HUNTS THE CGR. Garden City, 1944	40	60	60
Thompson, (James) Maurice. HOOSIER MOSAICS. New York, 1875	75	125	100
Thompson, Ruth Plumly. THE PRINCESS OF COZY TOWN. Chicago, 1922. Issued in box	—	600	750
Thomson, James. THE CITY OF DREADFUL NIGHT +. London, 1880. (40 large-paper copies)	500	750	1,000
Regular edition	125	250	250
Thomson, June. NOT ONE OF US. New York, 1971	—	—	40
Thomson, Virgil. THE STATE OF MUSIC. New York, 1939	60	100	125
Thoreau, Henry David. A WEEK ON THE CONCORD AND MERRI-	1,250	10K	15K

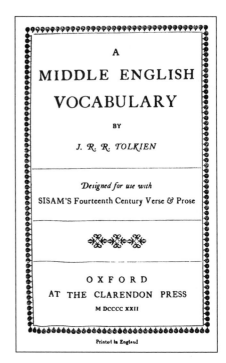

	1986	1995	2000
MACK RIVERS. Boston, 1849. (405 copies.) With 3 lines at bottom of p. 396 written in by Thoreau			
Without lines written in	—	—	10K
Boston, 1862. First edition sheets with new title page	—	1,250	3,000
Boston, 1868. (Includes all Thoreau's changes)	—	300	400
Thornton, Lawrence. IMAGINING ARGENTINA. New York, 1987	—	—	50
Thorp, Roderick. INTO THE FOREST. New York (1961)	—	50	50
Thorpe, T(homas) B(angs). THE MYSTERIES OF THE BACKWOODS. Philadelphia, 1846	—	500	500
THOUGHTS IN THE CLOISTER AND THE CROWD. (Sir Arthur Helps.) London, 1835	150	250	200
Thubron, Colin. MIRROR TO DAMASCUS. London, 1967	—	75	100
THE GOD IN THE MOUNTAIN. London, 1977. Author's first novel	—	—	75
Thurber, James. IS SEX NECESSARY? Written with E. B. White. New York, 1929	350	1,000	1,500
London (1930)	200	500	750
THE OWL IN THE ATTIC. New York, 1931 (Also 6 musical scores between 1922 and 1924, all for Ohio State's Scarlet Mark Club.)	250	750	1,000
Thurman, Wallace. NEGRO LIFE IN NEW YORK'S HARLEM. Little Blue Book #494. Girard, Kansas, no date. Wraps	150	150	250
THE BLACKER THE BERRY. New York, 1929	300	1,000	2,500
Thwaites, Anthony. THE FANTASY POETS NO. 17. Eynsham (England), 1952. Wraps	50	150	150
HOME TRUTHS. London, 1957	—	60	60
Thwaites, Reuben Gold. HISTORIC WATERWAYS . . . Chicago, 1888	100	175	150
Tidyman, Ernest. FLOWER POWER. New York (1968). Wraps	—	75	35
Tietjens, Eunice. PROFILES FROM CHINA. Chicago, 1917	125	175	150
Tilghman, Christopher. IN A FATHER'S PLACE. New York (1990). (Advance excerpt preceded)	—	40	40
Timlin, William M. THE SHIP THAT SAILED TO MARS. London (1923). Half vellum. 48 colored plates. In dustwrapper	1,500	2,500	3,500
New York (1923)	1,250	1,750	2,500
Timrod, Henry. POEMS. Boston, 1860	150	150	150

	1986	1995	2000
Tinker, Chauncey Brewster. DR. JOHNSON AND FANNY BURNEY . . . New York, 1911	60	125	75
Tiphaigne de la Roche, Charles François. GIPHANTIA, OR . . . WHAT WILL PASS, IN THE WORLD. London, 1761. First book to predict photography	—	—	3,500
Todd, Charles. A TEST OF WILLS. New York (1996).	—	—	100
Todd, Mabel (Loomis). FOOTPRINTS. Amherst, 1883. Wraps	200	300	300
Todd, Marilyn. I CLAUDIA. London, 1995	—	—	100
Todd, Ruthven. OVER THE MOUNTAIN. London (1939)	100	150	450
New York, 1939	—	—	200
LAUGHING MULATTO . . . London (1939 or 1940?) (May have preceded.)	—	150	350
Todhunter, John. LAURELLA +. London, 1876. Ads at rear dated Oct. 1876	—	—	250
Tolkien, J(ohn) R(onald) R(euel). A MIDDLE ENGLISH VOCABULARY. Oxford, 1922. Wraps. First issue: ads dated October 1921. 186 ornaments in cover design	850	850	850
Second issue: ads undated; "Printed in England" at bottom of title page, 184 ornaments	400	400	400
Tolkin, Michael. THE PLAYER. New York (1988)	—	75	60

	1986	1995	2000
Toller, Ernest. MASSES AND MAN. London, 1923. (First English translation.) Do not believe in dustwrapper	125	150	150
Tolson, Melvin B. RENDEZVOUS WITH AMERICA. New York, 1944	60	100	100
Tolstoy, Leo. CHILDHOOD AND YOUTH. London, 1862. (First English translation)	500	750	750
New York (1886)	—	—	150
TOM BROWN'S SCHOOL DAYS. (Thomas Hughes.) Cambridge, 1857. First issue: "nottable" for "notable" p. 24:15	350	750	1,000
TOM CRINGLE'S LOG. (Michael Scott.) Edinburgh, 1833. 2 volumes	200	450	450
Boston, 1833. 2 volumes	—	200	250
Tomkins, Calvin. INTERMISSION. New York, 1951	35	35	50
Tomlinson, Charles. RELATIONS AND CONTRARIES. Aldington [England] (1951). Wraps	75	75	125
Tomlinson, H(enry) M(ajor). THE SEA AND THE JUNGLE. London (1912)	100	200	150
New York, 1913	60	100	75
Tooker, Richard. THE DAY OF THE BROWN HORDE. New York: Payson & Clarke, 1929	75	125	125
Brewer & Warren. New York, 1929	50	100	100
Toole, John Kennedy. A CONFEDERACY OF DUNCES. Baton Rouge, 1980. (2,500 copies)	175	750	1,250
(London, 1981.) (1,500 copies)	75	350	450
Toomer, Jean. CANE. New York, 1923	2K	5K	12.5K
Without dustwrapper	—	—	2,000
TOPSYS AND TURVEYS. (Peter Newell.) New York, 1893. Pictorial boards	250	500	500
Torres, Edwin. CARLITO'S WAY. New York (1975)	—	—	75
Torrey, Bradford. BIRDS IN THE BUSH. Boston, 1885	50	50	50
Tourgee, Albion W. BOOK OF FORMS. (Raleigh, 1868.) Wraps *Also see* Henry Churton	200	250	350
Tourtel, Mary. A HORSE BOOK. London, 1901	—	250	350
Towle, Tony. AFTER DINNER WE TAKE A DRIVE INTO THE NIGHT. New York, 1968. Wraps. 20 signed and numbered copies	—	175	200
250 numbered copies	—	50	75

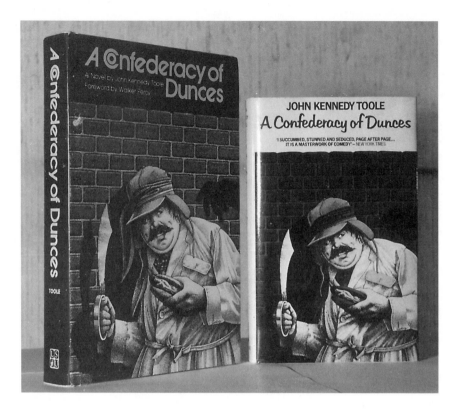

	1986	1995	2000
Toynbee, Arnold J. GREEK POLICY SINCE 1882. London, 1914. Wraps	100	125	100
Tracy, Honor. KAKEMANO ... London, 1950	—	100	100
Train, Arthur (Chesney). McALLILSTER AND HIS DOUBLE. New York, 1905	50	75	100
Traven, B. THE DEATH SHIP. London, 1934. (First English Translation by Eric Sutton)	450	750	2,500
New York, 1934. (English translation by Traven, revised)	350	750	1,750
Traver, Robert. (John Donaldson Voelker.) TROUBLE-SHOOTER. New York, 1943	125	150	175
Travers, P(amela) L(yndon). MARY POPPINS. (London, 1934)	350	500	750
New York (1934)	250	400	450
TREATISE OF HUMAN NATURE, A. (David Hume.) London, 1739–40. 3 volumes	9K	20K	35K
Tree, Iris. POEMS. Nassau, 1917. Wraps	75	400	400

	1986	1995	2000
Treece, Henry. 38 POEMS. London (1940)	100	125	150
Trelawny, Edward John. *See* ADVENTURES OF A YOUNGER SON			
Tremayne, Sydney. FOR WHOM THERE IS NO SPRING. London, 1946. Wraps	50	50	40
Treuer, David. LITTLE. Saint Paul (1995).	—	—	30
Trevanian. (Rodney Whitaker.) THE EIGER SANCTION. New York (1972)	40	75	100
Trevelyan, R. C. MALLOW AND ASPHODEL. London, 1898	—	—	200
Trevor, William. (William Trevor Cox.) A STANDARD OF BEHAVIOR. London (1958)	350	750	1,000
THE OLD BOYS. London (1964)	150	300	350
New York (1964)	—	150	175
TRIBUNE BOOK OF OPEN AIR SPORTS, (THE). (Henry Hall.) New York, 1887. (Hall edited this book, believed to be the first printed from machine-set type.)	250	250	300
Trillin, Calvin. AN EDUCATION IN GEORGIA . . . New York (1964)	35	75	75
Trilling, Diana. CLAREMONT ESSAY. New York (1964)	25	60	60
Trilling, Lionel. MATTHEW ARNOLD. New York (1939)	75	75	50
Trocchi, Alexander. *See* Frances Lengel			
Trocheck, Kathy Hogan. EVERY CROOKED NANNY. New York (1992)	—	100	150
Trollope, Anthony. THE MACDERMOTS OF BALLY-CLORAN. London, 1847. 3 volumes	4K	12.5K	20K
London, 1848	—	—	1,500
Trollope, T(homas) Adophus. A SUMMER IN BRITTANY . . . London, 1840. 2 volumes	250	450	450
Trotsky, Lev Davydovich. FROM THE WORKERS MOVEMENT . . . Geneva, 1900	350	750	1,250
Troupe, Quincy. EMBRYO. New York (1972).	—	—	50
Trowbridge, John Townsend. *See* Paul Creyton			
THE OLD BATTLEGROUND. New York, 1860	—	—	300
Troy, Judy. MOURNING DOVES. New York (1993)	—	—	35

	1986	1995	2000
TRUE COPIES OF THE LETTERS BETWEEN . . . IOHN BISSHOP OF SARUM AND D. COLE . . . (THE). (Bishop John Jewel.) London (1560)	—	—	4,500
Trumbo, Dalton. ECLIPSE. London (1935)	1,000	2,500	3,000
WASHINGTON JITTERS. New York, 1936. (Noted in both blue and yellow cloth–priority unknown)	100	250	250
Tryon, Thomas. THE OTHER. New York, 1971	25	75	100
Tuchman, Barbara. *See* Barbara Wertheim			
Tucker, Wilson. THE CHINESE DOLL. New York, 1946	—	100	150
London (1948)	—	—	75
Tuckerman, Frederick Goddard. POEMS. Boston, 1864	—	—	300
Tully, Jim. EMMETT LAWLER. New York (1922)	150	250	350
Turbyfill, Mark. THE LIVING FRIEZE. Evanston (1921). 350 numbered copies *Also see* Samuel Putnam	100	150	125
Turgenev, Ivan. RUSSIAN LIFE IN THE INTERIOR . . . Edinburgh, 1855. First English translation	—	—	1,000
Turner, Frederick Jackson. THE CHARACTER AND INFLUENCE OF THE FUR TRADE . . . (Madison, 1889.) Wraps	500	500	350
Turow, Scott. ONE L. New York, 1977	—	175	250
Turpin, Waters Edward. THESE LOW GROUNDS. New York, 1937	—	350	125
Tuten, Frederic. THE ADVENTURES OF MAO ON THE LONG MARCH. (New York, 1971)	—	50	75
Tutuola, Amos. THE PALM-WINE DRINKARD. London, 1952	50	75	100
New York, 1953	40	60	75
Twain, Mark. (Samuel Langhorne Clemens.) THE CELEBRATED JUMPING FROG OF CALAVERAS COUNTY. New York, 1867. First issue: ad before title page; p. 66 last line "life" unbroken; p. 198, last line "this" unbroken	4K	17.5K	17.5K
Second issue: lacks ads and type noted above either broken or worn	—	3,000	3,500
London, 1867. Wraps	1,500	3,500	3,500
TWO PHILOSOPHERS, THE. (John Jay Chapman.) Boston (1892). Wraps	200	200	200

	1986	1995	2000
TWO YEARS BEFORE THE MAST. (Richard Henry Dana.) New York, 1840. Presumed first issue: perfect "i" in the word "in," first line of copyright	2,000	5,000	5,000
Second issue: no dot above the letter "i." BAL notes two bindings: black cloth and muslin, no priority. (Also noted in brown cloth.) Three states of the muslin. Ads in back for Harper's Family Library. First state lists nos. 1–105; second state lists nos. 1–121; and third state lists nos. 1–129	—	1,750	2,500
Boston, 1869. Revised. Adds chapter	—	200	300
Tyler, Anne. IF MORNING EVER COMES. New York (1964)	400	1,500	2,000
London, 1965	—	—	600
Tyler, Parker. *See* Charles Ford			
Tynan, Katherine. (K. T. Hinkson.) LOUIS DE LA VALLIERE +. London, 1885	90	150	150
Tynan, Kenneth. HE THAT PLAYS THE KING. London, 1950. One of 50 Copies	50	75	200

U

	1986	1995	2000
Ullman, Doris. *See* Doris V. Jaeger			
Ullman, James Ramsey. MAD SHELLEY. Princeton, 1930. Wraps	30	100	50
Underhill, Evelyn. A BAR—LAMB'S BALLAD BOOK. London, 1902	—	100	100
Unger, Douglas. LEAVING THE LAND. New York (1984)	—	100	35
Unsworth, Barry. THE PARTNERSHIP. London (1966)	—	150	350
Untermeyer, Louis. FIRST LOVE. Boston, 1911	50	75	50
Updike, D. B. (Printer.) VEXILLA REGIS QUOTIOE. Boston, 1893. 100 copies	150	350	350
Updike, John (Hoyer). THE CARPENTERED HEN. New York (1958). First dustwrapper with "two children" in biographical information	350	750	850
HOPING FOR A HOOPEE. London, 1959. (New title)	75	100	125
Upfield, Arthur W(illiam). THE HOUSE OF CAIN. London (1928)	600	4,500	6,000
New York, 1928	200	1,500	3,500
Upson, William Hazlett. THE PIANO MOVERS. St. Charles, Illinois, 1927	60	75	125
Upward, Allen. SONGS IN ZIKLAG. London, 1888	200	150	150

	1986	1995	2000
Upward, Edward. JOURNEY TO THE BORDER. London: Hogarth Press, 1938 (Previous verse work in 1924.)	150	300	350
Urdang, Constance. CHARADES AND CELEBRATIONS. New York, 1965. Wraps	30	40	30
Uris, Leon. BATTLE CRY. New York (1953) London, 1953	100 50	350 150	350 150
Urquart, Jane. WHIRLPOOL. Toronto, 1990. Wraps Boston (1990)	- —	125 —	250 100
Ustinov, Peter (Alexander). HOUSE OF REGRETS. London (1943)	50	100	200
Uttley, Alison (Alice Jane). THE SQUIRREL, THE HARE AND THE LITTLE GREY RABBIT. London, 1929. Issued in glassine wraps	—	350	350

V

	1986	1995	2000
Vachss, Andrew H. FLOOD. New York (1985)	—	60	75
Vail, Amanda. (Warren Miller.) LOVE ME LITTLE. New York (1957). (Second book) *Also see* Warren Miller	25	30	35
Valentino, Rudolph. DAY DREAMS. New York, 1923. Issued without dustwrapper London, 1923	— —	300 —	350 350
Valin, Jonathan. THE LIME PIT. New York, 1980	35	75	125
Van, Melvin. (Melvin Van Peebles.) THE BIG HEART. San Francisco, 1957	40	75	75
Van de Wetering, Janwillem. THE EMPTY MIRROR. London, 1973 Boston, 1974	— —	— —	75 40
OUTSIDER IN AMSTERDAM. Boston, 1975. First mystery	—	—	75
Van Der Post, Lawrence. IN A PROVINCE. London, 1934. (1,250 copies) New York (no date)	150 100	200 125	250 150
Van Dine, S. S. (Willard Huntington Wright.) THE BENSON MURDER CASE. New York, 1926. (First Under This Name)	400	4,500	4,500
Van Dore, Wade. FAR LAKE. New York, 1930	50	50	75
Van Doren, Carl. THE LIFE OF THOMAS LOVE PEACOCK. Boston, 1911 London, 1911	150 100	100 75	125 100

	1986	1995	2000
Van Doren, Mark. HENRY DAVID THOREAU. Boston, 1916	150	100	125
Van Dyke, Henry. LADIES OF THE RACHMANINOFF EYES. New York (1965)	40	75	75
Van Gieson, Judith. NORTH OF THE BORDER. New York (1988)	—	350	400
London (1990). Wraps	—	—	50
Van Gulik, Robert (Hans). AN ENGLISH-BLACKFOOT VOCABULARY BASED ON MATERIAL FROM THE SOUTHERN PEIGANS. Amsterdam, 1930. Written with C. C. Uhlenbeck. 2 volumes. Wraps	—	600	1,250
DEE GOONG AN. Tokyo, 1949. 1,200 signed and numbered copies. Issued without dustwrapper	750	1,000	1,250
THE CHINESE MAZE MURDERS. The Hague, 1956	400	400	500
London, 1957	300	300	400
Van Loon, Hendrik Willem. THE FALL OF THE DUTCH REPUBLIC. Boston, 1913	100	150	350
Van Lustbader, Eric. THE SUNSET WARRIOR. Garden City, 1977	—	100	60
Van Peebles, Melvin. *See* Melvin Van			
Van Vechten, Carl. MUSIC AFTER THE GREAT WAR. New York, 1915	75	100	100
(Previous musical score and promotional pamphlet.)			
Van Vogt, A. E. SLAN. Sauk City, 1946	150	250	250
Vance, Jack. (John Holbrook.) THE DYING EARTH. (1950.) Wraps	150	250	300
San Francisco/Columbia, 1976. (First hardcover)	—	150	150
Vanderhaeghe, Guy. MAN DESCENDING. Toronto (1982).	—	—	75
Vargas Llosa, Mario. THE TIME OF THE HERO. New York, 1966. First English translation	40	75	150
London (1967)	—	100	100
Varley, John. THE OPHIUCHI HOTLINE. New York, 1977	—	40	75
Veblen, Thorstein. THE THEORY OF THE LEISURE CLASS. London, 1899	400	600	750
New York, 1899	250	500	600
Vega, Janine Pommy. POEM TO FERNANDO. San Francisco (1968). Wraps	—	—	30
Velikovsky, Immanuel. WORLDS IN COLLISION. New York, 1950	50	150	150

	1986	1995	2000
Verdelle, A. J. THE GOOD NEGRESS. Chapel Hill, 1995	—	—	35
Verne, Jules. FIVE WEEKS IN A BALLOON. New York, 1869. (First English)	200	500	2,000
London, 1870	—	—	1,250
VERSES. (Edith Wharton.) Newport, Rhode Island; 1878. Wraps	25K	50K	60K
VERSES BY TWO UNDERGRADUATES. (Van Wyck Brooks and John Hall Wheelock.) (Cambridge, 1905.) Wraps	500	500	600
Very, Jones. ESSAYS AND POEMS. Boston, 1839	—	300	400
Vesey, Paul. (Samuel Allen.) ELFENBEIN ZÄHNE/IVORY TUSKS. Heidelberg (1956). English/German text	300	300	350
Vestal, Stanley. FANDANGO . . . Boston, 1927	150	175	200
Vidal, Gore. WILLIWAW. New York, 1946	175	400	750
Vidocq, François Eugène. MEMOIRS OF VIDOCQ . . . London, 1828–30. 4 volumes	600	1,500	1,750
Viereck, Georg Sylvester. GEDICHTE. New York, 1904. Wraps. 300 numbered copies	—	300	300
Viertel, Peter. THE CANYON. New York (1940)	—	150	200
Villa, José García. FOOTNOTE TO YOUTH. New York, 1933	75	125	125
Vinal, Harold. WHITE APRIL. New Haven, 1922. Stiff wraps	40	75	100
Viramontes, Helena Maria. THE MOTHS +. Houston (1985). Wraps. (No hardbound edition)	—	—	100
Virginian, A. (William Alexander Caruthers.) THE KENTUCKIAN IN NEW YORK. New York, 1834. 2 volumes	300	450	450
Visiak, E. H. BUCCANEER BALLADS. London, 1910. Introduction by John Masefield	40	75	75
Visscher, William Lightfoot. BLACK MAMMY . . . Cheyenne, 1885	250	350	450
Vliet, R. G. EVENTS AND CELEBRATIONS. New York, 1966	—	—	150
London (1967)	—	—	75
Vliet, Russ. A MANUAL OF WOODSLORE SURVIVAL. (Cimarron, 1949.) Wraps	—	200	350
Voigt, Ellen Bryant. CLAIMING KIN. Middletown (1976). Cloth	—	—	50
Wraps	—	—	25

	1986	1995	2000
Vollmann, William T. YOU BRIGHT AND RISEN ANGELS. (London, 1987)	—	250	150
New York, 1987	—	150	125
THE CONVICT BIRD. San Francisco, 1987. (100 copies) Wraps	—	—	250
Vonnegut, Kurt, Jr. PLAYER PIANO. New York, 1952. "A" and seal on copyright page	300	1,000	1,250
London, 1953	200	500	500
Voynich, E. L. THE GADFLY. London, 1897	30	50	75

W

	1986	1995	2000
W., E. B. (E. B. White.) THE LADY IS COLD. New York, 1929. First issue: Plaza Hotel statue on cover, spine lettered in gold	300	400	450
Second issue: city skyline on cover, spine lettered in green	250	350	350
Waddell, Helen. THE SPOILED BUDDHA. Dublin, 1919. Wraps (Previous translation.)	35	100	100
Waddington, Miriam. GREEN WORLD. Montreal, 1945. Stiff wraps and dustwrapper	250	250	200
Wade, Henry. (Henry Lancelot Aubrey-Fletcher.) THE VERDICT OF YOU ALL. London, 1926	100	175	350
Wagoner, David. DRY SUN, DRY WIND. Bloomington, 1953	75	125	100
Wagstaff, Theophile. (William Makepeace Thackeray.) FLORE ET ZEPHYR. London, 1836. (Wrapper folio with 9 unnumbered plates by Thackeray)	1,500	3,000	3,500
Wahlöö, Per. THE ASSIGNMENT. New York, 1966	—	100	50
WAIKNA . . . (Ephraim G. Squier.) New York, 1855	—	150	125
Wain, John (Barrington). MIXED FEELINGS: NINETEEN POEMS. University of Reading for Subscribers. 1951. Wraps. 120 numbered copies	250	400	400
HURRY ON DOWN. London, 1953	100	100	125
BORN IN CAPTIVITY. New York, 1954. (New Title)	50	50	60
Wainwright, John. DEATH IN A SLEEPING CITY. London, 1965	—	50	50
Waite, A. E. A LYRIC OF THE FAIRY LAND +. London, 1879	—	500	750
Wakefield, Dan. ISLAND IN THE CITY. Boston, 1959	30	40	50
Wakefield, H(erbert) R(ussell). GALLIMAUFRY. London (1928)	150	250	450

	1986	1995	2000
THEY RETURN AT EVENING. New York, 1928. (First fantasy)	125	250	500
Wakeman, Frederic. SHORE LEAVE. New York (1944)	—	50	60
Wakoski, Diane. JUSTICE IS REASON ENOUGH. (Berkeley), 1959. Privately printed. (50 mimeographed copies)	1,500	500	500
COINS AND COFFINS. (New York, 1962.) Wraps	100	150	100
Walcott, Derek. IN A GREEN NIGHT. London, 1962. (First outside Caribbean)	200	300	400
SELECTED POEMS. New York, 1964. (First U.S. publication)	—	150	175
Waldman, Anne. ON THE WING. New York, 1967. Wraps. 25 signed and numbered copies	75	150	150
475 numbered copies	35	50	60
GIANT NIGHT. (New York, 1968.) Stapled wraps. (100 copies)	35	100	100
New York, 1970	15	25	25
Waley, Arthur. *See* CHINESE POEMS			
Walker, Alice. ONCE. New York (1968)	200	850	1,250
Walker, Margaret (Abigail). FOR MY PEOPLE. New York, 1942	150	350	750
Walker, Mary Willis. ZERO AT THE BONE. New York (1991).	—	—	1,000
Walker, Ted. THESE OTHER GROWTH. Leeds, 1964. Wraps	—	50	50
Wallace, Alfred Russel. PALM TREES OF THE AMAZON. London, 1853. (250 copies)	—	1,500	1,750
Wallace, David Foster. THE BROOM OF THE SYSTEM. New York (1987). Cloth	—	75	750
Wraps	—	20	75
Wallace, (Richard Horatio) Edgar. THE MISSION THAT FAILED. Cape Town, 1898. Wraps	500	600	750
Wallace, Irving. THE FABULOUS ORIGINALS. New York, 1955	50	50	35
London, 1956	40	40	35
Wallace, Lew(is). THE FAIR GOD. Boston, 1873. First issue: sheets bulk 1″ scant, signature mark "k" on p. 161	100	125	300
Second issue: sheets bulk ¹⁵⁄₁₆″, signature mark "k" on p. 161 lacking	—	40	100
Wallant, Edward Lewis. THE HUMAN SEASON. New York (1960)	75	75	125

	1986	1995	2000
Waller, Mary Ella. THE ROSE BUSH OF HILDESHEIM. Boston (1889)	100	100	100
Waller, Robert James. JUST BEYOND THE FIRELIGHT. Ames, Iowa, 1988	—	150	100
Walpole, Sir Hugh Seymour. THE WOODEN HORSE. London, 1909. With the original Smith Elder binding and title page	50	150	150
Walrond, Eric. TROPIC DEATH. New York, 1926	150	150	350
Walsh, Chad. THE FACTUAL DARK. Prairie City (1949)	75	75	100
Walsh, Ernest. POEMS AND SONNETS. New York (1934)	150	250	300
Walters, Minette. THE ICE HOUSE. London (1992). Trial/proof dustwrapper with two heads under ice. Supposedly only 6 copies printed	—	—	2,500
One head under ice	—	600	1,000
New York (1992)	—	300	400
Walton, Izaak. *See* THE COMPLEAT ANGLER . . .			
Walton, Todd. INSIDE MOVES. Garden City, 1978	25	35	75
Wambaugh, Joseph. THE NEW CENTURIONS. Boston (1970)	25	50	100
London, 1971	25	30	50
Wandrei, Donald. ECSTASY. Athol, 1928. Issued in plain tissue wrapper	400	400	450
Waniek, Marilyn Nelson. FOR THE BODY. Baton Rouge, 1978. Cloth	—	40	150
Wraps	—	—	25
Wantling, William. SEARCH. (New York, 1964). Wraps	—	—	75
Ward, Frederick William Orde. *See* PESSIMUS			
Ward, Gregory. CARPET KING. Toronto, 1991	—	100	75
Ward, Lynd. GOD'S MAN. New York (1929). 409 signed copies. Issued in slipcase	400	500	1,000
Trade edition	150	200	250
Ward, Mary Jane. THE TREE HAS ROOTS. New York (1937)	—	100	100
Ward, Robert. SHEDDING SKIN. New York (1972)	—	—	35
Ware, Eugene Fitch. *See* RHYMES OF IRONQUILL			
Warga, Wayne. HARDCOVER. New York (1985)	—	—	35

	1986	1995	2000
Warhol, Andy. LOVE IS A PINK CAKE CORKIE & ANDY. [New York, 1953.] 23 leaves in folder. Quarto spiral-bound	250	600	750
Waring, Robert Lewis. AS WE SEE IT. Washington, 1910	75	75	200
Warner, Charles Dudley. THE BOOK OF ELOQUENCE. Cazenovia. New York, 1852	—	150	150
MY SUMMER IN A GARDEN. Boston, 1871	75	100	75
Warner, Rex (Ernest). THE KITE. Oxford, 1936	125	150	125
Warner, Susan. *See* Elizabeth Wetherell			
Warner, Sylvia Townsend. THE ESPALIER. London, 1925	175	250	250
New York, 1925	—	—	150
Warren, Charles Marquis. ONLY THE VALIANT. New York, 1943	—	50	50
Warren, Robert Penn. JOHN BROWN. New York, 1929	750	1,250	1,500
Warren, Samuel. *See* PASSAGES FROM THE DIARY . . .			
Washington, Booker T(aliaferro). DAILY RESOLVE. London/New York, 1896. "Booker T. Washington" on title page	400	2,500	3,000
BLACK BELT DIAMONDS. New York, 1898	400	1,250	1,500
THE FUTURE OF THE OF THE AMERICAN NEGRO. Boston, 1899	250	600	750
Washington, Doris V. YULAN. New York (1964)	—	40	60
Washington, George. THE JOURNAL OF MAJOR GEORGE WASHINGTON . . . Williamsburg, 1754. Without map	—	—	150K
London, 1754. With map	—	—	40K
Wasserstein, Wendy. UNCOMMON WOMEN AND OTHERS. New York (1978)	—	—	25
Waterhouse, Keith. THE CAFE ROYAL . . . London, 1955. (Written with Guy Deghy)	75	100	100
THERE IS A HAPPY LAND. London, 1957	50	75	75
Waterman, Andrew. LIVING ROOM. London, 1974. Wraps	—	40	40
Waters, Frank. FEVER PITCH. New York (1930)	400	750	1,250
Waters, (William Russell). RECOLLECTIONS OF A POLICEMAN. New York, 1852	—	300	500
RECOLLECTIONS OF A DETECTIVE POLICE OFFICER. London, 1856	—	750	1,000

	1986	1995	2000
Watkins, Paul. NIGHT OVER DAY OVER NIGHT. London, 1988	—	100	200
New York, 1988	—	—	50
Watkins, Vernon (Phillips). BALLAD OF THE MARILWYD +. London (1941)	75	100	100
Watson, Colin. COFFIN SCARCELY USED. London, 1958	—	150	200
New York, 1967	—	75	100
Watson, Ian. JAPAN: A CAT'S EYE VIEW. No place, 1969. Wraps	—	150	150
THE EMBEDDING. London, 1973	—	250	250
New York, 1973	—	—	35
Watson, Lawrence. IN A DARK TIME. New York (1980)	—	100	250
Watson, Sheila. THE DOUBLE HOOK. Toronto, 1959	—	350	350
Watson, Wilfred. FRIDAY'S CHILD. London (1955)	35	35	35
Watson, William. THE PRINCE'S QUEST. London, 1880	75	75	125
Watts, Alan W. AN OUTLINE OF ZEN BUDDHISM. London (1932). Wraps	125	150	250
BUDDHISM IN THE MODERN WORLD. London [1933]. Wraps	50	75	150
Watts-Dunton, Theodore. JUBILEE GREETING AT SPITHEAD . . . London, 1897. Wraps	—	150	200
Waugh, Alec. THE LOOM OF YOUTH. London, 1917	100	150	200
New York [1917]	60	100	100
Waugh, Auberon. THE FOXGLOVE SAGA. London, 1960	35	40	40
New York, 1961	25	30	30
Waugh, Evelyn. (Arthur St. John.) THE WORLD TO COME. (Privately printed) 1916	7.5K	10K	12.5K
P.R.B. AN ESSAY ON THE PRE-RAPHAELITE BROTHERHOOD. (Privately printed) 1926	2,500	4,000	6,000
ROSSETTI—HIS LIFE AND WORKS. London, 1928	1,000	2,000	2,500
New York, 1928	600	1,250	1,500
DECLINE AND FALL. London, 1928. "Published . . . 1928" on copyright page and pp. 168 and 169 have "Martin Gaythorne-Brodie" and "Kevin Saunderson," respectively	600	3,000	4,000
Second issue has "The Hon. Miles Malpractice" and "Lord Parakeet"	—	—	3,500
Garden City: Doubleday, 1929	—	—	1,500
New York: Farrar & Rinehart, 1929. Remainder sheets	—	—	1,000
Waugh, Frederic J. THE CLAN OF MUNES. New York, 1916	400	400	400

	1986	1995	2000
WAVERLEY . . . (Sir Walter Scott.) Edinburgh, 1814. 3 volumes. First issue: "our" vs. "your" in first line of volume 2, p. 136	—	3,000	3,500
Second issue	—	—	2000
New York, 1815. 3 volumes	—	1,000	1,250
Weaver, John V. IN AMERICA POEMS. New York, 1921	50	50	25
Webb, Charles. THE GRADUATE. (New York, 1963)	40	125	125
London (1964)	—	—	75
Webb, Francis. A DRUM FOR BEN BOYD. Sydney, 1948	—	125	125
Webb, James. FIELDS OF FIRE. Englewood Cliffs (1978)	35	60	75
Webb, Mary. THE GOLDEN ARROW. London, 1916	125	200	200
Weber, Max. CUBIST POEMS. London, 1914. Cloth and boards. 100 numbered copies	250	450	500
Blue pictorial cloth	200	250	300
Wraps	100	200	200
Webster, John White. A DESCRIPTION OF THE ISLAND OF ST. MICHAEL. Boston, 1821	200	200	300
Weedon, Howard. SHADOWS ON THE WALL. New York, 1898	50	350	350
Weegee. (Arthur Fellig.) NAKED CITY. New York (1945). First issue: rough and heavy gray-green buckram	250	250	250
Second issue: smooth tan cloth	—	200	200
Weidman, Jerome. I CAN GET IT FOR YOU WHOLESALE. New York, 1937	250	350	450
Weinbaum, Stanley G(rauman). DAWN OF FLAME. (Jamaica, New York, 1936.) Issued without dustwrapper. First issue: introduction by Palmer. (7 copies)	1,750	2,500	2,500
Second issue: introduction by Keating. (250 copies)	1,000	1,500	1,500
Weir, Hich C. MISS MADELYN MACK, DETECTIVE. Boston, 1914	—	200	250
Weiss, Ehrich. *See* Harry Houdini			
Weissmuller, Johnny. SWIMMING THE AMERICAN CRAWL. Boston, 1930	125	150	150
Weissner, Carl. MANIFESTO FOR THE GREY GENERATION. No place,1966. (Written with D. Georgakas and Poessnecker)	35	40	40
Welch, Denton. MAIDEN VOYAGE. London, 1943	200	250	400
New York, 1945	60	100	125

	1986	1995	2000
Welch, James. RIDING THE EARTHBOY FORTY. World. New York/Cleveland (1971). Reportedly not distributed	40	250	150
New York: Harper, (1976). Revised	20	125	100
Welch, Lew. WOBBLY ROCK. (San Francisco) 1960. Wraps. (500 copies)	60	75	150
Weldon, Fay. THE FAT WOMAN'S JOKE. London (1967)	30	100	200
AND THE WIFE RAN AWAY. New York, 1968	—	60	100
Welles, Orson. EVERYBODY'S SHAKESPEARE: THREE PLAYS. (Written with Roger Hill.) Woodstock, Illinois (1934)	—	250	300
Welles, Winifred. THE HESITANT HEART. New York, 1919	40	40	50
Wellesley, M. A. (Dorothy). EARLY POEMS. London, 1913	—	60	75
Wellman, Manly Wade. THE INVADING ASTEROID. New York (1932). Wraps	100	125	125
Wells, Carolyn. (Mrs. Hadwin Houghton.) THE STORY OF BETTY. New York, 1899	125	175	200
Wells, H(erbert) G(eorge). TEXT BOOK OF BIOLOGY. London (1893). 2 volumes (Previous doctoral dissertation.)	600	1,000	1,250
SELECT CONVERSATIONS WITH AN UNCLE. London, 1895	350	450	750
New York, 1895	250	350	350
Welsh, Irvine. PAST TENSE . . . South Queensferry [1992]. (300 copies)	—	—	250
TRAINSPOTTING. London, 1993. Cloth	—	—	1,500
Wraps	—	—	400
New York (1996). Wraps	—	—	75
Welty, Eudora. THE KEY. (Garden City, 1941.) Wraps	2,000	2,500	2,500
A CURTAIN OF GREEN. Garden City, 1941 More if dustwrapper unfaded.	750	1,000	1,250
Wentworth, Patricia (Dora Amy Elles). THE ASTONISHING ADVENTURES OF JANE SMITH. London, 1923. First mystery	—	—	450
Boston, 1923	—	—	350
Wertheim, Barbara. (Barbara Tuchman.) THE LOST BRITISH POLICY. London, 1938. Stiff wraps	—	300	400
WERTHER'S YOUNGER BROTHER . . . (Michael Fraenkel.) New York/Paris (1931). Stiff wraps	100	175	200

	1986	1995	2000
Wescott, Glenway. THE BITTERNS. Evanston (1920). Wraps. (200 copies)	500	600	600
West, Anthony. GLOUCESTERSHIRE. London, 1939	—	150	150
ON A DARK NIGHT. London (1949)	—	75	75
THE VINTAGE. Boston, 1950	30	35	35
West, Christopher. DEATH OF A BLUE LANTERN. London (1994)	—	—	50
West, Dorothy. LIVING IS EASY. Boston, 1948	200	600	1,000
West, Jessamyn. THE FRIENDLY PERSUASION. New York (1945)	—	100	125
West, Mae. BABE GORDON. New York, 1930	75	200	300
West, Morris. *See* Julian Morris			
West, Nathanael. (Nathanael W. Weinstein.) THE DREAM LIFE OF BALSO SNELL. Paris (1931). (500 copies) 15 copies in cloth	1,750	7,500	7,500
485 copies in wraps	1,000	1,500	2,000
West, Paul. (POEMS.) Fantasy Poets No. 7. Eynsham, 1952. Wraps	—	75	350
West, Rebecca. (Cicily Isabel Fairfield Andrews.) HENRY JAMES. London, 1916	60	150	125
New York, 1916	40	125	75
THE RETURN OF THE SOLDIER. New York, 1918	60	75	75
London, 1918. First issue: blue cloth stamped in green and gilt	50	60	60
Westcott, Edward Noyes. DAVID HARUM. New York, 1898. First issue: perfect "J" in "Julius" penultimate line p. 40	60	100	75
Westlake, Donald E(dwin). THE MERCENARIES. New York (1960)	125	250	500
London, 1961	75	150	200
Weston, Edward. EDWARD WESTON. New York, 1932. 550 signed and numbered copies. Issued without dustwrapper (Exhibition brochure preceded.)	1,250	2,000	2,500
Weston, Patrick. (Gerald Hamilton.) DESERT DREAMERS. London (1914). (250 copies)	125	125	250
Westwood, Thomas. POEMS. London, 1840	60	150	175
Wetherell, Elizabeth. (Susan Bogert Warner.) THE WIDE, WIDE WORLD. New York, 1851. 2 volumes. First issue: p. 157 in volume 1 and p. 34 in volume 2 have numbers misplaced	—	750	1,250

	1986	1995	2000
Weyman, Stanley. THE HOUSE OF THE WOLF. London, 1890	75	100	125
Whalen, Philip. THREE SATIRES. (Portland, Oregon, 1951.) Wraps	400	450	450
SELF-PORTRAIT FROM ANOTHER DIRECTION. (San Francisco), 1959. Wraps	35	50	40
Whaler, James. HALE'S POND +. New York, 1927	35	40	40
Wharton, Edith Newbold Jones. *See* VERSES			
THE DECORATION OF HOUSES. (Written with O. Codman.) New York, 1897	350	600	1,500
London, 1898	250	500	1,000
THE GREATER INCLINATION. New York, 1899	125	300	400
Wharton, Will. GRAPHITI FROM ELSINORE. Prairie City (1949)	75	75	100
Wharton, William. BIRDY. New York, 1979	35	75	75
London, 1979	35	50	50
Wheatley, Dennis (Yates). THE FORBIDDEN TERRITORY. London (1933)	75	300	350
New York (1933)	—	150	250
Wheatley, Phillis. POEMS ON VARIOUS SUBJECTS, RELIGIOUS AND MORAL. London, 1773	2K	6K	15K
Philadelphia, 1786	1,000	3,500	7,500
Wheeler, Ella (Wilcox). DROPS OF WATER. New York, 1872	50	75	125
Wheeler, Kate. NOT WHERE I STARTED FROM. Boston, 1993	—	—	40
Wheelock, John Hall. *See* VERSES BY TWO UNDERGRADUATES			
THE HUMAN FANTASY. Boston, 1911	75	150	150
Wheelwright, John Brooks. NORTH ATLANTIC PASSAGE. (Florence, Italy, 1924)	750	1,000	1,000
Whicher, George Frisbie). ON THE TIBUR ROAD. Princeton, 1911	50	50	50
Whigham, Peter. CLEAR LAKE COMES FROM ENJOYMENT. London (1959). Written with Denis Goacher	—	75	100
Whistler, James Abbott McNeill. WHISTLER V. RUSKIN. Chelsea, 1878. Wraps. First edition: duodecimo	350	600	600
Second edition: quarto	200	300	300
White, Antonia. FROST IN MAY. London (1933)	200	250	500

	1986	1995	2000
White, E(lwyn) B(rooks). *See* Sterling Finney, James Thurber *and* E.B.W.			
White, Edmund. FORGETTING ELENA. New York (1973)	40	100	100
White, Edward Lucas. NARRATIVE LYRICS. New York and London, 1908	30	30	50
White, Eric Walter. THE ROOM +. London, 1927. Issued without dustwrapper	—	50	50
White, Grace Miller. A CHILD OF THE SLUMS. Ogilvie, 1904. Wraps	200	250	250
White, Lionel. THE SNATCHERS. New York (1953). Wraps	—	—	100
White, Michael. A BROTHER'S BLOOD. New York (1996)	—	—	50
White, Owen P. JUST ME +. El Paso, 1924. Stiff wraps. (Carl Hertzog's first typography.) 275 numbered copies	—	350	350
White, Patrick. (Victor Martindale.) THE PLOUGHMAN +. Sydney, 1935	1,000	2,500	6,000
HAPPY VALLEY. London, 1939	600	1,500	3,500
New York, 1940	300	850	1,500
White, Randy Wayne. *See* Randy Striker			
SANIBEL FLATS. New York (1990)	—	—	850
White, Stewart Edward. THE BIRDS OF MACKINAC ISLAND. New York, 1893. Wraps	400	750	1,000
THE WESTERNERS. New York, 1901	—	—	200
THE CLAIM JUMPERS. New York, 1901	75	200	200
Wraps. (Town and Country Library)	60	150	150
White, T(erence) H(anbury). THE GREEN BAY TREE. (Cambridge, 1929.) Wraps	350	400	250
LOVED HELEN +. London (1929)	300	500	250
White, T(heodore) H. THUNDER OUT OF CHINA. New York, 1946. Written with Annalee Jacoby	25	40	40
White, Walter F(rancis). THE FIRE IN THE FLINT. New York, 1924	150	200	500
White, William Allen. RHYMES BY TWO FRIENDS. Fort Scott (1893). (Written with A. B. Paine.) (500 copies)	75	150	150
THE REAL ISSUE. Chicago, 1896	40	50	60

	1986	1995	2000
White, W(illiam) L(indsay). WHAT PEOPLE SAID. New York, 1936	35	35	35
White Rabbit Press. LAMENT FOR THE MAKERS. Oakland, 1962. Wraps. (By Jack Spicer. First book of the press)	300	300	750
Whitehead, E. A. THE FOURSOME. London (1972)	30	30	30
Whitehead, Henry S(t.Clair). JUMBEE +. (Sauk City) 1944	175	300	300
Whitehead, James. JOINER. New York, 1971	—	—	30
Whitlock, Brand. THE 13TH DISTRICT . . . Indianapolis (1902)	25	30	50
Whitman, Sarah Helen (Power). POEMS. (Providence, 1847.) Wraps	50	150	250
HOURS OF LIFE +. Providence, 1853	—	150	200
Whitman, Walt(er). FRANKLIN EVANS: OR, THE ENEBRIATE. (New York, 1842.) Wraps. First issue: price 12½ cents	5K	8.5K	25K
Second issue: price 6½ cents	4,000	5,000	20K
Rebound or disbound without covers	—	—	3,500
New York, 1929. 700 Copies	—	150	200
Also see LEAVES OF GRASS			
Whittemore, Edward. QUIN'S SHANGHAI CIRCUS. New York, 1974	35	75	100
Whittemore, (Edward) Reed. HEROS AND HEROINES. New York (1946)	50	75	75
Whittier, John Greenleaf. LEGENDS OF NEW ENGLAND. Hartford, 1831. First issue: last line p. 98 "The go" for "They go." In original cloth	250	750	350
Whyte-Melville, George John. DIGBY GRAND. London, 1853. 2 volumes	200	300	350
Wideman, John Edgar. A GLANCE AWAY. New York (1967)	75	200	250
Wiebe, Rudy. PEACE SHALL DESTROY MANY. Toronto, 1962	—	60	60
WIELAND . . . New York, 1798. (Charles Brockden Brown)	—	1,500	2,000
Wiener, Norbert. CYBERNETICS . . . New York (1948) (Preceded by two pure mathematics titles.)	125	350	400
Wieners, John (Joseph). THE HOTEL WENTLY POEMS. (San Francisco) 1958. Wraps. First issue: censored	50	100	200
Second issue: unexpurgated (press listed at "1334 Franklin Street")	30	40	50

	1986	1995	2000
Wiesel, Elie. NIGHT. Paris, 1958	75	200	300
New York (1960)	—	150	200
Wiggin, Kate Douglas. *See* Kate Douglas Smith			
Wilbur, Richard (Purdy). THE BEAUTIFUL CHANGES +. New York (1947). (750 copies)	250	350	400
Wilcox, James. MODERN BAPTISTS. Garden City, 1983.	—	—	75
Wilde, Oscar. (Fingal O'Flahertie Wills.) RAVENNA. Oxford, 1878. Wraps. First issue: Oxford University arms on title and cover	600	1,000	1,500
Wilder, Amos N(iven). BATTLE-RETROSPECT +. New York, 1923	150	200	200
Wilder, Isabel. MOTHER AND FOUR. New York (1933)	—	100	125
Wilder, Laura Ingalls. LITTLE HOUSE IN THE BIG WOODS. New York, 1932	—	400	1,000
Wilder, Thornton. THE CABALA. New York, 1926. First issue: "conversation" for "conversion" on p. 196:13, "explaininn" for "explaining" p. 202:12. Blue patterned cloth reportedly scarcer than red	250	350	400
London, 1926	75	150	175
Wiley, Richard. SOLDIERS IN HIDING. Boston, 1986	—	—	100
Wilhelm, Kate. MORE BITTER THAN DEATH. New York, 1963	50	75	100

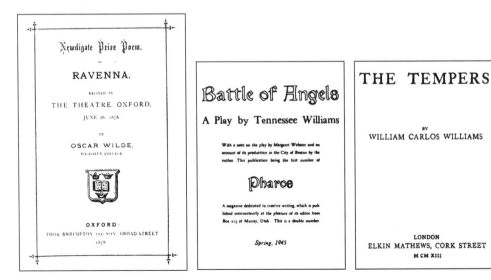

	1986	1995	2000
Wilkins, Mary E. (Mary E. W. Freeman.) DECORATIVE PLAQUES. Boston (1883). (Written with George F. Barnes)	600	2,000	2,000
Wilkinson, Sylvia. MOSS ON THE NORTH SIDE. Boston, 1967	60	60	75
Will, George. THE PURSUIT OF HAPPINESS +. New York, 1979	35	75	35
Willeford, Charles. PROLETARIAN LAUGHTER. Yonkers, 1948. Wraps. 1,000 Copies	125	150	200
Williams, Alfred. SONGS IN WILTSHIRE. London, 1909. (500 copies)	40	40	75
Williams, Ben Ames. ALL THE BROTHERS WERE VALIANT. New York, 1919. In N. C. Wyeth dustwrapper	50	400	600
Williams, C(harles) K(enneth). A DAY FOR ANNE FRANK. Philadelphia (1968). Wraps	40	75	400
LIES. Boston, 1969	—	75	200
Williams, Charles. HILL GIRL. New York (1951). Wraps	—	—	40
Williams, Charles (Walter). THE SILVER STAIR. London, 1912	300	300	450
Williams, Heathcote. THE SPEAKERS. London, 1964	35	35	35
Williams, Joan. THE MORNING AND THE EVENING. New York, 1961	25	50	60
London, 1962	25	40	40
Williams, John. NOTHING BUT THE NIGHT. Denver, 1948	50	75	75
Williams, John A(lfred). THE ANGRY ONES +. New York (1960). Wraps	50	75	150
Williams, Jonathan (Chamberlain). PAINTING & GRAPHICS. Highlands, 1950. (Exhibition folder) (Previous pamphlet may exist.)	500	500	500
Williams, Joy. STATE OF GRACE. Garden City, 1973	25	100	75
Williams, Margery. THE LATE RETURNING. London, 1902	—	100	250
THE VELVETEEN RABBIT . . . London, 1922. First children's book	—	350	10K
New York (1922) *Also see* Margaret Bianco	—	200	3,500
Williams, Oscar. THE GOLDEN DARKNESS. New Haven, 1921. Wraps over boards	60	125	125
Williams, Philip Lee. HEART OF A DISTANT FOREST. New York (1984).	—	—	75

	1986	1995	2000
Williams, Sherley Anne. GIVE BIRTH TO BRIGHTNESS. New York, 1972	—	125	150
Wraps	—	—	35
Williams, Tad. TAILCHASER'S SONG. New York (1985)	—	—	35
Williams, Tennessee (Thomas Lanier). BATTLE OF ANGELS. Murray, Utah, 1945. Published as Pharos Nos. 1 and 2. Wraps	350	750	750
Williams, Terry Tempest. THE SECRET LANGUAGE OF SNOW. New York: Sierra Club (1984). Written with Ted Major	—	—	300
PIECES OF WHITE SHELL. New York (1984)	—	75	125
Williams, Thomas. CEREMONY OF LOVE. Indianapolis (1955)	40	75	125

	1986	1995	2000
Williams, William Carlos. POEMS. (Rutherford, New Jersey), 1909. Wraps. (100 copies) First issue: 2 known copies. Line 5 of first poem reads "of youth himself, all rose-y-clad"	15K	30K	35K
Second issue: fewer than 15 known copies. Line 5 of first poem reads "of youth himself all rose-y clad"	—	17.5K	20K
THE POEMS. London, 1913	800	1,500	2,000
Williamson, Henry. THE BEAUTIFUL YEARS. London, 1921. (750 copies)	300	750	750
Williamson, Jack. THE GIRL FROM MARS. New York (1929). Wraps. (Written with Dr. M. Breuer)	75	100	150
THE LEGION OF SPACE. Reading, 1947. 500 signed and numbered copies	90	150	150
Trade edition	35	75	75
Willingham, Calder (Bayard). END AS A MAN. New York (1947). First issue: no text on back panel of dustwrapper	75	150	150
Second issue: text on back panel of dustwrapper	—	75	75
Willington, James. (Oliver Goldsmith.) MEMOIRS OF A PROTES- TANT. London, 1758	2,000	3,000	3,000
Willis, George. TANGLEWEED. Garden City, 1943	35	50	75
Willis, N(athaniel) P(arker). SKETCHES. Boston, 1827	100	200	150
Willocks, Tim. BAD CITY BLUES. London (1991)	—	—	250
Wills, Garry. CHESTERTON. New York (1961)	50	75	50
Willson, Meredith. AND THERE I STOOD WITH MY PICCOLO. New York, 1948	50	60	75
Wilson, A(ndrew) N(orman). THE SWEETS OF PIMLICO. London (1977)	—	350	350
Wilson, Adrian. PRINTING FOR THE THEATRE. San Francisco, 1957. (250 copies)	—	1,250	1,250
Wilson, Angus. (Frank Johnstone.) THE WRONG SET +. London, 1949	60	75	100
Wilson, Augusta Jane Evans. *See* INEZ . . .			
Wilson, Carroll Atwood. VERDANT GREEN. No place, 1933. Wraps	40	75	75
Wilson, Colin (Henry). THE OUTSIDER. London, 1956.	75	200	250
Boston, 1956. First has the date on title page. At least 3 different binding variants without date, but stating "First American Edition" on copyright page have been seen	40	100	150

	1986	1995	2000
Wilson, Derek. THE TRIARCHS. London (1994)	—	—	50
Wilson, Edmund. THE UNDERTAKER'S GARLAND. New York, 1922. (Written with J. P. Bishop.) 50 Copies for "Bookseller Friends." Issued without dustwrapper	250	250	250
Trade edition in dustwrapper	350	350	450
DISCORDANT ENCOUNTERS. New York (1927)	350	500	1,000
Wilson, Harry Leon. ZIG ZAG TALES FROM EAST TO WEST. New York, 1894. Wraps	100	200	300
Cloth	75	125	150
Wilson, John Morgan. SIMPLE JUSTICE. New York (1996)	—	—	30
Wilson, Lanford. BALM IN GILEAD +. New York, 1965. Wraps	35	75	35
Wilson, William S. WHY I DON'T WRITE LIKE FRANZ KAFKA. New York (1977)	—	—	25
Wilson, (Thomas) Woodrow. CONGRESSIONAL GOVERNMENT. Boston, 1885. First issue: publisher's monogram on spine	100	250	350
Wiltz, Chris. THE KILLING CIRCLE. New York, 1981	—	60	35
Windham, Donald. YOU TOUCHED ME. New York (1947). (Written with Tennessee Williams.) 506 hardcover in white pictorial dustwrapper	—	400	600
Cream-colored wraps with preliminary price of $.75	—	200	250
Gray wraps printed in black with 85-cent price. (All subsequent printings in bright orange)	75	150	150
THE HITCHHIKER. (Florence, 1950.) 250 signed and numbered copies. Wraps	125	125	125
Wingfield, R. D. FROST AT CHRISTMAS. Toronto, 1987. Wraps	—	—	300
London (1989)	—	—	300
Wingfield, Sheila. POEMS. London (1938)	—	75	75
Winogrand, Garry. THE ANIMALS. New York, 1969. Oblong wraps	—	75	100
Winslow, Don. A COOL BREEZE ON THE UNDERGROUND. New York (1991)	—	50	150
Winsor, Justin. A HISTORY OF THE TOWN OF DUXBURY ... Boston, 1849	150	250	300
Winsor, Kathleen. (Herwig Shaw Porter.) FOREVER AMBER. New York, 1944	60	75	100
Winter, William. POEMS. Boston, 1855	150	200	200

	1986	1995	2000
WINTER IN THE WEST, A. By a New Yorker. (Charles Fenno Hoffman.) New York, 1835. 2 volumes	150	650	600
WINTER SHIP, A. (Sylvia Plath.) Edinburgh, 1960. Wraps	1,000	1,000	2,000
Winters, Yvor. DIADEMS AND FAGOTS. Sante Fe (1920). (Translation by Winters of Olavo Bilac's book.) (50 copies)	500	600	750
THE IMMOBILE WIND. Evanston (1921). Wraps	450	500	600
Winterson, Jeanette. ORANGES ARE NOT THE ONLY FRUIT. London (1985). Wraps	—	200	450
New York (1987). Wraps with $6.95 price and stating "First American edition, September, 1987."	—	75	100
Wishart, David. I, VIRGIL. London, 1995	—	—	60
Wister, Owen. THE LADY OF THE LAKE. (Cambridge) 1881. (Chorus book)	200	300	400
THE NEW SWISS FAMILY ROBINSON. (Cambridge, 1882)	250	500	750
Witwer, Harry Charles. FROM BASEBALL TO BOCHES. Boston (1918)	40	40	35
Wodehouse, P(elham) G(renville). THE POTHUNTERS. London, 1902. First issue: silver cup on front	1,750	3,500	4,000
Second issue: finish line on front, with 8 pages of ads ending with MIKE	—	750	850
Woiwode, Larry. WHAT I'M GOING TO DO . . . New York (1969)	40	50	75
London, 1970	40	40	50
Wolfe, Bernard. REALLY THE BLUES. New York (1946). Written with Milton Mezzrow	75	75	150
LIMBO. New York (1952)	75	75	100
Wolfe, Gene. OPERATION ARES. New York (1970)	—	40	40
London, 1977. First hardcover	—	50	75
Wolfe, George C. THE COLORED MUSEUM. New York (1988)	—	—	50
Wolfe, Humbert. THE OLD MAN OF KOENIGSBERG . . . Holy Well, 1907	—	300	300
THE COUNT OF SALDEYNE. London, 1915	50	100	100
Wolfe, Susan. THE LAST BILLABLE HOUR. New York, 1989	—	175	200
Wolfe, Thomas (Clayton). THE CRISIS IN INDUSTRY. Chapel Hill, 1919. Wraps	6,000	7,500	7,500

	1986	1995	2000
LOOK HOMEWARD, ANGEL. New York, 1929. First issue: dustwrapper has author's picture on back	1,500	2,500	7,500
Second issue: author's picture not on back of dustwrapper	750	1,250	1,500
London, 1930. (Few textual changes)	650	750	750
Wolfe, Tom. THE KANDY-KOLORED . . . New York (1965)	60	175	250
Wolfert, Ira. TUCKER'S PEOPLE. New York, 1943. Pictorial dustwrapper	—	75	200
Printed, nonpictorial dustwrapper	—	—	150
BATTLE FOR THE SOLOMONS. Boston, 1943	—	75	75
Wolff, Geoffrey. BAD DEBTS. New York, 1969	20	35	75
Wolff, Maritta M. WHISTLE STOP. New York (1941)	40	40	100
Wolff, Tobias. UGLY RUMOURS. London (1975)	—	500	1,000
IN THE GARDEN OF THE NORTH AMERICAN MARTYRS. New York (1981). Cloth in dustwrapper that has not been price clipped	40	100	350
In price-clipped dustwrapper	—	—	150
Wraps	—	35	40
Wolheim, Donald A(llen). THE SECRET OF SATURN'S RINGS. Philadelphia (1954)	35	125	150

(Previous edited anthologies.)

	1986	1995	2000
Womack, Jack. AMBIENT. New York (1987)	—	—	60
Wood, Charles Erskine Scott. IMPERIALISM VS. DEMOCRACY. New York, 1899. (Offprint from "Pacific Monthly")	100	150	150
A MASQUE OF LOVE. Chicago, 1904	60	75	75
Wood, Clement. GLAD OF EARTH. New York, 1917	40	60	60
Wood, Ted. SOMEBODY ELSE'S SUMMER. Toronto, 1973	—	—	150
DEAD IN THE WATER. Toronto, 1983 (First mystery)	—	200	250
New York, 1983	—	35	50
Woodberry, George Edward. THE RELATIONS OF PALLAS ATHENE TO ATHENS. Privately printed [1877]. Wraps	—	300	300
HISTORY OF WOOD-ENGRAVING. New York, 1883	125	150	150
THE NORTH SHORE WATCH. New York, 1883. 200 copies	—	150	150
THE NORTH SHORE WATCH +. Boston, 1890	—	75	75
Woodcock, George. SIX POEMS. London, 1938. Single sheet folded. One of 100 signed copies	—	750	600
Woodford, Jack. EVANGELICAL COCKROACH. New York, 1929	60	75	100
Woodman, Richard. AN EYE OF THE FLEET. London (1981)	—	—	200
Woodrell, Daniel. UNDER THE BRIGHT LIGHTS. New York (1986)	—	—	50
Woods, Sara (Sara Bowen-Judd) BLOODY INSTRUCTIONS. London, 1962	—	100	100
New York, 1963	—	40	40
Woods, Stuart. CHIEFS. New York, 1981. First mystery	—	125	200
Woodward, C(omer) Vann. TOM WATSON: AGRARIAN REBEL. New York, 1938	—	200	150
Woodward, W(illiam) E. BUNK. New York, 1923	60	75	100
Woody, Elizabeth. HAND INTO STONE. New York (1988). Wraps.	—	—	30
Woolf, Douglas. THE HYPOCRITIC DAYS. Divers Press, 1955. Wraps	50	75	100

	1986	1995	2000
Woolf, L(eonard) S. THE VILLAGE IN THE JUNGLE. London (1913)	250	350	500
Woolf, Virginia. THE VOYAGE OUT. London, 1915. Green cloth	500	1,500	1,500
Red cloth (trial binding?)	400	1,500	1,500
New York (1920). Text revised by Woolf. In dustwrapper	—	2,000	2,500
Woollcott, Alexander. MRS. FISKE . . . New York, 1917. First issue: author's name misspelled on title page	50	50	50
Woolly Whale, Press of. LE CHAPEAU IMMORTEL. (New York, 1928.) 350 copies. (First "Book" of press a broadside by Earl H. Emmons)	75	75	75
Woolner, Thomas. MY BEAUTIFUL LADY. London, 1863	—	250	350
Woolrich, Cornell. COVER CHARGE. New York, 1926	750	2,000	2,500
Wordsworth, William. AN EVENING WALK. London, 1793	5K	5K	35K
Wouk, Herman. THE MAN IN THE TRENCH COAT. New York (1941). Wraps	750	1,250	1,500
AURORA DAWN. New York, 1947	100	175	250
London, 1947	75	100	100
Wright, Austin Tappan. ISLANDIA. New York (1942). With INTRODUCTION TO ISLANDIA by Basil Davenport. 2 volumes	300	400	450
Wright, Charles. THE DREAM ANIMAL. Toronto, 1968. Issued without dustwrapper	—	200	250
Wraps	—	35	35
THE GRAVE OF THE RIGHT HAND. Middletown (1970). Cloth	35	75	75
Wraps	—	30	30
Wright, Charles (Stevenson). THE MESSENGER. New York (1963)	40	75	50
Wright, Eric. THE NIGHT THE GODS SMILED. Toronto (1983)	—	—	75
London (1983)	—	—	60
New York (1983)	—	—	35
Wright, Frank Lloyd. THE JAPANESE PRINT. Chicago, 1912. Orange wraps	—	—	4,000
Printed boards. One of 35 on Japan vellum	600	3,000	3,000
Trade	—	2,000	2,000
New York, 1967. Issued in slipcase	—	300	350

	1986	1995	2000
Wright, Harold Bell. THAT PRINTER OF UDELL'S. Chicago, 1903	40	60	75
Wright, James (Arlington). THE GREEN WALL. New Haven, 1957	250	350	350
Wright, Jay. DEATH AS HISTORY. (New York): Milbrook (1967). Wraps. (200 copies)	—	150	150
Wright, Judith. THE MOVING IMAGE. Melbourne (1946)	100	125	150
Wright, L. R. THE SUSPECT. Toronto, 1985	—	100	100
New York (1985)	—	—	50
Wright, Richard (Nathaniel). UNCLE TOM'S CHILDREN. New York, 1938	600	1,250	1,500
New York (1938). Enlarged edition	—	600	750
Wright, Richard B. ANDREW TOLLIVER. Toronto, 1965	—	125	150
THE WEEKEND MAN. Toronto, 1970	—	75	50
New York (1971)	30	40	30
Wright, S(ydney) Fowler. THE AMPHIBIANS. London (1925)	100	350	350
Wright, Sarah E. GIVE ME A CHILD. (Written with Lucy Smith.) Philadelphia (1955). Wraps	50	200	200
THIS CHILD'S GONNA LIVE. (New York, 1969)	35	75	75
London, 1969	—	—	40
Wright, Stephen. MEDITATIONS IN GREEN. New York, 1983	—	50	75
Wright, Willard Huntington. SONGS OF YOUTH. New York, 1913 *Also see* S. S. Van Dine	60	500	500
Wurlitzer, Rudolph. NOG. New York (1968)	35	50	40
THE OCTOPUS. London, 1969. (New title)	30	30	40
Wylie, Elinor (Hoyt). *See* INCIDENTAL NUMBERS			
NETS TO CATCH THE WIND. New York, 1921. First issue: unwatermarked paper	300	300	250
London, 1928	—	150	125
Wylie, Philip (Gordon). HEAVY LADEN. New York, 1928	150	250	350
Wyndham, Francis. OUT OF THE WAR. London, 1974	—	50	35

	1986	1995	2000
Wyndham, John (John Beynon Harris). *See* John Beynon			
THE DAY OF THE TRIFFIDS. Garden City, 1951. (First novel)	150	300	450
London (1951). (Contains textual revisions)	200	400	600

Y

	1986	1995	2000
Yarbro, Chelsea Quinn. TIME OF THE FOURTH HORSEMAN. Garden City, 1976	—	30	30
Yates, Edmund Hodgson. MY HAUNTS AND THEIR FREQUENTERS. London, 1854. Wraps	125	150	200
Yates, Elizabeth. QUEST IN THE NORTH-LAND. New York, 1940	35	50	35
Yates, Richard. REVOLUTIONARY ROAD. Boston (1961)	60	150	200
(London, 1962)	50	75	100
Yeats, Jack B(utler). JAMES FLAUNTY. London (1901). Wraps	200	350	400
Yeats, W(illiam) B(utler). MOSADA. Dublin, 1886. (100 copies)	35K	75K	85K
THE WANDERINGS OF OISIN +. London, 1889. (500 copies)	1,000	3,000	3,000
Yellen, Samuel. IN THE HOUSE AND OUT +. Bloomington, 1952	—	40	40
Yerby, Frank (Garvin). THE FOXES OF HARROW. New York, 1946	60	100	200
Yevtushenko, Yevgeny. SELECTED POEMS. New York, 1962. (First English translation)	—	75	75
Yglesias, José. A WAKE IN YBOR CITY. New York (1963) (Previous translations.)	30	40	40
Yorke, Henry Vincent. *See* Henry Green	150	200	125
Young, Al. DANCING. New York (1969). Wraps. 50 signed and numbered copies			
Regular edition	30	50	35
Young, Andrew. SONG OF NIGHT. London [1910]	200	200	200
Young, Art. *See* R. Palasco Drant			
Young, Marguerite. PRISMATIC GROUND. New York, 1937	50	50	100
Young, Stark. THE BLIND MAN AT THE WINDOW +. New York, 1906 /	100	200	200
Young Lady, A. *See* AGNES DE CASTRO			
Yount, John. WOLF AT THE DOOR. New York, 1967	40	75	75

MOSADA.

A Dramatic Poem.

BY

W. B. YEATS.

WITH A

Frontispiece Portrait of the Author

By J. B. YEATS.

Reprinted from the DUBLIN UNIVERSITY REVIEW.

DUBLIN:
PRINTED BY SEALY, BRYERS, AND WALKER,
94, 95 AND 96 MIDDLE ABBEY STREET.
1886.

	1986	1995	2000
Yurick, Sol. THE WARRIORS. New York (1965)	40	60	100

Z

Zabor, Rafi. THE BEARS COMES HOME. New York, 1987.	—	—	100
Zagat, Arthur Lee. SEVEN OUT OF TIME. Reading, 1949	25	35	40
Zangwill, I. THE BACHELOR'S CLUB. London, 1891	150	300	300
New York, 1891	—	—	100

Previous collaboration.

Zanuck, Darryl F. HABIT +. Los Angeles, 1923	—	150	150
Zaroulis, N(ancy) L. THE POE PAPERS. New York (1977)	—	75	50
Zaturenska, Marya. THRESHOLD AND HEARTH. New York, 1934	—	150	150
Zeitlin, Jake. FOR WHISPERS AND CHANTS. San Francisco, 1927. (500 numbered copies)	200	175	125
Zelazny, Roger. THIS IMMORTAL. New York (1966). Wraps	—	—	50
London, 1967. First hardback edition	—	—	600
Zimler, Richard. THE LAST KABBALIST OF LISBON. Woodstock / New York (1998)	—	—	100
Zimmer, Paul. A SEED ON THE WIND. San Francisco, 1960. One of 200 signed, numbered copies in wraps	—	—	125
THE RIBS OF DEATH. New York, 1967. Author's first regularly published book	—	—	50
Zindel, Paul. THE PIGMAN. New York (1968)	35	50	40
Zindell, David. NEVERNESS. New York, 1988	—	35	150
London (1989)	—	—	75
Zugsmith, Leane. ALL VICTORIES ARE ALIKE. New York, 1929	100	100	100

Zukofsky, Louis. *See* Anton Reiser

LE STYLE APOLLINAIRE. Paris, 1934. Wraps	4,000	4,000	2,000
FIRST HALF OR 'A'—9. New York, 1940. 55 mimeographed signed copies	1,500	2,000	2,000

Appendix A

Pseudonyms

The following is a list of author names and pseudonyms. The sources include practically all the reference works listed in the Selected Bibliography, plus individual bibliographies.

The list has been arbitrarily limited to pseudonyms used by the authors when publishing books and does not include pseudonyms used in magazine appearances.

The names are listed alphabetically. Those in **boldface** type are the real names of the authors.

A.	**Matthew Arnold**
A., T.B.	**Thomas Bailey Aldrich**
Abbott, Anthony	**Fulton Oursler**
Abbott, John	**Evan Hunter**
Acre, Stephen	**Frank Gruber**
Adams, William Taylor	Warren T. Ashton; Oliver Optic
Ai	**Florence Anthony**
Akers, Floyd	**L. Frank Baum**
Alcott, Louisa May	A. M. Barnard
Aldrich, Thomas Bailey	T.B.A.
Alger, Horatio	Arthur Lee Putnam; Julian Starr
Allbeury, Ted	Richard Butler; Patrick Kelly
Allen, Grace	Allen Weston (with **Alice Mary Norton**)
Allen, Hervey	Hardly Alum
Allen, Steve	William Allen Stevens; William Christopher Stevens
Allingham, Margery	Maxwell March
Alum, Hardly	**Hervey Allen**
Ambler, Eric	Eliot Reed (with **Charles Rodda**)
Amis, Kingsley	Robert Markham; William Tanner
Anderson, Maxwell	John Nairne Michaelson

Anderson, Poul

Andrezel, Pierre
Anstey, F.
Anthony, C. L.
Anthony, Florence
Anthony, Peter
Antoninus, Brother (Dominican
lay brother, 1951–69)
Ard, William

Arden, William
Armstrong, Terence Ian Fytton
Arnold, Matthew
Arno, Peter
Arnow, Harriette
Ashdown, Clifford

Ashe, Gordon
Ashton, Warren T.
Asimov, Isaac
Aston, James
Atherton, Gertrude
Aubrey-Fletcher, Henry Lancelot
Auchincloss, Louis
August, John
Auster, Paul
Austin, Mary H.
Axton, David

B., E.C.
B., J.K.
Bachman, Richard
Bagby, George
Baker, Asa
Bancroft, Laura
Bangs, John Kendrick
Banshuck, Grego
Baraka, Imamu Amiri
(legal name change)
Barbellion, W.N.P.
Barbette, Jay
Barclay, Bill
Barnes, Julian
Barnsley, Alan
Barr, Robert
Baum, L. Frank

Bax, Roger
Baxter, George Owen

A.A. Craig; Michael Karageorge;
Winston P. Sanders
Karen Blixen
Thomas Anstey Guthrie
Dodie Smith
Ai
Peter and Anthony Shaffer
William Everson

Ben Kerr; Mike Moran; Jonas Ward;
Thomas Wills
Dennis Lynds
John Gawsworth
A.
Curtis Arnoux Peters
Harriett Simpson
R. Austin Freeman and John
James Pitcairn
John Creasey
William Taylor Adams
George E. Dale; Paul French
T. H. White
Frank Lin
Henry Wade
Andrew Lee
Bernard De Voto
Paul Benjamin
Gordon Stairs
Dean R. Koontz

Edmund Blunden
John Kendrick Bangs
Stephen King
Aaron Marc Stein
Davis Dresser
L. Frank Baum
J.K.B.
Hugo Gernsback
Leroi Jones

Bruce Frederick Cummings
Bart Spicer (with Betty Spicer)
Michael Moorcock
Dan Kavanagh
Gabriel Fielding
Luke Sharp
Floyd Akers; Laura Bancroft;
John Estes Cook; Edith Van Dyne
Paul Winterton
Frederick Faust

Baxter, John	**Howard Hunt**
Beaton, George	**Gerald Brenan**
Beaumont, Charles	**Charles Nutt**
Beecher, Harriet	**Harriet Beecher Stowe** (married name)
Bell, Acton	**Ann Brontë**
Bell, Currer	**Charlotte Brontë**
Bell, Ellis	**Emily Brontë**
Bell, Eric Temple	John Taine
Benjamin, Paul	**Paul Auster**
Benson, A.C.	Christopher Carr
Bentley, E.C.	E. Clerihew
Berkeley, Anthony	Francis Iles
Berne, Victoria	**M.F.K. Fisher** and **Dillwyn Parrish**
Betjeman, John	Richard M. Farren
Beynon, John	**John Wyndham P.L.B. Harris**
Bierce, Ambrose	Dod Grile; William Herman
Bigby, Cantell A.	**George W. Peck**
Birdwell, Cleo	**Don DeLillo**
Birney, Earle	E. Robertson
Black, Mansell	**Elleston Trevor**
Blair, Eric Arthur	George Orwell
Blaisdell, Anne	**(Barbara) Elizabeth Linington**
Blake, Nicholas	**C. Day Lewis**
Bland, E.	**E. Nesbit**
Bland, Fabian	**E. Nesbit**
Bleeck, Oliver	**Ross Thomas**
Bliss, Reginald	**H. G. Wells**
Blixen, Karen	Pierre Andrezel; Isak Dinesen; Osceola
Block, Lawrence	Lesley Evans; Chip Harrison; Sheldon Lord; Andrew Shaw (and God only knows how many more—Block won't say how many pseudonyms he uses)
Blood, Matthew	**Davis Dresser** (with **Ryerson Johnson**)
Blunden, Edmund	E.C.B.
Boston, Charles K.	**Frank Gruber**
Boucher, Anthony	**William Anthony Parker White**
Bowen, Marjorie	George R. Preedy; Joseph Shearing
Box, Edgar	**Gore Vidal**
Boyd, Nancy	**Edna St. Vincent Millay**
Boyle, Kay	Mrs. Laurence Vail
Boz	**Charles Dickens**
Bradbury, E. P.	**Michael Moorcock**
Bradley, Marion Zimmer	Lee Chapman; Miriam Gardner
Bramah, Ernest	**Ernest Bramah Smith**
Brand, Christianna	**Mary Christianna Lewis**
Brand, Max	**Frederick Faust**
Brawner, Helen	Geoffrey Coffin (with **F. Van Wyck Mason**)
Brenan, Gerald	George Beaton
Bright, Mary Chavelita (Dunne)	George Egerton
Brock, Rose	**Joseph Hansen**

Brontë, Ann	Acton Bell
Brontë, Charlotte	Currer Bell
Brontë, Emily	Ellis Bell
Brown, Frederic	Felix Graham
Brown, Zenith Jones	Leslie Ford; David Frome
Bruce, Leo	**Rupert Croft-Cooke**
Brunner, John	Gill Hunt
Bryan, Michael	**Brian Moore**
Buchanan, Eileen-Marie Duell	Clare Curzon; Rhona Petrie
Buck, Pearl S.	John Sedges
Burgess, Anthony	**John Anthony Burgess Wilson**
Burgess, Trevor	**Elleston Trevor**
Burke, Leda	**David Garnett**
Burn, Tex	**Louis L'Amour**
Burnett, W. R.	James Updyke; John Monahan
Burroughs, William	William Lee
Burton, Miles	**Cecil John Charles Street**
Butler, Gwendoline	Jennie Melville
Butler, Richard	**Ted Allbeury**
Butler, Walter C.	**Frederick Faust**
Butler, William Vivian	J. J. Marric (continuation of series originally written by **John Creasey**)
Bynner, Witter	Emanuel Morgan
Cain, Paul	**George Sims**
Campbell, R. T.	**Ruthven Todd**
Campbell, William Edward March	William March
Canning, Victor	Alan Gould
Cannon, Curt	**Evan Hunter**
Carco, Francis	**Jean Rhys**
Carr, Christopher	**A. C. Benson**
Carr, John Dickson	Carr Dickson; Carter Dickson; Roger Fairbairn; Torquemada
Carroll, Lewis	**Charles Lutwidge Dodgson**
Carter, Nick	**Dennis Lynds; Martin Cruz Smith**
Cary, Arthur	Joyce Cary
Cary, Joyce	**Arthur Cary**
Cauldwell, Frank	**Francis King**
Cawthorn, Jim	Desmond Reid (with **Michael Moorcock**)
Challis, George	**Frederick Faust**
Chapman, Lee	**Marion Zimmer Bradley**
Charles, Will	**Charles Willeford**
Charteris, Leslie	**Leslie C.B. Lin**
Chaucer, Daniel	**Ford Madox Ford**
Chester, Miss Di	**Dorothy Sayers**
Christie, Agatha	Mary Westmacott
Clark, Alfred A. G.	Cyril Hare
Clark, Curt	**Donald Westlake**
Claude	**Claude Durrell**
Clemens, Samuel Langhorne	Mark Twain

Clement, Hal	**Harry Clement Stubbs**
Clerihew, E.	**E. C. Bentley**
Clerk, N. W.	**C. S. Lewis**
Coe, Tucker	**Donald Westlake**
Coffey, Brian	**Dean R. Koontz**
Coffin, Geoffrey	**F. Van Wyck Mason** (with **Helen Brawner**)
Coffin, Peter	**Jonathan Latimer**
Coleman, Emmett	**Ishmael Reed**
Coles, Cyril H.	Manning Coles (with **Adelaide Manning**); Francis Gaite
Coles, Manning	**Adelaide Manning** and **Cyril H. Coles**
Collins, Hunt	**Evan Hunter**
Collins, Michael	**Dennis Lynds**
Colton, James	**Joseph Hansen**
Colvin, James	**Michael Moorcock**
Conrad, Joseph	**Theodor Jósef Konrad Korzeniowski**
Cook, John Estes	**L. Frank Baum**
Cooper, James Fenimore	Jane Morgan
Cooper, William	H. S. Hoff
Cornwell, David J.M.	John le Carré
Corvo, Baron	**Frederick William Rolfe**
Costler, A.	**Arthur Koestler**
Coward, Noel	Hernia Whittlebot
Cox, William Trevor	William Trevor
Cozzens, Frederick S.	Richard Haywarde
Craig, A.A.	**Poul Anderson**
Crane, Stephen	Johnston Smith
Crayon, Geoffrey	**Washington Irving**
Creasey, John	Gordon Ashe; Norman Deane; Robert Caine Frazer; Michael Halliday; Kyle Hunt; Peter Manton; J. J. Marric; Richard Martin; Anthony Morton; Ken Ranger; William K. Reilley; Tex Riley; Jeremy York
Crews, Judson	Mason Jordon Mason
Creyton, Paul	**John T. Trowbridge**
Crichton, Michael	Michael Douglas; Jeffrey Hudson; John Lange
Crispin, Edmund	**Robert Bruce Montgomery**
Croft-Cooke, Rupert	Leo Bruce
Cross, Amanda	**Carolyn Gold Heilbrun**
Crowe, John	**Dennis Lynds**
Crowfield, Christopher	**Harriet Beecher Stowe**
Crowley, Aleister	Leo Vincey
Culver, Kathryn	**Davis Dresser**
Culver, Timothy J.	**Donald Westlake**
Cummings, Bruce Frederick	W.N.P. Barbellion
Cunningham, E. V.	**Howard Fast**
Curzon, Clare	**Eileen-Marie Duell Buchanan**
D., H.	**Hilda Doolittle**
Dale, George E.	**Isaac Asimov**

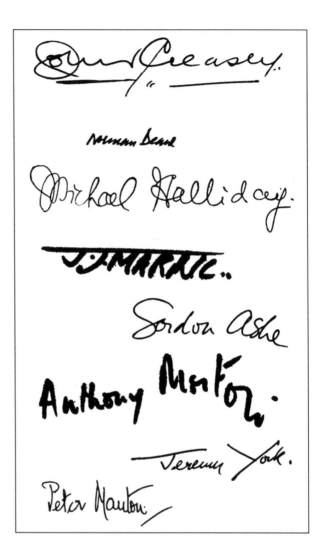

Dana, Freeman	**Phoebe Atwood Taylor**
Dannay, Frederic	Ellery Queen; Barnaby Ross (both
	with **Manfred B. Lee**); Daniel Nathan
Davidson, Lawrence H.	**D. H. Lawrence**
Daviot, Gordon	**Elizabeth Mackintosh**
Davis, Don	**Davis Dresser**
Davis, Gordon	**Howard Hunt**
Day-Lewis, Cecil	Nicholas Blake
de la Mare, Walter	Walter Ramal
DeLillo, Don	Cleo Birdwell
Deane, Norman	**John Creasey**
Debrett, Hal	**Davis Dresser**
Deghy, Guy	Herald Froy; Lee Gibb (both with
	Keith Waterhouse)

Delacorta

Daniel Odier

Derleth, August

Stephen Grendon; Eldon Heath; Tally Mason

De Voto, Bernard

John August

Dickens, Charles

Boz

Dickson, Carr

John Dickson Carr

Dickson, Carter

John Dickson Carr

Dietrich, Robert

Howard Hunt

Dinesen, Isak

Karen Blixen

Dodge, Mary Abigail

Gail Hamilton

Dodgson, Charles Lutwidge

Lewis Carroll

Dominic, R. B.

M. Latsis and **M. Henissart**

Donovan, Dick

Joyce E.P. Muddock

Dooley, Mr.

Finley Peter Dunne

Doolittle, Hilda

H.D.; John Helforth

Douglas, Ellen

Josephine Haxton

Douglas, Michael

Michael Crichton

Douglas, Norman

Normyx

Downes, Quentin

Michael Harrison

Doyle, John

Robert Graves

Dresser, Davis

Asa Baker; Matthew Blood (with **Ryerson Johnson**); Kathryn Culver; Don Davis; Hal Debrett; Brett Halliday; Anthony Scott; Anderson Wayne

Drinan, Adam

Joseph MacLeod

Dudley-Smith, T.

Elleston Trevor

Duke, Will

Wm. Campbell Gault

Dunne, Finley Peter

Mr. Dooley

Dunne, Mary Chavelita
(married name **Bright**)

George Egerton

Dunsany, Lord (title)

Edward John M. Drax Plunkett

Durrell, Claude

Claude

Durrell, Lawrence

Charles Norden

Dwyer, Deanna

Dean R. Koontz

Dwyer, K. R.

Dean R. Koontz

E., A.

George Russell

Earle, William

W. E. John

Early, Jon

W. E. John

Eddy, Mary Baker

Mary Baker Glover (first marriage)

Egerton, George

Mary Chavelita Dunne (married name **Bright**)

Eisner, Simon

Cyril M. Kornbluth

Ellison, Harlan

Paul Merchant

Engelhardt, Frederick

L. Ron Hubbard

Epernay, Mary

Kenneth Galbraith

Ericson, Walter

Howard Fast

Esse, James

James Stephens

Evans, Evan

Frederick Faust

Evans, Lesley

Lawrence Block

Evans, Margiad

Peggy Whistler

Everson, William	Brother Antoninus (Dominican lay brother, 1951–69)
Ewing, Frederick R.	Theodore Sturgeon
F, Inspector	William Russell
F., M.T.	Katherine Anne Porter
Fair, A. A.	Erle Stanley Gardner
Fairbairn, Roger	John Dickson Carr
Farjeon, Eleanor	Tom Fool
Farmer, Philip José	Kilgore Trout
Farrell, James T.	Jonathan Titulesco Fogarty
Farren, Richard M.	John Betjeman
Fast, Howard	E. V. Cunningham; Walter Ericson
Faulkner, William	Ernest V. Trueblood
Faust, Frederick	George Owen Baxter; Max Brand; Walter C. Butler; George Challis; Evan Evans; John Frederick; Frederick Frost; David Manning; Peter Henry Morland
Feikema, Feike	Frederick Manfred
Feinstein, Isidor	I. F. Stone
Ferguson, Helen	Helen Woods
Field, Gans T.	Manly Wade Wellman
Fielding, Gabriel	Alan Barnsley
Finney, Jack	Walter B. Finney
Finney, Walter B.	Jack Finney
Fips, Mohammed Ulysses Socrates	Hugo Gernsback
Fish, Robert L.	Robert L. Pike
Fisher, M.F.K.	Victoria Berne (with Dillwyn Parrish)
Flapdoodle, Phineas	Henry Miller
Fleming, Oliver	Philip MacDonald
Fogarty, Jonathan Titulesco	James T. Farrell
Follett, Ken	Simon Myles; Zachary Stone
Fool, Tom	Eleanor Farjeon
Ford, Ford Madox (legal name change)	Ford Madox Hueffer; Daniel Chaucer; Fenil Haig
Ford, Leslie	Zenith Jones Brown
Forester, Frank	Henry William Herbert
Forrest, Felix C.	Paul Linebarger
Frazer, Robert Caine	John Creasey
Frederick, John	Frederick Faust
Freedgood, Morton	John Godey; Stanley Morton
Freeman, R. Austin	Clifford Ashdown (with John James Pitcairn)
French, Paul	Isaac Asimov
Frome, David	Zenith Jones Brown
Frost, Frederick	Frederick Faust
Froy, Herald	Keith Waterhouse (with Guy Deghy)
Fuller, Henry Blake	Stanton Page

Gaite, Francis	**Cyril H. Coles**
Galbraith, Kenneth	Mark Epernay
Galsworthy, John	John Sinjohn
Galt, Walter	**Talbot Mundy**
Gardner, Erle Stanley	A. A. Fair; Carleton Kendrake
Gardner, Miriam	**Marion Zimmer Bradley**
Garnett, David	Leda Burke
Garrett, Randall	Robert Randall (with **Robert Silverberg**)
Garth, Will	**Henry Kuttner**
Garve, Andrew	**Paul Winterton**
Gash, Jonathan	Graham Gaunt
Gashbuck, Greno	**Hugo Gernsback**
Gault, William Campbell	Will Duke
Gaunt, Graham	**Jonathan Gash**
Gawsworth, John	**Terence Ian Fytton Armstrong**
Geisel, Theodor Seuss	Dr. Seuss
Gernsback, Hugo	Grego Barshuck; Mohammed U.S. Fips; Greno Gashbuck; Gus N. Habergock
Gibb, Lee	**Keith Waterhouse** (with **Guy Deghy**)
Gibson, Walter	Maxwell Grant
Gibson, Walter B.	Maxwell Grant
Glover, Mary Baker (first marriage)	**Mary Baker Eddy**
Godey, John	**Morton Freedgood**
Goldman, William	S. Morgenstern; Harry Longbaugh
Goldsmith, Oliver	James Willington
Goodrich, S. G.	Peter Parley
Gopaleen, Myles Na	**Brian O'Nolan**
Gorey, Edward	Ogdred Weary
Gottschalk, Laura (first married name; later **Laura Jackson**)	**Laura Riding**
Gould, Alan	**Victor Canning**
Graham, Felix	**Frederic Brown**
Graham, James	**Jack Higgins**
Graham, John	**David Graham Phillips**
Graham, Tom	**Sinclair Lewis**
Grainger, Francis Edward	Headon Hill
Grant, Maxwell	**Dennis B. Lynds**
Grant, Maxwell	**Walter B. Gibson**
Grantland, Keith	**Charles Nutt**
Graves, Robert	John Doyle; (ghostwriter for) **Frank Richards;** Barbara Rich (with **Laura Riding**)
Green, Hannah	**Joanne Greenburg**
Green, Henry	**Henry Vincent Yorke**
Greenburg, Joanne	Hannah Green
Gregory, J. Dennis	**John A. Williams**
Grendon, Stephen	**August Derleth**

Gribben, William L.
Grieve, C. M.
Grile, Dod
Gruber, Frank

Guthrie, Thomas Anstey

H., H.
Habergock, Gus N.
Haig, Fenil
Haines, William
Hale, Edward Everett
Hall, Adam
Halliday, Brett
Halliday, Michael
Hamilton, Clive
Hamilton, Gail
Hannon, Ezra
Hansen, Joseph
Harbage, Alfred B.
Hare, Cyril
Harris, Johnson
Harris, John Wyndham
   Parkes Lucas Beynon
Harrison, Chip
Harrison, Michael
Haxton, Josephine
Haywarde, Richard
Heath, Eldon
Heilbrun, Carolyn Gold
Heinlein, Robert A.
Helforth, John
Henissart, Martha

Henry, Edgar
Henry, O.
Herbert, Henry William
Herman, William
Hext, Harrington
Heyen, William
Heyer, Georgette
Hibbert, Elizabeth Alice
Higgins, Jack
Highsmith, Patricia
Hill, Headon
Hill, John
Hill, Reginald
Hilton, James
Hirschfield, Magnus
Hoff, H. S.

Talbot Mundy
Hugh Mac (or Mc or M') Diarmid
Ambrose Bierce
Stephen Acre; Charles K. Boston;
   John K. Vedder
F. Anstey

Helen Hunt Jackson
Hugo Gernsback
Ford Madox Ford
William Heyen
Frederic Ingham
Elleston Trevor
Davis Dresser
John Creasey
C. S. Lewis
Mary Abigail Dodge
Evan Hunter
Rose Brock; James Colton
Thomas Kyd
Alfred A.G. Clark
John Wyndham P.L.B. Harris
John Beynon; Johnson Harris; Lucas
   Parkes; John Wyndham
Lawrence Block
Quentin Downes
Ellen Douglas
Frederick S. Cozzens
August Derleth
Amanda Cross
Simon York
Hilda Doolittle
R. B. Dominic; Emma Lathen (with
   M. Latsis)
Albion W. Tourgée
William Sydney Porter
Frank Forester
Ambrose Bierce
Eden Phillpotts
William Haines
Mrs. George R. Rougier
Jean Plaidy
James Graham; Harry Patterson
Claire Morgan
Francis Edward Grainger
Dean R. Koontz
Patrick Ruell
Glen Trevor
Arthur Koestler
William Cooper

Holmes, H. H.	William Anthony Parker White
Holmes, Raymond	Raymond Souster
Holt, Samuel	Donald Westlake
Honeyman, William C.	James McGovan
Hooker, Richard	**H. Richard Hornberger**
Hopley, George	**Cornell Woolrich**
Hornberger, H. Richard	Richard Hooker
Houdini, Harry	**Ehrich Weiss**
Houghton, Claude	**Claude Houghton Oldfield**
Howard, Robert E.	Sam Walser
Hubbard, L. Ron	Frederick Engelhardt; René Lafayette
Hudson, Jeffrey	**Michael Crichton**
Hudson, Stephen	**Sydney Schiff**
Hueffer, Ford Madox	**Ford Madox Ford** (legal name change)
Hunt, Gill	**John Brunner**
Hunt, Howard	John Baxter; Gordon Davis; Robert Dietrich; David St. John
Hunt, Kyle	**John Creasey**
Hunter, Evan (born Salvatore Lombino)	John Abbott; Curt Cannon; Hunt Collins; Ezra Hannon; Richard Marsten; Ed McBain
Huntley, Lydia	**Lydia Sigourney**
Iles, Francis	**Anthony Berkeley**
Ingham, Frederic	**Edward Everett Hale**
Innes, Michael	**John Innes M. Stewart**
Inspector F	**William Russell**
Irish, William	**Cornell Woolrich**
Iron, Ralph	**Olive Schreiner**
Irving, Washington	Geoffrey Crayon; Diedrich Knickerbocker; Launcelot Langstaff
Jackson, Helen Hunt	H.H.
Jackson, Laura (second marriage)	**Laura Riding** (maiden name); **Laura Gottschalk** (first marriage)
Jakes, John	Alan Payne; Jay Scotland
John, W. E.	William Earle; Jon Early
Johnson, Benj. F.	**James Whitcomb Riley**
Johnson, Ryerson	Matthew Blood (with **Davis Dresser**)
Jones, Edith Newbold (maiden name)	**Edith Wharton**
Jones, James Athearn	Matthew Murgatroyd
Jones, Leroi	**Imamu Amiri Baraka** (legal name change)
Judd, Cyril	**Cyril M. Kornbluth**
K., R.A.	**Ronald Knox**
Kain, Saul	**Siegfried Sassoon**
Kaler, Otis J.	James Otis
Karageorge, Michael	**Poul Anderson**
Kavan, Anna	**Helen Woods**

Kavanagh, Dan | **Julian Barnes**
Kell, Joseph | **John Anthony Burgess Wilson**
Kelley, Martha | Q. Patrick (with **Richard W. Webb**)
Kelly, Patrick | **Ted Allbeury**
Kendrake, Carleton | **Erle Stanley Gardner**
Kerr, Ben | **William Ard**
King, Francis | Frank Cauldwell
King, Stephen | Richard Bachman
Kingsmill, Hugh | Hugh Lunn
Knickerbocker, Diedrich | **Washington Irving**
Knight, Clifford | Reynolds Knight
Knight, Reynolds | **Clifford Knight**
Knox, Ronald | R.A.K.
Koestler, Arthur | A. Costler; Magnus Hirschfield
Koontz, Dean R. | David Axton; Brian Coffey; Deanna Dwyer; K. R. Dwyer; John Hill; Leigh Nichols; Anthony North; Richard Paige; Owen West; Aaron Wolfe
Kornbluth, Cyril M. | Simon Eisner; Cyril Judd (with Judith Merril); Jordan Park
Korzeniowski, Theodor Jósef Konrad | Joseph Conrad
Kosinski, Jerzy | Joseph Novak
Kurnitz, Harry | Marco Page
Kuttner, Henry | Will Garth; Lewis Padgett (and many others with **C. L. Moore**)
Kyd, Thomas | **Alfred B. Harbage**
Kyle, Robert | **Robert Terrall**
Lafayette, René | **L. Ron Hubbard**
L'Amour, Louis | Tex Burn
Lange, John | **Michael Crichton**
Langstaff, Launcelot | **Washington Irving**
Lathen, Emma | **M. Latsis** and **M. Henissart**
Latimer, Jonathan | Peter Coffin
Latsis, Mary J. | R. B. Dominic; Emma Lathen (both with **M. Henissart**)
Lawless, Anthony | **Philip MacDonald**
Lawrence, D. H. | Lawrence H. Davidson
Lawrence, T. E. | J. H. Ross; L. H. Ross; T. E. Shaw
Lear, Peter | **Peter Lovesey**
le Carré, John | **David J.M. Cornwell**
Lee, Andrew | **Louis Auchincloss**
Lee, Manfred B. | Ellery Queen; Barnaby Ross (both with **Frederic Dannay**)
Lee, William | **William Burroughs**
Lemke, Henry E. | **Richard Tooker**
Lessing, Doris | Jane Somers
Lewis, C. S. | N. W. Clerk; Clive Hamilton

Lewis, Mary Christianna	Christianna Brand
Lewis, Sinclair	Tom Graham
Lin, Frank	**Gertrude Atherton**
Lin, Leslie C.B.	Leslie Charteris
Linebarger, Paul	Felix C. Forrest; Cordwainer Smith
Linington, (Barbara) Elizabeth	Anne Blaisdell; Dell Shannon
Locke, David Ross	Petroleum V. Nasby
Logan, Jake	**Martin Cruz Smith**
Longbaugh, Harry	**William Goldman**
Lord, Sheldon	**Lawrence Block**
Lothrup, Harriet Mulford Stone	Margaret Sidney
Lovecraft, H. P.	Lewis Thoebold, Jr.
Lovesey, Peter	Peter Lear
Lucas, Victoria	**Sylvia Plath**
Ludlum, Robert	Jonathan Ryder; Michael Shepherd
Lunn, Hugh	**Hugh Kingsmill**
Lynds, Dennis	William Arden; Nick Carter; Michael Collins; John Crowe; Maxwell Grant; Mark Sadler
Lyre, Pynchbeck	**Siegfried Sassoon**
M., S.W.	**S. Weir Mitchell**
Mac (or Mc or M') Diarmid, Hugh	**C. M. Grieve**
Macdonald, John (and John Ross)	**Kenneth Millar**
MacDonald, Phillip	Oliver Fleming; Anthony Lawless; Martin Porlock
Macdonald, Ross	**Kenneth Millar**
Machen, Arthur	Leolinus Siluriensis
Mackin, Edward	**Ralph McInerny**
Mackintosh, Elizabeth	Gordon Daviot; Josephine Tey
MacLeod, Fiona	**William Sharp**
MacLeod, Joseph	Adam Drinan
Madge, Kathleen	**Kathleen Raine**
Manfred, Frederick	Feike Feikema
Manning, Adelaide	Manning Coles (with **Cyril H. Coles**)
Manning, David	**Frederick Faust**
Manton, Peter	**John Creasey**
Mara, Bernard	**Brian Moore**
March, Maxwell	**Margery Allingham**
March, William	**William Edward March Campbell**
Markham, Robert	**Kingsley Amis**
Marric, J. J.	**John Creasey** (series later written by **William Vivian Butler**)
Marsten, Richard	**Evan Hunter**
Martin, Richard	**John Creasey**
Marvil, Ik	**Donald Grant Mitchell**
Mason, F. Van Wyck	Geoffrey Coffin (with **Helen Brawner**); Frank W. Mason; Ward Weaver
Mason, Frank W.	**F. Van Wyck Mason**
Mason, Mason Jordon	**Judson Crews**

Mason, Tally	**August Derleth**
Matheson, Richard	Logan Swanson
McBain, Ed	**Evan Hunter**
McGivern, William Peter	Bill Peters
McGovan, James	**William C. Honeyman**
McInerny, Ralph	Edward Mackin; Monica Quill
McNeile, Herman C.	Sapper
Melville, Jennie	**Gwendoline Butler**
Merchant, Paul	**Harlan Ellison**
Mertz, Barbara G.	Barbara Michaels; Elizabeth Peters
Meynell, Alice	A. C. Thompson
Michaels, Barbara	**Barbara G. Mertz**
Michaelson, John Nairne	**Maxwell Anderson**
Middleton, Arthur	**Edward J. O'Brien**
Millar, Kenneth	John Macdonald; John Ross
	Macdonald; Ross Macdonald
Millay, Edna St. Vincent	Nancy Boyd
Miller, Henry	Phineas Flapdoodle
Miller, Warren	Amanda Vail
Mitchell, Donald Grant	Ik Marvil
Mitchell, S. Weir	S.W. M.
Monahan, John	**W. R. Burnett**
Montgomery, Robert Bruce	Edmund Crispin
Moorcock, Michael	Bill Barclay; E. P. Bradbury; James Colvin;
	Desmond Reid (with **Jim Cawthorn**)
Moore, Brian	Michael Bryan; Bernard Mara
Moore, Catherine Lucille	Lewis Padgett (with **Henry Kuttner**)
Moore, Edward	**Edwin Muir**
Moran, Mike	**William Ard**
Morecamp, Arthur	**Thomas Pilgrim**
Morgan, Claire	**Patricia Highsmith**
Morgan, Emanuel	**Witter Bynner**
Morgan, Jane	**James Fenimore Cooper**
Morgenstern, S.	**William Goldman**
Morland, Peter Henry	**Frederick Faust**
Morris, Julian	**Morris West**
Morton, Anthony	**John Creasey**
Morton, Stanley	**Morton Freedgood**
Muddock, Joyce E.P.	Dick Donovan
Muir, Edwin	Edward Moore
Mundy, Talbot	Walter Galt; William L. Gribben
Munro, Hector Hugh	Saki
Murgatroyd, Matthew	**James Athearn Jones**
Myles, Simon	**Ken Follett**
Nabokoff-Sirin, V.	**Vladimir Nabokov**
Nabokov, Vladimir	V. Nabokoff-Sirin; V. Sirin
Nasby, Petroleum V.	**David Ross Locke**
Nathan, Daniel	**Frederic Dannay**
Nesbit, E.	E. Bland; Fabian Bland

Nichols, Leigh	**Dean R. Koontz**
Norden, Charles	**Lawrence Durrell**
Normyx	**Norman Douglas**
North, Andrew	**Alice Mary Norton**
North, Anthony	**Dean R. Koontz**
Norton, Alice Mary	Andrew North; Andre Norton; Allen Weston (with **Grace Allen**)
Norton, André	**Alice Mary Norton**
Norway, Nevil Shute	Nevil Shute
Novak, Joseph	**Jerzy Kosinski**
Nutt, Charles	Charles Beaumont; Keith Grantland
Oates, Joyce Carol	Rosamond Smith
O'Brien, Edward J.	Arthur Middleton
O'Brien, Flann	**Brian O'Nolan**
O'Casey, Sean	P. O'Cathasaigh
O'Cathasaigh, P.	**Sean O'Casey**
O'Connor, Frank	**Michael O'Donovan**
Odier, Daniel	Delacorta
O'Donovan, Michael	Frank O'Connor
Oldfield, Claude Houghton	Claude Houghton
Oliver, George	Oliver Onions
Onions, Oliver	**George Oliver**
O'Nolan, Brian	Myles Na Gopaleen; Flann O'Brien
Oppenheim, E. Phillips	Anthony Partridge
Optic, Oliver	**William Taylor Adams**
Orwell, George	**Eric Arthur Blair**
Osceola	**Karen Blixen**
Otis, James	**Otis J. Kaler**
Oursler, Fulton	Anthony Abbott
Padgett, Lewis	**C. L. Moore** and **Henry Kuttner**
Page, Marco	**Harry Kurnitz**
Page, Stanton	**Henry Blake Fuller**
Paige, Richard	**Dean R. Koontz**
Palmer, Stuart	Jay Stewart
Pargeter, Edith	Ellis Peters
Park, Jordan	**Cyril M. Kornbluth**
Parkes, Lucas	**John Wyndham P.L.B. Harris**
Parley, Peter	**S. G. Goodrich**
Parrish, Dillwyn	Victoria Berne (with **M.F.K. Fisher**)
Partridge, Anthony	**E. Phillips Oppenheim**
Patrick, Q.	**Richard W. Webb** (alone and with **Martha Kelley**)
Payne, Alan	**John Jakes**
Peck, George W.	Cantell A. Bigby
Pennington, Patience	**Elizabeth Pringle**
Pentecost, Hugh	**Judson Phillips**
Percy, Charles Henry	**Dodie Smith**
Perse, St. John	**Aléxis St. Léger**
Peters, Bill	**William Peter McGivern**

Peters, Curtis Arnoux	Peter Arno
Peters, Elizabeth	**Barbara G. Mertz**
Peters, Ellis	**Edith Pargeter**
Petrie, Rhona	**Eileen-Marie Duell Buchanan**
Phillips, David Graham	John Graham
Phillips, Judson	Hugh Pentecost
Phillpotts, Eden	Harrington Hext
Pike, Robert L.	**Robert L. Fish**
Pilgrim, Thomas	Arthur Morecamp
Pitcairn, John James	Clifford Ashdown (with **R. Austin Freeman**)
Plaidy, Jean	**Elizabeth Alice Hibbert**
Plath, Sylvia	Victoria Lucas
Plunkett, Edward J.M.D.	**Lord Dunsany** (title)
Porlock, Martin	**Philip MacDonald**
Porter, Eleanor H.	Eleanor Stuart
Porter, Katherine Anne	M.T.F.
Porter, William Sydney	O. Henry
Preedy, George R.	**Marjorie Bowen**
Pringle, Elizabeth W.A.	Patience Pennington
Putnam, Arthur Lee	**Horatio Alger**
Q	**Arthur Quiller-Couch**
Queen, Ellery	**Frederic Dannay** and **Manfred B. Lee**
Quentin, Patrick	**Richard W. Webb** and **Hugh C. Wheeler**
Quill, Monica	**Ralph McInerny**
Quiller-Couch, Arthur	Q
Quinn, Martin (and Simon)	**Martin Cruz Smith**
R., C.G.	**Christine G. Rossetti**
Raine, Kathleen	Kathleen Madge
Ramal, Walter	**Walter de la Mare**
Rampling, Anne	**Anne Rice**
Randall, Robert	**Randall Garrett** and **Robert Silverberg**
Randolph, Georgiana Ann	Craig Rice; Daphne Sanders; Michael Venning
Ranger, Ken	**John Creasey**
Rattray, Simon	**Elleston Trevor**
Reed, Eliot	**Eric Ambler** and **Charles Rodda**
Reed, Ishmael	Emmett Coleman
Reid, Desmond	**Michael Moorcock** (with **Jim Cawthorn**)
Reilly, William K.	**John Creasey**
Rendell, Ruth	Barbara Vine
Rhode, John	**Cecil John Charles Street**
Rhys, Jean	Francis Carco
Rice, Anne	Anne Rampling; A. N. Roquelaure
Rice, Craig	**Georgiana Ann Randolph**
Rich, Barbara	**Laura Riding** and **Robert Graves**
Richards, Frank	**Robert Graves** (ghostwriter)
Riding, Laura	**Laura Gottschalk** (first married name; later **Laura Jackson**)
Riley, James Whitcomb	Benj. F. Johnson

Riley, Tex
Robertson, E.
Rodda, Charles
Rohmer, Sax
Rolfe, Frederick William
Roquelaure, A. N.
Ross, Barnaby
Ross, J. H. and L. H.
Rossetti, Christine G.
Rougier, Mrs. George R.
Ruell, Patrick
Ruric, Peter
Russell, George
Russell, William
Ryder, Jonathan

John Creasey
Earle Birney
Eliot Reed (with **Eric Ambler**)
Arthur Henry S. Ward
Baron Corvo
Anne Rice
Frederic Dannay and **Manfred B. Lee**
T. E. Lawrence
C.G.R.
Georgette Heyer
Reginald Hill
George Sims
A.E.
Inspector F; Waters
Robert Ludlum

S., E.W.
S., S.H.
Sadler, Mark
S(ain)t John, David
Saki
Sanders, Daphne
Sanders, W. Franklin
Sanders, Winston P.
Sanford, John
Sapper
Sassoon, Siegfried
St. Léger, Aléxis
Sayers, Dorothy
Scarlett, Susan
Schiff, Sydney
Schreiner, Olive
Scotland, Jay
Scott, Anthony
Scott, Evelyn
Scott, Warwick
Sedges, John
Seuss, Dr.
Shaffer, Anthony
Shaffer, Peter
Shannon, Dell
Shapiro, Julian L.
Sharp, Luke
Sharp, William
Shaw, Andrew
Shaw, T. E.
Shearing, Joseph
Shepherd, Michael
Sherman, E. W.
Shute, Nevil

E. W. Sherman
Siegfried Sassoon
Dennis Lynds
Howard Hunt
Hector Hugh Munro
Georgiana Ann Randolph
Charles Willeford
Poul Anderson
Julian L. Shapiro
Herman C. McNeile
Saul Kain; Pynchbeck Lyre; S.H.S.
St. John Perse
Miss Di Chester
Noel Streatfield
Stephen Hudson
Ralph Iron
John Jakes
Davis Dresser
Ernest Souza
Elleston Trevor
Pearl S. Buck
Theodor Seuss Geisel
Peter Anthony (with **Peter Shaffer**)
Peter Anthony (with **Anthony Shaffer**)
(Barbara) Elizabeth Linington
John Sanford
Robert Barr
Fiona MacLeod
Lawrence Block
T. E. Lawrence
Marjorie Bowen
Robert Ludlum
E.W.S.
Nevil Shute Norway

Sidney, Margaret	Harriet Mulford Stone Lothrup
Sigourney, Lydia	Lydia Huntley
Siluriensis, Leolinus	**Arthur Machen**
Silverberg, Robert	Robert Randall (with **Randall Garrett**)
Sim, Georges	Georges Simenon
Simenon, Georges	**Georges Sim**
Simpson, Harriet	Harriette Arnow
Sims, George	Paul Cain; Peter Ruric
Sinjohn, John	**John Galsworthy**
Sirin, V.	**Vladimir Nabokov**
Smith, Cordwainer	**Paul Linebarger**
Smith, Dodie	C. L. Anthony; Charles Henry Percy
Smith, Ernest Bramah	Ernest Bramah
Smith, Johnston	**Stephen Crane**
Smith, Kate Douglas	Kate Douglas Wiggin
Smith, Martin Cruz	Nick Carter; Jake Logan; Martin Quinn; Simon Quinn
Smith, Rosamond	**Joyce Carol Oates**
Somers, Jane	**Doris Lessing**
Somers, Paul	**Paul Winterton**
Souster, Raymond	Raymond Holmes
Souza, Ernest	**Evelyn Scott**
Spicer, Bart	**Betty Spicer** and **Jay Barbette**
Spicer, Betty	Bart Spicer (with **Jay Barbette**)
Stagge, Jonathan	**Richard W. Webb** and **Hugh Wheeler**
Stairs, Gordon	**Mary H. Austin**
Stark, Richard	**Donald Westlake**
Starr, Julian	**Horatio Alger**
Stein, Aaron Marc	George Bagby; Hampton Stone
Stephens, James	James Esse
Stevens, William Allen (and William Christopher)	**Steve Allen**
Stewart, Jay	**Stuart Palmer**
Stewart, John Innes M.	Michael Innes
Stone, Hampton	**Aaron Marc Stein**
Stone, I. F.	**Isidor Feinstein**
Stone, Zachary	**Ken Follett**
Stowe, Harriet Beecher	**Harriet Beecher** (maiden name); Christopher Crowfield
Streatfield, Noel	Susan Scarlett
Street, Cecil John Charles	Miles Burton; John Rhode
Stuart, Eleanor	**Eleanor H. Porter**
Stubbs, Harry Clement	Hal Clement
Sturgeon, Theodore	Frederick R. Ewing
Swanson, Logan	**Richard Matheson**
Taine, John	**Eric Temple Bell**
Tanner, William	**Kingsley Amis**
Taylor, Phoebe Atwood	Freeman Dana; Alice Tilton
Terrall, Robert	Robert Kyle

Tey, Josephine	**Elizabeth Mackintosh**
Thackeray, William Makepeace	M. A. Titmarsh; Theophile Wagstaff
Theobold, Lewis, Jr.	**H. P. Lovecraft**
Thomas, Ross	Oliver Bleeck
Thompson, A. C.	**Alice Meynell**
Tilton, Alice	**Phoebe Atwood Taylor**
Titmarsh, M. A.	**William Makepeace Thackeray**
Todd, Ruthven	R. T. Campbell
Tooker, Richard	Harry E. Lemke
Torquemada	**John Dickson Carr**
Torsvan, Berick Traven	B. Traven
Tourgée, Albion W.	Edgar Henry
Traven, B.	**Berick Traven Torsvan**
Traver, Robert	**John Donaldson Voelker**
Trevanian	**Rodney Whitaker**
Trevor, Elleston	Mansell Black; Trevor Burgess; T. Dudley-Smith; Adam Hall; Simon Rattray; Warwick Scott
Trevor, Glen	**James Hilton**
Trevor, William	**William Trevor Cox**
Trout, Kilgore	**Philip José Farmer**
Trowbridge, John T.	Paul Creyton
Trueblood, Ernest V.	**William Faulkner**
Twain, Mark	**Samuel Langhorne Clemens**
Updyke, James	**W. R. Burnett**
Vail, Amanda	**Warren Miller**
Vail, Mrs. Laurence	**Kay Boyle**
Van, Melvin	**Melvin Van Peebles**
Van Dine, S. S.	**Willard Huntington Wright**
Van Dyne, Edith	**L. Frank Baum**
Van Peebles, Melvin	Melvin Van
Vedder, John K.	**Frank Gruber**
Venning, Michael	**Georgiana Ann Randolph**
Vidal, Gore	Edgar Box
Vincey, Leo	**Aleister Crowley**
Vine, Barbara	**Ruth Rendell**
Voelker, John Donaldson	Robert Traver
W., E.B.	**E. B. White**
Wade, Henry	**Henry Lancelot Aubrey-Fletcher**
Wagstaff, Theophile	**William Makepeace Thackeray**
Walser, Sam	**Robert E. Howard**
Ward, Arthur Henry S.	Sax Rohmer
Ward, Jonas	**William Ard**
Waterhouse, Keith	Herald Froy; Lee Gibb (both with **Guy Deghy**)
Waters	**William Russell**
Wayne, Anderson	**Davis Dresser**

Weary, Ogdred	**Edward Gorey**
Weaver, Ward	**F. Van Wyck Mason**
Webb, Richard W.	Q. Patrick (alone and with **Martha Kelley**) and others; Patrick Quentin and Jonathan Stagge (with **Hugh Wheeler**)
Weiss, Ehrich	Harry Houdini
Wellman, Manly Wade	Gans T. Field
Wells, Carolyn	Roland Wright
Wells, H. G.	Reginald Bliss
West, Morris	Julian Morris
West, Owen	**Dean R. Koontz**
Westlake, Donald	Curt Clark; Tucker Coe; Timothy J. Culver; Samuel Holt; Alan Marshall; Richard Stark
Westmacott, Mary	**Agatha Christie**
Weston, Allen	**Grace Allen and Alice Mary Norton**
Wharton, Edith	**Edith Newbold Jones** (maiden name)
Wharton, William	**?** (undisclosed)
Wheeler, Hugh Callingham	Patrick Quentin; Jonathan Stagge (both with **Richard W. Webb**)
Whistler, Peggy	**Margiad Evans**
Whitaker, Rodney	Trevanian
White, E. B.	E.B.W.
White, T. H.	James Aston
White, William Anthony Parker	Anthony Boucher; H. H. Holmes
Whittlebot, Hernia	**Noel Coward**
Wiggin, Kate Douglas	**Kate Douglas Smith**
Wilde, Oscar	Fingal O'Flahertie Wills
Willeford, Charles	Will Charles; W. Franklin Sanders
Williams, John A.	J. Dennis Gregory
Willington, James	**Oliver Goldsmith**
Wills, Fingal O'Flahertie	**Oscar Wilde**
Wills, Thomas	**William Ard**
Wilson, John Anthony Burgess	Anthony Burgess; Joseph Kell
Winterton, Paul	Roger Bax; Andrew Garve; Paul Somers
Wolfe, Aaron	**Dean R. Koontz**
Woods, Helen	Helen Ferguson; Anna Kavan
Woolrich, Cornell	George Hopley; William Irish
Wright, Roland	**Carolyn Wells**
Wright, Willard Huntington	S. S. Van Dine
Wyndham, John	**John Wyndham P.L.B. Harris**
York, Jeremy	**John Creasey**
York, Simon	**Robert A. Heinlein**
Yorke, Henry Vincent	Henry Green

Appendix B

Book Dealers

The following is a list of book dealers who issue catalogs, primarily of literary (fiction, poetry, drama, detective, science fiction, etc.) first editions. Also included, when they sent us their catalogs, are those dealers who issue catalogs in other areas of collecting interest. It is certainly not complete, but represents the dealers who keep our name on their mailing lists. The asterisk (*) denotes dealers that are members of the International League of Antiquarian Booksellers (ILAB) through their countries' organizations, and/or the Antiquarian Booksellers' Association of America (ABAA), in the United States.

The ABAA was formed in 1949 to encourage interest in rare books and manuscripts and to maintain the highest standards in the antiquarian book trade. To be a member of the ABAA, the bookseller must have been in business for five years, have a sufficient inventory, maintain a suitable reference library, be sponsored by four current full-time members of the ABAA, and be willing to adhere to the ABAA code of ethics.

To receive a copy of the ABAA Membership Directory—which provides members' addresses, telephone, fax and e-mail, homepage and specialties—call the ABAA headquarters at (212) 944-8291. Leave your postal address on the tape if there is no answer. You can also fax your address to (212) 944-8293, or e-mail the information: abaa@panix.com. You must supply your postal address—the directory is too large to e-mail. The ABAA address is 20 West 44th Street, 4th floor, New York, NY 10036. We highly recommend the ABAA booksellers that are listed in this directory.

About Books, 83 Harbord Street, Toronto, Ontario M5S-1G4, Canada*
Adjala Bookshop, 252 Cottingham Street, Toronto, Ontario M4V-1C6 Canada
Charles Agvent, 291 Linden Road, Mertztown, PA 19539*
Allen and Patricia Ahearn, see Quill & Brush*
Alder Books, 13743 Lakeside Drive, Clarksville, MD 21029
Aldredge Book Shop, 2909 #1A Maple Street, Dallas, TX 75201
Alphabet Bookshop, 145 Main Street West, Port Colborne, Ontario L3K-3V3, Canada*
American Dust Co., 47 Park Court, Staten Island, NY 10301

Am Here Books, P.O. Box 574, Philo, CA 95466

The Americanist, 1525 Shenkel Road, Pottstown, PA 19464*

Ampersand Books, P.O. 674 Cooper Station, New York, NY 10276

Anacapa Books, 3090 Claremont Avenue, Berkeley, CA 94705

Annex Books, 1083 Bathurst Street, Toronto, Ontario M5R-3G8, Canada*

Hugh Anson-Cartwright, 229 College Street, Toronto, Ontario M5T-1R4, Canada*

Antic Hay Rare Books, P.O. Box 2185, Asbury Park, NJ 07712*

Antipodean Books Maps & Prints, P.O. Box 189, Cold Spring, NY 10516*

Any Amount of Books, 62 Charing Cross Road, London WC2H-0BB, United Kingdom

Argosy Book Store, 116 East 59th Street, New York, NY 10022*

Ash Rare Books, 25 Royal Exchange, Threadneedle Street, London EC3V-3LP, United Kingdom

Ashlar Books, P.O. Box 964, Wilder, VT 05088

The Associates, P.O. Box 4747, Falls Church, VA 22044*

Authors of the West, 191 Dogwood Drive, Dundee, OR 97115

Bert Babcock, 9 East Derry Road, P.O. Box 1140, Derry, NH 03038*

The Backlist, P.O. Box 791, Doylestown, PA 18901

Bartleby's Books, P.O. Box 15400, Chevy Chase, MD 20825

Bauman Rare Books, 1215 Locust Street, Philadelphia, PA 19107

Bay Side Books, P.O. Box 57, Soquel, CA 95073

Beasley Books, 1533 West Oakdale, Chicago, IL 60657*

Gordon Beckhorn, 497 Warburton Avenue, Hastings-on-Hudson, NY 10706

Bell, Book & Radmall, 4 Cecil Court, London WC2N-4HE, United Kingdom*

Bella Luna Books, 4697 Stone Canyon Ranch Road, Castle Rock, CO 80104

Steven C. Bernard, 15011 Plainfield Lane, Darnestown, MD 20874*

Between the Covers, 35 W. Maple Avenue, Merchantville, NJ 08109*

Biblioctopus, 2142 Century Park Lane, Century City, CA 90067*

Bishop of Books, 328 Market Street, P.O. Box 579, Steubenville, OH 43952

Black-Bird Books, 24 Grampion Gardens, London NW2-1JG, United Kingdom

Black Sun Books, 157 East 57th Street, New York, NY 10022*

Blackwell's Rare Books, 38 Holywell Street, Oxford OX1-3SW, United Kingdom*

Blue Mountain Books and Manuscripts, Ltd., P.O. Box 363, Catskill, NY 12414

Bolerium Books, 2141 Mission Street, #300, San Francisco, CA 94110*

Nelson Bond, 4724 Easthill Drive, Sugarloaf Farms, Roanoke, VA 24018*

The Book Block, P.O. Box 11090, Greenwich, CT 06831*

The Book Shelf, 1308 Sussex Lane, Newport Beach, CA 92660

Bookpress, Box KP, Williamsburg, VA 23187*

Books & Autographs, 287 Goodwin Road, Eliot, ME 03903*

Books Etc., 298 Fourth Avenue, #395, San Francisco, CA 94118

Books West Southwest, 2452 North Campbell Avenue, Tucson, AZ 85719

The Bookshop, 400 West Franklin Street, Chapel Hill, NC 27516

Boston Book Company & Book Annex, 705 Centre Avenue, Jamaica Plain, MA 02130*

Bowie & Company, 314 First Avenue South, Seattle, WN 98104*

Marilyn Braiterman, 20 Whitfield Road, Baltimore, MD 21210*

The Brick Row Bookshop, 49 Geary Street, Suite 235, San Francisco, CA 94108*

Bromer Booksellers, 607 Boylston Street, Boston, MA 02116*

Bromlea & Jonkers Rare Books, 24 Hart Street, Henley on Thames, Oxfordshire, United Kingdom RG9 2AU*

Brunswick Press, P.O. Box 2244, Cathedral City, CA 92235

Buckingham Books, 8058 Stone Bridge Road, Greencastle, PA 17225
Buddenbrooks, 31 Newbury Street, Boston, MA 02116*
Burke's Book Store, 1719 Poplar Avenue, Memphis, TN 38104
Nicholas and Helen Burrows, 32 Woodlands Avenue, New Malden, Sussex KT3 3UQ, United Kingdom
Harold M. Burstein & Company, 36 Riverside Drive, Waltham, MA 02154*
By the Way Books, P.O. Box 255869, Sacramento, CA 95865
Andrew Cahan, 3000 Blueberry Lane, Chapel Hill, NC 27516*
Caliban Book Shop, 416 South Craig Street, Pittsburgh, PA 15213*
Caney Booksellers, 1 Cherry Hill Road, Suite 220, Cherry Hill, NJ 08002*
The Captain's Book Shelf, 31 Page Avenue, Asheville, NC 28801*
Cardinal Books, 4010 NE 136th Street, Vancouver, WA 98686
Bev Chaney, Jr., 73 Croton Avenue, Ossining, NY 10562
Chapel Hill Rare Books, P.O. Box 456, Carrboro, NC 27510*
Chloe's Books, P.O. Box 2249, Loomis, CA 95650
Clearwater Books, St. Bartholomew Cottage, Green Hayes, Shipton Gorge, Near Bridport, Dorset DT6 4LU United Kingdom*
Cold Tonnage Books, 22 Kings Lane, Windlesham, Surrey GU20 6JQ, United Kingdom
Conundrum, 679 Mayfield Avenue, Stanford, CA 94305
Cornstalk Bookshop, P.O. 336, Glebe, New South Wales 2037, Australia
Country Lane Books, P.O. Box 47, Collinsville, CT 06022*
N. A. Cournoyer Books, 1194 Bank Street, Ottawa, Ontario K1S-3Y1, Canada
William Cowan Books, Ards Cottage, Connel, Argyll PA37 1PT, Scotland, United Kingdom
Charles Cox, Middle Barn, Colliehole Farm, Changford, Devon TQ13 8DY, United Kingdom
Claude Cox Old and Rare Books, 3 & 5 Silent Street, Ipswich 1P1 1TF, United Kingdom
Cultured Oyster Books, P.O. Box 404 Planetarium Station, New York, NY 10024-0404
James Cummins, 699 Madison Avenue, New York, NY 10021*
L. W. Currey, P.O. Box 187 (Water Street), Elizabethtown, NY 12932*
G. Curwen Books, 1 West 67th Street, #710, New York, NY 10023
D & D Galleries, P.O. Box 8413, Somerville, NJ 08876*
Robert Dagg, 49 Geary Street, Suite 225, San Francisco, CA*
Dalian Books, 81 Albion Drive, London Fields, London E8-4LT, United Kingdom
Tom Davidson, 37-3 Avenue L, Brooklyn, NY 11210
Decline and Fall, P.O. Box 659, Stevens Point, WI 54481
Joseph A. Dermont, 13 Arthur Street, P.O. Box 654, Onset, MA 02558
Detering Book Gallery, 2311 Bissonnet, Houston, TX 77005*
Dinkytown Antiquarian Bookstore, 1316 SE 4th Street, Minneapolis, MN 55414*
John Dinsmore & Associates, 1037 Castleton Way South, Lexington, KY 40517
Thomas Dorn, 10230 Oak Way, Canton, GA 30114
Duga's Books, 610 Aldama Ct., Ocoee, FL 32761
Dunn and Powell, The Hideaway, Bar Harbor, ME 04609-1714
I. D. Edrich, 17 Selsdon Road, Wanstead, London E11-2QF, United Kingdom
Francis Edwards, The Old Cinema, Castle Street, Hay-on-Wye, via Hereford HR2-5DF, United Kingdom
Else Fine Books, P.O. Box 43, Dearborn, MI 48121*
Elsey's Books, 206 19th Avenue, Vero Beach, FL 32962
Estates of Mind, 2175 Shoreward Drive, Great Neck, NY 11021*
Euclid Books, 227 Euclid Street, Santa Monica, CA 90402
The Fine Books Co., 781 E. Snell Road, Rochester, MI 48306*

Fireproof Books, 13598 Oakland Place, Minnetonka, MN 55305

First Folio, 1206 Brentwood, Paris, TX 38242-3804*

Nelson Freck at Second Story Books, 12160 Parklawn Drive, Rockville, MD 20852*

Robert Gavora, 108 South Front Street, P.O. Box 448, Talent, OR 97540*

R. A. Gekoski, 15a Bloomsbury Square, London WC1A-2LP, United Kingdom*

Michael Ginsberg, Box 402, Sharon, MA 02067*

Gloucester Road Bookshop, 123 Gloucester Road, London SW7 4TE, United Kingdom

Thomas A. Goldwasser, 49 Geary Street, Suite 244, San Francisco, CA 94108*

Charles E. Gould, Jr., P.O. Box 543, Kent, CT 06757

Gregor Books, 3407 California Avenue, Seattle, WA 98116*

Hawthorn Books, 7 College Park Drive, Westbury-on-Trym, Bristol BS10-7AN, United Kingdom*

Heirloom Bookstore, P.O. Box 16336, Hooksett, NH 03106

Susan Heller/Pages for Sages, 22611 Halburton Road, Beachwood, OH 44122*

Heritage Bookshop, 8540 Melrose Avenue, Los Angeles, CA 90069*

The Hermitage Bookshop, 290 Filmore Street, Denver, CO 80206-5020*

Historicana, 1200 Edgehill Drive, Burlingame, CA 94010*

Richard L. Hoffman, 420 12th Street, Apt. F3R, Brooklyn, NY 11215

David Holloway, 7430 Grace Street, Springfield, VA 22150

Holly Books, P.O. Box 75, Storrs, CT 06268

David J. Holmes, P.O. Box 548, Collinswood, NJ 08108*

Glenn Horowitz, 19 East 76th Street, Suite 712, New York, NY 10021

George Houle, 7260 Beverly Boulevard, Los Angeles, CA 90036*

John Hudak, 184 Columbia Heights #1D, Brooklyn, NY 11201

Idlewood Rare Books, 6420 West 50 South, Lebanon, IN 46052

In Our Time, P.O. Box 390386, Cambridge, MA 02139

James S. Jaffe, 367 W. Lancaster Avenue, P.O. Box 496, Haverford, PA 19041*

Janus Books, P.O. Box 40787, Tucson, AZ 85717

Jarndyce Antiquarian Books, 46 Great Russell Street, London, WC1B-3PA United Kingdom

Joseph the Provider Books, P.O. Box 90, Santa Barbara, CA 93102*

Priscilla Juvelis, 1166 Massachusetts Avenue, Cambridge, MA 02138*

Katonah Book Scout, 75 Meadow Lane, Katonah, NY 10536

Kemp Booksellers, 5b Vicar Lane, Howden, Goole, East Yorkshire DN14 7BP, United Kingdom

Key West Island Bookstore, 513 Fleming Street, Key West, FL 33040

Kingfisher Books, 124 Caya Avenue, West Hartford, CT 06110

Gerry Kleier, 322 Manhattan Drive, Vallejo, CA 94591

John W. Knott, Jr., 8453 Early Bud Way, Laurel, MD 20707

Ralph Kristiansen, P.O. Box 1309, Boston, MA 02217*

Kubik Fine Books, 3474 Clar-Von Drive, Dayton, OH 45430*

Kugleman & Bent, 3000 East Colfax, Suite 174, Denver, CO 80206

Lakin & Marley Rare Books, P.O. Box 1209, Mill Valley, CA 94942

Lame Duck Books, 355 Boylston Street, Boston, MA 02116*

Larsen Books, Middle Road, Exeter, New South Wales 2579, Australia

James & Mary Laurie, 921 Nicolett Mall, Minneapolis, MN 55402*

John Le Bow, 117 Langford Road, P.O. Box 737, Candia, NH 03034

Leaves of Grass, 2433 Whitmore Lake Road, Ann Arbor, MI 48103*

Lee-Gannon Booksellers, P.O. Box 80516, San Marino, CA 91118

The Legacy Co., P.O. Box 1303, Iowa City, IA 52244

Barry R. Levin, 720 Santa Monica Boulevard, Santa Monica, CA 90401*

Loblolly Books, 2601 College Avenue, #201, Berkeley, CA 04704
Ken Lopez, 51 Huntington Road, Hadley, MA 01035*
Stephen Lupack, 449 Hanover Avenue, S. Meriden, CT 06451
T. N. Luther, P.O. Box 429, Taos, NM 87571
MacDonnell Rare Books, 9307 Glenlake Drive, Austin, TX 78730*
George S. Macmanus Co., 1317 Irving Street, Philadelphia, PA 19017*
Robert A. Madle, 4406 Bestor Drive, Rockville, MD 20853
Maggs Brothers Ltd, 50 Berkeley Square, London, W1X-6EL, United Kingdom*
Magic Lantern Books, 107 Broyles Drive, Johnson City, TN 37601
Main Street Fine Books & Manuscripts, 301 S. Main Street, Galena, IL 61036
Maple Ridge Books, 17 Bristol Sands Crescent, Stouffville, Ontario, L4A 7X4, Canada
Jeff Maser, 1055 Pine Street, #5, Menlo Park, CA 94025
David Mason, 342 Queen Street West, 2nd floor, Toronto, M5V-2A2, Canada*
David Mayou, 82 Gordon Road, London W5 2AR, United Kingdom*
McClintock Books,1454 Sheridan Avenue NE, Warren, OH 44483
McGowan Book Company, P.O. Box 4226, Chapel Hill, NC 27515*
Ian McKelvie, 45 Hertford Road, London N2-9BX, United Kingdom
R. McLaughlin, 1613 Monterey Drive, Livermore, CA 94550
Ming Books, 10 Harcran House, Gibbs Couch, Carpenders Park, Watford, Herts WD1 5EZ,
  United Kingdom
George Robert Minkoff, 26 Rowe Road, Alford, MA 01230*
Hartley Moorhouse Books, 10 Ashchurch Terrace, London W12 9SL, United Kingdom
Mordida Books, P.O. Box 79322, Houston, TX 77279
Howard S. Mott, 170 South Main Street, P.O. Box 309, Sheffield, MA 02157*
Mysterious Bookshop, 129 W. 56th Street, New York, NY 10019
Mystery & Imagination Bookshop, 238 N. Brand Boulevard, Glendale, CA 91203
Nineteenth Century Shop, 1047 Hollins Street, Baltimore, MD 21223
Nouveau, P.O. Box 12471, 5005 Meadow Oaks Park Drive, Jackson, MS 39211
Oak Knoll Books, 310 Delaware Street, New Castle, DE 19720*
Old New York Book Shop, 660 Spindlewick Drive, Atlanta, GA 30350*
The Old Paperphiles, P.O. Box 135, Tiverton, RI 02878
Jan and George O'Nale, Route 2, Box 1293, New Castle, VA 24127
David L. O'Neal, 234 Clarenden Street, Boston, MA 02116*
James F. O'Neil, 160 Commonwealth Avenue, #521, Boston, MA 02116
Orpheus Books, 11522 NE 20th Street, Bellevue, WA 98004
Out of Atlanta, 1036 Eulalia Road, Atlanta, GA 30319
Parnassus Books, 3707 Fifth Avenue, #337, San Diego, CA 92103
James Pepper Rare Books, 2026 Cliff Drive, Suite 224, Santa Barbara, CA 93109*
Lee Perron Fine Books, 2125 Siesta Lane, Santa Rosa, CA 95404
R. & A. Petrilla, P.O. Box 306, Roosevelt, NJ 08555
Phoenix Bookshop South, P.O. Box 1018, St. Michaels, MD 21663
James M. Pickard, Pendragon, 21 Grenfell Road, Leicester LE2-2PA, United Kingdom
Philip J. Pirages, P.O. Box 504, 2205 Nut Tree Lane, McMinnville, OR 97128*
Polyanthos Books, 600 Park Avenue, P.O. Box 343, Huntington, NY 11743
Nicholas Pounder's Bookshop, P.O. Box 451, Kings Cross, New South Wales, 2011, Australia*
John William Pye, 79 Hollis Street, Brocton, MA 02402
Quill & Brush, 1137 Sugarloaf Mountain Road, Dickerson, MD 20842*
Paul Rassam, Flat 5, 18 East Heath Road, London NW3-1AJ, United Kingdom*
Red Snapper Books, 17 Ethelbert Close, Bromley, Kent RB1-1JR, United Kingdom
David Rees, 18A Prentis Road, London SW16-1QD, United Kingdom

William Reese Co., 409 Temple Street, New Haven, CT 06511*

Jo Ann Reisler, Ltd., 360 Glyndon Street N.E., Vienna, VA 22180*

L. & T. Respess Books, P.O. Box 1604, Charlottesville, VA 22902*

Revere Books, P.O. Box 420, Revere, PA 18953

Ridge Books, P.O. Box 58, Stone Ridge, New York, NY 12484

Alice Robbins, 3002 Roundhill Road, Greensboro, NC 27408

Robert Frost Books, P.O. Box 719, Rensselaer, NY 12144

Bertram Rota, 31 Long Acre, Covent Garden, London WC2E-9LT, United Kingdom*

The Rue Morgue, P.O. Box 4119, 946 Pearl Street, Boulder, CO 80306

Rulon-Miller Books, 400 Summit Avenue, St. Paul, MN 55102*

Rykken and Scull, P.O. Box 1979, Guerneville, CA 95446*

Sawtooth Booksellers, 5004 Lake's Edge Place, Boise, ID 83703

Bud Schweska, P.O. Box 1222, Port Washington, NY 11050

Andrew Sclanders, 11 Albany Road, Stroud Green, London N4-4RR, United Kingdom

Second Life Books, P.O. Box 242, 55 Quarry Road, Lanesborough, MA 01237*

Second Story Books, 12160 Parklawn Drive, Rockville, MD 20852*

Serendipity Books, 1201 University Ave., Berkeley, CA 94702*

Sherwood Fine Books, 5911 East Spring Street, Suite 402, Long Beach, CA 90808

Anthony Sillem, 9 Tackleway, Old Town, Hastings, East Sussex TN34-3DE, United Kingdom

Ralph Bruno Sipper, 10 West Micheltorena, Santa Barbara, CA 93101*

Skyline Books, P.O. Box T, Forest Knolls, CA 94933*

Ed Smith Books, 20 Paget Road, Madison, WI 53704*

Southern First Editions, P.O. Box 50192, Columbia, SC 29250

Monroe Stahr Books, 4420 Ventura Canyon Avenue, #2, Sherman Oaks, CA 91423

Peter L. Stern & Co., Inc., 355 Boylston Street, 2nd Floor, Boston, MA 02116*

Summer & Stillman, P.O. Box 973, Yarmouth, ME 04096*

Sylvester & Orphanos, 2484 Cheremoya Avenue, P.O. Box 2567, Los Angeles, CA 90078-2567

A Tale of Two Sisters, 2509 Stone Hollow Drive, Bedford, TX 76021

Tall Tales, 2141 Mission Street, Suite 301, San Francisco, CA 94110

Tamerlane Books, P.O. Box C, Havertown, PA 19083*

Taugher Books, 2550 Somerset Drive, Belmont, CA 94002-2926

Robert Temple, 65 Mildway Road, London N1-4PU, United Kingdom

Steven Temple Books, 489 Queen Street West, Toronto, Ontario M5V-2B4, Canada*

Michael John Thompson, 4376 West 10th Avenue, Vancouver, British Columbia V6R- 2H7, Canada*

Michael R. Thompson, 8312 West Third Street, Los Angeles, CA 90048*

Time and Again, 320 East 46th Street, #34G, New York, NY 10017

TLC Books, 9 N. College Avenue, Salem, VA 34153

Henry E. Turlington, P.O. Box 190, Carrboro, NC 27510*

Turtle Island Booksellers, 2067 Center Street, Berkeley, CA 94704*

Ulysses Bookshop, 40 Museum Street, London WC1A-1LH, United Kingdom*

Len Unger Rare Books, P.O. Box 5858, Sherman Oaks, CA 91413*

John Updike Rare Books, 7 St. Bernard's Row, Edinburgh EH4 1HW, Scotland, United Kingdom

Vagabond Books, 11706 San Vicente Boulevard, Brentwood, CA 90049*

Versetility Books, P.O. Box 1133, Farmington, CT 06034

Virgo Books, "Little Court," South Wraxall, Bradford-on-Avon, Wilts. BA15-2SE, United Kingdom

Waiting for Godot Books, P.O. Box 331, Hadley, MA 01035

Rob Warren, 13 West 18th Street, New York, NY 10011

Watermark West, 149 N. Broadway, Wichita, KS 67202

Water Row Books, P.O. Box 438, Sudbury, MA 01776
Waverly Books, 948 Ninth Street, Santa Monica, CA 90403
Wessel & Lieberman, 121 First Avenue South, Seattle, WA 98104
E. Wharton & Co., 3232 History Drive, Oakton, VA 22124
Wheldon & Wesley, Ltd., Lytton Lodge, Codicote, Hitchin, Herts. SG4-8TE, United Kingdom
Jett W. Whitehead, 1412 Center Avenue, Bay City, MI 48708
Wilder Books, P.O. Box 762, Elmhurst, IL 60126
Nigel Williams, 22 and 25 Cecil Court, London WC2N 4HE, United Kingdom*
John Windle Antiquarian Bookseller, 49 Geary Street, Suite 233, San Francisco, CA 94108*
J. Howard Woolmer—Rare Books, P.O. Box 179, Revere, PA 18953*
Words Etcetera, 2 Cornhill, Dorchester, Dorset DT1-1BA, United Kingdom*
Robert Wright Books, 479 Queen Street West, Second Floor, Toronto, Ontario M5V 2A9, Canada
Wrigley-Cross Books, 8001 A SE Powell, Portland, OR 97206
Herb Yellin, 10973 Los Alamos Street, Northridge, CA 91326
Yesterday's Books, 25625 Southfield Road, Suite 104, Southfield, MI 48075

Appendix C

Auction Houses

Baltimore Book Auction, 2112 North Charles Street, Baltimore, MD 21201. Catalogs by subscription.

Christie's, 502 Park Avenue at 59th Street, New York, NY 10022. Catalogs by subscription.

Christie's East, 219 East 67th Street, New York, NY 10021. Catalogs by subscription.

Samuel T. Freeman and Co., 1808 Chestnut Street, Philadelphia, PA 19103. Catalogs by subscription.

Kane Antiquarian Auction, 1525 Shenkel Road, Pottstown, PA 19464. Catalogs by subscription.

Richard E. Oinonen Book Auctions, Box 470, Sunderland, MA 01375. Catalogs by subscription.

Pacific Book Auction Galleries, 139 Townsend Street, Suite 305, San Francisco, CA 94107. Catalogs by subscription.

Phillips, Sons & Neale, Inc., 406 East 79th Street, New York, NY 10021. Catalogs by subscription.

Sotheby Parke Bernet, Inc., 1334 York Avenue, New York, NY 10021. Catalogs by subscription.

Swann Galleries, 104 East 25th Street, New York, NY 10010. Catalogs by subscription.

Waverly Auctions, 4931 Cordell Avenue, Suite AA, Bethesda, MD 20814. Catalogs by subscription.

Appendix D

Selected Bibliography of Works Consulted

The following is a listing of individual author bibliographies, general bibliographies that include several authors, and our own *Author Price Guides* (which are priced bibliographic checklists and are available from us at 1137 Sugarloaf Mountain Road, Dickerson, MD 20842, or through e-mail at firsts@qb.com). We have broken this section into two areas: "General Bibliographies Consulted" and "Individual Bibliographies Consulted."

The second section ("Individual Bibliographies Consulted") is self-explanatory, except that where the author, press, or subject was included in a general bibliography, we have noted where this information may be found (e.g., under the listing for Malcolm Cowley, you will find "see FPAA #4" and know that this information is in volume 4 of *First Printings of American Authors*). The general bibliographies we refer to the most are APG (*Author Price Guides*), BAL (*Bibliography of American Literature*), Currey (*Science Fiction and Fantasy Authors . . .*), FPAA (*First Printings of American Authors*), and Johnson (*American First Editions*). Full bibliographic information for APG, BAL, etc. can be found in the "General Bibliographies Consulted" section.

GENERAL BIBLIOGRAPHIES CONSULTED

Abbey, J. R. *Travel . . .* (2 vols.) | *Scenery . . .* | *Life . . .* San Francisco: Alan Wofsy Fine Arts, 1991.

Adams, Ramon F. *The Rampaging Herd.* Cleveland: Zubal, 1982.

Adams, Ramon F. *Six-Guns and Saddle Leather.* Cleveland: Zubal, 1982.

Ahearn, Allen and Patricia. *Author Price Guides.* Dickerson, MD: Quill & Brush, 1992–99. (APG)

Ahearn, Allen and Patricia. *Collected Books: The Guide to Values.* 1998 Edition. New York: G. P. Putnam's Sons (1998).

American Book Prices Current. New York: Bancroft–Parkman, 1975–98.

Blanck, Jacob. *Bibliography of American Literature.* New Haven: Yale University, 1953–73. (7 volumes). 1990–91 (volumes 8 & 9 edited and completed by Michael Winship). (BAL)

Blanck, Jacob. *Peter Parley to Penrod.* Waltham, MA: Mark Press, 1974.

Bleiler, E. F. *The Checklist of Science-Fiction and Supernatural Fiction.* Glen Rock, N.J.: Firebell Books, 1978.

Bradley, Van Allen. *The Book Collector's Handbook of Values, 1982–83.* New York: G. P. Putnam's Sons, 1982. (VAB)

Bruccoli, Matthew J.; Clark, C. E. Frazer, Jr.; Layman, Richard; and Franklin, Benjamin V. (editors). *First Printings of American Authors.* 5 vols. Detroit: Gale Research, 1977–89. (FPAA)

CASANOVA Booksellers' Checklists of Twentieth Century Authors. Second Series, Milwaukee: 1933 (Richard Aldington, Martin Armstrong, Aldous Huxley, James Joyce, and Christopher Morley); Third Series, Milwaukee: 1935 (Erskine Caldwell, Frank Harris, Robert Nathan, A. Edward Newton, and Gertrude Stein).

Currey, L. W. *Science Fiction and Fantasy Authors: A Bibliography of First Printings . . .* Boston: G. K. Hall (1979).

Cutler, B. D., and Stiles, Villa. *Modern British Authors.* New York: Greenberg Publisher (1930).

Dykes, Jeff. *Western High Spots.* No place: Northland Press, 1977.

Fabes, Gilbert H. *The First Editions of A. E. Coppard, A. P. Herbert and Charles Morgan.* London: Myers & Co., 1933.

Ford, Hugh. *Published in Paris . . .* London: Garnstone Press, 1975.

Franklin, Colin. *The Private Presses.* Chester Springs: Dufour Editions, 1969.

Gawsworth, John. *Ten Contemporaries: Notes Toward Their Definitive Bibliography.* London: Ernest Benn, 1932.

Howes, Wright. *U.S. Iana (1650–1950).* New York: Bowker, 1962.

Hubin, Allen J. *Crime Fiction 1749–1980: A Comprehensive Bibliography.* New York: Garland Publishing, 1984.

Johnson, Merle. *American First Editions.* Revised and Enlarged by Jacob Blanck. Waltham, MA: Mark Press, 1969.

Kirkpatrick, D. L., ed. *Twentieth-Century Children's Writers.* 2d ed. New York: St. Martin's Press, 1983.

Kirkpatrick, D. L., and Vinson, James, eds. *Contemporary Novelists.* 4th ed. New York: St. Martin's Press, 1986.

Kunitz, Stanley J., ed. *Twentieth Century Authors First Supplement: A Biographical Dictionary of Modern Literature.* New York: H. W. Wilson, 1945.

Kunitz, Stanley J., and Haycraft, Howard, eds. *Twentieth Century Authors: A Biographical Dictionary of Modern Literature.* New York: H. W. Wilson, 1942.

Lepper, Gary M. *A Bibliographical Introduction to Seventy-five Modern American Authors.* Berkeley: Serendipity Books, 1976.

McGrath, Ann F., ed. *Bookman's Price Index.* (Vols. 47–51). Detroit: Gale Research, 1993–1996.

Morrison, Shelley. *Texana Catalogue Prices: 1994/1995.* Austin: W. M. Morrison Books, 1995/1996.

Morrison, Shelley. *Western Americana Catalogue Prices: 1994/1995.* Austin: W. M. Morrison Books, 1995/1996.

Phillips, John C. *A Bibliography of American Sporting Books: Sport–Natural History–Hunting Dogs–Trapping–Shooting–Early American . . .* New York: James Cummins Bookseller, 1991.

Ransom, Will. *Private Presses and Their Books.* New York: Bowker, 1929.

Rees, David. *Brian Moore, Alasdair Gray, John McGahern: A Bibliography of Their First Editions.* London: Colophon Press, 1991.

Rees, David. *Bruce Chatwin, Martin Amis, Julian Barnes: A Bibliography of Their First Editions.* London: Colophon Press, 1992.

Rees, David. *Muriel Spark, William Trevor, Ian McEwan: A Bibliography of Their First Editions.* London: Colophon Press, 1992.

Reilly, John M., ed. *Twentieth-Century Crime and Mystery Writers.* 2d ed. New York: St. Martin's Press, 1985.

Sadleir, Michael. *XIX Century Fiction.* 2 vols. Cambridge: Maurizio Martino Publisher, no date (reprint of original 1951 edition).

Schwartz, Dr. Jacob. *1100 Obscure Points.* Bristol, England: Chatford House Press, 1931.

Smith, Curtis C., ed. *Twentieth-Century Science-Fiction Writers.* New York: St. Martin's Press, 1981.

Streeter, Thomas W. *Bibliography of Texas 1795–1845.* Cambridge: Harvard University Press, 1960.

Vinson, James, and Kirkpatrick, D. L., eds. *Contemporary Poets.* 4th ed. New York: St. Martin's Press, 1985.

Wagner, Henry R., and Camp, Charles L. *The Plains & the Rockies.* San Francisco: John Howell Books, 1982.

Zemple, Edward N. and Linda A. *Book Prices: Used and Rare, 1996.* Peoria: Spoon River Press, 1996.

Zemple, Edward N. and Linda A. *First Editions: A Guide to Identification.* 2d ed. Peoria: Spoon River Press, 1989.

INDIVIDUAL BIBLIOGRAPHIES CONSULTED

(ABBEY) Maxwell, Spencer. *Collecting Abbey: A Checklist of the First Editions of Edward Abbey.* Santa Fe, N.M.: Vinegar Tom Press (1991).
See also APG.

(ABBEY PRESS) See Ransom.

(ABERCROMBIE) Cooper, Jeffrey. *A Bibliography and Notes on the Works of Lascelles Abercrombie.* (London) Archon Books, 1969.
See also Gawsworth.

(ACE SCIENCE FICTION DOUBLES) Corrick, James A. Brooklyn: 1991.

(ACTON) Ritchie, Neil. *A Bibliography of Harold Acton.* Florence: no publisher, 1934.

(ADAMIC) Christian, Henry A. *Louis Adamic: A Checklist.* (Kent, Ohio): Kent State University Press (1971).

(ADAMS, A.) See FPAA #4.

(ADAMS, H.) See BAL #1, and Johnson.

(ADAMS, J. T.) See BAL #4, and FPAA #4.

(ADAMS, L.) See FPAA #4.

(ADAMS, O. F.) See BAL #1.

(ADE) Russo, Dorothy Ritter. *A Bibliography of George Ade, 1866–1944.* Indianapolis: Indiana Historical Society, 1947.
See also FPAA #2, and Johnson.

(AFRICAN-AMERICAN) Saifer. *A Century of Fiction by American Negroes.* 1974.

(AGEE, J.) See APG, and FPAA #1.

(AIKEN) Bonnell, F. W. and F. C. *Conrad Aiken: A Bibliography, (1902–1978).* San Marino, Calif.: Huntington Library, 1982.
See also FPAA #4, and Johnson.

(ALBEE, E.) Green. *Edward Albee: A Bibliography,* 1980.
See also APG, and FPAA #3.

(ALCOTT, A. B.) See BAL #1.

(ALCOTT) Gulliver, Lucille. *Louisa May Alcott: A Bibliography.* Boston: Little Brown, 1932.
See also BAL #1, and Johnson.

(ALDERBRINK PRESS) See Ransom.

(ALDERGATE PRESS) See Ransom.

(ALDINGTON) Kershaw, Alister. *A Bibliography of the Works of Richard Aldington from 1915 to 1948.* London: The Quandrant Press, 1950.
See also *Casanova.*

(ALDISS, B.) Manson, Margaret. *Brian Aldiss: A Bibliography, 1954–62.* (Birmingham: Dryden Press, 1962.)
See also Currey.

(ALDRICH, T. B.) See BAL #1, and Johnson.

(ALGER) Gardner, Ralph D. *Road to Success: A Bibliography of the Works of Horatio Alger.* Mendota, Ill.: Wayside Press, 1971.

See Also FPAA #5, and Lepper.

(ALGREN) Bruccoli, Matthew J. *Nelson Algren: A Descriptive Bibliography.* (Pittsburgh) University of Pittsburgh Press, 1985.

See Also APG, FPAA #1, and Lepper.

(ALLEN, E. A.) See BAL #1.

(ALLEN, H.) See Johnson.

(ALLEN, J. L.) See BAL #1, and Johnson.

(ALLEN, P.) See FPAA #4.

(ALLEN, W.) See APG.

(ALLSTON, W.) See BAL #1.

(ALSOP, R.) See FPAA #1.

(ALWIL PRESS) See Ransom.

(AMIS, K.) Gohn, Jack Benoit. *Kingsley Amis: A Checklist.* (Kent, Ohio) Kent State University Press (1976).

(AMIS, M.) See Rees.

(AMMONS, A. R.) See FPAA #1.

(ANDERSON, M.) See FPAA #1.

(ANDERSON, P.) See Currey.

(ANDERSON, S.) Sheehy, Eugene P., and Lohf, Kenneth A. *Sherwood Anderson: A Bibliography.* Los Gatos: Talisman Press, 1960.

See also APG, FPAA #2, and Johnson.

(ANDREWS) Webber, William Hallam. *William Loring Andrews: A Study and Bibliography.* Rockville, Md.: no publisher, 1980.

See also FPAA #2, and Johnson.

(ANGEL ALLEY PRESS) See Ransom.

(ANOUILH, J.) Kelly. *Jean Anouilh: A Bibliography,* 1973.

(ANTIN, M.) See FPAA #5.

(ANTONINUS, B.) See Everson.

(APPLEDORE PRESS) See Ransom.

(AQUILA PRESS) See Ransom.

(ARGONAUT PRESS) See Ransom.

(ARIES PRESS) See Ransom.

(ARMSTRONG) See *Casanova.*

(ARNOLD) Smart, Thomas Burnett. *The Bibliography of Matthew Arnold.* Reprinted. New York: Burt Franklin (1968).

(ARNOW, H. S.) See FPAA #2.

(ASHBERY) Kermani, David K. *John Ashbery: A Comprehensive Bibliography.* New York: Garland Publishing, 1976.

See also FPAA #1, and Lepper.

(ASHENDENE PRESS) See Franklin, and Ransom.

(ASIMOV) Miller, Marjorie M. *Isaac Asimov: A Checklist of Works Published in the United States, March 1939–May 1972.* No place: Kent State University Press (1972).

See also Currey.

(ATHERTON, G.) McClure, Charlotte. *Gertrude Atherton.* Twayne, 1979.

See also Johnson.

(ATTAWAY, W.) See FPAA #2.

(ATWOOD) Horne, Alan J. *A Preliminary Checklist of Writings By and About Margaret Atwood.* In the *Malahat Review* No. 41. Victoria, British Columbia, Canada: University of Victoria, 1977.

(AUCHINCLOSS, L.) Bryer, Jackson. *Louis Auchincloss and His Critics,* Hall, 1977.
See also FPAA #1, and Lepper.

(AUCHINLECK PRESS) See Ransom.

(AUDEN) Bloomfield, B. C., and Mendelson, Edward. *W. H. Auden: A Bibliography, 1924–1969.* Charlottesville: University of Virginia (1972).

(AUDUBON, J. J.) See FPAA #1, and Johnson.

(AUSTEN) Gilson, David. *A Bibliography of Jane Austen.* Winchester / New Castle: St. Paul's / Oak Knoll, 1997.
Keynes, Geoffrey. *Jane Austen: A Bibliography.* London: Nonesuch Press, 1929.
See also Schwartz.

(AUSTER, P.) See APG.

(AUSTIN, J. G.) See BAL #1, and Johnson.

(AUSTIN, M.) Fink, Augusta. *I, Mary: A Bibliography.* 1983.
See also Johnson.

(BACHELLER, I.) See Johnson.

(BACON, D. S.) See BAL #1.

(BAGBY, G. W.) See BAL #1.

(BAKER, D.) See FPAA #2.

(BAKER, E.) See FPAA #1.

(BALDWIN, J.) See APG, FPAA #5, and Lepper.

(BALDWIN, J. G.) See BAL #1.

(BALLANTINE BOOKS) Aronovitz, David. *Ballantine Books: the First Decade.* Rochester, Mich.: Bailiwick Books, (1987).

(BALLANTYNE) Quayle, Eric. *R. M. Ballantyne: A Bibliography of First Editions.* London: Dawsons of Pall Mall, 1968.

(BALLARD, J. G.) See Currey.

(BANCROFT, G.) See BAL #1.

(BANDER-LOG PRESS) See Ransom.

(BANGS, J. K.) See BAL #1, and Johnson.

(BARING) Chaundy, Leslie. *A Bibliography of the First Editions of the Works of Maurice Baring.* London: Dulau, 1925.
See also Cutler and Stiles.

(BARKER, J. N.) See BAL #1.

(BARLOWE, J.) See BAL #1.

(BARNES, D.) Messeri, Douglas. *Djuna Barnes: A Bibliography.* (New York) David Lewis, 1975.
See also FPAA #1.

(BARNES, J.) See APG, and Rees.

(BARRIE) Cutler, B. D. *Sir James M. Barrie: A Bibliography.* New York, 1931.
Garland, Herbert. *A Bibliography of the Writings of Sir James Matthew Barrie.* London: Bookman's Journal, 1928.

(BARTH) Weixlmann, Joseph. *John Barth: A Descriptive . . . Bibliography.* New York: Garland, 1976.
See also APG, FPAA #2, and Lepper.

(BARTHELME) Klinkowitz, Jerome; Pieratt, Asa; and Davis, Robert Murray. *Donald Barthelme: A Comprehensive Bibliography.* (Hamden, Conn.) Archon Books, 1977.
See also APG, FPAA #2, and Lepper.

(BARTRAM, W.) See FPAA #4.

(BASKIN, L.) See Gehenna Press.

(BASSLER, T. J.) See Currey.

(BASSO, H.) See FPAA #2.

(BATES, H.) See Currey.

(BATES, H. E.) Eads, Peter. *A Bibliographical Study.* Winchester: St. Paul's Bibliographies, 1990.

(BAUM) See Oz.

(BAYLEY, B.) See Currey.

(BEAGLE, P. S.) See Currey, and FPAA #2.

(BEARDSLEY) Gallatin, A. E. *Aubrey Beardsley, Catalogue of Drawings and Bibliography.* Mamaroneck, N.Y.: Paul Appel (no date).

(BEATTIE, A.) See APG.

(BEAUMONT PRESS) See Ransom.

(BECKETT) Lake, Carlton, et al. *No Symbols Where None Intended.* (Samuel Beckett). Austin: Humanities Research Center, University of Texas (1984).

(BEEBE) Berra, Tim. *William Beebe: An Annotated Bibliography.* (Hamden, Conn.) Archon Books, 1977.

> See also Johnson.

(BEER, T.) See FPAA #2.

(BEERBOHM) Gallatin, A. E., and Oliver, L. M. *A Bibliography of the Works of Max Beerbohm.* London: Rupert Hart-Davis, 1952.

> See also Cutler and Stiles.

(BELDORNIE PRESS) See Ransom.

(BELKNAP, J.) See BAL #1.

(BELL, E. T.) See Currey.

(BELLAMY, E.) See BAL #1, and Johnson.

(BELLOC) Cahill, Patrick. *The English First Editions of Hilaire Belloc.* London: privately published, 1953.

(BELLOW, S.) See APG, and Lepper.

(BEMELMANS) Pomerance, Murray. *Ludwig Bemelmans: A Bibliography.* New York: James Heineman, 1993.

(BENÉT, S. V.) See Johnson.

(BENÉT, W. R.) See Johnson.

(BENFORD, G.) See Currey.

(BENJAMIN, P.) See BAL #1.

(BENNETT) Pound. *Arnold Bennett: A Bibliography.* 1953.

(BENNETT, E.) See BAL #1.

(BENNETT, G.) See Currey.

(BENSON, MILDRED WIRT) See Drew.

(BERGER, T.) See APG, FPAA #2, and Lepper.

(BERRIGAN, D.) See Lepper.

(BERRIGAN, T.) See Lepper.

(BERRY, W.) Freedman, Russell. G. *Wendell Berry: A Bibliography.* Lexington: University of Kentucky Libraries, 1998.

> See also Lepper.

(BERRYMAN) Stefanik, Ernest C., Jr. *John Berryman: A Descriptive Bibliography.* (Pittsburgh) University of Pittsburgh Press, 1974.

> See also FPAA #1, and Lepper.

(BESTER, A.) See Currey.

(BETJEMAN) Stapleton, Margaret L. *Sir John Betjeman: A Bibliography of Writings By and About Him.* Metuchen, N.J.: Scarecrow Press, 1974.

(BIANCHI, M. G.) See FPAA #2.

(BIERCE) Starrett, Vincent. *Ambrose Bierce: A Bibliography*. Philadelphia: The Centaur Book Shop, 1929.

See also BAL #1, Johnson, and Schwartz.

(BIGGLE, L.) See Currey.

(BILLINGS, J.) See BAL #1.

(BINDER, O. O.) See Currey.

(BIRD, R. M.) See BAL #1, and Johnson.

(BIRDS) See Sitwell.

(BISHOP) MacMahon, Candace. *Elizabeth Bishop: A Bibliography, 1927–1979*. Charlottesville: University Press of Virginia (1980).

See also FPAA #2.

(BISHOP, J. P.) See FPAA #1.

(BISHOP, M.) See Currey.

(BLACK, A. AND C.) Inman, Colin. *Colour Books*. London: Werner Shaw Ltd, 1990.

(BLACK, M.) See FPAA #2.

(BLACKBURN, P.) See Lepper.

(BLACKMORE, R. D.) Sutton. *R. D. Blackmore: A Bibliography*. 1979.

(BLACK SPARROW PRESS) Minkoff, George Robert. *A Bibliography of the Black Sun Press*. Great Neck: G. R. Minkoff, 1970.

Morrow & Cooney. *A Bibliography 1966–78*. 1981.

See also Ransom.

(BLAINE, M.) Legman, G. *The Art of Mahlon Blaine*. No place: Peregrine Books, 1982.

(BLAKE, W.) Lindsay. *William Blake*. 1978.

(BLAKENEY PRESS) See Ransom.

(BLECHMAN, B.) See FPAA #2.

(BLEEKER, A. E.) See FPAA #4.

(BLISH, J. B.) See Currey.

(BLIXEN, K.) See Dineson, Isak.

(BLOCH, R.) Larson, Randall D. *The Complete Robert Bloch*. Sunnyvale, Calif.: Fandom Unlimited, 1986.

See also Currey.

(BLOCK, L.) *Lawrence Block: Bibliography 1958–1993*. (A.S.A.P. Press, Mission Viego, Calif.) 1993.

(BLUE SKY PRESS) See Ransom.

(BLUNDEN) Kirkpatrick, Brownlee. *A Bibliography of Edmund Blunden*. Oxford: Clarendon Press, 1979.

(BLY) Roberson, William H. *Robert Bly: A Primary and Secondary Bibliography*. Metuchen, N.J., and London: The Scarecrow Press, 1986.

See also Lepper.

(BODMAN, M.) See FPAA #4.

(BOGAN, L.) See FPAA #1.

(BOKER, G. H.) See BAL #1.

(BOND, N.) See Currey.

(BOOTH, P. E.) See FPAA #2.

(BORGES) Loewenstein, C. Jared. *A Descriptive Catalogue of the Jorge Luis Borges Collection at the University of Virginia Library*. Charlottesville: University Press of Virginia (1993).

(BORROW) Collie, Michael, and Fraser, Angus. *George Borrow: A Bibliographical Study*. Hampshire: St. Paul's Bibliographies, 1984.

(BOURJAILY, V.) See FPAA #1.

(BOVA, B. W.) See Currey.

(BOWLES, J.) Dillion. See FPAA #5.

(BOWLES, P.) Miller, Jeffrey. *Paul Bowles: A Descriptive Bibliography*. Santa Barbara: Black Sparrow, 1986. See also Lepper.

(BOWLING GREEN PRESS) See Ransom.

(BOX, E.) (Vidal) See FPAA #3.

(BOYD, J.) See Johnson.

(BOYESEN, H. H.) See BAL #1.

(BOYLE, K.) See FPAA #3.

(BRACE, G. W.) See FPAA #2.

(BRACKENRIDGE, H. H.) See BAL #1, and Johnson.

(BRACKETT, L.) See Currey.

(BRADBURY) Nolan, William F. *The Ray Bradbury Companion*. Detroit: Bruccoli Clark/Gale Research, 1975.
See also APG, FPAA #1, and Currey.

(BRADFORD, G.) See Johnson.

(BRADFORD, R.) See Johnson.

(BRADFORD, W.) See FPAA #3.

(BRADLEY, M. E.) See Currey.

(BRADSTREET, A.) See FPAA #3.

(BRAINARD, J. G.) See BAL #1.

(BRAND) Richardson, Darrell C. *Max Brand (Frederick Faust): The Man and His Work*. Los Angeles: Fantasy Publishing (1952).

(BRAUTIGAN) Barber, John F. *Richard Brautigan: An Annotated Bibliography*. Jefferson, N.C., and London: McFarland (1990).
See also Lepper.

(BRENNAN, J. P.) See Currey.

(BRESLIN, J.) See FPAA #2.

(BRIGGS, C. F.) See BAL #1.

(BRODEUR, P.) See FPAA #1.

(BROMFIELD, L.) See FPAA #4, and Johnson.

(BRONK, W.) See FPAA #3.

(BRONTË) Wise, Thomas J. *A Bibliography of the Writings . . . of the Brontë Family*. London: Dawsons of Pall Mall (1917).

(BROOKE, R.) Keynes, Geoffrey. *A Bibliography of the Works of Rupert Brooke*. London: Rupert Hart-Davis, 1964.

(BROOKS, C. T.) See BAL #1.

(BROOKS, G.) Luff, J. N. *Gwendolyn Brooks: A Bibliography*.
See also APG.

(BROOKS, M. G.) See BAL #1.

(BROOKS, V. W.) Nelson. *Van Wyck Brooks: A Writer's Life*.
See also FPAA #5.

(BROOKS PRESS) See Ransom.

(BROSSARD, C.) See APG, and FPAA #2.

(BROWN, A.) See FPAA #3.

(BROWN, C. B.) See BAL #1, and Johnson.

(BROWN, F.) Baird, Newton. *A Key to Frederic Brown's Wonderland*. Georgetown, Calif.: Talisman Literary Research, 1981.
See also APG, and Currey.

(BROWN, R. G.) See Currey.

(BROWN, W. H.) See BAL #1, and FPAA #1.

(BROWNE, C. F.) See BAL #1.

(BROWNELL, H. H.) See BAL #1.

(BROWNING, E. B.) Barnes, Warner. *A Bibliography of Elizabeth Barrett Browning.* (Austin) University of Texas Press (1967).

See also Schwartz.

(BROWNING, R.) Wise, Thomas J. *A Bibliography of the Writings . . . of Robert Browning.* London: Dawsons of Pall Mall, 1971.

See also Schwartz.

(BROWNSON, O. A.) See FPAA #4.

(BRUNNER, J. K.) See Currey.

(BRYAN, C.D.B.) See FPAA #2.

(BRYANT, E.) See Currey.

(BRYANT, W. C.) Scribner. *William Cullen Bryant: A Bibliography.* 1971.

See also BAL #1, and Johnson.

(BUCHAN, J.) Blanchard, Robert G. *The First Editions of John Buchan.* (Hamden, Conn.) Archon Books, 1981.

(BUCK, P.) See Johnson.

(BUDRYS, A. J.) See Currey.

(BUECHNER, F.) See FPAA #1.

(BUKOWSKI, C.) Dorbin, Sanford. *A Bibliography of Charles Bukowski.* Los Angeles: Black Sparrow, 1969.

Fogel, Al. *Charles Bukowski: A Comprehensive Checklist.* (Miami: Sole Proprietor Press, 1982).

Fogel, Al. *Under the Influence: A Collection of Works by Charles Bukowski, Illustrated with Original Drawings by the Author.* Sudbury, Mass.: Jeffrey H. Weinberg Books, 1984.

See also Lepper.

(BULFINCH, T.) See FPAA #4.

(BULMER, H. K.) See Currey.

(BULWER, L.) See Sadleir.

(BUNNER, H. C.) See BAL #1, and Johnson.

(BUNTING, B.) Guedalla, Roger. *Basil Bunting: A Bibliography of Works and Criticism.* Norwood, Pa.: Norwood Editions, 1973.

(BURDETTE, R. J.) See BAL #1.

(BURGESS, A.) Brewer, Jeutonne. *Anthony Burgess: A Bibliography.* Metuchen, N.J., and London: The Scarecrow Press, 1980.

(BURGESS, G.) See Johnson.

(BURGESS, T.) Dowhan, Michael W., Jr. *Thornton W. Burgess, Harrison Cady: A Book, Magazine and Newspaper Bibliography.* New York: Carlton Press (1990).

Wright, Wayne W. *Thornton W. Burgess: A Descriptive Book Bibliography.* Sandwich, Mass.: Burgess Society, 1979.

(BURKE, E.) Todd, William B. *A Bibliography of Edmund Burke.* (Surrey, England) St. Paul's Bibliographies, 1982.

(BURKE, J. L.) See APG.

(BURNETT, F. H.) See BAL #1.

(BURNS, R.) (Gibson, James). *The Bibliography of Robert Burns . . .* Reprinted. New York: Kraus, 1969.

(BURROUGHS, E. R.) Heins, Henry Hardy. *A Golden Anniversary Bibliography of Edgar Rice Burroughs.* (Revised). West Kingston, R.I.: Donald Grant, 1964.

Zeuschner, Robert B. *Edgar Rice Burroughs: The Exhaustive Scholar's and Collector's Descriptive Bibliography.* Jefferson. North Carolina / London: McFarland and Company (1996).

See also Currey.

(BURROUGHS, J.) See BAL #1, and Johnson.

(BURROUGHS, W.) Maynard, Joe, and Miles, Barry. *William S. Burroughs: A Bibliography, 1953–73.* Charlottesville: University of Virginia Press (1978).

See also APG, FPAA #5, and Lepper.

(BURTON, R.) Penzer, Norman M. *An Annotated Bibliography of Sir Richard Francis Burton.* New York: Burt Franklin (1970).

(BUSCH, F.) See FPAA #2.

(BUTLER, S.) Harkness, Stanley B. *The Career of Samuel Butler (1835–1902): A Bibliography.* London: The Bodley Head (1955).

Hoppe, A. J. *A Bibliography of the Writings of Samuel Butler.* New York: Burt Franklin (1968).

See also Schwartz.

(BUTLER, W. A) See BAL #1.

(BUTLER, W. H.) See BAL #1.

(BYLES, M.) See FPAA #1.

(BYNNER, E. L.) See BAL #1.

(BYNNER, W.) See Johnson.

(BYRD, W.) See FPAA #4.

(BYRNE, D.) Wetherbee, Winthrop, Jr. *Donn Byrne: A Bibliography.* New York: New York Public Library, 1949.

See also BAL #1, and Johnson.

(BYRON, L.) Wise, Thomas J. *A Bibliography of the Writings in Verse and Prose of George Gordon Noel, Lord Byron.* 2 vols. London: Dawsons of Pall Mall, 1972.

See also Schwartz.

(CABELL, J. B.) Brussel I. R. *James Branch Cabell: A Revised Bibliography.* Philadelphia: Centaur Book Shop, 1932.

See also FPAA #2, and Johnson.

(CABLE, G. W.) See BAL #2, and Johnson.

(CAHAN, A.) See FPAA #2.

(CAIN, J. M.) See FPAA #1.

(CAIN, P.) See FPAA #4.

(CALDWELL, E.) See *Casanova,* FPAA #2, and Johnson.

(CALIFORNIA LITERATURE) Gaer. *Bibliography Pre Gold Rush.* 1970.

(CALISHER, H.) See FPAA #2, and Lepper.

(CALVERT, G. H.) See BAL #2.

(CAMUS, A.) Roeming. *Albert Camus: A Bibliography.* 1968.

(CANTWELL, R.) See FPAA #5.

(CAPOTE, T.) See APG, and Lepper.

(CARADOC PRESS) See Franklin.

(CARLETON, W.) See BAL #2.

(CARLYLE, T.) Dyer, Isaac Watson. *A Bibliography of Thomas Carlyle's Writings . . .* New York: Burt Franklin (1968).

Tarr, Rodger L. *Thomas Carlyle: A Descriptive Bibliography.* (Pittsburgh) University of Pittsburgh Press, 1989.

(CARMAN, B.) See BAL #2, Johnson.

(CARREFOUR PRESS) See Ford.

(CARROLL, L.) Williams, Sidney Herbert. *A Bibliography of the Writings of Lewis Carroll.* (Charles Lutwidge Dodgson.) London: *Bookman's Journal,* 1924.

See also Cutler and Stiles.

(CARROLL, P.) See FPAA #2.

(CARRUTH, H.) See FPAA #2.

(CARRYL, G. W.) See BAL #2.

(CARSON, R.) See FPAA #3.

(CARTER, H.) See FPAA #4.

(CARUTHERS, W. A.) See BAL #2.

(CARY, A.) See BAL #2.

(CARY, P.) See BAL #2.

(CASTLEMON) Blanck, Jacob. *Harry Castlemon Boy's Own Author.* Waltham, Mass.: Mark Press, 1969.

(CATHER, W.) Crane, Joan. *Willa Cather: A Bibliography.* Lincoln: University of Nebraska Press (1982).
   See also APG, FPAA #4, and Johnson.

(CATHERWOOD, M.) See BAL #2.

(CATTLE INDUSTRY) See Adams.

(CAWEIN, M.) See BAL #2.

(CENTAUR PRESS) See Ransom.

(CERVANTES) Grismer, Raymond L. *Cervantes: A Bibliography.* Reprinted. New York: Kraus, 1970.

(CHANDLER, R.) Bruccoli, Matthew. *Raymond Chandler: A Descriptive Bibliography.* (Pittsburgh) University of Pittsburgh Press, 1979.
   See also APG, and FPAA #1.

(CHANNING, W. E.) See BAL #2, and FPAA #4.

(CHARTERIS, L.) See APG.

(CHATWIN, B.) See APG, and Rees.

(CHEEVER, J.) See APG, FPAA #5, Lepper.

(CHEKHOV) Meister, Charles W. *Chekhov Bibliography: Works in English by and About Anton Chekhov; American, British and Canadian Performances.* Jefferson, N.C., and London: McFarland (1985).

(CHESNUTT, C.) See APG, FPAA #3, and Johnson.

(CHESTERTON, G. K.) Sullivan, John. *G. K. Chesterton: A Bibliography.* Warwick Square, London: University of London Press (1958).

(CHILD, L. M.) See BAL #2.

(CHILDREN S BOOKS) Blanck, Jacob. *Peter Parley to Penrod.* Waltham, Mass.: Mark Press, 1974.
   Kirkpatrick, D. L., ed. *Twentieth-Century Children's Writers.* 2d ed. New York: St. Martin's Press (1983).

(CHIVERS, L. M.) See BAL #2, and Johnson.

(CHOPIN, K.) See BAL #2.

(CHRISTIE, A.) See APG.

(CHURCHILL, W.) Woods, Frederick. *A Bibliography of the Works of Sir Winston Churchill.* (London) St. Paul's Bibliographies (1975).
   See also APG, and Johnson.

(CIARDI, J.) See FPAA #2.

(CITY LIGHTS) Cook, Ralph T. *The City Lights Pocket Poets Series: A Descriptive Bibliography.* La Jolla, Calif.: Laurence McGilvery/Atticus Books, 1982.

(CIVIL WAR) Menendez, Albert. *Civil War Novels: An Annotated Bibliography.* New York and London: Garland, 1986.

(CLANCY, T.) See APG.

(CLARK, E.) See FPAA #4.

(CLARK, J. F.) See FPAA #4.

(CLARK, T.) See Lepper.

(CLARK, W. G.) See BAL #2.

(CLARK, W. V.) See FPAA #5.

(CLARKE, J. F.) See FPAA #4.

(CLARKE, M.) See BAL #2.

(CLAVELL, J.) See APG.

(CLEMENS, S.) See BAL #2, and Johnson.

(CLERK'S PRESS) See Ransom.

(COATES, R. M.) See FPAA #4.

(COBB, E.) See Johnson.

(COBB, H.) See FPAA #3.

(COBB, I. S.) See Johnson.

(COKER, E.) See FPAA #4.

(COLERIDGE) Haney, John Louis. *A Bibliography of Samuel Taylor Coleridge*. Philadelphia: Privately printed, 1903.

(COLLINS, W.) Beetz, Kirk H. *Wilkie Collins: An Annotated Bibliography, 1889–1976*. Metuchen, N.J., and London: The Scarecrow Press, 1978.

(COLLINS CRIME CLUB) Foord, Peter, and Williams, Richard. *Collins Crime Club: A Checklist of the First Editions*. South Humberside (England): Dragonby Press, 1987.

(CONDON, R.) See FPAA #2.

(CONNELL, E.) See FPAA #2.

(CONRAD, J.) Cagle, William. *A Bibliography of Joseph Conrad*. (Unpublished.)
Wise, Thomas J. *A Bibliography of the Writings of Joseph Conrad (1895–1921)*. (London) Dawsons of Pall Mall, 1972.
See also APG, Cutler and Stiles, and Schwartz.

(CONROY, J.) See FPAA #1.

(CONROY, P.) See APG.

(CONTACT EDITIONS) See Ford.

(COOKE, J. E.) See BAL #2, and Johnson.

(COOKE, R. T.) See BAL #2.

(COOPER, J. F.) Spiller, Robert E., and Blackburn, Philip C. *A Descriptive Bibliography of the Writings of James Fenimore Cooper*. New York: Bowker, 1934.
See also BAL #2, and Johnson.

(COOPER, S. F.) See BAL #2.

(COOVER, R.) See FPAA #1, and Lepper.

(COPPARD, A. E.) Schwartz, Jacob. *The Writings of Alfred Edgar Coppard*. London: The Ulysses Bookshop, 1931.
See also Fabes.

(CORMAN, C.) See Lepper.

(CORNFORD, F.) Anderson, Alan. *A Bibliography of the Writings of Frances Cornford*. Edinburgh: Tragara Press, 1975.

(CORNWELL, P.) See APG.

(CORSO, G.) Wilson, Robert. *A Bibliography of Works by Gregory Corso, 1954–1965*. New York: The Phoenix Book Shop, 1966.

(CORVO, F. R.) Woolf, Cecil. *A Bibliography of Frederick Rolfe Baron Corvo*. London: Rupert Hart-Davis, 1957.

(COTTON, J.) See FPAA #4.

(COWBOY) See Adams.

(COWLEY, A.) Perkin, M. R. *Abraham Cowley: A Bibliography*. (Kent, England) Dawson (1977).

(COWLEY, M.) See FPAA #4.

(COX, P.) Dickerson, Richard E. *A Brownie Bibliography: The Books of Palmer Cox 1840–1924*. Second edition. (Pasadena, Calif.) Golden Pippin Press, 1995.

(COZZENS) Bruccoli, Matthew. *James Gould Cozzens: A Descriptive Bibliography*. (Pittsburgh) University of Pittsburgh Press, 1981.
See also FPAA #1.

(cozzens, f. s.) See BAL #2.

(cranch, c.) See BAL #2.

(crane, h.) Schwartz, Joseph, and Schweik, Robert C. *Hart Crane: A Descriptive Bibliography.* (Pittsburgh) University of Pittsburgh Press (1972).

See also FPAA #1.

(crane, s.) Stallman, R. W. *Stephen Crane: A Critical Bibliography.* Ames: Iowa State University Press, 1972.

Williams, Ames W., and Starrett, Vincent. *Stephen Crane: A Bibliography.* Glendale, Calif.: John Valentine, 1948.

See also BAL #2, FPAA #1, and Johnson.

(crapsey, a.) See BAL #2.

(crawford, f. m.) See BAL #2.

(creasey, j.) *John Creasey: Master of Mystery.* (London: Hodder & Stoughton) No date.

John Creasey in Print. (London: Hodder & Stoughton, 1969.)

(creeley, r.) Novik, Mary. *Robert Creeley: An Inventory, 1945–1970.* No place: Kent State University Press (1973).

See also FPAA #3, and Lepper.

(cresset press) See Ransom.

(crews, h.) Hargraves, Michael. *Harry Crews: A Bibliography.* (Westport, Conn.) Meckler, (1986).

See also APG, and FPAA #2.

(crumb) Fine, Donald M. *R. Crumb Checklist of Works and Criticism . . .* Cambridge: Boatner Norton Press, 1981.

(crosby, c.) See FPAA #4.

(crosby, h.) See FPAA #2.

(crosby gaige press) See Ransom.

(crumley, j.) See APG.

(cuala press) See Ransom.

(cullen, c.) See APG.

(cummings, e. e.) Firmage, George J. *E. E. Cummings: A Bibliography.* (Middletown, Conn.) Wesleyan University Press (1960).

See also Johnson.

(cummins, m.) See BAL #2.

(cunningham, j. v.) Gullans, Charles. *A Bibliography of the Published Works of J. V. Cunningham.* Los Angeles: University of California Library, 1973.

(curtis, g. w.) See BAL #2, and Johnson.

(cushing, e. l.) See FPAA #5.

(d., h. [hilda doolittle]) Boughn, Michael. *H. D.: A Bibliography 1905–1990.* Charlottesville/London: Bibliographical Society of the University of Virginia/University of Virginia Press (1993).

(dabbs, j. m.) See FPAA #4.

(dahlberg, e.) Billings, Harold. *A Bibliography of Edward Dahlberg.* Austin: University of Texas Press (1971).

See also FPAA #1.

(dana, r. h., sr.) See BAL #2, and Johnson.

(daniel press) See Franklin, and Ransom.

(darrow, c.) Hunsberger, Willard D. *Clarence Darrow: A Bibliography.* Metuchen, N.J.: Scarecrow Press, 1981.

(darwin, c.) Freeman, R. B. *The Works of Charles Darwin: An Annotated Bibliographical Handlist.* (Hamden, Conn.) Dawson-Archon Books (1977).

(DAVENPORT, G.) Crane, Joan. *Guy Davenport: A Descriptive Bibliography.* Haverford: Greenshads, 1996.

(DAVIDSON, D.) Young, Thomas D., and Inge, Thomas. *Donald Davidson: An Essay and Bibliography.* Nashville: Vanderbilt University Press, 1965.

(DAVIDSON, J.) See Cutler and Stiles.

(DAVIES, RHYS) See Gawsworth.

(DAVIES, ROBERTSON) Ryrie, John. *Robertson Davies: An Annotated Bibliography.* (Downsview, Ontario: Stong College, York University, 1981.)
   See also APG.

(DAVIES, W. H.) Harlow, Sylvia *W. H. Davies: A Bibliography.* Winchester, England: St. Paul's Bibliographies, and New Castle, Del.: Oak Knoll Books, 1993.

(DAVIS, C. A.) See BAL #2.

(DAVIS, R. H.) Quinby, Henry Cole, A. M. *Richard Harding Davis: A Bibliography.* New York: E. P. Dutton (1924).
   See also BAL #2, FPAA #5, and Johnson.

(DAWES, R.) See BAL #2.

(DAWSON, F.) See FPAA #5.

(DAY-LEWIS, C.) Handley-Taylor, Geoffrey, and Smith, Timothy d'Arch. *C. Day-Lewis the Poet Laureate: A Bibliography.* Chicago and London: St. James Press, 1968.

(DE CAMP, L. S.) Laughlin, Charlotte, and Levack, Daniel J. H. *An L. Sprague De Camp Bibliography.* San Francisco, Calif./Columbia, Pa.: Underwood/Miller, 1983.

(DE FOREST, J. W.) See BAL #2.

(DEIGHTON, L.) Milward-Oliver, Edward. *Len Deighton: An Annotated Bibliography, 1954–1985.* (Kent, England) The Sammler Press (1985).

(DELAND, M.) See Johnson.

(DELILLO, D.) See APG, and FPAA #1.

(DELL, F.) See FPAA #3.

(DELL PAPERBACK) Lyles, William. *Putting Dell on the Map 1942–1962.* Two volumes.

(DENNIE, J.) See BAL #2.

(DERBY, G. H.) See BAL #2.

(DEREKSEN, D.) See Stacton.

(DERLETH, A.) *100 Books by August Derleth.* Sauk City (Wisc.): Arkham House, 1962.
   Wilson, Alison M. *August Derleth: A Bibliography.* Metuchen, N.J., and London: Scarecrow Press, 1983.

(DERRYDALE PRESS) Frazier, Don, and Koch, Jo. *Derrydale Press Books.* Long Valley, N.J.: Calderwoods Books, circa 1984.

(DE VRIES, P.) Bowden, Edwin T. *Peter De Vries: A Bibliography, 1934–1977.* Austin: University of Texas (1978).
   See also FPAA #4.

(DEWEY, J.) See FPAA #1.

(DEXTER, C.) See APG.

(DIBDIN, T. F.) O'Dwyer, E. J. *Thomas Frognall Dibdin: Bibliographer & Bibliomaniac Extraordinary 1776–1847.* Pinner (Middlesex, England): Private Libraries Association, (1967).

(DICK, P. K.) Levack, Daniel J. H. *PKD: A Philip K. Dick Bibliography.* San Francisco/Columbia, Pa.: Underwood/Miller, 1981.

(DICKENS, C.) Carr, Sister Lucille. *A Catalog of the Vanderpoel Dickens Collection . . .* Austin: University of Texas Press (1968).
   Eckel, John C. *The First Editions of the Writings of Charles Dickens and Their Values: A Bibliography.* London: Chapman & Hall, 1913.
   Podeschi, John B. *Dickens and Dickensiana: A Catalogue of the Richard Gimbel Collection . . .* New Haven: Yale University Library, 1980.

Smith, Walter E. *Charles Dickens in the Original Cloth: A Bibliographical Catalogue. Part I: The Novels with Sketches by Boz.* Los Angeles: Heritage Book Shop, 1982.

Smith, Walter E. *Charles Dickens in the Original Cloth: A Bibliographical Catalogue. Part II: The Christmas Book and Selected Secondary Novels.* Los Angeles: Heritage Book Shop, 1982.

See also Sadleir.

(DICKEY, J.) Bruccoli, Matthew J., and Baughman, Judith S. *James Dickey: A Descriptive Bibliography.* (Pittsburgh) University of Pittsburgh Press, 1990.

See also FPAA #1, Lepper.

(DICKINSON, E.) Myerson, Joel. *Emily Dickinson: A Descriptive Bibliography.* (Pittsburgh) University of Pittsburgh Press, 1984.

See also BAL #2, and Johnson.

(DIDION. J.) See APG, and FPAA #2.

(DINESEN, I.) Henriksen, Liselotte. *Isak Dinesen: A Bibliography.* (Viborg, Denmark) Gyldendal (1977).

(DIPRIMA, D.) See Lepper.

(DISCH, T. M.) Stephens, Christopher. *A Checklist of Thomas M. Disch.* (Hastings-on-Hudson, N.Y.) Ultramarine, 1991.

(DOBIE, J. F.) McVicker, Mary Louise. *The Writings of J. Frank Dobie: A Bibliography.* Lawton (Okla.): Museum of the Great Plains (1968).

(DOBSON) Dobson, Alban. *A Bibliography of the First Editions . . .* New York: Burt Franklin (1970). A reprint of the 1925 edition with a preface by Edmund Gosse.

(DOCTOROW, E. L.) See APG, and FPAA #1.

(DODGE, M. A.) See BAL #1.

(DODGE, M. M.) See BAL #2, and Johnson.

(DONLEAVY, J. P.) See FPAA #2.

(DONNELLY, I.) See BAL #2.

(DOOLITTLE, HILDA.) See D., H.

(DORN, E.) Streeter, David. *A Bibliography of Ed Dorn.* New York: The Phoenix Bookshop, 1973. See also FPAA #3, and Lepper.

(DOS PASSOS, J.) Sanders, Harvey. *John Dos Passos: A Comprehensive Bibliography.* New York and London: Garland Publishing, 1987.

See also APG, FPAA #1, and Johnson.

(DOUGLAS, N.) McDonald, Edward D. *A Bibliography of the Writings of Norman Douglas.* Philadelphia: The Centaur Book Shop, 1927.

See also Schwartz.

(DOVES PRESS) See Franklin, and Ransom.

(DOWSON, E.) See Cutler and Stiles, and Schwartz.

(DOYLE, A. C.) Green, Richard Lancelyn, and Gibson, John Michael. *A Bibliography of A. Conan Doyle.* Oxford: Clarendon Press (1983).

(DRAKE, J. R.) See BAL #2, and Johnson.

(DREISER, T.) McDonald, Edward D. *A Bibliography of the Writings of Theodore Dreiser.* New York: Burt Franklin (1968).

See also APG, FPAA #4, Schwartz, and Johnson.

(DREW, N.) Farah, David. *Farah's Price Guide to Nancy Drew Books and Collectibles.* Seventh Printing. No place: Farah's Books (1990).

(DRIFTWIND PRESS) See Ransom.

(DRINKWATER, J.) See Cutler and Stiles.

(DUGAN, A.) See FPAA #2.

(DUGANNE, A.J.H.) See BAL #2.

(DUNBAR, P. L.) See BAL #2.

(DUNCAN, R.) Bertholf, Robert J. *Robert Duncan: A Descriptive Bibliography.* Santa Rosa, Calif.: Black Sparrow Press, 1986.
See also FPAA #3, and Lepper.

(DUNLAP, W.) See BAL #2.

(DUNNE, F. P.) See Johnson.

(DUNSANY, L.) See Cutler and Stiles.

(DURRELL, L.) Fraser, G. S., and Thomas, Alan G. *Lawrence Durrell: A Study.* London: Faber & Faber (1968).

(DWIGHT, THEODORE) See FPAA #1.

(DWIGHT, TIMOTHY) See BAL #2.

(DYKE, H. V.) See FPAA #2.

(DYKEMAN, W.) See FPAA #4.

(E., A.) Denson, Alan. *Printed Writings by George W. Russell (A.E.): A Bibliography.* Evanston: Northwestern University Press, 1961.

(EASTLAKE, W.) See APG, and FPAA #2.

(EBERHART, R.) See FPAA #1.

(EDGERTON, G.) See Gawsworth.

(EDMONDS, W. D.) See Johnson.

(EGGLESTON, E.) See BAL #3, and Johnson.

(EIGNER, L.) Wyatt, Andrea. *A Bibliography of Works by Larry Eigner.* Berkeley: Oyez, 1970.

(ELIOT, G.) Lake, Brian, and Nassau, Janet. *George Eliot in Original Cloth: A Bibliographical Catalogue.* (Bloomsbury/London): Jarndyce Antiquarian Books (1988).
See also Sadleir.

(ELIOT, T. S.) Gallup, Donald. *T. S. Eliot: A Bibliography.* London: Faber & Faber (1970).
See also APG, and Schwartz.

(ELKIN, S.) See FPAA #1.

(ELLIOTT, G. P.) See FPAA #4, and Lepper.

(ELLIOTT, W.) See FPAA #1.

(ELLISON, R.) See FPAA #3.

(ELY, D.) See FPAA #2.

(EMERSON, R. W.) Myerson, Joel. *Ralph Waldo Emerson: A Descriptive Bibliography.* (Pittsburgh) University of Pittsburgh Press, 1982.
See also BAL #3, FPAA #2, Johnson, and Schwartz.

(ENGLISH, T. D.) See BAL #3.

(EPSTEIN, S.) See FPAA #1.

(ERAGNY PRESS) See Franklin, and Ransom.

(ESHLEMAN, C.) See FPAA #3, and Lepper.

(ESSEX HOUSE) See Franklin, and Ransom.

(EVANS, WALKER) Kingston, Rodger. *Walker Evans in Print.* (Belmont, Mass.): R. P. Kingston, 1995.

(EVERSON, W.) Sipper, Ralph. *William Everson: A Collection of Books & Manuscripts.* Santa Barbara: Joseph the Provider (1987).
See also Lepper.

(EXLEY, F.) See FPAA #3.

(FAIRFIELD, S. L.) See BAL #3.

(FANFROLIC PRESS) See Ransom.

(FARRELL, J. T.) Branch, Edgar. *A Bibliography of James T. Farrell's Writings 1921–1957.* Philadelphia: University of Pennsylvania Press (1959).
See also FPAA #5, and Johnson.

(FAULKNER, W.) Brodsky, Louis Daniel, and Hamblin, Robert *W. Faulkner: A Comprehensive Guide to the Brodsky Collection.* Jackson: University Press of Mississippi (1982).

Petersen, Carl. *Each in Its Ordered Place: A Faulkner Collector's Notebook.* Ann Arbor: Ardis (1975).

Massey, Linton R. *"Man Working," 1919–1962: William Faulkner.* Charlottesville, Va.: Bibliographical Society of the University of Virginia (1968).

See also APG, FPAA #1, and Johnson.

(FAUST, I.) See FPAA #1.

(FAWCETT, E.) See BAL #3.

(FAY, T.) See BAL #3.

(FEARING, K.) See FPAA #1.

(FEIBLEMAN, P.) See APG.

(FERBER, E.) See Johnson.

(FERLINGHETTI, L.) See Lepper.

(FERRINI, V.) See FPAA #3.

(FIELD, E.) See BAL #3, and Johnson.

(FIELDS, J. T.) See BAL #3.

(FIRBANK, R.) Benkovitz, Miriam J. *A Bibliography of Ronald Firbank.* London: Rupert Hart-Davis, 1963.

Benkovitz, Miriam J. *Supplement to a Bibliography of Ronald Firbank.* London: Enitharmon Press, 1980.

See also Cutler and Stiles.

(FISHER, V.) See Johnson.

(FISKE, J.) See BAL #3.

(FITCH, C.) See BAL #3.

(FITZGERALD, E.) Prideaux, Colonel W. F. *Notes for a Bibliography of Edward FitzGerald.* New York: Burt Franklin (1968).

(FITZGERALD, F. S.) Bruccoli, Matthew J. *F. Scott Fitzgerald: A Descriptive Bibliography.* (Pittsburgh) University of Pittsburgh Press, 1987.

See also APG, and FPAA #1.

(FITZGERALD, Z.) See FPAA #2.

(FLANNER, J.) See FPAA #4.

(FLEMING, I.) Campbell, Iain. *Ian Fleming: A Catalogue of a Collection.* Liverpool: Iain Campbell (1978).

See also APG.

(FLETCHER, J. G.) Morton, Bruce. *John Gould Fletcher: A Bibliography.* No place: Kent State University Press (1979).

(FLEURON PRESS) See Ransom.

(FLINT, T.) See BAL #3.

(FLORENCE PRESS) See Ransom.

(FLOWERS) See Sitwell.

(FOOTE, S.) See FPAA #2.

(FORD, F. M.) Harvey, David Dow. *Ford Madox Ford 1873–1939.* New York: Gordian Press, 1972.

(FORD, P. L.) See BAL #3, and Johnson.

(FORESTER, C. S.) See APG.

(FORESTER, F.) See Herbert, H. W.

(FORSTER, E. M.) Kirkpatrick, B. J. *A Bibliography of E. M. Forster.* Oxford: Clarendon Press, 1985.

(FORTUNE PRESS) See Ransom.

(FOSTER, H.) See BAL #3.

(FOWLES, J.) See APG.

(FOX, J., JR.) See BAL #3, and Johnson.

(FOX, W. P.) See FPAA #1.

(FRANCIS, D.) See APG.

(FRANKLIN, B.) Ford, Paul Leicester. *A List of Books Written by, or Relating to Benjamin Franklin.* Reprinted. New York: Burt Franklin (1968).

(FRANKLIN PRESS) See Ransom.

(FREDERIC, H.) See BAL #3, and Johnson.

(FREEMAN, M.E.W.) See BAL #3, and Johnson.

(FRENEAU, P.) See BAL #3, and Johnson.

(FRIEDMAN, B. J.) See FPAA #4, and Lepper.

(FROST, R.) Crane, Joan St. C. *Robert Frost: A Descriptive Catalogue of Books and Manuscripts in the Clifton Waller Barrett Library.* Charlottesville: University Press of Virginia (1974).
See also APG, FPAA #1, Johnson, and Schwartz.

(FUCHS, D.) See FPAA #1.

(FULLER, H. B.) See BAL #3, and Johnson.

(FULLER, M.) Myerson, Joel. *Margaret Fuller: A Descriptive Bibliography.* (Pittsburgh) University of Pittsburgh Press, 1978.
See also BAL #3, and FPAA #1.

(FULLER, S. M.) See BAL #3, and FPAA #1.

(GADDIS, W.) See APG, and FPAA #1.

(GAINES, E.) See APG, and FPAA #1.

(GALLAGHER, W. D.) See BAL #3.

(GALSWORTHY, J.) Fabes, Gilbert H. *John Galsworthy His First Editions: Points and Values.* London: W. and G. Foyle (1932).
See also Cutler and Stiles, and Schwartz.

(GARCÍA MÁRQUEZ, G.) See APG.

(GARDNER, J.) Howell, John M. *John Gardner: A Bibliographical Profile.* Carbondale and Edwardsville: Southern Illinois University Press (1980).
See also FPAA #3, and Lepper.

(GARLAND, H.) See Johnson.

(GARRETT, G.) Wright, Stuart. *George Garrett: A Bibliography, 1947–1988.* (Huntsville, Tex.) Texas Review Press, Sam Houston State University, 1989.
See also FPAA #2.

(GASCOYNE, D.) Benford, Colin T. *David Gascoyne: A Bibliography of His Works (1929–1985).* Isle of Wight: Heritage Books, no date.

(GASKELL, MRS.) See Sadleir.

(GASS, W. H.) See APG, FPAA #4, and Lepper.

(GEHENNA PRESS) Franklin, Colin; Baskin, Hosea; and Baskin, Leonard. *The Gehenna Press: The Work of Fifty Years, 1942–1992.* No place: The Birdwell Library, and The Gehenna Press (1992).

(GELLHORN, M.) See FPAA #4.

(GIBBINGS, R.) Kirkus, A. Mary. *Robert Gibbings: A Bibliography.* London: J. M. Dent (1962).

(GIBSON, WILFRID) See Gawsworth.

(GIBSON, WILLIAM) See FPAA #5.

(GILBRETH, F. B.) See FPAA #3.

(GILDER, R. W.) See BAL #3.

(GILL, B.) See FPAA #3.

(GILL, E.) Gill, Evan R. *Bibliography of Eric Gill.* (Revised by D. Steven Corey and Julia MacKenzie.) Second edition. St. Paul's Bibliographies. Wincester/Omnigraphics. Detroit: 1991.

(GINSBERG, A.) Dowden, George. *A Bibliography of Works by Allen Ginsberg.* (San Francisco): City Lights Books (1971).

(GISSING, G.) Collie, Michael. *George Gissing: A Bibliography.* (Toronto and Buffalo) Dawson (1975).

(GLASGOW, E.) Kelly, William W. *Ellen Glasgow: A Bibliography*. Charlottesville: The Bibliographical Society of the University of Virginia (1964).

See also FPAA #2, and Johnson.

(GOLD, H.) See FPAA #1, and Lepper.

(GOLDEN COCKEREL PRESS) See Franklin.

(GOLF) Donovan, Richard E., and Murdoch, Joseph S. F. *The Game of Golf and the Printed Word 1566–1985: A Bibliography of Golf Literature in the English Language*. Endicott, N.Y.: Castalio Press, 1988.

(GOODMAN, P.) See Lepper.

(GORDIMER, N.) See APG.

(GORDON, C.) See FPAA #1.

(GORES, J.) See FPAA #3.

(GOREY, E.) Toledano, Henry. *Goreyography: A Divers Compendium of and Price Guide to the Works of Edward Gorey*. San Francisco: Word Play Publications (1996).

(GOVER, R.) See FPAA #2.

(GOYEN, W.) Wright, Stuart. *William Goyen: A Descriptive Bibliography, 1938–1985*. (Westport, Conn.) Meckler (1986).

See also APG, FPAA #4, and Lepper.

(GRABHORN PRESS) See Ransom.

(GRAFTON, S.) See APG.

(GRAHAM, S.) See FPAA #3.

(GRAU, S.) See APG, FPAA #4, and Lepper.

(GRAVES, R.) Higginson, F. H., and Williams, William P. *Robert Graves: A Bibliography*. (Hampshire, England) St. Paul's Bibliographies, 1987.

See also APG.

(GRAY, ALASDAIR) See Rees.

(GREEN, A. K.) See FPAA #4, and Johnson.

(GREEN, B. K.) Wilson, Robert A. *Ben K. Green: A Descriptive Bibliography of Writings By and About Him*. Flagstaff: Northland Press (1977).

(GREENAWAY, K.) Engen, Rodney. *Kate Greenaway: A Biography*. New York: Schocken Books, 1981. Kiger, Robert, ed. *Kate Greenaway: Catalogue of an Exhibition of Original Artworks and Related Materials . . .* Pittsburgh: Hunt Institute for Botanical Documentation, Carnegie-Mellon University, 1980.

(GREENBERG, J.) See FPAA #2.

(GREENE, G.) Wobbe, R. A. *Graham Greene: A Bibliography and Guide to Research*. New York and London: Garland, 1979.

See also APG.

(GREGOR, A.) See FPAA #2.

(GREGYNOG PRESS) See Franklin, and Ransom.

(GREY, Z.) Myers, Edward and Judith. *A Bibliographical Check List of the Writings of Zane Grey*. Collinsville, Ct.: Country Lane Books, 1986.

See also APG, and FPAA #5.

(GRIMES, M.) See APG.

(GRISWOLD, R. W.) See BAL #3.

(GROSSMAN, A.) See FPAA #4.

(GRUBB, D.) See APG.

(GRUMBACH, D.) See APG.

(GUEST, B.) See FPAA #5.

(GUINEY, L.I.) See BAL #3, and Johnson.

(GUNN) Hagstrom, Jack W. C., and Bixby, George. *Thom Gunn: A Bibliography 1940–78*. London: Bertram Rota (1979).

(HAGGARD, H. R.) McKay, George L. *A Bibliography of the Writings of Sir Rider Haggard*. London: The Bookman's Journal, 1930.

Scott, J. E. *Sir Henry Rider Haggard 1856–1925*. Takeley (England): Elkin Mathews, 1947.

(HALE, N.) See FPAA #1.

(HALE, S. J.) See BAL #3.

(HALL, B. R.) See BAL #3.

(HALL, D.) See Lepper.

(HALL, J.) See BAL #3.

(HALL, J. N.) See FPAA #3.

(HALLECK, F.) See BAL #3, and Johnson.

(HALPINE, C. G.) See BAL #3.

(HAMMETT, D.) Layman, Richard. *Dashiell Hammett: A Descriptive Bibliography*. (Pittsburgh) University of Pittsburgh Press, 1979.

See also APG, and FPAA #1.

(HANLEY, J.) Gibbs, Linnea. *James Hanley: A Bibliography*. Vancouver: William Hoffer, 1980.

(HARDY, A. S.) See BAL #3.

(HARDY, J. E.) See FPAA #2.

(HARDY, T.) Purdy, Richard Little. *Thomas Hardy: A Bibliographical Study*. Reprinted. Oxford: Clarendon Press (1978).

Webb, A. P. *A Bibliography of the Works of Thomas Hardy 1865–1915*. New York: Burt Franklin (1968).

See also Cutler and Stiles, and Sadleir.

(HARLAND, H.) See BAL #3.

(HARRIS, F.) See *Casanova*.

(HARRIS, G. W.) See BAL #3.

(HARRIS, J. C.) See BAL #3, and Johnson.

(HARRIS, M.) See FPAA #1.

(HARRISON, C.) See BAL #3.

(HARRISON, J.). See APG.

(HARRISON OF PARIS) See Ford.

(HARTE, B.) See BAL #3, and Johnson.

(HASSLER, J.) Powers, Michael. *An Interview with Jon Hassler*. With a bibliography by Larry Dingman. Minneapolis: Dinkytown Antiquarian Bookstore, 1990.

(HAWKES, J.) See FPAA #1, Gawsworth, and Lepper.

(HAWTHORNE, N.) Clark, C. E. Frazer, Jr. *Nathaniel Hawthorne: A Descriptive Bibliography*. (Pittsburgh) University of Pittsburgh Press, 1978.

See also BAL #4, FPAA #1, Johnson, and Schwartz.

(HAY, J.) See BAL #4, and Johnson.

(HAYNE, P. H.) See BAL #4.

(HAZO, S.) See FPAA #2.

(HAZZARD, S.) See FPAA #4.

(HEARN, L.) Perkins, P. D. and Ione. *Lafcadio Hearn: A Bibliography of His Writings*. Boston and New York: Houghton Mifflin, 1934.

See also BAL #4, and Johnson.

(HEDGE, F. H.) See FPAA #3.

(HEINLEIN, R. A.) Owings, Mark. *Robert A. Heinlein: A Bibliography*. Baltimore: Croatan House (1973). See also APG.

(HELLER, J.) See APG, FPAA #2, and Lepper.

(HELLMAN, L.) See FPAA #2.

(HEMINGWAY, E.) Hanneman, André. *Ernest Hemingway: A Comprehensive Bibliography*. Princeton, N.J.: Princeton University Press, 1967.

Hanneman, André. *Supplement to Ernest Hemingway: A Comprehensive Bibliography*. Princeton, N.J.: Princeton University Press, 1975.

See also APG, FPAA #1, and Johnson.

(HENRY, O.) See Porter, BAL #7, and Johnson.

(HENTY, G. A.) Dartt, Robert L. *G. A. Henty: A Bibliography*. Cedar Grove (N.J.): Dar-Web and Altricham (England): John Sherratt (1971).

Dartt, Robert L. *A Companion to G. A. Henty: A Bibliography*. (Cedar Grove, N.J.: Robert L. Dartt, 1972.)

(HERBERT, A. P.) See Fabes.

(HERBERT, F.) Levack, Daniel J. H. *Dune Master: A Frank Herbert Bibliography*. (Westport, Conn.) Meckler (1988).

(HERBERT, H. W.) Van Winkle, William Mitchell. *Henry William Herbert [Frank Forester]: A Bibliography of His Writings 1832–1858*. Portland, Ore.: Southworth-Anthoesen Press, 1936.

See also BAL #4, and Johnson.

(HERBST, J.) See FPAA #1.

(HERFORD, O.) See Johnson.

(HERGESHEIMER, J.) Swire, H.L.R. *A Bibliography of the Works of Joseph Hergesheimer*. Philadelphia: Centaur Book Shop, 1922.

See also Johnson, and Schwartz.

(HERLIHY, J. L.) See FPAA #5.

(HEWLETT, M.) See Cutler and Stiles.

(HEYEN, W.) See FPAA #2.

(HEYWARD, D.) See FPAA #3, and Johnson.

(HIGGINS, G. V.) See FPAA #1.

(HIGGINSON, T. W.) See BAL #4.

(HILLERMAN, T.) *Collecting Tony Hillerman: A Checklist of the First Editions of Tony Hillerman*. Santa Fe, N.M.: Vinegar Tom Press (1992).

Heib, Louis A. *Tony Hillerman: A Bibliography*. Tucson: Press of the Gigantic Hound, 1990.

See also APG.

(HILLHOUSE, J. A.) See BAL #4.

(HIMES, C.) See APG.

(HIRSHMAN, J.) See Lepper.

(HODGSON, R.) Sweetser, Wesley D. *Ralph Hodgson: A Bibliography*. New York and London: Garland, 1980.

(HOFFMAN, C. F.) See BAL #4, and Johnson.

(HOFFMAN, D.) See FPAA #2.

(HOGARTH PRESS) Woolmer, J. Howard. *A Checklist of The Hogarth Press 1917–1946*. Revere, Pa.: Woolmer/Brotherson, 1986.

(HOLLAND, J. G.) See BAL #4.

(HOLLEY, M.) See FPAA #4.

(HOLMES, J.) See FPAA #5.

(HOLMES, J. C.) Ardinger, Richard K. *An Annotated Bibliography of Works by John Clellon Holmes*. Pocatello: Idaho State University Press, 1979.

See also FPAA #2.

(HOLMES, M. J.) See BAL #4.

(HOLMES, O. W.) Currier, Thomas Franklin. *A Bibliography of Oliver Wendell Holmes.* New York: New York University Press; London: Oxford University Press; 1953.

See also BAL #4, Johnson, and Schwartz.

(HOOKER, T.) See FPAA #4.

(HOPKINS, G. M.) Dunne, Tom. *Gerard Manley Hopkins: A Comprehensive Bibliography.* Oxford: Clarendon Press, 1978.

(HOPLEY, G.) See FPAA #3, and Woolrich.

(HORGAN, P.) Horgan, Paul. *Approaches to Writing.* New York: Farrar, Straus & Giroux (1973).

(HOSMER, W.H.C.) See BAL #4.

(HOUGH, E.) See BAL #4, and Johnson.

(HOUSMAN, A. E.) Carter, John, and Sparrow, John. *A. E. Housman: A Bibliography.* Second edition. Revised by William White. (Suffolk, England) St. Paul's Bibliographies, 1982.

Ehrsam, Theodore G. *A Bibliography of Alfred Edward Housman.* Boston: F. W. Faxon, 1941.

(HOVEY, R.) See BAL #4, and Johnson.

(HOWARD, R. E.) Lord, Glenn. *The Last Celt: A Bio-Bibliography of Robert Ervin Howard.* West Kingston (R.I.): Donald M. Grant, 1976.

(HOWE, E. W.) See FPAA #2.

(HOWE, J. W.) See BAL #4.

(HOWELLS, W. D.) Gibson, William M., and Arms, George. *A Bibliography of William Dean Howells.* New York: New York Public Library (1971).

See also BAL #4, Johnson.

(HUDSON, S.) See Gawsworth.

(HUDSON, W. H.) Payne, John R. *W. H. Hudson: A Bibliography.* (Hamden, Conn.) Archon Books (1977).

See also Schwartz, Cutler and Stiles.

(HUGHES, L.) Dickinson, Donald C. *A Bio-bibliography of Langston Hughes 1902–1967.* (Hamden, Conn.) Archon Books, 1972.

See also APG, and FPAA #3.

(HUGHES, T.) Sagar, Keith, and Tabor, Stephen. *Ted Hughes: A Bibliography 1946–1980.* (London) Mansell (1983).

(HUNT, LEIGH) Brewer, Luther A. *My Leigh Hunt Library: The First Editions.* New York: Burt Franklin (1970). A reprint of the 1932 edition.

(HUMPHREY, W.) See FPAA #1.

(HUNEKER, J.) See BAL #4, and Johnson.

(HURSTON, Z. N.) See APG, and FPAA #1.

(HUXLEY, A.) Eschelbach, Claire John, and Shober, Joyce Lee. *Aldous Huxley: A Bibliography 1916–1959.* Berkeley: University of California Press, 1961.

See also *Casanova,* and Cutler and Stiles.

(INGE, W.) See FPAA #2.

(INGERSOLL, R. G.) Stein, Gordon. *Robert G. Ingersoll: A Checklist.* No place: Kent State University Press (1969).

(INGRAHAM, J. H.) See BAL #4.

(IRISH, W.) See Woolrich.

(IRVING, J.) See APG.

(IRVING, W.) Langfeld, William R. *Washington Irving: A Bibliography.* New York: New York Public Library, 1933.

Williams, Stanley T., and Edge, Mary Allen. *A Bibliography of the Writings of Washington Irving: A Check List.* Reprinted. New York: Burt Franklin (1970).

See also BAL #5, and Johnson.

(ISHERWOOD, C.) Westby, Selmer, and Brown, Clayton M. *Christopher Isherwood: A Bibliography.* Los Angeles: California State College at Los Angeles Foundation, 1968.

(ISHIGURO, K.) See APG.

(JACKSON, C.) See FPAA #3.

(JACKSON, H. H.) See BAL #5, and Johnson.

(JACKSON, S.) See FPAA #2.

(JACOBS, W. W.) Edel, Leon, and Laurence, Dan H. *A Bibliography of Henry James.* Oxford: Clarendon Press, 1982.

Lamerton, Chris. *W. W. Jacobs: A Bibliography.* (Margate, Kent) Greystone Press (1988).

Philips, LeRoy. *A Bibliography of the Writings of Henry James.* New York: Coward McCann, 1930. See also BAL #5, and Johnson.

(JAMES, P. D.) See APG.

(JAMES, W.) See Johnson.

(JANVIER, T. A.) See BAL #5, Johnson.

(JARRELL) Wright, Stuart. *Randall Jarrell: A Descriptive Bibliography 1929–1983.* Charlottesville: University Press of Virginia (1986).

See also FPAA #4.

(JEFFERIES, R.) See Sadleir.

(JEFFERS, R.) Alberts, S. S. *A Bibliography of the Works of Robinson Jeffers.* Rye, N.Y.: Cultural History Research, 1961.

See also APG, FPAA #3, and Johnson.

(JEWETT, S. O.) See BAL #5, and Johnson.

(JOHNSON, J.) See FPAA #5.

(JOHNSON, O.) See FPAA #5.

(JOHNSON, S.) Courtney, William Prideaux, and Smith, David Nichol. *A Bibliography of Samuel Johnson.* With *Johnsonian Bibliography: A Supplement to Courtney,* by R. W. Chapman and Allen Hazen. (New Castle, Del.) Oak Knoll Books and Gerald M. Goldberg, 1984.

See also FPAA #3.

(JOHNSTON, M.) See Johnson.

(JOHNSTON, R. M.) See BAL #5.

(JONES, J.) Hopkins, John R. *James Jones: A Checklist.* Detroit: Gale Research, 1974.

See also FPAA #1.

(JONES, J. B.) See BAL #6.

(JONES, L.) Dace, Letitia. *LeRoi Jones (Imamu Amiri Baraka): A Checklist of Works By and About Him.* London: Nether Press, 1971.

See also FPAA #1.

(JONES, M. P.) See FPAA #1.

(JONES, R. F.) See Currey.

(JONG, E.) See FPAA #1.

(JOSEPHSON, M.) See FPAA #1.

(JOYCE, J.) Slocum, John J., and Cahoon, Herbert. *A Bibliography of James Joyce.* Westport, Conn.: Greenwood Press (1953).

See also APG, and *Casanova.*

(JUDAH, S.B.H.) See BAL #5.

(JUDD, S.) See BAL #5.

(KAFKA, F.) Flores, Angel. *A Kafka Bibliography 1908–1976.* New York: Gordian Press, 1976.

(KAHN, R.) See FPAA #5.

(KEATS, J.) MacGillivray, J. R. *Keats: A Bibliography and Reference Guide with an Essay on Keats' Reputation.* Canada: University of Toronto Press (1949).

See also Schwartz.

(KELLER, D. H.) See Currey.

(KELLEY, E. S.) See FPAA #1.

(KELLEY, R.) See Lepper.

(KELLEY, W. M.) See FPAA #2.

(KELLY, W.) See FPAA #4.

(KELMSCOTT PRESS) Peterson, William S. *A Bibliography of the Kelmscott Press.* Reprinted with corrections. Oxford: Clarendon Press, 1985.

See also Franklin, and Ransom.

(KENNEDY, J. P.) See BAL #5, and Johnson.

(KENNEDY, W.) See APG.

(KENNEDY, X.) See FPAA #1.

(KENNEDY, X. J.) See FPAA #2.

(KENT, R.) See Johnson.

(KEROUAC, J.) Charters, Ann. *A Bibliography of Works by Jack Kerouac.* New York: Phoenix Bookshop, 1975.

See also APG, and FPAA #1.

(KESEY, K.) See APG, and FPAA #1.

(KEY, F. S.) See BAL #5.

(KEYES, D.) See Currey.

(KILLENS, J. O.) See FPAA #2, and Lepper.

(KILMER, J.) See BAL #5, and Johnson.

(KING, S.) See APG, and Currey.

(KINNELL, G.) See FPAA #2.

(KIPLING) Livingston, Flora V. *Bibliography of the Works of Rudyard Kipling.* New York: Burt Franklin (1968).

Livingston, Flora V. *Supplement to a Bibliography of the Works of Rudyard Kipling.* New York: Burt Franklin (1968).

See also Cutler and Stiles.

(KIRKLAND, C. M.) See BAL #5.

(KIRKLAND, J.) See BAL #5.

(KLASS, P. J.) See Currey.

(KLINE, O. A.) See Currey.

(KNEALE, T. N.) See Currey.

(KNIGHT, D. F.) See Currey.

(KNOWLES, J.) See FPAA #3.

(KOCH, K.) See Lepper.

(KOESTLER, A.) Merrill, Reed, and Frazier, Thomas. *Arthur Koestler: An International Bibliography.* Ann Arbor: Ardis (1979).

(KOONTZ, D. R.) Stephens, Christopher P. *A Checklist of Dean R. Koontz.* Hastings-on-Hudson, N.Y.: Ultramarine, 1987.

(KORNBLUTH, K. M.) See Currey.

(KOSINSKI, J.) See FPAA #4.

(KUNITZ, S.) See FPAA #1.

(KUTTNER, H.) See Currey.

(LAFFERTY, R. A.) See Currey.

(LAMANTIA, P.) See Lepper.

(LAMB, C.) Livingston, Luther S.; Thomson, J. C.; and Roff, Renée (compiler). *A Bibliography of the Writings of Charles and Mary Lamb.* Bronxville, N.Y.: Nicholas T. Smith (1979).

(LANDON, M. D.) See BAL #5.

(LANDOR, W. S.) Wise & Wheeler. *Walter Savage Landor: A Bibliography.* London: 1979.

(LANGE, J. F.) See Currey.

(LANIER, SIDNEY) See BAL #5, and Johnson.

(LANIER, STERLING) See Currey.

(LARCOM, L.) See BAL #5.

(LARDNER, R.) Bruccoli, Matthew J., and Richard Layman. *Ring W. Lardner: A Descriptive Bibliography.* (Pittsburgh): University of Pittsburgh Press (1976).
See also FPAA #1, and Johnson.

(LARKIN, P.) Bloomfield, B. C. *Philip Larkin: A Bibliography 1933–1976.* London and Boston: Faber & Faber (1979).

(LARNER, J.) See FPAA #2.

(LATHROP, G. P.) See BAL #5.

(LAUMER, J. K.) See Currey.

(LAWRENCE, D. H.) Roberts, Warren. *A Bibliography of D. H. Lawrence.* Second edition. Cambridge: Cambridge University Press (1982).
See also APG, Cutler and Stiles, and Schwartz.

(LAWRENCE, T. E.) O'Brien, Philip M. *T. E. Lawrence: A Bibliography.* Boston: G. K. Hall (1988).
See also APG.

(LAZARUS, E..) See BAL #5.

(LEACOCK, S.) Lomer, Gerhard R. *Stephen Leacock: A Check-list and Index of His Writings.* Ottawa: National Library of Canada, 1954.
Spadoni, Carl. *A Bibliography of Stephen Leacock.* (Toronto) ECW Press (1998).

(LEAVIS, F. R.) McKenzie, D. F., and Allum, M-P. *F. R. Leavis: A Check-list 1924–1964.* London: Chatto & Windus, 1966.

(LECARRÉ, J.) See APG.

(LEGALLIENNE, R.) See Cutler and Stiles.

(LE GUIN, U.) Cogell, Elizabeth Cummins. *Ursula K. Le Guin: A Primary and Secondary Bibliography.* Boston: G. K. Hall (1983).
See also Currey.

(LEIBER, F.) Morgan, Chris. *Fritz Leiber: A Bibliography 1934–1979.* Selly Oak, Birmingham, England: Morgenstern, 1979.
See also Currey.

(LELAND, C. G.) See BAL #5.

(LEONARD, E.) Stephens, Christopher P. *A Checklist of Elmore Leonard.* (Hastings-on-Hudson, N.Y.: Ultramarine 1991.)
See also APG.

(LESSING, D.) Brueck, Eric T. *Doris Lessing: A Bibliography of Her First Editions.* (London) Metropolis (Antiquarian Books), 1984.

(LEVERTOV, D.) Wilson, Robert. *A Bibliography of Denise Levertov.* New York: Phoenix Bookshop, 1972.
See also FPAA #3, and Lepper.

(LEVIN, I.) See FPAA #2.

(LEWIS, A. H.) See BAL #5.

(LEWIS, C. S.) Christopher, Joe R., and Ostling, Joan K. *C. S. Lewis: An Annotated Checklist of Writings About Him and His Works.* (Rochester): Kent State University Press, no date.
See also Currey.

(LEWIS, J.) See FPAA #4.

(LEWIS, S.) Pastore, Stephen R. *Sinclair Lewis: A Descriptive Bibliography.* New Haven: Yale Books, 1997.
See also FPAA #3, and Johnson.

(LEWIS, W.) Morrow, Bradford, and Lafourcade, Bernard. *A Bibliography of the Writings of Wyndham Lewis.* Santa Barbara: Black Sparrow Press, 1978.

(LEY, R. A.) See Currey.

(LIMITED EDITIONS CLUB) See APG.

(LINCOLN, A.) Smith, William H., Jr. *A Priced Lincoln Bibliography*. New York: privately published, 1906.

(LINDSAY, D.) See Currey.

(LINDSAY, V.) See Johnson.

(LINEBARGER, P.) See Currey.

(LIPPARD, G.) See BAL #5.

(LOCKE, D. R.) See BAL #5.

(LODGE, G. C.) See FPAA #1.

(LOEB, H.) See FPAA #1.

(LOEWINSOHN, R.) See Lepper.

(LONDON, J.) Sisson, James E., III, and Martens, Robert W. *Jack London First Editions*. Oakland: Star Rover House, 1979.

   Walker, Dale L., and Sisson, James E., III. *The Fiction of Jack London: A Chronological Bibliography*. El Paso: Texas Western Press, 1972.

   Woodbridge, Hensley C.; London, John; and Tweney, George H. *Jack London: A Bibliography*. Georgetown (Calif.): Talisman Press, 1966.

   See also APG, BAL #5, and Johnson.

(LONG, F. B.) See Currey.

(LONG, H.) See FPAA #5.

(LONGFELLOW) Livingston, Luther S. *A Bibliography of the First Editions . . . of Henry Wadsworth Longfellow*. New York: Burt Franklin (1968).

   See also BAL #5, Johnson, and Schwartz.

(LONGFELLOW, S.) See FPAA #3.

(LONGSTREET, A. B.) See BAL #6, and FPAA #1.

(LOOS, A.) See FPAA #3.

(LOVECRAFT, H. P.) Owings, Mark, with Chalker, Jack L. *The Revised H. P. Lovecraft Bibliography*. Baltimore: Mirage Press, 1973.

   See also Currey.

(LOWELL, A.) See BAL #6, and Johnson.

(LOWELL, J. R.) Chamberlain, Jacob Chester, and Livingston, Luther S. *A Bibliography of the First Editions in Book Form of the Writings of James Russell Lowell*. New York: privately printed, 1914.

   See also BAL #6, and Johnson.

(LOWELL, R.) See FPAA #1.

(LOWELL, R.T.S.) See BAL #6.

(LOWNDES, R. A.) See Currey.

(LOWRY, M.) Woolmer, J. Howard. *Malcolm Lowry: A Bibliography*. Revere, Mass.: Woolmer/Brotherson, 1983.

(LUDLUM, R.) See APG.

(LUMPKIN, G.) See FPAA #2.

(LUPOFF, R. A.) See Currey.

(LURIE, A.) See FPAA #5.

(LYON, H. M.) See FPAA #4.

(LYTLE, A.) Wright, Stuart. *Andrew Nelson Lytle: A Bibliography 1920–1982*. Sewanee (Tenn.): University of the South, 1982.

   See also FPAA #1.

(MACDONALD, J. D.) Shine, Walter and Jean. *A MacDonald Potpourri—Being a Miscellany of Post-perusal Pleasures of the John D. MacDonald Books . . .* Gainesville, Fla.: University of Florida Libraries, 1988.

   See also APG.

(MACDONALD, R.) Bruccoli, Matthew J. *Ross Macdonald/Kenneth Millar A Descriptive Bibliography.* (Pittsburgh) University of Pittsburgh Press, 1983.
See also APG, and FPAA #1 (Millar).

(MACGREGOR, J. M.) See Currey.

(MACHEN, A.) Danielson, Henry. *Arthur Machen: A Bibliography.* London: Henry Danielson, 1923.
Goldstone, Adrian, and Sweetser, Wesley. *A Bibliography of Arthur Machen.* New York: Haskell House, 1973.

(MACLEAN, K. A.) See Currey.

(MACLEISH, A.) Mullaly, Edward J. *Archibald MacLeish: A Checklist.* No place: Kent State University Press (1973).
See also Johnson.

(MACNEICE, L.) Brown, Terence, and Reid, Alec. *Time Was Away: The World of Louis MacNeice.* (Dublin) Dolmen Press (1974).

(MAILER, N.) See APG, FPAA #5, and Lepper.

(MAJOR, C.) See BAL #6.

(MALAMUD, B.) Kosofsky, Rita Nathalie. *Bernard Malamud: An Annotated Checklist.* No place: Kent State University Press (1969).
See APG, FPAA #5, and Lepper.

(MALZBERG, B. N.) See Currey.

(MANSFIELD, K.) Kirkpatrick, J. *A Bibliography of Katherine Mansfield.* Oxford: Clarendon Press, 1989.

(MARCH, W. E.) See FPAA #3.

(MARKFIELD, W.) See FPAA #1.

(MARKHAM, E.) See Johnson.

(MARKSON, D.) See APG.

(MARQUAIS, D.) See Johnson.

(MARQUAND, J. P.) See FPAA #1.

(MARSH, N.) Gibbs, Rowan, and Williams, Richard. *Ngaio Marsh: A Bibliography of English Language Publications in Hardback and Paperback.* South Humberside, England: Dragonby Press, 1990.

(MARSHALL, P.) See APG.

(MARTIN, G.R.R.) See Currey.

(MARVEL, I.) See Johnson.

(MASEFIELD, J.) Handley-Taylor, Geoffrey. *John Masefield, O.M. The Queen's Poet Laureate.* London: Cranbrook Tower Press (1960).
Simmons, Charles H. *A Bibliography of John Masefield.* New York: Columbia University Press, 1930.
See also Cutler and Stiles.

(MASON, D. R.) See Currey.

(MASSON, D. I.) See Currey.

(MASTERS, E. L.) See FPAA #2, and Johnson.

(MATHESON, R.) See APG, and Currey.

(MATHEWS, C.) See BAL #6.

(MATTHIESSEN, P.) Nicholas, D. *Peter Matthiessen: A Bibliography 1951–1979.* Canoga Press, Calif.: Orirana Press (1979).
See also FPAA #1.

(MAUGHAM, W. S.) Stott, Raymond Toole. *A Bibliography of the Works of W. Somerset Maugham.* Edmonton: University of Alberta Press, 1973.

(MAXWELL, W.) See APG.

(MCALMON, R.) See FPAA #1.

(MCCAFFREY, A. I.) See Currey.

(MCCARTHY, CORMAC.) See APG, and FPAA #1.

(MCCARTHY, M.) Goldman, Sherli Evens. *Mary McCarthy: A Bibliography.* New York: Harcourt, Brace & World (1968).

See also FPAA #4.

(MCCLURE, M.) Clements, Marshall. *A Catalog of Works by Michael McClure 1956–1965.* New York: Phoenix Bookshop (1965).

See also Lepper, and *Six Poets.*

(MCCOY, H.) See FPAA #1.

(MCCULLERS, C.) Shapiro, Adrian M.; Bryer, Jackson R.; and Field, Kathleen. *Carson McCullers: A Descriptive Listing and Annotated Bibliography of Criticism.* New York and London: Garland, 1980.

See also FPAA #2.

(MCCUTCHEON, G. B.) See BAL #6, and Johnson.

(MCELROY, J.) See APG.

(MCEWAN, I.) See Rees.

(MCFEE, W.) Babb, James T. *A Bibliography of the Writings of William McFee.* Garden City: Doubleday, Doran, 1931.

See also Johnson.

(MCGAHERN, J.) See Rees.

(MCGUANE, T.) See APG, and FPAA #5.

(MCHENRY, J.) See BAL #6.

(MCILWAIN, D.) See Currey.

(MCINTYRE, V.) See Currey.

(MCMURTRIE, D. C.) Bruntjen, Scott, and Young, Melissa L. *Douglas C. McMurtrie: Bibliographer and Historian of Printing.* Metuchen, N.J., and London: Scarecrow Press, 1979.

(MCMURTRY, L.) See APG, FPAA #4, and Lepper.

(MCPHEE, J.) See APG.

(MELTZER, D.) Kherdian, David. *David Meltzer: A Sketch from Memory and Descriptive Checklist.* Berkeley: Oyez, 1965.

See also Lepper.

(MELVILLE, H.) See BAL #6, Johnson, and Sadleir.

(MENCKEN, H. L.) Adler, Betty, and Wilhelm, Jane. *H. L. M.: The Mencken Bibliography.* Baltimore: Enoch Pratt Free Library (1961).

Frey, Carroll. *A Bibliography of the Writings of H. L. Mencken.* Philadelphia: The Centaur Book Shop, 1924.

Schrader, Richard J. (with the assistance of Thompson, George H., and Sanders, Jack R.) *H. L. Mencken: A Descriptive Bibliography.* (Pittsburgh) University of Pittsburgh Press (1998).

See APG, Johnson, and Schwartz.

(MEREDITH, G.) Collie, Michael. *George Meredith: A Bibliography.* (Toronto and Buffalo) University of Toronto Press (1974).

Forman, Maurice Buxton. *A Bibliography of the Writings in Prose and Verse of George Meredith.* New York: Haskell House, 1971.

Forman, Maurice Buxton. *Meredithiana, Being A Supplement to the Bibliography of Meredith.* New York: Haskell House, 1971.

(MEREDITH, W.) See FPAA #2.

(MERRIL, J.) See Currey.

(MERRILL, J.) See FPAA #2.

(MERRITT, A.) See Currey.

(MERRYMOUNT PRESS) See Ransom.

(MERTON, T.) Breit, Marquita E. *Thomas Merton: A Comprehensive Bibliography.* New edition. New York and London: Garland, 1986.

See also APG.

(MERWIN, W. S.) See FPAA #1.

(METCALF, P.) See FPAA #3.

(MICHENER, J.) Groseclose, David A. *James A. Michener: A Bibliography.* Austin: State House Press, 1996.

See also APG.

(MILES, J.) See Lepper.

(MILL, JOHN STUART) MacNinn, Ney, et al. *Bibliography of the Published Writings of John Stuart Mill.* Evanston: Northwestern University, 1945.

(MILLAR, K.) See FPAA #1.

(MILLAY) Yost, Karl. *A Bibliography of the Works of Edna St. Vincent Millay.* New York and London: Harper & Brothers. 1937.

See also FPAA #4, and Johnson.

(MILLER, A.) Jensen, George H. *Arthur Miller: A Bibliographical Checklist.* (Columbia, S.C.) J. Faust (1976).

See also APG, and FPAA #1.

(MILLER, H.) Moore, Thomas H. *Bibliography of Henry Miller.* (Minneapolis): Henry Miller Literary Society, 1961.

Porter, Bern. *Henry Miller: A Chronology and Bibliography.* (Baltimore: Waverly Press, 1945.)

Shifreen, Lawrence J., and Jackson, Roger. *Henry Miller: A Bibliography of Primary Sources.* (Ann Arbor, Mich., and Glen Arm, Md.: Roger Jackson, and Lawrence J. Shifreen) 1993.

(MILLER, J.) See BAL #6, and Johnson.

(MILLER, WALTER M.) See Currey.

(MILLER, WARREN.) See Lepper.

(MILNE, A. A.) See Cutler and Stiles.

(MITCHELL, D.) See BAL #6, and Johnson.

(MITCHELL, I.) See BAL #6.

(MITCHELL, J. A.) See BAL #6.

(MITCHELL, S. W.) See BAL #6, and Johnson.

(MOLLOY, R.) See FPAA #4.

(MOODY, W. V.) See BAL #6, and Johnson.

(MOORCOCK, M.) See Currey.

(MOORE, B.) See Rees.

(MOORE, C. C.) See BAL #6.

(MOORE, C. L.) See Currey.

(MOORE, G.) Gilcher, Edwin. *A Bibliography of George Moore.* Dekalb: Northern Illinois University Press (1970).

See also Cutler and Stiles.

(MOORE, JULIA) Greely, A. H. *The Sweet Singer of Michigan Bibliographically Considered.* New York: The Bibliographical Society of America, 1945.

(MOORE, M.) Abbott, Craig S. *Marianne Moore: A Descriptive Bibliography.* (Pittsburgh) University of Pittsburgh Press, 1977.

See also FPAA #1.

(MORGAN, C.) See Coppard.

(MORLEY, C.) Lee, Alfred P. *A Bibliography of Christopher Morley.* Garden City: Doubleday, Doran, 1935.

Lyle, Guy R., and Brown, H. Tatnall, Jr. *A Bibliography of Christopher Morley.* Washington, D.C.: The Scarecrow Press, 1952.

See also *Casanova,* and Johnson.

(MORMON) Flake, Chad J. *A Mormon Bibliography, 1830–1930.* Salt Lake City: University of Utah Press, 1978.

(MORRIS, G. P.) See BAL #6.

(MORRIS, W.) Pye, John William. *A Bibliography of the American Editions of William Morris Published by Roberts Brothers, Boston, 1867–1898.* Brockton, Mass.: John William Pye Rare Books, 1993. See also FPAA #5, and Lepper.

(MORRISON, T.) See APG.

(MORTON, S. W.) See BAL #6, and FPAA #2.

(MOSKOWITZ, S.) See Currey.

(MOSS, H.) See FPAA #2.

(MOTLEY, J. L.) See BAL #6.

(MOTLEY, W.) See FPAA #2.

(MOULTON, E. L.) See BAL #6.

(MUIR, E.) Mellown, Elgin W. *Bibliography of the Writings of Edwin Muir.* University: University of Alabama Press (1964).

(MUIR, J.) Kimes, William F. and Maymie B. *John Muir: A Reading Bibliography.* Fresno: Panorama West Books, 1986. See also BAL #6, and Johnson.

(MUIR, P. H.) *P. H. Muir: A Check List of His Published Work.* (No author listed.) Blakeney (Norfolk, England): Elkin Mathews, 1983.

(MUMFORD, L.) Newman, Elmer S. *Lewis Mumford: A Bibliography 1914–1970.* New York: Harcourt Brace Jovanovich (1971).

(MUNDY, T.) Grant, Donald M. *Talbot Mundy: Messenger of Destiny.* West Kingston (R.I.): Donald M. Grant, 1983.

(MURDOCH, I.) Tominaga, Thomas T., and Schneidermeyer, Wilma. *Iris Murdoch and Muriel Spark: A Bibliography.* Metuchen, N.J.: Scarecrow Press, 1976.

(MURFREE, M. N.) See BAL #6.

(MURRY, JOHN. M.) Lilley, George P. *A Bibliography of John Middleton Murry 1889–1957.* Toronto and Buffalo: University of Toronto Press (1974). See also Currey.

(MYERS, P. H.) See BAL #6.

(NABOKOV, V.) Juliar, Michael. *Vladimir Nabokov: A Descriptive Bibliography.* New York and London: Garland, 1986. See also APG, and FPAA #5.

(NASH, JOHN HENRY PRESS) See Ransom.

(NASH, O.) See FPAA #3.

(NATHAN, G. J.) See Johnson.

(NATHAN, R.) Laurence, Dan H. *Robert Nathan: A Bibliography.* New Haven: Yale University Library, 1960. See also *Casanova,* FPAA #2, and Johnson.

(NEAL, JOHN) See BAL #6.

(NEAL, JOSEPH C.) See BAL #6.

(NEIHARDT, J. G.) See Johnson.

(NEMEROV, H.) See FPAA #2.

(NEUGEBOREN, J.) See FPAA #5.

(NEWELL, R. H.) See BAL #6.

(NEWHOUSE, E.) See FPAA #2.

(NEWMAN, F.) See FPAA #1.

(NEW REVIEW PRESS) See Ford.

(NEWTON, EDWARD.) (Fleck, Robert). *A. Edward Newton: A Collection of His Work.* (New Castle, Del.) Oak Knoll Books, 1986. See also *Casanova,* and Johnson.

(NEWTON, SIR ISAAC.) Gray, George J. *A Bibliography of the Works of Sir Isaac Newton.* Second Edition, Revised and Enlarged. Cambridge: Bowes and Bowes, 1907. Facsimile edition. Mansfield Centre, Conn.: Martino Fine Books (1998).

(NICHOLS, R.) See Gawsworth.

(NIMS, J. F.) See FPAA #4.

(NIN, A.) Franklin, Benjamin, V. *Anaïs Nin: A Bibliography.* No place: Kent State University Press (1973).
See also FPAA #1.

(NIVEN, L.) See Currey.

(NOAH, M. M.) See BAL #6.

(NONESUCH PRESS) See Ransom.

(NORDHOFF, C. B.) See FPAA #3.

(NORRIS, F.) Lohf, Kenneth A., and Sheehy, Eugene P. *Frank Norris: A Bibliography.* Los Gatos (Calif.): The Talisman Press, 1959.
See also BAL #6, and Johnson.

(NORTON, A.) See Currey.

(NOURSE, A. E.) See Currey.

(NYE, B.) See BAL #6.

(OATES, J. C.) Lercangee, Francine. *Joyce Carol Oates: An Annotated Bibliography.* New York and London: Garland, 1986.
See also FPAA #5, and Lepper.

(OBELISK PRESS) See Ford.

(O'BRIEN, F.) See BAL #6.

(O'BRIEN, P.) See APG.

(O'CASEY, S.) Ayling, Ronald, and Durkan, Michael J. *Sean O'Casey: A Bibliography.* Seattle: University of Washington Press (1978).

(O'CONNOR, E.) See FPAA #5.

(O'CONNOR, FLANNERY) Farmer, David. *Flannery O'Connor: A Descriptive Bibliography.* New York and London: Garland, 1981.
See also APG, and FPAA #1.

(O'CONNOR, FRANK) Sheehy, Maurice. *Michael/Frank: Studies on Frank O'Connor.* Dublin: Gill & Macmillan (1969).

(OFFICINA BODINI PRESS) See Ransom.

(O'FLAHERTY, L.) Doyle, Paul A. *Liam O'Flaherty: An Annotated Bibliography.* Troy, N.Y.: Whitston, 1972.

(O'HARA, F.) Smith, Alexander Jr. *Frank O'Hara: A Comprehensive Bibliography.* New York and London: Garland, 1979.
See also FPAA #4, and Lepper.

(O'HARA, J.) Bruccoli, Matthew J. *John O'Hara: A Descriptive Bibliography.* (Pittsburgh) University of Pittsburgh Press, 1978.
See also FPAA #1.

(OLIVER, S. C.) See Currey.

(OLSON, C.) Butterick, George F., and Glover, Albert. *A Bibliography of Works by Charles Olson.* New York: Phoenix Bookshop, 1967.
See also FPAA #3.

(OLYMPIA PRESS) Kearney, Patrick J. *The Paris Olympia Press.* London: Black Spring Press (1987).

(O'NEILL, E.) Atkinson, Jennifer McCabe. *Eugene O'Neill: A Descriptive Bibliography.* (Pittsburgh) University of Pittsburgh Press, 1974.
See also FPAA #1, and Johnson.

(OPPENHEIMER, J.) See FPAA #3.

(O'REILLY, J. B.) See BAL #6.

(ORWELL, G.) Fenwick, Gillian. *George Orwell: A Bibliography*. New Castle: Oak Knoll Press, 1998. See also APG.

(OSGOOD, F. S.) See BAL #6.

(OSLER, W.) Golden, Richard L., M.D., and Roland, Charles G., M.D. *Sir William Osler: An Annotated Bibliography with Illustrations*. San Francisco: Norman, 1988.

(OZ) Martin, Dick; Haff, James E., and Greene, David L. *Bibliographia Oziana: A Concise Bibliographical Checklist of the Oz Books by L. Frank Baum and His Successors*. No place: International Wizard of Oz Club (1976).

(OZICK, C.) See APG.

(PAGE, T. N.) See BAL #6, and Johnson.

(PAINE, A. B.) See FPAA #5.

(PALEY, G.) See FPAA #2.

(PALMER, H. P.) See Gawsworth.

(PANGHORN, E.) See Currey.

(PANSHIN, A.) See Currey.

(PARIS) See Ford.

(PARKER, D.) See FPAA #4, and Johnson.

(PARKER, R.) See APG.

(PARKER, T.) See FPAA #4.

(PARKMAN, F.) See BAL #6, and Johnson.

(PARRISH, A.) See FPAA #4.

(PARSONS, T. W.) See BAL #6.

(PASTERNAK, B.) Holtzman, Irwin T. *A Check List of Boris Leonidovich Pasternak (1890–1960): Books in English*. (Southfield, Mich.: Irwin T. Holtzman, 1990.)

(PATCHEN, K.) Morgan, Richard G. *Kenneth Patchen*. Mamaroneck, N.Y: Paul P. Appel (1978).

(PATER, W.) See Cutler and Stiles.

(PAUL, E.) See FPAA #5.

(PAULDING, J. K.) See BAL #7, and Johnson.

(PAYNE, J. H.) See BAL #7.

(PEABODY, E. P.) See FPAA #3.

(PEAKE, M.) See Currey.

(PEARSON, E. L.) Webber, Hallum. "Edmund Lester Pearson." Not published.

(PEGASUS PRESS) See Ransom.

(PEGNANA PRESS) See Ransom.

(PERCIVAL, J. G.) See BAL #7.

(PERCY, W.) Hobson, Linda Whitney. *Walker Percy: A Comprehensive Descriptive Bibliography*. New Orleans: Faust, 1988.
  Wright, Stuart. *Walker Percy: A Bibliography: 1930–1984*. (Westport, Conn.): Meckler (1986). See also APG, and FPAA #2.

(PERCY, W. A.) See FPAA #2.

(PETERKIN, J.) See FPAA #1.

(PETRY, A.) See FPAA #1.

(PHILBRICK, C.) See FPAA #5.

(PHILLIPS, D. G.) See BAL #7.

(PIATT, J. J.) See BAL #7.

(PIKE, A.) See BAL #7.

(PINCKNEY, J.) See FPAA #2.

(PINKERTON, A.) See Johnson.

(PINKNEY, E. C.) See BAL #7.

(PIPER, H.) See Currey.

(PLAIN EDITIONS) See Ford.

(PLANTE, D.) See APG.

(PLATH, S.) See FPAA #2.

(POE, E. A.) Heartman, Charles F., and Canny, James R. *A Bibliography of First Printings of the Writings of Edgar Allan Poe.* Hattiesburg, Miss: The Book Farm, 1940.

Robertson, John W., M.D. *Bibliography of the Writings of Edgar A. Poe.* New York: Kraus, 1969.

See also BAL #7, Johnson, and Schwartz.

(POETRY BOOKSHOP) Woolmer, J. Howard. *The Poetry Bookshop 1912–1935: A Bibliography.* Revere, Pa.: Woolmer/Brotherson, and Winchester (England): St. Paul's Bibliographies, 1988.

(POHL, F.) See Currey.

(POLLINI, F.) See FPAA #2.

(POOL, M. L.) See FPAA #5.

(PORPOISE PRESS) See Ransom.

(PORTER, G. S.) MacLean, David G. *Gene Stratton-Porter.* Decatur (Ga.): (Americana Books) 1987.

(PORTER, K. A.) Waldrip, Louise, and Bauer, Shirley Ann. *A Bibliography of the Works of Katherine Anne Porter* and *A Bibliography of the Criticism of the Works of Katherine Anne Porter.* Metuchen, N.J.: Scarecrow Press, 1969.

See also FPAA #2, Johnson, and Schwartz.

(PORTER, W. S.) Clarkson, Paul S. *A Bibliography of William Sydney Porter (O.Henry).* Caldwell (Ida.): Caxton Printers, 1938.

See also BAL #7, and Johnson.

(PORTIS, C.) See FPAA #4.

(POTTER) Linder, Leslie. *A History of the Writings of Beatrix Potter.* London and New York: Frederick Warne (1971).

(POUND, E.) Gallup, Donald. *Ezra Pound: A Bibliography.* Charlottesville: University Press of Virginia (1983).

See also APG.

(POURNELLE, J.) See Currey.

(POWELL, A.) Lilley, George. *Anthony Powell: A Bibliography.* Winchester, (England): St. Paul's Bibliographies, and New Castle, Del.: Oak Knoll Books, 1993.

(POWELL, D.) See FPAA #5.

(POWERS, J. F.) See FPAA #5.

(POWYS, J. C.) Thomas, Dante. *A Bibliography of the Writings of John Cowper Powys: 1872–1963.* Mamaroneck, N.Y.: Paul P. Appel, 1975.

(POWYS, T. F.) Riley, Peter. *A Bibliography of T. F. Powys.* Hastings: R. A. Brimmell, 1967.

See also Cutler and Stiles.

(PRATT, F.) See Currey.

(PRESCOTT, W. H.) See BAL #7.

(PRICE, R.) Wright, Stuart, and West, James L.W., III. *Reynolds Price: A Bibliography 1949–1984.* Charlottesville: University Press of Virginia (1986).

See also APG, FPAA #1, and Lepper.

(PRIEST, C.) See Currey.

(PRINGLE, E. W.) See FPAA #2.

(PURDY, J.) See FPAA #2, and Lepper.

(PUTNAM, H. P.) See FPAA #2.

(PUZO, M.) See FPAA #5.

(PYLE, H.) See BAL #7, and Johnson.

(PYNCHON, T.) Mead, Clifford. *Thomas Pynchon: A Bibliography of Primary and Secondary Materials.* (Elmwood Park, Ill.) Dalkey Archive Press (1989).

See also APG, FPAA #1, and Walsh and Northouse.

(PYNSON PRESS) See Ransom.

(QUILLER-COUCH) Brittain, F. *Arthur Quiller-Couch: A Biographical Study of Q.* Cambridge: Cambridge University Press, and New York: Macmillan, 1948.

(QUINN, S. G.) See Currey.

(RACKHAM, A.) Latimore, Sarah Briggs, and Haskell, Grace Clark. *Arthur Rackham: A Bibliography.* Jacksonville, Fla.: San Marco Bookstore, 1936.

(RAND) Perinn, Vincent L. *Ayn Rand: First Descriptive Bibliography.* (Rockville, Md.) Q & B (Quill & Brush), 1990.

See Author Price Guides.

(RANDALL, M.) See Currey.

(RANDOM HOUSE) See Ransom.

(RANSOM) Young, Thomas Daniel. *John Crowe Ransom: Critical Essays and a Bibliography.* Baton Rouge: Louisiana State University Press (1968).

See also FPAA #5.

(RANSON, J. C.) See FPAA #5.

(RAWLINGS, M. K.) See FPAA #2.

(READ, T. B.) See BAL #7.

(READE, C.) See Sadleir.

(RECHY, J.) See FPAA #3.

(REED, I.) See FPAA #2.

(REMINGTON, F.) See BAL #7, and Johnson.

(REPPLIER, A.) See Johnson.

(REXROTH, K.) Hartzell, James, and Zumwinkle, Richard. *Kenneth Rexroth: A Checklist of His Published Writings.* Los Angeles: Friends of the UCLA Library, 1967.

(REYNOLDS, D. M.) See Currey.

(RICCARDI PRESS) See Ransom.

(RICHTER, C.) See FPAA #1.

(RICKETTS, C.) Barclay, Michael Richard. *Catalogue of the Works of Charles Ricketts R.A. (from The Collection of Gordon Bottomley.)* Stroud Glos (England): Catalpa Press, 1985.

(RIDING, L.) Wexler, Joyce Piell. *Laura Riding: A Bibliography.* New York and London: Garland, 1981.

See also APG.

(RIIS, J. A.) Fried, Lewis, and Fierst, John. *Jacob A. Riis: A Reference Guide.* Boston: G. K. Hall (1977).

(RILEY, J. W.) Russo, Anthony J. and Dorothy R. *A Bibliography of James Whitcomb Riley.* Indianapolis: Indiana Historical Society, 1944.

See also BAL #7, and Johnson.

(RIPLEY, G.) See FPAA #3.

(ROBERTS, E. M.) See FPAA #2, and Johnson.

(ROBERTS, K. J.) See Currey.

(ROBERTS, K. L.) Murphy, P. *Kenneth Lewis Roberts: A Bibliography.* Privately printed (1975).

See also FPAA #2, and Johnson.

(ROBINSON, E. A.) Hogan, Charles Beecher. *A Bibliography of Edwin Arlington Robinson.* New Haven: Yale University Press, and London: Oxford University Press, 1936.

See also FPAA #2, Johnson, and Schwartz.

(ROBINSON, F. M.) See Currey.

(ROBINSON, P.) See Currey.

(ROBINSON, R. E.) See BAL #7, and Johnson.

(ROE, E. P.) See BAL #7.

(ROETHKE, T.) McLeod, James Richard. *Theodore Roethke: A Bibliography.* No place: Kent State University Press, 1973.

See also FPAA #1.

(ROGERS, B.) See Ransom.

(ROOSEVELT, T.) Wheelock, John Hall. *A Bibliography of Theodore Roosevelt.* New York: Charles Scribner's Sons, 1920.

See also Johnson.

(ROSS, SIR RONALD) See Gawsworth.

(ROTH, H.) See APG.

(ROTH, P.) See Lepper.

(ROTHENBERG, J.) See FPAA #4, and Lepper.

(ROVING EYE PRESS) See Ford.

(ROWSON, S. H.) See BAL #7, and Johnson.

(ROYALL, A. N.) See BAL #7.

(ROYCROFT PRESS) See Ransom.

(RUDGE, W. P.) See Ransom.

(RUMAKER, M.) See FPAA #3.

(RUSHDIE, S.) See APG.

(RUSKIN, J.) *The Bibliography . . . Arranged in Chronological Order of the Published Writings in Prose and Verse of John Ruskin, M. A. (From 1834 to 1881).* London: Eliot Stock, no date.

Wise, Thomas J., and Smart, James P. *A Complete Bibliography of the Writings in Prose and Verse of John Ruskin, LL.D.* Reprinted. 2 volumes. Folkestone and London: Dawsons of Pall Mall, 1974.

(RUSS, J.) See Currey.

(RUSSELL, C. M.) Yost, Karl, and Renner, Frederic G. *A Bibliography of the Published Works of Charles M. Russell.* Lincoln: University of Nebraska Press (1971).

(RUSSELL, E. F.) See Currey.

(RUSSELL, G. W.) See A.E.

(RUSSELL, I.) See BAL #7.

(RYAN, A. J.) See BAL #7.

(SABERHAGEN, F. T.) See Currey.

(SACKVILLE-WEST, V.) See APG.

(SALINGER) Starosciak, Kenneth. *J. D. Salinger: A Thirty-Year Bibliography, 1938–1968.* No place: no publisher, no date.

See also APG, and FPAA #1.

(SALTUS, E. E.) See BAL #7, and Johnson.

(SANBORN, F. B.) See FPAA #4.

(SANDBURG, C.) See Johnson.

(SANDOZ, M.) See FPAA #2.

(SANDY, S.) See FPAA #5.

(SANTAYANA, G.) See Johnson.

(SARGENT, E.) See BAL #7.

(SAROYAN) Kherdian, David. *A Bibliography of William Saroyan 1934–64.* San Francisco: Roger Beacham (1965).

(SARTRE, J-P.) Belkind, Allen. *Jean-Paul Sartre: Sartre and Existentialism in English, A Bibliographical Guide.* No place: Kent State University Press (1970).

(SASSOON, S.) Farmer, David. *Siegfried Sassoon: A Memorial Exhibition.* Austin: Humanities Research Center, University of Texas, 1969.

(SAXE, J. G.) See BAL #7.

(SAYERS, D.) Gilbert, Colleen B. *A Bibliography of the Works of Dorothy L. Sayers.* Hamden, Conn.: Archon Books, 1978.

(SCHMITZ, J. H.) See Currey.

(SCHULBERG, B.) See FPAA #1.

(SCHWARTZ, D.) See FPAA #1.

(SCORTIA, T. N.) See Currey.

(SCOTT, E.) See APG, and FPAA #5.

(SCOTT, SIR W.) Bodd, William B., and Bowden, Ann. *Sir Walter Scott: A Bibliographical History 1796–1832.* (New Castle, Del.) Oak Knoll Press (1998).

(SCOTT, W. T.) See FPAA #5.

(SEDGWICK, C. M.) See BAL #7.

(SEEGER, A.) See BAL #7.

(SEIZEN PRESS) See Ford.

(SENDAK) Hanrahan, Joyce Y. *Works of Maurice Sendak 1947–1994.* Portsmouth, N.H.: Peter E. Randall Publisher, 1995.

(SERVIRE PRESS) See Ford.

(SERVISS, G. P.) See Currey.

(SETON, E. T.) See Johnson.

(SETTLE, M.) See APG.

(SHAKESPEARE & CO.) See Ford.

(SHAKESPEARE HEAD) See Franklin.

(SHAKESPEARE HEAD PRESS) See Franklin.

(SHAPIRO, K.) See FPAA #1.

(SHAW, B.) See Currey.

(SHAW, G. B.) See Cutler and Stiles.

(SHAW, H. W.) See BAL #7.

(SHAW, I.) See FPAA #5.

(SHECKLEY, R. E.) See Currey.

(SHEED, W.) See FPAA #4.

(SHELDON, A.) See Currey.

(SHELLEY, M. & P.) See Schwartz.

(SHERMAN, F. D.) See BAL #7.

(SHIEL, M. P.) Morse, A. Reynolds. *The Works of M. P. Shiel.* Los Angeles: Fantasy Publishing, 1948. See also Gawsworth.

(SHILLABER, B. P.) See BAL #7.

(SHUTE) Giffuni, Cathy. *Nevil Shute: A Bibliography.* Adelaide: Auslip Press, 1988.

(SIGOURNEY, L. H.) See BAL #7.

(SILL, E. R.) See BAL #7.

(SILLITOE, A.) Gerard, David. *Alan Sillitoe: A Bibliography.* (London) Mansell, 1988.

(SILVERBERG, R.) See Currey.

(SIMAK, C.) See Currey.

(SIMENON, G.) Foord, Peter; Williams, Richard; and Swan, Sally. *Georges Simenon: A Bibliography of the British First Editions . . . and of the Principal French and American Editions.* South Humberside, England: Dragonby Press, 1988.

(SIMMS, W.) See BAL #7, FPAA #1, and Johnson.

(SIMPSON, L.) See FPAA #2.

(SINCLAIR, U.) See FPAA #5.

(SINGER, I. B.) See APG.

(SITWELL, E., O. AND S.) Fifoot, Richard. *A Bibliography of Edith, Osbert and Sacheverell Sitwell.* London: Rupert Hart-Davis, 1963.

   See also Gawsworth.

(SLADEK, J. T.) See Currey.

(SLOANE, W. M.) See Currey.

(SMITH, B.) See FPAA #3.

(SMITH, C. A.) Sidney-Fryer, Donald, and Hands, Divers. *Emperor of Dreams, A Clark Ashton Smith Bibliography.* West Kingston, R.I.: Donald M. Grant, 1978.

   See also Currey.

(SMITH, E. E.) See Currey.

(SMITH, E. H.) See FPAA #1.

(SMITH, F. H.) See BAL #7, and Johnson.

(SMITH, G. O.) See Currey.

(SMITH, R. P.) See BAL #7.

(SMITH, S. F.) See BAL #7.

(SMITH, SEBA) See BAL #7.

(SMITH, STEVIE) Barbera, Jack, et al. *Stevie Smith: A Bibliography.* London: Mansell (1987).

(SMITH, T.) See APG.

(SMITH, W. G.) See FPAA #2.

(SNELLING, W. J.) See BAL #7.

(SNODGRASS, W. D.) See FPAA #1.

(SNYDER, G.) Kherdian, David. *Gary Snyder: A Biographical Sketch and Descriptive Checklist.* Berkeley: Oyez, 1965.

   McNeil, Katherine. *Gary Snyder: A Bibliography.* New York: The Phoenix Bookshop, 1983.

   See also Lepper.

(SOHL, G.) See Currey.

(SOLZHENITSYN, A.) Fiene, Donald M. *Alexander Solzhenitsyn: An International Bibliography of Writings By and About Him.* Ann Arbor: Ardis (1973).

   See also APG.

(SONTAG, S.) See FPAA #1.

(SORRENTINO, G.) See FPAA #1.

(SPACKMAN, W. M.) See APG.

(SPARKS, M.) Tominaga, Thomas T., and Schneidermeyer, Wilma. *Iris Murdoch and Muriel Spark: A Bibliography.* Metuchen, N.J.: Scarecrow Press, 1976.

(SPEICHER, J.) See FPAA #2.

(SPENCER, E.) See APG.

(SPENDER, S.) Kulkarni, H. B. *Stephen Spender Works and Criticism: An Annotated Bibliography.* New York and London: Garland, 1976.

(SPICER, J.) See Lepper.

(SPINRAD, N. R.) See Currey.

(SPOFFORD, H. P.) See BAL #7.

(SPRINGS, E. W.) See FPAA #1.

(ST. CLAIR, M.) See Currey.

(STABLEFORD, W. O.) See Currey.

(STACTON, D.) See FPAA #3.

(STANFORD, A.) See FPAA #2.

(STAPLETON, O.) See Currey.

(STEADMAN, R.) Dinsmore, John, and Pilarz, John. *Ralph Steadman Bibliography.* (Lexington) Blue & Green Press (1996).

(STEDMAN, E. C.) See BAL #7.

(STEGNER, W.) Colberg, Nancy. *Wallace Stegner: A Descriptive Bibliography*. Lewiston, Ida.: Confluence Press (1990).

(STEIN, G.) Wilson, Robert A. *Gertrude Stein: A Bibliography*. Rockville, Md.: Quill & Brush, 1994. See also *Casanova*, and FPAA #1.

(STEINBECK, J.) Goldstone, Adrian H., and Payne, John R. *John Steinbeck: A Biographical Catalogue of the Adrian H. Goldstone Collection*. Austin: University of Texas Press (1974). See also APG, FPAA #1, and Johnson.

(STERLING, G.) See BAL #7, and Johnson.

(STEVENS, W.) Edelstein, J. M. *Wallace Stevens: A Descriptive Bibliography*. (Pittsburgh) University of Pittsburgh Press, 1973. See also FPAA #1.

(STEVENSON, R. L.) Prideaux, Colonel W. F. *A Bibliography of the Works of Robert Louis Stevenson*. New York: Burt Franklin (1968). See also Cutler and Stiles.

(STEWART, D. O.) See FPAA #1.

(STOCKTON, F. R.) See BAL #7, and Johnson.

(STODDARD, C. W.) See BAL #8.

(STODDARD, E. D.) See BAL #8.

(STODDARD, R. H.) See BAL #8.

(STONE, R.) Lopez, Ken, and Chaney, Bev. *Robert Stone: A Bibliography, 1960–1992*. Hadley, Mass.: Numinous Press, 1992. See also APG.

(STORY, W. W.) See BAL #8.

(STOUT, R.) Townsend, Guy M. *Rex Stout: An Annotated Primary and Secondary Bibliography*. New York and London: Garland, 1980. See also APG.

(STOWE, H. B.) Hildreth, Margaret Holbrook. *Harriet Beecher Stowe: A Bibliography*. (Hamden, Conn.) Archon Books, 1976. See also BAL #8, and Johnson.

(STRATTON-PORTER, G.) See Porter.

(STRAWBERRY HILL PRESS) See Ransom.

(STRIBLING, T. S.) See FPAA #4, and Johnson.

(STUART, J.) See FPAA #4.

(STUBBS, H. C.) See Currey.

(STURGEON, T.) See Currey.

(STYRON, W.) See APG, FPAA #4, and Lepper.

(SUMMERS, H.) See FPAA #2.

(SUMMERS, M.) Smith, Timothy d'Arch. *Montague Summers: A Bibliography*. Wellingborough, Northamptonshire (England): The Aquarian Press (1983).

(SWADOS, H.) See Lepper.

(SWANN, T. B.) See Currey.

(SWIFT, J.) Teerink, H. *A Bibliography of the Writings of Jonathan Swift*. Second edition, revised and corrected. Philadelphia: University of Pennsylvania Press (1963).

(SWINBURNE, A. C.) Wise, Thomas J. *A Bibliography of the Writings in Prose and Verse of Algernon Charles Swinburne*. Vols. 1 and 2. London: Dawsons of Pall Mall, 1966. See also Schwartz.

(SYMONDS, J. A.) Babington, Percy L. *Bibliography of the Writings of John Addington Symonds*. New York: Burt Franklin (1968). See also Cutler and Stiles.

(SYMONS, J.) Walsdorf, John J. *Julian Symons: A Bibliography*. New Castle (Del.), Oak Knoll Press, and Winchester (England): St. Paul's Bibliographies, 1996.

(TABB, J. B.) See BAL #8, and Johnson.

(TAGGARD, G.) See FPAA #1.

(TARKINGTON, B.) Currie, Barton. *Booth Tarkington: A Bibliography*. Garden City, N.Y.: Doubleday, Doran, 1932.

Russo, Dorothy Ritter, and Sullivan, Thelma L. *A Bibliography of Booth Tarkington, 1869–1946*. Indianapolis: Indiana Historical Society, 1949.

See also FPAA #1, and Johnson.

(TATE, A.) Falwell, Marshall Jr. *Allen Tate: A Bibliography*. New York: David Lewis, 1969.

See also FPAA #4.

(TATE, J.) See FPAA #2.

(TAYLOR, B.) See BAL #8.

(TAYLOR, E.) Gefvert, Constance J. *Edward Taylor: An Annotated Bibliography, 1668–1970*. No place: Kent State University Press (1971).

See also FPAA #5.

(TAYLOR, P.) Wright, Stuart. *Peter Taylor: A Descriptive Bibliography, 1934–87*. Charlottesville: University Press of Virginia (1988).

See also APG, and FPAA #1.

(TEASDALE, S.) See Johnson.

(TENNYSON, A.) Shepherd, Richard Herne. *The Bibliography of Tennyson*. New York: Haskell House Publishers, 1970.

Tennyson, Charles, and Fall, Christine. *Alfred Tennyson: An Annotated Bibliography*. Athens: University of Georgia Press (1967).

See also Schwartz.

(TERHUNE) Rais, Kathleen. *Albert Payson Terhune: A Bibliography of Primary Works*. Phoenixville, Pa.: Kathleen Rais, 1997.

(THACKERAY, W. M.) Van Duzer, Henry Sayre. *A Thackeray Library*. New York: Burt Franklin (1971).

See also BAL #8.

(THAXTER, C.) See BAL #8.

(THEROUX, A.) See APG.

(THEROUX, P.) See APG.

(THOMAS, D.) Maud, Ralph. *Dylan Thomas in Print: A Bibliographical History*. London: J. M. Dent (1970).

Rolph, J. Alexander. *Dylan Thomas: A Bibliography*. New York: New Directions (1956).

See also APG.

(THOMAS, E.) Eckert, Robert P. *Edward Thomas: A Biography and a Bibliography*. London: Dent & Sons (1937).

(THOMAS, F.) See BAL #8.

(THOMAS, R.) See APG.

(THOMPSON, D. P.) See BAL #8, and Johnson.

(THOMPSON, F.) See Cutler and Stiles.

(THOMPSON, H.) See APG.

(THOMPSON, JIM.) Stephens, Christopher P. *A Checklist of Jim Thompson*. (Hastings-on-Hudson, N.Y.) Ultramarine, 1991.

(THOMPSON, M.) See BAL #8, and Johnson.

(THOMPSON, S. E.) See Johnson.

(THOMPSON, W. T.) See BAL #8.

(THOMSON, JAMES.) See Cutler and Stiles.

(THOMSON, M. N.) See BAL #8.

(THOREAU, H. D.) Borst, Raymond R. *Henry David Thoreau: A Descriptive Bibliography*. (Pittsburgh) University of Pittsburgh Press, 1982.

See also BAL #8, FPAA #3, Johnson, and Schwartz.

(THORPE, T. B.) See BAL #8.

(THREE MOUNTAINS PRESS) See Ransom, and Ford.

(THURBER, J.) Bowden, Edwin T. *James Thurber: A Bibliography*. Columbus: Ohio State University Press (1968).

See also FPAA #1.

(THURMAN, W.) See FPAA #4.

(TICKNOR & FIELDS.) Pye, John William. *The 100 Most Significant Books Published by Ticknor & Fields 1832–1871: A Guide Book for Collectors*. Brockton, Mass: John William Pye Rare Books, 1995.

(TIMROD, H.) See BAL #8, and FPAA #1.

(TOLKIEN, J.R.R.) Hammond, Wayne G., and Anderson, Douglas A. *J.R.R. Tolkien: A Descriptive Bibliography*. Winchester (England): St. Paul's Biographies, and New Castle, Del.: Oak Knoll Press, 1993.

See also Currey, and Lewis.

(TORREY, B.) See FPAA #3.

(TOURGEE, A.) See BAL #8, and FPAA #1.

(TOYNBEE, A. J.) Morton, S. Fiona. *A Bibliography of Arnold J. Toynbee*. Oxford: Oxford University Press, 1980.

(TRAVEN, B.) See FPAA #1.

(TREVOR, W.) See Rees.

(TRILLING, L.) See FPAA #5.

(TROLLOPE, A.) Sadleir, Michael. *Trollope: A Bibliography*. (Kent, England): Dawson, 1977.

See also Sadleir.

(TROWBRIDGE, J. T.) See BAL #8, and FPAA #4.

(TRUMBULL, J.) See BAL #8, and FPAA #4.

(TUBB, E. C.) See Currey.

(TUCKER, A. W.) See Currey.

(TUCKER, N. B.) See BAL #8.

(TUCKER, ST. G.) See FPAA #4.

(TUCKERMAN, H. T.) See BAL #8.

(TUDOR) Hare, William John, and Hare, Priscilla T. *Tasha Tudor: A Bio-Bibliography*. New Castle (Del.): Oak Knoll Press (1998).

(TWAIN, M.) Johnson, Merle. *A Bibliography of the Work of Mark Twain*. New York and London: Harper & Brothers, 1910.

McBride, William M. *Mark Twain: A Bibliography of the Collections of the Mark Twain Memorial and the Stowe-Day Foundation*. Hartford: McBride (1984).

See also APG, and Schwartz.

(TYLER, A.) See APG.

(TYLER, R.) See FPAA #4.

(UPDIKE, J.) See APG, FPAA #5, and Lepper.

(URIS, L.) See FPAA #4.

(VALE PRESS) See Franklin, and Ransom.

(VAN DYKE, H.) See FPAA #2.

(VAN LOON, H. W.) See Johnson.

(VAN VECHTEN) Kellner, Bruce. *A Bibliography of the Work of Carl Van Vechten*. Westport, Conn., and London: Greenwood Press (1980).

See also Schwartz.

(VAN VOGT, A. E.) See Currey.

(VARLEY, J.) See Currey.

(VERNE, J.) Gallagher, Edward J.; Mistichelli, Judith A.; and Van Eerde, John A. *Jules Verne: A Primary and Secondary Bibliography*. Boston: G. K. Hall (1980).

Myers, Edward and Judith. *Jules Verne: A Bibliography*. New Hartford, Conn.: Country Lane Books, 1989.

(VERY, J.) See FPAA #3.

(VIDAL, G.) See FPAA #3.

(VLIET, R. G.) Freedman, Russell. *A Bibliography of the Writings of R. G. Vliet*. In *At Paisano*, by R. G. Vliet. Lanesborough, Mass.: Second Life Books, 1989.

(VOELKER, J. D.) See FPAA #3 (under Traver).

(VONNEGUT, K.) Pieratt, Asa B., Jr.; Huffman-Klinkowitz, Julie; and Klinkowitz, Jerome. *Kurt Vonnegut: A Comprehensive Bibliography*. (Hamden, Conn.): Archon Books, 1987.

See also APG, FPAA #1, and Currey.

(WAKEFIELD, H. R.) See Currey.

(WAKOSKI, D.) See Lepper.

(WALKER, A.) See APG, and FPAA #2.

(WALKER, M.) See FPAA #2.

(WALLACE, E.) Kiddle, Charles. *A Guide to the First Editions of Edgar Wallace*. Motcombe, Dorset (England): The Ivory Head Press (1981).

Lofts, W.O.G., and Adley, Derek. *The British Bibliography of Edgar Wallace*. London: Howard Baker (1969).

(WALLACE, L.) See BAL #8, and Johnson.

(WALLANT, E. L.) See FPAA #1, and Lepper.

(WALPOLE, H.) Hazen, A. T. *A Bibliography of Horace Walpole*. Folkestone, England: Dawsons of Pall Mall, 1973.

(WALTON, E.) See Currey.

(WAMBAUGH, J.) See FPAA #5.

(WANDREI, D.) See Currey.

(WARD, E.S.P.) See BAL #8.

(WARNER, A. B.) See BAL #8.

(WARNER, C. D.) See BAL #8.

(WARNER, S. B.) See BAL #8.

(WARREN, R. P.) Grimshaw, James A., Jr. *Robert Penn Warren: A Descriptive Bibliography, 1922–79*. Charlottesville: University Press of Virginia (1981).

See also APG, and FPAA #1.

(WATERS, F.) Tanner, Terence A. *Frank Waters: A Bibliography*. Glenwood, Ill.: Meyerbooks (1983).

(WATSON, I.) See Currey.

(WAUGH, E.) Davis, Robert Murray; Doyle, Paul A.; Gallagher, Donat; Linck, Charles E.; and Bogaards, Winifred M. *A Bibliography of Evelyn Waugh*. Troy, N.Y.: Whitston, 1986.

See also APG.

(WEAVER, J.V.A.) See FPAA #5.

(WEINBAUM, S. G.) See Currey.

(WELCH, L.) See Lepper.

(WELLMAN, M. W.) See Currey.

(WELLS, H. G.) Chappell, Fred A. *Bibliography of H. G. Wells*. Chicago: Covici-McGee, 1924.

Feir, Gordon D. *The Collector's Bibliography of the Works of H. G. Wells*. Houston/Vancouver: Southern Maple (1992).

Wells, Geoffrey H. *A Bibliography of the Works of H. G. Wells 1893–1925 (With Some Notes and Comments)*. Reprinted. New York: Burt Franklin (1968).

H. G. Wells Society (compilers). *H. G. Wells: A Comprehensive Bibliography.* Second edition, revised. London: H. G. Wells Society (1968).

See also Currey, and Cutler and Stiles.

(WELTY, E.) Polk, Noel. *Eudora Welty: A Bibliography of Her Work.* Jackson: University Press of Mississippi (1994).

See also APG, and FPAA #1.

(WEST, N.) White, William. *Nathanael West: A Comprehensive Bibliography.* No place: Kent State University Press (1975).

See also FPAA #1.

(WESTCOTT, E. N.) See BAL #9, and Johnson.

(WESTCOTT, G.) See Johnson.

(WHALEN, P.) See Lepper.

(WHARTON, E.) Davis, Lavinia. *A Bibliography of the Writings of Edith Wharton.* Portland, Me.: The Southworth Press, 1933.

Garrison, Stephen. *Edith Wharton: A Descriptive Bibliography.* (Pittsburgh) University of Pittsburgh Press, 1990.

Melish, Lawson McClung. *A Bibliography of the Collected Writings of Edith Wharton.* New York: The Brick Row Book Shop, 1927.

See also FPAA #3, and Johnson.

(WHEELER, M.) See Ford.

(WHEELWRIGHT, J. B.) See FPAA #5.

(WHIGHAM, P.) Sipper, Ralph B. *A Checklist of the Works of Peter Whigham: With a Memoir of the Poet.* Santa Barbara, Calif.: Joseph the Provider, no date.

(WHISTLER, J.A.M.) See BAL #9, and Johnson.

(WHITE, E. B.) Hall, Katherine Romans. *E. B. White: A Bibliographical Catalogue of Printed Materials in the Department of Rare Books, Cornell University Library.* New York and London: Garland, 1979.

(WHITE, J.) See Currey.

(WHITE, P.) Lawson, Alan. *Patrick White.* London and Melbourne: Oxford University Press (1974).

(WHITE, S. E.) See FPAA #5, and Johnson.

(WHITE, T. H.) Gallix, Francois. *T. H. White: An Annotated Bibliography.* New York and London: Garland, 1986.

(WHITE, TERENCE H.) See Currey.

(WHITE, THEODORE E.) See Currey.

(WHITE, W. A.) See FPAA #2, and Johnson.

(WHITEHEAD, H. S.) See Currey.

(WHITEMAN, S. H.) See BAL #9, and FPAA #3.

(WHITMAN, S. H.) See BAL #9, and FPAA #3.

(WHITMAN, W.) Myerson, Joel. *Walt Whitman: A Descriptive Bibliography.* Pittsburgh: University of Pittsburgh Press, 1993.

Shay, Frank. *The Bibliography of Walt Whitman.* New York: Friedmans', 1920.

Wells, Carolyn, and Alfred F. Goldsmith. *A Concise Bibliography of the Works of Walt Whitman.* New York: Burt Franklin (1968).

See also BAL #9, Johnson, and Schwartz.

(WHITTEMORE, R.) See FPAA #1.

(WHITTIER, J. G.) See BAL #9, and Johnson.

(WHYTE-MELVILLE, G. J.) See Sadleir.

(WIENERS, J.) See Lepper.

(WIGGIN, K. D.) See BAL #9.

(WILBUR, R.) See FPAA #2.

(WILDE, O.) Mason, Stuart. *Bibliography of Oscar Wilde*. London: T. Werner Laurie Ltd. (1914). See also Cutler and Stiles, and Schwartz.

(WILDER, A.) See FPAA #3.

(WILDER, T.) See FPAA #3, and Johnson.

(WILHELM, K.) See Currey.

(WILLIAMS, C.) Glenn, Lois. *Charles W. S. Williams: A Checklist*. No place: Kent State University Press (1975).
See also Currey.

(WILLIAMS, J.) Jaffe, James S. *Jonathan Williams: A Bibliographical Checklist of His Writings, 1950–1988*. Haverford, Penn.: No publisher, 1989.

(WILLIAMS, JOHN A.) See FPAA #2.

(WILLIAMS, T.) Gunn, Drewey Wayne. *Tennessee Williams: A Bibliography*. Metuchen, N.J., and London: The Scarecrow Press, 1980.
Tennessee Williams: A Catalogue. New York: Gotham Book Mart, no date.
See APG.

(WILLIAMS, W. C.) Wallace, Emily Mitchell. *A Bibliography of William Carlos Williams*. Middletown, Conn.: Wesleyan University Press (1968).
See also APG, and FPAA #3.

(WILLIAMSON, J.) See Currey.

(WILLINGHAM, C.) See FPAA #1.

(WILLIS, N. P.) See BAL #9.

(WILSON, A. J.) See BAL #9.

(WILSON, C.) Stanley, Colin. *The Work of Colin Wilson: An Annotated Bibliography and Guide*. San Bernardino: The Borgo Press, 1989.
See also APG.

(WILSON, E.) See APG.

(WILSON, H. L.) See Johnson.

(WILSON, M.) See FPAA #5.

(WILSON, W.) See Johnson.

(WINTER, W.) See BAL #9.

(WINTERS, Y.) See FPAA #2.

(WINTHORP, T.) See BAL #9.

(WISE, J.) See FPAA #4.

(WISTER, O.) See FPAA #4, and Johnson.

(WODEHOUSE, P. G.) Jasen, David A. *A Bibliography and Reader's Guide to the First Editions of P. G. Wodehouse*. (London) Greenhill Books (1970).
McIlvaine, Eileen; Sherby, Louise S.; and Heineman, James H. *P. G. Wodehouse: A Comprehensive Bibliography and Checklist*. New York: James H. Heineman, and Detroit: Omnigraphics (1990).
See also APG.

(WOIWODE, L.) See FPAA #2.

(WOLFE, G.) See Currey.

(WOLFE, T.) Johnston, Carol. *Thomas Wolfe: A Descriptive Bibliography*. (Pittsburgh) University of Pittsburgh Press, 1989.
See also APG, FPAA #1, and Johnson.

(WOLLHEIM, D. A.) See Currey.

(WOLLSTONECRAFT, M.) Todd, Janet M. *Mary Wollstonecraft: An Annotated Bibliography*. New York and London: Garland, 1976.

Windle, J. R. *Mary Wollstonecraft (Godwin): A Bibliography of Her Writings.* Los Angeles (John Windle), 1988.

(WOODBERRY, G. E.) See BAL #9.

(WOODWARD, W.) See Currey.

(WOODWORTH, S.) See BAL #9.

(WOOLF, L.) Luedeking, Leila, and Edmonds, Michael. *Leonard Woolf: A Bibliography.* Winchester (England): St. Paul's Bibliographies, and New Castle, Del.: Oak Knoll Press, 1992.

(WOOLF, V.) Kirkpatrick, B. J., and Clarke, Stuart N., *A Bibliography of Virginia Woolf.* Fourth edition. Oxford: Clarendon Press, 1997.

See also APG.

(WOOLRICH, C.) See FPAA #3.

(WOOLSON, C. F.) See BAL #9.

(WORDSWORTH, W.) Wise, Thomas J. *A Bibliography of the Writings in Prose and Verse of William Wordsworth.* London: printed for private circulation, 1916.

(WOUK, H.) See FPAA #1.

(WRIGHT, A. T.) See Currey.

(WRIGHT, H. B.) See FPAA #2.

(WRIGHT, J.) See FPAA #1.

(WRIGHT, R.) See FPAA #1.

(WRIGHT, S. F.) See Currey.

(WURLITZER, R.) See FPAA #2.

(WYLIE, E.) See BAL #9, and Johnson.

(WYLIE, P.) See Currey.

(YEATS, W. B.) Wade, Allan. *A Bibliography of the Writings of W. B. Yeats.* London: Rupert Hart-Davis, 1958.

See also Cutler and Stiles, and Schwartz.

(YOUD, C.) See Currey.

(YOUNG, M.) See FPAA #2.

(YOUNG, R. F.) See Currey.

(ZUKOFSKY) Zukofsky, Celia. *A Bibliography of Louis Zukofsky.* Los Angeles: Black Sparrow Press, 1969.

Appendix E

First-Edition Identification
by Publisher

In the case of titles published before 1900, the key to first-edition identification is often the date on the title page. The vast majority of first editions published before 1900 had the year of publication on the title page (this is true for fiction and nonfiction titles). The presence of a date on the title page alone may identify books published prior to the mid-1800s as first editions. A matching date on the copyright page (or the back of the title page) often identifies a book published in the mid- to late 1800s as a first edition. Since 1900, a number of publishers have not put the date on the title page of their first editions.

In the early 1900s, many publishers began to identify the first edition on the copyright page. A variety of statements have been used and continue to be used to denote a first edition, such as "First Edition," "First Printing," "First Impression," "First published [Year, or Month and Year]," or simply "Published [Year, or Month and Year]." A few publishers have placed or place their logo, colophon, or a code (generally "1" or "A") on the copyright page of the first edition. Publishers who did not or do not use a first-edition statement, in most cases, note subsequent printings on the copyright page. For these publishers, the absence of a later printing statement is the key to identifying a first edition.

Over the past few decades, the majority of publishers have used a number row on the copyright page to identify a book's printing and occasionally the date of publication. Sometimes the number row is accompanied by a first edition-statement (often it is not). It is important to note that regardless of the order of the numbers in the row, the lowest number indicates the printing. The presence of the numeral 1 (with few exceptions) indicates a first printing. Some examples follow:

1 2 3 4 5 6 7 8 9 10
10 9 8 7 6 5 4 3 2 1 *and*
1 3 5 7 9 10 8 6 4 2
all indicate a first edition.

76   77   78   79   80   10   9   8   7   6   5   4   3   2
indicates a second printing published in 1976.

3   4   5   6   7   8   9   10   90   89   88   87   86
indicates a third printing published in 1986.

1   3   5   7   9   11   13   15   17   19   H/C   20   18   16   14
12   10   8   6   4   2
indicates a first printing, manufactured by "H" in a cloth binding
(used by Scribners)

Unfortunately, publishers sometimes fail to omit a first-edition
statement from subsequent printings:

First Edition

3   4   5   6   7   8   9   10

and

First Printing
10   9   8   7   6   5   4   3   90   89   88   87   86   85   84

both indicate third printings.

The list below provides at-a-glance information for first-edition identification by publisher. For more detailed information on identifying first editions by a wide range of publishers, we recommend the 1995 edition of Edward N. Zempel and Linda A. Verkler's *First Editions: A Guide to Identification* (The Spoon River Press, 2319-C West Rohmann Avenue, Peoria, IL 61604). This superb reference provides publishers' verbatim statements, collected over nearly seventy years, on their practices for identifying first editions and later printings. In addition, we highly recommend the occasional series "A Collector's Guide to Publishers" featured in the monthly magazine for book collectors *Firsts* (4493 N. Camino Gacela, Tucson, AZ 85718; telephone 520-529-5847). This interesting and informative series provides a history, some notable writers and books published, and standard practices for first-edition identification (and, in some cases, notable exceptions), for the publishers profiled—more than thirty major publishers to date. We used our experience over the last thirty years, our stock, and both of the above-mentioned references to compile the list below.

A final, important note: It is always prudent to consult a bibliography for conclusive first-edition identification; see Appendix D, Selected Bibliography of Works Consulted, for a comprehensive list of bibliographies.

D. Appleton & Co. Used a numerical identification, in parentheses or brackets, at the foot of the last page: "(1)" = first printing, "(2)" = second printing, etc. (May have occasionally used a "first edition" statement instead of the numerical identification.)

D. Appleton-Century Co. Prior to the 1980s, used a numerical identification, in parentheses or brackets, at the foot of the last page: "(1)" = first printing, "(2)" = second printing, etc. (May have occasionally used a "first edition" statement instead of the numerical identification.) Since the 1980s, have used a number row to indicate year of publication and printing.

Arkham House/Arkham House Publishers, Inc. With the exception of collected works of H. P. Lovecraft, did not reprint titles and, as late as the 1980s, always included a colophon at the back of each book (reprints would be noted there). According to the publisher, began using a first-edition statement and noting later printings on the copyright page sometime in the late 1970s to early 1980s.

Atheneum. States first edition on copyright page. Began using a number row in the mid-1980s.

Atlantic Monthly Press. Prior to 1925, did not use a first-edition statement (or put the publication date on the title page of first editions as was the case for many publishers in the late 1800s to early 1900s) and did not consistently list later printings on the copyright page. See Little, Brown for books published after 1925 (Little, Brown began publishing the Atlantic Monthly Books in 1925 and using their methods for first-edition identification).

Avalon Books. Does not normally reprint books, but according to the publisher, later printings would be noted.

Ballantine Books. In general, hardcover editions stated "First edition [Month, Year]" or "First printing [Month, Year]"; paperback originals carried no statement on the copyright page for first printings; later printings were noted.

Robert A. Ballou. No consistent practice.

A. S. Barnes. According to the publisher, have noted later printings on the copyright page since at least 1976. Prior to this, designation of later printings was erratic. (Does not use a first-edition statement.)

Ernest Benn. States "First published in [Year]" on the copyright page of first editions; or sometimes omits the "first published" statement and puts the year of publication on the title page with their imprint to designate a first edition. In either case, subsequent printings are noted.

William Blackwood. No statement on first editions, but subsequent printings noted. (According to the publisher, in the early 1900s may have designated some first editions "second edition" as a marketing tool.)

Blakison. Reprint publisher.

Bobbs-Merrill. Prior to the 1920s, sometimes used a bow-and-arrow design on the copyright page of their first editions; after 1920, generally stated "First edition" or "First printing" (but not consistent in either practice).

Bodley Head. States "First published [Year]" or "First published in Great Britain [Year]"; subsequent printings would presumably be noted.

Albert & Charles Boni. No statement on first editions, but subsequent printings noted.

Boni & Liveright. May have occasionally stated first edition, but in general, the absence of a later printing statement indicates a first edition.

Book Supply Co. Uses a first-edition statement; subsequent printings presumably noted.

Brentano's. Prior to 1928, no statement on first editions; subsequent printings noted. In 1928, began stating "First printed [Year]" on copyright page of first editions and continued noting subsequent printings.

Edgar Rice Burroughs, Inc. Published only the books of Edgar Rice Burroughs. No statement on books published prior to 1933; began using a first edition statement sometime in 1933. (Although both were published in 1933, there is no statement on the first edition of *Apache Devil*, but *Tarzan and the City of Gold* states first edition on the copyright page.)

A. L. Burt. Primarily a reprint publisher, but published the first U.S. edition of P. G. Wodehouse's *Man with Two Left Feet* (states first edition on the copyright page). For those authors whose first editions have become very high-priced, A. L. Burt reprints in dust jackets closely matching the first editions are sometimes desirable.

Calder & Boyars. States "First published [Year]" or "First published in Great Britain [Year]"; subsequent printings would presumably be noted.

Jonathan Cape. States "First published [Year]" or "First published in Great Britain [Year]" on copyright page of first editions; subsequent printings noted.

Jonathan Cape & Harrison Smith. States "First published [Year]" or "First published in America [Year]"; subsequent printings would presumably be noted.

Cassell & Co. Prior to the early 1920s, put the year of publication on the title page of the first edition and left the copyright page blank; subsequent printings would presumably be noted or carry a later date on the copyright page. In the early 1920s, began stating "First published [Year]" or "First published in Great Britain [Year]" on copyright page of first editions; subsequent printings noted.

Caxton Printers. No statement on first editions, but subsequent printings noted.

Century Co. No consistent practice.

Chapman & Hall. Either stated "First published [Year]" or made no statement on first editions; subsequent printings noted.

Chatto & Windus. In general, no statement on first editions, although sometimes states "Published by Chatto & Windus" (without a date); subsequent printings noted. May have added a number row in the early 1990s.

Clarke, Irwin. No statement on the first edition; subsequent printings presumably noted.

Collier. In our limited experience with this publisher, no statement on the first edition; subsequent printings presumably noted.

Collins (U.K.). No statement on the first edition; presumably subsequent printings would be noted (with either a statement, or a date subsequent to the copyright date).

Contact Editions. Limited editions included a colophon page. Did not generally use a first-edition statement on trade editions, but subsequent printings would presumably be noted.

Pascal Covici. May have occasionally stated first edition, but in general the absence of a later printing statement indicates a first edition.

Covici-Friede. No statement on first editions, but subsequent printings noted.

Covici McGee. No statement on the first edition, but presumably later printings would be noted.

Coward-McCann. Not consistent in their practices for identifying first editions, but in general subsequent printings noted. (Until mid-1930s, usually placed a colophon with a torch design on the copyright page of first editions and removed the torch portion of the colophon on subsequent printings. After 1935, stated "first American edition" on the copyright page of books first published outside the United States, but made no statement on books first published in the United States.)

Coward, McCann and Geoghehan. No statement on first editions, but subsequent printings noted.

Creative Age. No statement on first editions, but subsequent printings noted.

Crime Club (U.K.). *See* Collins.

Crime Club (U.S.). *See* Doubleday, Doran & Co.

Thomas Y. Crowell. No statement on first editions, but subsequent printings noted. May have used a number row to indicate printings as early as the 1940s.

Crown Publishers. Prior to the 1970s, no statement on first editions, but subsequent printings noted. Began using a number row and first-edition statement in the 1970s.

John Day Co. / John Day in association with Reynal and Hitchcock [1935–38] / John Day & Co. First few years (beginning in 1928) may have stated "First Published [Month, Year]" on first editions and noted later printings. In the 1930s, switched to designating only later printings (no statement on first editions). In the 1970s, began using a number row. (In the late 1970s, may have added a first-edition statement to the number row.)

Delacorte Press/Seymour Lawrence. Presently uses a number row; previously stated "first printing" or "first American printing."

Devin-Adair. Although may have consistently stated "First Edition" in recent years, in general first editions can be identified by the absence of a later printing statement.

Dial Press. Although occasionally stated "First Printing" prior to the mid-1960s, did not list subsequent printings. In general, first editions published prior to the mid-1960s can be identified by the presence of the same date on the title page and the copyright page (also true for books published before the mid-1930s with the imprint "Lincoln MacVeagh/The Dial Press"). In the late 1960s, began stating "First Printing [Year]" on first editions and noting subsequent printings. Currently uses a number row.

Dillingham. In our limited experience with this publisher, no statement on the first edition; subsequent printings would presumably be noted.

Dodd, Mead. Prior to 1976, no statement on first editions, and often subsequent printings were not noted. In late 1976, added a number row to most titles (occasionally deleting the row from subsequent printings and replacing it with a later printing statement). Note: According to *Firsts* magazine, in the 1970s first-printing dustwrappers of some mystery titles were issued without a price on the flap, making them appear to be book-club editions.

George H. Doran. Generally placed a colophon with the initials "GHD" on the copyright page of the first edition (but not consistently until the early 1920s). Occasionally, stated "first printing." Merged with Doubleday in 1927.

Doubleday & Co. States "first edition" on copyright page; no statement on later printings.

Doubleday, Doran & Co. States "first edition" on copyright page; no statement on later printings.

Doubleday & McClure Co. In general, the date on the title page should match last date on the copyright page of a first edition.

Doubleday, Page & Co. Before the early 1920s, no statement on the first edition. In early 1920s, began stating "first edition," but may not have used any statement on books first published outside the U.S. (no statement on later printings).

Duell, Sloan and Pearce. In general, either stated "First Edition" or placed a Roman numeral I on the copyright page of first editions. Later printings were usually denoted similarly—e.g., "Second Printing" or Roman numeral II.

E. P. Dutton. Prior to 1929, the date on the title page should match the last date on the copyright page of a first edition. In the 1930s, began stating "First edition" or "First printing." In recent years, added a number row (they adjust the numbers for subsequent printings, but often fail to remove the first edition statement).

Editions Poetry. States "First published [Year]" on the copyright page of the first edition; subsequent printings would presumably be noted.

Egoist Press. Limited editions included a colophon page. Did not generally use a first-edition statement on trade editions, but subsequent printings would presumably be noted.

Eyre & Spottiswoode. Either printed the year of publication under their name at the bottom of the title page of first editions, or stated "This book, first published [Year], is printed . . ." on the copyright page; subsequent printings were noted.

Faber & Faber, Ltd. States "First Published [Month, Year]" on copyright page and notes subsequent printings. Prior to 1968, the year of publication was in roman numerals; beginning in 1968, switched to arabic numerals. Since World War II, the month has generally been omitted from the first-edition statement. Recently added a number row to most publications.

Faber & Gwyer, Ltd. Stated "First published by Faber & Gwyer in [Month, Year]" on copyright page of first editions; noted subsequent printings.

Fantasy Press. States "First Edition" on copyright page; may have occasionally left "First Edition" statement of original publisher on offset reprints with their imprint.

Farrar, Rinehart. Publisher's logo appears on the copyright page of first editions; no statement on subsequent printings. Very rarely stated "first edition" (in place of the logo).

Farrar, Straus. Publisher's stylized initials (FS) appear on the copyright page of first editions; no statement on subsequent printings.

Farrar, Straus & Cudahy. States either "First published [Year]" or "First printing" on the copyright page of first editions.

Farrar, Straus & Giroux. States either "First published [Year]," "First printing [Year]," or "First edition [Year]" on the copyright page of first editions.

Farrar, Straus & Young. Used either a first-edition statement or a colophon on the copyright page of first editions.

Fawcett. Uses a number row to designate printings.

Four Seas. In general, no statement on first editions, but subsequent printings noted.

Funk & Wagnalls. Used a roman numeral I on the copyright page of first editions. According to the publisher's statements, beginning in 1929, stated "First published [Month, Year]" on first editions and noted subsequent printings (presumably no statement on first editions published prior to 1929). But the first edition of John Cheever's *The Enormous Radio,* published in 1953, has the roman numeral I and does not have a first-edition statement.

Lee Furman. Made no attempt to identify first editions or subsequent printings.

Gambit, Inc. States "First printing" on the copyright page of first editions; subsequent printings are noted.

Bernard Geis. States "First printing" on the copyright page of first editions; presumably subsequent printings are noted.

Gnome Press. States "First Edition" on copyright page; may have occasionally left "First Edition" statement of original publisher on offset reprints with their imprint.

Victor Gollancz, Ltd. Prior to 1984, no statement on first editions, but subsequent printings noted [e.g., "First published [Year] | Second impression [Year]"]. In 1984, began stating "First published in [Year]" on the copyright page of first editions.

Grosset & Dunlap. Primarily a reprint house, but some notable first editions have been published by Grosset & Dunlap: *King Kong* (photoplay); Nancy Drew and Hardy Boys series; Fran Striker's "Lone Ranger" series; and Zane Grey's *The Redheaded Outfield and Other Stories.* In addition, Grosset & Dunlap's "photoplay" editions (illustrated with stills from motion pictures) are collectible. In our experience, there is no statement of edition or printing on Grossett & Dunlap publications. It is, however, possible to eliminate obvious later printings by checking the list of other books published in the series. A later printing would probably list titles that were published after the book in hand. (Note: For those authors whose first editions have become very high-priced, Grosset & Dunlap reprints in dust jackets closely matching the first edition's are sometimes desirable).

Grove Press. First editions and subsequent printings are always noted on the copyright page; currently uses a number row. Later-printing dustwrappers are identifiable by small letter code on the rear panel (e.g., "ii" designates a second-printing dustwrapper).

Robert Hale. Prior to 1958, either no statement on first editions or stated "First published [Year]," but in both cases subsequent printings were noted. Beginning in 1958, stated "First published in Great Britain in [Year]" on first editions; continued to identify subsequent printings. According to the publisher, a number row was adopted in 1994 for nonfiction titles only.

Hamish Hamilton. States "First published [Year]" or "First published in Great Britain in [Year]" on copyright page; notes subsequent printings. Added a number row in 1988.

Harcourt, Brace & Co. (1921–1960.) From 1921 to about 1931 did not identify first printings.

In about 1931 started specifying "First Edition" or "First American Edition" on the copyright page. In many instances, did not identify later printings, but removed the first-edition statement after the first printing. Occasionally, through the 1940s, numeral 1 used on first printings, then removed for later printings.

Harcourt, Brace & Howe. (1919–1921.) Usually placed the numeral 1 on the copyright page of first printings, 2 on second printings, and so on. Occasionally stated "Published [Month] [Year]" on the copyright page of first printings, and noted later printings.

Harcourt Brace Jovanovich. (Established 1970.) Stated "first edition" or "first American edition" on the copyright page of first editions, or "First Edition/ABCDE," except during 1973–1983, when the "A" was not used ("First Edition/BCDE"). In both cases, "First Edition" and the applicable letter(s) dropped on later printings.

Harcourt, Brace & World. (1960–1970.) Stated "first edition" or "first American edition" on the copyright page. Succeeded by Harcourt Brace Jovanovich in 1970.

Harper & Brothers. Prior to 1912, the date on the title page should match the last date on the copyright page. Began stating "First Edition" on the copyright page in 1922. A letter code for the month and year of publication was introduced in 1912. In most cases for first editions published between 1912 and 1922, the letter code for the year on the copyright page should match the date on the title page.

Months (The letter J was not used.)

A = January	**D** = April	**G** = July	**K** = October
B = February	**E** = May	**H** = August	**L** = November
C = March	**F** = June	**I** = September	**M** = December

Years (The letter J was not used.)

M = 1912	**B** = 1927	**R** = 1942	**G** = 1957
N = 1913	**C** = 1928	**S** = 1943	**H** = 1958
O = 1914	**D** = 1929	**T** = 1944	**I** = 1959
P = 1915	**E** = 1930	**U** = 1945	**K** = 1960
Q = 1916	**F** = 1931	**V** = 1946	**L** = 1961
R = 1917	**G** = 1932	**W** = 1947	**M** = 1962
S = 1918	**H** = 1933	**X** = 1948	**N** = 1963
T = 1919	**I** = 1934	**Y** = 1949	**O** = 1964
U = 1920	**K** = 1935	**Z** = 1950	**P** = 1965
V = 1921	**L** = 1936	**A** = 1951	**Q** = 1966
W = 1922	**M** = 1937	**B** = 1952	**R** = 1967
X = 1923	**N** = 1938	**C** = 1953	**S** = 1968
Y = 1924	**O** = 1939	**D** = 1954	
Z = 1925	**P** = 1940	**E** = 1955	
A = 1926	**Q** = 1941	**F** = 1956	

HarperCollins. (Harper & Row changed its name to HarperCollins in 1990.) States "First Edition" and uses a number row that indicates the year of publication and printing (may sometimes fail to remove the "First Edition" statement from later printings).

Harper & Row. States "First Edition" on the copyright page (also see month and date code above). In 1969, added a number row to the bottom of the last page (directly before the rear free endpaper) but often failed to remove the "First Edition" statement from later printings. By 1975, the number row was usually placed on the copyright page (still often failed to remove "First Edition" statement from later printings).

Hart-Davis, MacGibbon Limited. States "Published . . . [Year]" on first editions; subsequent printings are noted.

Rupert Hart-Davis. Although usually stated "First published [Year]" on copyright page of first editions, sometimes placed the publication date on the title page of first editions (with no statement on the copyright page); in both cases, subsequent printings were noted.

Harvard University Press. Places the year of publication on the title page of first editions, removing it from subsequent printings and adding a notice to the copyright page. In addition, may have used a number row in the 1980s.

W. Heinemann, Ltd./William Heinemann, Ltd./William Heinemann. From 1890 to 1921, placed the year of publication on the title page of first editions, removing it from subsequent printings and adding a notice to the copyright page (very occasionally, books reprinted in the year of initial publication may not have a notice on the copyright page). In the 1920s, began stating "First published [Year]" or "First published in Great Britain [Year]" on copyright page of first editions; continued to note subsequent printings.

Heritage Press. Publishes reprints or "trade editions" of the Limited Editions Club.

Hodder & Stoughton Ltd. Prior to the 1940s, had no consistent practice for identifying first editions or later printings. In the 1940s, may have begun to state "First Printed [Year]" on first editions and to note subsequent printings. By 1976, were consistent in stating "First published in [Year]" on first editions and noting subsequent printings.

Hogarth Press. No statement on first editions; subsequent printings are identified on the title page and/or copyright page. Currently use a number row.

Henry Holt. Prior to 1945, first editions can generally be identified by the lack of a later printing statement on the copyright page. Beginning in 1945, usually placed a first-edition statement on the copyright page of books produced in the United States (no statement on books produced outside the United States). After 1985, began using a first-edition statement and number row.

Holt, Rinehart & Winston. Prior to the 1970s, may have used a first-edition statement (with the exception of books produced outside the United States). Presumably in the 1970s began using a first-edition statement and number row.

Houghton, Mifflin. Almost invariably places the date, in arabic numerals, on the title page of first printings, removing it on subsequent printings. Additionally, in the late 1950s, began consistently placing a "first printing" statement on the copyright page. In the early 1970s, replaced the "first printing" statement with a number row, which includes a manufacturer code.

B.W. Huebsch. No statement on first editions; subsequent printings noted.

Hurst. Reprint publisher.

Hutchinson & Co. States "First published [Year]" or "First published in Great Britain [Year]" on copyright page of first editions. (May be no statement on books published early in this century).

Michael Joseph Ltd. Since at least the mid-1930s, has stated "First published . . . [Month, Year]" on copyright page of first editions, and noted subsequent printings. In the late 1980s and early 1990s, a number row was added to the printing statement.

Alfred A. Knopf. Until 1933–1934, sometimes stated "Published [Month or Year]" on the copyright page of first editions; later printings were noted. Since 1933–1934 have consistently stated "First Edition" (with the possible exception of children's books). Books with "First and second printings before publication" on the copyright page are second printings (e.g., booksellers' demand warranted a second printing prior to the publication date).

John Lane. Prior to 1925, no statement on first editions, but subsequent printings were noted.

Since 1925, have stated "First Published in [Year, or Month and Year]" on first editions and continued to note subsequent printings.

Limited Editions Club. Does not reprint titles (see Heritage Press for "trade" editions), and always includes a colophon at the back of each book. In general, limited to 1,500 copies; issued in fine bindings and slipcases or boxes. Nearly all the titles are signed by the illustrator, and occasionally by the author or others.

J. B. Lippincott. Until mid-1920s, the date on the title page should match the date on the copyright page, but in the case of "fall titles," the date on the title page may predate the one on the copyright page by one year. Beginning in roughly 1925, sometimes placed a first-edition statement on the copyright page but always indicated later printings (or "impressions"). In the mid-1970s, added a number row to the first-edition statement.

Lippincott and Crowell. States "First Edition" and uses a number row.

Little, Brown. Prior to the early 1930s, no statement on first editions, but subsequent printings noted. In the 1930s, stated "Published [Month] [Year]" on the copyright page of first editions; later printings were normally indicated. Since 1940, have stated "First Edition" or "First Printing," and added a number row in the late 1970s.

Horace Liveright, Inc./Liveright Publishing Corp. Prior to the 1970s, in general, no statement on first editions, but subsequent printings noted (may have occasionally used a first-edition statement). In recent years, may have used a number row in addition to stating "First Edition."

John Long. No statement on first editions, but subsequent printings noted.

Longmans, Green Co. (U.K.). Prior to the late 1920s, no statement on the first edition, but subsequent printings noted. Since the late 1920s, have stated "First Published [Year]" on the copyright page of first editions; subsequent printings are noted.

Longmans, Green Co. (U.S.). Prior to the late 1920s, no statement on the first edition; subsequent printings are presumably noted or carry a date on the copyright page later than the date on the title page. Since the late 1920s, have stated "First Edition" on the copyright page and noted subsequent printings.

The Macaulay Co. No statement on first editions; subsequent printings generally noted.

The Macmillan Co./Macmillan Publishing Co., Inc. (U.K.). Prior to the mid-1920s, no statement on the first edition, but subsequent printings noted. Since the mid-1920s, have stated "First Published [Year]" on the copyright page of first editions.

The Macmillan Co./Macmillan Publishing Co., Inc. (U.S.). Prior to the late 1800s, the date on the title page should match the last date on the copyright page for first editions (did not always designate later printings, but did change the date on the copyright page). Also, beginning sometime in the late 1800s, usually placed the statement "Set up and electrotyped. Published [Month, Year]" on first editions, and generally indicated subsequent printings. Mid-year 1936, began stating "First printing" on the copyright page; added a number row in the 1970s.

Macmillan of Canada. Does not designate first editions.

Robert M. McBride. Stated "First Published [Month, Year]," "Published [Month, Year]," or more recently "First Edition" on the copyright page of first editions; subsequent printings were noted.

McClure, Phillips. Either no statement or "Published [Month, Year, occasionally followed by a letter code]" on the copyright page of the first edition; subsequent printings presumably noted with either a statement or a later date.

A. C. McClurg. Stated "Published in [Year]" on the first edition, but may have failed to change this notice on later printings.

McDowell, Obolensky. No statement on the first edition or sometimes stated "First printing"; subsequent printings would presumably be noted.

McGraw-Hill. Until 1956, may not have used a first-edition statement. Since 1956, have used a first-edition statement and noted subsequent printings.

Methuen & Co. Since 1905, have stated "First published in [Year]" or "First published in Great Britain [Year]" on the copyright page of first editions, and noted subsequent printings. Prior to 1905, no statement on first editions, but subsequent printings noted (sometimes with a "thousands" statement on the title page such as "43rd Thousand").

Metropolitan Books. No statement on the first edition; subsequent printings presumably noted.

Modern Library. Reprint series published by Random House (prior to 1925 published by Boni & Liveright). Early titles in the series, especially in dust jacket, "Modern Library Giants," and titles with new forewords by the author or original publisher are collectible. Since 1925, have stated "First Modern Library Edition" on the copyright page of the first edition (only haphazardly prior to 1925); occasionally left the first-edition statement on subsequent printings, but the presence of later-published titles within the book in hand will often identify it as a later edition. Note: Later-issue dust jackets are often found on the first editions.

William Morrow. Prior to 1973, only sometimes placed "First Printing [Month, Year]" on the copyright page but always indicated later printings. Since 1973, have used a number row and sometimes a first-edition statement (occasionally fail to remove first-edition statement from later printings).

Museum of Modern Art. No statement on first editions, but subsequent printings are noted.

Mycroft & Moran. *See* Arkham House.

New American Library. Uses a first-edition statement and number row.

New Directions. Not consistent in using a first-edition statement or identifying subsequent printings, and often bound up first-editions sheets later, so binding variations are important in first-edition identification.

New English Library. States "First published by New English Library in [Year]" or "First published in Great Britain [Year]" on the copyright page of first editions. In general, the year in the "first published" notice should match the copyright year.

George Newnes. No statement on first editions.

W. W. Norton. In past years, usually used a first-edition statement, but did not indicate later printings. Currently uses a first-edition statement and number row, but occasionally fails to remove the first-edition statement from subsequent printings.

Peter Owen. States "First published by Peter Owen [Year]" on the copyright page of first editions and notes subsequent printings.

Oxford University Press. (New York and U. K.). Until the late 1980s, no statement on first editions, but subsequent printings noted. Started using a number row in the late 1980s.

Pantheon Books, Inc. Until 1964, no statement on first editions, but subsequent printings noted (may have occasionally stated "First Printing"). Since 1964, have stated "First Edition." May have begun using a number row, in addition to the first-edition statement, in the late 1980s.

Payson & Clarke. No statement on first editions, but subsequent printings noted.

G. P. Putnam's Sons. Prior to 1985, no statement on first editions, but subsequent printings noted. Since 1985, have used a number row.

Random House. States "First Edition" on the first printing; does not indicate subsequent printings. In recent years, added a number row beginning with 2, i.e., "First Edition/23456789," to first editions, and removed the first-edition statement from subsequent printings (e.g., "23456789" without a first edition statement would indicate a second printing).

Rapp & Whiting. Generally stated "First published [Year]" on the copyright page of the first edition.

Reynal & Hitchcock. Until 1947, no statement on first editions, but subsequent printings noted. For books published after 1947, see Harcourt, Brace & Co.

Grant Richards. No statement on the first edition.

Rinehart & Co. Placed an R in a circle on first editions and removed from subsequent printings (subsequent printings not otherwise noted).

St. Martin's Press. Until the early 1980s, no first-edition statement, but subsequent printings noted. Since the early 1980s, have used a number row and a first-edition statement.

Scribners. Until 1930, the Scribners seal and the date of publication (month and year) generally appeared on first editions, and subsequent printings were usually noted (although did not strictly adhere to either practice). Since 1930, have used an A on the copyright page to denote the first edition, sometimes with the Scribner seal, and sometimes with a code representing the month and year of publication and the book's manufacturer (later printings were either not noted, or indicated with a B, etc.). In the 1970s, added a number row, which includes a letter code for the manufacturer and type of binding (at the center).

Martin Secker, Ltd. / Secker & Warburg. Prior to the 1940s, no statement on first editions or occasionally stated "First Published in . . . [Year]"; subsequent printings noted. In the 1940s, began stating "First published in . . . [Year]" on the copyright page of first editions; continued noting subsequent printings.

Simon & Schuster. Until 1952, no statement on first editions, but subsequent printings noted (possibly with symbols as, reportedly, a few titles in the 1930s carried a series of dots or asterisks on the copyright page to indicate additional printings). In 1952, began using a first-edition statement. In the early 1970s, began using a number row (occasionally with a first-edition statement).

William Sloane Associates. States "First Printing" on the copyright page of first editions, and notes subsequent printings.

Small, Maynard. No statement on the first edition.

Smith, Elder. No statement on the first edition.

Harrison Smith & Robert Haas. Not consistent in use of a first-edition statement, but subsequent printings noted.

Stanton & Lee. *See* Arkham House.

Frederick A. Stokes Co. No statement on first editions, but subsequent printings noted.

Sun Dial. Reprint publisher.

Alan Swallow. No statement on the first edition; subsequent printings presumably noted.

Tower Books. *See* World Publishing Co.

Time Inc. / Time-Life Books. Until 1976, used a small hourglass design on the last page to designate the printing (i.e., one hourglass for the first printing, two for the second, etc.); since 1976, have stated the printing on the copyright page.

Triangle. Reprint publisher.

Trident Press. In our limited experience with this publisher, no statement on the first edition; subsequent printings presumably noted.

United Book. In our limited experience with this publisher, no statement on the first edition; subsequent printings presumably noted.

T. Fisher Unwin. Prior to 1914, no statement on the first edition. Since 1914, states "First published in [Year]" on the copyright page of the first edition.

Vanguard. No statement on first editions, and sometimes failed to note subsequent printings. In the 1970s, instituted a number row (but may have abandoned it in the mid-1980s).

Viking Press. Until the late 1930s, no first edition statement, but subsequent printings noted. In 1937, began stating "First Published by Viking in [Year]" or "Published by Viking in [Year]" on first editions, and continued the practice of noting subsequent printings. In the 1980s, added a number row to later printings only.

Villard Books. *See* Random House.

Vintage Books. *See* Random House.

Walker and Co. States "First Published . . . [Year]" on first editions, and uses a number row to indicate subsequent printings.

Ward, Lock. Prior to the 1930s, generally placed the year of publication on the title page of first editions and removed it from subsequent printings. Beginning in the mid-1930s, generally stated "First published in . . ." on the copyright page of first editions.

Weidenfeld & Nicolson. Either states "First published in . . ." or no statement on first editions, but subsequent printings are generally noted.

Wesleyan University. States "First Edition" or "First Printing" on first editions, and notes subsequent printings.

John Wiley & Sons. Prior to 1969, no statement on first editions, but subsequent printings noted. Have used a number row since 1969.

John C. Winston. Until the 1940s, no statement on either first editions or subsequent printings. Started stating the printing some time in the 1940s.

World Publishing Co. States "First Edition" or "First Printing" on the copyright page of the first edition. Note: World's "Tower Books" are reprints, with the exception of two Raymond Chandler first editions: *Red Wind* and *Spanish Blood* (both state "First Printing [Month, Year]".

CONDITION AND EDITION
ARE VERY IMPORTANT

Important: The section on First Edition Identification by publisher (Appendix E) is applicable to each entry unless otherwise stated. Check the date on the title page carefully. If the entry herein does not have the date in parentheses, the date must be on the title page. Compare your book's condition with the conditions listed below. All prices in this volume are for books in the following condition:

Books published before 1800: Rebound in the nineteenth century unless otherwise stated. Copies in original bindings (even extensively repaired) or contemporary bindings would have a much higher value.

Books published from 1800 to 1839: Rebound at some early date after the date of publication unless otherwise stated. Binding is clean and intact. The original binding would greatly increase the value.

Books published from 1840 to 1919: In original leather, cloth (cloth-covered boards), boards (paper-covered boards), or wraps unless otherwise stated. Books published from 1840 to 1879 are in good to very good condition with only minor edge wear or loss and still tight and clean. Books published from 1880 to 1919 are clean and bright with no loss or tears on the edges. Copies in fine to very fine condition would bring much more.

Books published from 1920 to 1949: Must be in very good to fine condition with only minimal (if any) soiling. In original dustwrapper (unless in wraps or in limited-edition slipcase) that is clean, with only minimal soiling or fading, and only a few *small* chips and closed tears. If the dustwrapper is missing, the value is greatly reduced (75 percent on fiction and 20 percent or more on nonfiction).

Books published after 1950: Those published from 1950 to 1975 must be in fine condition, in original dustwrapper that shows only very minor wear, fading, or soiling and that may or may not be price-clipped. Those published from 1975 until the present must, like their dustwrapper, look new, and the dustwrapper must not be price-clipped.